AN INTRODUCTION TO WESTERN PHILOSOPHY

AN INTRODUCTION TO

WESTERN PHILOSOPHY

IDEAS AND ARGUMENT
FROM PLATO TO
SARTRE

ANTONY FLEW

THE BOBBS-MERRILL COMPANY, INC.
INDIANAPOLIS · NEW YORK

First American edition 1971
The Bobbs-Merrill Company, Inc.
Indianapolis · New York

© 1971 A. G. N. FLEW

Printed and bound in Great Britain

Library of Congress Catalog Card No. LC 74-142179

CONTENTS

IV Survival and Immortality

PART TWO

V Aquinas and the Synthesis of Faith and Reason

VI The Existence of God and the Limits of Explanation

VII Predestination, Freewill, and Determinism

CONTENTS

PART THREE

VIII Descartes and the Cartesian Revolution

IX Philosophical Doubt and Cartesian Certainty

X Perception and 'the External World'

XI Rationalism and Empiricism

EPILOGUE

XII *Words and the World*

Conventions and Acknowledgements

This book is an introduction to philosophy which, as is explained more fully in Chapter I, synthesizes two methods: that of beginning with readings from the classics; and that of the ordinary textbook, written as such. One fundamental aim has been to ensure continuous readability; while at the same time providing both an Index of Notions and an Index of Names, intended to facilitate a different sort of reading for later revision and reinforcement. It is in accordance with this fundamental aim that the readings from the classics are worked into a single continuous book, and not segregated into a separate supplementary part. Three further consequences of the same fundamental policy are: that there are no footnotes or other devices requiring the reader to read the book in several places at once; that all the necessary translations have been, in so far as the limitations of my own linguistic equipment and of copyright permitted, made by me; and that the punctuation, typography and spelling of all quotations from authors writing before the present century have been assimilated to the style followed in the rest of the book.

Footnotes have been avoided by working the essential references into the text, and by providing fuller bibliographical information in an appendix of 'Particulars of books mentioned'. For the substantial extracts the references are given by mentioning the author and the title of the particular work before the extract begins, and adding a more precise indication of source in brackets at the end. Since these works are usually found in many editions with different paginations I use edition-neutral methods of reference whenever one with sufficient precision is available. For instance: with Plato the final parentheses contain only the Stephanus numbers; thus, (§§64A–66E); while those after extracts from Locke's *Essay concerning Human Understanding* give simply the Book, Chapter, and Section numbers; thus, (II(xx)4). Where, as with the work of Russell, there is no such edition-neutral method of reference page numbers are given and the further details of the particular edition used will be found in the appendix of 'Particulars'. Other references are given in brackets after the quotation; thus, (Waismann (2), p. 480). My intention when I first started work on this book was always to employ translations already made by other people. But, although excellent translations are available of most of the works quoted, I soon found that to use these in a book of this sort required a lot of tiresome and distracting annotation and rephrasing. Also, quite apart from these considerations of smoothness, which do not affect the sense at all, there are some cases where widely current translations fail to do full justice to philosophical points.

On the conventions of typography and punctuation the main thing to be said is that, having only three devices available to do many more than three semantically important jobs, I have tried to avoid any further and unnecessary overloading. I use double inverted commas to mark verbatim quotations. Single inverted commas have four different jobs. They mark the titles of articles or chapters in books. They indicate quotations within quotations. They are a sign of direct speech not attributed to any particular real person. And they give warning that the word or expression thus escorted is being employed in some atypical or otherwise suspect way. Italics have two tasks. They are employed to distinguish the titles of books and journals. But they are also employed to indicate that a word or expression is not being used in a discussion but is itself the topic. The point of this philosophically important distinction will be explained later (see especially Ch. VI, §2). Its importance is here only mentioned in order to suggest one reason why I have been careful not myself to require italics for either emphasis or proclaiming the foreignness of foreign words; although, of course, in quoting from our contemporaries I have to follow whatever conventions they have chosen. Most of the words and expressions commonly employed which are customarily marked off in this fashion are in any case immigrants of doubtful value: there is, for instance, surely no vacancy for the Latin *mutatis mutandis* which is not already satisfactorily filled by the English *with appropriate alterations*. The two exceptions which I have found indispensable are *apriori* and *aposteriori*. But these valuable citizens have lived with us for so long that it is now overtime to treat them, as I do, as both single native words.

My debts of gratitude are of two kinds. The first is to Mrs Winifred May who, while simultaneously meeting all the other secretarial demands of an unusually active department, managed both to type the entire manuscript and to remain good-tempered with the writer about his successive alterations. The second is to the various authors and publishers who have granted permission for quotation. The list below is arranged in order of the first citation of each individual work.

My thanks therefore to: Bertrand Russell, and to both George Allen and Unwin Ltd, and Simon and Schuster, Inc., as publishers of *Human Society in Ethics and Politics*; the Wittgenstein Executors, and to Basil Blackwell, Publisher, as publishers of *The Blue Book*; the Executors of H. J. Paton as translator, and to the Hutchinson Publishing Group as publishers of *The Moral Law*, and to Harper and Row, Inc., as publishers of its U.S.A. edition as *Immanuel Kant, Groundwork of the Metaphysic of Morals*, trans. H. J. Paton; the G. E. Moore Executors, and to the Cambridge University Press as publishers of *Principia Ethica*; Bertrand Russell, and to the Clarendon Press, Oxford, as publishers of *Religion and Science*; the Executors of J. M. Keynes, and to both Rupert Hart-Davis Ltd and August M. Kelley Inc., & Clarke, Irwin, Inc., and to the Turtle Bay Bookshop as publishers of *Two Memoirs*; the Albert Einstein Executors, and to both Thames and Hudson Ltd and The Philosophical Library, New York, as publishers of *Out of my Later Years*; R. M. Hare, and to the Clarendon Press, Oxford, as publishers of *The Language of Morals*; the Executors of Louis MacNeice and to Faber and Faber Ltd, as publishers of *The Agamemnon of Aeschylus*, translated by Louis MacNeice; R. D. Hicks, and to the Cambridge University Press as publishers of *Aristotle's de Anima*; N. J. Dawood as translator, and to Penguin Books as publishers of *The Koran*, trans. N. J. Dawood; the Executors of Norman Kemp Smith as translator, and to Macmillan and Co. of London, the St Martin's Press, Inc., of New York and the Macmillan Company of Canada as publishers of *Immanuel Kant's Critique of Pure Reason*, trans. N. Kemp Smith; H. Butterfield, and to George Bell and Sons Ltd, as publishers of *The Origins of Modern Science*; M. Friedländer as translator, and to both Routledge and Kegan Paul Ltd, and Dover Publications, Inc., as publishers of *The Guide for the Perplexed* by Moses Maimonides, trans. M. Friedländer; R. B. Parry, and to Little, Brown and Co., as publishers of *The Thought and Character of William James*; The Society of Authors as the literary representative of the Estate of A. E. Housman, and to both Jonathan Cape Ltd and Holt, Rinehart and Winston, Inc., as publishers of A. E. Housman's *Collected Poems*; C. C. Gillispie, and to both the Oxford University Press and the Princeton University Press as publishers of *The Edge of Objectivity*; the Executors of Norman Kemp Smith, and to both Macmillan and Co. of London, St Martin's Press, Inc., of New York, and the Macmillan Company of Canada as publishers of *The Credibility of Divine Existence*; the Executors of T. S. Eliot, and to both Faber and Faber Ltd and Harcourt, Brace and World, Inc., as publishers of *Four Quartets*;

J. C. Eccles, and to the Free Press of Glencoe as publishers of *The Critical Approach to Science and Philosophy*, ed. M. Bunge; C. Hartshorne and P. Weiss as editors, and to the Belknap Press of the Harvard University Press as publishers of *The Collected Papers of C. S. Peirce*; the Executors of A. N. Whitehead, and to the Cambridge University Press as publishers of *Science and the Modern World*; Henry Reed, and to both Jonathan Cape Ltd and Harcourt, Brace and World, Inc., as publishers of *A Map of Verona*; P. G. Lucas as translator, and to the Manchester University Press as publishers of *Kant's Prolegomena*, trans. P. G. Lucas; Bertrand Russell, and to both George Allen and Unwin Ltd and Simon and Schuster, Inc., as publishers of *The Analysis of Matter*; Lord Brain, and to Basil Blackwell, Publisher, as publishers of *Mind, Perception and Science*; R. Carnap, and to the Open Court Publishing Co., as publishers of *The Philosophy of R. Carnap*, edited by P. A. Schilpp; the Wittgenstein Executors and to the Executors of C. K. Ogden as translator, and to both Routledge and Kegan Paul Ltd and the Humanities Press as publishers of *Tractatus Logico-Philosophicus*; the Executors of J. L. Austin as translator, and to Basil Blackwell, Publisher, as publishers of *Frege's Foundations of Arithmetic*; Philip Mairet as translator, and to both Methuen and Co. and the Philosophical Library, New York, as publishers of *Existentialism and Humanism* by J. P. Sartre, from which I quote by courtesy of its French publishers, Editions Nagel; W. Kaufmann as translator, and to World Publishing Co., as publishers of a translation from Nietzsche's *The Gay Science*, which first appeared in their *Existentialism from Dostoievsky to Sartre* by W. Kaufmann; Martin Milligan as translator, and to International Publishers, Inc., as publishers of *Karl Marx: The Economic and Philosophic Manuscripts of 1844*; and, finally, to the Executors of J. L. Austin, and to both the Clarendon Press, Oxford, and the Harvard University Press as publishers of *How to Do Things with Words*.

Introductory

CHAPTER I

Making Progress in Philosophy

§ 1 *The peculiar form of this book*

It would be silly to pretend that there are not already many books designed
to serve as textbooks for introductory courses in, and generally, as introductions to, philosophy; and it would be ungenerous as well as silly to
suggest that there are not among these several which are of their kinds
excellent. One way of filling the need which these books are intended to
meet is to produce a collection of readings from classical sources, keeping
the editorial material to the minimum. A good specimen of this sort is
A Modern Introduction to Philosophy by Paul Edwards and Arthur Pap.
Another method is simply to write a more or less elementary book. Within
this second method we can distinguish two manners. The author may, like
John Hospers in *An Introduction to Philosophical Analysis*, strive to be not
only fair to all points of view but also in some measure detached. Alternatively, he may, like Michael Scriven in *Primary Philosophy*, equally fair-
mindedly attempt to establish his own conclusions even in areas which
have been and are controversial.

The first thing to be remarked about the present volume is that it tries
to integrate the first with the second method, while inclining to the second
of the two manners of following the second method. A little less than half
of the total space is given to passages from classical sources. But these are
not segregated into a separate and not quite equal part. Instead the classical
philosophers make their contributions as and when it seems to the author
that some particular one of them has something immediately relevant and
especially good to say. This form of presentation is bound to displease
those who like to keep all the recognized specialisms and sub-specialisms
strictly separate; and those who insist that the men of old may reappear
only as history, and then always in due chronological order. My offence in
their eyes will surely be compounded by willingness to quote poetry, and

to refer to issues of contemporary moral and political dispute: 'As if it were not bad enough to refuse to divide the history of his subject from his subject, the man even betrays interests in things which are not his subject at all!'

Such departmental-mindedness is quite out of place in philosophy generally, and it is doubly out of place in the particular context for which this book is designed (Ch. I, § 3). It is out of place generally, because philosophy is an activity which can have connections in all directions, and because in philosophy a point classically made may be perennially relevant. (I am, by the way, using the difference between the small and the capital letter to mark the distinction between the broad sense of *classical*, indicating the achievement of an accepted standard of excellence, and the narrow, in which *Classical* refers to a certain period of Greco-Roman civilization. Compare the distinctions between saying that a man is conservative, or a republican, or a democrat; and saying that he is – in Britain – Conservative, or – in the United States – a Republican or a Democrat.)

That philosophy is an activity which can have connections in all directions is, indeed, one of the grounds of its claim for a place in any programme of liberalizing and integrative studies. For the philosopher above all it is scandalous to be misguided by something which merits a mnemonic pillory label, *The Specialist Fallacy*. This is the fallacy of inferring: from the premise that I am only paid to know about, and to be interested in, this; the conclusion that I am paid to know about, and be interested in, this only. That philosophy does have such connections can only be shown later and at length. For the moment it must suffice simply to say that it is both a fault in the presentation of philosophy as philosophy, and a betrayal of such wider educational intentions, not to draw attention to some of these links.

It is, for example, effectively to misrepresent Descartes to refuse to notice his contribution to the development of modern science, and to ignore the impact upon his own thinking of Harvey's discovery of the circulation of the blood. (See, for example, Ch. VIII, § 5 and Ch. XI, § 3.) Again, it is to diminish St Thomas Aquinas, and all those others who have offered what they took to be philosophical proofs of the existence of God, not to take account of the fact that the claim that this conclusion can indeed be known without benefit of revelation has now been defined as one of the essential doctrines of the Roman Catholic faith (Ch. V, § 2 and Ch. VI). Nor again is it sensible for anyone who wants to understand either Plato's thought or our own world to neglect the hint by Bertrand

Russell in his *The Practice and Theory of Bolshevism*, written in 1920 after returning from a private study tour in Soviet Russia: "Far closer than any actual historical parallel is the parallel of Plato's *Republic*" (pp. 28–29). For Plato's dream like the Leninist actuality is of an élite political order guided in the exercise of absolute power by its supposed insight into essential reality (Ch. II, §2 and Ch. III, §1).

The immediate relevance of all this is that the great advantage of my method of working the extracts from the classics into the text is that this makes it far easier to show, and not merely to say, that and how in philosophy classical contributions remain perennially relevant and alive.

One possible disadvantage is that an image, a distinction, an argument is often employed in a way in which its originator would not or could not have used it himself. But wherever I recognize that my use of materials is flagrantly different from that of their inventor I say so. Furthermore, there is not, and there should not be, any copyright in philosophical ideas. All philosophers are entitled to appropriate from the public domain whatever can be made to serve their own proper purposes. Again, the method of integration must involve that the authorities cited do not appear as they would in a work aiming specially to describe and assess the thought of individuals. This second possible disadvantage can to some small extent be offset by systematic use of the Index of Names: the impact of the sum as thus collected is likely to be different from that of its several parts appearing successively. Incidentally, such systematic use of the Index of Notions as well as of the Index of Names provides also an excellent method of reinforcement in learning; and it is primarily for this that both indices are designed. However, for full satisfaction you obviously must turn to books with different intentions: *A Critical History of Western Philosophy*, for instance, edited by D. J. O'Connor, provides substantial accounts of twenty-one major individual figures and of eight schools or periods; and consultations of *The Encyclopaedia of Philosophy*, edited by Paul Edwards, can always be recommended to those fortunate enough to have access to it.

Whatever disadvantages my method may be thought to have there is certainly no call to direct any apologies towards the classical philosophers themselves. It cannot be too often emphasized, especially in university circles, that just as Aeschylus and Shakespeare were concerned to make plays for the theatre rather than to provide source materials for scholars of literature, so Plato and Kant were dedicated to the progress of philosophy and not to the production of subjects for the antiquarian of ideas. Had

17

they, or any of the others who deserved their accolades as great classical philosophers, been alive today they themselves would have wanted to share in the continuing inquiries, not to withdraw to some institute for the study and propagation of their own complete and marmoreal revelations.

§2 *What counts as progress in philosophy*

The second main point to be made about the present volume is that it is an expression of the conviction that there can be, has been, and ought to be, progress in philosophy. It seems often to be assumed, it is sometimes in books which purport to be introductory in as many words said, that philosophical problems are as such necessarily insoluble. In particular, and congenially to the spirit of a scientific age, it is suggested that from time to time issues which had previously been unprofitably philosophical become at last definitely settlable; and that these issues then by that token fall within the province of some, usually some new, science.

Certainly there is some true foundation for this last misconception. For the word *philosophy* as an academic label was once used in a far wider sense than it now is. When a writer of the 1600's spoke of "the new philosophy" he was referring to modern science, to work such as that of Galileo (1564–1642) and Newton (1642–1727). This older and wider sense of the word *philosophy* is still preserved, fossilized, in the official titles of some of the older chairs of physics in Old World Britain. Thus the senior professor of physics in the ancient universities of Scotland is by tradition Professor of Natural or Experimental Philosophy. Again, it is only in the last hundred years that psychology has established itself as an autonomous discipline, and the critical interpreter of such earlier writers as Locke or Hume or Kant will find it both difficult and essential to insist on making and pressing unmade distinctions between psychological and philosophical theses. (In Britain this emancipation of psychology as a science from philosophy as philosophy was not universally recognized by university administrations until the decade after World War II. Often previously psychologists were brigaded into Departments of Philosophy.)

However, although there has been this progressive narrowing of the scope of the word *philosophy*, it would be wrong to think that the changes involved have been purely verbal; and still more wrong to assume that the word is now properly so employed that philosophical problems must be insoluble, by definition. The very growth of science, which has been marked by the development of a series of autonomous scientific disciplines quite separate from philosophy, has forced philosophers to recognize more clearly than ever before that and how philosophical questions differ from scientific. It is not that the former by becoming answerable are transformed into the latter. The questions which can now be answered by the sciences always were scientific; and any question which ever was (in the present, more restricted, sense) philosophical remains what it was, whether or not it can be satisfactorily answered. It is, obviously, one of the vital tasks of the present book to explain this distinction between, on the one hand, philosophical issues, and, on the other, scientific and other sorts of problems. But it is a task which is best performed with reference to particular cases of possible confusion met as we go along. (Compare, for instance, Ch. VII, § 1 and Ch. XII, §§ 2–3.)

A further reason frequently given for believing that there is no progress in philosophy points to the way in which in the sciences matters which used to be in dispute seem to get definitively settled. The findings are put into the archives, and the focus of interest among the professionals moves elsewhere. This observation is indeed one made by Immanuel Kant, who both knew what science is and was concerned that there should be progress in philosophy also. Thus in his *Critique of Practical Reason* he commends "the systematic process by which a science is established . . . matters which have been decided ought only to be cited and not again discussed".

By contrast, it is said, the philosophers continue apparently everlastingly discussing their supposedly great (but really often trivial or absurd) questions without ever achieving consensus about what any of the answers are. Again, it is often urged that in philosophy it is never possible to prove to someone who disagrees with you that you are right and he is wrong; nor yet for him to prove the opposite to you. What may appear to be the same point has been put with more style and refinement by one who was himself a distinguished philosopher: "No philosophic argument ends with a Q.E.D. However forceful it never forces. There is no bullying in philosophy, neither with the stick of logic nor with the stick of language" (Waismann (2), p. 480).

As before there is sufficient truth in these objections to make it instructive to consider precisely how much, and precisely what conclusions must follow. Certainly it cannot be denied that science does make progress in the way suggested; and this notwithstanding that all its findings – no matter how revered their place in the archives – are in principle, and sometimes in practice, subject to revision, amendment, and correction in the light of the further progress of enquiry. Certainly too philosophical discussions often seem, and sometimes are, like those of the fallen angels in Pandemonium who, as Milton tells us (*Paradise Lost*, II, 558–561):

> *. . . reason'd high*
> *Of Providence, Foreknowledge, Will, and Fate,*
> *Fixt Fate, free will, foreknowledge absolute,*
> *And found no end, in wandring mazes lost.*

But that fallen angels, or even people, do or do not fail or refuse to agree is a plain matter of fact about what with fallen angels, or with people, is so; whereas a contention about whether or not agreement would in this case be justified involves a totally different sort of claim, a claim about what ought or ought not to be so. To argue directly from any premise or collection of premises purely of the first sort to any conclusion which is even partly of the second kind must be, as we shall explain more fully in Chapter III, fallacious. The nerve of the argument proceeds from the facts, or the alleged facts, of the existence of a consensus, or the lack of it, immediately to the conclusion that such agreement, or disagreement, is as it ought to be (in as much as this is what is rationally warranted). But any such argument is as unsound, and as common, as the inference which moves from the true observation that there is a great diversity of moral opinion directly to the conclusion that none of these opinions can properly be said – much less be known – to be either true or false. In both cases the factual, or would-be factual, observations about what people happen to believe have to be reinforced by something else before we become entitled to draw these radically different conclusions about the absence or the impossibility of knowledge.

Of course, here and always, to insist upon the invalidity of some form of argument is not at all the same thing as to say or even to suggest that the conclusion being drawn from that argument must be false. Notoriously, a valid argument from false premises may, but does not necessarily, lead to false conclusions; while an argument which is in fact invalid can be employed to support some conclusion which happens to be true. Suppose we were to urge, however implausibly, first, that philosophers are always lifelong bachelors, and, second, that King Henry VIII of England was a philosopher. Then it would follow necessarily from these two false premises that that in fact much-married king must have been a lifelong bachelor. Suppose now we replace the second premise by the claim that

President Buchanan was a philosopher. The form of the argument remains the same. It is, therefore, still valid. The replacement second premise is in fact as false as the original which it replaces. Yet the new conclusion, that President Buchanan was a lifelong bachelor, happens to be true. Again, to argue that because, first, all Communists disapprove of racial discrimination, and because, second, that man disapproves of racial discrimination, therefore that man must be a Communist, is to argue fallaciously. And the argument will remain just as fallacious notwithstanding that the person in question may happen to be an authentic, card-carrying, fully paid up, believing and practising Bolshevik.

A fallacy, by the way, is not just any vagary of belief. Someone who erroneously believed that Henry VIII never married or that President Buchanan did would not, in the strict and economical usage invariably observed in philosophy, be involved in a fallacy. By contrast anyone employing any argument of the second of the two forms just illustrated would be committing what is named officially but not very memorably *The Fallacy of the Undistributed Middle*. This was by some in the heyday of Senator Joseph McCarthy more pointedly nicknamed the Unamerican Fallacy.

It is, therefore, clear that we cannot construe the absence of consensus in philosophy as an independently sufficient demonstration that the subject does not make progress. We have next to consider the suggestion that in philosophy it is never possible to prove to someone that you are right and he is wrong. The essential distinction, here unhappily confounded by the employment of this wretched expression *prove to*, is that between producing a proof and persuading a person. A man may be persuaded by an abominable argument, just as he may remain unconvinced by one which ought to be accepted. In persuasion a second person is always involved; and it is, so to speak, up to that second person whether or not he is persuaded successfully. Yet whether or not some candidate argument does indeed constitute a valid proof is not a matter to be settled by reference to any actual consensus. There might be a proof which no one had ever recognized as such, just as it is possible for a fallacy to be detected in an argument which was once universally mistaken to be sound. Creative mathematicians are for ever discovering proofs which, precisely because they are mathematical discoveries, were never recognized previously; while from time to time, though far more rarely, they also unearth fallacies in what their predecessors had passed as legitimate theorems.

The effect of confounding the notion of proof with that of persuasion in this talk of proving something to a person is to suggest that no proof can be, much less be known to be, valid unless it is possible to persuade all comers of its validity. Since this never – or almost never – is possible, to accept so irrelevant and preposterous a criterion of validity would be to make not just philosophical but almost any other sort of knowledge unattainable. It may very well be, for instance, that no one can prove to – that is to say persuade – spokesmen of the Soviet Bloc, whether professional or amateur, that Russian tanks were sent into Hungary in 1956, into Czechoslovakia in 1968, and wherever next, in order to preserve the world's largest and most unyielding empire. But that is in itself no good reason for saying that what such spokesmen thus refuse to admit is not both true and known to be true.

This same confusion between the ideas of proof and persuasion can in a more subtle form be seen even in the work of so distinguished a philosopher as Bertrand Russell (1872–1970), albeit in one of his less distinguished books. It may well be, as I shall myself later urge (Ch. III, § 6), that there is something peculiar about moral arguments and moral conclusions. But if this is so it is not, as seems to be the implication of the following very representative passage from *Human Society in Ethics and Politics*, that these arguments or these conclusions are uniquely ineffective in winning universal assent:

> I do not know how, by any purely logical argument, to refute a man who maintains that only the desires of Germans should be considered. This view has been refuted on the battlefield, but can it be refuted in the study? When I say that it has been refuted on the battlefield, am I admitting that if Germany had been victorious the view would have been valid? I am naturally reluctant to say this, and I do not believe it, so let us see what there is to be said on the other side.
>
> If the concept of 'objective rightness' is to serve any purpose, it must satisfy two conditions, one theoretical and the other practical. The theoretical condition is that there must be some way of knowing what kinds of act are 'objectively right'; the practical condition is that, at least for some people, the fact that an act is recognized as objectively right must be a motive prompting its performance.
>
> Let us first take the view that *objectively right* is indefinable. . . . I can say: 'Sir, . . . Ethical intuition is a notable faculty . . . it is a faculty which teaches disinterestedness, which requires you to . . . view the world with God-like impartiality . . .'
>
> I can make this speech, with such embellishments as my rhetorical

skill may suggest, but will it carry conviction to my interlocutor? It may do if he already has a profound respect for me, or if he is a schoolboy exposed for years to my subtle propaganda. But if he is a Nazi and I am his prisoner, he will merely subject me to torture and semi-starvation until I admit that he is the best of the argument. For this I may hate and despise him, but I cannot refute him. (pp. 80–81)

The attempt, which we have been examining, to show that there is no philosophical knowledge by simply urging that there is always someone who can be relied on to remain unconvinced, should be regarded as a special case of a remarkably common fallacy. Since it is so common, and hence presumably so seductive, it becomes worth while to have a label for it. Having such mnemonic labels helps us to be on guard against the fallacies so labelled. This particular fallacy involves a changing of the subject, from an original issue of whether what has been said is true or supported by good reasons, to the quite different and here irrelevant question of whether everyone can be convinced that this is indeed so. I therefore docket it as the *But-there-is-always-someone-who-will-never-agree Diversion*.

This Diversion, in the form just considered, constitutes a second attempt to dismiss any idea of progress in philosophy by appealing to a lack of consensus. The third claim, that "No philosophic argument ends with a Q.E.D. However forceful it never forces", is quite different. Most importantly it is different in being relevant. It is relevant because it appeals to what is supposed to be the essential logical character of philosophical arguments rather than to putative psychological facts about the intractability of some people's beliefs. What is wrong with this third objection is, that in so far as it does pick out a characteristic of philosophical arguments it is one which is equally characteristic of all others and, furthermore, that it is anyway not something which rules out the possibility of progress in philosophy and of philosophical knowledge.

It is characteristic, it is indeed the defining characteristic, of a valid deductive argument that if you assert the premises you cannot then deny the conclusion without thereby contradicting yourself. Take, just for once and for the sake of piety, the example hallowed by immemorial tradition. If, first, all men are mortal, and, second, Socrates is a man, then it follows necessarily, third, that Socrates is mortal. This uninteresting argument is, obviously, valid. Certainly too it does force. For clearly it shows, in virtue of the very principle of its validity, that you cannot assert the first and the second propositions and yet deny the third without thereby contradicting yourself. Yet it does not thereby force us, on pain of self-contradiction, to accept the conclusion. For it is another practically as well as theoretically important characteristic of such arguments that they are always reversible. Allowing, as we must, that an argument of the form of that given is compulsively valid, we are still not thereby compelled to accept it as proof of its conclusion. It always remains theoretically possible, and is often practically correct, to receive it rather as a disproof of at least one of its premises.

The practical importance of this characteristic of reversibility is best illustrated by referring to the logic of the falsification of hypotheses. On the hypothesis that the burglary was an outside job, and granted that the building could only have been entered by the doors or the windows, then it follows that one of these must have been opened. But suppose we know that this conclusion is in fact false. And suppose we also know, as we do, that we have here a valid deductive inference. Then we are in a position to recognize that we have, not a proof of the truth of the conclusion of that argument – a conclusion which is not true but false – but instead a proof of the falsity of at least one of the two premises. It is this pattern of argument which is always and necessarily involved in the testing of hypotheses in the sciences. There the terms will be more technical and less lighthearted than those employed in our illustration. But though the content is different the essential form of the argument is the same.

What this brief but fundamental consideration of the essential nature of valid deduction should bring out is that every sound argument 'forces', in the sense that it limits the available options even though no argument can ever be 'completely compulsive', if by that were to be meant – what never is meant – that it blocks up literally every alternative to accepting its conclusion. For, in the first resort, any valid deductive argument can as such be either a proof of its conclusions or a disproof of one of its premises; while, in the last resort, however sound and however complete the argument offered, no argument can of its nature force men to be rational. Every argument always leaves at least one alternative of irrationality, the acceptance of the penalty of self-contradiction. In this, incidentally, there is an important analogy between the compulsions of a compulsive argument and other less metaphorical pressures. When the bank manager excuses his action in opening the strong room for the bank robbers by saying, 'I had no alternative. They would have killed me had I refused', he is not claiming, what would not be true, that he had literally no alternative at all. He could and, had it been a life-and-death matter of the survival of his country or his family, should and perhaps would have told them to shoot away and let his knowledge of the combination die with him. When he claims that he acted under compulsion, that he had no alternative, what he means is that in the particular circumstances there was no alternative which it would have been reasonable for him to accept. But of this more below (Ch. VII, especially § 1).

We must not, therefore, be led to despair of making progress in philosophy, either by the seductions of the But-there-is-always-someone-who-will-never-agree Diversion, or by the fact that arguments in philosophy are not compulsive in some way in which no other argument is either. Yet to beat off some suggestions that progress in philosophy is impossible is not to show that there can be, much less that there has been, such progress. To show this is, as I have indicated already, a main aim of the present book. The very fact that it is so widely believed that progress in philosophy is impossible, either practically or in virtue of the implicit definition of the expression *philosophical problem*, makes it vital to demand of any introduction that it shall provide evidence to the contrary. For what is the reader supposed to be reading it for if it is not in order to know more at the end than he did at the beginning? This basic requirement could, of course, be met by an introduction to a subject to which the idea of progress was scarcely if at all applicable. We could learn a lot from a good introduction to sculpture without its having to labour to establish that the work of Michelangelo somehow rendered all Cycladic carvings obsolete. But whatever could be the point of puzzling our heads with philosophical problems if such problems were inherently insoluble, and if even the notion of making progress towards a correct resolution were entirely out of place?

This is a demand which we have to concede unreservedly to be legitimate. However much and however rightly we shall want to emphasize the differences between progress in philosophy and progress in the sciences, we cannot jettison the idea of progress here without thereby abandoning all claims to be furthering a genuine subject of enquiry. In particular there has to be some difference, and some difference relevant to the advancement of philosophical investigations, between the man who has and the man who has not had the benefit of a good grounding in philosophy. So in composing the present book I have constantly asked myself what would be, or what should be, the elements of the intellectual equipment of a person so trained. Of what fundamental distinctions must he be aware, what special ideas and vocabulary does he need to have mastered, of what insights should he be seized, of what important arguments must he have taken the measure, against what mistakes will he be most on his guard? It is my answers to questions of this sort which have largely determined my decisions on what had to be included within the treatments of the different areas selected for attention in the present book.

Some very pedestrian examples of such philosophical rudiments have appeared already in this chapter. I have, for instance, found occasion to bring out the essential nature of deductive argument; to insist on the distinction between questions about the validity or invalidity of arguments and questions about the truth or falsity of their premises or conclusions; to indicate the strict usage of the term *fallacy*; to identify, to elucidate, and to label the But-there-is-always-someone-who-will-never-agree Diversion; and to say something about what compulsion is and what it is not. Before I proceed to mention a third feature of the present book let us consider another and more exciting specimen, which also constitutes an illustration of the way in which it is possible to take philosophical profit from the classics.

This example comes from what must surely be one of the earlier dialogues of Plato (*circa* 427–347 BC). This dialogue, *Euthyphro*, is devoted to the typically Socratic question: 'What is holiness (or piety)?' The character 'Socrates' plays a leading part in all these earlier Platonic dialogues, dominating most. Plato certainly knew, and was in some way influenced by Socrates (469–399 BC). But it is, as might be expected, a matter of scholarly dispute how closely the historical Socrates resembled Plato's Socratic persona. However, we do have Aristotle's word for it that the quest for definitions was authentically Socratic (*Metaphysics* 1078B27 ff.); and Aristotle (384–322 BC), who studied for many years in Plato's Academy before founding his own Lyceum, should have been in a position to know. The passage quoted begins where 'Socrates' has led 'Euthyphro' to recognize the definition implicit in what he has been saying:

EUTHYPHRO – Well, I would say that the holy is this, what all the gods love, and the opposite, what all the gods hate, is unholy.
SOCRATES – We shall soon know better, my dear fellow. Just consider this argument. Is the holy loved by the gods because it is holy, or is it holy because it is loved?
EUTHYPHRO – I do not understand what you are saying, Socrates.
SOCRATES – Then I will try to say it more clearly. We speak of being carried and of carrying, of being led and leading, of being seen and

seeing; and you understand in all such cases that and how the one thing differs from the other?

EUTHYPHRO – I think I do.

SOCRATES – Then there is being loved, and loving is something different from this?

EUTHYPHRO – Of course.

SOCRATES – Then tell me, is what is being carried what is being carried because someone is carrying it, or for some other reason?

EUTHYPHRO – No, for that reason.

SOCRATES – And what is being led is what is being led because someone is leading it, and what is seen is what is seen because someone is seeing it?

EUTHYPHRO – Certainly.

SOCRATES – Then someone does not see it because it is being seen but, on the contrary, because someone sees it it becomes something which is being seen. Again, someone does not lead something because it is being led but it becomes something led in virtue of the fact that someone is leading it. So is it quite clear, Euthyphro, what I want to say?

EUTHYPHRO – Certainly.

SOCRATES – Now then, what shall we say about the holy, Euthyphro? It is, according to your account, what is loved by all the gods?

EUTHYPHRO – Yes.

SOCRATES – For this reason, because it is holy, or for some other reason?

EUTHYPHRO – No, for this reason.

SOCRATES – It is loved because it is holy, not holy because it is loved?

EUTHYPHRO – So it seems.

SOCRATES – But surely, that which is loved and that which is god-beloved is loved and god-beloved in virtue of the gods loving it?

EUTHYPHRO – Of course.

SOCRATES – Then the god-beloved is not the holy, Euthyphro, nor is the holy the god-beloved, as you were saying, but the one is different from the other.

EUTHYPHRO – How is that, Socrates?

SOCRATES – Because we agree, do we not, that the holy is loved because it is holy, rather than that it is holy because it is loved?

EUTHYPHRO – Yes.

SOCRATES – Also that what is god-beloved is god-beloved because it is loved by gods, that is, by reason of this love, rather than that they love it because it is god-beloved?

EUTHYPHRO – You are right.

SOCRATES – So if the god-beloved and the holy were the same thing,

27

my dear Euthyphro, and if the holy were loved in virtue of being holy then the god-beloved would be loved in virtue of being god-beloved; and if the god-beloved were god-beloved in virtue of being loved by gods, then the holy would be holy because it is loved. But you now see that the opposite is the case, in that both are entirely different from each other. For the one is beloved in virtue of being loved, whereas the other is loved because it is worthy to be loved. And it looks as if you, Euthyphro, when you were asked what the holy is were unwilling to reveal its essence to me, but instead mentioned an accident of this the holy – being loved by all gods. You have not yet said what it really is. If you please, then, do not hide it from me but begin over again from the beginning and tell me what the holy is. Forget about whether it is loved by gods or any other accident, for that is not the point at issue. Now, tell me frankly, what is the holy and what the unholy? (§§9E–11B)

To this question the dialogue never succeeds in finding any satisfactory answer. The passage quoted is nevertheless one to reread, and to take to heart. For it can serve both as a paradigm of distinctively philosophical argument and as an illustration of the way in which definite progress can be made in philosophy, even without settling the question originally raised. 'Socrates' is labouring to distinguish between possible accidents, and the essence, of the holy. The former is a matter of what may or may not happen to be true of holy things, even perhaps true universally of all holy things; but which even if it were thus universally true it would still be possible to question without actually contradicting yourself. The latter is a matter of what is part or the whole of the meaning of the word *holy*, and which therefore could not be denied to the holy without self-contradiction. To see why the distinction matters in this sort of case we have to turn from Plato to the German Gottfried Leibniz (1646–1716). Although Leibniz was concerned not with gods but with God, and not with the holy in particular but with goodness in general, neither of these differences diminishes the crucial relevance to him of the challenge: "Is the holy loved by the gods because it is holy or is it holy because it is loved?" Like any question which matters it matters because of what hinges on the answer. In his *Discourse on Metaphysics* Leibniz brings out one of the things which is at stake, while himself firmly opting for the first of the two alternative answers:

Thus I am far removed from those who maintain that there are no rules of goodness and of perfection in the nature of things . . . and that the works of God are only good by definition, because God has made them. For if that were so, God, knowing that he was the author of things, had no need to look at them afterwards and to find them good, as Holy Scripture testifies that he did. It seems to have employed this anthropomorphic expression in order to teach us that their excellence can be known by looking at them as they are in themselves, and even when we do not consider at all under this bald description who it is who causes them. . . . So in saying that things are not good by any rule of goodness, but sheerly by the will of God, it seems to me that one destroys, without realizing it, all the love of God and all his glory. For why praise him for what he has done if he would be equally praiseworthy in doing exactly the contrary? Where will be his justice and his wisdom if there only remains a certain despotic power, if will takes the place of reason, and if, according to the tyrants' definition, that which is pleasing to the most powerful is, as such, just?   (§ 11)

The way in which Leibniz employs Holy Scripture, even with its careful cautioning about "anthropomorphic expression", may strike some modern readers as quaint. Nevertheless he does decisively make his point that if you choose to define the word *good* by reference to the wishes or affections of God, then in your mouth the attempt to praise your God for his goodness becomes empty. It must be empty because, on the definition suggested, to say that what God does is always good is to say only and precisely that God always does exactly what he wants, while to say that he loves the good is to say nothing more nor less than that he loves just what he does love. These remarks may very well be true. Indeed, in so far as on the definition suggested they become tautologies, they must be true. But they scarcely constitute grounds for praise, much less worship; and this, surely, is not all that believers have intended in worshipping their God as perfectly good. In his horrified rejection of the implications of choosing this sort of answer to the challenge Leibniz was representative of the dominant tradition in Christian thought; even if he was, unfortunately, by no means equally representative in his seeing and never forgetting what these implications are.

Here, if not sooner, someone may want to protest that all this is not philosophy but theology. It is a fair objection, to which it is instructive to reply. The first and less important part of the answer is that the antithesis employed is false. Something can be, and this is, properly classifiable as both philosophy and theology. Indeed there are whole books in the area of what is called philosophical theology which librarians – who have to make decisions on these often unrewarding jurisdictional issues – may equally well shelve as either philosophy or theology. Again, and perhaps slightly more interestingly, there are stretches of theoretical argument within the sciences with the same ambiguous status. Einstein, as usual, knew what he was talking about when, speaking of the key step required for the development of his Special Theory of Relativity, he wrote: "The type of critical reasoning which was required for the discovery of this central point was in my case advanced above all by reading the philosophical writings of David Hume and Ernst Mach" (Einstein, p. 53).

The second and more important part of the answer to the complaint that what has just been going on is of merely theological interest appeals to that same distinction between the form and content of arguments which was tacitly employed earlier to excuse the seeming irrelevance to the serious business of philosophy of some rather lighthearted illustration. Just as the challenge originally raised by 'Socrates' in terms of the holy and gods remains relevant to those who are thinking, instead, of goodness and God, so it survives even a total de-theologizing. The crux is the general form, not any particular content of the argument. Thus any attempt to define *good* or any other general word of commendation in terms of the actual or possible wishes, decisions, likes, or dislikes of any human person, or group, or institution is equally exposed to an appropriate particular version of the same general challenge. Suppose, for instance, that you want to say that for you the word *justice* simply means *what the law prescribes*, then by this token you waive all rights to denounce as unjust any arrangements whatsoever which may happen to be legally laid down. Or, again, suppose that – with or without some reference to the alleged teachings of sociology or anthropology – you maintain that the word *good* is straightforwardly equivalent to *what is socially approved,* then you thereby abandon the privilege of being able on occasion to reject as bad some established norm of your own society.

The alternative which Leibniz rejected with a shudder was brazenly embraced by his older but bolder contemporary, the Englishman Thomas Hobbes (1588–1679). With his usual lack of inhibition Hobbes urges in Chapter XXXI of his *Leviathan* that

> the right of nature whereby God reigneth over men, and punisheth those that break his laws, is to be derived not from his creating them, as if he required obedience as of gratitude for his benefits, but from his irresistible power. . . . To those therefore whose power is irresistible the dominion of all men adhereth naturally by their excellence of power;

and, consequently, it is from that power that the kingdom over men and the right of afflicting them at his pleasure belongeth naturally to God almighty, not as creator and gracious, but as omnipotent. And though punishment be due to sin only, because by that word is understood affliction for sin, yet the right of afflicting is not always derived from men's sin but from God's power.

This question, 'Why evil men often prosper and good men suffer adversity?' has been much disputed . . . and is the same with this of ours, 'By what right God dispenses the prosperities and adversities of this life?' and is of that difficulty as it hath shaken the faith not only of the vulgar but of philosophers, and, which is more, of the saints, concerning the divine providence. 'How good', said David, 'is the God of Israel to those that are upright in heart, and yet my feet were almost gone . . . for I was grieved at the wicked, when I saw the ungodly in such prosperity.' And Job, how earnestly does he expostulate with God for the many afflictions which he suffered notwithstanding his righteousness. This question in the case of Job is decided by God himself not by arguments derived from Job's sin but his own power. For whereas the friends of Job drew their arguments from his affliction to his sin, and he defended himself by the conscience of his innocence, God himself taketh up the matter; and, having justified the affliction by arguments drawn from his power, such as this, 'Where wast thou when I laid the foundations of the earth?', and the like, both approved Job's innocence and reproved the erroneous doctrine of his friends.

To anyone who follows Hobbes in choosing this alternative there can be no theological Problem of Evil; or, if you prefer it, there is a problem but one which has a simple Gordian solution. The theological Problem of Evil is to show, or to try to show, that there is really no inconsistency: between asserting, on the one hand, that there is an omnipotent, omniscient, and perfect creator God; while on the other hand admitting, as we must, that our world – his supposed creation – is far from flawless. To Leibniz who, as we have seen, accepted the other alternative, and who also insisted upon believing in a God with the characteristics specified, this Problem of Evil was inescapable. He presented his treatment in his *Theodicy*. Although we shall not in this book be much concerned with this Problem of Evil, which only arises for the theist or the would-be theist, it is worth mentioning by the way that the key notion in the candidate solution proposed by Leibniz is – as in any competent treatment it surely must be – that of all actual evils as somehow the logically, as opposed to causally, necessary preconditions of higher goods. The idea is that all the actual evils of the world are necessary to the occurrence of more than compensating goods: in the way in which there necessarily has to be an injury if there is to be forgiveness; and not in the way in which, in the world as it in fact is but might not have been, there has to be hard training if there is to be a first-class athletics team.

The paragraphs to be quoted now from the *Theodicy* provide some variations on the theme of the earlier citation from the *Discourse on Metaphysics*. For those who have no time for theology, and even for those who have, it will be a salutary exercise to adapt the arguments of Leibniz to some parallel secular case, such as that of the Nazi "Right is what is good for Germany":

Those who believe that God has established good and evil by an arbitrary decree ... deprive God of the designation *good*. For what reason could one have to praise him for what he does, if in doing something quite different he would have done equally well? I have very often been surprised that various Supralapsarian theologians, as for instance Samuel Rutherford, a Professor of Theology in Scotland ... could have been involved in so strange an idea. Rutherford ... says positively that nothing is unjust or morally bad in God's eyes before he has forbidden it. Thus without this prohibition it would be a matter of indifference whether one murdered or saved a man, loved God or hated him, praised or blasphemed him.

Nothing is so unreasonable as that. One may teach that God established good and evil by a positive law, or one may assert that there was something good and just before his decree, but that he is not required to conform to it, and that nothing prevents him from acting unjustly and perhaps condemning the innocent. But it all comes to the same thing, offering almost equal dishonour to God. For if justice was established arbitrarily and without any cause, if God came upon it by a kind of chance, as if it were a matter of drawing lots, then his goodness and his wisdom are not manifested in it and there is nothing at all to attach him to it. If it is by a purely arbitrary decree, without any reason, that he has established or created what we call justice and goodness, then he can annul them or change their nature. The result would be that one would have no reason to assume oneself that he will observe them always, as on the assumption that they are founded on reasons it would be possible to say that he will observe them. The same would hold good more or less if his justice were different from ours, if, for example, it were written in his code that it is just to make the innocent eternally unhappy. Also, according to these principles nothing would oblige

God to keep his word or would guarantee us its fulfilment. For why should the law of justice, which states that reasonable promises must be kept, be more inviolable for him than any other laws?   (§ 176)

All this consideration of the nature and implications of the challenge put by 'Socrates' was introduced – it may easily have been forgotten – to show how something becomes part of the progress of philosophy. Interesting and important as it is in itself it also is a good illustration for this purpose. For it is the sort of point which, once well and truly made and developed, cannot properly be ignored. No one with any pretensions to philosophical competence now has any business to argue in any of the areas to which it is relevant without recognizing this kind of challenge, and trying to come to terms with it. This is not to say that mere competence now by the same token also demands some one particular response. Leibniz, as we have been seeing, was scandalized at any suggestion of an answer other than that God approves of what is good for the reason that it is good. Hobbes, on the other hand, unflinchingly accepts the implications of the opposite position. What they have in common is that both see that the challenge first put by 'Socrates' in the *Euthyphro* is relevant, where it is, and both see that the opposite answers carry the implications which they do carry.

It is precisely and only because it is in this and other ways possible to assess philosophical expertise independently of any judgement of the truth or falsity of some particular position that we are able to conduct non-partisan university examinations which set questions in philosophy as opposed to questions asking only what some philosopher as a matter of fact said. Nevertheless, although generally distinctions can be seen to be relevant or irrelevant and arguments to be valid or invalid independent of any categorical assessment of the truth or falsity of premises or conclusions, in a particular case a collection of premises may be known to be true; and then, given also suitable valid arguments, we may claim to know the conclusions thus derived from these premises. If from this and that the other follows necessarily, then we may have a choice of taking the argument as either a proof of the other or a disproof of either this or that. But suppose the other is known to be false, then no similar choice remains. It is for this sort of reason that it is possible to hope not just to make progress towards, but actually to reach, some philosophical answers.

I conclude the present section with a passage suggesting an analogy. The image sketched here illustrates the way in which in philosophy there may be progress without finality. Also, to cite a passage containing such an image is to suggest another albeit relatively minor way in which progress is made. Hume in his first *Inquiry* remarked: "In all abstract reasonings there is one point of view which, if we can happily hit, we shall go further towards illustrating the subject than by all the eloquence and copious expression in the world" (§ VII(ii)). Certainly no one could claim to have been sufficiently initiated into philosophy who had never met and felt the power of – say – Plato's great image of The Cave (Ch. II, § 2). The example which follows does not approach that in haunting fascination, but it does satisfy Hume's specification. The passage comes from *The Blue Book* of Ludwig Wittgenstein (1889–1951). This was the first work, printed only posthumously, of the second period of one of the two or three most influential philosophers of our own century:

> Imagine that we had to arrange the books of a library. When we begin the books lie higgledy-piggledy on the floor. Now there would be many ways of sorting them and putting them in their places. One would be to take the books one by one and put each on the shelf in its right place. On the other hand we might take up several books from the floor and put them in a row on a shelf, merely in order to indicate that these books ought to go together in this order. In the course of arranging the library this whole row of books will have to change its place. But it would be wrong to say that therefore putting them together on the shelf was no step towards the final result. In this case, in fact, it is pretty obvious that having put together books which belong together was a definite achievement, even though the whole row of them had to be shifted. But some of the greatest achievements in philosophy could only be compared with taking up some books which seemed to belong together, and putting them on different shelves; nothing more final about their positions than that they no longer lie side by side. The onlooker who doesn't know the difficulty of the task might well think in such a case that nothing at all had been achieved. – The difficulty in philosophy is to say no more than we know. E.g., to see that when we have put two books together in their right order we have not thereby put them in their final places. (pp. 44–45)

§ 3 *An introduction for the lay majority*

In the first section of this chapter I explained how I proposed to compound two approaches to the problem of effecting an introduction to philosophy. In the second I confessed that the whole book is an expression of the conviction that there can be, has been, and ought to be, progress in philosophy; and I developed and defended this perhaps paradoxical notion. The third main point to be made about the project is that I have throughout tried to keep it in mind that the vast majority of those who are introduced to philosophy will not in fact be pursuing this first acquaintance much further, if at all. If the introduction is made publicly in a university or other institution of tertiary education then the chances are, that it will be through some course forming one element in a programme which is not primarily philosophical, and that the inclusion of an element of philosophy in this programme will be justified largely by references to the sharpening of wits and the widening of horizons. If on the other hand the introduction is made privately it will, again in most cases, presumably be to someone who wants to learn something about philosophy in much the same way as he might also want to learn something about astronomy or something about biology. If so he will not be aspiring to be a philosopher, any more than he is hoping to be an astronomer or to be a biologist.

Granted that this is right about introductory courses and introductions to philosophy, and surely it is, then there are several morals not all of which are always taken to heart by everyone responsible for the design and operation of such courses. In the first place, a very obvious but none the less important point, it must be wrong to include more than a strict minimum of material the benefits of which can only be enjoyed by those who go further. One should not ask people laboriously to lay foundations for a building which will never be erected. It is, for instance, as sensible as it is necessary to demand that students starting to learn another language should do a lot of hard memory work of a kind which no one in his senses would try to justify as worth while in itself; and to point to the rewards to come once the initial grind is done with. It becomes perfectly preposterous if – with the defenders of the elementary Latin admission requirement of the older English universities – you demand this of people who you know will not be continuing to collect the post-dated rewards.

In the second place, a deliberate and constant effort needs to be made to ensure that the people concerned, and above all precisely those who will not be nourishing their first acquaintance with philosophy into a lifelong friendship, do actually get some of the advantages which advocates of such courses claim for them. Thus it is said of philosophy, as it is said of every other not obviously utilitarian and career-oriented study, that it can be a mental training invaluable in any walk of life whatever. This claim is in fact made with equal assurance for all such studies, and for others too. It is made despite the accumulation of psychological evidence suggesting that there really is no such thing as the supposed phenomenon of the transfer of training, by which a skill acquired in one area would ease the acquisition or improvement of other quite different skills in other areas.

However, the spokesman for philosophy has no call to be disturbed by such psychological evidence. He can make this claim for philosophy without thereby presupposing any psychologically questionable doctrine. For philosophy, as the word is understood here, is concerned first, last and all the time with argument. (It is, incidentally, because most of what is labelled *Eastern Philosophy* is not so concerned – rather than for any reasons of European parochialism – that this book draws no materials from any sources east of Suez. Such works of the classical Chinese Sages as the *Analects* of Confucius are in their own kind great. But that does not make them in the present sense philosophy.) Since this is in large part what philosophy is, a training in philosophy must involve a training both in arguing soundly and in assessing the soundness of arguments. To apply a training of this sort on another field is not a matter of somehow having been by acquiring it made more apt to learn how to do something totally different, but only of applying this very training to other arguments in some other area.

Since this possibility of application elsewhere provides the main subsidiary justification for studying philosophy at all, the study needs to be pursued in such a way as to make the most of the possibility. It is with this in mind that I make a point of picking out and labelling patterns of argument, and particularly fallacies, which it is important to recognize not only in philosophy but also in all the other contexts where they occur. It would, for instance, be a very easy yet worthwhile field exercise to collect from extra-curricular discussions a few specimens of the But-there-is-always-someone-who-will-never-agree Diversion, carefully rejecting as not genuine any of these where the reference to insurmountable disagreement happens in fact to be relevant to the question at issue. Again, it is with the same ulterior aim also in view that I persistently insist on the strict usage of certain non-technical, or at most only semi-technical, key terms such as *fallacy, valid* or *invalid, true* or *false, know* and *refute*.

The sloppy common abusage of these terms is a mark not of a venial informality of expression but of a blunt and clumsy imprecision of thought. The crucial points about the first five in the list just given have been made already. But these cruces are so fundamental as to bear reiteration. A fallacy is, strictly, a defect in argument. It is thus incorrect to speak of the assertion that the planet Venus is populated by androids as a fallacy. Certainly any such assertion would be in error. But what precisely is wrong is that it is false and not true. Since it is not itself an argument it cannot be invalid or, for that matter, valid. About knowledge and refutation the first step towards precision of thought is to insist that *know* is not a synonym for *believe,* nor *refute* simply equivalent to *deny.* To say that Hegel knew this, or that Descartes refuted that, is to lay yourself open to challenge about the adequacy of their warrants for claiming to know the one thing, or to have refuted the other. 'No doubt Hegel did behave as if he knew, but had he really got sufficient reason to warrant his conviction; and, furthermore, was his belief actually true at all?' 'Perhaps Descartes did deny it, yet did he succeed in showing that it is false?' And of course, here as always, perfectly correct verbal usage may be observed in an utterance which is not in its content and its implications itself correct. Words may indeed be precisely used precisely in order to say or to suggest things which are, and are perhaps even by the user known to be, false. Thus, shortly after the Six Day War of 1967, the Moscow newspaper *Izvestia* sadly editorialized that many of the countries of black Africa had "not yet come to know that Israeli aggression is directed against the whole anti-colonialist movement in that continent".

Mental training is all very well. Nevertheless, however relevant and powerful we may make the main subsidiary justification in those terms, the essential and primary reason for doing philosophy must always be an interest in the solution of philosophical problems. If this primary reason is to be made relevant to the great majority of those who actually are introduced to philosophy, then the questions selected for treatment must be those which either already do or can fairly easily be made to interest intellectually lively laymen. To some this might, especially perhaps in our time, suggest a concentration on moral and political or, more widely, social philosophy. I could, I think, one day be persuaded to produce a book on the present lines in that area. But such a book would have to leave out too much of what even the briefest introduction to philosophy in general must contain. Thus it could scarcely find place for more than one of Kant's famous trio of great philosophical topics – God, freedom, and immortality. Here all three have their chapters (Ch. VI, VII, and IV). Again, social philosophy cannot compass 'Perception and "the External World" ' (Ch. X); and yet, thanks largely to Descartes, it is part of everyone's stereotype of the philosopher that he pretends to doubt the most certain deliverances of common sense and common experience (Ch. IX).

37

The one indispensable which such a different book would also have to contain is a discussion of 'The Nature of Value', of how far ethical and other norms are subjective or relative and how far objective or absolute (Ch. III).

Another consideration affecting the choice of areas to be covered in the present general introduction, and carrying rather more weight in determining the manner of their treatment, is the desire to give some hearing both to all the very greatest figures and to certain main opposing traditions. A similar book confined to social philosophy would naturally give a lot of space to Hegel and Rousseau, who are in the present production seen only in the wings, but could only very artificially find any place at all for Descartes, from whom the modern period in philosophy is now considered to have begun. One of these pairs of opposing traditions is provided for within the framework of the chapter on 'Survival and Immortality': we have there to contrast Platonic or Platonic-Cartesian with Aristotelian views of the nature of man. Another, the contrast between 'Rationalism and Empiricism', demands a separate chapter (Ch. XI).

Since there appears to be no natural succession determining a single order in which these almost self-selected topics need to be taken I have imposed a rather artificial grouping of chapters into three parts. In Part One the link is Plato's Theory of Forms (or Ideas). The three topics of Part Two were all matters of special concern to the philosopher theologian St Thomas Aquinas. Part Three starts, as did the whole modern period in philosophy, from Descartes (Ch. VIII). The three Parts may thus seem to correspond with the triadic division, ancient, medieval, and modern. So in a very limited way they do. Yet any idea of a radical separation on these lines, and still more any notion of a smooth and steady advance in this succession, would be wholly mistaken. Although, as we argued in the previous section, there can be and is progress in philosophy, it is not such that Kant renders Locke obsolete or Berkeley becomes too antique to have anything to say to Mill. The fact that the discussions of the first Part both collectively and singly start from Plato does not mean either that later writers are disqualified from participation, or that the subjects of these earlier chapters belong to a reserve labelled *Ancient Philosophy*. To the question, 'When shall we be getting on to contemporary philosophy?' the appropriate answer comes in the manner of a Chinese Sage, 'When shall we not be doing contemporary philosophy?'

Part One

CHAPTER II

Plato and the Theory of Forms

§1 *Starting with Plato*

A. N. Whitehead is often quoted, or misquoted, as saying that the whole later development of Western philosophy can be regarded as a series of extended footnotes to Plato. This is, of course, an exaggeration; while in any case all such claims about what can be seen as what leave open the possibility of other and perhaps better points of view. Nevertheless it is a good exaggeration from which to begin. First, for the pedestrian but fundamental reason that he is the first philosopher in our sense of the word to have left a substantial body of writing which is in fact still extant. Plato's works have all survived, and printed together they make a bumper volume.

By contrast Plato's martyred hero Socrates apparently wrote nothing. So for any knowledge of Socrates we depend upon whatever scholars may be able to infer from other evidence. In fact this evidence is mainly that of Plato himself. Almost all Plato's writings are in dialogue form and, as has been noticed already in Chapter I, in most of these the character 'Socrates' makes the running. But it is scarcely possible to doubt that this 'Socrates' is often a mouthpiece for Plato rather than a faithful representation of the historical Socrates. Of the Pre-Socratic philosophers we possess only fragments whose interpretation is often disputable, or at any rate disputed. Thus from the Classical atomists Leucippus and Democritus we have at first hand only broken extracts measurable in lines – in the case of the former one fragment only, and that doubtfully authentic. Again, our knowledge of Zeno and his famous paradoxes is similarly based on short accounts by others, chiefly Aristotle, and a few quoted fragments. We have, for instance, nothing from Zeno's own pen decisively to settle the question whether he himself construed these paradoxes as proofs of their apparent conclusion, the unreality of motion, or whether, reversing the arguments, he did actually recognize them to be disproofs of some premise doctrine from which they follow as a consequence.

Second, because – partly just for the first reason that they have in fact survived – the works of Plato possess an uniquely strong historic claim to constitute a paradigm by reference to which the word *philosophy* may be defined. It is perhaps putting it a little too strongly to insist, with the Oxford author of the article 'Plato' in *The Concise Encyclopaedia of Western Philosophy and Philosophers*, that "To say that there is little philosophy in a major work by Plato is self-contradictory; or it expresses an arbitrary and improper change in the meaning of the word" (p. 296). Yet certainly, in face of the fact that Plato wrote such a dialogue as the *Theaetetus*, it is quite preposterous to urge that the analysis of the meaning of notions like knowledge is not truly philosophical; that this is somehow a betrayal – for the sake of a bastard philological substitute – of authentic, old-time, traditional philosophy.

A third reason for accepting Plato as our first starting-point is that his works possess an unexcelled literary elegance and charm. Whereas his great junior Aristotle writes – it would seem – only for those whose interest can be taken for granted, Plato has both the gift and the inclination to inspire. Thus, where Aristotle employs illustrations sparingly, and these always tightly harnessed to the immediate expository purposes of the moment, Plato paints verbal pictures which haunt the imagination. And while Aristotle lectures to an anonymous company with no felt surroundings, Plato's dialogues are conducted between three-dimensional characters in settings vividly hinted. Plato's charm indeed is so great that the reader needs constantly to be on his guard. If he is not he may discover, or perhaps more likely not discover, that he has accepted from Plato what he would accept from no one else.

A fourth claim of Plato's works to serve as a paradigm of philosophy is that their author's thought obviously was not static. Since there is no reliable method of dating his compositions which is altogether independent of ideas about Plato's development, questions about the progress of his thought are inevitably to some extent speculative. Yet some inconsistencies between different dialogues are so flagrant that it becomes perverse to attempt to present their author as a lifelong Platonist, presenting on successive appropriate occasions different parts and aspects of a single seamless system of truth long since grasped once and for all in its incorrigible entirety. For instance, whether the informed cosmological speculations of the *Timaeus* precede or follow the contemptuous rejection in

The Republic of all empirical science in favour of the developments of a hierarchy of branches of pure mathematics, the author who wrote both dialogues must certainly be allowed to have encompassed a drastic change of mind on a major issue. Still more striking is the evidence of Plato's willingness to criticize even his own distinctive notions severely. Of these, as we shall soon see, his Theory of Forms (or Ideas) is by common consent the most important and remarkable. Yet it is in Plato's own writings that we find the first statements of the classic difficulties for any such view. The fullest and most impressive of these is in the *Parmenides* where, as we shall be seeing (Ch. II, § 3), Plato puts into the mouth of the eponymous hero of the dialogue objections which the young 'Socrates' is unable to answer.

However, although it is wrong to think of Plato as an unteachable teacher his thought did have constant themes and tendencies. The most fundamental of these he characterizes in his own way in *The Sophist*, in what has become one of the classic epitomizing images of philosophy. *The Sophist* is almost universally agreed to have been one of Plato's latest dialogues. Although 'Socrates' does appear at the start the main participants are 'Theaetetus' and a 'Stranger' from Elea. The passage following comes immediately after an intricate technical argument against Parmenides who, like the 'Stranger', was an Eleatic:

STRANGER – We have not gone through all those who give a precise account of what is and what is not. However, let that suffice. Now we must turn our attention to those who speak on a different level, so that we can know from all sources that it is no easier to say what being than what not being is.

THEAETETUS – Very well then, we must go on to them.

STRANGER – Look then, for there seems to be a sort of Battle of the Gods and the Giants going on among them because of their dispute about existence.

THEAETETUS – How so?

STRANGER – One side drags down everything from heaven and the unseen to earth, rudely grasping rocks and trees in their hands. For they get their grip on all such things and they maintain that that alone exists which can be handled and touched. They define body and existence as the same thing, and if anyone says that one of the other things which does not have body exists they completely despise him and are unwilling to listen to another word.

THEAETETUS – Terrible men they are of whom you speak. I myself have met with a lot of them in my time.

STRANGER – For that reason those who battle against them defend themselves very carefully from somewhere above in the unseen, contending that true existence consists in certain incorporeal Forms which are objects of the mind. But they pound the bodies of their opponents and what these call truth into small pieces in their arguments, denouncing it as a sort of motion and becoming. There is always, Theaetetus, an interminable battle going on between the two camps about these issues.
THEAETETUS – True. ($\S\S$ 245E–246C)

It would be ideally appropriate to contrast this report from the side of the Greek Gods with some manifesto by one of the Pre-Socratic Giants, such as Leucippus or Democritus. But since unhappily no such manifesto is extant take instead a memorably militant paragraph from Hobbes. It comes from Chapter XLVI of *Leviathan*, in Part IV, 'The Kingdom of Darkness'. In this Part the general aim is to discredit certain crucial and characteristic doctrines of the Roman Catholic Church, several of which are seen by Hobbes as "tenets of vain philosophy" entering into "the universities, and thence into the Church, partly from Aristotle, partly from blindness of understanding." At this point it is sufficient to know of Abstract Essences and Substantial Forms only that they were supposed to be real things yet without body, and of School Divinity (or Scholasticism) that it was the philosophy and theology done in the Schools (or Universities) of medieval European Christendom:

From these metaphysics, which are mingled with the Scripture to make School Divinity, we are told there be in the world certain Essences separated from bodies, which they call Abstract Essences and Substantial Forms: for the interpretation of which jargon there is need of somewhat more than ordinary attention. . . . The world (I mean not the earth only, that denominates the lovers of it worldly men, but the universe, that is the whole mass of all things that are) is corporeal, that is to say body; and hath the dimensions of magnitude, namely, length, breadth, and depth. Also every part of body is likewise body and hath the like dimensions; and, consequently, every part of the universe is body; and that which is not body is no part of the universe. And because the universe is all, that which is no part of it is nothing; and, consequently, nowhere. Nor does it follow from hence that spirits are nothing. For they have dimensions, and are therefore really bodies, though that name in common speech be given to such bodies only as are visible or palpable, that is, that have some degree of opacity. But for spirits, they call them incorporeal; which is a name of more honour, and may with more piety be attributed to God himself – in whom we consider not what attribute expresseth best his nature, which is incomprehensible, but what best expresseth our desire to honour him.

There is no better statement of metaphysical materialism – the creed of the Giants – than that contained in that last paragraph. In this context materialism has of course, as Hobbes hints, no necessary connection with worldliness or carnality. It is a metaphysical thesis about what there ultimately is; that all there is is, in the last analysis, stuff; and that whatever is not stuff is nonsense. The word *metaphysics* has been and still is used and abused in many ways. It derives from the title of Aristotle's *Metaphysics*, which was itself originally so called simply because it followed after his *Physics*. (*Meta,* here, is Greek for *after*.) In one tolerably precise and useful employment the word refers to the investigation of being, to the study of what there ultimately is, and what it means to say of different sorts of things that they exist. Since this employment fits sufficiently well what Aristotle was doing in his *Metaphysics*, and since the usage involved seems to be in fact the dominant one, it is regularly observed in the present book.

Against such Giants the Gods do indeed have to "defend themselves very carefully". What they require for victory is examples of things which while undoubtedly incorporeal can nevertheless be shown to exist. This is where "certain incorporeal Forms which are objects of the mind" come in. And once any incorporeal objects are admitted – whether Plato's Forms or any others – then not only are the extreme negative claims of the Giants defeated but the door is also ajar for the admission of yet further incorporeals belonging "somewhere above in the unseen". Thus St Augustine (354–430) in his *Confessions* tells how he himself drew this moral:

But then, having read those books of the Platonists, and having been taught by them to seek incorporeal truth, I descried Your invisibilities, understood through the creation; and though cast back, I perceived what it was which through the darkness of my mind I was hindered from contemplating. I became certain that You exist, are infinite, and yet not diffused over finite or infinite space; that You truly exist, being always Yourself the same, in no part and in no motion another or different, and that all other things are truly from You for this single surest reason that they are. (VII § 20)

§ 2 *The theory of Forms*

There is no single passage in Plato's writings to provide us with either his own complete account of what the Theory of Forms involved or his own full case for believing that something of this sort must be true. Usually he takes for granted that his assumptions will be at least in outline familiar, and that he can therefore proceed at once to apply, to develop, or to criticize them. We, consequently, have to piece together from the materials which he provided on various occasions and with various other purposes in view our substitutes for what he does not give us. Again, as we have indicated already, Plato appears to have come to see great force in several objections; and so, presumably, he found himself holding different versions at different times – bolder or less bold perhaps, more or less comprehensive, Special or General as it were. I shall present the most comprehensive version which Plato's texts permit, and shall construe these texts in their boldest possible sense. This happens to be, in this case very reasonably, the traditional established interpretation. Aristotle, who must surely have known what he was talking about, gives a succinct account in his *Metaphysics*:

> The Theory of Forms occurred to its spokesmen because they were persuaded of the truth of the Heracleitean doctrine that all things accessible to the senses are always in a state of flux, so that if knowledge or thought is to have an object there must besides things accessible to the senses be certain other entities which persist; for there is no knowledge of things which are in a state of flux. Socrates occupied himself with the moral virtues, and was the first to look for general definitions in this area. . . . There are two things which may fairly be ascribed to Socrates, arguments by analogy and general definitions, both of which are concerned with the starting-point of knowledge. But whereas Socrates made neither the universal nor the definitions exist separately, others gave them a separate existence and this was the sort of thing to which they gave the name of Forms. So for them it followed by almost the same argument that there are Forms for everything to which general words apply. . . . (1078 B13–35)

Several of Plato's dialogues present a 'Socrates' who fits this description. Typically in these he forces the eponymous hero of the dialogue to recognize that though by common consent that hero provides a splendid example of some particular virtue he nevertheless does not know what that, or any, virtue is. Thus in the *Charmides* 'Charmides' is a model of temperance. Yet he is at a loss to meet the challenge of 'Socrates' to tell him, by producing an adequate definition of *temperance*, what temperance is. In the *Euthyphro*, from which we quoted in Chapter I, 'Euthyphro' is a (remarkably unattractive) specimen of piety. So what that dialogue fails properly to define is the term *piety*. Again and similarly in the *Laches* the fine old soldier 'Laches' is shown to be quite unable satisfactorily to meet this challenge to say, in a definition of *courage,* what courage is. So, 'Socrates' urges, until and unless we know the true answers to questions of this sort, we cannot be in a position to know anything else about either these particular virtues or virtue in general. "For", as he is made to say in the final sentence of Book I of *The Republic*, "when I do not know what justice is I can scarcely know whether it is a virtue or not, and whether he that possesses it is unhappy or happy." This curiously seductive falsism, the wiles of which we shall try to discover later (Ch. IX, § 3), is also urged in the *Meno*:

MENO – Can you tell me, Socrates, whether virtue can be taught? Or is it not taught but acquired by practice? Or is it neither acquired by practice nor learnt, but something which comes to men by nature or in some other way? . . .

SOCRATES – . . . I reproach myself with a total ignorance about virtue. When I do not know what something is, how could I know about its attributes? Or do you think that it is possible for someone who is totally ignorant who Meno is to know whether he is handsome or rich or nobly born, or the opposite of these? . . . In heaven's name, Meno, what do you say virtue is? . . .

MENO – But there is no difficulty, Socrates. In the first place, if you want the virtue of a man, it is easy. This is the virtue of a man, to be competent to manage the affairs of his city state, in managing them to serve his friends well and his enemies ill, and to take good care to avoid suffering harm himself. If you want the virtue of a woman it is not difficult to run through it. She needs to order her household well, looking after things indoors and being obedient to her husband. . . .

SOCRATES – I seem to have been very lucky, Meno, since in seeking one virtue I have discovered a whole swarm of virtues in your keeping. Now, to keep to this image of the swarms, suppose I were to ask you about the real nature of the bee and you said that they are many and various, what would you reply if I asked you, 'Do you say that they are many and various and different one from the other in respect of their being bees? Or do they differ not at all in this but in something else, for

47

example, beauty or size or something else of that sort?' Tell me, what
would you answer if you were questioned in this way?

MENO – This. that there is no difference at all in respect of being bees
between one and another.

SOCRATES – If then I went on to say, 'Well now tell me this, Meno,
what do you say this is in respect of which there is no difference at all
but they are all the same?' You would, I imagine, have something to say
to me?

MENO – Indeed I would.

SOCRATES – And so too with the virtues. Even if they are many and
various they all have one common character whereby they are virtues,
and to which one would be wise to look when one is answering someone
who has asked you to explain what virtue actually is. You do understand
what I am saying?

MENO – I think I do at any rate. . . .

SOCRATES – . . . You appreciate of course that the same applies in every
case. . .?

MENO – Certainly.   (§§ 70A, 71B and E, 72A–D, and 74B)

There is no suggestion here that what the many and various instances
allegedly have in common, that character or characteristic which they all
supposedly share, and their presumed possession of which makes them
instances of whatever it may be, is something separate or separable from
these instances. So I have rendered the Greek word which would elsewhere be translated by the technical term *Form* simply as character. No
doubt the original function of the Forms was, as Aristotle says, to offer
suitably unchanging and incorporeal objects for thought and knowledge.
But obviously at some stage Plato was led to think of them as also providing the answers to all 'What is X?' questions. (These are the questions
which ask 'What is justice?', 'What is piety?', 'What is figure?', or what
have you.) The next passage comes from the *Phaedo*. It will serve to explain
and to verify Aristotle's statement: "But whereas Socrates made neither
the universals nor the definitions exist separately, others gave them a
separate existence and this was the sort of thing to which they gave the
name of Forms." The dramatic setting of the *Phaedo* is the prison in which
'Socrates' is waiting to drink the hemlock. Plato here sets his doctrine of
Forms to work to assist in his attempt to prove the immortality of another
class of putative incorporeal objects, namely, human souls:

SOCRATES – Well, this is what I mean. It is nothing new, but what I
have never stopped saying both in our previous discussion and on other

occasions. For I am going to try to show you the Form of the cause with which I have been concerned. I shall go back to those much spoken of objects and begin from them, assuming that there is such a thing as the Beautiful itself, and the Good, and the Great and all the rest of them. If you grant me this and agree that these things exist I hope starting from these to explain cause to you, and to prove that the soul is immortal.

CEBES – Well, you may indeed take it that I do grant this and go on.

SOCRATES – Then see if you agree with me in the next step. For it seems to me that if anything else is beautiful besides the Beautiful itself it is beautiful for no other reason whatever but that it participates in that Beautiful; and I say the same in all cases. Do you agree with this sort of cause?

CEBES – I do.

SOCRATES – So I still do not understand and cannot grasp these other clever causes. If anyone tells me that what makes something beautiful is having a gorgeous colour or shape or anything else of that sort I take no notice, for I am confused by all those other things. I hold in a simple, unsophisticated, and perhaps foolish way that nothing else makes it beautiful other than the presence or the communion or whatever you like to call it of that thing the Beautiful, wherever or however it comes in. I am not insisting on this last as yet, but only on the point that all beautiful things become beautiful through the Beautiful. For this seems to me to be the safest answer to give to myself and to another person, and if I cleave to this I think I shall never have a fall. It is safe for me or for anyone else to give this answer that beautiful things are beautiful through Beauty. Or do you not agree?

·CEBES – I do.

SOCRATES – And through Greatness great things are great and greater things are greater, while through Smallness smaller things are smaller.

CEBES – Yes. . . .

SOCRATES – Well, then, if one were added to one or if one were divided into two you would be careful not to say that the addition or the division was the cause of the becoming two, would you not? You would speak up loud to say that you know no other way in which an individual can come into existence than by participating in the peculiar being of each Form in which it participates. And so you allow no other cause of becoming two than participation in Duality. Things which are going to be two must participate in this, while whatever is going to be one must participate in Unity. You would ignore these divisions and additions and other such subtleties, leaving them to be explained by wiser men than yourself. You would be afraid of your inexperience and,

49

as the saying goes, of your own shadow. So you would cleave to that safe principle and answer accordingly. And if anyone attacked the principle itself you would see him off, and would not give your answer until you had examined its consequences to see whether they agree with one another or not; and when you had to give a reason for it you would provide this by laying down as another principle whichever of those from the next higher order seemed best, and so on till you came to something sufficient. You would not if you wanted to discover any of the realities jumble things up together, as sophistical debaters do, by discussing both the first principle and its consequences at the same time. (Perhaps they do not give one moment's thought or concern to this, for they are so clever that they can mix everything up and still be able to have a good conceit of themselves.) But you, if you are a philosopher, would I think do as I say. (§§ 100B–E, and 101C–102A)

A first line of approach to the Forms thus becomes clear. The Socratic quest for definitions is epitomized in the 'What is X?' question form. The search for the answer to such questions is seen as the search for what is the same in all cases of X, what all the instances to which the word X is correctly applied have in common, the thing which makes them all X's. The argument which proceeds thus from the many to the one is traditionally labelled the One over Many Argument. In so far as this argument is sound the presumption is that there must be a One for every many – a point which is clearly taken by the 'Socrates' of *The Republic*: "We have regularly assumed a Form for all the manys to which we apply the same name, one Form for each many" (§ 596A).

A second line of approach to the Forms, which Aristotle has told us was originally the first, is traditionally and this time less happily labelled the Argument from the Sciences. Whereas the One over Many Argument proceeds from the facts of predication – the possibility of saying things about things – the Argument from the Sciences is concerned with what are thought to be the presuppositions of knowledge – with what, that is, supposedly has to be so if there is to be true knowledge. Most of the dialogue *Cratylus* is a curiosity of arbitrary etymology and conjectural linguistics. But at the end 'Socrates' puts this Argument from the Sciences to 'Cratylus', who is represented as a follower of the Pre-Socratic Heracleitus:

SOCRATES – Now, my dear Cratylus, consider what I often dream about. Shall we say that there are the Beautiful itself, the Good, and all the rest of them? Or not?

CRATYLUS – I think there are, Socrates.

SOCRATES – Then let us consider the absolute, not whether a particular face is beautiful or something of that sort or even whether it seems that all these things are in a state of flux. Is not the Beautiful itself, in our opinion, always such as it is?

CRATYLUS – Necessarily.

SOCRATES – So how could that which is never in the same state be anything? For if it ever is in the same state then clearly, at any rate at that time, it is not changing. But if it is always in the same state and is the same how could it ever change or move, without abandoning its form?

CRATYLUS – Not at all.

SOCRATES – No, indeed, nor could it be known by anyone. For at the very moment when the man who is going to know it approaches, it would become something else and different, so that it could not be known what sort of thing it is and in what condition. Certainly there is no knowledge which knows what is in no condition.

CRATYLUS – It is as you say.

SOCRATES – And furthermore, Cratylus, we cannot even say that there is Knowledge if all things are changing and nothing remains. For if Knowledge itself does not change from being Knowledge then Knowledge would always remain and would be Knowledge. But if even the Form of Knowledge changed then at the very moment of the change into another Form of Knowledge there would be no Knowledge, and if it is always changing then there would always be no Knowledge. The consequence is that there would be neither knowing nor known. But if there is always that which knows and that which is known, if the Beautiful, the Good, and all the rest of the realities exist, then I do not see how these conditions of which we are now speaking have any resemblance at all to flux and motion. . . .   (§§ 439C–440B)

What is perhaps fundamentally the same argument is presented also in the *Timaeus*. But there the emphasis is epistemological rather than ontological. (Ontology is concerned with what there is, whereas epistemology is the study of how we know, if we know, and what we know.) The argument in the *Timaeus* takes its start from the curious assumption, which Plato elaborated somewhat less enigmatically in *The Republic*, that different cognitive powers or modes – such things as knowledge, ignorance, opinion, and so on – must have each their own different objects (Ch. X, § 5). There is no explicit reference here, as there is in the *Cratylus*, to the doctrine of Heracleitus that everything which exists is in a state of flux. However, since in any case an epistemological argument is being used with the aim of establishing an ontological conclusion, both passages can also be seen as showing how extremely artificial this formidably labelled distinction often is. The speaker is 'Timaeus'; and I have, in the interests of intelligibility, translated rather more freely than usual:

> Is there a Form of Fire, and do all the other several Forms of which we are always speaking exist? Or are the only things which exist those which we see or otherwise perceive through the body, having reality of that kind? Is there nothing at all besides these anywhere, and is it idle talk and no more than a catchphrase when we say that there is always an intelligible Form for everything? . . .
>
> If rational knowledge and true opinion are two categories then certainly these Forms – which we cannot perceive, which are objects of thought only – do exist in their own right. But if on the contrary, as some people believe, there is no difference between rational knowledge and true opinion then we must take the whole lot of things which we perceive through the body as the surest. However, these two must be declared to be two, because they originate separately and remain unlike. For the one of them arises in us by teaching, the other by indoctrination. The one is always accompanied by sound reasons, whereas the other is groundless. The one cannot be shifted by propaganda, whereas the other can. And, while we have to allow that all men have a share in the latter, only the gods and a small class of men participate in rational knowledge.
>
> This being so we must agree that one category involves Form existing in its own right, without beginning and without end . . . unseen and unsensed in other ways; for this is the province of rational knowledge. The second province is one in which things have the same names as, and resemble, things in the first – the sphere of the sensible, of the generated, of what is always being moved about, of things originating in one place and then perishing in another; and this is accessible to opinion aided by perception. . . .   (§§ 51B–52A)

A third line of approach to the Forms is seen in Plato's doctrine of recollection. This is perhaps more immediately interesting than either of the former two, simply because it involves what are supposed to be proofs of the pre-existence of the soul. Since the soul is thought of as the person, albeit construed as being essentially incorporeal, this conclusion is the proposition that we all existed even before we were conceived. We shall have something to say about this remarkable thesis for its own sake in Chapter IV. Here our concern is with that doctrine considered as a pointer to the Forms. Let us in that aspect call it the Argument from Recollection.

There are two versions, of which the following comes in the *Phaedo* where it forms part of an extended case for the immortality of the soul:

SOCRATES – Now consider if this is how it is. We say, do we not, that there is such a thing as Equality? I do not mean of one piece of wood to another or of one stone to another or anything like that, but something else additional to and different from that – Equality itself. Shall we say that there is such a thing? Or not?

SIMMIAS – We shall, my goodness, say that there is. Yes indeed.

SOCRATES – And do we know what it is?

SIMMIAS – Certainly.

SOCRATES – From where did we get our knowledge of it? Is it not from the things we were just this moment speaking of, from seeing equal pieces of wood or stone or what have you? Did we not think it up from these as something different from them? Or do you not agree that it is different? Look at it in this way too. Do not equal stones and equal pieces of wood sometimes, though remaining the same, seem equal to one person but not to another?

SIMMIAS – Surely.

SOCRATES – Well then, did absolute equals ever seem to you unequal; I mean, did Equality ever appear to you to be Inequality?

SIMMIAS – To me it never did, Socrates.

SOCRATES – Well then, from these equal things, which are not the same as Equality itself, you have none the less thought that up and acquired knowledge of it?

SIMMIAS – What you say is very true.

SOCRATES – So it is either like them or unlike them?

SIMMIAS – Quite.

SOCRATES – It makes no difference. Whenever seeing one thing leads you to think of another, whether or not the one is like the other, that must necessarily be recollection.

SIMMIAS – Surely.

SOCRATES – Well then, is this the sort of thing which happens to us in the case of the pieces of wood and the other instances of equality of which we were speaking just now? Do they seem to us to be equal as Equality is equal, or do they somehow fall short of being like Equality?

SIMMIAS – They fall a long way short of it.

SOCRATES – So are we agreed that whenever someone on seeing something thinks 'The thing I can see now wants to be like something else, but falls short of and cannot be the same and is inferior to that something else', then he who thinks this must necessarily have had previous knowledge of the thing he says the other resembles albeit as an inferior?

SIMMIAS – Necessarily.

SOCRATES – Well then, is not this our own situation with regard both to instances of equality and to Equality itself?

SIMMIAS – Absolutely.

SOCRATES – Then necessarily we must have had knowledge of Equality itself before that time when we first saw equal things, and entertained the notion that all such instances aspire yet fail to be the same as Equality itself?

SIMMIAS – That is so.

SOCRATES – And, furthermore, we are agreed that we have not acquired knowledge of it, and that it is impossible to acquire such knowledge except by sight, or touch, or some other sense, for I regard all these as the same?

SIMMIAS – It is all the same, Socrates, at least for the purposes of this argument.

SOCRATES – Then it is from the senses we have to learn that all sensible objects both aspire after Equality, and fall short of it. Is that our view?

SIMMIAS – It is.

SOCRATES – So before we began to see and to hear and to perceive in other ways, we must somehow have acquired knowledge of Equality itself; if we were going to compare the instances of equality provided by the senses with that and to appreciate that these are all eager to be like that, but are inferior to it.

SIMMIAS – This follows necessarily from what has been said before, Socrates.

SOCRATES – And we saw and heard and had the other senses as soon as we were born?

SIMMIAS – Certainly.

SOCRATES – Yet we said we must have acquired knowledge of Equality before these?

SIMMIAS – Yes.

SOCRATES – Then it seems we must have acquired it before we were born?

SIMMIAS – That is how it seems.

SOCRATES – Now if we had acquired that knowledge before we were born, and were born with it, then we knew both before we were born and immediately then, not only Equality, and the Greater and the Less, but all such things? For our present argument is concerned with Equality no more than with the Beautiful and the Good and the Just and the Holy and, in a word, with all those things which we stamp with the seal of 'That which is' when we ask questions in our questionings and give answers in our answerings. So, necessarily, we must have acquired the knowledge of all these things before we were born.

SIMMIAS – That is so.

SOCRATES – And if in each case after acquiring it we have not forgotten we must have been born knowing them and we must know them throughout our lives. For to know is to have acquired knowledge, to have it, and not to have lost it. And is not this loss of knowledge, Simmias, what we mean by forgetting?

SIMMIAS – Absolutely so, Socrates.

SOCRATES – But suppose that we acquired it before we were born and lost it at birth, and suppose that later by the use of our senses we regained that knowledge of these which we had previously possessed, then would not what we call learning be recovering our own knowledge? And should we not be speaking correctly if we called this recollection?

SIMMIAS – Yes indeed. . .

SOCRATES – Then is not this, Simmias, how things stand? If as we are always saying the Beautiful exists, and the Good, and all that sort of being, and if we refer all the deliverances of the senses to this, finding that it existed before and is now ours, and if we liken these things to it, does it not follow necessarily that just as these Forms exist so our souls existed before we were born? And if the Forms do not exist then the account we have given must be all wrong. Is this how things stand, and is it equally certain both that these things exist and that our souls existed even before we were born; whereas if they do not, neither did our souls?

SIMMIAS – That is splendid, Socrates. It seems to me that there is the same certainty, and that our argument comes to the fine conclusion both that our souls existed before we were born and likewise that the sort of things of which you speak do exist. For there is nothing so manifest to me as this, that all such things quintessentially are – the Beautiful, and the Good, and all the others which you were speaking of just now. And it seems to me that this has been adequately demonstrated.
(§§ 74A–75E and 76D–77A)

We have now followed three main lines of argument which all converge on the Forms. The movements of thought should be clear even if – to those who are by temperament Giants rather than Gods – not fully convincing. The presentation of these movements serves at the same time as the most intelligible characterization of Plato's conclusions. Thus the One over Many Argument urges that wherever we apply one general word to many particular instances there must be one thing which makes all these particulars instances of whatever it may be; while, surely, to enquire after the nature of Goodness itself is not the same as to investigate a lot of individual cases in which we can apply the word *good*. Plato construes this making as some sort of causation. Correspondingly, he interprets the difference as a matter of Goodness itself being another and very special sort of object – inevitably an incorporeal object. Next, in the Argument from the Sciences, it is maintained that if there is to be knowledge it can only be of the unchanging. But, while all ordinary things are subject to change, Goodness, Justice, Equality, Twoness, and so on cannot change. Plato is inclined to make acquaintance with a person – knowing who Meno is – his paradigm for knowledge. Hence truly to know is to be acquainted with the eternal Forms. Finally, in the *Phaedo* version of the Argument from Recollection, the contention is that it is a presupposition of our capacity to recognize that in all actual instances in which everyday things are said to be equal really they are only approximately equal, that we must have been antecedently acquainted with Equality itself.

It is important to notice that Plato wants to make his Form of Equality, or whatever it may be, a criterion which is at the same time an ideal exemplar. The Form of Equality must be perfectly equal, the Form of the Good must be pre-eminently good, and so on: "For it seems to me that if anything else is beautiful besides the Beautiful itself it is beautiful for no other reason whatever but that it participates in that Beautiful; and I say the same in all cases" (*Phaedo*, § 100C).

This suggests a fourth line of approach to the Forms. If there are Forms such as have been described then it should be possible to settle any question whether this here should or should not be characterized as a such and such by reference to the appropriate Form: "It was agreed that each of the Forms exists, and that the other things which partake of these get their names from them" (*Phaedo*, § 102B). So if we are in doubt about the justice of some piece of conduct or the beauty of some physical object then we have only to compare the supposed instance with the Form itself in order to settle the issue once and for all. Certainly one large element in the appeal to Plato of his doctrine of Forms was their promise to provide simultaneously both stable, knowable standards of value and ideally perfect exemplars of those values. Also, granted always that we do know some moral or other value truths, and granted too that some Argument from the Sciences is sound, then perhaps we might be able to infer the existence of some value Forms as the necessary presuppositions of such knowledge.

Whatever may be thought of this as a suggested proof of the existence of Forms there is no doubt but that Plato himself made the most of this aspect of his theory. Above all it provided the basis for his consciously paradoxical thesis that philosophers should rule, and that rulers should be philosophers. For the word *philosopher* is being implicitly redefined to mean "one who knows the Forms", and it is precisely and only in virtue of this knowledge that the philosopher's philosophy becomes his qualification for government. So Plato's first utopia *The Republic* is to be ruled strictly and austerely by the largely hereditary caste of Guardians, and these Guardians become qualified to serve in a self-perpetuating, salaried oligarchy because, thanks to their special talents and training, they are privileged to enjoy this the only true knowledge:

SOCRATES – Unless either philosophers begin to rule as kings in the cities or those who are now called kings and bosses start doing philosophy genuinely and adequately, until there is a conjunction of these two things – philosophy and political power – while the motley crew of those who at present pursue one or the other separately is compulsorily excluded, until then there will be no end to troubles for our states, my dear Glaucon, nor, I think, for the human race either. Nor will this constitution which we have just been describing be – as far as it can be – realized and see the light of the sun. Now this is the thing which made me hesitate so long to speak, because I saw that it would be a very paradoxical saying. For it is hard to see that no one will be happy in either their private or their public life in any other way. . . .

(§§ 473D–474A)

GLAUCON – Whom do you mean then by the true philosophers?
SOCRATES – Those who love to contemplate the spectacle of truth.
GLAUCON – That is right enough, but how do you construe this?
SOCRATES – It would not be by any means easy to explain it to someone else. But I think you will grant me something of this sort.
GLAUCON – What?
SOCRATES – Since the Fair is opposite to the Foul, they are two.
GLAUCON – Of course.
SOCRATES – So since they are two, each is one.
GLAUCON – That also.
SOCRATES – And about the Just and the Unjust, and the Good and the Bad and all the Forms the same statement holds, that in itself each is one

but that through their communion with activities and bodies and one another each appears to be many aspects everywhere?

GLAUCON – Right.

SOCRATES – This then is my division. I put on one side those of whom you were just now speaking, the lovers of spectacles and lovers of crafts and practical men. And I put on the other side again those with whom our argument is concerned, those whom alone it would be correct to call philosophers.

GLAUCON – What do you mean?

SOCRATES – The one lot, the lovers of spectacles and lovers of sounds delight in fine voices and colours and shapes and everything that art fashions from things of that sort. But their minds are incapable of seeing and delighting in the nature of the Beautiful itself.

GLAUCON – Yes, that is how it is.

SOCRATES – The others, capable of approaching the Beautiful itself and seeing it in itself, would be a mere handful, would they not?

GLAUCON – Yes indeed.

SOCRATES – He, then, who believes in beautiful things but neither believes in Beauty itself nor is capable of following should anyone lead him towards knowledge of it, do you think he lives awake or in a dream? Just consider. Is not to dream this, for someone to think that something which is like something is not like it but is the very thing which it resembles; and this regardless of whether he is asleep or awake?

GLAUCON – I should certainly say that that is what dreaming is.

SOCRATES – Well then, take the opposite case of the man who believes in a Beautiful itself and is capable of distinguishing it and the things which participate in it, and who neither believes that the things which participate are it nor that it is the things which participate. What about this one? Do you think he lives awake or in a dream?

GLAUCON – He is very much awake.

SOCRATES – We should, therefore, be right to call his mental condition knowledge, as the condition of one who knows, but that of the other man opinion, as the condition of one who opines?

GLAUCON – Absolutely ...   (§§ 475E–476E)

SOCRATES – So now, Glaucon, after a long and weary journey our argument has at last made clear who are the philosophers, or lovers of wisdom, and who are not. . . . Since the philosophers are those who are capable of grasping what is eternal and unchanging, while those who are not but wander amid all sorts of aspects of all sorts of things are not philosophers, which of two ought to be the leaders of the state?

GLAUCON – What would be a fair statement of the case?

SOCRATES – Whichever appear capable of guarding the laws and practices of the state, these we should establish as Guardians.

GLAUCON – Right.

SOCRATES – Is this then clear, whether the guardian who is to keep watch over anything ought to be blind or sharp-sighted?

GLAUCON – How could it fail to be clear?

SOCRATES – Then do you think that there is any difference between the blind and those who are deprived of the true knowledge of the essences of things, and who have no vivid pattern in their souls, and who cannot, like painters, look away at the perfect truth as their model, and always with reference to and in the exactest possible contemplation of it establish in this world too the norms of the beautiful, the just and the good, where they need to be established, and where they are established to guard them and keep them safe?

GLAUCON – No, in heaven's name there is not much difference.

(§§ 484A–484D)

If all that has gone before about the existence and the nature of Forms is granted, and in particular if it is allowed both that for every many there must be a One and that each of these Ones must itself possess in pre-eminent degree that characteristic of which it is the Form, then – it surely follows – there will have to be a further supreme Form bearing to all the many Forms the same relation which each of these Ones bears to its own many particular instances. For, according to the theory, all the many Forms exist, and they all constitute actual ideal realizations of whatever it is of which each is the Form. So the supreme Form must be at the same time the Form of both existence and perfection. Also, since every Form is thought of as in some way causing the particular instances of whatever it may be to be what they are, this supreme Form of existence and perfection must in its turn in the same not fully intelligible way be the ultimate source of all goodness and reality. It is thus by the internal logic of the theory itself that Plato is driven onwards and upwards to the Form of the Good as the necessary unifying principle – the coping stone for the whole construction. And it is because he has already, and very naturally, taken it for obvious that every Form must be the pre-eminent exemplar of that of which it is the Form that this supreme Form becomes the Form of both the Good and the Real. Once Plato has arrived by this route at an eternal unchanging, incorporeal object which is both supremely good and supremely real, and which is at the same time the ultimate cause and origin of all goodness and being, it becomes neither surprising nor incongruous that he should speak of this his Form of the Good in many of the terms in which mystics tend to speak of their God.

The passages in *The Republic* about the Form of the Good have had a remarkable influence. It was from them that Plotinus in the 200's of our era derived the central notion of the philosophy which was later to become known as Neo-Platonism, and the ideas of Plotinus for centuries played a part in shaping the intellectual traditions first of Christianity and then of Islam. It is sometimes asserted, mainly by those influenced by Neo-Scholastic and Scholastic ideas, that it is an axiom of metaphysics "that *goodness* and *being* are convertible terms", that is to say, are synonyms. This strange claim will become more intelligible, though remaining both false and in its eternity-serving implications obnoxious, if we are able to recognize and to understand its ultimate source in Plato's conception of the Form of the Good. This is introduced in *The Republic* as that object above all which the Guardians will need to know if they are to do their job as philosopher kings:

SOCRATES – ... For you have often heard that the greatest object of knowledge is the Form of the Good, by which just and all other things become useful and beneficial. And now you are almost certain that I am going to talk about this, and to say about it that we have no adequate knowledge of it. But if we do not know this, then even if we knew everything else but this perfectly, you appreciate that it would profit us nothing; exactly like possessing something without possessing the good. Or do you think there is any advantage in possessing everything except what is good, or in understanding everything except the good – understanding nothing that is fine and good?
GLAUCON – Heavens no, I do not ...
SOCRATES – But, furthermore, you know this too, that to the vulgar pleasure seems to be the good, and to the more refined, understanding.
GLAUCON – Of course. ....   (§ 505 A–B)

SOCRATES – So it is apparent that there are many and great disputes about it?
GLAUCON – Certainly.
SOCRATES – Again, it is apparent that while many would in practice, possession, and opinion choose what seemed, even if it were not, just and fine, no one would be satisfied to have what only seemed good. Instead in this case they pursue reality, and everyone despises appearance.
GLAUCON – Just so.
SOCRATES – Then can we say that the best men in the state, those to

whom we are going to entrust everything, ought to be kept in the dark about something of this kind and this importance – something which every soul pursues and for the sake of which he does everything he does? Everyone has an intuition of its reality, but is baffled and unable to get an adequate grasp of what it is or to acquire about it a stable conviction as about other things; and so fails to get any profit even from the other things.

GLAUCON – These men least of all.

SOCRATES – Certainly I think that just and fine things would not have got a guardian who was worth much if he did not know how these are good; and my guess is that no one will know them properly until he knows that.

GLAUCON – You guess well.

SOCRATES – So our constitution will only be perfectly organized when a guardian who knows these things oversees it?

GLAUCON – Necessarily. . . .   (§§ 505D–506B)

SOCRATES – We say that there are many beautiful things, and many good things, and so on; and we distinguish these in our arguments.

GLAUCON – We do.

SOCRATES – And we postulate the Beautiful itself, and the Good itself, and so on, in all the cases where previously we spoke of many; and having turned about and postulated a single Form on the basis of each many being One we call that what it is.

GLAUCON – That is so.

SOCRATES – And we say that the one lot of things can be seen but not thought, while the other – the Forms – can be thought but not seen.

GLAUCON – Absolutely, yes.

SOCRATES – Then with what of ourselves do we see visible things?

GLAUCON – With sight.

SOCRATES – And audible things with hearing, and all other sensible things with all the other senses?

GLAUCON – Surely.

SOCRATES – Have you ever considered how the maker of the senses has lavished by far his greatest efforts on making it possible to see and to be seen?

GLAUCON – I confess that I have not.

SOCRATES – Well, look at it like this. Do sound and hearing stand in need of anything else for one to be heard and for the other to hear, in the absence of which third element the one will not be heard and the other will not hear?

GLAUCON – They stand in need of nothing.

SOCRATES – And I do not think that many of the others, though I do not say all, stand in need of any such element. Or can you think of one?

GLAUCON – No, I cannot.

SOCRATES – But do you not appreciate that sight and what is seen do stand in this need?

GLAUCON – How is that?

SOCRATES – Although the eyes have sight and although the man who has it attempts to use it, and although there is colour in the objects, you appreciate that without the presence of a third thing specifically and naturally directed to this the sight will see nothing and the colours will be unseen.

GLAUCON – What is this thing of which you speak?

SOCRATES – What you call light.

GLAUCON – What you say is true.

SOCRATES – The sense of sight and the capacity to be seen are linked together by a bond which is by very much more admirable than those which unite the others if, that is, light is admirable.

GLAUCON – It certainly is, very much so.

SOCRATES – Which of the gods in heaven can you hold responsible as the one in charge, whose light makes our sight see best and make the things which are seen seen?

GLAUCON – Why, the one which you and everyone else have in mind. For it is clear that you are asking about the sun.

SOCRATES – Is not this the relation of sight to this god?

GLAUCON – What?

SOCRATES – Neither sight nor that in which it lies, what we call the eye, is the sun.

GLAUCON – No.

SOCRATES – But it is, I think, the most sunlike of all the organs of sense.

GLAUCON – By far.

SOCRATES – And does it not hold the power which it possesses, issued from the sun, as something adventitious?

GLAUCON – Certainly, that is so.

SOCRATES – Is it not also true that the sun is not sight, yet, as the cause of it, is seen by sight itself?

GLAUCON – Yes.

SOCRATES – This then you must understand me to have meant by the offspring of the Good which the Good sired as like itself: the relation which the Good has in the world of thought to thought and the objects of thought, this has in the world of sight to sight and the things which are seen.

GLAUCON – How so? Tell me more.

SOCRATES – You appreciate that eyes when you no longer direct them at things whose colours are held in the light of day are dim and like those of the blind, and it is as if they did not have clear sight.

GLAUCON – Yes indeed.

SOCRATES – But, I take it, when it is at things which the sun illuminates they see clearly and sight seems to reside in these same eyes.

GLAUCON – Certainly.

SOCRATES – Now then, think of the case of the soul too in the same way. On the one hand when it has cloven to what truth and reality illuminates it apprehends and knows it and appears to possess reason. But, on the other hand, when it is dealing with what is mingled with darkness – the world of becoming and passing away – it is dim, and conjectures, and shifts its opinions this way and that, and now seems like something lacking reason.

GLAUCON – That is what it does seem like.

SOCRATES – This then, which gives their truth to the objects of knowledge and to the knower his power of knowing, call the Form of the Good, and think of it as the cause of knowledge and of the truth in so far as it is known. Fine as knowledge and truth are you will be right to think of it as something else even finer than these. Just as in the other case it is correct to regard light and sight as sunlike, but not correct to believe that they are the sun, so here it is correct to regard both of these – knowledge and truth – as goodlike, but not correct to believe either of them is the Good. For the possession of the Good is even more admirable.

GLAUCON – You are speaking of an unthinkable fineness if it is the source of knowledge and truth and yet itself exceeds them in fineness. Surely you do not mean that this is pleasure?

SOCRATES – Hush! Consider the likeness of it further in this way.

GLAUCON – How?

SOCRATES – The sun provides, I presume you would say, for the things which are seen not only the power to be seen but also generation, increase and sustenance – though it is not itself generation.

GLAUCON – Yes.

SOCRATES – So, similarly, say that the things which are known not only derive from the Good their being known, but from it comes to them their being and existence also; though the Good is not being but transcends being in dignity and power. (§§ 507B–509B)

The extracts just given are more than usually worth re-reading. It is important to master the argument which apparently demands that the

Theory of Forms be completed with a Form of Forms from which all those many Forms – the only true realities – must derive the characteristics which they themselves share; and to appreciate how this supreme Form of the Good comes to be, along with so much else, the Form of the Real also. It is important too to savour the simile of the sun: this is one of the great Platonic images, and it is one which – as has been said – has had a historically remarkable appeal for the Neo-Platonists and for others. But it is even more important to appreciate that and how the philosophical argument and the poetic imagery are combined. For it is entirely characteristic of the genius of Plato that the supreme object of which he speaks only in the language of worship should have been inferred by him as the ultimate conclusion of a chain of reasoning which starts as an investigation of the supposed presuppositions of the possibilities of knowledge and predication. There can be no adequate introduction to philosophy which does not provide many such examples of the way in which apparently arid and technical matters may be connected with issues of world-outlook and metaphysical belief.

Again, it is worth noticing the contrast here between Plato's ritual genuflexions towards the established polytheism and his obviously authentic attitudes of worship directed towards a wholly different innovation of his own. 'Socrates' is made to ask: "Which of the gods in heaven can you hold responsible as the one in charge, whose light makes our sight see best and makes the things which are seen seen?"; and the phrasing perfectly expresses the established idea of a multiplicity of spatio-temporal gods, each with a particular area of special jurisdiction. The answer is, of course, the sun – supreme in and over the world of the corporeal. But for 'Socrates' the true realities are incorporeal, and their sun is the Form of the Good.

To anyone raised under the shadow of one of the three great theist religions – Judaism, Christianity, or Islam – the attributes of this Platonic object may seem very familiar. He will need to nudge himself to recognize that Plato is here an innovator. Even that final phrase of the last extract, a phrase which has confounded the commentators, may through sounding familiar too easily be taken to be intelligible. When 'Socrates' claims that "from it comes their being and existence also; though the Good is not being but transcends being in dignity and power", the last clause may seem to echo half-remembered theses from some such much-mentioned theologian as Paul Tillich: "God does not exist. He is being-itself beyond essence and existence. Therefore, to argue that God exists is to deny him" (Tillich, I

p. 227). Yet it is precisely from Plato – and indeed from this very passage as mediated through Aristotle, Plotinus, Aquinas and others – that the perplexing notion so strikingly expressed by Tillich himself chiefly derives.

The deceptive familiarity of much which Plato says about his Form of the Good makes it especially necessary carefully to distinguish this idea from that of a personal agent God. Certainly all (other) things are supposed to derive their existence and their excellence from the Form of the Good, and certainly it, like any other Form, must somehow make and cause whatever has these attributes to have them. Yet, equally certainly, it is not supposed actually to be personal; nor to be an agent which could appropriately be said to act in the history of the world, to answer prayers, or to redeem his people Israel. Two distinctions can conveniently be noticed and applied here. The first is that between this Form of the Good in *The Republic* and the Demiurge of the *Timaeus*. The second is between two senses of the word *creation*.

The *Timaeus* is, as has been remarked already, a dialogue of cosmological and scientific speculation. It purports to be an immediate sequel of at least the more political sections of *The Republic*. In it "our best astronomer", the eponymous 'Timaeus' of the dialogue, presents the changing universe as constructed out of already existing elements by a Great Craftsman – "the Maker and Father of the universe" (§ 28C: the universe here specifically does not include the eternal and unchanging Forms). This Great Craftsman has come to be known as a Demiurge, because the Greek word for craftsman was *demiourgos,* and because a technical word was felt to be needed for this sort of idea of a maker of the universe. Although it must be doubtful how far Plato himself would have wanted to accept in a literal sense the talk of a Demiurge which he puts into the mouth of 'Timaeus', this Demiurge is certainly spoken of both as personal and as a very superior agent. In these respects the Demiurge is like the Jehovah of the Old Testament and quite unlike the Form of the Good. But a Demiurge is also by definition not a creator: he does not create the universe out of nothing, but fashions it from materials already available.

The two senses of *creation* can be distinguished as the layman's and the theologian's. In the layman's sense to say that the universe is a or the creation entails that it must have had a beginning. In this interpretation of the word it would not be inconsistent to say that the Creator created the universe but that he then left it entirely to its own devices; as a watchmaker might (not create but) make a watch, and then cease to have any further connection with the product. In the theologian's sense the heart of the matter is not a beginning out of nothing but a constant and absolute dependence. In this interpretation it would not be inconsistent to say both that the universe is God's creation and that it had no beginning and will have no end. For a universe that was without beginning and would be without end could nevertheless be always at every moment totally dependent upon God for its existence; and any universe thus sustained by the indispensable ontological underpropping of its Creator must as such be, in the theologian's sense, a creation. Though the Form of the Good cannot be rated as strictly Creator, for the sufficient reason that it is not thought of as in any way personal, still the relation between it and all other existence would seem to be of precisely the sort which is supposed to obtain between Creator and creation: "The sun . . . for the things which are seen provides not only the power to be seen but also . . . generation, increase, and sustenance. . . . So similarly . . . the things which are known not only derive from the Good their being known, but from it comes their being and existence also . . ." (*The Republic*, § 509B).

The present section can be rounded off appropriately with another and perhaps the most famous and haunting of Plato's great images. Like the Battle of the Gods and the Giants in *The Sophist*, the Cave in *The Republic* has become a perennial symbol of one of the constant themes in Plato, and hence in philosophy. But whereas the former represents the continuing confrontation between metaphysical materialists and those who believe in other, higher, and incorporeal realities this latter is intended to illustrate the difficulties of moving from concern with the world of the sensible to a vision of the intelligible. It is at least as much through such images as by his arguments that Plato became and remains the primal philosophical spokesman for all those who consider our everyday world of common sense and common experience to be less real and less important than some other and immaterial sphere. Both in his arguments and in his images there recur again and again the contrasts which are in this context to re-echo down the centuries. On the one hand there are the corporeal, the visible, the sensible, the changing, the coming to be and passing away; while over against these on the other side there stand the invisible, the intelligible, the unchanging, the eternal without end and without beginning. The former is the illusion to the latter's reality, the shadow to its substance, the truth to its falseness; while to see only the former is really to be blind, to mistake unstable opinion for certain knowledge, to be dreaming yet thinking one is awake:

66

SOCRATES – Next compare our nature as regards education and the lack of it with a situation like this. Picture men as living in an underground cave with a long entrance open to the light across the whole width of the cave. Imagine them as being chained in this since childhood by their legs and their necks so that they have to remain there and see only what is in front of them, and unable because of their fetters to turn their heads. Imagine the light from a fire burning further up and behind them, and between the fire and the prisoners and above them a road along which a low wall has been built – as the exhibitors of puppet-shows have screens in front of the men and display the puppets over these.

GLAUCON – I am imagining it.

SOCRATES – Then imagine men carrying along beside this wall all sorts of apparatus which rises above the wall – statues of men and other living things made out of wood and stone and every sort of material, and probably some of the men who are carrying talking and some silent.

GLAUCON – A strange image you are describing, and strange prisoners.

SOCRATES – They are like us. For in the first place do you think that men like these would have seen anything of themselves and one another except the shadows cast on to the wall of the cave in front of them by the fire?

GLAUCON – How could they, if they had been compelled to keep their heads motionless throughout their lives?

SOCRATES – And what about the objects being carried past them? Would not the same be true?

GLAUCON – Surely.

SOCRATES – So if they were able to talk with one another do you not think that they would believe that in naming what they saw they were naming the passing objects?

GLAUCON – Inevitably.

SOCRATES – Then if the prison had an echo from the wall opposite them whenever one of the people carrying uttered do you think that they would believe that the utterer was anything but the passing shadow?

GLAUCON – Heavens no, I do not.

SOCRATES – So people in such a situation could not but believe that the only true thing was the shadows of the apparatus.

GLAUCON – Quite inevitably.

SOCRATES – Consider then what their release from bonds and cure of folly would be like; if such a thing happened to them in the course of nature. When one was set loose and made to stand up suddenly and turn his neck round and walk and look up towards the light, and when in doing all this he felt pain and when because he was dazzled he was unable to discern the things whose shadows he saw formerly, what do you think he would say if someone said to him that what he had seen previously was nonsense, but that now he was nearer to reality and turned towards things which were more real, he was seeing more correctly? And what if also someone were to show him each of the things that were passing by, and to force him by questioning to answer what it was? Do you not think that he would be at a loss, and would believe that the things he used to see were more real than those he was now being shown?

GLAUCON – He would believe that they were far more real.

SOCRATES – If, therefore, someone were to compel him to look towards the light itself his eyes would hurt and he would turn and flee away to the things which he was able to see properly, would he not, believing that these were really clearer than the things he was being shown?

GLAUCON – That is so.

SOCRATES – And if someone were to heave him by force from there up the rough and steep ascent, and not let him go until he had dragged him out into the light of the sun, do you not think that he would be distressed and angry at being hauled along? And when he came to the light would he not with his eyes full of its radiance be unable to see even one of the things now called real?

GLAUCON – No he would not, not right away.

SOCRATES – So he would, I imagine, need to get used to things if he was going to see the things above. And at first he would discern shadows most easily, and after that the reflections of men and other things in water, and later the things themselves. From these he would go on to contemplate things in the heavens and the heavens themselves, more easily by night – looking at the light of the moon and the stars – than by day, looking at the sun and the sun's light.

GLAUCON – Of course.

SOCRATES – Then finally, I suppose, he would be able to look on the sun – not on its reflections in water or in some other alien setting but on the sun itself by itself in its own place – and to contemplate it as it is.

GLAUCON – Inevitably.

SOCRATES – And after this he would reason about it that this it is which provides the seasons and the years, and which presides over all things in the sphere of the visible, and is somehow the cause of all that they saw.

GLAUCON – Obviously he would come to this after all that.

SOCRATES – Well then, if he remembered his first home and what passed for wisdom there and his fellow prisoners of those days, do you not think he would count himself happy in the change and pity them?

GLAUCON – He would indeed. (§§ 514A–516C)

§3 Plato's own criticism of that theory

In the first section of the present chapter I said that, though he seems always to have sided with the Gods as opposed to the Giants, Plato was no lifelong Platonist – no unteachable teacher, one-sidedly instructing others while himself frozen into intellectual immobility. This can now be shown by quoting some of Plato's criticism of his own most distinctive philosophical contribution, the Theory of Forms. It is tempting to cite the *Theaetetus* where, in the course of an enquiry into the nature of knowledge, 'Socrates' almost casually insists on the falsehood of what is in fact the main assumption of the Argument from the Sciences – at least in the *Timaeus* as opposed to the *Cratylus* version (*Theaetetus*, §§ 195E–196C). This is the assumption, much elaborated in *The Republic*, that knowledge and other cognitive faculties or modes are to be distinguished one from another by the fundamental differences between their several supposed peculiar objects. The temptation is, however, to be resisted. For the point made in the *Theaetetus* is not explicitly made against that Argument from the Sciences and its assumptions. We have, therefore, no sufficient positive reason for insisting that Plato himself saw this bearing of his point, much less for attributing to him a creditable wish to draw attention to a decisive objection. Too many thinkers have provided the materials for their own refutation unwittingly for the cautious interpreter to credit them all, for this reason only, with any such intention! But in Plato's *Parmenides* we can find quite unequivocal evidence of radical self-criticism. The young Socrates is presented as confronting his much respected senior Parmenides, accompanied by that most brilliant follower of Parmenides the Zeno of the paradoxes:

PARMENIDES – What an admirable drive for argument you have, Socrates. Tell me, did you invent this distinction which you are using yourself – between the Forms themselves, on the one hand, and the things which partake of these, on the other? And do you believe that there is such an entity as Likeness itself apart from the likeness which we possess, and One, and all the lot of which you heard Zeno speaking just now?

SOCRATES – Yes, I do.

PARMENIDES – And such entities as an abstract Form of the Just, and of the Beautiful, and of the Good, and of all things of this sort too?

SOCRATES – Yes.

PARMENIDES – And what about a Form of Man apart from us and all like us, is there an abstract Form of Man, or of Fire, or even of Water?

SOCRATES – I have often been perplexed, Parmenides, about these, wondering whether I had to say the same about them or to say something else.

PARMENIDES – And are you perplexed too, Socrates, about the ones which would seem ridiculous, like Hair and Mud and Dirt or anything else which is very beastly and worthless – whether you have to say that there is a separate Form for each of these which is again different from what we have to do with, or not?

SOCRATES – By no means, no. These things at any rate are as we see them and it would be quite absurd to believe that there is a Form for any of them. And yet I am sometimes troubled by the thought that the same thing may apply to all cases. Then whenever I find myself in this position I run away from it, being afraid lest I should ruin myself by falling into some abyss of nonsense. So whenever I reach those things which we said just now do have Forms I stay and busy myself with them.

PARMENIDES – Because you are still young, Socrates, and philosophy has not yet got that grip on you which I believe it will get one day. Then you will not despise them, but now because of your youth you still take notice of what people think. Now tell me this. Do you believe, as you say, that there are Forms, and that these other things which partake of them are named after them – for instance that those which partake of Likeness become like, of Greatness great, of Beauty and Justice, beautiful and just?

SOCRATES – Absolutely.

PARMENIDES – Well then, does each individual which partakes partake of the whole Form or of part? Or could there be some other kind of participation over and above these?

SOCRATES – How could there be?

PARMENIDES – So do you believe that the whole Form, being one, is in each of the many, or what?

SOCRATES – Yes it is, for what is to stop it being in them, Parmenides?

PARMENIDES – Then notwithstanding that it is one and the same it is simultaneously and as a whole in many separate entities, and so it would itself be separate from itself.

SOCRATES – No it would not, not if it were like day which is one and the same everywhere, is in many places at once, and is none the less not separate from itself. If it were like this with Forms each one though one and the same might be in the lot simultaneously.

PARMENIDES – Delicious, Socrates; you make one and the same thing to be in many places simultaneously, just as if after spreading a sail over many people you were to say that one whole was over many. Or do you not think that that is about what you are saying?

SOCRATES – Perhaps it is.

PARMENIDES – Would the whole sail be over each person or one part over one and one over another?

SOCRATES – Part over each.

PARMENIDES – Then, Socrates, the Forms themselves are divisible into parts and what partakes of them would partake of a part; and so in each of these it would no longer be the whole Form but only part.

SOCRATES – So it appears.

PARMENIDES – Are you willing, Socrates, to say that the single Form is for us truly divided into parts and yet that it will still be one?

SOCRATES – By no means.

PARMENIDES – No, for consider. Suppose you divide up Greatness itself, then each of the many great things will be great by a smaller part of Greatness than Greatness itself, and will that not appear unreasonable?

SOCRATES – Certainly.

PARMENIDES – Again, will anything, by acquiring a small part of the Equal, possess something by which – while it is less than the Equal itself – what has it will be equal to something else?

SOCRATES – Impossible.

PARMENIDES – Again, suppose one of us has part of the Small, the Small will be greater than this since this is a part of it, and so the Small itself will surely be greater. Yet that to which the subtracted part is added will be smaller, and not greater, than before.

SOCRATES – This could never be.

PARMENIDES – In what way will other things partake in these Forms of yours, Socrates, if they cannot partake either through parts or through the wholes?

SOCRATES – For heaven's sake, that sort of question seems to me by no means easy to settle.

PARMENIDES – Well then, how about this one?

SOCRATES – What is this?

PARMENIDES – I imagine that this is the sort of reason why you think that each Form is one, that whenever you believe that there are many particular great things maybe it seems to you as you review them all that there is some one and the same Form, and you therefore think that the Great is one.

SOCRATES – You are right.

PARMENIDES – Yet if you took the Great itself along with all the other things which are great and reviewed all these in the same way in your mind's eye, would not a further Great appear which must make all these to appear great?

SOCRATES – So it would seem.

PARMENIDES – That is, another Form of Greatness will make its appearance alongside Greatness itself and the things partaking in that; and another in addition to all these through which all these will be great; and so each of your Forms will no longer be one, but they will be infinite in number.   (§§ 130B–132B)

I apologize for interrupting the flow of a most elegant and classical deployment of philosophical criticism. But it is necessary to mention that that last movement – opening with the question of Parmenides "Well then, how about this one?" – has a name, and important to emphasize that in it we have another of those contributions which though short, simple, ancient, and – if you like – negative, are nonetheless decisive and parts of the progress of philosophy. The name of this movement, a name already well established by the time of Aristotle, is *The Third Man Argument*. This name derives from another version which works with a more straight-forward example. Suppose we allow that the One over Many Argument shows that for every many particular instances there has to be a one Form, and suppose we also allow – as would seem natural and obvious – that any Form must itself possess in pre-eminent degree that characteristic of which it is the Form, then both the Form of Man and any particular flesh-and-blood man must be men. But now, by the One over Many Argument, there must be a Third Man – a second Form of Man – to account for the fact that both the flesh-and-blood man and the original Form of Man are correctly described as men. Clearly the regress is infinite so long as each new Form of Man shares the characteristic of manhood first with all flesh-and-blood particular men and next with all previous Forms of Man. Almost equally clearly the regress is also vicious, since the Form as somehow the cause of its particulars must be in some way prior to them.

It is probably impossible to determine precisely what Plato himself considered that the Third Man Argument proved, and at which stages of his own development. But since the intellectual prime mover of the whole

Theory of Forms is the One over Many Argument, and since it is the conjunction of this with the assumption that the One must always itself exemplify the characteristic shared by the many which generates the vicious infinite regress, the correct conclusion must surely be that if anything is to be saved this assumption at least has to go.

It is perhaps a surprising conclusion, and even disturbing. Some inchoate awareness of the Third Man Argument and of this implication may well have been stirring beneath the surface of Plato's mind when he wrote in *The Republic*: "So, similarly, say that the things which are known not only derive from the Good their being known, but from it comes to them their being and existence also; though the Good is not being but transcends being in dignity and power" (§ 509B). For this argument shows that the Form of the Good could not itself be, as Plato had wished and believed, exemplary in goodness; while if and in so far as it is correct to urge that it must also be the Form of Existence and Reality then, by the same token, it cannot itself exist. These conclusions threaten, in particular, Plato's Theory of Forms. But more generally they also threaten the notions of all those who hanker after a God or a God-substitute which (or who) shall be both Goodness itself and yet itself (or himself) pre-eminently good, Existence itself and yet itself (or himself) superlatively existent.

They threaten the Theory of Forms as a whole because it is essential to that theory that Forms should exist separately and in addition to their particulars. But to do that they surely must themselves possess some characteristics. Yet, if – as we surely must – we continue to apply that One over Many Argument which generated the Theory of Forms in the first place, we have to insist that there must be further Forms to account for whatever characteristics the Forms themselves possess. And so on. The same conclusions obviously threaten such theological aspirations; and it is an indication that the threat is recognized, even if it is not actually met, when a radical theologian proclaims paradoxically in a passage quoted once earlier: "God does not exist. He is being-itself. . . . Therefore, to argue that God exists is to deny him" (Tillich, I p. 227: and compare, for criticism, Hook and Edwards).

When we take up the *Parmenides* again where we left off we find Plato's 'Socrates' putting, and 'Parmenides' meeting, an objection to the apparently decisive Third Man Argument. This objection is interesting both for its own sake and because it constitutes a very early example of an extremely common philosophical move, the attempt to show – or often simply to assume – that what must apply in the public physical world does not necessarily apply in the same way, if at all, in the private psychological worlds of human minds:

SOCRATES – But, Parmenides, each of these Forms may be a thought which can exist only in minds. In that case each would be one without being exposed to the consequences which were described just now.

PARMENIDES – Come now, is each of the thoughts one, but a thought of nothing?

SOCRATES – But that is impossible.

PARMENIDES – Then of something?

SOCRATES – Yes.

PARMENIDES – Of something that is or of something that is not?

SOCRATES – Of something that is.

PARMENIDES – And is it not of a single something which that thought thinks of as belonging to all, as being a single idea?

SOCRATES – Yes.

PARMENIDES – Then will not this thing which is thought to be one, being always the same in all cases, be a Form?

SOCRATES – That again seems inescapable.

PARMENIDES – Well then, does not the necessity which compels you to say that all other things partake of Forms oblige you to believe: either that each particular thing is made of thoughts, and that everything thinks; or that being thoughts they are without thought?

SOCRATES – This too seems unreasonable. But, Parmenides, I think the most likely view is this. These Forms exist in nature as patterns, all other things resemble them and are imitations of them, and the participation of all other things in the Forms is nothing else but assimilation to them.

PARMENIDES – Then if anything resembles the Form can that Form be unlike the thing assimilated to it to the extent that that thing has been made to resemble the Form; or is there any way in which the like can be unlike the like?

SOCRATES – There is not.

PARMENIDES – And is it not overwhelmingly necessary that the like should partake of one and the same Form with its like?

SOCRATES – It is.

PARMENIDES – And would not that by partaking of which like things are like be the Form itself?

SOCRATES – Absolutely.

PARMENIDES – So it is not possible for anything to be like the Form, or for the Form to be like anything. Otherwise some further Form will always make its appearance alongside the first, and if that is like anything another again. And the process of a fresh Form always appearing will never stop if the Form is like the thing which partakes of it.

SOCRATES – Perfectly true.

PARMENIDES – Then it is not by likeness that other things partake of Forms; we must look for some other kind of partaking.

SOCRATES – So it seems.

PARMENIDES – Do you see then, Socrates, how great the difficulty is for anyone who maintains that there are Forms existing in their own right?

SOCRATES – Indeed I do.

PARMENIDES – You may be sure, if I may say so, that you have not yet grasped the magnitude of the difficulty involved in your contention that there is in every case a single Form separate from the particulars.

(§§ 132B–133B)

'Parmenides' now proceeds, more tentatively, to develop some seeming consequences of insisting on a really radical difference between abstract Forms (or Ideas) and concrete particular things. Plato, it might here be proposed, has not up till now in making this distinction been drastic enough. By treating *Goodness* as the name of a peculiar and quintessentially good object, or *Manhood* as the caption for some hypothetical everlasting ideal Superman, he is still construing abstract general ideas as if they were concrete particular things. As such the former could indeed stand in relations to, and be engaged in causal transactions with, the latter. Yet really the members of the two categories are so fundamentally different that they never could in any such way meet. Furthermore, and consequently, to know members of the one and their mutual relations must be wholly different from knowing some of the others and theirs. 'Parmenides' even urges that either sort of knowledge must actually be incompatible with the other. From this he draws the further consequence that a God – who would presumably possess the higher kind of knowledge of the higher kind of objects – must be totally detached from, impotent in, and ignorant of, our world. It is worth quoting the central paragraphs of the main argument, while omitting the corollary. For though it is not essential to master either in order to get a good grasp of both the Theory of Forms and Plato's own critique of that theory, this passage does constitute a good specimen of a fairly difficult and sophisticated philosophical argument:

PARMENIDES – So all those Forms which are what they are in relation to other things depend for their existence upon the Forms themselves, in which we partake and from which our several denominations derive.

They are not dependent upon the likenesses – or whatever anyone may choose to call them – which belong to our world; while these things in our world which share the same names with those Forms are also relative to themselves and not to the Forms, and belong to themselves and not to the similarly named Forms.

SOCRATES – What do you mean?

PARMENIDES – It is like this. Suppose one of us is master or slave to someone, he is slave not of Master in the abstract but of the man who is master, or he is master not of Slave in the abstract but of the man who is slave. Both are relations of man with man. But Mastery in the abstract is what it is in relation to Slavery in the abstract, while Slavery similarly is Slavery in the abstract relative to Mastery in the abstract. The things in our world do not have their powers relative to those things, nor those theirs relative to us. But they, as I say, belong to themselves and are relative to themselves, while the things in our world are correspondingly relative to their own kind. You understand what I am saying, do you not?

SOCRATES – Certainly, I understand.   (§§ 133C–134A)

'Parmenides' is in the end willing to allow that these and other massive difficulties inherent in the Theory of Forms may be superable. But his reason for insisting that it is essential to salvage something is not presented as a reason for maintaining the bold original Theory of Forms, as that was expounded in the second section of the present chapter, and as it was being interpreted in the previous criticism. Nevertheless, before that criticism it obviously could have been so presented – and presumably was. In this clearly possible employment it can conveniently be labelled the Argument from Meaning. Aristotle no doubt had his own polemical reasons for mentioning – along with the One over Many Argument and the Arguments from the Sciences – only one specific variety of this general Argument from Meaning: "But according to the argument that we have some conception of what has been destroyed there will be Forms of corruptible things. . . ." (*Metaphysics*, 1079A10). I have, for the reason indicated earlier in the present paragraph, sometimes in this final extract from the *Parmenides* rendered words elsewhere translated by the technical *Form* quite untechnically and noncommittally as *idea*:

SOCRATES – But surely this is an excessively paradoxical argument if it is going to deprive God of knowledge.

PARMENIDES – And yet, Socrates, these difficulties and many more besides are inseparable from the Forms, if these ideas of things exist and each Form is to be treated as a separate object. So the hearer is baffled, and maintains that they do not exist, and even if they do they absolutely must be unknowable by man; and he thinks that in saying this he has a point, and – as I was saying a moment ago – he is mightily hard to convince. It takes a very good man to be able to understand that everything has a class and an abstract essence, and a still more wonderful man to discover and to teach other people all these things after he has analysed them properly.

SOCRATES – I agree with you, Parmenides, for what you say is very much in accord with my own thinking.

PARMENIDES – But on the other hand, Socrates, if in view of all these recent objections and others of the same sort anyone refuses to allow that there are ideas of things, and will not admit any sort of general idea under which each particular is classed, he will not know how to direct his understanding. For he denies that there are ideas – which are always the same – of everything, and in this way he will altogether destroy the possibility of carrying on a discussion. You seem to me to have seized this sort of point very firmly.

SOCRATES – Quite true.

PARMENIDES – Then what will you do about philosophy? Where can you turn if these things are unknown?

SOCRATES – I do not see my way at all, at least at the present moment.

(§§ 134E–135C)

CHAPTER III

The Nature of Value

§ 1 *Plato and the longing for objective values*

"Plato grew up in a period when the established order and accepted standards seemed on the verge of dissolution under the pressure of political events and theoretical criticism. . . . he turned to philosophical speculation as the only direction from which help might come. From one point of view, indeed, the chief aim of Plato's philosophy may be regarded as the attempt to re-establish standards of thought and conduct for a civilization that seemed on the verge of dissolution" (Field, p. 91). No such single point of view can embrace the full richness and complexity of Plato; and, of course, to Plato – as to any other conservative – things always seemed to be going downhill more generally and more swiftly even than they are. But with these provisos this judgement from an excellent survey of *Plato and his Contemporaries* can be accepted as epitomizing one aspect of the appeal of the Theory of Forms. For if, as the 'Socrates' of the *Parmenides* would have it, there are "such entities as an abstract Form of the Just, and of the Beautiful, and of the Good, and of all things of this sort" (§ 130B), then values and ideals are as objective, as absolute, as unchangingly eternal as any heart could desire. And if too this theory, as the 'Socrates' of *The Republic* urges, draws us on by its own inherent logic to an ultimate and supreme Form of the Good and the Real, then not only are these the true values and ideals intrinsic to the unseen yet fundamental structure of the universe but they are also as it were supported and endorsed by the source itself of all goodness and reality. No philosophical spokesman of the objectivity of value could be more thoroughly entrenched.

But before Plato is confronted by any opposite view it is well to have a glimpse of what that "pressure of political events and theoretical criticism" was, both because this will illustrate one way in which philosophical enquiries may be stimulated by concerns which were not originally philosophical at all, and because – at least as regards these particular pressures – "Plato was the child of a time which is still our own" (Popper (1), I p. 173). To set the stage I will quote two famous passages, one from each of the two great Athenian historians of the Classical period. The first, from Herodotus, is a record of and comment on some of the outrages of the Persian King Cambyses:

He did many such mad deeds against the Persians and their allies. While he was living in Memphis he opened up the ancient tombs and examined the corpses. In the same way he came into the temple of Hephaestus and made mock of the image. . . . Also he entered the temple of the Cabeiri into which no one but the priest is allowed to go. . . . It seems to me altogether clear that Cambyses was very mad, otherwise he would never have set himself to ridicule matters of religion and custom. For if anyone put it to all men telling them from all customs to pick out the finest, each would after investigation choose those of his own people. So strong is everyone's belief that the customs of his own people are by far the finest. It is, therefore, not likely that anyone but a madman would make mock of such things. That all men do hold this belief about their customs can be established by this piece of evidence, among many others. Darius when he was King summoned those Greeks who were with him and asked them what sum of money would induce them to make a meal of their dead fathers. And they said that nothing would induce them to do this. Darius then summoned the so-called Callatian Indians, who do eat their parents, and, in the presence of the Greeks (who understood what was said through an interpreter), asked them how much money they would take to burn their dead fathers in a fire. And they raised a great uproar, telling him not to speak of such a thing. So firmly rooted are these matters of habitual usage; and I consider that the poet Pindar was quite right to say that custom is the universal king. (III 37–38)

This characteristic and dramatic tale of a confrontation staged at the court of the Great King of Persia has become a traditional paradigm of the influence upon lively minds of the knowledge that sincerely held notions of what it is proper to do have varied and do vary enormously. There is, therefore, good reason to give further currency to the term *Herodotage,* which has sometimes been employed as a convenient shorthand general word for all anthropological material appearing in comparisons of this sort. Such deservedly popular books as Ruth Benedict's *Patterns of Culture,* and Margaret Mead's *Growing up in New Guinea, Coming of Age in Samoa,* or *Sex and Temperament in Three Primitive Societies,* are specimens of the best

Herodotage of our own time. All Herodotage, from the original archetype to the latest paperback to hit the bookstands, provokes the same fundamental questions, about the possible plasticity of human nature and the limits to this plasticity, and about the status of value in the universe. The first of these two questions is clearly a matter of science rather than of philosophy, since it is straightforwardly a question of what the facts are and would be. But for the Greeks of the Classical period both issues were seen as involved in a favourite antithesis between nature (*phusis,* from which we get our word *physics*) and law or custom or convention (*nomos,* hence such formidable jargon terms as *nomothetic* and *nomological*). Plato in *The Republic* responds to the first of these two questions implicitly in his proposals for the social and political arrangements of a supposedly perfect state, while explicitly giving his answer to the second in terms of the Theory of Forms.

The second quotation from a Classical historian comes from Thucydides on the Peloponnesian War. This war – between Athens and her allies and Sparta and hers – began before Plato was born, lasted with one short intermission until his early manhood, and at Athens was followed first by an oligarchic revolution and later by a decisively successful democratic counter-revolution. This war – like World War II – was in one aspect an international civil conflict: there were in most of the city states involved both oligarchic and democratic factions, the former inclined to look to Sparta and the latter to Athens for outside support. Plato, though an Athenian, was no democrat. He had indeed close family and personal connections with members of the oligarchic junta – "the Thirty Tyrants" – although, according to his Seventh Letter, he was disillusioned by their outrageous behaviour in power. The commentary of Thucydides upon the events which he narrates, given both in his own person and in the form of speeches appropriate to the occasion attributed to other participants, constitutes a treasury of extremely tough-minded political wisdom. It was this which attracted Hobbes to make a translation of Thucydides his first published work, and which led him to praise the historian as "the most politic historiographer that ever writ". The passage quoted here is part of a general consideration occasioned by the savage civil strife at Corcyra (the modern Corfu), the first and pace-setting civil campaign within the general Peloponnesian War:

And so many terrible things happened to cities through civil conflict, things which happen and always will happen so long as the nature of men is the same, but which are worse or milder and differ in their forms according to the variations of the circumstances in each case. In periods of peace and prosperity both states and individuals maintain better dispositions, because they do not fall under necessities against their will. But war, which robs people of the easy supply of their daily wants, is a violent schoolmaster matching most men's tempers to their conditions.

There was, then, civil conflict; and those of the cities which were involved later, through hearing of what had happened earlier, pushed on to further extremes of innovation both in the ingenuity of their schemes for seizing power and in the extravagance of their reprisals. They altered the accepted usage of words in relation to deeds as they thought fit. Reckless audacity was termed courageous loyalty to party; prudent hesitation, specious cowardice; moderation, a cover for spinelessness; and ability to understand all sides, total inertia. Fanatical enthusiasm was rated a man's part; and cautious deliberation, an euphemism for desertion. (III 82–83)

§2 *What* objectivism *and* subjectivism, *in our broad senses, do and do not involve*

Such shifts are, as Thucydides foresaw, still altogether familiar in our own time; especially, although certainly not exclusively, as they are found in the official propaganda of totalitarian regimes. It could be instructive in more than one way to make a collection for oneself, from all sources. Such a collection might perhaps begin with such textbook samples as Adolf Hitler's claim before World War II that National Socialism was true democracy, or the denunciation by the USSR, shortly after that war, of Switzerland as a fascist state; and it could then proceed to add more recent specimens, sometimes – disquietingly – from nearer home. But the immediate reason for mentioning such things is to make the longing for objective values more intelligible and more sympathetic.

The opposite kind of account, the subjectivist, holds that value is not intrinsic to the universe around us, but is somehow some sort of function, or manifestation, or expression, of human desires and human inclinations. From this camp the best champion for our present purposes will be Hume. Certainly predecessors and contemporaries of Plato, especially some of the travelling professional lecturers known as Sophists, advanced various views which were in this wide sense subjectivist. For instance, a view of this sort must have been at least part of what Protagoras meant by his famous slogan: "Man is the measure of all things". But what knowledge we can have of the Sophists has to be founded upon secondary sources, mainly the not always sympathetic and sometimes perhaps plain unreliable representations provided by Plato himself. (Plato wrote whole dialogues named for Hippias of Elis, Gorgias of Leontini, and Protagoras of Abdera; the *Theaetetus* too gives a lot of attention to views attributed to the last-named; and presumably Sophistical ideas are found on the lips of other characters elsewhere.)

However, it is worth delaying a little longer before introducing Hume, in order to remove some very popular misconceptions about what is and is not necessarily being implied by describing a view as, in the senses presently attached to these terms, either objectivist or subjectivist. Anyone who has seized all the main points about what does not follow will already have advanced more deeply here than most.

First, neither *subjectivism* nor *objectivism* is an accepted technical term referring to one specific view. Both are words which always have to be, and are here being, given a particular use before they can be profitably set to work. It will not do, notwithstanding that it is too often done, to announce dashingly and out of the blue that you are a subjectivist about values or about whatever else it may be, as if that made your position perfectly clear to yourself and everyone else. With these terms you have yourself to provide an explanation of the meanings which you are proposing to attach.

Second, both words are in their present employment very general indeed. An extremely wide variety both of specific accounts and of sorts of accounts can be subsumed under each. Examples of other sorts of objectivism besides that of Plato will be displayed in § 4 of this chapter.

Third, this distinction is not to be identified with that between relative and absolute; nor, incidentally, is it true to say that there can never be a categorical correct or incorrect about what is essentially relative. Certainly motion is essentially relative in that it makes no sense to speak of something as being in motion absolutely and not relatively to anything at all. (Whatever Newton and other scientific defenders of absolute motion meant they were certainly not defending the idea in this nonsensical interpretation.) But this essential relativity of motion does not prevent its being the case that, if once a reference point is specified or given by the context, then any statement that something is in motion is either true or false; and no three ways about it.

So it would be quite unsound, if you had concluded that all value judgements are essentially relative, to go on immediately to infer that about these there can, therefore, be no correct or incorrect. It is, on the contrary, perfectly consistent: both, on the one hand, to allow that what, on any particular occasion, I ought to do must in part at least depend on the nature of that occasion; and, on the other hand, to insist that, relative to the actual specifications of all the variables on some given occasion, it may become unambiguously and absolutely right to act in this one particular way. It must now appear obvious too that someone who believes that ethical values are objective can, with entire consistency, insist that the courses of conduct which these values determine must vary partly according to the particular occasions; and hence be relative to them. So the two distinctions are by no means the same.

Fourth, to say that a view is subjectivist is neither to say nor to imply that all valuations must be either in some depreciatory sense merely subjective, or arbitrarily conventional, or matters of purely personal taste important only to the individual. Let us examine these three supposed implications in turn.

Consider first the move from subjective to merely subjective. The first thing to notice is that it is a move. Anyone who says to an audience that value is not objective but subjective, or that people are composed of chemicals and nothing else, or that our brains are enormously complex and sophisticated machines, or anything of the such, must expect to be misreported as having said that values are merely subjective, that people are merely chemicals, that the brain is merely a sophisticated machine, and so on. This must be a misreporting since by the insertion of the little word *merely* statements which were not necessarily disparaging become precisely that.

The second thing to remark is that *merely* and the synonymous *nothing but* are essentially negative qualifications. Anyone who urges that this is merely that by these words exposes himself to the challenge – which ought to be pressed more often than it is – to answer what exactly he is intending thereby to suggest that that is not. Thus to say that people are merely chemicals is no doubt correct if the *merely* is to be construed as denying only that there is any component in a person of a kind not known to chemistry. But if this utterance is to be taken as denying that there is anything more to be said about people than what the chemist can tell us of their chemical composition, then the statement is obviously false. If too it is to be taken to imply that people may properly be treated as one might handle a load of chemicals, then the suggestion is monstrous. Again, and most immediately relevant, one is of course entitled to say of any subjectivist that he is necessarily committed to the thesis that values are merely subjective; provided that that *merely* is saying only and uninterestingly that a subjectivist cannot as such be an objectivist. But it is quite another thing if it is to be taken to imply that because values are not objective therefore valuations have to be either capricious, or unimportant, or both.

The truth is that the line of division between the subjective and the objective just does not coincide with that between the important and the unimportant. Plenty of differences are embedded in the structure of the things around us without this objectivity providing us with any reason why we should care; whereas human cries of distress do constitute urgent grounds of concern, not in spite but because of the fact that they spring immediately from the condition of men.

Our paradigm subjectivist will be the Scottish philosopher and historian David Hume (1711–1776). He was the first major thinker of the modern period to develop a world-outlook which was through and through secular, this-worldly, and man-centred. So for Hume to claim that moral values are rooted in fundamental needs and inclinations of our universal human nature was not to say that they are unimportant. It was, on the contrary, to insist that they must matter to us as much as anything possibly could: ". . . these principles, we must remark, are social and universal; they form, in a manner, the party of humankind against vice or disorder, its common enemy . . ." (*Inquiry concerning the Principles of Morals*, § IX).

Consider next the suggestion that subjectivism necessarily involves that what is subjective must be arbitrarily conventional. The two points to fix here are that not all conventions are arbitrary, and that conventions are not all to be dismissed as mere matters of convention. Both are points which a moment's thought should make obvious. This however seems to be one of the many occasions for adding the comment which the poet A. E. Housman made in one of his scholarly editions of a Classical text: "But thought is a painful process, and a moment is a long time."

The trite but sufficient example to work with is the convention, now embodied in the laws of the land, that you drive on the right-hand side of the highway; or, in Britain and a diminishing minority of other countries, on the left. Certainly, in terms of the old Greek antithesis, this is a matter of law or custom or convention rather than of nature. Certainly too it is an arbitrary matter which side it should be, in the sense that if you could start again from the beginning with a clean slate there would be absolutely no good reason why you should choose one rather than the other: it would be a textbook case of an issue which could appropriately be settled by spinning a coin. But there would be nothing similarly arbitrary about the prior decision to have one or other of these alternative conventions, as opposed to none at all. The same example can also be employed to show that what is a matter of convention, whether to have a convention or not, can be literally a matter of life and death. With only a little more ingenuity a case can be found where this is also true of the question whether to follow one particular convention rather than another. For even in the same area of traffic control conventions can be either safe or lethal.

Turn now to the notion that to say that values are subjective, in our present sense, is to say that they are entirely a matter of individual taste or caprice. The point of urging this, the reason why the suggestion is both pressed and rejected vigorously, is that the second proposition is taken to involve both that value judgements concern no one but the individual who does the valuing and that no values can be in any way independent of the particular likes and dislikes of that individual. Difficult though it is for anyone to draw a satisfactory precise line of demarcation the subjectivist is surely not as such required to deny that there is a vital difference between those affairs which are the proper business of "the party of humankind" and those which concern only each one of us alone. The capricious artistic taste which I manifest in my private study has indeed nothing to do with you; but you may have a preference for kinds of "vice or disorder" which, as threats to the public peace, are everybody's business. Again, the value of anything, construed as its open market price, is certainly not definable in terms of the whims and wishes of any particular individual. Yet, equally certainly, it is in the present sense subjective and not objective. For market prices are "not intrinsic to the universe around us", being in truth indisputably "some sort of function, or manifestation, or expression of human desires and human inclinations".

Consider a further pair of extracts from Hobbes, a writer whose trenchant audacity and tersely brilliant style earns him a place in a book such as this more prominent than might be thought warranted by his relative weight as anything but a political thinker. The first, from Chapter VI of *Leviathan*, is a statement of an extremely radical subjectivist view. This maintains that some (though in Hobbes' view certainly not all) value words are wholly definable in terms of the reactions and inclinations of the particular individual employing these words. For some the term *subjectivist* means exclusively a defender of this kind of extreme and individualist position. This is an entirely legitimate employment of the word;

from which, of course, some of what I have been arguing not to be consequences of its use in our wider sense surely will follow after all. What is not legitimate is to equivocate between the wider and the narrower sense. Commonly this is done by launching an onslaught effective against the scarcely defensible Hobbist outpost and then mistaking it to have disposed of every variety of subjectivism in our wider sense. Hobbes wrote:

But whatsoever is the object of any man's appetite or desire, that is it which he for his part calleth *good*; and the object of his hate and aversion, *evil*; and of his contempt, *vile* and *inconsiderable*. For these words of good, evil, and contemptible are ever used with relation to the person that useth them; there being nothing simply or absolutely so, nor any common rule of good and evil to be taken from the nature of the objects themselves but from the person of the man (where there is no commonwealth), or (in a commonwealth) from the person that representeth it, or from an arbitrator or judge whom men disagreeing shall by consent set up and make his sentence the rule thereof.

The Latin tongue has two words whose significations approach to those of good and evil but are not precisely the same, and those are *pulchrum* and *turpe*. Whereof the former signifies that which by some apparent signs promiseth good, and the latter that which promiseth evil. But in our tongue we have not so general names to express them by. But for *pulchrum* we say in some things *fair*, in others *beautiful*, or *handsome*, or *gallant*, or *honourable*, or *comely*, or *amiable*; and for *turpe*, *foul, deformed, ugly, base, nauseous*, and the like, as the subject shall require. All which words in their proper places signify nothing else but the mien or countenance that promiseth good and evil. So that of good there be three kinds; good in the promise, that is *pulchrum*; good in effect as the end desired, which is called *jucundum* – delightful; and good as the means, which is called *utile* – profitable. And as many for evil: for evil in promise is that they call *turpe*; evil in effect and end is *molestum* – unpleasant, troublesome; and evil in the means *inutile* – unprofitable, hurtful.

It is worth noting that Hobbes is not making here any distinction between moral and aesthetic values. As we shall see better later with Hume it is a good tactic for any kind of subjectivist, remembering that it is proverbial that beauty lies in the eyes of the beholder, to start from the aesthetic and then to try to show that it is the same with other sorts of value. The second Hobbes passage is from Chapter X of *Leviathan*. Here, in his own way, Hobbes introduces values which though still in the wide sense subjective are independent of that individual caprice which he has earlier supposed to be involved essentially in all determinations of good and evil:

> The value, or worth, of a man is as of all other things his price; that is to say, so much as would be given for the use of his power; and therefore is not absolute, but a thing dependent on the need and judgement of another. An able conductor of soldiers is of great price in a time of war present, or imminent, but in peace, not so. A learned and uncorrupt judge is much worth in time of peace, but not so much in war. And as in other things so in men not the seller but the buyer determines the price. For let a man – as most men do – rate themselves at the highest value they can; yet their true value is no more than it is esteemed by others.
>
> The manifestation of the value we set on one another is that which is commonly called honouring, and dishonouring. To value a man at a high rate is to honour him, at a low rate to dishonour him. . . . The public worth of a man, which is the value set on him by the commonwealth, is that which men commonly call dignity. And this value of him by the commonwealth is understood by offices of command, judicature, public employment; or by names and titles, introduced for distinction of such value.
>
> To pray to another for aid of any kind is to honour, because a sign we have an opinion he has power to help, and the more difficult the aid is the more is the honour. To obey is to honour, because no man obeys them whom they think have no power to help or hurt them. And, consequently, to disobey is to dishonour. To give great gifts to a man is to honour him, because it is buying a protection and acknowledging of power. To give little gifts is to dishonour, because it is but almes and signifies an opinion of the need of small helps. To be sedulous in promoting another's good, also to flatter, is to honour – as a sign we seek his protection or aid. To neglect is to dishonour. . . . To show any sign of love, or fear, of another is to honour. For both to love and to fear is to value.

§3 *The subjectivism of Hume*

Hobbes offered the account of value just quoted only by the way. For *Leviathan*, though it contains pungent and seminal remarks on almost everything else as well, is primarily a re-presentation of the Hobbist theory of the nature and function of the state. That theory was regarded by Hobbes as a major contribution to the new science. It was supposed to constitute a political science strictly comparable with the physics of Galileo and the anatomy of Harvey. (Immodestly Hobbes wrote, in the Preface to his *de Corpore*: "Galileus ... was the first that opened to us the gate of natural philosophy universal", while "the science of man's body ... was first discovered . . . by our countryman Dr Harvey"; but "civil philosophy is no older than my own book *De Cive*.")

A century later Hume too thought of himself as doing what we should now call science rather than philosophy. His *Treatise of Human Nature* is subtitled "An Attempt to introduce the experimental method of reasoning into moral subjects". It is easy to be confused by differences of terminology, since the expression *moral subjects* was in Hume's day equivalent to *human studies*. It covered all investigations of man and society. Furthermore, Hume in his Introduction goes out of his way to make the misguided claim that true experiment is impossible in these subjects – albeit without drawing the moral that for him the word should in that case be not *experimental* but rather *experiential*. A key concept of the *Treatise*, and for us at this stage the key concept, is that of a sort of Copernican revolution in reverse. Whereas the astronomy of Copernicus (1473–1543) had shifted the earth – and hence, apparently, man – from the centre of the universe, the new moral science being opened up by Hume promised to restore humanity to the middle of the map of knowledge: ". . . all the sciences have a relation, greater or less, to human nature. . . . It is impossible to tell what changes and improvements we might make in these sciences were we thoroughly acquainted with the extent and force of human understanding, and could explain the nature of the ideas we employ, and of the operations we perform in our reasonings" (*Treatise,* Introduction).

The notion of studying the nature, and especially the limitations, of our human understanding had been introduced by the very English Englishman John Locke (1632–1704). It was the original and structuring idea of his *Essay concerning Human Understanding*. (See Ch. IX § 3, below.) But Hume's special model for the way in which the discoveries of a new science of man might reshape the map of knowledge was provided by what he – and everybody else – took to be the discoveries of physics about the difference between primary and secondary qualities. This distinction, like many great antitheses, has both had a long history and taken many forms. Its core is a contrast between, on the one hand, those qualities (called primary) which things are supposed truly to have in themselves, and, on the other hand, those other only so-called qualities (termed secondary) which are really only reactions in us occasioned by other and primary characteristics.

A distinction of this sort seems to have been developed first by the Classical Greek atomists. Certainly Galileo makes much of it, and it became one of the commonplaces of the new science — what Hume calls "modern philosophy". Since it was Hume's first ambition, as that of several others later, to become the Newton of the moral sciences it is appropriate to take our illustration here from the *Opticks*:

> The ... light and rays which appear red, or, rather, make objects appear so I call rubrific or red-making; those which make objects appear yellow, green, blue, and violet, I call yellow-making, green-making, violet-making, and so of the rest. And, if at any time I speak of light and rays as coloured or endued with colours, I would be understood to speak not philosophically and properly, but grossly, and according to such conceptions as vulgar people in seeing all these experiments would be apt to frame. For the rays, to speak properly, are not coloured. In them there is nothing else than a certain power and disposition to stir up a sensation of this or that colour. For as sound in a bell, or musical string, or other sounding body, is nothing but a trembling motion, and in the air nothing but that motion propagated from the object, and in the sensorium it is a sense of that motion under the form of sound; so colours in the object are nothing but a disposition to reflect this or that sort of rays more copiously than the rest. In the rays they are nothing but their dispositions to propagate this or that motion into the sensorium, and in the sensorium they are sensations of those motions under the form of colours.
>
> (I (ii), Definition to the second Theorem under the second Proposition. The word *sensorium* means literally *the thing of sensing*. No harm will come of interpreting it here as equivalent to *mind*.)

This then is the model for Hume's subjectivism. It is a model which leaves no room for individual caprice. If I am looking at an orange I do not choose what colour I see it as having. Also, the presumption will be in favour of some fundamental uniformity. For though some people cannot see at all, and others suffer from various disorders of colour vision, the overwhelming majority see the same things as having the same colours. And this presumption is one which, as we have seen, Hume was in fact prepared to defend. His first statement of his subjectivism comes in the *Treatise*:

> But can there be any difficulty in proving that vice and virtue are not matters of fact, whose existence we can infer by reason? Take any action allowed to be vicious: wilful murder, for instance. Examine it in all

lights, and see if you can find that matter of fact, or real existence, which you call vice. In whichever way you take it, you find only certain passions, motives, volitions and thoughts. There is no other matter of fact in the case. The vice entirely escapes you, as long as you consider the object. You never can find it, till you turn your reflexion into your own breast, and find a sentiment of disapprobation, which arises in you, towards this action. Here is a matter of fact, but it . . . lies in yourself, not in the object. So that when you pronounce any action or character to be vicious, you mean nothing, but that, from the constitution of your nature you have a feeling or sentiment of blame from the contemplation of it. Vice and virtue, therefore, may be compared to sounds, colours, heat and cold, which, according to modern philosophy, are not qualities in objects, but perceptions in the mind. And this discovery in morals, like that other in physics, is to be regarded as a considerable advancement of the speculative sciences; though, like that too, it has little or no influence on practice. Nothing can be more real, or concern us more, than our own sentiments of pleasure and uneasiness; and if these be favourable to virtue, and unfavourable to vice, no more can be requisite to the regulation of our conduct and behaviour.   (III (i) 1)

Immediately after this Hume adds a paragraph drawing a fundamental distinction which, he insists, "is . . . of the last consequence". It is indeed, and the paragraph will be quoted later. But since Hume himself does not put this crucial distinction visibly to work it is better to look first at his argument as he presents it in the second version of his account. The *Treatise*, in Hume's own much repeated words, "fell dead-born from the press". Partly for this reason he later recast whatever he then regarded as most valuable into what were in the event two fresh books: the one – *An Inquiry concerning Human Understanding*, with its title deliberately echoing that of Locke's *Essay* – is known as the first *Inquiry*; and the other – *An Inquiry concerning the Principles of Morals* – correspondingly as the second. A sentence at the end of the first strikes the keynote for the second: "Morals and criticism are not so properly objects of the understanding as of taste and sentiment. Beauty, whether moral or natural, is felt more properly than perceived. Or if we reason concerning it, and endeavour to fix the standard, we regard a new fact, to wit, the general taste of mankind, or some such fact which may be the object of reasoning and inquiry" (XII (iii)). Given this clue the old-fashioned contrasts between judgement or reason and sentiment should be no hindrance to grasping the main theme of this passage from the second *Inquiry*:

The various circumstances of society, the various consequences of any practice, the various interests which may be proposed; these, on many occasions, are doubtful, and subject to great discussion and inquiry. . . . And a very accurate reason, or judgement, is often requisite to give the true determination amidst such intricate doubts arising from obscure or opposite utilities.

But though reason, when fully assisted and improved, be sufficient to instruct us in the pernicious or useful tendency of qualities and actions; it is not alone sufficient to produce any moral blame or approbation. Utility is only a tendency to a certain end; and were the end totally indifferent to us, we should feel the same indifference towards the means. It is requisite a sentiment should here display itself, in order to give a preference to the useful above the pernicious tendencies. This sentiment can be no other than a feeling for the happiness of mankind, and a resentment of their misery; since these are the different ends which virtue and vice have a tendency to promote. Here therefore reason instructs us in the several tendencies of actions, and humanity makes a distinction in favour of those which are useful and beneficial. . . .

No, say you, the morality consists in the relation of actions to the rule of right; and they are denominated good or ill, according as they agree or disagree with it. What then is this rule of right? In what does it consist? How is it determined? By reason, you say, which examines the moral relations of actions. So that moral relations are determined by the comparison of action to a rule. And that rule is determined by considering the moral relations of objects. Is not this fine reasoning?

All this is metaphysics, you cry. That is enough; there needs nothing more to give a strong presumption of falsehood. Yes, reply I, here are metaphysics surely; but they are all on your side, who advance an abstruse hypothesis, which can never be made intelligible, nor quadrate with any particular instance or illustration. The hypothesis which we embrace is plain. It maintains that morality is determined by sentiment. It defines *virtue* to be 'whatever mental action or quality gives to a spectator the pleasing sentiment of approbation', and *vice*, the contrary. We then proceed to examine a plain matter of fact, to wit, what actions have this influence. We consider all the circumstances in which these actions agree, and thence endeavour to extract some general observations with regard to these sentiments. If you call this metaphysics, and find anything abstruse here, you need only conclude that your turn of mind is not suited to the moral sciences. . . .

This doctrine will become still more evident, if we compare moral beauty with natural, to which in many particulars it bears so near a resemblance. It is on the proportion, relation, and position of parts, that all natural beauty depends; but it would be absurd thence to infer that the perception of beauty, like that of truth in geometrical problems, consists wholly in the perception of relations, and was performed entirely by the understanding or intellectual faculties. In all the sciences, our mind from the known relations investigates the unknown. But in all decisions of taste or external beauty, all the relations are beforehand obvious to the eye; and we thence proceed to feel a sentiment of complacency or disgust, according to the nature of the object, and disposition of our organs.

Euclid has fully explained all the qualities of the circle; but has not in any proposition said a word of its beauty. The reason is evident. The beauty is not a quality of the circle. It lies not in any part of the line, whose parts are equally distant from a common centre. It is only the effect which that figure produces upon the mind, whose peculiar fabric of structure renders it susceptible of such sentiments. In vain would you look for it in the circle, or seek it, either by your senses or by mathematical reasoning, in all the properties of that figure.

Attend to Palladio and Perrault, while they explain all the parts and proportions of a pillar. They talk of the cornice, and frieze, and base, and entablature, and shaft, and architrave; and give the description and position of each of these members. But should you ask the description and position of its beauty, they would readily reply, that the beauty is not in any of the parts or members of a pillar, but results from the whole, when that complicated figure is presented to an intelligent mind, susceptible to those finer sensations. Till such a spectator appear, there is nothing but a figure of such particular dimensions and proportions: from his sentiments alone arise its elegance and beauty.

Again; attend to Cicero, while he paints the crimes of a Verres or a Catiline. You must acknowledge that the moral turpitude results, in the same manner, from the contemplation of the whole, when presented to a being whose organs have such a particular structure and formation. The orator may paint rage, insolence, barbarity on the one side; meekness, suffering, sorrow, innocence on the other. But if you feel no indignation or compassion arise in you from this complication of circumstances, you would in vain ask him, in what consists the crime or villainy, which he so vehemently exclaims against? At what time, or on what subject it first began to exist? And what has a few months afterwards become of it, when every disposition and thought of all the actors is totally altered or annihilated? No satisfactory answer can be given to any of these questions, upon the abstract hypothesis of morals; and we must at last acknowledge, that the crime or immorality is no particular fact or relation, which can be the object of the understanding, but arises entirely from the sentiment of disapprobation, which, by the structure of human nature, we unavoidably feel on the apprehension of barbarity or treachery. . . .

It appears evident that the ultimate ends of human actions can never, in any case, be accounted for by reason, but recommend themselves entirely to the sentiments and affections of mankind, without any dependence on the intellectual faculties. Ask a man why he uses exercise; he will answer because he desires to keep his health. If you then enquire, why he desires health, he will readily reply, because sickness is painful. If you push your enquiries farther, and desire a reason why he hates pain, it is impossible he can ever give any. This is an ultimate end, and is never referred to any other object.

Perhaps to your second question, why he desires health, he may also reply, that it is necessary for the exercise of his calling. If you ask, why he is anxious on that head, he will answer, because he desires to get money. If you demand, 'Why?' 'It is the instrument of pleasure', says he. And beyond this it is an absurdity to ask for a reason. It is impossible there can be a progress in infinitum; and that one thing can always be a reason why another is desired. Something must be desirable on its own account, and because of its immediate accord or agreement with human sentiment and affection.

Thus the distinct boundaries and offices of reason and of taste are easily ascertained. The former conveys the knowledge of truth and falsehood: the latter gives the sentiment of beauty and deformity, vice and virtue. The one discovers objects as they really stand in nature, without addition or diminution: the other has a productive faculty, and gilding or staining all natural objects with the colours borrowed from internal sentiment, raises in a manner a new creation. Reason, being cool and disengaged, is no motive to action, and directs only the impulse received from appetite or inclination, by showing us the means of attaining happiness or avoiding misery. Taste, as it gives pleasure or pain, and thereby constitutes happiness or misery, becomes a motive to action, and is the first spring or impulse to desire and volition. From circumstances and relations, known or supposed, the former leads us to the discovery of the concealed and unknown: after all circumstances and relations are laid before us, the latter makes us feel from the whole a new sentiment of blame or approbation.   (Appendix I)

There is one possibly vital difference to be noticed between the *Treatise* version and that in the second *Inquiry*. In the former Hume seems to be suggesting that certain moral terms have to be construed in a Hobbist way as referring only to the feelings of the user: ". . . . when you pronounce any action or character to be vicious, you mean nothing, but that from the constitution of your nature you have a feeling or sentiment of blame from the contemplation of it." In the latter what is actually said to be a definition introduces the very different notion of a spectator; who is, presumably, supposed as such to be disinterested and impartial. In so far as this presumption is correct the introduction of the spectator constitutes a change of kind. For whereas the former refers only to the actual reactions of the actual speaker, the latter is in this interpretation in terms of the hypothetical response of a theoretical ideal. The significance of the remaining paragraph of the *Treatise* version will perhaps be appreciated more easily now:

> I cannot forbear adding to these reasonings an observation, which may, perhaps, be found of some importance. In every system of morality which I have hitherto met with I have always remarked that the author proceeds for some time in the ordinary way of reasoning, and establishes the being of a God, or makes observations concerning human affairs; when of a sudden I am surprised to find that, instead of the usual copulations of propositions, *is* and *is not*, I meet with no proposition that is not connected with an *ought*, or an *ought not*. This change is imperceptible; but is, however, of the last consequence. For as this *ought*, or *ought not*, expresses some new relation or affirmation, it is necessary that it should be observed and explained; and at the same time that a reason should be given, for what seems altogether inconceivable, how this new relation can be a deduction from others, which are entirely different from it. But as authors do not commonly use this precaution, I shall presume to recommend it to the readers; and am persuaded that this small attention would subvert all the vulgar systems of morality, and let us see, that the distinction of vice and virtue is not founded merely on the relations of objects, nor is perceived by reason.
>
> (III (i) 1)

§4 *A Humean critique applied to four kinds of subjectivism*

Hume, though insisting that the distinction between *is* and *ought* was "of the last consequence" never himself put it visibly to work. It is nevertheless not hard to appreciate the decisive relevance of this seminal paragraph once it is set correctly into its original context of a value subjectivism modelled upon the scientific antithesis between primary and secondary qualities. And this decisive relevance is, of course, altogether independent of all the recently much disputed questions of how fully he himself recognized and exploited the consequences of his own insight, and of what precisely he intended us to understand by the opprobrious phrase "all the vulgar systems of morality".

So consider first its implications for a value objectivism based on the Theory of Forms. This theory could scarcely be rated a vulgar system; unless, as is very possible, Hume himself intended his ban to include everything pre-Humean – and hence, in this context and in his view, pre-scientific. Yet a Platonic objectivism does lie wide open to objection in terms of this crucial and fundamental distinction. For, even if we were to allow that the Theory of Forms could survive the criticism deployed in the *Parmenides*, still a Guardian contemplating or reporting on the Form of the Good, or of the Just, or of the Obligatory, would still be contemplating or reporting on a matter of fact – or alleged fact – about what supposedly is the case. And if it is proposed, as it was, to derive from such contemplation conclusions about what not merely is but ought to be, then it is to the point to demand "that a reason should be given, for what seems altogether inconceivable, how this new relation can be a deduction from others, which are entirely different from it."

Against this it might be replied that Plato did not think in these Humean terms; that such Forms constitute a synthesis which transcends Hume's antithesis; and that it is, therefore, entirely appropriate that Plato does not actually proceed by first making wholly neutral and detached reports on the state of the Form, and then from these invalidly inferring conclusions about what ought to be. This response will repay careful examination, for to learn what is wrong with it is to learn several lessons which have wider applications.

First, we must not be deceived by Hume's dramatic irony. Of course he is not wanting foolishly to maintain that his predecessors and opponents always made the appropriate distinction, yet universally failed to recognize the significance of what they were so scrupulously doing. His contention is, rather, not that this distinction in fact is but instead that it needs to be made every time. It is, therefore, altogether beside the point to aspire to discredit Hume's claim by producing words, or expressions, or whole utterances which either are ambiguous as between, or simultaneously combine, both sorts of meaning. If you respond in this way you will be labouring to show that the distinction is not always made. But Hume's thesis is not that it is but that it can and should be. So by successfully showing what you are trying to show you will have demonstrated, not that Hume was wrong, but that if he was right what he said was worth saying.

From all this it follows, second, that it is no sort of reply to protest that Plato did not think in such Humean terms. Of course he did not. Precisely that is where he is so instructively wrong. Certainly if we wish to understand what and how Plato thought then we have to be aware that distinctions of this kind did not appear to him to be so obvious and so fundamental as we are able to see them to be. But when it is a question not of how Plato in fact did think but of whether what he thought is sound, then to say that Plato did not think in these terms may be tantamount to an admission that he was not adequately seized of something quite fundamental. This, though it may be both true and entirely understandable and excusable, is not a rebuttal of an objection which presupposes exactly what is here admitted. Such pseudo-rebuttals in the defence of respected classical and contemporary writers are so common that it is worth inventing a label for this bogus intellectual judo move. Let us call it the *That-is-his-blind-spot-so-he-is-not-vulnerable-there Transformation*.

Third, this is one of many cases where talk of a synthesis transcending an antithesis simply tends to conceal the confounding of a crucial distinction. For, once the distinction has been firmly and clearly made, it is quite obvious that there is a world of difference between saying that something is actual and saying that it is ideal, between saying that it is the case and saying that it ought to be. Certainly one may be able to say both of these radically different things in the same form of words. But this is a reason for insisting that the distinction is one which we need carefully to draw rather than for saying that it is one which is in such hybrid forms of expression transcended. There are indeed many terms in which we need to distinguish two elements of meaning: the one purely descriptive – referring quite neutrally to what, as it happens, allegedly is the case; the other normative – in some way prescribing what it is supposed ideally ought, or ought not, to be. For instance, a usual expression is *to commit suicide*. To employ this is both to refer to self-killing and simultaneously and very differently to imply that such self-killing is wrong.

So the upshot is that, even if there were Forms, and even if he could contemplate them and report his observations, still Plato must lie wide open to the objection that all this would be so much information about what is the case, from which alone he necessarily could not validly deduce any of his desired conclusions about what ought to be. We can now proceed to the opening paragraphs of Aristotle's *Nicomachean Ethics*:

Every craft and every form of inquiry, and likewise every practical activity and choice, seems to aim at some good; hence it has been well said that the good is that at which everything aims. (It is true that there is a distinction among the ends: some are the activities themselves; the others are works over and beyond these. Where there are such further ends beyond the activities the works are naturally better than the activities.) But as there are many practical activities and crafts and forms of knowledge there are also many ends; for instance, that of medicine is health; that of shipbuilding, a ship; that of generalship, victory; and that of economic management, wealth. Wherever several of such are subordinate to some single capacity – as bridlemaking and the other trades concerned with harness are subordinate to horsemanship, and this and every other military pursuit to generalship, and others to others – in all these cases the ends of the master arts certainly are more to be preferred than those of the arts subordinate to these. (And it makes no difference whether the ends of the pursuits are the activities themselves or something else beyond these, as in the case of the sorts of knowledge mentioned.)

If there is some end of our actions which we want for its own sake while the others are means, and if we do not choose everything for the sake of something else (which would involve that they would proceed to infinity, with the consequence that all desire would be empty and vain), it is clear that this must be the good – indeed the supreme good. Will not knowledge of it have a great practical bearing, and if like archers we have it as our target are we not more likely to fulfil our proper aim? And if this is so we ought to try to comprehend at least in outline what it is, and of which of the capacities or forms of knowledge it is the object.

Now it would seem that it must be the end of the most sovereign, of the one which is pre-eminently the master one. This is obviously politics. For politics prescribes which forms of knowledge must exist in states, and which each individual is to learn and up to what point; and we notice that even the most highly esteemed of the capacities – like generalship, economic management, and oratory – are subordinate to this. Inasmuch then as this employs the rest of the forms of knowledge, and lays down the law about what people must do and refrain from doing, the end of this one must embrace the ends of all the others. So it must be the good of man. For even if this is the same for the individual and for the state, obviously that of the state is greater and more perfect both to attain and to preserve. To achieve this even for one individual is enough to be going on with. But it is finer and more divine to do it

97

for a people and for a state. Since our investigation has these aims it is a sort of politics.

Now our treatment will be adequate if it achieves that degree of elucidation which is appropriate to its subject matter. One must not look for precision in all areas of inquiry alike, any more than one would in all manufactured products. Fineness and justice, which are what politics is about, are subject to a great deal of deviation and dispute – so much so that they are sometimes believed to exist only by convention and not in nature. Good things are involved in the same sort of going astray because in many cases they happen to have harmful consequences. For people have before now been ruined by wealth, and others by courage. We must therefore be content if dealing with such a subject and starting with such premises we succeed in presenting a rough outline of the truth: when one is talking about and proceeding from what holds for the most part conclusions too will be of the same kind. Accordingly everything which is said must be received in the same way; for it is a mark of the educated man to look for that degree of precision in each kind which the nature of the subject admits. To accept probable reasonings from a mathematician is just like demanding strict demonstration from an orator. (1094A1–1094B28)

The immediate purpose of citing Aristotle is to summon a second champion to confront Hume's challenge. But I have quoted more than would be essential for this, mainly in order to include Aristotle's maturely sophisticated observations on the differences between different kinds of inquiry. In the light of Hume the most remarkable things about the previous passage are, that in all the alert richness of his other distinguishings Aristotle does not notice the crucial difference between saying that an end is in fact pursued and claiming that it ought to be, and that he does not make a division between politics as a matter of prescribing and political science as a descriptive and explanatory study of what does in fact – for better or for worse – actually happen.

Yet surely it must be unsound in principle for, for example, an anthropologist to argue that "since giving and receiving are the activities which are desired the most, we can safely assume that they represent the Trobriand idea of what is good" (Lee, p. 366). It is equally but more subtly unsound to presume that because various lower-order skills and capacities are included as subordinates within corresponding higher-order ones these in their turn must in a strictly analogous way be subordinate to a highest-order form of knowledge, whose business it is to prescribe how and when and how far all those other skills ought to be employed.

In this presumption Aristotle is following in the footsteps of Plato, who constantly urged that, since we should in so far as we were prudent entrust our ships to expert seamen, and employ expert generals to win our battles, so we must find expert rulers and give them full powers to govern us. But all such analogies break down at precisely the point which is crucial. For the expert seaman, the expert general, the expert in economic management, even the expert political operator – 'the wheeler-dealer' – are all expert, if expert at all, in knowing what means will in fact lead to what ends. But the postulated expert in ruling is required to know, not what are the levers which have to be pulled in order to bring about which effects, but what are the ends which ideally ought to be pursued. He would have to know (and as such also have to be committed to striving wholeheartedly for), not just what is instrumentally good – good as a means – but what is absolutely good, good as the proper end which categorically ought to be pursued. The philosopher kings must be by profession experts about ends.

That expression *categorically ought* refers to a famous distinction introduced by Immanuel Kant (1724–1804). It occurs in a short work uncompromisingly entitled *The Foundations of the Metaphysics of Morals*. The translation is by H. J. Paton, from his own edition in *The Moral Law* (pp. 82–83: italics removed). It is from the original German. For although the city in which Kant spent his entire life is now the Russian Kaliningrad it was before 1945 Koenigsberg, the capital of East Prussia:

All imperatives command either hypothetically or categorically. Hypothetical imperatives declare a possible action to be practically necessary as a means to the attainment of something else that one wills (or that one may will). A categorical imperative would be one which represented an action as objectively necessary in itself apart from its relation to a further end. ... If the action would be good solely as a means to something else, the imperative is hypothetical; if the action is represented as good in itself ... then the imperative is categorical. ... A hypothetical imperative thus says only that an action is good for some purpose or other, either possible or actual. In the first case it is a problematic practical principle; in the second case an assertoric practical principle. A categorical imperative, which declares an action to be objectively necessary in itself without reference to some purpose – that is, even without any further end – ranks as an apodeictic practical principle.

Everything that is possible only through the efforts of some rational being can be conceived as a possible purpose of some will; and consequently there are in fact innumerable principles of action so far as action is thought necessary in order to achieve some possible purpose which can be effected by it. All sciences have a practical part consisting of problems which suppose that some end is possible for us and of imperatives which tell us how it is to be attained. Hence the latter can in general be called imperatives of skill. Here there is absolutely no question about the rationality or goodness of the end, but only about what must be done to attain it. A prescription required by a doctor in order to cure his man completely and one required by a poisoner in order to make sure of killing him are of equal value so far as each serves to effect its purpose perfectly. (II)

Obviously Hume's *ought* will in the light of this later distinction have to be read as categorical. For a hypothetical imperative, like "If you want to arrive in Whitehorse by train you have to ride the White Pass and Yukon Railroad", is essentially a neutral description of what are the possible means to what possible ends.

Our third representative of a form of value objectivism, after Plato and Aristotle, will be St Thomas Aquinas (*c.* 1225–1274). For Aquinas, Aristotle was always "The Philosopher". From him Aquinas learnt and borrowed immensely more than from all other philosophical predecessors. This exploitation was an appropriate tribute to the great range, high quality, and recent availability of Aristotle's works. But it is also true and relevant that some of Aristotle's most characteristic ideas were more congenially suggestive to a devotedly Christian thinker than would have been those of, for instance, the Classical atomists.

Thus we have just watched Aristotle starting from the notion of everything having an end, which is its good. This conception of ends as fulfilments is one which he applies universally: it is as essential to his science as to his ethics. Yet it is hard to think, as he did, of ends as possibly distinct from purposes. But the idea of purpose is logically bound to that of an agent harbouring and understanding the purpose. So if all things are categorically to have ends or fulfilments which may be independent of actual human purposes it may well seem, though to Aristotle himself it did not, that they must be endowed with these by a personal and purposive God. This is a suggestion which Aquinas was understandably happy to accept and to develop.

Again, Aristotle connects his conception of the proper and inherent ends or fulfilments of things with one of his fundamental metaphysical distinctions – one which was to become fundamental for Aquinas also. This is the distinction between potency, or potentiality, and actuality, or act; and it is explained in, appropriately enough, the *Metaphysics*:

Actuality is the presence of the thing, and not in the way we mean when we speak of something being there potentially. We speak of something being there potentially like Hermes in a block of wood or the half in the whole, because it can be separated out; and of someone being potentially a scholar even when he is not engaged in study, because he is capable of study. The opposite of this is actuality. What we mean becomes clear by abstracting from the particular instances. There is no need to search for a definition always. There is also the possibility of grasping the analogy between instances, that it is the relation of actually building to what is suitable for building, of being awake to being asleep, of seeing to what has its eyes shut but possesses the power of sight, of that which is formed out of matter to the matter, and of the finished article to the raw material. Let actuality be distinguished by reference to one element in each of these antitheses and potentiality by reference to the other. (1048A31–1048B7)

Aristotle further argues that actualities are in every way prior and superior to their corresponding potentialities. Thus, the actuality has to be mentioned in any definition of the potentiality – because that is what it is a potentiality to become. But this does not apply the other way about – because you do not have to imply anything about origins in a statement of what now actually is. Again, the actuality is the end or fulfilment for the sake of which the potentiality exists: the essential point of the power of sight is to be realized in actual seeing, and so on. Hence, since any potentiality implies the possibility of change to the actuality, which is in every way better, there could be no unrealized potentialities in a perfect being; for a perfect being would, by definition, be one which could not conceivably be better. It is by this route that we arrive at the quite often mentioned but perhaps rather less frequently understood notion of God as pure actuality, or pure act.

It will now, after these Aristotelian preliminaries, be easier to comprehend the following passages from the *Summa Theologica* of Aquinas:

We have to say that goodness and being are in reality the same, differing in idea only. The proof is as follows. The principle of goodness consists in this, that it is something desirable. Hence The Philosopher, in Book I of the *Ethics*, says that "the good is that at which all things aim." And it is obvious that a thing is desirable in so far as it is perfect, for all things aim at their own perfection. But a thing is perfect in so far as it is actual. Hence it is clear that in so far as there is being there is something good, for to be is the actuality of everything. . . . It is, therefore, clear that goodness and being are the same in reality. But the word *good* states the principle of desirability, which *being* does not.

(I, Q5A1)

We have to say that every being is as such good. For every being is as such in actuality, and by that token perfect, because every actuality is a form of perfection, and perfection implies desirability and goodness – as is clear from what has been said before (in Q5A1, above). Hence it follows that every being is as such good.

(I, Q5A3)

Is every human action good, or are some bad? I reply that we have to say that we should give the same account of goodness and badness in actions as we give of goodness and badness in things. And in things everything has as much goodness as it has being; for *goodness* and *being* are convertible terms, as was said in Book I (Q5AA1 and 2).

(I (ii), Q18A1)

It is just worth noticing that that final clause of the third of these three short passages is strictly incorrect. For a glance back at the last two sentences of the first will show that Aquinas originally maintained something less obviously indefensible: his point was precisely not that the two notions are the same "in idea", but rather that they become equivalent "in reality" because – for the reasons given – it emerges that they both refer to the same things. It is this metaphysical equation, and the reasons given in its support, which is the important thing. Any such equation is, as I urged when it was first mentioned (Ch. II § 2, above), scandalous. For it appears to be an epitome of cosmic complacency: whatever was or is or will be is ultimately as it should be. Certainly it raises immediately the question of how any such ultimate equation can possibly be squared with all the obvious deficiencies of things. This question is, if anything, not less but more urgent for the philosopher who is also a Christian theologian concerned elsewhere to stress that there are indeed in the actual universe certain damnable defects; to wit, mortal sins. We shall not here try to follow the attempts of Aquinas to meet this challenge. Consider instead his account of the nature of moral imperatives, again from the *Summa Theologica*:

Now it is evident, granted that the world is ruled by Divine Providence . . . that the entire system of the universe is governed by Divine Reason. And so the very idea of the government of things in God as the Ruler of the universe contains the idea of law. And since the Divine Reason conceives not in time but eternally, as *Proverbs* 8: 23 says, it is therefore proper to call this sort of law eternal.

(II (i), Q91A1)

Hence, since all things which are subject to Divine Providence are measured and regulated by eternal law – as is obvious from what has just been said – it is evident that all things in some way participate in eternal law; in as much, that is, as it is from its imprint that they get their dispositions to their proper ends and fulfilments. Now among all these other things a rational creature lies under the Divine Providence in a more excellent way, in as much as it itself shares in the providence by being provident for itself and others. Hence it itself has a share in the Eternal Reason by which it has a natural disposition towards its required end and fulfilment; and this sort of sharing in the eternal law which occurs in a rational creature is called the law of nature. Hence the Psalmist, after saying (*Psalms* 4: 6), "Offer the sacrifices of righteousness", adds, as though he were replying to people asking what the works of righteousness are: "Many there are that say 'Who will show us good?'", and replying to this question he says, "Lord, the light of thy countenance is sealed upon us". It is as much as to say that the light of natural reason, by which we discern what is good and what evil – which is what concerns the law of nature – is nothing but an imprint of the Divine Light upon us. Hence it is clear that the law of nature is nothing but the participation by a rational creature in the eternal law.

(II (i), Q91A2)

The references to *Proverbs* and *Psalms* may remind us that the *Summa Theologica* is, and was always intended to be, primarily theological. Nevertheless, despite these and other possibly unfamiliar features of his presentation, what Aquinas is saying in these second two passages is, surely, as clear as it was in the first three. The same fundamental distinction needs to be applied to both positions. In his first version of the former Aquinas himself was quite clear that to state that something exists is not to state that it is desirable. But neither, to move from "idea" to "reality", are we compelled to go along with his far-fetched insistence that "a thing is perfect in so far as it is actual". There can be wretched specimens of anything you care to mention, just as there are innumerable possibilities which it would be most undesirable to have realized either well or badly. Nor, furthermore, would it be at all plausible – even if it were fully intelligible – to suggest that in all these cases the things must be good as existing and defective only through a shortage of existence. To anyone who urges that this equation of goodness and being is an essential of metaphysics the short answer is, 'So much the worse for metaphysics!'

The application of the same fundamental distinction to the latter position requires slightly more subtlety, but is correspondingly more profitable. We have to distinguish two senses of the word *law* and of expressions such as *law of nature*. In the one the law is prescriptive, laying down norms as to what should be done. In the other it is descriptive, stating what as a matter of fact always is the case. There is no contradiction in suggesting that a prescriptive law may be defied; whereas a descriptive law of nature cannot correctly be said to be broken. I may break the laws of some state by helping someone to procure an abortion, or to achieve euthanasia; but if an event occurs inconsistent with what was thought to be a descriptive law of nature, then that occurrence is by itself sufficient to show that either no such law holds or its scope has been exaggerated.

This is a distinction which has become established only since and through the rise of modern science. The fact that it is not employed by Aquinas in a context in which it would be, for one of our contemporaries, sheerly incompetent to neglect it is an index of progress in philosophy. The eternal law of Aquinas must be both always prescriptive, since in it God directs what should be, and yet usually at the same time descriptive, since presumably almost everything in the universe invariably albeit unconsciously obeys its – and His – prescriptions. The one exception, however, arises at precisely the point which is presently crucial. Aquinas introduces his notion of the law of nature as if this could be just the same eternal law, but in the special case where it is obeyed consciously. This might perhaps be perfectly acceptable if Aquinas were willing to say that in their conscious actions – whether or not they are themselves aware of this – all men always do obey this eternal law of God. But, of course, Aquinas is prepared to say no such thing. For in his view it is only when and in so far as we act as we should act that we act in accordance with the eternal law of God. So, whereas in its reference to the rest of creation this law may be at one and the same time both descriptive of what always does happen and prescriptive of what properly should happen, as applied to men it can at most lay down what we ought to do; and in this exceptional case such prescriptions will, notoriously, not be entirely congruent with descriptions of what actually does occur.

The crux is both fundamental and inescapable. For the whole point of appealing to a prescriptive law of nature is to find warrant for saying that this, which is done, constitutes a violation, while that, which is not done, would have represented a proper fulfilment. But wherever a descriptive law of nature obtains there can be no violation of that law. If any such descriptive laws do apply to human conduct they must cover equally both the actions which fulfil and the actions which violate any prescriptive law.

It is, therefore, radically misguided to confound one sort of law with the other, and to try to deduce proposed prescriptions of what ought to happen from descriptions of what supposedly does occur or tend to occur.

Aquinas offers a characteristically sophisticated version of this suggestion that what is natural is right. Yet the nub of the objection to any such notion is crudely simple. Unnatural vice is, for some people, doing what comes naturally; just as is natural vice for the rest of us. What has been called artificial contraception may be (but is not) essentially wrong. But it is no more, and no less, unnatural than having a polio shot or driving a truck. The Chinese Sage Lao Tzu is said, similarly, to have denounced the first bridges as unnatural. Hume's assessment of such misguided but perennial attempts is summed up in the *Treatise*, significantly only a few pages after the passages quoted earlier:

> Meanwhile it may not be amiss to observe ... that nothing can be more unphilosophical than those systems which assert that virtue is the same with what is natural, and vice with what is unnatural. For in the first sense of the word *nature* – as opposed to miracles – both vice and virtue are equally natural; and in the second sense – as opposed to what is unusual – perhaps virtue will be found to be the most unnatural. At least it must be owned that heroic virtue, being unusual, is as little natural, as the most brutal barbarity. As to the third sense of the word, it is certain that both vice and virtue are equally artificial, and out of nature. For, however it may be disputed whether the notion of a merit or demerit in certain actions be natural or artificial, it is evident that the actions themselves are artificial, and are performed with a certain design and intention; otherwise they could never be ranked under any of these denominations. It is impossible, therefore, that the character of natural and unnatural can ever, in any sense, mark the boundaries of vice and virtue.
>
> (III (i) 2)

So far in the present section Hume's challenge has been offered to three kinds of objectivism about value. In the first what was supposed to be objective was actual ideal standards, the Platonic Forms; in the second it was ends or fulfilments; and in the third a sort of law of nature. In the fourth and last kind to be considered the key notions are those of qualities and relations. The suggestion is that things have certain qualities, or are in certain relations, such that certain consequences follow about what ought to be recognized as valuable and what ought and ought not to be done. The essentials of this kind of objectivism can be found in the poet John Donne:

If they were good it would be seen,
Good is as visible as green,
And to all eyes itself betrays ('Community')

But our spokesman here must be the Cambridge philosopher G. E. Moore (1873–1958), writing at the very beginning of this century in his *Principia Ethica*:

> 'Good', then, if we mean by it that quality which we assert to belong to a thing, when we say that the thing is good, is incapable of any definition, in the most important sense of that word. The most important sense of 'definition' is that in which a definition states what are the parts which invariably compose a certain whole; and in this sense *good* has no definition because it is simple and has no parts. It is one of those innumerable objects of thought which are themselves incapable of definition, because they are the ultimate terms by reference to which whatever *is* capable of definition must be defined. That there must be an indefinite number of such terms is obvious, on reflection; since we cannot define anything except by an analysis, which, when carried as far as it will go, refers us to something, which is simply different from anything else. . . . There is, therefore, no intrinsic difficulty in the contention that 'good' denotes a simple and indefinable quality. There are many other instances of such qualities.
>
> Consider yellow, for example. We may try to define it, by describing its physical equivalent; we may state what kind of light-vibrations must stimulate the normal eye, in order that we may perceive it. But a moment's reflection is sufficient to show that those light-vibrations are not themselves what we mean by yellow. *They* are not what we perceive. Indeed we should never have been able to discover their existence, unless we had first been struck by the patent difference of quality between the different colours. . . .
>
> Yet a mistake of this simple kind has commonly been made about 'good'. It may be true that all things which are good are *also* something else, just as it is true that all things which are yellow produce a certain kind of vibration in the light. . . . But far too many philosophers have thought that when they named those other properties they were actually defining 'good'; that these properties, in fact were simply not other, but absolutely and entirely the same with goodness. This view I propose to call 'the naturalistic fallacy' . . . .   (pp. 9–10: italics original)

It is tempting to develop epistemological objections against Moore. For even allowing that we can have such knowledge of values we surely do not acquire it by a sort of perception. The suggested analogy with literal seeing breaks down at every point which is crucial. There is no variation in the findings of sight comparable with the Herodotean differences in the discoveries of the supposed moral sense. In Rudyard Kipling's words:

> . . . the wildest dreams of Kew are the facts of Khatmandhu.
> And the crimes of Clapham chaste in Martaban

('In the Neolithic Age')

And, whether or not disagreements about values are susceptible of definitively correct resolutions, it certainly cannot be demonstrated that someone's 'moral sense' is defective in any ways at all analogous with those in which the colour-blind man can be shown to be unable to perform tasks which present no difficulty to the fully sighted person. (Two instructive exercises here would be: first, to plan a demonstration, which a colour-blind person would be equipped to appreciate, to show that colour-blindness is a discriminatory deficiency and not just a personal eccentricity; and, second, to work out what would be required to make good a claim to possess an extra discriminatory capacity, which others lack, and which could properly be rated as a further sense.)

But though it is tempting to pursue such epistemological questions further our present concern is rather with ontology; with whether values are or could be in our sense objective, rather than with whether, and if so how, truths about such putative values could be known. In this context Moore too has to meet the Humean challenge to warrant his inference, from the claim that certain objects or situations do or would in fact possess this simple and indefinable quality of goodness, to the conclusion that such objects ought to be cherished and such situations ought to be brought about. And, once again, this cannot be done. For a prescriptive and normative conclusion is necessarily no part of any purely descriptive, neutral, and detached statement of alleged fact. Hence, equally necessarily, the former cannot be inferred validly from the latter.

Moore's position is a curiosity of the history of ideas. For, having taken goodness to be the primary concept in valuing, he insists that it is radically unsound to identify goodness with any of the ordinary characteristics of whatever might be said to be good. He then goes on later to distinguish these as "natural" from goodness, which he calls "non-natural". Yet he still thinks of goodness as a quality which can be possessed by things in themselves, and his supposed non-natural qualities have by others understandably been construed as intimations of a supernatural. If Moore were right we could sensibly and without contradiction entertain the supposition that a good thing and a bad thing might be in all other respects identical; which surely is preposterous. And precisely by this making goodness a characteristic of things in themselves he ensures that the alleged fact that something possesses it could not be sufficient to warrant conclusions about what ought to be. He thereby himself commits the Naturalistic Fallacy. For this expression, which Moore coined, has since come to be understood by reference to that Parthian paragraph of Hume – an author nowhere mentioned in *Principia Ethica*.

§ 5 *Subjectivism, in a narrower sense, refuted*

The upshot of the last two sections seems, therefore, to be that Hume did indeed forge the absolute weapon against objectivism in ethics. It must be fallacious to infer conclusions about what categorically ought or ought not to be from any statement or collection of statements detachedly describing what was or is or will be. It must be fallacious since the latter are essentially neutral; whereas the former, equally essentially, constitute an intervention. To say in your own person and in direct speech that this is categorically wrong necessarily is – whatever else it may be as well – to take sides, to make a commitment; whereas to say that among the Arapesh this would be right may be only a misleading way of reporting non-committally what the Arapesh believe, which is not as such to commit yourself.

But of course there is more to it than this. That a word is employed for one purpose does not prevent its being used simultaneously for other not incompatible tasks – as we have seen already in the case of the expression *to commit suicide*. There are, as Aristotle glimpsed long ago, innumerable multi-purpose verbal hybrids of this kind: "Indeed the very names of some have badness built in" (*Nicomachean Ethics*, 1107A10–11).

I want in what remains of the present chapter to indicate some of what that essential more to it must be. Let us begin this end by looking at the subjectivism which Plato puts into the mouth of his 'Thrasymachus' in Book I of *The Republic*. It is in reaction to this that in the remaining nine Books Socrates develops his own objectivism:

THRASYMACHUS – Listen, then. For I maintain that justice is nothing else but the advantage of the stronger. Well, why are you not showing your approval? But you will not be willing to.
SOCRATES – Well, let me first understand what you mean. For as it is I do not yet know. You maintain that the advantage of the stronger is

just. Yet whatever do you mean by this, Thrasymachus? For surely you
are not maintaining anything like this, that if Polydamas the athlete is
stronger than we are and if ox meat is advantageous for his body this
food will be both advantageous and just for us who are weaker than
him.

THRASYMACHUS – You are odious, Socrates, and you are interpreting
me in the sense in which you can do most damage to my argument.

SOCRATES – Not at all, my dear chap. But tell me more clearly what
you mean.

THRASYMACHUS – Do you not know then that some states are ruled
by dictators, others are democracies, and others are aristocracies?

SOCRATES – Of course I do.

THRASYMACHUS – So is not this what is strong in each state, the
ruling element?

SOCRATES – Certainly.

THRASYMACHUS – And each form of government lays down laws
for its own advantage, a democracy laws for the benefit of the pop-
ulace, a dictatorship laws for the benefit of the dictator, and the
others likewise. By legislating in this way they make it plain that
their advantage is justice for their subjects, and they punish anyone
who gets out of line with this as a lawbreaker and an unjust man.
So this is what I mean, you splendid fellow, that justice is in all states
the same, and it is the advantage of the established government. For
this, you agree, is strong; so that if you work it out correctly justice
is everywhere the same – the advantage of the stronger.

SOCRATES – I now grasp what you mean. Whether it is true or not I
shall attempt to discover.   (§ 338C–339A)

The critique developed by 'Socrates' is inept and unpersuasive. But
Hume in his second *Inquiry* pointed the way to a refutation which would
be both decisive and illuminating:

When a man denominates another his *enemy*, his *rival*, his *antagonist*,
his *adversary*, he is understood to speak the language of self-love and to
express sentiments peculiar to himself and arising from his particular
circumstances and situation. But when he bestows on any man the
epithets of *vicious* or *odious* or *depraved*, he then speaks another language
and expresses sentiments in which he expects all his audience are to
concur with him. He must here, therefore, depart from his private and
particular situation and must choose a point of view common to him
with others: he must move some universal principle of the human frame
and touch a string to which all mankind have an accord and symphony.
If he mean, therefore, to express that this man possesses qualities whose

109

tendency is pernicious to society, he has chosen this common point of view and has touched the principle of humanity in which every man, in some degree, concurs. . . . And though this affection of humanity may not generally be esteemed so strong as vanity or ambition, yet being common to all men, it can alone be the foundation of morals or of any general system of blame or praise. One man's ambition is not another's ambition, nor will the same event or object satisfy both; but the humanity of one man is the humanity of everyone; and the same object touches this passion in all human creatures. . . . The distinction, therefore, between these species of sentiment being so great and evident, language must soon be moulded upon it and must invent a peculiar set of terms in order to express those universal sentiments of censure or approbation which arise from humanity, or from views of general usefulness and its contrary. *Virtue* and *vice* become then known: morals are recognized; certain general ideas are framed of human conduct and behaviour; such measures are expected from men in such situations: this action is determined to be conformable to our abstract rule; that other, contrary. And by such universal principles are the particular sentiments of self-love frequently controlled and limited.

It seems certain . . . that a rude, untaught savage regulates chiefly his love and hatred by the ideas of private utility and injury, and has but faint perceptions of a general rule or system of behaviour. . . . But we, accustomed to society, and to more enlarged reflections correct, in some measure, our ruder and narrower passions. And though much of our friendship and enmity be still regulated by private considerations of benefit and harm, we pay at least this homage to general rules, which we are accustomed to respect, that we commonly pervert our adversary's conduct by imputing malice or injustice to him, in order to give vent to those passions which arise from self-love and private interest. When the heart is full of rage, it never wants pretenses of this nature. . .   (§ IX)

Hume's speculations about psychology and origins are no present business of ours. But his distinction between two ranges of terms – the one suited to express only the reactions and interests of the user, and the other implicitly appealing to some general rule or some wider concern – indicates why any such definition as that advanced by 'Thrasymachus' must be wrong. It must be wrong, because the point of employing words from the second category rather than from the first lies precisely in their reference to general principle and to an impartial standpoint independent of all particular individual or group interests or desires. This, like much else in philosophy, is obvious; but obvious only if and when an insight has been made obvious by a clear and persuasive statement. What 'Thrasymachus' is made to say is not muzzily or just marginally in error. It is diametrically the opposite of the truth. The whole point of speaking about justice precisely is to appeal to some standard or standpoint or principle independent of particular individual or group interests and wishes. So however the word *just* is correctly to be defined it is at least certain that it cannot be in the sort of way represented by 'Thrasymachus'. And, furthermore, it is only and exactly in so far as there is some genuine and original concern for justice that there can be anything for disingenuous and factitious pretences to such a virtue to exploit. This point too was made, in his own way, by Hume in his second *Inquiry*:

> From the apparent usefulness of the social virtues it has readily been inferred by sceptics, both ancient and modern, that all moral distinctions arise from education, and were at first invented, and afterwards encouraged, by the art of politicians in order to render men tractable and subdue their natural ferocity and selfishness, which incapacitated them for society. This principle, indeed, of precept and education must so far be owned to have a powerful influence that it may frequently increase or diminish, beyond their natural standard, the sentiments of approbation or dislike. . . . But that all moral affection or dislike arises from this origin will never surely be allowed by any judicious enquirer. Had nature made no such distinction, founded on the original constitution of the mind, the words *honourable* and *shameful*, *lovely* and *odious*, *noble* and *despicable* had never had place in any language, nor could politicians, had they invented these terms, ever have been able to render them intelligible or make them convey any idea to the audience. So that nothing can be more superficial than this paradox of the sceptics; and it were well if, in the abstruser studies of logic and metaphysics, we could as easily obviate the cavils of that sect as in the practical and more intelligible sciences of politics and morals. (§ V)

There is, unfortunately, no warrant whatsoever for crediting Plato with either of the insights which we have just been drawing from two passages of Hume. Nevertheless Plato's 'Thrasymachus' can be seen, most illuminatingly, as the type of the embittered debunker; a man sceptical only in the sense of not believing what – rightly or wrongly – he takes to be a pretence. He is the type of the man who, having seen through the fine but fraudulent phrases, tells us that when those two speak of a spiritual relationship, what they really mean is four legs in a bed; or that, when that lot advocates a true and socialist democracy, what they really mean is the absolute rule of a self-perpetuating oligarchy of party bureaucrats; or that, when that whited sepulchre prates of justice, what he really means is the interests of his own country, or of his own class, or simply of himself. In every such case the justification for the indignation, the ground for the suggestion of hypocrisy, is that what is said to be really meant precisely is not what the words actually used do really mean.

Suppose that it were in fact true that the expression *spiritual relationship* was synonymous with *regular sexual intercourse,* or that the slogan *socialist democracy* was by one and all intended and taken to mean the unchecked absolutism of Communist functionaries, or that the word *justice* was strictly and straightforwardly definable in terms of the interests of some particular individual or group; then there would be nothing false or hypocritical about using the former where the latter certainly would be correct. Both, if they were in truth synonymous, must be equally in place wherever either is: that is what *synonymous* means. But if this were so, and if there were not such essential meaning gaps between what the hypocrite actually does say, and what he would say if he were completely ingenuous, both the occupation of the hypocrite and that of his debunker would be gone. It is a sound and shrewd saw which states: 'Hypocrisy is the tribute which vice pays to virtue.'

It is worth remarking incidentally that parallel objections are correspondingly decisive against the kind of definitions suggested by passages quoted earlier from Hobbes and from Hume's *Treatise* (Ch. III §§ 2 and 3, above): "... whatsoever is the object of any man's appetite or desire is it which he for his part calleth *good* ..."; and "... when you pronounce any action or character to be vicious, you mean nothing, but that, from the constitution of your nature you have a feeling or sentiment of blame from the contemplation of it." I say *definition suggested* and not *definition given* because it seems more plausible to interpret at least Hume as reporting an alleged matter of psychological fact about the feeling or sentiments which accompany the employment of moral terms, rather than as offering an analysis of what as words these terms mean.

Suppose that *This is what ought to be done* or *That would be morally outrageous* really were simply reports of the condition of the speaker – and hence on all fours with *I feel sick* and *I've got earache* – then what to the uninstructed appear to be disagreements about what ought to be done, or about what would be morally scandalous, would really be confrontations at cross-purposes. It would be as if I said, challengingly, *I visited Moscow in 1964* and you responded, with equal vigour, *No, I did not. Never!* Furthermore, and similarly, if such an extreme subjectivist account of the meaning of moral terms were correct then any attempt to distinguish fundamentally between what I would like to do and what I believe ought to be done must be radically preposterous. It must be like insistence that only gifts are acceptable, but not donations; or that my beer mug is half full, but not half empty.

The upshot of the first four sections of the present chapter was that, in the widest senses carefully explicated in the second of those sections, every sort of value must be subjective as opposed to objective. But the arguments deployed in this fifth section are equally, and more swiftly, decisive against any perverse idea that moral words may be defined simply in terms of either the interests or the psychological reactions of particular interested or agitated individuals or groups. This further fundamental lesson can be underlined with another quotation from the *History* of Thucydides. It comes from the famous Melian Dialogue, a reconstruction of exchanges between the representatives of a great power – Athens – and those of a tiny island state, Melos. The Athenians wish with as little fuss as possible to subjugate this neutralist state, which falls unambiguously within their traditional sphere of influence:

ATHENIANS – So be it then. We on our side will not offer a lengthy speech which no one would believe, with a lot of fine talk about how it is our right to have an empire because we defeated the Persians, or that we are coming against you now because we have been wronged; and we do not expect you to think to persuade us that the reason why you did not join our camp was that you are kith and kin of the Spartans who originally settled Melos, or that you have done us no injury. Rather we expect you to try to do what is possible on the basis of the true thoughts of both parties, since you know and we know that it is part of the human condition to choose justice only when the balance of power is even, and that those who have an advantage do what they have the power to do while the weak acquiesce.

MELIANS – Well, we consider that it is expedient that you should not destroy something which is for the general good. (The word has to be *expedient* since you have in this way laid down that we must speak of advantage rather than justice.) For anyone who falls into danger there should be fair play and just dealing; and he should be able to convince with, and get the benefit of, arguments which fall a bit short of strict proof. And this is something which concerns you as much as us, for if you fall you would suffer a great vengeance and become an example to others.

ATHENIANS – But we, supposing our empire does come to an end, are not dismayed about the outcome. For it is not those who rule over others, as the Spartans do (though our present quarrel is not with the Spartans), who are a terror to the vanquished, but rather subject peoples who may some time attack and get the better of their rulers. . . .

MELIANS But do you not think that there is safety in the other course? For here also it is necessary, since you have forced us to abandon considerations of justice and are persuading us to give ear to what is in your interests, for us too to tell you what is to our advantage, and if your interests happen to be the same to try to persuade you.　　(V 89–90)

§6 *Ultimate ends and intrinsic values*

Had it been correct to define the word *just* in terms of the interests of the stronger party then the Athenians could have had no reason to forbid the Melians to appeal to considerations of justice, while the Melians in their turn would have lacked all incentive so to do. The truth is – and it is a truth which will bear a deal of reiteration – that it is of the essence of notions both of justice in particular and of morality in general that to appeal to such considerations is to appeal to principles logically independent of all particular individual or group interests or tastes. (To speak here of a logical independence is, of course, not to deny the obvious fact that the claims of justice may from time to time happen to coincide with the demands of some sectional interest. Rather it is to insist that when such coincidings do occur they must be logically coincidental, and not guaranteed by definition.)

It follows as a further consequence of this fundamental truth that claims about what ought or ought not to be, about what is just or unjust, or right or wrong, cannot be first assimilated to statements or expressions of individual or group likes or dislikes and then on that ground only cast out beyond the pale of possible reasoned discussion. The putative corollary cannot be so derived for the simple but sufficient reason that the attempted assimilation is itself radically mistaken and perverse. Yet, especially to anyone who fails to distinguish our wider from narrower senses of (*ethical*) *subjectivism* this regrettably obscurantist conclusion may seem to be an implication of any sort of subjectivism. Consider, for instance, the account of value offered by Bertrand Russell in the penultimate chapter of his *Religion and Science*:

Those who maintain the insufficiency of science . . . appeal to the fact that science has nothing to say about 'values'. This I admit; but when it is inferred that ethics contains truths which cannot be proved or disproved by science, I disagree. . . . Questions as to 'values' – that is to say, as to what is good or bad on its own account, independently of its effects – lie outside the domain of science, as the defenders of religion emphatically assert. I think that in this they are right, but I draw the further conclusion, which they do not draw, that questions as to 'values' lie wholly outside the domain of knowledge. That is to say, when we assert that this or that has 'value', we are giving expression to our own emotions, not to a fact which would still be true even if our personal feelings were different. . . . When a man says 'this is good in itself', he *seems* to be making a statement, just as much as if he said 'this is square' or 'this is sweet'. I believe this to be a mistake. I think that what the man really means is: 'I wish everybody to desire this', or rather, 'Would that everybody desired this'. If what he says is interpreted as a statement, it is merely an affirmation of his own personal wish; if, on the other hand, it is interpreted in a general way, it states nothing, but merely desires something. . . . The theory which I have been advocating is a form of the doctrine which is called the 'subjectivity' of values. This doctrine consists in maintaining that, if two men differ about values, there is not a disagreement as to any kind of truth, but a difference of taste. If one man says 'oysters are good' and another says 'I think they are bad', we recognize that there is nothing to argue about. The theory in question holds that all differences as to values are of this sort, although we naturally do not think so when we are dealing with matters that seem to us more exalted than oysters. The chief ground for adopting this view is the complete impossibility of finding any arguments to prove that this or that has intrinsic value. If we all agreed, we might hold that we know values by intuition. We cannot *prove*, to a colour-blind man, that grass is green and not red. But there are various ways of proving to him that he lacks a power of discrimination which most men possess, whereas in the case of values there are no such ways, and disagreements are much more frequent than in the case of colours. Since no way can even be imagined for deciding a difference as to values, the conclusion is forced upon us that the difference is one of tastes, not one as to any objective truth. The consequences of this doctrine are considerable. . . . I conclude that, while it is true that science cannot decide questions of value, that is because they cannot be decided at all, and lie outside the realm of truth and falsehood. Whatever knowledge is obtainable, must be attained by scientific methods; and what science cannot discover, mankind cannot know.   (pp. 223, 230, 235–236, 237–238, and 243: italics original)

The same conclusion that values are beyond the scope of rational discussion can also be derived from the very type of objectivist intuitionism which Russell is here at pains to reject. This point can be appreciated most piquantly by considering an account of the impact on the Bloomsbury Circle of the ethical doctrine of G. E. Moore, a doctrine noticed already at the end of § 4 of the present chapter. This further reference is the more apt since Russell knew and admired Moore, and was also at least acquainted with most members of the Bloomsbury Circle. The account comes from one of *Two Memoirs* by the economist John Maynard Keynes:

> How did we know what states of mind were good? This was a matter of direct introspection, of direct unanalysable intention about which it was useless and impossible to argue. In that case who was right when there was a difference of opinion? . . . It might be . . . that some people had an acuter sense of judgement, just as some people can judge a vintage port and others cannot. On the whole, so far as I remember, this explanation prevailed. In practice, victory was with those who could speak with the greatest appearance of clear, undoubting conviction and could best use the accents of infallibility. Moore at this time was a master of this method – greeting one's remarks with a gasp of incredulity – *Do* you *really* think *that*, an expression of face as if to hear such a thing said reduced him to a state of wonder verging on imbecility, with his mouth wide open and wagging his head in the negative so violently that his hair shook. *Oh!* he would say, goggling at you as if either you or he must be mad; and no reply was possible.
>
> (pp. 84–85; italics original)

To avoid any such seemingly obscurantist conclusion was one of the main motives behind classical Utilitarianism, the doctrine that the supreme good is the greatest happiness of the greatest number. This "greatest-happiness principle" gained its name and first fame through the work of Jeremy Bentham (1748–1832). The present point is made in an essay on 'Bentham' by Bentham's subtler disciple John Stuart Mill (1806–1873):

> Whether happiness be or be not the end to which morality should be referred – that it should be referred to an *end* of some sort, and not left in the dominion of vague feeling or inexplicable internal conviction, that it be made a matter of reason and calculation, and not merely of sentiment, is essential to the very idea of moral philosophy; is, in fact, what renders argument or discussion on moral questions possible. That the morality of actions depends on the consequences which they tend to produce, is the doctrine of rational persons of all schools; that the good

or evil of those consequences is measured solely by pleasure or pain is all of the doctrine of the school of utility which is peculiar to it.

This Utilitarian doctrine – it is worth underlining – was first introduced as, and still remains, a doctrine for benevolent reformers. For Bentham and for his immediate followers it provided the criterion by which to test established laws and institutions, and to find them very often and very badly wanting. Applied to morality it is best understood similarly, not as a rationale for existing principles and standards, but rather as a proposal for systematic reform. Certainly there are various norms widely accepted as moral which, it would seem, must be hard to justify by reference to the classical Utilitarian standard: the tabus, for instance, against homosexual relations between consenting adults or, much more importantly, against voluntary euthanasia. (These are examples of what J. S. Mill, but not Bentham, would have called secondary principles; which have all as such in his view to be justified, or rejected, by reference to the primary principle of the greatest happiness of the greatest number.)

The main reason, however, for mentioning classical Utilitarianism here is as a reminder of the enormous importance of arguments and investigations about means to ends. Even if we were to accept either what Russell says or what Moore says as giving the correct story about "what is good or bad on its own account, independently of its effects" (Russell), still we ought to protest against presentations which suggest that all matters of evaluation must be in some way ultimate and beyond reason. It is a mistake – and a mistake which may have practically serious consequences – to slide, as Russell does, from talking exclusively about "intrinsic value" to the comprehensive conclusion that "questions of value . . . cannot be decided at all, and lie outside the realm of truth and falsehood." For even if what he says and suggests is true about intrinsic value – what is valuable on its own account – it will not by the same token necessarily be true also about instrumental value – what is valuable as a means to something else. The point is aptly made in his *Out of My Later Years* by Einstein, who took broadly the same view as Russell about intrinsic value:

> I know that it is a hopeless undertaking to debate about fundamental value judgements. For instance, if someone approves, as a goal, the extirpation of the human race from the earth, one cannot refute such a viewpoint on rational grounds. But if there is agreement on certain goals and values, one can argue rationally about the means by which these objectives may be obtained. (p. 12)

A second point to notice is that Russell's position in *Religion and Science* incorporates a distinction of which his classical predecessors had not made use. We have already seen how subjectivism in the wide sense defended in the present chapter cannot be equated with, and does not entail, the narrow and extreme version which would construe value utterances as statements about the psychology of the speaker. With appropriate alterations the same can be said about the relations – or lack of relations – between subjectivism, again widely interpreted, and Russell's new, more sophisticated, version of the narrow form. This new version – which Russell may have taken from A. J. Ayer's *Language, Truth and Logic* – construes value utterances as ejaculations rather than as statements; and hence as expressions, rather than reports, of the reactions of the utterer. The official label for this view is *emotivism*. But the well-established nickname *The Boo-Hooray Theory* is to be preferred as being at the same time more specific, more informative, and more memorable.

The third comment on Russell's account of intrinsic value is provided by a passage from the chapter 'Decisions of Principle' in R. M. Hare's *The Language of Morals*, though Hare was not directing his argument at any one particular target:

> The truth is that, if asked to justify as completely as possible any decision, we have to bring in both effects – to give content to the decision – and principles, and the effects in general of observing those principles, and so on until we have satisfied our enquirer. Thus a complete justification of a decision would consist of a complete account of its effects, together with a complete account of the principles it observed, and the effects of observing those principles – for, of course, it is the effects (what obeying them in fact consists in) which give content to the principles too. Thus, if pressed to justify a decision completely, we have to give a complete specification of the way of life of which it is a part. This complete specification it is impossible in practice to give; the nearest attempts are those given by the great religions, especially those which can point to historical persons who carried out the way of life in practice. Suppose, however, that we can give it. If the enquirer still goes on asking 'But why *should* I live that?' then there is no further answer to give him, because we have already, *ex hypothesi*, said everything that could be included in this further answer. We can only ask him to make up his own mind which way he ought to live; for in the end everything rests upon such a decision of principle. He has to decide whether to accept that way of life or not; if he accepts it, then we can proceed to justify the decisions that are based upon it; if he does not accept it, then

let him accept some other, and try to live by it. The sting is in the last clause. To describe such ultimate decisions as arbitrary, because *ex hypothesi* everything which could be used to justify them has already been included in the decision, would be like saying that a complete description of the universe was unfounded, because no further fact could be called upon in corroboration of it. This is not how we use the words 'arbitrary' and 'unfounded'. Far from being arbitrary such a decision would be the most well-founded of decisions, because it would be based upon a consideration of everything upon which it could possibly be founded.   (pp. 68–69: italics original)

§7 *Making room for moral argument*

Even if The Boo-Hooray Theory, or something like it, did – or does – constitute the correct account of talk about intrinsic value it must still be quite wrong to suggest that most or even much discussion about what ought or ought not to be done reaches such questions of ultimate justification. It is indeed a serious fault in the presentations of that theory both by Russell here and by Ayer earlier that they give the impression that something which may or may not be true in the last analysis is supposed to be a fact with which we are always and everywhere confronted, not ultimately but immediately. One reason why there must be a gap between the first and any such last analysis has been indicated already: it is that there are so many immediately practical problems of how to achieve results which it is agreed would be desirable, or to prevent others which it is acknowledged would be deplorable. But another and much more interesting reason refers to a different kind of argument. This kind, which is more distinctively moral, is concerned not with ends and means but with consistency and inconsistency in attitudes and in the use of moral terms.

The Athenians on Melos were as wise as they were wicked when they refused absolutely to entertain any considerations of justice. For by this refusal they avoided giving purchase to moral arguments, which might have been embarrassingly forceful notwithstanding the obvious determination of the Athenians not to allow any such considerations to be effectively persuasive. Back in § 2 of Chapter I (pp. 22–23) I quoted another passage from Russell. The immediate aim was to underline the distinction between proving and persuading. But now we can draw further lessons from a second reading.

Russell began: "I do not know how, by any purely logical argument, to refute a man who maintains that only the desires of Germans should be considered. This view has been refuted on the battlefield, but can it be refuted in the study?" In the light of all that has been said in the present chapter about *ought* and *is* it should be obvious that Russell is confounding two interpretations of the word *should*. What has been decided on the battlefield is that some desires other than those of Germans will in fact carry weight. What has to be refuted, presumably in the study, is the quite different claim that only the desires of Germans ought to be considered. And if someone tells us that we cannot expect a convinced National Socialist to accept any refutation we must insist on a parallel distinction between prescriptive and descriptive senses of the word *expect*. We may expect (prescriptive) certain standards of this or that without being so foolish as to expect (descriptive) that these standards will always and everywhere be in fact observed. (Nelson's signal before Trafalgar was impressive partly because it used the word in both senses at once: "England expects that every man will do his duty.")

All this about refutation, however, applies to every sort of argument equally. The apparent peculiarity of (one main kind of) moral argument is that it would seem to be theoretically possible, and possible without irrationality, to avoid accepting any moral conclusions by simply refusing to offer any moral premises. In so far as this really is so, and in so far as, if so, it really is a peculiarity, (this form of) moral argument is essentially person to person in a way in which – say – proof in mathematics is not.

For to refuse to accept a matter of fact as being indeed such, when there are available sufficient reasons for holding that it actually is, is, surely, irrational; while, quite certainly, if you do accept premises it must be irrational to refuse to accept conclusions validly deduced therefrom. But it is at the very least not obvious that it has to be similarly irrational to refuse to accept any genuinely moral premises at all; and hence it is not obvious either that it must be irrational to refuse to accept, as genuinely binding, conclusions validly deduced from such premises. Of course, those qualifications *genuinely moral* and *genuinely binding* are essential. To refuse to allow that (at least some) people do have moral notions, and do acknowledge some moral claims as binding, would be to fly in the face of manifest fact. What is in question is how far it is possible, and at what price, to eschew commitment to such notions and claims as binding on oneself.

In practice any such theoretical possibility is most unlikely to be completely and perfectly actualized. Those – such as the Athenians at Melos – who on some particular occasion, or within some particular sphere of life, refuse to entertain any moral considerations will elsewhere commit themselves morally; and through this commitment give purchase to moral argument. They will find themselves expressing indignation and outrage at something done to themselves or to their friends. They will thereby be implying that such conduct is wicked and unjust. Yet to imply this, as we saw in the previous section, is to appeal to impartial general standards essentially independent of all individual or group interests and animosities.

The commitment to such standards once made, the way is wide open for argument about their systematic and consistent application. For it is both of the essence of morality and a presupposition of moral argument that moral notions must apply generally and impartially to all relevantly similar cases; although, and consequently, the question of what is relevantly similar remains perennially disputatious. We all know – or we should all know, since such hypocrisy is excruciatingly common – what to think of the so-called 'moral indignation' which is felt and expressed only against enemies. We are, for instance, altogether familiar with that pretended moral revulsion against the use of poison gas which is scandalized by its employment, but only when it is used in Vietnam by white men against communist guerrillas, or only when it is used in the Yemen by Arab socialists suppressing "reactionary feudal elements". Whatever such highly selective partisan revulsions may be they are as such precisely not authentically moral. Nevertheless even such pretences are still important as giving purchase. For, once again: 'Hypocrisy is the tribute which vice pays to virtue.'

In the previous section I quoted from the second *Inquiry* a passage in which Hume contrasted the functions of terms like *enemy* with those of such moral words as *vicious*. Hume's emphasis was on the difference between expressing the speaker's "particular circumstances and situation", and appealing to "some universal principle". The same essential feature of moral concepts is stressed by Kant also, but his emphasis is logical rather than psychological. Having argued that moral norms are, in his terminology, categorical as opposed to hypothetical imperatives Kant proceeds, still in his own altogether distinctive way, to develop this theme that impartiality and universality are built into the very idea of morality. The translation is again drawn from H. J. Paton's *The Moral Law,* and Kant's exuberant typography has as before been sobered down:

... we wish first to enquire whether perhaps the mere concept of a categorical imperative may not also provide us with the formula containing the only proposition that can be a categorical imperative; for even when we know the purport of such an absolute command, the question of its possibility will still require a special and troublesome effort, which we postpone to the final chapter.

When I conceive a hypothetical imperative in general, I do not know beforehand what it will contain – until its condition is given. But if I conceive a categorical imperative, I know at once what it contains. For since besides the law this imperative contains only the necessity that our maxim should conform to this law, while the law, as we have seen, contains no condition to limit it, there remains nothing over to which the maxim has to conform except the universality of a law as such; and it is this conformity alone that the imperative properly asserts to be necessary.

There is therefore only a single categorical imperative and it is this: 'Act only on that maxim through which you can at the same time will that it should become a universal law.'

Now if all imperatives of duty can be derived from this one imperative as their principle, then even although we leave it unsettled whether what we call duty may not be an empty concept, we shall still be able to show at least what we understand by it and what the concept means.

(p. 88)

Kant goes on almost immediately to illustrate this purely formal point by attempting to show how the key idea – Suppose everyone else were to do the same – can be put to use to generate more substantial conclusions. I will quote only one of these none too happy attempts, and then conclude the section and chapter with something less exceptionable from another source:

A man feels sick of life as the result of a series of misfortunes that has mounted to the point of despair, but he is still so far in possession of his reason as to ask himself whether taking his own life may not be contrary to his duty to himself. He now applies the test 'Can the maxim of my action really become a universal law of nature?' His maxim is 'From self-love I make it my principle to shorten my life if its continuance threatens more evil than it promises pleasure.' The only further question to ask is whether this principle of self-love can become a universal law of nature. It is then seen at once that a system of nature by whose law the very same feeling whose function is to stimulate the furtherance of life should actually destroy life would contradict itself, and consequently could not subsist as a system of nature. Hence this maxim cannot possibly hold as a universal law of nature, and is therefore entirely opposed to the supreme principle of all duty. (p. 89)

It is easy, and modestly instructive, to think of a few examples from natural history of instincts "whose function is to stimulate the furtherance of life" but which nevertheless do on occasion lead the animal to its own destruction. But the point which has to be made is that, since the notion of impartiality is essential to morality, any appeal to moral ideas may expose the appellant to charges of inconsistency. Thus once I commit myself to saying or suggesting that, for instance, to deny opportunities to otherwise qualified persons on the grounds of their race is morally wrong I become wide open to such charges if I then refuse to apply condemnation as much to blacks discriminating against whites or Asians as to whites discriminating against blacks. As a paradigm of such person-to-person moral argument, consider Nathan's rebuke to King David for his treatment of Uriah the Hittite (II *Samuel*, 11–12, King James' Authorized Version):

> And it came to pass in an eveningtide, that David arose from off his bed, and walked upon the roof of the king's house: and from the roof he saw a woman washing herself; and the woman was very beautiful to look upon. And David sent and enquired after the woman. And one said, 'Is not this Bathsheba, the daughter of Eliam, the wife of Uriah the Hittite?' And David sent messengers, and took her; and she came in unto him, and he lay with her. . . . And the woman conceived, and sent and told David, and said, 'I am with child' . . . And it came to pass in the morning, that David wrote a letter to Joab, and sent it by the hand of Uriah. And he wrote in the letter, saying, 'Set ye Uriah in the forefront of the hottest battle, and retire ye from him, that he may be smitten, and die. And it came to pass, when Joab observed the city, that he assigned Uriah unto a place where he knew that valiant men were. And the men of the city went out, and fought with Joab: and there fell some of the people of the servants of David; and Uriah the Hittite died also. . . . And the Lord sent Nathan unto David. And he came unto him, and said unto him, 'There were two men in one city; the one rich, and the other poor. The rich man had exceeding many flocks and herds. But the poor man had nothing, save one little ewe lamb, which he had bought and nourished up: and it grew up together with him, and with his children; it did eat of his own meat, and drank of his own cup, and lay in his bosom, and was unto him as a daughter. And there came a traveller unto the rich man, and he spared to take of his own flock and

of his own herd, to dress for the wayfaring man that was come unto him; but took the poor man's lamb, and dressed it for the man that was come to him.' And David's anger was greatly kindled against the man, and he said to Nathan, 'As the Lord liveth, the man that hath done this thing shall surely die: and he shall restore the lamb fourfold, because he did this thing, and because he had no pity.' And Nathan said to David, 'Thou art the man!'

CHAPTER IV

Survival and Immortality

§1 *Presuppositions of pre-existence and immortality*

SOCRATES – And yet we have not listed the greatest rewards and prizes offered for virtue.

GLAUCON – You must be thinking of something inconceivably great if there are other things greater than those of which you have spoken already.

SOCRATES – But what could become great in a small space of time? For surely the whole of this period from boyhood to old age must be small indeed compared with all time?

GLAUCON – Yes, nothing at all. So what?

SOCRATES – Do you think that an immortal object ought to be seriously concerned about so small a period, and not about all time?

GLAUCON – Of course I agree. But what have you in mind?

SOCRATES – Have you not appreciated that our souls are immortal and never perish?

GLAUCON – No, by Zeus, I have not. Can someone like you maintain this?

This exchange is found in Book X of Plato's *The Republic* (§ 608 C–D). It is perhaps most remarkable for the well-bred incredulity with which Plato presents Glaucon as responding to the idea of the immortality of the soul: "And he, looking at me in amazement, said . . . 'Can someone like you maintain this?' " Such a passage may be a salutary reminder that mortalism – the belief that all men die and that death is final – is not a peculiarly modern doctrine: it is, for instance, to be found in the Bible, not only in Ecclesiastes but very clearly and taken as obvious in the Psalms. The context in *The Republic* is that after the withdrawal of 'Thrasymachus' at the end of Book I, Plato's brothers 'Glaucon' and 'Adeimantus' enter the contest, and challenge 'Socrates' to show – among other things – that justice is always to the advantage of the man who acts justly. Now, halfway through the final Book, having already argued that even within our present life this is so, 'Socrates' proposes to press down the balance decisively by calling in an everlasting hereafter.

A practical concern of this kind has characterized most of the philosophical advocates of a doctrine of personal immortality. It is, for instance, in different versions perfectly clear and explicit in Descartes and Leibniz, in Berkeley and Kant. Locke's statement in *The Reasonableness of Christianity* is peculiar only in that it takes the robustly worldly form of investment advice, and in that Locke seems momentarily to have forgotten his Plato:

> The [Classical – A. F.] philosophers, indeed, shewed the beauty of virtue; ... but leaving her unendowed, very few were willing to espouse her. ... But now there being put into the scales on her side, 'an exceeding and immortal weight of glory'; interest is come about to her, and virtue is now visibly the most enriching purchase, and by much the best bargain. ... The view of heaven and hell will cast a slight upon the short pleasures and pains of this present state, and give attractions and encouragements to virtue, which reason and interest, and the care of ourselves, cannot but allow and prefer. Upon this foundation, and upon this only, morality stands firm, and may defy all competition. This makes it more than a name, a substantial good, worth all our aims and endeavours; and thus the gospel of Jesus Christ has delivered it to us.
>
> (p. 94)

In *The Republic* 'Socrates' presents one unpersuasive argument as a proof of the immortality of the soul, and then proceeds almost immediately to the Myth of Er. This is the story of Er, the son of Armenius, who was killed in battle but came back from the dead to report what happens to souls after death. Although Plato is certainly not asking us to accept this or any of his other myths as literally true it does embody two doctrines for which he offers elsewhere what are supposed to be philosophical demonstrations.

Number one is the immortality of the soul, which 'Socrates' takes to have been proved by the preceding argument. The second is the reverse but complementary doctrine of the eternal pre-existence of the soul. To those reared in a Christian or post-Christian culture the second but not the first of these is likely to seem outlandish. Yet – all questions of a possible revelation apart – they would appear to be a matching pair. If the soul, or the Universe, or God, or anything else, is thought to be everlasting then, surely, the presumption, in default of positive reason to the contrary, should be that what will be without end was also eternally without beginning; and the other way about likewise.

In the Myth of Er these complementary notions of pre-existence and immortality are combined with a doctrine of metempsychosis, the transmigration of souls. At the end of one life souls are despatched for reward or punishment as the case may be. But these rewards and punishments come to an end, and afterwards the souls have to start new lives in new bodies; and so on, indefinitely. Plato's entertainment of this bizarre doctrine was one of many marks of Pythagorean influence. Of Pythagoras and his followers more will be said later (Ch. XI, § 1). For the moment it must suffice to remark that he flourished in South Italy in the low 500's BC, and that there is no good reason for not crediting him with the invention of the Theorem of Pythagoras.

Transmigration was an idea which Plato perhaps did no more than entertain respectfully. Pre-existence and immortality he certainly at least at one stage asserted and thought that he had proved. Our main source here will be the *Phaedo*. But before looking at the crucial arguments there it is essential to get clear what is meant by the expression *the soul*, and what it is which is said to pre-exist and to be immortal.

The answer to this vital question is, in a word, the person. But now it has immediately to be added that the person is taken to be an incorporeal something. For Plato – as for so many others to this day – the soul is the person (but incorporeal). Both parts of this answer are equally indispensable for his arguments. If my soul were not me its immortality could not be my immortality: for by itself the mysterious supposed fact of its being incorporeal would give me no better reason for being urgently concerned about what might or might not become of it after my death than I have for interest in the ultimate destiny of my excised tonsils. If my soul were not allowed to be incorporeal then argument about its possible immortality could scarcely begin: Plato the lover of his poets knew as well as Aeschylus how "the money changer War, changer of bodies . . ."

Home from Troy refined by fire
Sends back to friends the dust
That is heavy with tears, stowing
A man's worth of ashes
In an easily handled jar. (*Agamemnon*, 437 and 440–444: tr. L. MacNeice)

These two essentials of Plato's concept of soul both come out in a piquant and memorable way towards the end of the *Phaedo*. It has been mentioned before that this dialogue is presented as a report on the last hours of Socrates, spent in prison discussing human immortality with his friends while waiting for his executioner to bring the draught of hemlock. We have to admire the boldness with which Plato not merely accepts but underlines the paradoxical consequences of his position. 'Crito' speaks first:

'Then we shall certainly try hard to do these things as you say,' he said, 'but how shall we bury you?' 'However you please', he replied, 'if you catch me and I do not give you the slip.' And he laughed, and then he turned to us quietly, and he said, 'I cannot persuade Crito, my friends, that I am this Socrates who is now conversing and arranging every bit of what is being said. He thinks that I am the thing which he will be seeing as a corpse in a short time, and he asks how to bury me. And all that I have been saying at great length just now about how when I drink the poison I shall no longer remain with you but shall go away to the joys of the blessed – that he seems to think was not what I really think but was said partly to encourage you and partly to encourage myself. So you', he said, 'go bail for me to Crito in the opposite sense from that in which he went bail to the court. For he gave surety that I would remain. But you must give surety that I shall not remain when I die but shall up and begone, in order that Crito may bear it more easily, and, when he sees my body either being burnt or being buried, not be distressed on my account as if I were suffering something terrible. And he must not say at the funeral that he is laying out Socrates, or carrying him out for burial, or burying him. For be sure', he said, 'my dear Crito, that to speak gauchely is not only jarring in itself. It infects the soul with something evil. No, you must keep your spirits up, and say that you bury my body – and bury it as you think fit, and as seems to you most proper.

(§ 115C–E)

§2 *From the Forms to immortality*

Section One has made it clear what souls are supposed to be. Plato offers several arguments for the conclusion that our souls survive death, and indeed that they are immortal. We shall concentrate on those which refer directly to the Theory of Forms. For Plato another of the many attractions of this theory surely was that it appeared to give support in more than one way to his conclusions about souls. It could, as was remarked in Chapter II, be in a very general way a mainstay of the Gods in their perennial battle against the Giants. More particularly, just as St

Augustine saw the existence of eternal and incorporeal Forms as opening the way for further incorporeal and eternal beings, so Plato wanted to argue that if there are Forms which are both then souls too can reasonably be expected to be eternal as well as incorporeal. He spells out this contention in the *Phaedo*:

SOCRATES – Well then, must we not ask ourselves something of this sort? What kind of thing naturally suffers dispersion? For what kind of thing is it appropriate to fear this, and for what not? And after this again we surely should enquire to which kind the soul belongs, and then be either confident or anxious about our souls according to what the answers are?

CEBES – What you say is true.

SOCRATES – So then, are not the compounded and the composite naturally liable to be decomposed in the same way in which they were put together? And if there is anything uncompounded is not that, if anything, naturally immune to decomposition?

CEBES – It seems to me that that is how it is.

SOCRATES – Then it is most probable that whatever things are always the same and unchanging are the uncompounded ones, and whatever are always different on different occasions and never the same are the compounded.

CEBES – Yes, I think so.

SOCRATES – Let us, then, turn to the things which we were discussing before. Is the Form of whose existence we give an account in our questions and answers always the same or different on different occasions? Equality, Beauty, any Form that is, do these things ever admit of any change whatsoever? Or does each of these Forms, being uniform and existing in its own right, remain the same and never anywhere in any way admit any change at all?

CEBES – It must necessarily remain the same, Socrates.

SOCRATES – Now how about the many things, for example men, or horses, or cloaks, or anything else of that sort, or equal things, or beautiful things, or all the things which have the same names as those Forms? Are they always the same? Or are they, in diametric opposition to those Forms, never the same as themselves or one another and, so to speak, just not the same?

CEBES – That is how it is. They are never the same.

SOCRATES – And you can touch, and see, and perceive these with the various senses, whereas the things which are always the same cannot ever be grasped by anything but the exercise of the understanding – such things are incorporeal and invisible.

CEBES – Certainly, what you say is true.

SOCRATES – Do you want us to postulate two kinds of existents, the visible and the incorporeal?

CEBES – Yes.

SOCRATES – And that the incorporeal is always the same, but the visible never?

CEBES – Yes again.

SOCRATES – Well then, do we not consist of two elements, the body and the soul?

CEBES – That is it.

SOCRATES – Now to which kind should we say that the body is more similar and more closely related?

CEBES – It is certainly obvious to everyone that it is to the visible.

SOCRATES – What about the soul? Visible or incorporeal? . . .

CEBES – It cannot be seen. . . .

SOCRATES – Then the soul is more like the incorporeal than the body is, and the body is more like the visible. . . . Consider the matter in another way too. When the body and the soul are joined together nature directs one to be the slave and to be ruled and the other to be the master and to rule. And this being the case, which seems to you like the divine and which like the mortal. . . .

CEBES – It is quite clear, Socrates, that the soul is like the divine while the body is like the mortal.

SOCRATES – Then consider, Cebes, whether this is our conclusion from all that has been said – that the soul is most like the divine, and the immortal, and the object of thought, and the uniform, and the indissoluble, and the eternally unchanging; while the body is most like the human, and the mortal, and the multiform, and what is not an object of thought, and the dissoluble, and what is never the same with itself. Is there anything else we can say to show that this is not so?

CEBES – No, there is not.

SOCRATES – Well, then, since this is how it is, is it not natural for the body to be dissolved quickly but for the soul to be entirely indissoluble or nearly so? (§§ 78B–79C and 80A–B)

Once granted its premises such an argument has a great deal of plausibility. Yet Plato would have wished to rest his case not on any mere considerations as to what is probable, but on what he clearly took to be a compulsive demonstration. The conclusion that the soul is immortal is apparently derived from the Theory of Forms; and, significantly and appropriately, it is drawn as the climax to the long exposition of that theory in the *Phaedo*. In the penultimate phase 'Socrates' is discussing logical incompatibilities, working with numbers and their characteristics as his example. Despite, or perhaps because of, his lack of a modern technical vocabulary his thesis should be sufficiently clear:

SOCRATES – The odd must always be labelled by this name odd, must it not?

CEBES – Certainly.

SOCRATES – Then is this the only thing – this is what I mean to ask – or is there something else, which is not the odd, but which must nevertheless be called this as well as by its own name because it is of such a nature that it is never separated from the odd? I mean, for instance, like the number three; and there are many others. Take the number three. Do you not agree that it can always be characterized by its own name and by that of the odd, which is not the same as the number three? Yet the number three and the number five and a full half of all the numbers are so constituted that without being the odd each of them is odd. And correspondingly the number two and the number four and the whole series of the alternate numbers are even, each one of them, without being the even. Do you go along with this, or not?

CEBES – Of course I do.

SOCRATES – So now see what I want to make plain. It is this, that it is not only the opposites which exclude one another but also all the things which while not being opposites eternally contain opposites. These too exclude the Form which is opposite to the one they contain, and when it approaches they either perish or withdraw. We have got to say, have we not, that the number three will be destroyed or will suffer anything else rather than submit to becoming, while still remaining the number three, even?

CEBES – Certainly.

SOCRATES – Yet the number two is not the opposite of the number three?

CEBES – No, it is not.

SOCRATES – Then it is not only opposite Forms which refuse to sustain each other's approach but certain others also. . . . Certainly you appreciate that of whatever the Form of three has possession must be not only three but also odd.

CEBES – Yes, indeed.

SOCRATES – So the Form opposite to the one which makes it that could not enter such a thing?

CEBES – No.

SOCRATES – But what made it that was the Form of the odd.

CEBES – Yes.

SOCRATES – And the opposite of this is the Form of the even?
CEBES – Yes.
SOCRATES – Then the Form of the even will never enter the number three?
CEBES – Certainly not. (§§ 103E–104E)

This discussion of the odd and the even is, as has been said, taken from the penultimate movement of a long argument. To understand the climax to which it is moving it is necessary to appreciate certain features of Greek, features which are of course paralleled in many other languages. The Greek word always translated by *soul* is *psuche*: this is the ultimate root from which English has derived a whole range of words beginning with *psych* – *psychic, psychology, psychoanalysis,* and so on. Now this word *psuche* both is and to a Greek must obviously appear to be etymologically related to others such as *empsuchos* (literally, 'ensouled'), meaning alive, and *lipopsuchein* (roughly, 'soul-leaving'), meaning to swoon or to die or just to fail in courage. It thus becomes overwhelmingly natural to think of the soul as being in some sense the principle of life; to think of being alive as a matter of being ensouled, having a soul; and to think of death as the loss or departure of the soul.

A concept of soul of this kind is radically different from that explained in § 1, in which the expression *the soul* becomes equivalent to *the person (but incorporeal)*. Yet this is a distinction which Plato, and not only Plato, failed to make. What he did do was for a philosopher the next best thing. He provided, in *The Republic*, a perfect occasion for making this distinction decisively obvious. 'Socrates' has just defined the work or function of a thing as that for which it is the indispensable instrument, or the best. He has gone on to urge that every such function has its appropriate excellence and its corresponding defect: the excellence is that of fulfilling the function well, the defect is the opposite:

SOCRATES – Right. Then next consider this. Has the soul some function which you could not fulfil with anything else at all? Take management, rule, deliberation, and everything of the such – is there anything else but the soul to which we could properly allocate these and say that they belonged to that?
THRASYMACHUS – There is nothing else.
SOCRATES – And what about being alive? Shall we say that that is a function of the soul?
THRASYMACHUS – That above all.

SOCRATES – And do we not therefore say that there is some excellence appropriate to the soul?

THRASYMACHUS – We do.

SOCRATES – Well then, Thrasymachus, will the soul fulfil its functions well if it lacks its own proper excellence, or is this impossible?

THRASYMACHUS – It is impossible.

SOCRATES – Of necessity then the bad soul must rule and manage badly while the good does all these things well.

THRASYMACHUS – Of necessity.

SOCRATES – And did we not agree that the excellence of the soul is justice and the defect injustice?

THRASYMACHUS – Yes, we did.

SOCRATES – So the just soul and the just man will live well and the unjust badly.

THRASYMACHUS – So it appears, by your reasoning.

SOCRATES – And, furthermore, the person who lives well is blessed and happy, and he who does not the contrary.

THRASYMACHUS – Of course.

SOCRATES – So the just man is happy and the unjust is miserable.

(§§ 353D–354E)

The fact that this conclusion, unless it is in some way drastically qualified, manifestly is not true should drive us back to make some unmade distinctions. One must be between *living well*, in the sense of enjoying life, and other senses of *living well*, in which to live well does not necessarily guarantee that anyone enjoys doing so. But what is relevant here is that "management, rule, deliberation, and everything of the such" are prerogatives of persons. Hence, if these are the function or functions of the soul in either of the two senses so far distinguished, they must belong to "the person (but incorporeal)". Being alive, however, is a totally different matter, and is no prerogative of persons: it is, surely, significant both that 'Socrates' has to mention this separately and that it is this which 'Thrasymachus' takes to be the pre-eminent function of the soul. We are now, at last, in a position to understand the grand finale of the argument of the *Phaedo*:

SOCRATES – Now, answer. What is it which by being in the body makes it alive?

CEBES – The soul.

SOCRATES – Is this always how it is?

CEBES – Of course.

SOCRATES – So of whatever the soul takes possession this it always approaches bringing life?

CEBES – It does.

SOCRATES – Is there or is there not something which is the opposite of life?

CEBES – There is.

SOCRATES – What is it?

CEBES – Death.

SOCRATES – Now, as we have agreed before, soul will never admit the opposite of what it brings with it?

CEBES – Absolutely not.

SOCRATES – Right. Now what do we call that which does not admit the Form of the even?

CEBES – Odd, or uneven. . . .   (§ 105C–D)

SOCRATES – Well then, what do we call that which would not admit death?

CEBES – Immortal.

SOCRATES – And the soul does not admit death?

CEBES – No.

SOCRATES – Then the soul is immortal.

CEBES – It is.

SOCRATES – Well. Shall we say that this is proved? What do you think?

CEBES – Yes indeed, Socrates, it is sufficient.   (§ 105E)

SOCRATES – All would agree, I think, that God, and the Form of life, and anything else there may be which is immortal, never perishes. . . . Since the immortal is also indestructible would not soul, if it is immortal, be imperishable too?

CEBES – Absolutely necessarily.

SOCRATES – Then when death comes to a man it seems that the mortal part of him dies while the immortal part goes away, safe and imperishable. In the face of death it withdraws.

CEBES – So it seems.

SOCRATES – It is, therefore, Cebes, certain that soul is immortal and imperishable; and our souls will go on existing in another world.

(§§ 106D–107A)

It is comparatively easy now, when the crucial distinction has been made already, to discern one fatal flaw in this argument. Although the situation is complicated by Plato's attempt to treat the soul as not itself being, but only being necessarily linked with, the principle of life let us here take Plato's own half-heartedness in this attempt as our excuse to simplify by ignoring the complication. Taking this simplification as made, it becomes obvious that Plato's argument revolves around an equivocation: in the conclusion the word *souls* is construed as meaning "persons (but incorporeal)"; whereas at the beginning the expression *the soul* refers to that "which by being in the body makes it alive". This pedestrian objection is, of course, by itself quite decisive. But it barely touches the features of the argument which make it an instructive landmark in the history of ideas.

Consider that first exchange: "'What is it which by being in the body makes it alive?' – 'The soul'." In the context of the Theory of Forms what this must mean is that whatever can be described as alive is alive in virtue of the fact that it participates in the Form of Life (or Soul), that that Form has possession of it. But now, if that is what it is for soul or the soul to be in the body – and in this present context it surely must be – then we are dealing not with the many particular souls but with the necessarily unique Form. So not only is the intended conclusion going to construe the word *soul* in a radically different sense from that given to it in the premise, but this same conclusion will be about all the individual souls, whereas that premise referred to the one only. Granted the Theory of Forms, and this theory is the basis of the whole operation, it must be both redundant and irrelevant to urge that "the Form of Life . . . never perishes": redundant because according to the theory the same is universally true of all Forms, including – presumably – even the Form of Death; and irrelevant because what is supposed to be being proved is the immortality of all the many particular individuals, who – again according to that theory itself – must be presumed to be ephemeral and changing, and who quite certainly cannot be identified with the unique Form.

To this it would be at best a very partial and quite inadequate reply to say that Plato thought individual souls had an intermediate status, like Forms both eternal and incorporeal, but unlike them not each one essentially unique. That he did. But this reply would be partial and inadequate because it takes up only an incidental in the objection, and does nothing at all to save the main argument. Far worse, it is precisely this affirmation of an impossible intermediate status which constitutes a landmark, the signpost pointing down an endless sidetrack of delusion.

Back in Chapter II I gave some first indications of how it seems perennially tempting, and yet why it must be utterly impossible, to identify any abstraction or Form – even the supreme Form of the Good – with any agent individual acting in space and time. This applies whether, like the Demiurge of the *Timaeus*, the latter is only a shaper or whether, like the

God of the children of Israel, a creator. Though Plato did at one stage believe that Goodness is a unique individual, which not merely may but must be itself pre-eminently good, he nevertheless remained most careful not to identify this supreme Form with his Demiurge. Yet here in his account of souls he makes a mistake similar to that which he there avoids. For, while he does not actually equate particular souls with the unique Form of Life, he does insist that souls must have an attribute which is really a prerogative of abstractions; and in doing this he can be seen as pointing the way towards innumerable later attempts to make some bodiless abstraction one flesh with an agent.

One cannot hope to achieve all at once full understanding of everything which is involved here. It is enough now to master two further distinctions. Plato maintains that both his Forms and his souls are eternal, immortal, and imperishable. But, in so far as we may speak of abstractions as eternal, it is because it would make no sense to predicate temporal attributes of these; whereas to say that a person is immortal is to say that, while no doubt it would make perfectly good sense to suggest that he might die one day, in actual fact he never will. It makes perfectly good sense, though it goes against everything we know about nature, to suggest that a man might survive to be older than the legendary Methusaleh – or even live for ever. But it is a nonsense even to ask what Goodness or the Form of Life may have been doing or not doing while the Founding Fathers were busy drafting the American Constitution.

The first distinction, which is needed to explain the second, is that between rejecting something as strictly unintelligible, because it is self-contradictory or nonsensical, and rejecting as simply false, because things are not or were not or will not be as it intelligibly but erroneously maintains. This distinction is indispensable to philosophy: one identifying peculiarity of the philosopher is that he is apt to offer arguments designed to demonstrate conclusions of the former sort.

The second distinction is between two senses of *eternal*. Let us label these as *eternal (everlasting)* and *eternal (non-temporal)*, respectively. It is good practice when making such distinctions always to provide mnemonic descriptive labels, and equally good practice to demand that others do the same. (People commonly complain that some term is ambiguous when it is really only vague or thought to be in some other way troublesome: no one has any business to talk of ambiguity unless they are ready to explain what the two different senses are.) In the present case the desired conclusion is that souls are eternal (everlasting), that as a matter of fact they never do perish. But abstractions are capable only of eternity, in the sense of being non-temporal. So the eternity of the Forms must be totally different from the temporal everlastingness which may, or may not, characterize people like us.

§ 3 *The soul and the person*

The argument just examined constitutes the philosophical climax of the *Phaedo*. But there are further fundamental lessons to be learnt now from Plato before ultimately we turn to Aristotle as the protagonist of another tradition of thought about the nature of man. In § 1 Plato's *soul* was construed as "person (but incorporeal)". This is, roughly, correct. But the word *psuche* was not freshly coined by Plato in order to attach to it his chosen meaning by simple stipulation. Nor was it a word with one single clear-cut established acceptation. (The same applies with appropriate alterations to its near, and not so near, equivalents in other languages.) In consequence what should ideally have been understood and presented as questions about what concept of soul to employ, or whether – in this particular interpretation of the word *soul* – there are such things, appear instead as investigations of some sort into the nature of the soul. Thus, much earlier in the *Phaedo* and in reply to the contentions of which the first passage in § 2 formed a part, 'Simmias' objects:

> Well, someone might apply the same argument to harmony and to the lyre with its strings, saying that the harmony in the well-attuned lyre is something invisible and incorporeal and all-beautiful and divine, whereas the lyre itself and its strings are bodies and corporeal and composite and earthy and related to the mortal. So suppose someone were to use the same argument as you and, when someone smashes the lyre or cuts and breaks the strings, to maintain that that harmony cannot have perished but must still exist? For it would be unthinkable that the lyre and its strings, which are of mortal kind, should still exist with the strings broken when it, which is related to the divine and the immortal and of the same nature with it, has perished before the mortal. He would say that the harmony must still exist somewhere, and that the wood and the strings would have to rot away before anything could happen to that. And I think myself, Socrates, that it must have occurred to you that we do understand the soul to be something very much like this, that our body is strung up and held together by heat and cold and dry and wet and the like, and our soul is a mixture and a harmony of these

same elements when they are well mixed in the correct relative proportions. If then the soul is a sort of harmony, it is obvious that, when our body is untunefully strung up or relaxed by diseases and other evils, the soul must immediately perish no matter how divine it is, just like the other harmonies both in sounds and in all the works of craftsmen, whereas the remains of each material thing will last a long time till they are burnt or decayed. Now what shall we say to this argument, if anyone claims that the soul, being a mixture of the components of the body, is the first to perish in what we call death? (§§ 85E–86D)

This objection, as 'Socrates' at once allows, embodies a vital point. This point can be generalized by saying that, if my soul is to survive my death and dissolution it must be, in one of the senses of a philosophically overworked word, a substance. It must, that is to say, be the sort of thing which can significantly be spoken of as existing separately and in its own right. The explanation of this meaning of the term *substance* once again presupposes the fundamental general distinction between rejecting some suggestion because it is strictly unintelligible (and, hence, perhaps strictly not a suggestion at all), and rejecting it as being in fact false. Good, because both apt and memorable, illustrations can be found in Lewis Carroll. Thus although one might say that the talk of a treacle well in *Alice's Adventures in Wonderland* was a piece of nonsense, it is certainly not strictly nonsensical. For the suggestion is perfectly intelligible notwithstanding that there are in fact no natural springs or reservoirs of treacle available to be tapped by wells. The case is altogether different with the subtraction sum in *Through the Looking Glass*:

> 'Nine from eight I can't, you know', Alice replied very readily: 'but –'
> 'She can't do Subtraction', said the White Queen. 'Can you do Division? Divide a loaf by a knife – what's the answer to that?'
> 'I suppose' – Alice was beginning, but the Red Queen answered for her. 'Bread-and-butter, of course. Try another Subtraction sum. Take a bone from a dog: what remains?'
> Alice considered. 'The bone wouldn't remain, of course, if I took it – and the dog wouldn't remain; it would come and bite me – and I'm sure I shouldn't remain!'
> 'Then you think nothing would remain?' said the Red Queen.
> 'I think that's the answer.'
> 'Wrong, as usual', said the Red Queen: 'the dog's temper would remain.'
> 'But I don't see how –'

'Why, look here!' the Red Queen cried. 'The dog would lose its temper, wouldn't it?'

'Perhaps it would', Alice replied cautiously.

'Then if the dog went away, its temper would remain!' the Queen exclaimed triumphantly.

Alice said, as gravely as she could, 'They might go different ways.' But she couldn't help thinking to herself, 'What dreadful nonsense we *are* talking!' (Ch. IX: italics in original)

Alice's unspoken comment was, of course, correct. What makes the passage nonsense is its treating of *temper* as if this were a word for a substance (logical). By thus talking as if losing a temper were precisely on all fours with losing a bone the Red Queen was talking as if both tempers and bones could sensibly be said to exist in their own right; whereas in truth although bones are, tempers are not, substances (logical). In the particular case presented by 'Simmias' the harmony is like the temper, while the lyre and its strings are comparable with the bone. To the challenge of this suggested analogy 'Socrates' responds by referring back to their previous agreement "that our souls existed before we were born": this was one of the two "fine conclusions" of the Argument from Recollection as cited already (Ch. II, § 2):

SOCRATES – What, then, do you want to say about that argument in which we maintained that learning is recollection and that, since this is so, our soul must necessarily have been somewhere else before it was imprisoned in the body?

CEBES – I was wonderfully convinced by it at the time and I still remain more persuaded by it than by any other.

SIMMIAS – I too am the same, and I should be very surprised if about this I were ever to change my mind.

SOCRATES – But you must change your mind, my Theban friend, if you remain of the opinion first that a harmony is a matter of composition and second that the soul is some sort of harmony formed from the arrangement of elements in the body. For surely you will not accept, and yourself assert, that a harmony existed before the elements out of which it has to be composed; or will you?

SIMMIAS – No, indeed I will not, Socrates.

SOCRATES – Then do you see that this is what you are saying when you maintain both, on the one hand, that the soul exists before it enters the bodily form of a man and, on the other hand, that it is composed from elements which do not yet exist? Harmony is not like the sort of thing with which you are comparing it, for the lyre and the strings and the sounds are prior to the harmonization, while the harmony is the last thing to emerge and the first to disappear. So however will you get this line of reasoning to harmonize with that?

SIMMIAS – I cannot at all.

SOCRATES – And yet if there is going to be harmony in any argument it is fitting that it should be in that about harmony.

SIMMIAS – It surely is.

SOCRATES – Well, there is no harmony in yours. Now see which you prefer, that learning is recollection or that the soul is a harmony.

SIMMIAS – The former, Socrates, by far. For the latter came to me without demonstration. It seemed in a way reasonable and fitting, which is why many other people hold it too. But I am conscious that lines of reasoning which establish their conclusions on probabilities are charlatans, and if one is not on one's guard against them they will deceive us badly both in geometry and in everything else. The theory of learning and recollection has, however, been established on a sound foundation. For it was agreed that our souls existed even before they entered the body, just as do the realities to which we give the name of Forms. And I am persuaded that these I have accepted on sufficient and correct grounds. So, it seems to me, I must not accept from myself or from anyone else the statement that the soul is a harmony.   (§§ 91E–92E)

Granted what everyone at this stage in the *Phaedo* does grant, the desired and vital conclusion surely follows. Yet that this is so should be seen rather as a reason for examining the Argument from Recollection more closely than as a demonstration that the soul must indeed be in the present sense a substance. In the *Phaedo* version, which is the version in which it is confidently put forward as a proof of human pre-existence, the nerve of the argument is this. We certainly never do perceive, for instance, perfect Equality. Nor do we ever perceive any perfectly equal things. Yet those imperfectly equal things with which we are acquainted can all be seen by us not only as being more or less like perfect Equality, but also as aspiring to this while nevertheless falling short. Now, to say that something is like something, or that it falls short of it, is to presuppose that you already have some sort of knowledge of whatever it is which that something is said to be like, or to fall short of. Hence we must infer that "before we began to see and to hear and to perceive in other ways, we must somehow have acquired knowledge of Equality itself."

A first point in this connection is that the priority of an assumption to the contention which logically presupposes that assumption is not temporal. To say that this contention presupposes that, is not to say that anyone who maintains the former must previously either publicly assert or privately believe the latter: often indeed the point of saying this will be precisely to draw someone's attention to the subsistence of a logical connection of which he had himself been altogether unaware. To confound temporal with logical priority is to make a mistake of the same sort, and as important, as that of assimilating the eternal (everlasting) to the eternal (non-temporal).

The second and main objection to the present employment of the Argument from Recollection is that it presupposes the conclusion which it is now supposed to be proving. Certainly if we did exist before we were born we cannot be a harmony, or any other sort of function, of the elements which compose our bodies. But if anyone in order to explain some present phenomena suggests that these involve remembering things with which we were acquainted before we were born, then the immediate response must be, simply and blankly, that before we were born – or, to be precise, before we were conceived – we did not exist to be acquainted with anything.

In this formulation this reply itself assumes that people are, as they surely are, corporeal: that people are objects which eat and excrete, which can be and are photographed and weighed, as well as being objects which think and act and – sometimes – control themselves. This objection does not occur to Plato in this form because he is here taking for granted the opposite: that we people are not as such corporeal but are, rather, in-corporeal souls. He is thus committed to discussing the question whether we, who are assumed to be incorporeal, are or are not, always on this assumption, (logical) substances. It is, of course, only on this special assumption that there is a question demanding investigation: people, in so far as people are allowed to be corporeal, are quite obviously (logical) substances. Equally it may seem that it can only be on this same peculiar assumption that there is any call to investigate the question whether we survive death and dissolution, either for a limited period or for ever: if we are indeed creatures of flesh and blood the answer is, it would appear, obviously negative. Nevertheless, even on Plato's own assumption, we must insist on having some good independent reason for taking in-corporeal souls to be substances (logical), before we can accept Plato's argument that his 'recollection' phenomena must be due to actual recollec-tion of knowledge acquired by souls before conception. For this theory presupposes, and hence can scarcely be employed to prove, that very thesis which 'Simmias' was challenging.

Earlier in the present § 3 I hinted at one reason why views about souls are rarely developed systematically and from the beginning. It is one mark of the extraordinary genius of Plato that he unlike the great majority does provide materials for a complete and systematic development. Thus in his *Alcibiades I*, a dramatically poor dialogue which has sometimes been challenged as spurious, we find 'Socrates' arguing for what appears elsewhere as the assumption that people are their souls:

SOCRATES – With whom are you talking now? To me, is it not?
ALCIBIADES – Yes.
SOCRATES – And I correspondingly to you?
ALCIBIADES – Yes.
SOCRATES – Then the person who is talking is Socrates?
ALCIBIADES – Of course.
SOCRATES – And the person who is listening is Alcibiades?
ALCIBIADES – Yes.
SOCRATES – And Socrates uses speech in taking?
ALCIBIADES – Surely.
SOCRATES – And talking and using speech you rate as the same thing, I suppose?
ALCIBIADES – Of course.
SOCRATES – But the user and what he uses are different, are they not?
ALCIBIADES – How do you mean?
SOCRATES – As, for instance, a shoemaker cuts with a shoemaker's knife, and with a splitting knife, and with other tools.
ALCIBIADES – Yes.
SOCRATES – So the cutter as the person who uses is different from the instruments which he uses in cutting?
ALCIBIADES – Of course he is.
SOCRATES – And in the same way the person who plays the harp would be different from the things which the person who plays the harp uses in playing the harp?
ALCIBIADES – Yes.
SOCRATES – Well then, this is what I was asking just now – whether you think that the person who uses and the things which he uses are always different.
ALCIBIADES – I think so.
SOCRATES – So what are we to say about the shoemaker? Does he cut only with his tools, or with his hands as well?
ALCIBIADES – With his hands as well.
SOCRATES – So he uses these too?
ALCIBIADES – Yes.

SOCRATES – Does he use his eyes too in his shoemaking?

ALCIBIADES – Yes.

SOCRATES – But we are agreed that the user and the things which he uses are different?

ALCIBIADES – Yes.

SOCRATES – Then the shoemaker and the harpist are different from the hands and eyes with which they do their work?

ALCIBIADES – So it seems.

SOCRATES – So a man uses his whole body?

ALCIBIADES – Surely.

SOCRATES – But the user and what he uses are different?

ALCIBIADES – Yes.

SOCRATES – Then a man is different from his own body?

ALCIBIADES – It seems so.

SOCRATES – Then whatever is the man?

ALCIBIADES – I do not know what to say.

SOCRATES – But you do – that he is what uses the body.

ALCIBIADES – Yes.

SOCRATES – Can that user of it then be anything but the soul?

ALCIBIADES – Nothing else.

SOCRATES – And thus the ruler?

ALCIBIADES – Yes.

SOCRATES – Now here is a remark with which I think no one would disagree.

ALCIBIADES – What is it?

SOCRATES – That man must be one of three things.

ALCIBIADES – What things?

SOCRATES – Soul, or body, or both together as a whole.

ALCIBIADES – So what?

SOCRATES – So we have agreed that what actually rules the body is the man.

ALCIBIADES – Yes, we have.

SOCRATES – Then does the body rule itself?

ALCIBIADES – By no means.

SOCRATES – For we said that it is ruled.

ALCIBIADES – Yes.

SOCRATES – Then this cannot be what we are looking for.

ALCIBIADES – It seems not.

SOCRATES – Well then, does the combination of the two rule the body, and is it this which is the man?

ALCIBIADES – Perhaps it is.

SOCRATES – That is out of the question, for if one of the two does not share in the rule it is out of the question that the combination of both rules.

ALCIBIADES – You are right.

SOCRATES – But then, since neither the body nor the combination of both is the man we are reduced, I suppose, to this: either man is nothing at all; or, if something, he turns out to be nothing else but soul.

(§§ 129B–130C)

Since the context of this inquiry in the *Alcibiades I* is a consideration of the interpretation of the famous maxim, "Know yourself", inscribed on the temple at Delphi, 'Socrates' eventually draws out an appropriate moral:

SOCRATES – It is, therefore, well to take the view that you and I are conversing with one another using words soul to soul.

ALCIBIADES – Quite so.

SOCRATES – Well, that is what we suggested a few moments back – that Socrates in using words to talk to Alcibiades is, it would seem, uttering the words not to your face but to Alcibiades; that is to say the soul.

ALCIBIADES – That is my opinion.

SOCRATES – Then he who bids us know ourselves is telling us to become acquainted with the soul.

ALCIBIADES – So it seems.

SOCRATES – And so anyone who gets to know something belonging to the body knows things which belong to him but not himself.

ALCIBIADES – That is so.

SOCRATES – So no doctor knows himself in virtue of his being a doctor, nor any trainer in virtue of being a trainer.

ALCIBIADES – It seems not.   (§§130D–131A)

It is no part of the purpose of 'Socrates' in the *Alcibiades I* to go beyond the proposition that we are incorporeal souls by further maintaining directly that these souls are (logical) substances. But, since he does even there insist that the soul rules the body, the next passage from the *Phaedo* can be regarded as bringing out a corollary implicit in the conclusion supposedly established in the *Alcibiades I*:

SOCRATES – Did we not then agree previously that it could never, granted that it is a harmony, sing a song opposed to the tensions and relaxations and vibrations and other conditions of the elements of which it is composed; but that it would follow them and never lead?

SIMMIAS – Yes, we did agree that; of course.

SOCRATES – Well then, do we now find the complete contrary, that the soul operates, leading all those elements of which it is said to consist, and opposing them in almost everything throughout life, and tyrannizing over them in every way – sometimes inflicting rather harsh and painful punishments (those of gymnastics and medicine), and sometimes milder ones; and that it is sometimes threatening and sometimes giving advice, conducting a dialogue with the desires and the passions and fears as if it were distinct from them and they from it? It is as Homer said in *The Odyssey*, when he wrote of Odysseus (XX, 17–18):

> He smote his breast and rebuked his heart,
> 'Endure it, heart: you have endured worse than this . . .'

Do you suppose that when he wrote these words he was thinking of it as a harmony and as the sort of thing which would be determined by the conditions of the body, rather than as the sort of thing to lead and to master these and itself a far more divine thing than a harmony?

SIMMIAS – By Zeus, Socrates, I think the latter. (§ 94C–E)

We can therefore credit Plato both with recognizing the importance of, and with offering argument for, two doctrines: first, that we people are incorporeal souls; and, second, that these souls are – in a general terminology which was not his – (logical) substances. To conclude this third section we must notice also both the bizarre implausibility of the first doctrine and yet how commonly and how easily it is in the present context taken for granted. Plato – typically of the well-educated Greek of his day – appealed to the authority of the still earlier epic poet Homer. So it is perhaps excusable to mention that Homer in the passage cited was not in fact talking about souls, and does not employ the word *psuche* or any of its derivatives. His Odysseus goes on immediately to refer to that more bitter day when the "Cyclops ate my mighty comrades" (not – pace 'Socrates' – merely their bodies); after which Homer describes how Odysseus "himself lay tossing this way and that" (not his body only, and with no mention of any soul directing the agitations).

We can also infer that the post-Homeric contemporaries of Socrates and Plato would have found these suggestions that people are incorporeal remarkably incongruous; for in his play *The Clouds* Aristophanes makes fun of the "wise souls" in the "thinking shop" of Socrates (line 94: cf. *The Birds*, 11.1535 ff.). It may perhaps seem that such references must be irrelevant, or worse. For, surely, it is no fault in a great creative thinker either that his guiding ideas are not in fact to be found in the epics of his forefathers, or that they could by the most brilliant satirist among his own contemporaries be made to sound ridiculous? Was not Galileo in his own time even persecuted for his premature Copernicanism? Why then should we now allow an appeal from the arguments of Plato to the prejudices of common sense?

The answer to this challenge has an importance extending far beyond the present case. The first thing to emphasize is that Plato as a philosopher is precisely not a scientist reporting newly discovered facts about people or adducing fresh theories to explain already familiar facts of human behaviour. Had Plato been, for instance, a physiologist explaining the functions of the heart it would indeed have been quite ridiculous for someone to try to dismiss his findings by insisting that the common sense embodied in familiar idioms knows nothing of the circulation of the blood, but only of the heart as the seat of the affections. Plato's philosophical arguments have, however, led him to two contentions of a quite different sort. That the second of these is a doctrine about what it would and would not make sense to say is immediately obvious from the definition of the word *substance* (logical). That the first is similarly concerned with meanings needs to be shown.

This can be shown fairly easily. Plato himself seems to be asserting it almost in as many words when in reply to the question, 'How shall we bury you?', he warns of the dangers of "speaking improperly". Clearly to say that the person is the soul is to assert some sort of identity; just as it would be if we were to say – using the time-hallowed example – that the morning star is the evening star. In that second, exemplary case the identity is an identity of denotation but not of connotation. A word or expression is said to denote whatever it can correctly be employed to refer to, whereas its connotation is what it means: this use of these two terms, which is not their only use, was introduced by John Stuart Mill. Thus the two expressions *the morning star* and *the evening star* both in fact denote one and the same planet, Venus. But that they have different connotations can be appreciated by reflecting that the discovery of this identity represented a (very minor) astronomical achievement, and that no process of purely semantic analysis without benefit of any observation of the heavens could be sufficient to vindicate the equation. (American English, by the way, substitutes *designation* for Mill's – and my – *connotation*.)

Now, suppose someone attempted to defend only the weaker claim that the words *person* and *soul* do as a matter of fact have the same denotation. His attempt must collapse the moment we remind him, and ourselves, of the actual denotations of the word *person*, and of all the other words which we may use to refer to persons. For, whatever difficulties we might have if we tried to define the connotation of the word, or in some other way to spell out verbally what it is to be a person, it is easy enough to indicate some specimens: it was, after all, by such ostensive or showing (as opposed to verbal or saying) definition that as children we must all have learnt our first person-words. But if that is what persons are, and it is, then they are visibly and tangibly corporeal. Since Platonic souls are essentially incorporeal the suggested equation must collapse completely. For in as much as persons and souls have not merely different but formally incompatible characteristics the terms *persons* and *souls* cannot enjoy even the same denotation, much less share equivalent connotations.

Of course, to insist that people are after all corporeal, that person-words do not have the sort of meanings which Plato apparently persuaded himself that they did have, is only the first step – albeit the indispensable first step. Once we have reminded ourselves of this, which all of us – and Plato too – already in a way knew perfectly well, then we are ready for the more interesting and more difficult task of discovering what is wrong with the premises and the arguments leading to this false doctrine.

If we consider only the case presented in the *Alcibiades I* two distinctions appear to be crucial. The first of these is between two senses of the word *use*: one in which we may say that a man uses his tools, his car, and even his companions; and the other in which he might be said to use parts or even the whole of himself – as when, for instance, we assert that Italians are inclined to use their hands a lot in talking, or that a devotee uses himself as a mere instrument in the service of his cause. The nerve of the argument under examination runs from the premises: first, that a man may be said to use his whole body; and, second, that the user and what he uses are different; to the initial conclusion that a man must be different from his own body. But here the second premise is true only in the first sense of *use*, and the first only in the second.

The second crucial distinction is more subtle, and a variant on that made already between J. S. Mill's senses of *connotation* and *denotation*. Certainly it is true to say that a man must be different from his own body, if this statement is construed as meaning that such pairs of expressions as *Socrates the man* and *the body of Socrates* are not synonymous. The decisive illustration to show the lack of complete logical equivalence here is the contrast between *They brought John down from the Eiger* and *They brought*

John's body down from the Eiger: from the former we may reasonably infer that he was alive; from the latter that he was dead. But from this admitted fact of the logical non-equivalence of certain sorts of words and expressions we are not entitled to deduce that they must refer to different kinds of objects. It may be the case, and it surely is, that my talk about my body is not talk about some object – some logical substance – different from me – another logical substance. It could be the case, as it surely is, that all the various possible phrases in which expressions such as *his body* occur have various functions of enabling us to say things about just one enormously complex and centrally important kind of object: namely, people.

It seems, therefore, that we have here in the *Alcibiades I* one particular – and particularly important – instance of one of the perennial false assumptions of philosophy. This is the assumption, first formulated generally and systematically attacked by George Berkeley, that every substantive (noun) names – or, better, is the word for – a sort of logical substance. The passage quoted earlier from *Through the Looking Glass* provided an absurd example of making this mistake by taking *temper* as a substance-word. The list in the Mad Hatter's Tea-Party in *Alice's Adventures in Wonderland* includes two more:

'They were learning to draw', the Dormouse went on, yawning and rubbing its eyes, for it was getting very sleepy; 'and they drew all manner of things – everything that begins with an M —'

'Why with an M?' said Alice.

'Why not?' said the March Hare.

Alice was silent.

The Dormouse had closed its eyes by this time, and was going off into a doze; but, on being pinched by the Hatter, it woke up again with a little shriek, and went on: '– that begins with an M, such as mouse-trap, and the moon, and memory, and muchness – you know you say things are 'much of a muchness' – did you ever see such a thing as a drawing of a muchness?'

'Really, now you ask me', said Alice, very much confused, 'I don't think —'

'Then you shouldn't talk', said the Hatter. (Ch. VII)

Once seized of the strangeness of the doctrine that people are incorporeal we have also to notice how widely and how easily it is taken for granted. The form in which it is taken for granted is nowadays almost always Cartesian rather than Platonic. So this is a subject to which we shall be returning in Part Three (Ch. VIII, § 5). But in the meantime let us glance at the first chapter of Butler's *The Analogy of Religion Natural and Revealed to the Constitution and Course of Nature*. Joseph Butler (1692–1752), after his contemporary George Berkeley (1685–1753) the second most distinguished philosophical talent ever to adorn the bench of Bishops of the Anglican communion, wished in his *Analogy* to show that the world as we know it is such as to make the doctrines both of natural theology and even of the Christian revelation probable; for, as he characteristically insisted, though "Probable evidence, in its very nature, affords but an imperfect kind of information; and is to be considered as relative only to beings of limited capacities", nevertheless "to us probability is the very guide to life" (Introduction, § 4). I shall complete the present third section by quoting a few extracts only. But the whole of Butler's first chapter can be strongly recommended as a salutary challenge to anyone for whom the falsity of any Platonic view now appears too comfortably obvious:

... let us consider what the analogy of nature, and the several changes which we have undergone, and those which we may undergo without being destroyed, suggest as to the effect which death may, or may not, have upon us; and whether it may not be from thence probable that we may survive this change, and exist in a future state of life and perception.

From our being born into the present world in the helpless imperfect state of infancy, and having arrived from thence to mature age, we find it to be a general law of nature in our own species that the same creatures, the same individuals, should exist in different degrees of life and perception, with capacities of action, of enjoyment and suffering, in one period of their being, greatly different from those appointed them in another period of it. And in other creatures the same law holds. . . . Thus all the various and wonderful transformations of animals are to be taken into consideration here.

But the states of life in which we ourselves existed formerly, in the womb and in our infancy, are almost as different from our present in mature age as it is possible to conceive any two states or degrees of life can be. Therefore, that we are to exist hereafter in a state as different (suppose) from our present, as this is from our former, is but according to the analogy of nature. . . .

We know we are endued with capacities of action, of happiness and misery: for we are conscious of acting, of enjoying pleasure and suffering pain. Now that we have these powers and capacities before death, is a presumption that we shall retain them through and after death; indeed a probability of it abundantly sufficient to act upon, unless there be some positive reason to think that death is the destruction of those living powers. . . .

But we cannot argue from the reason of the thing, that death is the destruction of living agents, because we know not at all what death is in itself; but only some of its effects, such as the dissolution of flesh, skin, and bones. And these effects do in no wise appear to imply the destruction of a living agent. And besides, as we are greatly in the dark upon what the exercize of our living powers depends, so we are wholly ignorant of what the powers themselves depend upon. . . .

(§§ 1–4 and 6)

All presumption of death's being the destruction of living beings, must go upon supposition that they are compounded. . . . But since consciousness is a single and indivisible power, it should seem that the subject in which it resides must be so too. . . .

The simplicity and absolute oneness of a living agent cannot indeed, from the nature of the thing, be properly proved by experimental observations. But as these fall in with the supposition of its unity, so they plainly lead us to conclude certainly, that our gross organized bodies, with which we perceive the objects of sense, and with which we act, are no part of ourselves; and therefore show us, that we have no reason to believe their destruction to be ours: even without determining whether our living substances be material or immaterial. For we see by experience that men lose their limbs, their organs of sense, and even the greatest part of these bodies, and yet remain the same living agents. And persons can trace up the existence of themselves to a time, when the bulk of their bodies was extremely small, in comparison with what it is in mature age; and we cannot but think that they might then have lost a considerable part of that small body, and yet have remained the same living agents – as they may now lose a great part of their present body, and remain so.

And it is certain that the bodies of all animals are in a constant flux, from that never-ceasing attrition which there is in every part of them. Now things of this kind unavoidably teach us to distinguish, between these living agents ourselves, and large quantities of matter with which we are very nearly interested: since these may be alienated, and actually are in a daily course of succession, and changing their owners; whilst we are assured that each living agent remains one and the same permanent being. . . .

. . . We have already several times over lost a great part or perhaps the whole of our body, according to certain common established laws of nature; yet we remain the same living agents. When we shall lose as great a part, or the whole, by another common established law of nature, death, why may we not also remain the same? That the alienation has been gradual in one case, and in the other will be more at once, does not prove anything to the contrary. We have passed undestroyed through those many and great revolutions of matter, so peculiarly appropriated to us ourselves; why should we imagine death will be so fatal to us?

(§§ 10, 12–13, and 15: the standard edition of Butler's works, and the division into sections, is by the English Liberal statesman W. E. Gladstone)

§4 *Aristotle and a materialist view of man*

So far in this Chapter IV we have been treating mainly Plato, and taking him as the spokesman for one of the two great philosophical approaches to the question of the nature of man. It is time to introduce Aristotle as a protagonist for the other. His contribution is found in his treatise *On Soul*, or, in Latin, *de Anima*: curiously it is almost always referred to by the Latin rather than the English or the original Greek title. Typically of Aristotle this treatise is often technical and sometimes crabbed. To understand what is going on the first thing is to remember the notion of the soul as the principle of life: to the question, 'What makes living things alive?', the answer comes back pat and ready-made, 'It is being ensouled (or animate), having a soul (or anima).' Aristotle begins rather portentously:

> In our view knowledge is a thing of beauty and value, and one sort is more so than another either because it is exact or because it is knowledge of better and more wonderful objects. On both these grounds we may reasonably place the investigation of the soul among the highest. It seems too that knowledge of it contributes greatly towards truth as a whole, but especially that about nature. For the soul is, so to speak, the first principle of all animal life. Our aim is to contemplate and to understand its nature and essence, and then all the attributes it may acquire. Some of these seem to belong to the soul itself, but others apply to living animals on account of it. But everywhere and in every way it is one of the most difficult things to get hold of anything reliable about it. (I (i): 402A 1–11)

One of the many difficulties lies in what is here the exceptionally strongly felt temptation to construe a substantive *psuche* as the word for a sort of (logical) substances. Aristotle never recognized and formulated this temptation as being such, and his own technical use of the Greek word translated *substance* was confusingly different. (Had he himself thought in these terms he might have been less willing than he was to talk of the vegetative, or the sensitive, soul when what he is discussing is the capacities to grow, decay, feed, and reproduce, or the capacities to see and to desire, respectively.) But characteristically Aristotle provides an account of the views of his predecessors, who all, with the exception of Plato, appear to have taken it that soul must be some thing or things corporeal:

In our inquiry concerning soul . . . we must make a collection of the views of those of our predecessors who expressed themselves on the subject, in order that we may adopt what was right in their conclusions and be on our guard against their errors. The first step in the investigation is to present what are commonly thought to be its natural attributes. Now there are two things especially in which the living seems to differ from the lifeless, movement and perception; and it is roughly these two which we have received from our predecessors as characteristics of soul. There were some who said that soul is pre-eminently and primarily the cause of movement. But as they believed that what is not itself in motion cannot move something else, they took the soul to be something which is in motion. Hence Democritus maintains that it is a sort of fire and heat. The atoms . . . are infinite in number, and those which are spherical – he says – are fire and soul; they are like what we call motes in the air, which are seen in the sunbeams coming through windows. He maintains that the sum total of such seeds constitutes the elements of the whole of nature, and Leucippus likewise. Those which are spherical are soul, because such shapes are most able to slip through everything, and being themselves in motion to move other things. They assume that the soul is what makes animals move. . . . Democritus does not use the word *mind* (*nous*) for a faculty concerned with truth, but makes *soul* and *mind* synonymous. . . .

From the anecdotes which are told it would seem that Thales too understood the soul to be something which puts in motion; if, that is, he said that the lodestone has soul because it moves iron. Diogenes, however, like some others, thought it is air; because he believed that this is made up of the finest particles, and is the first principle. . . . Among the more vulgar thinkers some – Hippon, for instance – maintained that it is water; they seem to have become persuaded of this because the seed of all creatures is wet.

(I (ii): 403B20–404A9, 404A30–31, 405A19–20, and 405B1–3)

All these thinkers are among those conventionally labelled as the Pre-Socratic philosophers: Thales the Ionian from Miletus in Asia Minor, Democritus and Leucippus the founders of Classical atomism, Diogenes of Apollonia (who was not the later Diogenes the Cynic, said to have lived in a barrel), and even the unfortunately vulgar medical materialist Hippon. Nevertheless, and although no such sharp jurisdictional distinction was made in their day, these first philosophers seem to have been offering their highly speculative answers to what should now be seen as a scientific rather than a philosophical problem. The division can here best be drawn by reference to two interpretations of the question, 'What makes living things alive?' or 'What is the principle of Life?'

In one interpretation this is a request for the criterion for the application of the term *alive*, or for some other sort of definition or explanation of its meaning. To the question construed in this first sense Plato's Theory of Forms would certainly constitute an appropriate, even if ultimately mistaken, answer. But in the other interpretation what is being requested is some sort of account of what produces life. In this second sense the *makes* can be labelled as causal, as opposed to constitutive. In its causal, as opposed to constitutive, interpretation the usually correct answer to the question, 'What is the principle of intoxication in intoxicating drinks?' would be, 'Their alcoholic content'. To the same question construed in the first sense, in which the *makes* is taken as constitutive and not causal, the appropriate response is to supply some explanation of the meaning of *intoxicating* as applied to drinks.

Remembering now the verbal equation between being alive and having a soul, and in the light of the fundamental distinction just explained, it is easy to interpret these Pre-Socratic philosophers as offering their bold conjectures about the causes of life in the form of dark apophthegms on the nature of the soul. Although Aristotle was always interested in all such scientific issues, and although he too did not himself distinguish sharply between the philosophical and the scientific in our modern way, the central thesis of the *de Anima* is unequivocally philosophical.

This central thesis is presented in terms of some of his own distinctive and historically important notions. Thus he uses again here the antithesis between potentiality and actuality, explained already (Ch. III, § 4). Then we have the antitheses between form and matter, and between the subjects of predication or attribution and the predicates or attributes applied to them. Both of these should become sufficiently intelligible from the passage to be quoted. But it must be emphasized that the form of Aristotle, and hence of Aquinas, is totally different from the Form of Plato: I am marking the distinction systematically by giving the latter but never the former an initial capital. Of Aristotle's difficult, and perhaps radically confused, idea of substance the best thing which can be said tolerably briefly at this stage is that it cannot be straightforwardly identified with our substance (logical). Finally there is "the-what-it-is-to-be" of such and such a thing, an Aristotelian phrase which was later to give rise to the barbarous Latin abstract noun *quidditas* and its equally deplorable English equivalent *quiddity*. But the thing to do now is to plunge into the text, clinging for support to the illustrations provided by Aristotle himself:

So much for the theories of soul handed down by our predecessors. But now let us go back again as if we were starting from the beginning, trying to define what soul is and what would be the most comprehensive account of it. Now in our terminology one kind of existent things is substance; and this includes, on the one hand, matter, which is not in itself anything in particular; then, next, form or configuration, in respect of which a thing is called this particular thing; and, third, the whole constituted of these two. Matter is potentiality and form actuality; of which latter there are two senses, having knowledge providing an illustration of the one, and the exercise of knowledge of the other.

Now bodies seem to be quintessentially substances, especially those which are natural, for these are the first principles of everything else. Of natural objects some possess life, and some do not. By *life* we mean independent nourishment, growth, and decay. Consequently every natural object possessed of life must be a substance. . . . And since we have here an object characterized in a certain way, namely, as possessing life, the soul cannot be the object. For an object is not the sort of thing which is an attribute of a subject: instead it is a subject of attributes, matter. It follows necessarily that the soul is substance, in as much as it is the form of a natural object such as could be alive; and this sort of substance is the actuality of the object.

But this term is ambiguous, having knowledge providing an illustration of the one sense, and the exercise of knowledge of the other. Clearly here the analogy is with having knowledge; for the soul is present as much during sleep as during being awake, and, while being awake is comparable with the exercise of knowledge, being asleep is like possessing but not exercising it. Furthermore the possession of knowledge is in any individual in origin prior. The soul, therefore, is the actuality, in the first sense, of a natural object possessing the capacity of life; and this means anything which is organic, in the sense of possessing organs.

(Yes, for even the parts of plants are organs, though of a very simple sort: for instance, the leaf is a sheath of the pod, and the pod of the fruit. Roots, again, are analogous to the mouth, since both draw in nourishment.) So if we have to make a general statement covering every sort of soul, the soul must be the actuality, in the first sense, of a natural object endowed with organs.

This being so there is no need to enquire whether the soul and the object are one, any more than there is with a piece of wax and the imprint on it; or, in general, with the matter of anything and the thing of which it is the matter. For though the terms *one* and *to be* are used in many senses, the master notion is actuality.

It has now been stated in general terms what the soul is, namely, substance-as-a-concept. This is the-what-it-is-to-be of such and such an object [its 'quiddity' – A.F.]. Suppose some tool – an axe, for instance – were a natural object, then being an axe would be its substance, in this sense; would indeed be its soul. Deprived of this it would no longer be an axe – or only in a Pickwickian sense. But as it is, it is an axe. The soul, however, is not the notion and the-what-it-is-to-be [the quiddity] of an object of that kind; but of a natural object of a particular sort, one which has in itself the power to originate motion and rest.

We must consider what has been said with reference to parts of the body too. For if the eye were an animal its soul would be eyesight, since this is the substance-as-a-concept of the eye. The eye is the matter of eyesight, and deprived of this it would no longer be an eye – or only in a Pickwickian sense, like an eye in stone or in a picture.

(II (i): 412A1–412B22)

So it is perfectly obvious that the soul – or if it is divided into parts, certain of its parts – cannot be separated from the object. . . .

(II (i): 413A3–5)

Whatever else in this epoch-marking passage may reasonably remain perplexing this at least, once granted Aristotle's account of the nature of the soul, should indeed be perfectly obvious. Yet to the distraction of all his commentators Aristotle himself proceeds forthwith partially to repudiate his own insights: "Nevertheless there is no reason why some others, if they are not the actualities of any material object, should not be separable. And, furthermore, it is not obvious whether the soul is the actuality of the body as the sailor is of the ship" (II(i): 413A6–9).

It should be perfectly obvious that if the soul is to a natural object – to be specific, a person – as being an axe is to an artificial object – equally specifically, an axe – then the soul could no more be separated from the person than the being-an-axe could be separated from the axe. Once again this is not just a matter of what happens in fact to be the case but, more fundamentally and also more philosophically, a matter of what it makes sense to suggest. If and precisely in so far as Aristotle's own first illustrations are well chosen, then the soul cannot be in our crucial sense a substance. In that case to suggest that it might survive separation must be like suggesting that the dog might go away while its temper remained, or – to take another *Wonderland* illustration – like suggesting that the grin of the Cheshire Cat might outlast the face to which it must belong as an attribute:

> 'Did you say pig, or fig?' said the Cat.
> 'I said pig', replied Alice; 'and I wish you wouldn't keep appearing and vanishing so suddenly: you make one quite giddy.'
> 'All right', said the Cat; and this time it vanished quite slowly, beginning with the end of the tail, and ending with the grin, which remained some time after the rest of it had gone.
> 'Well! I've often seen a cat without a grin,' thought Alice; 'but a grin without a cat! It's the most curious thing I ever saw in all my life!'
>
> (Ch. VII)

Someone inclined to think that to be serious must always be to be solemn might by the lightheartedness of these analogies from Lewis Carroll be misled to believe that the point being made is itself trivial or impossible to overlook. For his benefit it is perhaps just worth saying that Carroll was not alone among the authors of great children's books in writing simultaneously and deliberately on two different levels, and that he himself had undoubtedly serious interests in both logic and mathematics. Indeed the story goes that Queen Victoria, charmed by one of the Alice books, let it be known that she would welcome the dedication of the author's next work; she was then more surprised than pleased when the arrival in her Balmoral retreat of a suitably inscribed copy of *An Elementary Treatise on Determinants* showed how literally a royal wish had been taken as a command.

That a crux such as that being illustrated can be overlooked may be appreciated by contemplating two sentences from the widely circulated popular work of a professional physiologist. In Professor V. H. Mottram's *The Physical Basis of Personality* we find the word *personality* defined, reasonably and unsurprisingly as "That . . . assemblage of qualities which makes a person what he is as distinct from other persons". In this sense a personality is clearly not a substance; and the *makes* must be constitutive not causal. Yet five pages later all this is neglected in the asking of the question, "Does the body determine the personality, or does the personality in any way determine the physical make-up of the person?" (pp. 4 and 9).

That and how Aristotle's thesis about the nature of the soul is indeed epoch-marking can be brought out by examining a comment of the author of the standard English-language edition of the *de Anima*. In his 'Introduction' to this R. D. Hicks writes:

> In reducing soul to the logical essence or form of body Aristotle, according to his own presuppositions, so far from favouring materialism, secures once and for all the soul's absolute immateriality. The living body has independent existence, has its own form and its own matter. Even a dead body or an inanimate thing is something existing independently, to which we can apply the pronoun 'this'. But the soul does not exist in the same way. Nor, again, is it a thing capable of being added to or subtracted from another thing, the body, any more than form in general is a thing which can in mechanical fashion be united to and separated from its appropriate matter. If a brazen sphere be melted down the brass remains. It is still 'this' something, 'this' mass of metal; but we cannot then say of its spherical shape that it is 'this' anything or that it any longer exists. The lifeless body is like the eye which cannot see or the axe which is spoilt for use. We may apply to them the same names as before; but, as the nature is no longer the same, the application is irrelevant, misleading, equivocal. But, though the lifeless body is still a concrete particular and a substance, the soul apart from its relation to the body is no such thing at all. Now the soul as form stands to the body as matter of the concrete individual precisely as the spherical shape to the brass, as vision to the eye, as cutting power to the axe. In every case the form is a quality predicable of the matter. But the body is not predicable of the soul, we cannot explain the soul in terms of body or make it a material thing, however fine the materials. . . . Soul and body . . . are not two distinct things, they are one thing presenting two distinct aspects. (pp. xliii–xliv)

In every detail this statement is sympathetic, illuminating and correct; it constitutes an ideal guide for a rereading of Aristotle's own words. Yet the general claim that Aristotle's central thesis "so far from favouring materialism, secures once and for all the soul's absolute immateriality" could be utterly misleading as to its true significance. For, regardless of whatever personal reservations he may have harboured, Aristotle here contributed a powerful new weapon to the arsenal of the Giants in Plato's archetypal Battle of the Gods and the Giants.

Certainly Aristotle's thesis does involve the total rejection of primitive materialistic ideas that the soul is (that *soul* is a word for) a sort of material object or a kind of stuff: we met some of these ideas in his own account of the views of his predecessors. But, equally certainly, it also involves the total rejection of the Platonic concept of the soul as an incorporeal substance – what is often called a spiritual, as opposed to a material, substance: this has just been made abundantly clear. The significance of Aristotle's contribution, a significance which perhaps he did not himself accept altogether without reservations, was that it pointed the way to a more sophisticated materialism.

It is not necessary to choose: between, on the one hand, saying that the soul, or the mind, or the personality, is (that *soul*, or *mind*, or *personality*, is a word for) a sort of material object or a kind of stuff; and, on the other hand, saying that these are (that these are words for) not material but spiritual substances. Instead we may, taking our cue from Aristotle, explore the possibilities of saying that these are (that these substantives are words for) neither material nor immaterial substances. To say that someone is keeping body and soul together, that he has a first-class mind, or that he has an abrasive personality, is surely not to imply anything about the presence of an extra component, whether elusively corporeal or mysteriously spiritual. It is ultimately to predicate something of, to attribute something to, a subject which is both visibly and tangibly corporeal, a natural object, a person.

Hobbes – our paradigm metaphysical materialist – rarely had a good word to say for Aristotle. So it is the more significant that here Hobbes followed in the general direction indicated by Aristotle. In Chapter XLIV of *Leviathan,* addressing a public which both knew its English Bible and did not need to be told that *anima* is the Latin for *soul* and *vivere* for *to live,* Hobbes argued:

> The *soul* in Scripture signifieth always either the life or the living creature; and *the body and soul* jointly, the body alive. In the first day of creation God said, 'Let the waters produce *reptile animae viventis,* the creeping thing that hath in it a living soul'; the English translates it, *that hath life.* And again, God created whales and *omnem animam viventem;* which in the English is *every living creature.* And likewise of man, God

made him of the dust of the earth, and breathed in his face the breath of life, *et factus est homo in animam viventem,* that is, *and man was made a living creature.*

Before we move on to examine Aristotle's own reservations about the possibility of a completely materialist account of man it will be convenient, with his antithesis between form and matter still fresh in mind, to take note of a further famous and influential doctrine. This is traditionally but unfortunately known as the doctrine of the Four Causes: Material, Formal, Efficient, and Final. The description is unfortunate because in English the word *cause* would by someone quite untouched by Aristotelian influences be applied only to the third. Although it remains necessary to know the traditional labels it is perhaps best to think of Aristotle here as distinguishing four fundamentally different sorts of questions, and their corresponding answers. The passage comes from the *Metaphysics*:

> *Cause* means: (1) that from which, as its constitutive material, something comes, e.g., the bronze of the statue, and the silver of the libation bowl, and the sorts of things of which these are instances; (2) the form or pattern, that is, the account of the-what-it-is-to-be . . .; (3) the source of the first beginning of change or rest, e.g., the man who resolves is a cause, and the father is cause of the child, and generally the producer of the thing produced, and that which brings about a change of that which suffers change; and (4) the end, that for the sake of which, e.g., as health is of walking around. ('Why is he walking around?', we say. 'In order to be healthy', and having said this we think we have given the cause.) . . .
>
> These are just about all the senses of the word *cause*, and since the term is multiply ambiguous there are regularly several causes of the same thing; for instance, the making of a statue and the bronze are causes of the statue, not in some other aspect but as the statue. They are not, however, causes in the same sense, since the one is material and the other efficient. (1013A24–1013B9)

§5 *Aristotle and Aquinas*

In the previous section we have seen the importance of Aristotle for the development of a sophisticated materialist view of the nature of man. His own complicating reservations have been almost equally important, although much more difficult to understand. These reservations refer to the intellect (nous): for, unlike Democritus, Aristotle does not "make *soul* and *mind* (nous) synonymous", but "uses the word *mind* for a faculty concerned with truth"; the which he then takes to be one element in the human, but only the human, soul. The key passages again come from the *de Anima*:

> As to the part of the soul by which it knows and thinks – whether that is physically separable or separable only in thought – we have to investigate what its distinctive character is and how ratiocination comes about. Now if ratiocination is analogous to perception it will be a matter of being acted on by the object of thought, or something else of this sort. So this part of the soul must be impassive, and receptive of the form and potentially like it but not the same as it; and as the faculty of perception is to the things perceived, so the faculty of intellect must be to its objects. The mind, therefore, since it is concerned with everything must needs – as Anaxagoras has it – be unmixed with anything if it is to rule, that is to say, if it is to know. By intruding any character of its own it would hinder and obstruct its different objects; hence it has no other nature of its own than this, that it is a capacity. The part of the soul which we call intellect, then, and I mean by *intellect* that whereby the soul thinks and understands, is not any sort of actuality until it ratiocinates. Hence we cannot even think of it as mixed with the physical object; for in that case it would acquire some quality, like cold or heat, or there would even be some organ, as there are with the faculty of perception. But as a matter of fact there is not.   (III (iv): 429A10–27)

But, on the contrary, as a matter of fact there is; and, of course, that there is is a fact not to be despised. We must, however, give Aristotle a slightly longer hearing if we are going to get a sufficient grasp of what his view was:

> And it is this intellect which is separable and impassive and unmixed, and which is essentially an activity.   (III (v): 430A17–18)

> Intellect would seem to be in us as an existent substance, and not to perish. . . . But . . . love and hatred are not attributes of the intellect but of the person who has it, in so far as he does. Hence when this person perishes he neither remembers nor loves, for these things never attached to the intellect but to the whole which has perished; whereas the intellect is no doubt something more divine and something impassive.
> (I (iv): 408B18–19 and 25–29)

Even with the help of simplifying excisions this is difficult. But the difficulty is, first, in sympathizing with Aristotle's reasons for thinking that he was entitled or required to make some sort of exception in favour of the intellect, and, second, in discovering what this supposed exception could amount to. Certainly, it is entirely clear that his was not a doctrine of personal or individual immortality. Equally certain, and perhaps more surprising, is the fact that, although for Aristotle there still remained a line of division between those realities which could and those which could not be achieved by or attributed to material things, this line had to be drawn neither between the living and the non-living, nor between the conscious and the not-conscious, but between the intellectual and everything else. The vitalist doctrine that life cannot be any sort of function or character-istic of exclusively material objects is now perhaps completely finished and forgotten. But the Cartesian notion that consciousness cannot be any sort of function or characteristic of physical stuff is still so familiar that it comes as a shock to realize that the question of their relation, or lack of relation, did not present itself to Plato or Aristotle as a great – or even as any – problem at all. Thus it is so obvious to Aristotle that eyesight attaches to the eye just as unperplexingly as being-an-axe attaches to the axe that both examples occur to him as suitably simple and uncontroversial illustrations of his main, more disputatious, thesis. Later, again, he is willing to offer, as an explanation of something else, that "The faculty of perception cannot occur without the body, whereas the intellect is separable" (III (iv): 429 B4–5).

The difficulty about the content of Aristotle's reservation – and *difficulty* is, surely, too charitable a word – is that what is supposed "to be in us . . . and not to perish" is something which "has no other nature of its own than this, that it is a capacity". But a capacity has to be attached, it has to be the capacity of someone or of something, it precisely cannot be in our and the presently crucial sense "an existent substance".

The difficulty about the reasons for Aristotle's reservation can be left to the specialists. Yet his procedure does raise a general question of method. It would, of course, be ridiculous to reproach the outstanding creative biologist of his time for not having known in the 300's BC about the functions of the brain what nowadays it would be quite easy for anyone to find out. But what is worth noticing is that, quite apart from any know-ledge of any particular organ involved, and apart too from the particular unsatisfactoriness of Aristotle's present conclusions about detachable and imperishable capacities, any argument leading to any similarly counter-evidential findings ought to be suspect.

For consider: Aristotle seems to be arguing that it is somehow impos-sible for the capacity for ratiocination to belong to any physical object, whether some partial organ or the person as a whole. Yet all the evidence we have points in the opposite direction, since the only instances of ratiocination known to us are instances of people ratiocinating. Again and similarly, someone – though not Aristotle – may want us to believe it unthinkable that anything wholly material could also be conscious. Yet all our evidence would appear to be, once again, quite decisively to the contrary. For every conscious being with which I am acquainted would seem, at least to the uninstructed observer, to be as much a creature of flesh and blood as I am myself. A third example, and one of which more will have to be said in Chapter VI, is the claim that it is somehow inconceivable that anything so complex and so integrated as the human eye could possibly come into existence without design. And yet, in this third case too, it would seem to naïve inspection that our eyes – unlike, say, our cars but like Topsy – have "just growed", and were not planned or designed by anyone at all.

The true moral to be drawn is certainly not that everything must be as it has been suggested that it should at first sight seem: for some or all these various intimations of impossibility may turn out to be correct. The true moral is simply that we first ought to notice that what they are claiming is impossible appears to be what regularly occurs, and that we should then review the claims with appropriate suspicion. Let us therefore make it easier to recognize further cases by introducing a suspicious and suitably solemn label – *Ostensibly Counter-evidential Intuition*.

The main historical importance of Aristotle's curious reservations about the intellect lies in the scope they afforded to Aquinas in his attempt to reconcile a generally Aristotelian view of man with the immortalist requirements of Catholic doctrine. Anyone aware that that doctrine specifies the resurrection of the body rather than the immortality of the soul might be tempted to think that there need be no problem. For could not Aquinas have appealed simply and directly to the sheer omnipotence of his God? Consider two very different statements: the first from Chapter XVII, 'The Night Journey', in the Koran, in the translation of N. J. Dawood; and the second an epitaph written by the young Benjamin Franklin, and now inscribed not on but near his grave in Christ Church Cemetery in Philadelphia:

Thus they shall be rewarded: because they disbelieved Our revelations and said: 'When we are turned to bones and dust, shall we be raised to life?'

Do they not see that Allah, who has created the heavens and the earth, has power to create their like? Their fate is preordained beyond all doubt. Yet the wrongdoers persist in unbelief.

> The body of B. Franklin, printer, like the cover of an old book, its contents torn out, and stripped of its lettering and gilding, lies here, food for worms. But the work shall not be lost; for it will, as he believed, appear once more in a new and more elegant edition corrected and improved by the Author.

Certainly there need be no doubt but that Omnipotence "has power to create their like". But for the punishments to be just, and for it to be "their fate", what is to be created must not just be "their like", not replicas however perfect, but them. For the same reason Franklin's analogy of the new and revised edition fails to fit. The new edition might, like the first, be a credit to its Author; but it would surely not be the original Founding Father. Aquinas took this point, which is made in several different ways in the initial Objections in the Article 'Whether it will be numerically the same man who rises again?' in the *Summa Theologica* (III Supp. Q79 A2). In the main body of that Article he insists, correctly and to his contemporaries no doubt persuasively, that to give a negative answer would be "heretical and derogatory to the truth of Scripture, which preaches resurrection (*John* 5: 25; *I Corinthians* 15: 51)". The nub of his answer comes in the Reply to the First Objection (his *subsistent thing* or *thing subsisting in its own right* is our *logical substance*):

> We may also say that the form of other things subject to generation and corruption is not subsistent in itself, and able to survive the dissolution of the whole. But in the case of the rational soul it is. . . . Consequently there is no interruption in the substantial being of the man to make it impossible, because of an interruption of his existence, for numerically the same man to come back. But this is how it is with other things which have been dissolved. Their being is altogether ended, since their forms do not survive while their matter continues under a different organization.

It is thus seen to be essential to have some logical substance bridging the gap between now and then if even Omnipotence itself is to be able at the Last Day to restore numerically the same man. But, as the commentary of Hicks brought out very clearly, an Aristotelian form cannot in general be such a substance. Aristotle's analysis of objects into their forms and their matter is – unlike a chemical analysis – one which can be executed only in thought. So Aquinas urgently needs to show that one sort of form is exceptional, those forms which are human souls. What I have regretted as Aristotle's backslidings Aquinas from his opposite standpoint takes as a hint. I quote the Article 'Whether the human soul is something subsistent?' complete, partly in order to display the form – in yet another sense of form! – of the whole *Summa Theologica*:

We proceed to the second article. It may appear that the human soul is not something subsistent.

Objection one. For what is subsistent is said to be *this particular thing*. But it is not the soul but the whole consisting of body and soul which is described as *this particular thing*. Therefore, the soul is not something subsistent.

Objection two. Furthermore, everything which is subsistent can be said to act. But the soul is not said to act: for, in the words of the *de Anima* (I (iv)), 'to say that the soul feels or understands is like saying that it weaves or builds'. Therefore, the soul is not something subsistent.

Objection three. Furthermore if the soul were something subsistent it would act in some way apart from the body. But apart from the body it does not act, it does not even understand: for understanding does not occur without mental imagery, and there is no mental imagery without the body. Therefore, the human soul is not something subsistent.

But, on the contrary, we have what Augustine says in the *de Trinitate* (X (vii)): 'Whoever appreciated the nature of the mind, both that it is a substance and that it is not corporeal, appreciates that those who hold the opinion that it is corporeal are in error because they associate with it things without which they are unable to think of anything – namely, mental images of physical objects'. Therefore, the human mind is naturally not only incorporeal but also substantial – which means that it is a subsistent thing.

I answer, that we have to say that the principle of intellectual actuality which we call the human soul is necessarily an incorporeal and subsistent principle. For it is clear that through the intellect man can have knowledge of all physical objects. But what is able to have knowledge of some sort of object cannot have anything of that sort in its own nature: for whatever was naturally in it would hinder it from knowing anything else of that kind. Thus we observe that the tongue of a sick man which is infected with a choleric and bitter humour cannot perceive anything sweet, everything seems bitter to it. So if the intellectual principle had in it the nature of a physical object it would not be able to have know-

ledge of all physical objects. But every physical object has some determinate nature. It is, therefore, impossible for the intellectual principle to
be corporeal.

And it is similarly impossible for it to understand by means of a bodily
organ: for the determinate nature of that bodily organ would stop it
having knowledge of all physical objects. Compare the case of determinate colour where liquid poured into a glass vase seems to be of the
same colour when it is not just the pupil of the eye but the glass which
is coloured.

Therefore the intellectual principle, called the mind or the intellect,
does act on its own account and independent of the body. But nothing
can act on its own account unless it subsists in its own right. For there
is no acting save in actuality: hence in as much as something acts it
exists. Which is why we do not say that heat, but the hot object, heats.
The conclusion is, therefore, that the human soul, which is called the
mind or intellect, is something incorporeal and subsistent.

So to the First we must say that *this particular thing* can be taken in
two senses: in one it refers to anything subsistent; in the other to something which is complete in some particular kind. In the first sense it
excludes the inherence of an attribute or of a material form. In the
second, it also excludes the imperfection of being a part. Hence a hand
can be called this particular thing in the first sense but not in the
second. Hence, similarly, since the human soul is part of the particular
human kind it can be called this particular thing in the first sense, in as
much as it is a subsistent thing, but not in the second, for in that sense it
is the whole consisting of body and soul which is said to be this particular thing.

To the Second we must say, as is obvious from the context, that
Aristotle is not speaking in his own person but is giving the opinion of
those who said that to understand is to be moved.

Or we must say that to act on its own account belongs to what exists
in its own right. But something can be said to exist in its own right,
even if it is a part, so long as it is not inherent as is an attribute or a
material form. Yet the correct application of *subsistent in its own right* is
to what is neither inherent in the way described nor a part. In this sense
the eye or the hand cannot be spoken of as subsistent in their own
right; nor, consequently, as acting on their own account. Hence too the
actions of the parts are attributed to the whole operating through the
parts. For we say that a man sees with the eye, and feels with the hand;
and that not in the same sense in which the hot object heats with its
heat: for, strictly speaking, heat does not make [causal as opposed to

constitutive – A.F.] things hot. It is, therefore, possible to say that the soul understands as the eye sees. But it is more proper to say that the man understands with his soul.

To the Third we must say that the intellect needs the body for its action not as the organ for such action but to provide its object: for mental imagery is to the intellect what colour is to sight. But to be in this way dependent on the body does not prevent the intellect from being subsistent: or else an animal could not be a subsistent thing, since it needs external objects of sense in order to perceive. (IQ 75A2)

Whether or not there is in a person, as Aquinas urged, some element which is both incorporeal and subsistent the Aristotelian tradition is surely correct, as against the Platonic, in insisting that people as such are corporeal. It is, therefore, appropriate to end the present chapter and part with some extracts from the Myth of Er. For in this myth, told at the end of *The Republic* immediately after what is supposed to be a demonstration of the immortality of the soul, Plato seems himself to be admitting, tacitly and unwittingly, and contrary to all his conscious arguments and intentions, that this insistence is correct. The Myth of Er can thus be seen as having a deep philosophical significance. For against Plato's will it illustrates the truth of Wittgenstein's claim, in the *Philosophical Investigations,* that "The human body is the best picture of the human soul" (p. 78):

Once upon a time Er the son of Armenius . . . died in battle. When the corpses were taken up on the tenth day already decayed he was taken up uncorrupted, was brought home, and was lying on the pyre with the funeral about to begin when he revived. Returning to life he related what he had seen in the world beyond. He said that when his soul emerged he was made to go on a journey with a large company, and they came to a strange place. . . . And there he saw souls after judgement departing by each opening, both the one of the heavens and that of the earth; while as for the other pair of openings, there were souls dusty and dirty from the one coming up from the earth, whereas from the other others came down pure from the heavens. And the souls which kept arriving always seemed to have come after a great journey, and they gladly went off to the meadow and camped there as at a festival. Acquaintances greeted one another, and those which had come from the earth enquired of the others about things up there, while those from the heavens did the same about those with the rest. They told their stories to each other, the one lot weeping and wailing as they recalled how many things they had seen and suffered and of what sort. . . .

(§§ 614B–615C)

['Where is Ardiaeus the Great?']. . . . Then savage men of fiery aspect, who were standing by and took notice of the voice, seized and led them away. They bound Ardiaeus and others hand and foot and head, they flung them down and flayed them, they dragged them along by the roadside carding them on thorn bushes, making known to those who were all the time passing by why it was being done and that they would be taken and thrown into Tartarus. . . . When seven days had passed for each lot of people in the meadow, they had to rise up on the eighth and journey on. . . . (§§ 615E–616B)

Now when they arrived they had to go before Lachesis . . . the maiden daughter of Necessity. 'Souls that live for a day, it is the beginning of another cycle of the mortal race which is the bringer of death. No guardian spirit will draw a lot for you, instead you will choose your own destiny. Let him who draws the first lot choose a life to which he will cleave by necessity. But excellence has no master over her, and each shall have more or less of her as he honours or dishonours her. The responsibility is on the chooser: God is not responsible.' (§ 617D–E)

Part Two

CHAPTER V

Aquinas and the Synthesis of
Faith and Reason

§1 *Impossibility and contradiction*

In the final section of the previous chapter it was taken as obvious that it is "essential to have some logical substance bridging the gap between now and then if even Omnipotence itself is to be able on the Last Day to restore numerically the same man". Yet it has not always been, and still is not, obvious to everyone that and why the requirements of logic must be for all discourse concerned with what is truly the case inescapable. Fully to grasp this reason why is to have made a substantial advance in philosophical understanding. The crucial point is made by Aquinas, in the main body of an article in the *Summa Theologica* on 'Whether God is omnipotent?' What he says has a much wider and also secular bearing:

> Yet if we consider the matter aright, since power is spoken of by reference to possibilities, when God is said to be able to do everything the correct interpretation is that he can do everything possible, and this is why he is spoken of as omnipotent.
>
> Now according to The Philosopher (*Metaphysics IV* (ii)) *possible* is used in two senses. In the first sense it is in relation to some power; for instance, whatever is within human powers is said to be possible for man. . . . The conclusion is, therefore, that God is spoken of as omnipotent in as much as he is able to do everything which is possible absolutely; and this is the other sense of the word *possible*. Something is said to be possible or impossible absolutely in virtue of the relations of terms: possible in as much as the predicate does not contradict the subject, as that Socrates is sitting; but impossible absolutely when the predicate does contradict the subject, as that a man is a donkey. . . .

Whatever does not imply a contradiction is, therefore, among those possibilities in virtue of which God is described as omnipotent. But what does imply a contradiction is not subsumed under the divine omnipotence; because these things are not in principle possible. So it is better to say that they are not possible than that God cannot do them. Nor is this contrary to the word of the angel saying, 'No word will be impossible with God'. For that which implies contradiction cannot be a word; since no intellect can conceive it. (1Q 25A3)

In its reverent employment both of Aristotle and of the Bible this passage is thoroughly representative. Yet it also and importantly and equally representatively displays the philosophical acuteness of the saint. For the central distinction between what would now be called factual and logical impossibilities is indeed fundamental; while to complete the resolution of his difficulty he does also need the further insight that contradictions refer to the significant or insignificant employment of words rather than to the objective realities or unrealities of things. The heart of the matter is that it is no limitation on God – or on anyone or anything else – that he or it cannot do the logically impossible: the deficiency lies rather with those who produce contradictory or otherwise senseless forms of words.

Returning to our example of what even Omnipotence could not do, we can know that this suggestion is logically impossible without knowing anything at all about what powers God does in fact possess and choose to exercise. We can even know it, as I myself do, without believing that there is any God who in fact possesses any powers. For our knowledge is based upon or, if you like, simply is knowledge of the meanings of the terms involved: to say that a perfect replica of the long dead Ardiaeus created on the Last Day would be the original Ardiaeus would be to contradict yourself.

Many people, at least when it suits them, are inclined to treat contradictions lightly; in the spirit of Walt Whitman's 'Song of Myself':

> *... Do I contradict myself?*
> *Very well then I contradict myself*
> *(I am large, I contain multitudes.)*

This may, in its context, be all very well in a poet. But in general and for anyone concerned about what is, or is not, the case it will not do. For to contradict oneself is both to affirm something and to deny it; and to anyone who cares what actually is true this must be intolerable.

It is, as we saw back in Chapter I, upon this same truth-concerned Principle of Non-contradiction that the validity of all deductive inference depends: "It is characteristic, it is indeed the defining characteristic, of a valid deductive argument that if you assert the premises you cannot then deny the conclusion without thereby contradicting yourself." The notions of logical possibility and logical impossibility, of non-contradiction and of self-contradiction, and of deductive validity and invalidity, are thus all essentially connected one with another. It is important to recognize that they are all also equally and by the same token connected with the concept of meaning. For the key Principle of Non-contradiction forbids us to assert anything while at the same time either in whole or in part denying that assertion; and what is the whole, or part, of an assertion is the whole, or part, of what that assertion means. Similarly, deductive argument, which depends essentially upon this Principle, should be seen as a formal means of bringing out what must be already covertly involved in the assertion of its premises: it was for this reason that John Stuart Mill remarked that all such arguments really begged the question.

Once all these key notions have been understood in their interconnectedness it should no longer be surprising to notice that all philosophers, in our sense of the term, and not just some supposed contemporary school of linguistic philosophers, are constantly appealing in one way or another to the meanings and hence to the correct usage of words. Thus, for instance, Aquinas in order to bring out that heat is not a logical substance remarks that "we do not say that heat, but the hot object, heats"; while in the passage just quoted the nerve of his argument rests upon a distinction between two meanings of the word *possible*. This same passage also hints, though it no more than hints, towards a still more general and fundamental insight. At the end of Chapter II we saw Plato's 'Parmenides' arguing that the young 'Socrates' had been after all still insufficiently wholehearted in his separation of the abstract world of the Forms from the concrete world of material things and persons; that truths about Slavery and Mastery in the abstract must be radically different from truths about flesh-and-blood masters and slaves. The insight is that the former, with all their attendant notions and distinctions, refer ultimately to the significant or insignificant employment of words; whereas the latter, along with their corresponding retinue, are concerned with what as a matter of fact happens in the universe around us. Of this more and more will continue to be made as the present book advances.

§2 *Faith and reason*

Immediately, however, the outcome of § 1 is to make it easy to appreciate that, even if we were to allow that all truths of any importance are known only to faith, we could still not escape from questions involving the whole cluster of concepts considered there. For in any collection of supposed truths of faith at least some are bound to be in apparent contradiction with others; and this appearance must, to anyone who takes the truth claims seriously, be a challenge. Again, and precisely in so far as the various items are believed to be both important and true, the believer is confronted with the inseparable questions of what exactly is their full meaning and what can be deduced from them; questions which arise the more urgently in the great historic systems of supposed revelation as original meanings get lost, and present consequences become harder and harder to determine.

It will not do, therefore, at least for anyone who takes seriously the question of the truth about what is in fact the case, to try to reserve here a sphere of faith within which reason can have absolutely no place at all. However, it may still seem as if there could be some region for which only faith could supply the necessary premises, and where the supplying itself requires no rational support. Yet this too would be wrong. Certainly there are many fields where we are not yet, and perhaps will never be, able by any ordinary means to know what is or is not so. Certainly it is always possible to commit yourself to beliefs without evidence, or even against the evidence. But if you are to escape the charge of total arbitrariness and frivolity you must have some presentable reasons: first, for committing yourself categorically where the available evidence is admittedly less than sufficient; and, second, for committing yourself in whatever particular sense you choose.

That the situation is as I have been saying is often concealed by the tacit or explicit use of an inept model. This is the model of faith as a road beginning at the railhead of reason. One is reminded of the signs reading 'Jeepers: Creepers' said to have been erected by U.S. forward units in the jungles of World War II. (The left arm pointed back along some track barely negotiable by a jeep; while the right pointed forward into the undergrowth.) This sort of model is inappropriate here in almost every respect. First, because it takes it for granted – as we have just seen, wrongly – that reason can have no place within the supposed sphere of faith. Second, because it assumes as already given some warrant for continuing the journey; whereas, surely, the defeasible presumption must be that we ought when faced with a shortage of evidence rather to suspend judgement than to commit ourselves unreservedly. Third, because it supposes – what is manifestly not true – that there is only one route of faith available; and, furthermore, that this can without benefit of reasons be known to lead to our destination – truth.

Certainly both the first and the third of these points were fully seized by Aquinas. The whole enormous *Summa Theologica* constitutes an overwhelming vindication of the first. But that *Summa* is only one of two. There is also an earlier and complete *Summa contra Gentiles*, which might by Thomist standards rate as almost 'a slim volume'. (*Thomist*, by the way, is the adjective of *St Thomas Aquinas*: which one needs to know, just as one needs to know that *Cartesian* is the adjective of *Descartes*.) Tradition has it that this earlier *Summa* was composed as a handbook for the conversion of the infidel – and especially of the Islamic Moors who were then in control of most of the peninsula which is now Spain and Portugal. The Arab world was at that time intellectually formidable, mainly thanks to the influence of Aristotle. It was as presented by Arabic-writing commentators that Aristotle's chief works first entered Western Christendom; and of these commentators the greatest was undoubtedly Averroës (1126–1198), born in Cordova in Spain. There were then also throughout the Arab world religious Jews, of whom by far the most distinguished intellectual representative was Moses ben Maimon (Maimonides, 1135–1204): he is for his *Guide for the Perplexed* described sometimes as 'the Jewish Aquinas'.

The following paragraphs from this remarkable missionary handbook by the Christian Aquinas first explain a different distinction, not between reason and faith, but between natural reason and revealed faith. Aquinas then proceeds, having taken our third point, to offer what he confidently believes to be adequate reasons for rating his own preferred candidate as an authentically veridical revelation:

> Not every truth is made known in the same way. For, as has been very well said by The Philosopher, 'it is the mark of an educated man to try to obtain as much certitude as the nature of the subject permits' (*Nicomachean Ethics* I (iii) 4); and Boethius brings this in (*de Trinitate* II). So we must show first how the truth with which we are concerned can be made known.
>
> Now there are two kinds of truths among those which we believe about God. For there are some truths about God which transcend all the abilities of human reason; for instance, that God is triune. But there

are some which even natural reason can attain; for instance, that God exists, that he is one, and the like. These truths about God the philosophers have proved demonstratively, guided by the light of natural reason.

That there are certain things which can be understood about God that entirely transcend the capacities of human reason is absolutely obvious. For since the principle of all the knowledge which the reason has about anything is an understanding of its essence (for, according to the teaching of The Philosopher, the principle of demonstration is 'the-what-a-thing-is': see the *Posterior Analytics* II (iii)), it must be that the way in which we understand the essence of a thing determines what is known about that thing. Hence if the human intellect comprehends the essence of something – for example, a stone or a triangle – nothing which can be understood about it transcends the abilities of human reason. But this is not how it is with us in the case of God. For the human intellect is not able to attain to the grasping of God's essence by its natural endowments: since the knowledge of our intellect, in the present life, takes its start from sense; and so those things which do not fall under the senses cannot be grasped by human intellect, except in so far as knowledge of them is gathered from sensible things. Now sensible things cannot lead our intellect to the point of seeing in them the nature of the divine essence, for they are effects which fall short of the merits of their cause. Nevertheless, our intellect is led from sensible things into knowledge of God, knowing of God that he exists, and other such things which must be attributed to the First Principle. There are, therefore, certain intelligible truths about God which are accessible to human reason; but there are others which altogether surpass the power of human reason. . . .

. . . it is fitting that each sort is divinely offered to man for his belief. This must be shown first with regard to the truth which is accessible to rational inquiry. Otherwise someone might think that since it is available to reason there was no point in presenting it for belief through supernatural inspiration.

Now suppose this sort of truth were left solely for rational inquiry, three awkward consequences would follow. The first is that few men would possess knowledge of God. . . . The second is that those who did arrive at the discovery of the aforementioned truth would attain it with difficulty after a long time. . . . The third is that generally the inquiries of human reason have an element of falsehood in them, because of the weakness of our intellect in judgement. . . . The result would be that many, ignorant of the force of demonstration, would remain in doubt about even those things which had most truly been demonstrated; especially since they can see that among those who are reputed wise each one has his own different teachings. . . .

So it is salutary that the divine mercy provided that it should instruct us to hold by faith even those truths which reason is capable of investigating. In this way all men could easily have a share in the knowledge of God, and this without uncertainty and error.

Hence it is written (*Ephesians* 4: 17–18): 'Henceforward you walk not as also the Gentiles walk in the vanity of their own senses, having their intellect darkened'; and again (*Isaiah* 54: 13): 'All thy children shall be taught by the Lord'.

Now perhaps some think that men ought not to be asked to believe what reason is insufficient to investigate. . . . A certain Simonides once exhorted people to give knowledge of God a miss, and to apply their talents to human affairs: he said, 'A man should be wise in human affairs and a mortal in mortal'. The Philosopher replied, 'Man ought to draw himself towards the immortal and the divine as much as he can'. . . .

But those who put their faith in this sort of truth . . . do not believe frivolously. . . . For these 'secrets of divine Wisdom' (*Job* 11: 6) the divine Wisdom itself, which knows all things to the full, has deigned to reveal to men. It displays its own presence, and the truth of its inspiration and teaching, by appropriate evidences. Thus in order to confirm those things which transcend natural knowledge it displays to view works which exceed all the capacity of nature: viz., wonderful cures of diseases, raisings of the dead, wonderful transformations of heavenly bodies, and – what is more wonderful – the inspiration of human minds so that simple and untutored people, filled with the gift of the Holy Spirit, in an instant compass the highest wisdom and eloquence. When these evidences were examined an innumerable throng not only of simple people but of the wisest men flocked to the Christian faith; led by the power of the aforementioned proof, not by force of arms, not by the promise of pleasures, and – what is the most marvellous thing of all – in the midst of the tyranny of persecutors. This is the faith in which things transcending every human intellect are preached, in which the pleasures of the flesh are curbed, and in which it is taught that all the things of the world are to be despised. For the minds of mortal men to assent to these things is both the greatest of miracles and an obvious work of divine inspiration. . . . Now that this has not happened on the spur of the moment or by chance, but through the dispositions of God is clear from the fact that God foretold in many pronouncements of the

Prophets beforehand that he would do this. (Their books are venerated among us, since they give witness for our faith.) . . .

Those, however, who founded sects which are in error proceeded in the opposite way. This is obvious in the case of Mohammed, who seduced the people with promises of the carnal pleasures for which carnal concupiscence goads us to long. . . . Nor did he produce any supernatural signs such as alone provide suitable evidence of divine inspiration; since a visible performance which can only be divine reveals an invisibly inspired teacher of truth. On the contrary, he said that he was sent in the power of his arms – signs which are not lacking to bandits and tyrants too. . . . And so it is clear that those who put their faith in his words do believe frivolously.

(I, iii–vi: all four chapters have been more or less abbreviated, as indicated)

I do not propose to examine here the sort of case offered by Aquinas for rating the Christian faith as a genuine revelation of God. The immediate tasks are, first, to get the hang of the distinction between natural reason and revealed faith, and, second, to appreciate why it must indeed be – to borrow Aquinas' own well-chosen word – frivolous to give assent to any faith which cannot offer adequate rational credentials. But it is both interesting and relevant to notice that two of the claims made by Aquinas were in the decrees of the First Vatican Council of 1869–1870 defined as essential and constitutive dogmas of the Roman Catholic faith itself. The first of these deals with natural theology, that knowledge of God which is supposed to be accessible to natural reason; while the second is concerned with the identification of revelation (Denzinger, §§ 1806 and 1813):

If anyone shall say that the one true God, our Lord and creator, cannot be known for certain through the creation by the natural light of human reason: let him be anathema.

If anyone shall say that miracles cannot be performed, and hence that all reports of them, even those included in Holy Scripture, must be dismissed as myth or fable; or if he says that miracles can never be known for certain and that the divine origin of the Christian religion cannot be properly proved by them; let him be anathema.

Nowadays it is very frequently said, by theists no less than by atheists, that everyone knows that it is impossible to prove the existence of God. To anyone inclined to accept this piece of the conventional wisdom the first of the two definitions just quoted may make illuminating reading. It may in truth be both impossible and (by some) known to be – as I myself maintain. But what you cannot say, so long as there are sincere and instructed Roman Catholics committed to its denial, is that this is an uncontroversial item of common knowledge. Another and much more dangerous item in our contemporary conventional wisdom is the notion that a reference to faith can constitute either a self-sufficient justification for believing or an adequate excuse for having no reasons at all. The purpose of the present chapter has been to try to dispose of such ideas, and this with the help of the greatest thinker of the Age of Faith. The chapter can appropriately be concluded with some reinforcing extracts from one of the classical philosophers who was a Protestant. They come from the treatment 'Of Knowledge and Probability' in Locke's *Essay concerning Human Understanding*:

There is another use of the word *reason*, wherein it is opposed to *faith*: which, though it be in itself a very improper way of speaking, yet common use has so authorized it that it would be folly either to oppose or hope to remedy it. Only I think it may not be amiss to take notice, that, however faith be opposed to reason, faith is nothing but a firm assent of the mind: which, if it be regulated, as is our duty, cannot be afforded to anything but upon good reason; and so cannot be opposite to it. He that believes without having any reason for believing, may be in love with his own fancies; but neither seeks truth as he ought, nor pays the obedience due to his Maker, who would have him use those discerning faculties He has given him, to keep him out of mistake and error. He that does not this to the best of his power, however he sometimes lights on truth, is in the right but by chance; and I know not whether the luckiness of the accident will excuse the irregularity of his proceeding. This at least is certain, that he must be accountable for whatever mistakes he runs into: whereas he that makes use of the light and faculties God has given him, and seeks sincerely to discover truth by those helps and abilities he has, may have this satisfaction in doing his duty as a rational creature, that, though he should miss truth, he will not miss the reward of it. For he governs his assent right, and places it as he should, who, in any case or matter whatsoever, believes or disbelieves according as reason directs him. He that doth otherwise, transgresses against his own light, and misuses those faculties which were given him to no other end, but to search and follow the clearer evidence and greater probability. . . .

I find every sect, as far as reason will help them, make use of it gladly: and where it fails them, they cry out, 'It is a matter of faith, and above reason' . . . .   (IV, (xvii) 24 and (xviii) 2)

CHAPTER VI

The Existence of God and the
Limits of Explanation

§ 1 *The Stratonician Presumption*

Natural theology, in the sense explained in the previous chapter, is by tradition and rightly reckoned to be part of philosophy; although by some it has been regarded as a province held under a sort of condominium with theology. Aquinas himself, thinking of philosophy and theology as being both similarly deductive in their methods, distinguished the two by reference to their premises: those of the former are supplied by natural reason and observation, and those of the latter by revelation.

Nevertheless, and reasonably, he included what he took to be philosophical demonstrations of the existence of God in both the *Summa contra Gentiles* and the *Summa Theologica*. If someone nowadays is going to conclude that no such demonstration can be sound then this involves that a positive natural theology is impossible. In an obvious sense such a conclusion is negative, where its opposite would be positive. But this must not mislead us to think that it would by the same token be trivial or self-frustrating. A moment's consideration of the implications of Chapter V, and especially of the first of the two decrees of the First Vatican Council quoted there, can show that it would not be trivial. And firmly to establish any conclusion, whether positive or negative, must represent progress not frustration in philosophy.

The ambitions of the present chapter are, however, more modest and less comprehensive. I shall attend here to only a few arguments of natural theology, selecting the most famous and those from which the most useful wider lessons can most easily be drawn. The first of these lessons is about beginning from the beginning. In societies in which theism is the demanded and even the actual norm, it is usually the atheist who is challenged to provide reasons for not believing. But in a really systematic natural theology the onus of proof must, surely, lie on the proposition. It is up to the theist: first, to introduce and explain his chosen concept of God; and, second, to produce reasons for believing that in the corresponding sense the word *God* does in fact have application – that is to say that, in his sense, there is a God. So consider the two Objections in answer to which Aquinas in the *Summa Theologica* deploys his Five Ways. (*The Five Ways* is the traditional label for his five supposed proofs.) Those who may understandably feel that they have had more than their fill of official spokesmen should in fairness remind themselves that Aquinas was the author of his Objections as well as of his Replies: his thought here is in a very literal sense conducted as a dialogue with himself:

> It seems that God does not exist. For if of two contrary things one were to exist without limit the other would be totally eliminated. But what is meant by this word *God* is something good without limit. So if God were to have existed no evil would have been encountered. But evil is encountered in the world. Therefore, God does not exist.
>
> Furthermore, what can be accounted for by fewer principles is not the product of more. But it seems that everything which can be observed in the world can be accounted for by other principles, on the assumption of the non-existence of God. Thus natural effects are explained by natural causes, while contrived effects are referred to human reason and will. So there is no need to postulate the existence of God.
>
> (I, Q2A3)

The first of these ground-floor Objections is a formulation of the theological Problem of Evil, described already (Ch. II, § 2). The Reply takes its cue from a statement of Augustine in the *Encheiridion*: "Since God is supremely good he would not allow any evil in his works unless he were sufficiently omnipotent and good to make good come even out of evil" (§ XI). The second Objection is a statement of Naturalism, the view that all the phenomena of the universe can and must be explained without reference to any principle or principles in any sense 'outside', or 'beyond'.

Let us call the presumption that this can be done, *The Stratonician Presumption*. Strato of Lampsacus (d. 269 BC) was next but one after its founder Aristotle as the head of the Lyceum. Certainly he must have been in many ways anticipated in his radical naturalism by the Classical atomists, by the Hippocratic doctors, and by other predecessors even of Aristotle. But thanks first to the Roman orator Cicero (106–43 BC), and then in the modern period thanks also to the sceptical French Protestant Pierre Bayle

(1647–1706), Strato has come to hold a special position as the archetypal spokesman. Above all he was seen as such by Hume, the modern paragon of a man-centred naturalism.

Bayle wrote, and for the next hundred years every intellectual leader read, an enormously successful *Historical and Critical Dictionary*. Cicero composed several philosophical dialogues in order to introduce to Rome some much-needed Greek culture. For us these uninspired and derivative Ciceronian exercises are a main source of information about real thinkers whose works have since perished. The first passage comes from *de natura Deorum* [On the Nature of the Gods] and the second from the *Academica* [Affairs of the Academy]:

> Nor is his pupil Strato, called 'the physicist', worthy of attention. He thinks that all divine power rests in nature, which contains in itself the causes of birth, growth, and decay, but is entirely devoid of conscious-ness. . . .
> (I (xiii) 35)

> You deny that anything can be produced without a god. Look how you have Strato of Lampsacus butting in to give that god exemption from a great labour (and seeing that the priests of the gods have holi-days how much fairer it is that the gods themselves should have them!). He denies that he has any use for divine activities in constructing the world. He teaches that everything there is is a product of nature, although not in the way of the man who maintained that all these things are composed of rough and smooth, hooked and barbed, atoms with some emptiness between. Strato considers that these are dreams on the part of Democritus, the work of a wishful thinker rather than of a teacher. But he himself, reviewing the various portions of the universe one by one, teaches that whatever exists or comes to be either comes about or has come about through natural weights and movements.
> (II (xxxviii) 121)

The immediate relevance of this to us is that a complete and systematic natural theology will surely have to accept the Stratonician Presumption as its starting-point. Of course in so doing it will be accepting this only as a defeasible presumption, and one which it aims by its own arguments to defeat. So if in the event anyone does succeed in developing a positive natural theology then necessarily this achievement will involve the rejec-tion of a Stratonician metaphysic. But this conclusion would still not retrospectively discredit his insistence on starting from the Stratonician Presumption; on taking it, that is, as the one to beat.

The reason why atheist naturalism must have at least this initial priority over theism is that it is the more economical view. The theist as such postulates more than the atheist; and, in consequence, the onus of proof must rest on him. It is, therefore, altogether appropriate that the first sentence in the second Objection in Aquinas constitutes an earlier version of the principle of economy known as Ockham's Razor. This is usually stated as, 'Entities must not be multiplied unnecessarily', although the maxim is not to be found in precisely this form in the extant works of William of Ockham (c. 1290–1349). The philosophically important distinction is: between, on the one hand, metaphysical versions which assure us that the universe operates thriftily – "Nature abhors the pomp of superfluous causes"; and, on the other hand, methodological varieties which prescribe an economy of postulation to investigators. Similar distinctions between metaphysical and methodological versions can and should be made with respect to many philosophical doctrines. For yet a third version here, the semantic, apply to the Wittgenstein of the *Tractatus* (Ch. XI, § 5, below).

§ 2 *The Ontological Argument*

First place among attempts to defeat the Stratonician Presumption must go to the Ontological Argument. This is not because it is valid, or even because it is likely to seem to the modern reader the most plausible. It certainly is not valid, notwithstanding that philosophers of the calibre of Descartes, Leibniz, and Spinoza all thought that it was. But it must come before all others here because it involves a claim that the existence of God is, in a sense, self-evident; its nerve is that from the very notion of God it follows necessarily that God must exist. This Ontological Argument was first clearly stated by St Anselm (1033–1109). It was immediately attacked by contemporaries, especially a monk called Gaunilo. Among the Scholastics it was, at least ostensibly, rejected by Aquinas. Duns Scotus (*c.* 1226–1308) accepted it, although insisting on a preliminary later to be required also by Leibniz. (It is, by the way, to the uninhibitedly polemical opponents of Duns Scotus that we owe our word *dunce*.) The Ontological Argument was reintroduced at the beginning of the modern period by René Descartes (1596–1650), who made no acknowledgement to any of his predecessors. This version comes from Part IV of his *Discourse on the Method*:

After that I wanted to seek for other truths and I put my mind to the subject matter of the geometers. . . . I went through some of their most simple demonstrations. And having noticed that the great certainty which everyone attributes to these is founded on nothing else but the fact that they are clearly conceived . . . I also noticed that there was nothing at all in them to assure me of the existence of their subject matter. For, for instance, I saw clearly that given a triangle then necessarily its three angles must be equal to two right angles. But none of this gave me any reason to believe that any triangle existed in the world. However, on reverting to the examination of the idea which I had of a perfect Being I found that existence was comprised in the idea in the way that that of a triangle contains the equality of its three angles to two right angles, or that of a sphere the equidistance of all the points on its surface from the centre – or even more obviously still. And so, consequently, it is at least as certain that God – this perfect Being – is, or exists, as any demonstration of geometry could possibly be.   (IV)

The geometrical form came naturally to Descartes, who was one of the greatest creative geometers of his or any time. But it is necessary to look also at the later version in his *Meditations on First Philosophy* in order to appreciate that existence is supposed to be essential to the concept of God not because this is the concept of a being but because this Being is specified by definition as perfect. ("First Philosophy" was Aristotle's own description of the subject of what we call his *Metaphysics*):

[The Ontological Argument] seems to have some appearance of being a sophism. For, being accustomed in every other case to make a distinction between essence and existence, I easily persuade myself that the existence of God can be separated from his essence, and that it is thus possible to conceive God as not existing in reality. . . . But there is a hidden sophism in this specious objection. For from the fact that I cannot conceive a mountain without a valley it does not follow that there is any mountain nor any valley in the world; only that, whether there is or whether there is not, mountain and valley cannot by any means be separated one from the other. On the other hand, simply from the fact that I cannot conceive God without existence, it follows that existence is inseparable from him, and hence that he exists in reality. It is not that my thought can bring it about that this is how things are, and that it imposes any necessity on things. But, on the contrary, it is because the necessity of the thing itself, namely, the existence of God, determines my thought to conceive it in this way. For it is not within my power to conceive of a God without existence (that is to say a Being

184

supremely perfect without a supreme perfection), as I am free to imagine a horse without wings or with wings. (V)

It is thus crucial for Descartes to rate as a species of perfection actual existence, existence not in thought but in the world of things. The same applies to the original in Anselm's *Proslogion*:

> . . . we believe that You are something than which nothing greater can be thought. Or is there then no such being since 'The fool hath said in his heart, "There is no God"'? (*Psalms*, 14: 1). But, surely, this same fool when he hears my words *something than which nothing greater can be thought* understands what he hears. . . .
>
> Hence, even the fool is convinced that something exists, in the understanding at least, than which nothing greater can be thought. . . . And, surely, that than which nothing greater can be thought cannot exist in the understanding alone. For, suppose it exists in the understanding alone, then it can be thought to exist in reality; which is greater.
>
> Therefore, if that than which nothing greater can be thought exists in the understanding alone, then the very being than which nothing greater can be thought is one than which a greater can be thought. But this is certainly impossible. Hence, there is no doubt that there exists something than which nothing greater can be thought; and both in the understanding and in reality. (II)

To this the response of Aquinas was characteristically subtle, acute, and ambivalent. In the main body of the Article 'Whether the proposition *God exists* is self-evident?' in the *Summa Theologica* he seems in general to accept that the nerve of the Ontological Argument is sound, although unfortunately to us useless. But then in particular and in answer to the unnamed Anselm he unleashes the decisive fundamental objection:

> We have to say that *self-evident* is used in two senses; in one it is self-evident in itself, but not to us; in the other it is self-evident in itself, and to us. For a proposition is self-evident when the predicate is part of what the subject means: for instance, that man is an animal since animal is part of the meaning of man. If therefore everyone knows the essence of the subject and the predicate the proposition will be self-evident to all. . . .
>
> So I maintain that this proposition *God exists* is self-evident in itself, since its subject and predicate are identical; for, as we shall see later, God is his own existence. . . .

Someone hearing the word *God* may not understand that it means 'something than which a greater cannot be conceived', since some have believed God to be body. Even granted that everyone does understand that by the word *God* is meant 'that than which a greater cannot be conceived', still it does not follow from this that what is understood by the word exists in reality, only that it exists as thought about. You cannot argue that it exists in reality unless you are given that there exists in reality something than which no greater can be conceived – and this is not granted by those who take it that God does not exist.   (I, Q2 A1)

Whether or not this Reply can be squared with the conclusion of the main body of the Article, it certainly has the heart of the matter in it. Once seized of the absolute impossibility of deducing this sort of conclusion from this sort of premise, we can go forward to make further philosophical gains, putting the Ontological Argument to uses of a sort never intended by its sponsors.

The first of these uses is as a memorably persuasive illustration of the need to have and to master a notation which can make absolutely and systematically clear the fundamental difference between, on the one hand, verbal and conceptual questions and, on the other, "matters of fact and real existence". For the premise of the Ontological Argument is the definition of a word, whereas the proposed conclusion would be the supreme fact of the universe. The prime need is to distinguish, and the corresponding notational need is for devices to mark the distinction, between: on the one hand, discussion of the concept or concepts of – say – God (talk about the meaning or meanings of the word *God*, and about the implications of its employment); and, on the other hand, discussion of the objects, if any, of these concepts (talk about the things to which these words do or would refer).

It is largely to the German mathematician Gottlob Frege (1848–1925) that our contemporary philosophy owes its obsessional sensitiveness to this difference. Frege himself distinguished it as that between concept and object; and he always insisted, in another equally important insight, that it is essential never to confuse, either here or elsewhere, the psychological with the logical. Thus, had he ever wished to speak of the concept of God, he would have spoken of the concept 'God' (putting the word between inverted commas); or else (following the different convention of the present book) of the concept *God*. In doing this he would have been talking about the use to which the word *God* is put; and this, of course, must be exactly the same as the use of any precisely equivalent term in any other language. (Frege, being a German writing in German, would have written *Gott*; and this difference is here quite irrelevant.) What he would specifically not have been talking about would have been any mental images, or other such phenomena, which may or may not come before the minds of those who utter or hear or read the word *God* (or its equivalents in languages other than English).

Philosophers since Frege have often preferred to make the same fundamental distinction by speaking of the word or the expression or the sentence rather than of the concept. This preference is, however, no sufficient ground for any observer to think that he has discovered a new branch or category of Linguistic Philosophy. For the philosopher who speaks of the use of the word *God* (*Dieu, Gott, Deus,* or what have you) is in his different vocabulary referring to the same thing as his colleague who talks of concept of God or the concept *God*. He is certainly not concerned about words in the tediously philological manner of the man who will tell us that the British English *lift, car,* and *transport* are shorter than the American English *elevator, automobile,* and *transportation*; or that *Gott* is a four-letter word. The philosopher discussing the use of the word *God* is said to be mentioning that term; whereas if he or anyone else employs it to make some claim about the supposed object of the concept *God,* then he is said to be using the word.

Once given the prime distinction between concept and object, and a corresponding notation, these can be and have been developed to illuminate the general nature of logical relations. The extended notational distinction is that between the Material Mode of Speech (MMS) and the Formal Mode of Speech (FMS). These labels were introduced by Rudolf Carnap (b. 1891), a charter member of the Vienna Circle of old original Logical Positivists (Ch. XI, § 2). The man who says that Threehood necessarily involves Oddness, that the idea of a triangle contains the idea of the equality of its three angles to two right angles, or that existence is part of – or is – the essence of God is thereby employing the Material Mode of Speech. The alternative Formal Mode is, as might be feared, much more long-winded: to say 'There are three of them' and to deny 'There are an odd number of them' would be to contradict yourself; to say 'This is a triangle' and to deny 'This has three angles equal to two right angles' would be to contradict yourself; and 'which exists' is part of – or is – the definition of the word *God*.

No one would be so foolish as to suggest that the Formal ought completely and generally to replace the Material Mode of Speech. Yet it is extremely important to be able, and on occasion willing, to transpose passages from one into the other. Two excellent exercises would be: first, to transpose into the Formal Mode the passages from Anselm and Descartes quoted already in this Chapter; and, second, to put the newly-mastered technique to work to deal elegantly, on the lines suggested in the first section of Chapter V, with some puzzle about whether an omnipotent God could create something which even he could not control. Then if anyone protests that a merely notational innovation cannot really matter the best first reply is to offer him too some exercises: perhaps starting with a few calculations to be done in Roman not Arabic numerals; and then continuing by asking for the development of a chemical argument purely in words and without benefit of the now standard symbolism invented by Berzelius.

A further and deeper level of response requires us to appreciate how an inferior notation may also encourage and express actually erroneous ideas. This is the reason for writing *transpose* rather than *translate*; for the FMS analogue may sometimes be a substantial improvement on, and hence not equivalent to, the MMS original. Thus talk about the idea or the concept may both embrace and strengthen that very confusion between the logical and the psychological which Frege was properly concerned to avoid. Certainly too most of those, from Aristotle onwards, who have spoken of the essences of things would have been reluctant to allow that all they were saying was expressed in some FMS statement about the definitions of the words; though they might have had even greater difficulty in explaining precisely what more they had in mind, and in justifying their beliefs about it. Clearly, for instance, Aquinas could scarcely have been content with any application of such a suggestion to his remarks about the essence and existence of God.

The second lesson which can be taken from an examination of the Ontological Argument concerns existence in general. Both Descartes and Anselm assume that this is an especially splendid characteristic which something might or might not happen to have much as you or I might unsplendidly be overweight. Descartes speaks of existence as a perfection explicitly. But the same assumption is equally basic to Anselm. It is only thinly veiled as the contention that "that than which nothing greater can be conceived cannot exist in the understanding alone", but must also "exist in reality, which is greater". For that final comparative clause, "which is greater", mistakes it that actual existence might be the last and consummating characteristic specified in a proper definition of the word *God*.

The classic attempt to bring out that this is indeed a mistake was made by Kant in his *Critique of Pure Reason*. This is his greatest but immensely difficult work. It is known also as the first *Critique*, since it was the first of three books with similar titles all belonging to his critical (as opposed to pre-critical) period. This period began, as he generously acknowledged, when, primarily through a reading of Hume, Kant was awoken from his "dogmatic slumbers". Hume himself had dismissed the Ontological Argument in very short order. (See Ch. XI, § 2, below.) Kant took more time in order to draw a useful general moral. The translation is by Norman Kemp Smith:

Being is obviously not a real predicate; that is, it is not a concept of something which could be added to the concept of a thing. It is merely the positing of thing. . . . Logically, it is merely the copula of a judgement. The proposition, *God is omnipotent*, contains two concepts, each of which has its object – God and omnipotence. The small word *is* adds no new predicate, but only serves to posit the predicate. . . . If, now, we take the subject (God) with all its predicates (among which is omnipotence), and say *God is*, or *There is a God*, we attach no new predicate to the concept of God, but only posit the subject . . . with all its predicates, and indeed postulate it as being an object that stands in relation to my concept. The content of both must be one and the same; nothing can have been added to the concept, which expresses merely what is possible, by my thinking its object . . . as given absolutely. Otherwise stated, the real contains no more than the merely possible. A hundred real thalers do not contain the least coin more than a hundred possible thalers. For as the latter signify the concept, and the former the object and the positing of the object, should the former contain more than the latter, my concept would not, in that case, express the whole object, and would not therefore be an adequate concept of it. My financial position is, however, affected very differently by a hundred real thalers than it is by the mere concept of them (that is, of their possibility). For the object, as it actually exists, is not analytically contained in my concept . . . and yet the conceived hundred thalers are not themselves in the least increased through thus acquiring existence outside my concept.

By whatever and by however many predicates we may think a thing . . . we do not make the least addition to the thing when we further declare that this thing exists. Otherwise it would not be exactly the same thing that exists, but something more than we had thought in the concept; and we could not, therefore, say that the exact object of my concept exists. . . . When, therefore, I think a being as the supreme reality, without any defect, the question still remains whether it exists or not. (A598–600: B626–628)

The fundamental point made by Kant in this classic and powerful statement has since been incorporated as one of the elements of modern logic. For in the symbolism introduced in the *Principia Mathematica* of Bertrand Russell and A. N. Whitehead one is required always to distinguish between, on the one hand, existential statements (such as, 'There is a so and so') and, on the other hand, predicative statements (such as, 'The so and so is such and such'). It is a curiosity very typical of the history of ideas that Kant himself in this epoch-marking passage did not make the distinction, which has since become an important logical commonplace, between the *is* of existence and the *is* of predication (sometimes called the copulative).

The third and last general lesson of the Ontological Argument can be taken from Leibniz. He himself, like Duns Scotus three centuries earlier, believed that this argument provided the basis for a valid proof; but that an unstated assumption had first to be warranted. The passage comes from a short paper of 1684, 'Reflections on knowledge, truth, and ideas':

It frequently happens that we mistakenly think that we possess concepts: this occurs when we mistake it that we have already explained certain words we are employing. It is false, or at any rate equivocal, to say as some do that we necessarily must have the idea of a thing in order to be able to express it in words, and to understand what we are saying. For certainly we often understand the individual words, or recall vaguely that we did once understand each one separately; but ... we can easily fall into a contradiction which may be contained in the composite notion. I was at one time provoked to make a more exact investigation of this question by the celebrated scholastic argument for the existence of God, which Descartes recently revived. ... In truth ... this argument permits us to conclude only that the existence of God follows if the possibility of God is already proved. For we cannot use a definition in an argument without first making sure that ... it contains no contradiction. From concepts which contain a contradiction we can draw conclusions contrary to one another; which is absurd.

I used to explain this with the example of the idea of the fastest motion containing an absurdity. Let it be assumed that a wheel is turning with the fastest motion. Then it is easy to see that if one of the wheel's spokes were lengthened to extend beyond the rim, its end point would be moving faster than a nail lying on the rim; the motion of which is, therefore, not the fastest: which contradicts the hypothesis. At first blush it might seem that we have the idea of the fastest motion, for we understand what we are saying. Yet the fact is that we cannot have an idea of impossible things. So it is not enough to say that we think the most perfect being in order to certify that we can have an idea of such a being, and in the proof which we have been talking about the soundness of the argument depends on proving or presupposing the possibility of the most perfect being.

For Leibniz the immediate moral of this elegant and decisive demonstration was that the possibility required to be proved. But for anyone who has learnt the first two lessons which we have drawn from the Ontological Argument the conclusion must be that the idea of God employed as the premise is another vicious specimen to put alongside that of the fastest (logically) possible motion. This idea has, of course, been shown to be vicious only in so far as perfection has to be interpreted – as by the spokesmen of the Ontological Argument it was – as entailing actual existence. The wider moral of any such demonstration is one which Leibniz also drew. If one at first sight sound idea can be shown to contain a contradiction, then surely there may be other conceptual impostors still to be unmasked.

§ 3 The First Mover

The development of the Five Ways in the *Summa Theologica* is breath-takingly brief, covering in all only two or three ordinary printed pages. Partly indeed for this very reason, but mainly because these supposed proofs involve so many Aristotelian and other notions now generally unfamiliar, it is for our purposes necessary nevertheless to be selective. Characteristically all five arguments start from what Aquinas takes to be manifest general facts about the universe around us. Way One runs:

We must say that it is possible to prove the existence of God in five ways. The first and more obvious way is the one which begins from motion. For it is certain, and plain to our senses, that some things in this world move. Now everything which moves is moved by something else. . . . So if that by which it is moved is itself being moved it must be being moved by something else, and that by something else again. But this process cannot proceed to infinity; because, if it did, there would be no first mover and, consequently, no other mover. For secondary movers do not move unless they are moved by a first mover; for example, the stick does not move unless it is moved by the hand. It is, therefore, necessary to arrive at some first mover which is moved by nothing else; and this all men understand to be God. (I, Q2 A3)

To understand this argument, and its companions, it is essential to recall the distinction made much earlier between theologian's and layman's senses of *creation* (Ch. II, § 2). Aquinas is not trying to prove that there must have been an unmoved First Mover, or unchanging First Changer, to start things off "in the beginning". That the universe had a beginning he certainly did believe, but as an item of revelation. What he maintained could be proved by natural reason, and what he thought he was here so proving, was the existence of a present sustaining cause – a Creator in what I have labelled the theologian's sense of that word. (It was in defence of a distinction of this sort and, more particularly, of his claims about what could and could not be proved here by natural reason that Aquinas wrote his *Concerning the eternity of the world: against the murmurers* – "the murmurers" being those who were accusing him of heresy.)

Once this aim is understood it begins to become clear why Aquinas chose the example of a man waving a stick, and did not refer – say – to someone launching a missile. It also becomes easier to appreciate the placing of the emphasis in the clause, "this process cannot proceed to infinity". He is, for the reasons just indicated, precisely not maintaining that there cannot be physical processes without beginning and without end. It would, therefore, be a peculiarly gross howler to interpret his Way Two, which is a parallel argument to a First Cause, as being the medieval forefather of a popular sophism which is itself peculiarly scandalous: the sophism, namely, that since everything must have a cause, and that since the series of causes could not go back indefinitely into the past, therefore there must have been a First Cause "in the beginning". (This remarkably popular argument is peculiarly scandalous in that its conclusion not merely does not follow from, but actually contradicts one of, its own premises.)

But, now we are seized of what Aquinas was and was not in fact trying to prove, we must recall Newton's First Law of Motion which we all learnt, or should have learnt, at our mother's knees: "Every body continues in its state of rest, or of uniform motion in a right [straight] line, unless it is compelled to change that state by forces impressed upon it." From the vantage point provided by Newtonian, as opposed to Aristotelian, physics we can see that there is no necessity in nor warrant for the principle that "everything which moves is moved by something else."

Aquinas here laboured to derive this conclusion from the Aristotelian notions of potentiality and actuality (Ch. III, § 4). These panting labours I omitted from our quotation, partly because they would be felt as paralysingly technical, but chiefly because they could at best show only – what at this late hour no longer needs to be shown – the scientific inadequacy of these and other Aristotelian concepts.

The questions which are, however, very much worth pursuing are, in particular, that of the relation here between Aristotelian and modern mechanics; and, in general, that of the acceptability or otherwise of different explanatory ultimates. On the former it is very roughly correct, and for present purposes adequate, to say that Aristotelian physics started from the commonsense idea that bodies are naturally at rest. Hence what requires explanation is not only any beginning but also any continuation of motion or change. Within this framework much imagination and ingenuity had to be, and was, exercised to explain why a missile continues to move after it has been released from the thrower's hand. This explanation was required to show that what was no longer being pushed by the thrower was nevertheless still being pushed by something else; otherwise it was believed that it could not be, as in fact it was, continuing to move. The scientific revolution effected under the leadership of Galileo and Newton reformed the framework by introducing the different fundamental idea embodied in the modern First Law of Motion: whereas any deviation from this new norm demands explanation, the continuation of uniform motion in a straight line – inertial motion – does not.

Historically it was one of the most important features of the Aristotelian framework that it did leave this opening for the postulation of one or many sustaining causes of all those actual motions which are not congruent with the approved standard of the brandished stick. When in the early 1200's Aristotle's philosophical and scientific works began to become available in the west his ideas appeared as a threat to Christendom. Intellectually he was incomparably superior to all the known competition – obviously "The Philosopher". Yet he had been himself a pagan, and came now into Christendom escorted by the infidel commentators of Islam. It was the great ambition of St Thomas to turn this threat to the positive advantage of his Church by incorporating into an orthodox synthesis all that was sound and true in Aristotle. To his more conservative contemporaries this aspiration looked unpromising and rash. But, as was suggested earlier (Ch. III, § 4), many of Aristotle's most characteristic ideas are congenially suggestive to the devoutly Christian thinker as those –

say – of the Classical atomists or of the Hippocratic doctors or of Strato "the physicist" would certainly not have been.

It is worth reinforcing this general point, in its particular application to Aristotelian physics, by quoting an appreciation by an historian of science who happens himself to be a Christian. It comes from Herbert Butterfield's *The Origins of Modern Science: 1300–1800*:

> We have not always brought home to ourselves the peculiar character of that Aristotelian universe in which the things that were in motion had to be accompanied by a mover all the time. A universe constructed on the mechanics of Aristotle had the door half-way open for spirits already; it was a universe in which unseen hands had to be in constant operation, and sublime Intelligences had to roll the planetary spheres around. . . . The modern law of inertia, the modern theory of motion, is the great factor which in the seventeenth century helped to drive the spirits out of the world and opened the way to a universe which ran like a piece of clockwork. Not only so – but the very first men who in the middle ages launched the great attack on the Aristotelian theory were conscious of the fact that this colossal issue was involved in the question. The first of the important figures, Jean Buridan, in the middle of the fourteenth century pointed out that his alternative interpretation would eliminate the need for the Intelligences that turned the celestial spheres. He even noted that the Bible provided no authority for these spiritual agencies. . . . Not much later than this, Nicholas of Oresme went further still, and said that on the new alternative theory God might have started off the universe as a kind of clock and left it to run of itself.
>
> (pp. 7–8)

Before proceeding to the second issue of the acceptability of alternative explanatory ultimates it is also worth noticing that the Jewish Aquinas found Aristotelian physics equally congenial; and he, unlike Buridan, was able to find Scriptural warrant for "the Intelligences". Maimonides indeed should be noticed much more often than he is, and such comparisons made much more often than they are. I myself in the previous chapter should perhaps have quoted his statement: "Thus we, Monotheists, do not consider it a defect in God, that He does not combine two opposites in one object, nor do we test His omnipotence by the accomplishment of any similar impossibility" (I (lxxv)). So now, in compensation, consider these extracts from his exploitation of Aristotle, written a century before Aquinas in Cairo – where a Jew then found greater tolerance. The translation, from the Arabic original, is by M. Friedlander:

We notice many objects consisting of a motor and a thing moved; i.e. objects which set other things in motion, and whilst doing so are themselves set in motion by other things; such is clearly the case as regards all the middle members of a series of things in motion. We also see a thing that is moved, but does not itself move anything, viz., the last member of the series; consequently a motor must exist without being at the same time a thing moved, and that is the Prime Motor, which, not being subject to motion, is indivisible, incorporeal, and independent of time, as has been shown in the preceding argument.

(II (i))

The theory of Aristotle in respect to the causes of the motion of the spheres led him to assume the existence of Intelligences. Although this theory consists of assertions which cannot be proved, yet it is the least open to doubt, and more systematic than any other. . . . It includes maxims which are identical with those taught in Scripture, and it is to a still greater extent in harmony with doctrines contained in well-known Midrashim, as will be explained by me. For this reason I will cite his views and his proofs, and collect from them what coincides with the teachings of Scripture, and agrees with the doctrine held by our Sages.

(II (iii))

Scripture supports the theory that the spheres are animate and intellectual, i.e. capable of comprehending things; that they are not, as ignorant persons believe, inanimate masses like fire and earth, but are, as the philosophers assert, endowed with life, and serve their Lord, whom they mightily praise and glorify; compare 'The heavens declare the glory of God' (*Psalms*, 19: 2), etc. It is a great error to think that this is a mere figure of speech; for the verbs *to declare* and *to relate*, when joined together, are, in Hebrew, only used of intellectual beings. (II (v))

We have already stated that the angels are incorporeal. This agrees with the opinion of Aristotle: there is only this difference in the names employed – he uses the term *Intelligences* and we say instead *angels*. His theory is that the Intelligences are intermediate beings between the Prime Cause and existing things, and that they effect the motion of the spheres, on which motion the existence of all things depends. This is also the view we meet in all parts of Scripture. . . . (II (vi))

So perhaps it is. However, this excursion into Maimonides was for us only a sidetrip. The main thing to be established was, that Way One takes as its premise the proposition that everything which moves is moved by something else, and that this claim is both seemingly in conflict with familiar fact and dependent upon the now discredited physics of Aristotle. We should notice too that Aquinas goes on to argue, fallaciously, that, since "secondary movers do not move unless they are moved by a first mover", therefore there must be one single First Mover which moves them all.

The same mistake, which modern logicians label *The Quantifier-shift Fallacy*, is repeated in other later Ways. It certainly is a fallacy: you might as well argue that, since all roads lead somewhere, therefore there must be some single place to which all roads lead – Rome, no doubt!

That this and some other arguments of Aquinas are in this respect fallacious seems to have been pointed out first by the classical commentator on the *Summa Theologica*, Thomas de Vio known as Cajetan (1468–1534). Cajetan was a Dominican who became Master-General of his order. Later as a Cardinal he was the Papal Legate deputed to hold conversations during the Diet of Augsburg with the turbulent Luther. Cajetan was the author also of *de Analogia Nominum,* the standard Scholastic treatise on analogy. This is a doctrine developed from Aristotelian materials in an attempt to meet the problem of explaining how human language, evolved within a finite world, can be got to say anything about an infinite God.

Many modern apologists, despairing to defend the actual Way One presented so confidently by Aquinas himself, have suggested that it should be reinterpreted in order hopefully to make it independent of any and every revolution in physics. Physics, it is then urged, may like other sciences do an excellent job in its own limited sphere. But we need in addition something else more fundamental. Thus in particular, besides all those various explanations of individual movements which it is the more menial task of the physicists to supply, we also require a general answer to the general question, 'Why is there any such thing as motion at all?' And this, they maintain, is what the Unmoved Prime Mover provides.

An important lesson about ultimates in explanation is to be learnt here. Consider a passage from Aristotle's *Metaphysics*:

> Leucippus, however, and his associate Democritus maintain that the elements are the Full and the Void; describing them as being and not-being, respectively. . . . These, they say, are the material causes of things. And just as those who make the underlying substance one generate other things by its modifications . . . so they maintain that the differences [in the atoms] are the causes of everything else. These differences, they hold, are three: shape, arrangement, and position. . . . Thus, A differs

from N in shape, AN from NA in arrangement, and Z from N in position. As for motion, whence and how it arises in things, they complacently neglected the problem, much as the others did. (985B 5–21)

This passage is all too typical of Aristotle's reports on earlier thinkers:
they are treated as if they had existed only to be his predecessors; and they
are made to dress themselves in the livery of such distinctively Aristotelian
concepts as Material Cause (Ch. IV, § 5). So we may with a very good
conscience speculate that it was not complacency but in part a profound
insight which led these Classical atomists not to attempt a general explanation of motion as such.

The crux is that it is in principle impossible to explain everything. The
point is so rarely mastered in its full implications that anyone who took
away only this from a first course in philosophy would not have been
wasting his time. It follows from the essential nature of explanation why
something is the case. Suppose, for instance, that we notice and are
puzzled by the fact that the new white paint above our gas cooker quickly
turns a dirty brown. The first stage is to discover that this is what always
happens, with that sort of stove, and that kind of paint. Pressing our
questions to a second stage we learn that this phenomenon is to be explained by certain wider and deeper regularities of chemical combination:
the sulphur in the gas fumes forms a compound with something in the
paint. Driving on still further we are led to see the squalor in our kitchen
as a consequence of the truth of an all-embracing atomic-molecular theory
of the structure of matter. And so on. At every stage explanation is and
has to be in terms of something else which, at least at that stage, is and has
to be accepted as a brute fact: that is just how it is.

It is important to see both what does and what does not follow from
this obviously preliminary and partial analysis. It does follow that however
far and however deep you go in the series of explanations you must always
be left with something which itself is not, precisely because it is that in
terms of which other things are, explained. It does not follow, either that
there is some particular specific point at which we have to stop, or that
there is some particular specific fact or sort of fact in terms of which we
have to explain all others. Consequently, it is not necessarily a fault in –
rather it is itself a necessary feature of – any theoretical explanation that it
leaves something unexplained. What would really be faults would be,
either to fail to compass what could and should have been accounted for,
or to pretend to explain absolutely everything.

We cannot, therefore, follow Aristotle in taking it as obvious that, if the Classical atomists omitted to construct an answer to the question why there is such a thing as motion, then this must have been a mark of scandalous negligence. Since every explanatory system must contain ultimates which are not and, at least within that system, cannot be themselves explained, it remains possible that Leucippus and Democritus – like Galileo and Newton – may have made motion one of these; perhaps as somehow inherent in matter in the void. Nor, again, can we follow that interpretation of Aquinas which urges that motion as such inexorably demands explanation. For no reason has yet been given for insisting that motion itself cannot be one of the ultimates.

Once this point about the inevitability of ultimates in explanation is fully grasped it becomes just a little less difficult to break out of a very common and insidious sort of intellectual parochialism; the parochialism, that is, of assuming that there can be no such ultimates other than your own. It was, as has been suggested already in the particular case of physics, one of the essential and constitutive achievements of the revolution through which modern science replaced Aristotelian that it abandoned one set of ultimates in favour of another. To grasp the dangers of this kind of parochialism is indispensably relevant to the main theme of the present chapter. For that theme is the attempt to defeat the Stratonician Presumption, and this itself is the presumption of the possibility of purely naturalistic ultimates.

The first extract quoted in § 1 shows that Aquinas acknowledged atheist naturalism as in some measure an intellectually considerable alternative to theism. But when we examine his Way One as an attempt to defeat an atheist presumption it soon appears that he has not taken the measure of the possible strength of this opposition. Living as he did before the rise of modern science, and in a place and a period totally dominated by one particular form of theism, it would have been most surprising if he had. But we now have no excuse for not seeing that the demand for a general explanation of why there is any motion at all cannot be a proper starting-point for an argument to defeat such a presumption. It cannot be, because it takes for granted that motion could not itself be one of the explanatory ultimates. But precisely this is what the Stratonician does not grant, but is denying. Of course he does not have to say in advance of the research that either motion or anything else actually is one of these ultimates. He is as a defender of the presumption committed only to insisting that he knows no sufficient reason for maintaining that they could not be naturalistic, as opposed to theistic. It seems, therefore, that even on the more charitable and more instructive interpretation "the first and more obvious way" really presupposes just that rejection of all purely naturalistic ultimates which it purports to validate. And if now the patient defender wants to suggest that this is inevitable in any argument to this conclusion, then the immediate response should be: 'If that is indeed so, then so much the worse for natural theology; and so much the worse also for all those committed to the defence of its possibility.'

§4 *Cosmological arguments*

Way Two of Aquinas is, as has been hinted, very similar to Way One. Way Three when correctly construed turns out to be of antiquarian interest only. But it has been and is widely misinterpreted. (See Patterson Brown.) It is mistaken to be a version of a or the Cosmological Argument. This in turn is often spoken of as if it were, like the Ontological, one argument. In fact Cosmological Arguments are of two radically different kinds, having only their starting-point in common. This starting-point is wonder and perplexity that there is any universe at all. (*Kosmos* is the Greek for *universe*.)

Such generalized amazement at the universe as a whole is often regarded as the prime source of all truly metaphysical concern. In the typically gnomic words of Wittgenstein's *Tractatus Logico-Philosophicus*: "Not how the world is, is the mystical, but that it is" (§ 6.44). This theme was developed, and given a characteristically pessimistic twist, by Arthur Schopenhauer (1788–1860), The extracts both came from the chapter 'On Man's Need of Metaphysics' in *The World as Will and Idea*, translated from the original German by R. B. Haldane and J. Kemp:

> With the exception of man, no being wonders at his own existence; but it is to them so much a matter of course that they do not observe it. . . . Only after the inner being of nature . . . has ascended . . . through the long and broad series of animals, does it attain at last to reflection for the first time on the entrance of reason, . . . in man. Then it marvels at its own works, and asks itself what it itself is. Its wonder however is the more serious, as it here stands for the first time consciously in the presence of death, and besides the finiteness of all existence, the vanity of all effort forces itself more or less upon it. With this reflection and this wonder there arises therefore, for man alone, the need for a metaphysic; he is accordingly a [metaphysical animal] . . . very early, with

the first dawn of reflection, that wonder already appears, which is some day to become the mother of metaphysics. In agreement with this Aristotle too says at the beginning of his *Metaphysics*, 'It is through wonder that men were first led to philosophize, as they are now.' Moreover, the special philosophical disposition consists primarily in this, that man is capable of wonder beyond the ordinary and everyday degree, and is thus induced to make the universal of the phenomenon his problem. . . . The lower a man stands in an intellectual regard the less of a problem is existence itself for him; everything, how it is, and that it is, appears to him rather as a matter of course . . . without doubt it is the knowledge of death, and along with this the consideration of the suffering and misery of human life, which gives the strongest impulse to philosophical reflection and metaphysical explanation of the world. If our life were endless and painless, it would perhaps occur to no one to ask why the world exists, and is just the kind of world it is; but everything would just be taken as a matter of course.   (II, pp. 359–360)

In fact, the pendulum which keeps in motion the clock of metaphysics, that never runs down, is the consciousness that the non-existence of this world is just as possible as its existence . . . what is more, we very soon apprehend the world as something the non-existence of which is not only conceivable, but indeed preferable to its existence. . . . Not merely that the world exists, but still more that it is such a wretched world, is the . . . problem which awakens in mankind an unrest that cannot be quieted by scepticism nor yet by criticism.

(II, pp. 374–375)

The first kind of Cosmological Argument proceeds from the incontestable premise that there are the things which there are, directly to the conclusion that these things must all be the work of one God. Cruder versions emphasize a supposed need for a temporally First Cause to start things off "in the beginning", whereas the subtler postulate instead a sustaining (theological) Creator, without whose continual controlling support the whole universe would instantly collapse into non-existence. In its richer forms the argument is adorned with contrasts between the changing world of ephemeral things and the unchanging eternal God, and so on. Considered however, not as an expatiation upon what is supposed to be known already on other grounds, but as an argument from a need for an explanation to the explanatory hypothesis required, this kind of Cosmological Argument is wide open to the objection which we have seen to lie against Way One. For it assumes without warrant both that the existence of the universe cannot, and that that of God must, be the ultimate in explanation. The whole exercise depends for its appeal entirely upon our being required to press the question 'What produces or sustains the universe?' while being forbidden to ask the same in turn about the approved answer, 'God'.

It will not do in the present context simply to assume that the existence of the universe, possessed of whatever fundamental general characteristics science may discover it to have, cannot be the last word. For precisely this is what the natural theologian has to show if he is to defeat the initial Stratonician Presumption. And, though it sounds pre-eminently profound to ask, 'Why is there anything at all?' it should surely be seen as preposterous and perverse in this way to start by taking it from the beginning that the non-existence of the universe is the norm, and that it is deviations from this which are what have to be explained. Nor, again, will it do here to try to choke off further questions: either by in some way specifying that God, in your sense of the word *God*, is to be ultimate by definition; or by appealing to an "idea which for theism is axiomatic; the existence of perfection requires no explanation, the existence of limited being requires explanation" (Farrer, p. 15). For the Stratonician is well placed to make a pre-emptive definitional strike by making the universe itself ultimate, "in my sense"; and he too could, if pressed, beg the question by calling his own position axiomatic.

In fact the Stratonician is better placed, and in a stronger position; for two reasons. First, because – as was stressed in § 1 – since his account would be more economical, the onus of proof must rest on his opponent. Thus, in the present case, if anything is to be arbitrarily defined as ultimate it is less arbitrary, because more economical, to make it the universe and stop here, rather than to postulate God as an extra, and then insist on stopping there. Second, because, since concepts of God are notoriously plagued with obscurities and riven by apparent or actual contradictions, it is wanton to introduce one unnecessarily. This point about concepts of God can be illustrated relevantly and instructively by reflecting for a moment on the definition of *God* as "a perfect Being". The assumption of the Ontological Argument that actual existence is a perfection we challenged in § 2. Yet even freed from this assumption the supposed idea of a perfect Being remains questionable as an idea. For, surely, what constitutes a perfect anything depends upon what that anything is, and often particularly upon what it is being judged as being for. A perfect sledgehammer needs to be relatively heavy, a perfect tack hammer relatively light; while what makes this ice-pick perfect as a murder weapon may be what is its major disadvantage for its ordinary domestic purpose. There thus seems to be some reason to suspect talk about a perfect Being in general, as opposed to talk of a perfect this or of a perfect that or of a thing perfect for some particular purpose; and hence a reason to remember that elegant proof by Leibniz of the impossibility of a fastest conceivable motion.

It is Leibniz again who provides our example of a Cosmological Argument of the second kind. It comes from 'The Principles of Nature and of Grace founded on Reason', written in 1714 in French:

> So far we have spoken only as natural scientists. Now we must raise ourselves up to metaphysics, and make use of the great principle – generally not much employed – that 'Nothing happens without sufficient reason'; in other words that nothing occurs without its being possible for someone who had a sufficient knowledge of things to provide a reason sufficient to determine why it is thus, and not otherwise. This principle given, the first question which we have a right to put will be 'Why is there something rather than nothing?' For nothing is simpler and easier than something. Next, given that things must exist, it must be possible to provide a reason, 'Why should they exist thus, and not otherwise?'
>
> Now this sufficient reason for the existence of the universe cannot be found in the procession of contingent things. . . . So the sufficient reason, which needs no further reason, must be outside this procession of contingent things, and is found in a substance which is the cause of that procession and which is a necessary being containing the reason for his existence in himself; otherwise we should not have a sufficient reason at which we could stop. And this final reason for things is called *God*.   (§ 7–8)

The difference between the first and this second kind of Cosmological Argument lies in the fact that the latter involves, and revolves around, the fundamental distinction between the necessary and the contingent. (To say that an assertion is logically necessary is to claim that its denial must involve a contradiction, whereas to say that it is logically contingent is to maintain that this would not be the case.) Typically the argument begins by seeing both the universe as a whole and all its parts as contingent, as just so many "might-not-have-beens". It is then urged that contingent being presupposes a necessary Being. The merit of this second kind of Cosmological Argument compared with the first is that such a logically necessary Being would appear to provide an explanatory ultimate which is not itself an unexplained brute fact. This is precisely what, with his usual succinct acuteness, Leibniz urges in its favour, in the second paragraph of the previous extract.

We also have here yet one more excellent illustration of the erratic course of progress in philosophy, and of how a sound argument may eventually be found a use opposite to that intended by its inventor (Ch. I, § 2). To anyone who accepts the critique of the Ontological Argument offered in § 2 of the present chapter the Cosmological Argument of Leibniz must be seen as a decisive reduction to absurdity of his own Principle of Sufficient Reason. For the latter argument in this Leibnizian form demonstrates that the vicious notion of a logically necessary actual being is a direct consequence of that great Principle.

The classic treatment of this second kind of Cosmological Argument is found in Kant's *Critique of Pure Reason,* immediately after the conclusion of his refutation of Descartes. (*Apriori,* which we print as a single and fully assimilated English word, is the opposite of *aposteriori,* and means 'in advance and independent of experience'.) Again the translation is by Kemp Smith:

> The attempt to establish the existence of a supreme being by means of the famous ontological argument of Descartes is, therefore, so much labour and effort lost; we can no more extend our stock . . . by mere ideas, than a merchant can better his position by adding a few noughts to his cash account. (A602: B630)

> To attempt to extract from a purely arbitrary idea the existence of an object corresponding to it is a quite unnatural procedure and a mere innovation of scholastic subtlety. Such an attempt would never have been made if there had not been antecedently . . . the need to assume as the basis of existence in general something necessary (in which our regress may terminate); and if, since this necessity must be unconditioned and certain apriori, reason had not, in consequence, been forced to seek a concept which would satisfy, if possible, such a demand, and enable us to know an existence in a completely apriori manner. Such a concept was supposed to have been found . . . and . . . was therefore used only for the more definite knowledge of that necessary being, of the necessary existence of which we were already convinced, or persuaded, on other grounds. (A603: B631)

We must interrupt Kant here in order to establish the essential distinction between logical and other senses of *necessary Being*. For it is at least partly, if not largely, because many "were already convinced, or persuaded, on other grounds" of the existence of a God necessary in some quite different sense that they have been as hospitable as they have to arguments purporting to establish that there is a logically necessary Being. Long before ever Anselm first thought up the Ontological Argument, long before even Christianity itself began, men had believed that there exists a God who is the indispensable cause of the entire universe. When the Psalmist spoke of the fool saying in his heart 'There is no God', the fool's supposed folly did not lie in denying a proposition which is logically necessary, and the denial of which must therefore involve him in self-contradiction. Rather it lay in ignoring the most important of all facts; a fact which conceivably might have been, but is not, otherwise: "Before the mountains were brought forth, or ever thou hadst formed the earth and the world, even from everlasting to everlasting, thou art God" (*Psalms*, 90: 2).

It is a conclusion of this quite different sort which is reached in the first kind of Cosmological Argument. Indeed, even to say that the two kinds conclude to the existence of Beings necessary in different senses of *necessary* is still to understate the difference. For logical necessity and logical contingency are not, strictly and in the first instance, possible properties of any actual being. These expressions are best seen as belonging to a secondary vocabulary for talk about talk rather than to the primary vocabulary of talk about things. So to say that God is a logically necessary Being is to say, in the Material Mode of Speech, what Aquinas put more formally when he claimed "that this proposition *God exists* is self-evident in itself". It is to say what, in the purest Formal Mode of Speech, would be expressed by saying that the proposition *God exists* is logically necessary, or that the proposition *There is no God* is self-contradictory. (*Proposition*, by the way, in the usage of philosophers – as opposed to that of propositioning businessmen – means 'whatever can be asserted or denied'.)

Kant now, having commended as "at any rate natural" the procedure of what we distinguish as the second kind of Cosmological Argument, goes on to insist nevertheless that it too is exposed to the basic criticisms deployed against the Ontological. His emphasis on experience is characteristic. It relates to the fact that his *Critique of Pure Reason* is one more, and the most profound, treatise in the tradition started by Locke's *Essay* (Ch. III, § 3):

This proof, termed by Leibniz the proof *a contingentia mundi* [from the contingency of the universe – AF], we shall now proceed to expound and examine.

It runs thus: If anything exists, an absolutely necessary being must also exist. Now I, at least, exist. Therefore an absolutely neccessary being exists. The minor premise contains an experience, the major premise the inference from there being any experience at all to the necessary. The proof therefore really begins with experience. . . . For this reason, and because the object of all possible experience is called the world, it is entitled the cosmological proof. Since, in dealing with the objects of experience, the proof abstracts from all special properties through which this world may differ from any other possible world, the title also serves to distinguish it from the physico-theological proof, which is based upon observations of the particular properties of the world disclosed to us by our senses. (A604–605 : B632–633)

The procedure of the cosmological proof is artfully designed to enable us to escape having to prove the existence of a necessary being . . . through mere concepts. Such proof would have to be carried out in the ontological manner. . . . Accordingly, we take as the starting point of our inference an actual existence (an experience in general) and advance, in such a manner as we can, to some absolutely necessary condition of this existence. We have no need to show the possibility of this condition. For if it has been proved to exist the question as to its possibility is entirely superfluous. If now we want to determine more fully the nature of this necessary being, we do not endeavour to do so in the manner that would be really adequate, namely, by discovering from its concept the necessity of its existence. For could we do that we should have no need of an empirical starting point. No, all we seek is the negative condition (*conditio sine qua non*) without which being would not be absolutely necessary. . . . But in the present case it unfortunately happens that the condition needed for absolute necessity is only to be found in one single being. This being must therefore contain in its concept all that is required for absolute necessity, and consequently it enables me to infer this necessity a priori. . . . If I cannot make this inference (as I must concede if I am to avoid admitting the ontological proof), I have come to grief in the new way I have been following, and am back again at my starting point. (A610–611: B638–639)

. . . an old argument is disguised as a new one, and . . . appeal is made to the agreement of two witnesses, the one with the credentials of pure reason and the other with those of experience. In reality the only witness is that which speaks in the name of pure reason; in the endeavour to pass as a second witness it merely changes its dress and voice. In order to lay a secure foundation for itself, this proof takes its stand on experience, and thereby makes profession of being distinct from the ontological proof, which puts its entire trust in pure ... concepts. But the cosmological proof uses this experience only for a single step in the argument, namely, to conclude the existence of a necessary being. (A606: B634)

§5 *Arguments to design*

What Kant calls "the physico-theological proof" is more usually known as the Argument from Design. But this label, though less splutteringly ponderous than Kant's coinage, is unhappy nevertheless. For, once granted that the universe is a work of design, we must immediately and with no possibility of dispute infer a Designer. It is, therefore, better to speak without prejudice of Arguments to Design. Way Five of Aquinas is certainly one:

> The fifth way begins from the guidedness of things. For we observe that some things which lack knowledge, such as natural bodies, work towards an end. This is apparent from the fact they always or most usually work in the same way and move towards what is best. From which it is clear that they reach their end not by chance but by intention. For those things which do not have knowledge do not tend to an end, except under the direction of someone who knows and understands: the arrow, for example, is shot by the archer. There is, therefore, an intelligent personal being by whom everything in nature is ordered to its end, and this we call God. (I, Q2A3)

Aquinas proceeds at once now to his Replies to the two initial Objections quoted in § 1. The Reply to the second Objection, his statement of what we call the Stratonician Presumption, is dependent most closely upon Way Five:

> To the second it has to be said that since nature works towards a determinate end under the direction of a superior agent, then necessarily those things which happen naturally must be referred to God as their first cause. In the same way too those things which come about by contrivance must be referred to some higher cause than human reasoning and will. For these are changeable and can cease to be and, as we have seen, everything which is changeable and can cease to be requires some first principle which is not subject to change or liable to cease to be. (I, Q2A3)

Way Five is as it stands so lamentable that the devout apologist is reduced quickly to pretending that Aquinas never thought of it as being, what he has just quite explicitly said that it is, a proof: "We must say that it is possible to prove the existence of God in five ways." If we waive value questions about the cosmic complacency expressed in the claim that things "always or most usually . . . move towards what is best", the first thing for us to notice is that Way Five like Way One is expressed in terms of a fundamental concept of Aristotelian science. In this case it is that of an end. Aristotle thought of everything as tending to its own appropriate natural end, in the way that we in our time might still see the natural end of an acorn as being to become an oak. So for Aristotle one universal sort of explanation becomes explanation in terms of ends (Greek, *tele*); teleological explanation. These ends are the Final Causes of things (Ch. IV, § 5); and, since all things have an inherent natural tendency to develop towards their ends, to refer some development to its Final Cause is to explain it in terms of an Aristotelian fundamental law.

But now, as Aquinas of course knew better than we, such Aristotelian ends are as such not supposed to be necessarily intended by anyone, neither man nor God. So Aquinas is moving beyond – indeed against – Aristotle in maintaining that "those things which do not have knowledge do not tend to an end, except under the direction of someone who knows and understands". Yet to claim this here, as Aquinas does, as one of his premises is both flagrantly to beg the question against the Stratonician and to fly in the face of apparent fact. For suppose we consider organisms, as the most plausible candidates for the application of teleological ideas. Still the apparent facts are that organisms, unlike artefacts, grow and are not made; and that, whereas the production of a computer requires "the direction of someone who knows and understands", the growth of an acorn or even of an oak does not. Certainly appearances may be, here as elsewhere, deceptive. But it must remain one of the most remarkable cases of the fascination of an Ostensibly Counter-evidential Intuition that Arguments to Design are so often based primarily on just those organic phenomena which at least appear to constitute a refutation of their conclusion.

The second thing for us to notice about Way Five is very much to the credit of Aquinas. Naturally and inevitably he operated within an Aristotelian framework which modern science has found good reason to reject. (Had he in his day done anything else he would indeed have been open to charges of backwardness and obscurantism on that account!) Yet his argument is not essentially linked to the limitations of one particular stage in the development of our scientific knowledge. For he does not rest his case here upon any rash claim that there is something not susceptible of explanation in terms of natural causes. Instead it ultimately depends precisely upon an appeal to observed natural regularities: things "always or most usually work in the same way". His contention is that the very regularities of nature themselves prove the existence of "an intelligent personal being by whom everything in nature is ordered. . . ." He could, therefore, have welcomed all the regularities uncovered in the exponential growth of scientific knowledge as further support for his conclusion. In particular he could have welcomed the work of Charles Darwin, as the author of the following could not:

Atheism is so senseless and odious to mankind that it never had many professors. Can it be an accident that all birds, beasts, and men have their right side and left side alike-shaped (except in their bowels); and just two eyes, and no more, on either side of the face; and just two ears on either side of the head; and a nose with two holes; and either two forelegs or two wings or two arms on the shoulders, and two legs on the hips, and no more? Whence arises this uniformity in all their outward shapes but from the counsel and contrivance of an Author?

Whence is it that the eyes of all sorts of living creatures are transparent to the very bottom, and the only transparent members in the body, having on the outside a hard transparent skin . . . with a crystalline lens in the middle and a pupil before the lens, all of them so finely shaped and fitted for vision that no artist can mend them? Did blind chance know that there was light, and what was its refraction, and fit the eyes of all creatures after the most curious manner to make use of it? These and suchlike considerations always have and ever will prevail with mankind to believe that there is a Being who made all things and has all things in his power, and who is therefore to be feared. . . .

The passage just quoted is in fact taken, not – as it might very well have been – from the famous *Natural Theology* of Archdeacon William Paley (1743–1805), but from 'A Short Scheme of the True Religion' by Sir Isaac Newton (Brewster, I, pp. 347–348). Yet this sort of Argument to Design is unsophisticated and essentially pre-Darwinian where Way Five of Aquinas is not. Although Hume was consciously in many ways a follower of Newton, Hume's attack on Arguments to Design was not, notwithstanding that this is often complacently assumed, limited to such versions. For Hume is spokesman for the idea that whatever order is found in things must be taken to be inherent in rather than impressed upon the universe; and this is the contrary of the principle of every version, including the most sophisticated.

In his first *Inquiry* he examined an Argument to Design under the description of "the religious hypothesis". For Hume, here following Newton, *hypothesis* is a bad word. Also, again because he was taking Newton as his tutor, Hume cherished a doubtless too austere estimate of the proper place of speculation and conjecture in scientific method. Nevertheless the objections made here are, surely, decisive: first, against the crediting the supposed Orderer with attributes more splendid than anything manifested in his alleged work; and, second and more radically, against any attempt to postulate God as the hypothetical explanation of either the existence or the orderliness of the universe. These objections are presented, with "abundant caution", in the form of a dialogue between Hume and an imaginary friend, the latter taking the part of the atomist Epicurus (342–270 BC):

'You find certain phenomena in nature. You seek a cause or author. You imagine that you have found him. You afterwards become so enamoured of this offspring of your brain that you imagine it impossible but he must produce something greater and more perfect than the present scene of things, which is so full of ill and disorder. You forget that this superlative intelligence and benevolence are entirely imaginary, or, at least, without any foundation in reason, and that you have no ground to ascribe to him any qualities but what you see he has actually exerted and displayed in his productions.'

'But allowing you to make experience (as indeed I think you ought) the only standard of our judgment concerning this and all other questions of fact, I doubt not but, from the very same experience to which you appeal, it may be possible to refute this reasoning. . . . If you saw, for instance, a half-finished building, surrounded with heaps of brick and stone and mortar, and all the instruments of masonry, could you not infer from the effect that it was a work of design and contrivance? And could you not return again, from this inferred cause, to infer new additions to the effect and conclude that the building would soon be finished and receive all the further improvements which art could bestow upon it? If you saw upon the seashore the print of one human foot, you would conclude that a man had passed that way, and that he has also left the traces of the other foot, though effaced by the rolling of the sands or inundation of the waters. Why, then, do you refuse to admit the same method of reasoning with regard to the order of nature? Consider the world and the present life only as an imperfect building from which you can infer a superior intelligence; and arguing from that superior intelligence, which can leave nothing imperfect, why may you not infer a more finished scheme of plan which will receive its completion in some distant point of space or time? Are not these methods of reasoning exactly similar? And under what pretense can you embrace the one while you reject the other?'

'The infinite difference of the subjects', replied he, 'is a sufficient foundation for this difference in my conclusions. In works of human art and contrivance, it is allowable to advance from the effect to the cause, and, returning back from the cause, to form new inferences concerning the effect, and examine the alterations which it has probably undergone or may still undergo. But what is the foundation of this method of reasoning? Plainly this: that a man is a being whom we know by experience, whose motives and designs we are acquainted with, and whose projects and inclinations have a certain connection and coherence according to the laws which nature has established for the government of such a creature. When, therefore, we find that any work has proceeded from the skill and industry of man, as we are otherwise acquainted with the nature of the animal, we can draw a hundred inferences concerning what may be expected from him; and these inferences will all be founded in experience and observation. . . .

'The case is not the same with our reasonings from the works of nature. The Deity is known to us only by his productions, and is a single being in the universe, not comprehended under any species or genus, from whose experienced attributes or qualities we can, by analogy, infer any attribute or quality in him. . . .

'The great source of our mistake on this subject and of the unbounded license of conjecture which we indulge is that we tacitly consider ourselves as in the place of the Supreme Being and conclude that he will, on every occasion, observe the same conduct which we ourselves, in his situation, would have embraced as reasonable and eligible. But besides that the ordinary course of nature may convince us that almost everything is regulated by principles and maxims very different from ours – besides this, I say, it must evidently appear contrary to all rule of analogy to reason from the projects and intentions of men to those of a Being so different and so much superior. In human nature there is a certain experienced coherence of designs and inclinations, so that, when from any fact we have discovered one intention of any man, it may often be reasonable, from experience, to infer another and draw a long chain of conclusions concerning his past or future conduct. But this method of reasoning can never have place with regard to a being so remote and incomprehensible, who bears much less analogy to any other being in the universe than the sun to a waxen taper, and who discovers himself only by some faint traces or outlines beyond which we have no authority to ascribe to him any attribute or perfection. What we imagine to be a superior perfection may really be a defect. Or were it ever so much a perfection, the ascribing of it to the Supreme Being, where it appears not to have been really exerted to the full in his works, savours more of flattery and panegyric than of just reasoning and sound philosophy. No new fact can ever be inferred from the religious hypothesis, no event foreseen or foretold, no reward or punishment expected or dreaded, beyond what is already known by practice and observation.'

'But there occurs to me' (continued I) 'with regard to your main topic a difficulty which I shall just propose to you, without insisting on it, lest it lead to reasonings of too nice and delicate a nature. In a word, I much doubt whether it be possible for a cause to be known only by its effect (as you have all along supposed) or to be of so singular and particular a nature as to have no parallel and no similarity with any other cause or object that has ever fallen under our observation. It is only when two species of objects are found to be constantly conjoined that we can infer the one from the other; and were an effect which was entirely singular and could not be comprehended under any known species, I do not see that we could form any conjecture or inference at all concerning its cause. If experience and observation, and analogy, be the only guides which we can reasonably follow in inferences of this nature, both the effect and cause must bear a similarity and resemblance to other effects and causes which we know. . . . I leave it to your own reflection to pursue the consequences of this principle. I shall just observe that as the antagonists of Epicurus always suppose the universe, an effect quite singular and unparalleled, to be the proof of a Deity, a cause no less singular and unparalleled, your reasonings upon that supposition seem at least to merit our attention. There is, I own, some difficulty how we can ever return from the cause to the effect and, reasoning from our ideas of the former, infer any alteration on the latter or any addition to it.' (§ XI)

What Hume said "I shall just propose to you" and "leave it to your own reflection to pursue the consequences" Kant, awoken by Hume from his "dogmatic slumbers", was later to elaborate into a major doctrine; Kant's crucial point being that we are not entitled to project our notions of cause and effect beyond the range of our possible experience. What Hume has himself provided is a neatly decisive answer to the fair question why the sort of argument to design which we should all apply to a derelict construction site cannot, equally reasonably, be applied to the universe as a whole. The answer is neat since it is derived directly from defining characteristics of the postulated cause and the supposed effect. Both the theist God and the universe itself are essentially unique. Since the universe as a whole is all there is (with the possible exception of God) we cannot have experience of what, if anything, produces universes. Since the theist God is a unique being "not comprehended under any species or genus" we cannot from our knowledge of other members of his kind deduce what he might do. When it was first suggested that gases were composed of so far unobserved particles it was possible by applying the calculations of classical mechanics to these hypothetical particles to deduce the consequences which would obtain if the Kinetic Theory of Gases were true; and, in fact they do. But precisely because of his essential uniqueness the unfathomable God of theism could not serve as the inferred entity in "the religious hypothesis".

For Hume this contribution was a first essay. His main treatment is in the deliberately posthumous *Dialogues concerning Natural Religion,* a work last lovingly corrected on his deathbed. It is here that he provides material bearing directly on the sort of Argument to Design deployed in Way Five. There is, of course, scholarly debate on which character most nearly expresses Hume's own final view. But for us what matters is the material presented. Peripatetics are Aristotle and his followers:

'Experience alone can point out ... the true cause of any phenomenon. Now, according to this method of reasoning, Demea, it follows ... that order, arrangement, or the adjustment of final causes is not, of itself, any proof of design; but only in so far as it has been experienced to proceed from that principle. For aught we can know apriori matter may contain the source or spring of order originally, within itself, as mind does. . . .'   (§ II)

'How therefore shall we satisfy ourselves concerning the cause of that Being, whom you suppose the Author of nature. . .? . . . But if we stop, and go no farther, why go so far? Why not stop at the material world? How can we satisfy ourselves without going on in infinitum? And after all, what satisfaction is there in that infinite progression? Let us remember the story of the Indian philosopher and his elephant. It was never more applicable than to the present subject. . . . It were better, therefore, never to look beyond the present material world.   (§ IV)

'It was usual with the Peripatetics, you know, Cleanthes, when the cause of any phenomenon was demanded, to have recourse to their faculties or occult qualities, and to say, for instance, that bread nourished by its nutritive faculty, and senna purged by its purgative. But it has been discovered that this subterfuge was nothing but the disguise of ignorance; and that these philosophers, though less ingenuous, really said the same thing with the sceptics or the vulgar, who fairly confessed that they did not know the cause of these phenomena. In like manner, when it is asked, what cause produces order in the ideas of the supreme Being, can any other reason be assigned . . . than it is a rational faculty, and that such is the nature of the Deity? But why a similar answer will not be equally satisfactory in accounting for the order of the world, without having recourse to any such intelligent creator as you insist on, may be difficult to determine. It is only to say, that such is the nature of material objects, and that they are originally possessed by a faculty of order and proportion. . . . An ideal system, arranged of itself, without precedent design, is not a whit more explicable than a material one, which attains its order in a like manner; nor is there any more difficulty in the latter supposition than in the former.'   (§ IV)

Hume's Philo, the mouthpiece of the last two of these three passages, rudely attributes the appeal of the former view to "its greater conformity to vulgar prejudices". Less harshly it must be granted that we, being ourselves conscious agents, do find a certain sympathetic attraction in arrangements which make an intelligent Will the ultimate in explanation. But they still provide no escape from the essential inexplicability of ultimate fact; a point apparently made, in a very different tone of voice from that of the ironic Hume and with a very different aim, by Maimonides. Again this comes from Friedlander's translation of *The Guide for the Perplexed*:

But of those who accept our theory that the whole universe has been created from nothing, some hold that the inquiry after the purpose of creation is necessary, and assume that the universe was only created for the sake of man's existence, that he might serve God. . . . The literal meanings of some passages in the books of the prophets greatly support this idea. Compare 'He formed it . . . to be inhabited' (*Isaiah* 45 : 18) . . . On examining this opinion as intelligent persons ought to examine all different opinions, we shall discover the ̣rrors it includes. . . . Even if the universe existed for man's sake and man existed for the purpose of serving God . . . the question remains, 'What is the end of serving God?' He does not become more perfect if all his creatures serve him and comprehend him as far as possible; nor would he lose anything if nothing existed beside him. It might perhaps be replied that the service of God is not intended for God's perfection; it is intended for our own perfection. . . . But then the question might be repeated, 'What is the object of our being perfect?' We must in continuing the inquiry as to the purpose of creation at last arrive at the answer, 'It was the will of God'. . . .   (III (xiii))

§6 *The appeal to personal experience*

A few paragraphs back I wrote: "Since the universe is all there is (with the possible exception of God) we cannot have experience of what, if anything, produces universes." Many believers would object to this that they do in fact have experience of God; and, furthermore, that their knowledge of God is founded upon precisely this direct personal experience. This is an understandably popular form of argument. It is also, incidentally, characteristically Protestant. It is popular because it appears to be so immediately and incontestably decisive: what need has anyone to trouble himself with laborious attempts to infer that foreign experts must have been training the Ruritanian tank crews if he himself has actually met these foreign experts at work? Its Protestant appeal lies in its assumption of the possibility of a confrontation between the individual and his God. In so far as I am personally acquainted with the Deity and his ways, there is no call for me to seek the mediation of priest or church.

Precisely because this approach is both attractive at first sight and widely popular we must learn to appreciate that, and some of the decisive reasons why, a knowledge of God cannot be based initially and entirely upon such an appeal to immediate individual experience. But at least for the moment it will have to suffice to insist on two crucial and, it should seem, rather obvious distinctions. It is significant that here we can find no philosopher of the first rank to serve as spokesman for the proposition.

The first distinction is that between, first, beliefs as such and, second, whatever it is to which those beliefs refer. It is one thing to say that someone believes that this is so (whether or not it is), and quite another to say that what he believes is so is indeed the case. But that he believes what he does believe is just as much a fact, which may have causal consequences, as it is a fact albeit a different one, which may also have causal consequences, that what he believes is the case or – as the case may be – not the case.

Now there is, of course, no doubt at all that at least some beliefs about God do make a difference and do have practical consequences. For people who believe in some God, and who believe various things about the nature and activities of their God, do often act very differently from those who have no such beliefs. Indeed, if they did not this would be a reason against accepting the claim that we were here dealing with genuine beliefs. In the words of Descartes in Part III of the *Discourse*: "I needed, in order to determine what people really believed, to notice what they did rather than what they said."

Nevertheless it should be obvious – at least once it has been pointed out – that none of this provides the slightest independent reason for saying that God is acting in or through these believers, nor yet any reason for attributing the effects of their beliefs to his agency. Yet there clearly is a temptation to mistake it that knowledge of the impact of beliefs about God in our own lives and in those of other people is, as such, knowledge of the actual operations of the God believed in.

The same applies in the intriguing special case where the God is some-how identified with an historical personage. For, though the life lived and even the death died by such a man may continue to have remote con-sequences in the lives of others long after, the truth that their own present beliefs have such and such present effects no more constitutes by itself a reason for saying that he still exists and is active, than does the parallel truth about the continuing long-term influence of Lenin. Consider the poster proclamation which I saw in Moscow in 1964: "Lenin's words and Lenin's ideas live; he is an inspiration to millions."

The first crucial distinction, between the truth that something is believed and the truth of that belief itself, is confounded whenever we allow talk of "psychological truth", or of "truth for him", as opposed to plain and simple truth. Such talk was much encouraged, especially in religious contexts, by the Swiss psychotherapist C. G. Jung (1875–1961). In this obscurantist sense of *truth* a belief becomes psychologically true if and only if it answers to some deep desire or need in the believer. To assert, therefore, the "psy-chological truth" or the "truth for him" of some belief is neither to assert nor to give any reason for asserting that it is – in the ordinary and straight-forward sense – true. Any attempt to establish such a second usage for the word *true* darkens counsel. For speech habits are just as much habits as any others, and just as hard to alter. So to describe a belief as (even only psychologically) true is sure to suggest that it actually is (quite straight-forwardly) true. This almost irresistible verbal association becomes the more dangerously misleading when the describer is someone who is thus made to seem – or who thus makes himself to seem – to be endorsing the belief in question with his authority as a sort of psychological guru.

The temptation to collapse the distinction between the truth that someone believes and the truth of his beliefs is especially strong in the context of religious studies; there have been sociologists of religion, and some others, who have even wanted explicitly to define such words as *God* wholly in terms of the influence on mankind of the religious beliefs held by men. The understandable, though not therefore acceptable, excuse for this lies in the apparent irrelevance of questions about the supposed activities of the Deity to the workaday business of secular investigation. Thus the military historian, for instance, in order to understand the battle or the campaign needs to discover not only where the Union and the Confederate commanders thought the various units were but also – what was often a very different thing – where they actually were; and the interplay of these two kinds of facts will be a perennial and vital theme in his story. The historian of religion, by contrast, seems to be neither able nor required to compare the actual doings of divine beings with possibly mistaken human beliefs about such doings; since, at least in his professional capacity, he has no access at all to the former.

The second crucial distinction is between, first, kinds of claim where the claimant seems to have some sort of special authority in virtue of an apparent privileged access and, second, those where he does not. If I claim that I had a dream or a vision, or that I am in pain, then both those primary claims and my further descriptions of the experiences involved appear to possess a peculiar authority. Short of challenging either my sincerity or my capacity to employ my language correctly it seems that you can have no possible basis for rejecting them. If and in so far as an appeal to experience involves no more than this, then perhaps my own honest and carefully chosen phrases do constitute incorrigible last words. In as much as such claims would be claims only about ongoings in the claimant's own mind let us speak of them as assertions about his subjective experience.

Ideas of privileged access and of the essential privacy of the mental are nowadays highly disputatious: hence the stilted caution of some of the expressions of the previous paragraph. This, and the reasons for it, will perhaps be more fully appreciated when we reach Part Three. Yet even if it proved possible to fight off all contemporary onslaughts on the idea that each individual must be the ultimate authority on what goes on in the privacy of his own mind, still this would not even begin to show that the special authority extended further. If this idea is indeed correct, and if you honestly report that you have had a dream or a waking vision of the Blessed Virgin Mary or of Shiva the Destroyer, then maybe we do have no option but to accept that you did. Let us, for the sake of the argument, admit that there is indeed no alternative.

The great temptation is to think that this gets you much further than it does. For in this context the expressions "of the Blessed Virgin Mary" and "of Shiva the Destroyer" have to be construed as simply describing the subjective experience. The moment they are taken to refer also to supposed causes 'outside the mind' you cease to have any special authority; and we, who have allowed that your subjective experience was as you said it was, may now very reasonably challenge a further contention that it was caused in the presumably supernatural way you have gone on to suggest. It is one thing to construe the *of* in these two expressions as meaning – roughly – 'resembling standard pictures described as'. It is quite another to interpret it as – equally roughly – 'caused by a presently actually existing'. (Notice, by the way, that the non-committal description of the features of subjective experience involved in the first case is called phenomenological. The idea of phenomenology as the attempt to elaborate and multiply such descriptions is linked especially with the name of Edmund Husserl (1859–1938).)

Usually when we speak of someone's experience of this or that we are not referring exclusively, primarily, or even at all, to his private and subjective experience. Instead we are making assertions about his knowledge of, based upon transactions with, the objects in question. Consider, for example, advertisements asking for people with experience of computer programming; or those blue books about woman's experience of the male; and so on. Let us label experience, in this undisputatious and untechnical sense of the word, objective experience.

Now from the fact, if it be a fact, that you have had subjective experience of Shiva it does not by any means follow that you, or anyone else, has had or could have had objective experience of that Hindu Destroyer. But, of course, granted that someone had had objective experience of God, then it would follow necessarily that there is a God of which he had had experience. In order, therefore, to establish the desired conclusion the appeal has to be to experience in the second and not just the first sense.

But here at any rate there is absolutely no question of any unchallengeable authority. For claims to have objective experience of something or other may in principle be not only insincere but also mistaken. Obviously in practice there are plenty of such claims which cannot be seriously challenged on either count. But this is precisely not so when their supposed object is, as here, God. There are in this case rich possibilities of honest error. For instance, as we have just shown, the effects of religious beliefs may be mistaken for the operations of their supposed objects; and, again, the believer who thinks of himself as face to face – perhaps even conversing – with his God appears to the detached and unbelieving observer merely to be wrapped up in his own imaginings.

Hobbes summed up in his own gratuitously but memorably offensive way in Chapter XXXII of *Leviathan*:

> For if a man pretend to me that God hath spoken to him supernaturally and immediately, and I make doubt of it, I cannot easily perceive what argument he can produce to oblige me to believe it. It is true that, if he be my Sovereign, he may oblige me to obedience, so as not by act or word to declare I believe him not; but not to think any otherwise than my reason persuades me. . . .
>
> For to say that God hath spoken to him . . . in a dream, is no more than to say that he dreamed that God spoke to him; which is not of force to win belief from any man that knows that dreams are for the most part natural, and may proceed from former thoughts. . . . To say he hath seen a vision, or heard a voice, is to say he hath dreamed between sleeping and waking. . . . To say he speaks by supernatural inspiration, is to say he finds an ardent desire to speak, or some strong opinion of himself, for which he can allege no natural and sufficient reason. So that though God almighty can speak to a man by dreams, visions, voice, and inspiration; yet he obliges no man to believe that he hath done so to him that pretends it; who (being a man) may err, and (which is more) may lie.

§7 *Pascal's Wager*

Finally, consider a quite different type of argument. All those examined so far have attempted to show that there actually is a God. But it is also possible to offer reasons for believing, not that this conclusion is true, but that it is a conclusion which, regardless of whether it is in fact true or false, it is somehow profitable or prudent for us to believe. The key distinction here is between giving reasons (evidencing) and giving reasons (inducing). But notice also that reasons (inducing) may be, and in the examples to be considered are, offered not as reasons for merely pretending but as reasons for somehow getting yourself to believe genuinely. This second difference is: between, on the one hand, the all too familiar business of offering such effectively persuasive reasons as the heavy threats of a Hobbist Sovereign state for pretending that you believe, or not making it obvious that you do not; and, on the other hand, offering similarly inducing reasons for trying to persuade ourselves that something actually is true, and perhaps even known to be true, notwithstanding that there is no, or no sufficient, evidence to support either conclusion.

The classic example here is an argument made notorious by the French mathematician and scientist Blaise Pascal (1623–1662). Pascal's Wager, as it is called, is found in his posthumous *Pensées* [Thoughts]:

> Let us examine this point then, and say, 'God is, or he is not'. But to which side shall we incline? Reason can decide nothing here. . . . What will you wager? According to reason, you can do neither one thing nor the other; according to reason, you cannot defend either of the two options. So do not reproach those who have made a choice with getting it wrong, for you know nothing about it.
>
> 'No, but I shall reproach them for having made not this choice but a choice . . . the right course is to make no wager.'
>
> 'Yes, but you have to wager. That is not a matter of choice, you are committed. So which option will you take? Let us see. Since you have to choose, let us see which is of less concern to you. . . . Let us weigh the gain and the loss in making your bet on the existence of God. Let us estimate these two possibilities. If you win, you win the lot. If you lose, you lose nothing. So, without hesitation, bet on the existence of God.'
>
> 'That is splendid. Yes, I must bet. But perhaps I am staking too much?'
>
> 'Let us see. Since there are equal chances of winning and of losing, if you had only to win two lives for one you could still bet. But if there were three to win you would have to play – since you are in a situation where you have to play – and you would be imprudent, since you are compelled to play, not to risk your life to gain three in a game in which the chances of winning and of losing are equal. . . . But here we have an infinity of infinitely happy life to win, a chance of winning against a finite number of chances of losing, and what you bet is finite. So there is no problem of decision: wherever the infinite is, and where there is no infinity of chances of losing against that of winning, there is nothing to weigh up, you have to give all. . . . And so our contention is of infinite force, when there is the finite to stake in a game in which the chances of winning and of losing are equal and there is the infinite to gain. That is demonstrative; and if men are capable of any truth, that's it.'

'I confess it. I admit it. But . . . I am the sort of person who is so made that I cannot believe. So what would you have me do?'

'True. But at any rate learn that your inability to believe is a product of your passions, since reason brings you to this and yet you nevertheless cannot. . . . You want to go to the Faith, and you do not know the route . . . learn from those who have been bound like you and who are now wagering all they have; these are people who know the road which you want to follow. . . . Follow the way in which they began; by acting as if they believed, by taking the holy water, by having masses said, and so on. In the natural course of things, that will make you believe, and make you dull.'

'But that is what I am afraid of.'

'And why? What have you to lose?'

(Brunschvicg arrangement, §233)

This will not do. The main objection bears against the assumption, which must not be read as necessarily representing Pascal's own convictions, first that there are only two possible ways to bet, and second that there is no evidential basis for saying that one of these is more probably correct than the other. For if we really are, as Pascal is here conceding, in a situation of total ignorance – "Reason can decide nothing here" – then the possible options must be taken not only as equiprobable but also as infinite. In particular, for every conceivable option promising eternal bliss for one way of life (and perhaps, correspondingly, eternal torment for all outsiders), there is another conceivable option promising the diametric opposite; the in-group of the one becomes the out-group of the other, and the other way about; and so on. But if the theoretically possible options are thus infinite, then in the assumed situation of total ignorance no one single option – such as Pascal's preferred Roman Catholicism – can be taken as equiprobable with the sum of all the rest.

We are apt to underestimate the logical force of this rebuttal since few of the infinite range of theoretically possible alternative options are for us psychologically live. This notion of a live option was introduced by the American psychologist William James (1842–1910). It occurs in one of his philosophical essays, 'The Will to Believe':

Let us give the name *hypothesis* to anything that may be proposed to our belief; and just as the electricians speak of live or dead wires, let us speak of any hypothesis as either live or dead. A live hypothesis is one which appeals as a real possibility to him to whom it is proposed. If I ask you to believe in the Mahdi, the notion makes no electric connection with your nature – it refuses to scintillate with any credibility at all. As an hypothesis it is completely dead. To an Arab, however (even if he is not one of the Mahdi's followers), the hypothesis is among the mind's possibilities: it is alive. This shows that deadness and liveness in an hypothesis are not intrinsic properties but relations to the individual thinker. They are measured by his willingness to act. . . .

Next, let us call the decision between two hypotheses an option. Options may be of several kinds. They may be (1) living or dead; (2) forced or avoidable; (3) momentous or trivial; and for our purposes we may call an option a genuine option when it is of the forced, living, and momentous kind. (§ I)

From these materials James proceeds to develop the influential doctrine that, in certain limited but specially important cases, our beliefs ought to be determined entirely by "our passional nature". To borrow a term which his philosophically superior friend, compatriot, and protégé C. S. Peirce (1839–1910) used of another of James' arguments, this is "suicidal" (R. B. Parry, II p. 438). For such reasoning can be effective only in so far as it is not understood. What "our passional nature" – what Pascal would have called "the reasons of the heart which reason knows not" – wants to believe is that the proposed belief is true, and known to be true. It is, therefore, at least and precisely in so far as you fully and clearly appreciate what is going on, no help at all to be assured that, where and in as much as there is no evidential reason to believe one thing rather than another, you are entitled to believe whatever you please. In *The Republic* Plato argued that it would be good if the citizens of his ideal state could be persuaded to believe a made-up myth about its origins – the 'Noble Lie'. But Plato was concerned that they should not be told, what James most frankly does tell us, that the beliefs proposed are wholly without evidential support:

The thesis I defend is, briefly stated, this: Our passional nature not only lawfully may, but must, decide an option between propositions, whenever it is a genuine option that cannot by its nature be decided on intellectual grounds; for to say, under such circumstances, 'Do not decide, but leave the question open', is itself a passional decision – just like deciding yes or no. . . . (§ IV)

CHAPTER VII

Predestination, Freewill, and Determinism

§ 1 *The elementary ideas*

"Nobody, certainly, will deny that the idea of the existence of an omnipotent, just, and omnibeneficent personal God is able to accord man solace, help and guidance; also by virtue of its simplicity it is accessible to the most undeveloped mind. But, on the other hand, there are decisive weaknesses attached to this idea in itself, which have been painfully felt since the beginning of history. That is, if this being is omnipotent then every occurrence including every human action, every human thought, and every human feeling and aspiration is also his work. How is it possible to think of holding men responsible for their deeds and thoughts before such an almighty Being?"

(Einstein (2), pp. 26–27)

Einstein, writing on 'Science and Religion' in *Out of my Later Years,* put this rhetorical question to support his thesis that "The main source of the present-day conflict between the spheres of religion and science lies in this concept of a personal God"; and proceeded to urge that we should think, as did Baruch Spinoza (1623–1677), of the universe itself as God – "God, or Nature". For us here Einstein's whole statement can serve as a first formulation of the philosophical problem of God's omnipotence and man's responsibility, which is the religious analogue of the secular philosophical problem of freewill and determinism.

The precondition for progress here is to start from formulations which make these both philosophical and problems. Philosophical questions may – indeed the most important usually do – arise out of assumptions, practices, speculations, and discoveries which are not themselves philosophical: that is at least part of the reason why for the philosopher "Specialization . . . is the mortal sin" (Popper (2), p. 136). But in order to be philosophical the questions arising have got to be about basic meanings; about logical presuppositions, implications, and incompatibilities. So, interpreting *determinism* to mean 'the contention that what happens could be subsumed under universal laws of nature', questions about how far and in what areas determinism is true belong to the sciences. On the other hand questions such as whether a completely deterministic account of human behaviour must logically preclude the commonsense claim that people often could do otherwise than they do are philosophical. A suitable mnemonic, as nearly correct as such natty slogans ever are, is: "Science asks, 'What happens, and why?'; and philosophy asks, 'If so, so what?' ".

The problem of presenting these particular much-canvassed philosophical problems not only as philosophical but also as problems arises because at first sight it seems to the uninitiated that the answer to any such questions must be, 'Yes, of course; quite obviously the two are incompatible'. Yet many if not most of those of the great philosophers of the past who have addressed themselves to these issues have concluded for some sort of Compatibility Thesis; and the same appears to be true also of our contemporaries. So even if an Incompatibility Thesis is going in the end to turn out to be true there is no excuse whatever for deliberately building it into our formulations at the beginning. To do this is simultaneously to prejudge and to suppress the philosophical question. The frequency of this offence among those who have had the opportunity to benefit from a philosophical training remains a present scandal. (It is, by the way, to such prejudgement, prior to a proper examination of arguments and evidence, that the word *prejudice* strictly refers: the bad habit of dismissing all strong convictions as necessarily prejudices is a revealing index of a prissy and anaemic shrinking from any possibly unpopular commitment.)

To avoid prejudice, and to ensure that our philosophical problem is so specified as genuinely to be such, we must studiously disallow arbitrary definitions making particular solutions immediately obvious. Thus it will not do in our specification to define *freewill* in a libertarian sense. For a philosophical, as opposed to a political, libertarian holds that in some or all actions agency is a matter of the operation of an uncaused cause; and, clearly, if there is any freewill in this sense then universal determinism must be in consequence false. Yet *freewill* in this interpretation certainly is not, notwithstanding that philosophical libertarians frequently mistake it to be, *freewill* as the meaning of that word is given by common usage. For in that untechnical meaning to say that George acted of his own freewill is simply to deny that he acted under compulsion. Thus, in the example discussed earlier (Ch. I, § 2), the Bank Manager who opened his safe at the point of a gun did not, in this the ordinary sense, act of his own freewill. Yet, as was argued there, to say this is not to say, equally untechnically, that he had literally no alternative. The philosophical libertarian would, I think, be best advised to offer his ideas as an analysis, not of the everyday notion of freewill, but rather of this different and more fundamental concept of having an alternative. For it is this which for all human action is the key concept, and it is presupposed equally both by everyday freewill and by its opposite.

With the same aim of avoiding prejudice *determinism* too has to be construed in an unaggressive way. It will not do, for example, to equate it immediately and explicitly with either fatalism or predestinationism. Thus for me to be a fatalist about something is for me to believe that my desires, my plans, my decisions, my actions, will not affect the outcome either one way or the other. But if that is so then these are neither the cause nor even partial causes of that outcome. Yet that I should be its cause, or at least its partial cause, is a necessary condition for my having any share in the responsibility for that outcome: even the uncaused cause postulated by the philosophical libertarian must be itself a cause. So a universal fatalism which would necessarily preclude this condition must necessarily, by the same token, preclude any human responsibility for anything.

Again, we must recognize what may be, and by many is, regarded as a crucial difference between determination and predestination. The determinist as such is committed only to saying that everything that happens theoretically could be subsumed under universal laws of nature; even if and where there is no practical possibility that this will in fact be done. Hence, presumably, he is also as such committed to saying both that everything that happens is in principle, though no doubt often not in practice, predictable; and that it is the outcome of causes which were in their turn fully caused. But to believe in predestination, in the useful sense in which the word is not just a superfluous synonym for *determination*, is to believe that this determination of our actions was at some stage itself arranged by some other personal or quasi-personal agent. This manifestly does make a difference even if that difference is not allowed to be decisive. For the predestiner surely must, at the very least, share responsibility for the actions the occurrence of which he arranges; in the way that if you hypnotize me, and put me under certain post-hypnotic suggestions, you must, at the very least, share responsibility with me for my later implementation of those suggestions.

Predestination is, therefore, a notion peculiar to the religious version of the problem; and although – or because – so much of the argument is common to both we have to beware any unexamined assumption that always what applies to the one must apply to the other. It is partly for this reason that I have been careful to speak of a rather than the Compatibility Thesis and an rather than the Incompatibility Thesis. The other part of the reason is that in this as in all cases where there is talk of a great or perennial philosophical problem what we actually have is not one specific and unitary question but a ramifying cluster of multiply interrelated issues. Thus we have here not merely two main versions, religious and secular, but a vast number of sub-questions within each; and someone who allowed that the freewill/compulsion contrast is by no means congruent with the determinism/indeterminism antithesis might nevertheless with some show of reason insist that there is a vital everyday concept of having an alternative which does presuppose a measure of indeterminism.

§2 *Aristotelian conservatism: splitting hairs not starting hares*

This very range and complexity of such great problems may mislead people to think that there neither is nor can be progress in philosophy. Yet not to have done everything is not necessarily to have done nothing. The aim in the present chapter, as throughout this book, is neither to complete everything nor to leave the reader with a general impression of obscure profundity and irresolvable conflict. Rather it is, in a modestly pedestrian way, to get at least some essentials firmly established.

Of these the first and perhaps the most important is a matter of method. If progress is to be made it will be made piecemeal, by care and precision, rather than wholesale, by talking largely and sloppily about wide issues never formulated satisfactorily. Our best first teacher is Aristotle. In the *Nicomachean Ethics*, in answer to his own unspoken guiding question 'When is a man not responsible?', he painstakingly elucidates the notion of responsibility by examining different kinds of extenuating circumstance and excuse. It is only at the end of this investigation – and after analysing the notions of choice, deliberation, and desire – that he even raises, still in his own characteristically down-to-earth and hardworking way, the issue whether responsibility as thus understood can be reconciled with determinism. Aristotle's work here was for so long so little appreciated that it has often been said that he either never truly recognized, or made no substantial contribution to dealing with, our present problem. He begins with a rather unfortunately labelled distinction between those cases where people are held responsible, and those where they are not. His terms are usually translated *voluntary* and *involuntary*. This is certainly awkward, since in English the opposite of voluntary is not involuntary but compulsory: attendance at the rallies of the ruling party may – in different countries – be either voluntary or compulsory, but scarcely involuntary; whereas the cries, starts, and twitches which are so typically involuntary could scarcely in any normal circumstances be said to be compulsory – or even voluntary. My own alternative translation is little better, since the fault here surely lies with Aristotle himself:

> Virtue is thus concerned with both feelings and actions. But it is only those that are willing which are praised and blamed, whereas those that are unwilling are pardoned and sometimes even pitied. So it seems to be necessary for the student of ethics to define the difference between the willing and the unwilling; and this will be useful also to the legislator in assigning both marks of honour and punishments.
>
> Well then, it seems that actions are unwilling when they occur under compulsion or through ignorance. An action is forced when its origin is from outside, being such that the agent or the person who is compelled has nothing to do with it: as, for example, if you were carried somewhere by the wind or by men who had you in their power. But there is some dispute about whether to count as unwilling or willing those cases where something is done out of fear of something worse or for the sake of something fine: suppose a tyrant who has a man's parents and children in his power orders him to do a foul thing, and they will be safe if he does it and killed if he does not. A somewhat similar case is the jettisoning of a cargo in a storm; for in ordinary circumstances no one jettisons, whereas in order to save himself and his shipmates anyone would. So such actions are a mixture, though they seem to have more in common with the willing. For at the time when they are done they are chosen; and, as the end of an action varies with the actual occasion, so the terms *willing* and *unwilling* should be applied with reference to when it is done. The agent acts willingly; for the origin of the movement of the parts of the body in such actions lies in him, and when the origin is in oneself it is in one's power to do it or not. Such actions, therefore, are willing; though perhaps apart from the circumstances unwilling, since no one would choose anything of the sort for its own sake.

Sometimes indeed people are actually praised for actions of this kind. . . . In other cases it is not a question of praise but of pardon, when someone does what ought not to be done under pressures which put too great a strain on human nature and which no one could sustain. But perhaps there are some things which it is not possible to plead that you were compelled to do, but where you should rather submit to the most terrible death. For instance, it seems ridiculous for Alcmaeon in Euripides to claim that he was compelled to murder his mother. But it is sometimes difficult to decide what should be chosen rather than what, and what should be endured in preference to what. And it is still more difficult to stay with the decision made, since generally in such cases the expected penalty is painful and what we are being pressed to do is disgraceful. Which is why praise and blame are awarded according as we do or do not yield to such pressure.   (1109B30–1110B2)

To describe what we do because it is splendid or because we enjoy doing it as done under compulsion – pretending that these things are outside us compelling – would be to make everything compulsory. For these are the motives for which everyone does everything. Again, to act unwillingly and under compulsion is painful, whereas what we do because it is splendid or because we enjoy doing it is pleasant. Also, it is ridiculous to blame external things and not ourselves for falling prey to their attractions; and ridiculous to take the credit oneself for one's good actions, but to put the blame for the disgraceful ones on pleasures.
                                                        (1110B9–1110B16)

An act done through ignorance is in every case not willing, but it is unwilling only when it leads to heart burning and regret. For the man who has done something in ignorance but is not at all sorry about what he has done has not acted willingly, because he did not know what he was doing, nor yet unwillingly, because he is not sorry about it. Acts done through ignorance fall, therefore, into two classes: if the agent regrets the action, it seems to be unwilling; but in the other case, if he does not regret it, let us call him not-willing, since where there is a difference it is better to have a special word for it.

Again, acting through ignorance seems to be different from acting in ignorance. For the man who is drunk or in a rage does not act because of ignorance, but because of the things mentioned, although he does not know and is in ignorance.   (1110B18–1110B28)

The man who is ignorant of some particular feature of the case is the man who acts unwillingly. So perhaps it will be no bad thing to specify the nature and number of these sorts of feature. They are (1) who the agent is, (2) what he is doing, (3) the scope of sphere of the action; and sometimes also (4) the instrument, (5) the end – saving someone's life, for instance, and (6) the manner – gently, for instance, or to excess.

Now no one could be ignorant of all these things unless he were mad; and obviously he will know (1) the agent – how could he fail when it is he himself? But a man may be ignorant of (2) what he is doing – as, for instance, when people say 'it slipped out as they were speaking'; or 'they did not know they were secret', as Aeschylus said of the Mysteries; or 'I let it off when I only meant to show how it worked', as the man said in the catapult case. Again (3) someone might mistake her son for an enemy, as Merope did; or (4) a pointed spear for one with a button on it, or a stone for a bit of pumice. Or (5) one might kill someone by giving them medicine with the intention of saving their life; or (6) in loose wrestling hit a man when you intended only to grasp his hand. Since ignorance is possible about all these features of an action, the man who is ignorant of one of them is held to have acted unwillingly. This is especially so if he was ignorant of the most important of them, and the most important seem to be (2) what he is doing and (5) the end. Granted ignorance of one of these sorts then it is still necessary for the action to cause heartburning and to be regretted if it is to be characterized as unwilling.

An unwilling act being one done under compulsion or through ignorance, a willing one would seem to be one the origin of which lies in an agent who knows the particular features of its occurrence.

(1111A3–1111A24)

In its simultaneous sensitivity both to the richness of the available nontechnical vocabulary and to the variety of the differences between actual cases this is a model of method for all those "sympathetic to a policy of splitting hairs to save starting them". And if it now appears to us that even Aristotle's tread occasionally falters, or that more might have been made – for instance – of the insight that what counts as compulsion depends largely upon what has to be excused, this shows only and satisfactorily that we have learnt his lesson well. The policy statement just quoted comes from John Austin (1911–1960); appropriately enough, since it was he who made the modern classic in this area 'A Plea for Excuses' (Austin (1), pp. 44 and 123–152).

Aristotle next proceeds to analyse choice, deliberation and desire. His account of deliberation is both basically relevant to the immediate business of the present chapter and generally a paradigm of how the thing should be done:

Now about deliberation. Do people deliberate about everything – is everything a possible object of deliberation – or are there some things about which deliberation is impossible? The expression *possible object of deliberation* must, presumably, be taken to cover not what some fool or madman might deliberate about but what the sensible person would.

Well, then, no one deliberates about things immutable, such as the order of the universe or the incommensurability of the side and the diagonal. Nor yet about things which are in motion but are always the same . . . such as the solstices and the sunrise. Nor about irregular occurrences, such as droughts and rains. Nor about the things which happen by luck, such as the finding of treasure. The reason why is that none of these things would be affected by our agency. We deliberate about the things which are within our control and can be brought about by action: (these are what is left . . .). But we do not deliberate about all human affairs – no Spartan, for instance, deliberates about the best way for Scythians to conduct their political affairs. Each lot of people deliberates about the things which can be brought about by its own actions. Again, there is no room for deliberation about exact and complete branches of knowledge. . . . But we deliberate about the things which we effect yet not in a completely uniform way; for example, questions of medicine and business; and more about navigation than about athletic training because the former has been less completely reduced to a science; and similarly with other things too . . .

Deliberation, then, occurs in matters where, though there are general rules which generally hold good, the issue is uncertain. . . .

And we deliberate not about ends but about means to those ends. A doctor does not deliberate about whether he shall heal, nor an orator whether he shall persuade, nor a statesman whether he shall secure good government, nor does anyone else deliberate about the end of his profession. Instead, having posited some end, they consider how and by what means it will be achieved. If they find that there is more than one way of achieving it they investigate which is the best and easiest. If there is only one way of accomplishing it they ask how it is to be done by that means, and how that means in turn is to be effected, until they reach the first cause; which in the order of discovery is the last. . . . And if they come up against an impossibility they give up – for instance, if it needs money and this cannot be provided; whereas if it appears to be possible they begin to act. By *possible* I mean 'whatever can come about through our agency'; and things done through the instrumentality of our friends are in a way 'through our agency', since the origin is in us.   (1112A18–1112B29)

A moment's reflection reveals that Aristotle's whole argument depends upon, and indeed is, an appeal to what we could, and could not, properly call deliberation. How else, indeed, could the conservative analysis of a concept proceed? No one who has so reflected will be surprised if, in reading – say – *The Concept of Mind* by Gilbert Ryle (b. 1900), he often feels as if he were reading Aristotle; albeit an Aristotle very much in modern dress. Certainly such similarities and continuities do not appear either accidental or surprising to those contemporary philosophers who know their Plato and their Aristotle; a class pre-eminently including both Ryle and Austin. Aristotle continues:

> It appears therefore, as has been said, that a man is the origin of his actions, and deliberation is concerned with those which it is within the power of the deliberator to perform. . . .   (1112B32–34)

Where it is in our power to act, it is in our power not to act; and where it is in our power to say 'No', it is in our power to say 'Yes'. So if we are responsible for doing a thing when this is right, we are also responsible for not doing it when that is wrong; and if we are responsible for rightly not doing a thing, then we are equally responsible for wrongly doing it. . . . And if this is obvious, and if we are unable to trace our actions back to any other origins than those in ourselves, then all those the origins of which are in ourselves are things which are under our control and willing.

This conclusion seems to be attested both by the way that individuals behave in private life and by the practice of the legislators themselves. For they punish and penalize those who do scoundrelly deeds (except the ones who act under compulsion, or through ignorance for which they were not themselves to blame), and they honour those who do good deeds – as a disincentive to the one and an incentive to the other. But no one provides incentives to do what is not willing and not within our power. For it is no use being persuaded not to feel heat or pain, or hunger or anything like that; because we shall feel them just the same.

And, furthermore, they punish ignorance itself if the agent seems to be responsible for his ignorance. For instance, the penalties are doubled for offenders who were drunk; since he could have avoided getting drunk, and that is the cause of his not knowing what he is doing. They also punish those who do not know some provision in the law, which they should and could without difficulty have known; and similarly in other cases where people seem to be ignorant through carelessness, on the ground that it was in his power not to be ignorant since he could have taken the trouble.

But, it may be objected, he is the sort of man not to have taken the trouble. Well, people are themselves responsible for becoming that sort, by living laxly; just as they are for being unjust or profligate when they do wrongs and spend their time in drinking and dissipation. For every regular activity produces a person of the corresponding sort. This is shown by the way people train for any contest or pursuit: practice makes perfect. Only a person without any sense at all can fail to know that character traits arise from the corresponding practice, and if a man knowingly acts in a way which will result in his becoming unjust he must be said to be unjust willingly.

Again, though it is unreasonable to say that the man who acts unjustly or who behaves in a profligate way does not want to be unjust or profligate, still this by no means implies that he can stop being unjust and become just at will; any more than a sick man can get well at will, even though perhaps his illness is willing – in the sense that it was due to an intemperate way of life and disobedience to doctor's orders. At that time he could have avoided the illness, but once he has let himself go he can do so no longer. In the same way once you have thrown a stone you cannot pull it back again; but you are none the less responsible for picking it up and throwing it, for the origin of the act was in you. So too with the unjust man and the profligate man: at the beginning they could have avoided becoming so, and therefore they are so willingly; but now they have become as they are it is no longer possible for them not to be so.   (1113B7–1114A22)

But suppose somebody says: 'All men seek what seems to them good but they cannot help its seeming so: every man's end is determined by his character, whatever that may happen to be. If you allow that, in a way, every man produces his traits and dispositions; then, in a way, he is responsible for what seems good to him. But if you do not, then no one is the cause of his own wrongdoing. For he does these things through ignorance of the proper end, believing that this is how the greatest good for him will come about. His aim at his end is not of his own choosing. A man needs to be born with this sort of vision, by which to judge correctly and to choose what is truly good . . .'

Now if this is true, how will virtue be any more willing than vice? For, for both the good man and the bad man alike, the given end is determined by nature or what have you, and for the rest they do whatever they do do by reference to this end. Whether then a man's end, whatever it may be, is not given by nature but is partly a matter for him; or whether, though the end is determined by nature, the good man then acts willingly and so makes his virtue willing; still vice must be no less willing, since the bad man too performs his own actions even if he does not choose his own end. If, therefore, as is said, our virtues are willing (and if we are in a way part causes of our traits and dispositions, and if we have a certain end because we are people of a certain kind), then by parity of reasoning our vices too are willing.   (1114A30–1114B26)

§3 *Radical onslaughts: (i) predestinationism*

Aristotle thus shows himself to have been conservative both in his temperament, and in his method, and in his conclusions. The methodological conservatism is easy to vindicate. For – here as elsewhere – it must be sensible first to see clearly where we are before beginning to consider whether we want to go somewhere else. It is silly – though not unheard of – to launch campaigns for revolution or reform without having some clear knowledge of what the existing set-up is, and how it works. Even if we were – or are – going to end by concluding that the whole idea of human responsibility is a chimera, still it must be prudent to begin by making sure what that idea would actually involve.

But to maintain conservative conclusions is a different and more difficult matter. Certainly Aristotle is right to insist that it will not do to argue that none of our faults are our fault, while still counting our merits to our credit. But his reply is no longer adequate for the conservative who is confronted by a consistent and wholehearted radical. For such a more formidable opponent will be ready to attack the basic assumptions involved in the claim that we are responsible agents: that we do often act, that whenever we do thus act in any one particular way we always could have acted otherwise, and that the ultimate origin of these our actions is truly in ourselves. He will not weaken the case by cheatingly applying his contention only to the bad but not to the good also.

Nor, again, will he wage a limited and peripheral campaign, attempting only to show in one way or another that many more things than people usually think are in fact done under compulsion or through ignorance. For, as we have seen, to say either of these sorts of thing presupposes that we are indeed agents who did what we did: to plead compulsion, for instance, is to admit that you did it, but to maintain that there was no alternative available which you could reasonably have been expected to choose. Instead the really bold and militant radical will – to borrow phrases from the 'Introduction' of Hume's *Treatise* – "leave the tedious lingering method . . . and, instead of taking now and then a castle or village on the frontier, . . . march up directly to the capital": the capital here being the concept of action, and the assumptions of its applicability.

The radical offensive has its greatest impetus when it is backed by and based upon theism. For, surely, if the universe is absolutely dependent for its existence upon a Creator as its first and sustaining cause then the ultimate origins of our actions cannot be in ourselves: rather we must say that "every occurrence including every human action, every human thought, and every human feeling and aspiration is his work" (Einstein). Precisely this is argued, with compelling force and lucidity, by Aquinas in the first of the three following passages from the *Summa contra Gentiles*:

> From this it is evident, next, that God is the cause of the operation of everything which operates. . . . Again, every operation which results from some power is reckoned to be the effect of the thing which gave it that power. . . . Now, every power in any agent comes from God as the first principle of all perfection. Therefore, since every operation results from some power, the cause of every operation must be God.

> Furthermore, it is obvious that every action which cannot continue after the support of some agent has stopped is of that agent. For instance, the manifestation of colours cannot happen after the sun has stopped its work of illuminating the air; and so there is no doubt but that the sun is the cause of the manifestation of colours. And the same thing is clear with violent motion, which ceases when the supporting violence which was keeping it going stops. But just as God not only gave being to things when they first began, but is also – as the conserving cause of being – the cause of their being as long as they last . . .; so he also not only gave things their operative powers when they were first created, but is always the cause of these in things. Hence, if this divine influence stopped every operation would stop. Every operation, therefore, of anything is traced back to him as its cause.   (III (lxvii))

Consistently with this clear-headed insistence upon the logical consequences of creation (theological) Aquinas proceeds emphatically to reject the suggestion that men enjoy freewill (libertarian). This next passage should be especially interesting to those who have allowed themselves to be persuaded that theism and philosophical libertarianism are natural allies:

> God alone can move the will, as an agent, without doing violence to it. Hence it is said (in *Proverbs*, 21: 1), 'The king's heart is in the hand of the Lord, and he will turn it whithersoever he wills' and (*Philippians*,

2: 13) 'It is God who works in us, to wish and to accomplish, according to his good will.'

Some people, as a matter of fact, not understanding how God can cause a movement of our will in us without prejudicing the freedom of the will, have tried to explain these authoritative texts wrongly: that is, they would say that God 'works in us, to wish and to accomplish' means that he causes in us the power of willing, but not in such a way that he makes us will this or that. This is how Origen interprets it (*de Principiis*, III (i)), when he is defending freewill [libertarian – AF] against the authoritative texts already given. . . . These people are, of course, opposed quite plainly by authoritative texts of Holy Writ. For it says in *Isaiah* (26: 2), 'Lord, you have worked all our works in us.' Hence we receive from God not only the power of willing but its employment also. (III (lxxxviii) and (lxxxix))

Finally, those who have been taught to believe that the scandalous doctrine of divine predestination is within Christendom confined to the followers of the Reformer John Calvin (1509–1564) will be instructively surprised by this account of further corollaries:

So, since it has been shown that some people by God's working are directed to their ultimate end aided by grace, whereas others deprived of that help of grace fail to attain the ultimate end, and since all things which are done by God are eternally foreseen and ordained through his wisdom, as again has been shown above; then necessarily that discrimination between men must have been ordained by God from eternity. Accordingly, therefore, because he has preordained certain people from eternity to be directed to their ultimate end he is said to have predestined them. . . . But those to whom he has from eternity arranged that he will not give his grace he is said to have reprobated, or to have held under his hatred. . . . By reason of this discrimination, in which he reprobated some and predestined others, we take note of God's election. So it is, therefore, clear that predestination, election, and reprobation are part of God's providence according to which men are by God's providence directed to their ultimate end. . . .

Moreover, that predestination and election are not occasioned by any human merits can not only be made obvious from this, that God's grace, which is the effect of predestination, is not preceded by merits but precedes all human merits, as has been shown. It can also be made obvious from this, that God's will and providence is the first cause of the things that are done, whereas there can be no cause of God's will and providence; although among the effects of providence, and of predestination likewise, one may be the cause of another. (III (clxiii))

Aquinas proceeds immediately to conclude his Book III with a prayer of praise to the God whom he supposes to have made these arrangements. It is not part of our present business to discuss them at length; though it is just worth noting that anyone who has mastered Chapter III of this book will want to distinguish the prescriptive sense given to *ultimate end* at the beginning of the first paragraph from the purely descriptive one into which Aquinas slips at the end. The immediate point for us is that what has so far been presented from Aquinas constitutes an apparently decisive case for the radical conclusion that the notion of divine creation leaves no room for that of responsible human action. For on that hypothesis the origin of every ostensible action must lie not in the ostensible human agent but in God. We must, therefore, all of us all the time be – as it were – subjects under the hypnotic control of the divine Hypnotist.

Against this it is merely diversionary to urge that the theist God cannot, strictly, predestinate; since he is 'outside time'. Such a move must be ineffective: first, because a God who – like the God of Islam and of traditional Judaism and Christianity – is to be himself an agent can at most be eternal (everlasting) and not eternal (non-temporal); and, second, because even if the anticipatory aspect of God's causality could somehow be neutralized such a God must still remain as a first and sustaining cause. Aquinas makes no such move; since he is, as we have seen, well content to maintain precisely those doctrines of predestination, of reprobation, and of election, which are so often wrongly thought to have been Calvinistic innovations.

But, of course, Aquinas – like almost any Christian theologian – does also want to hold that our sins, though not our merits, are our own; and sufficiently so to justify God's arrangements for the everlasting damnation of the reprobate. He is thus, from our present point of view, not "a consistent and wholehearted radical". So his position is exposed to the criticism of the last passage quoted in the previous section. The one significant difference is that there Aristotle's opponent by his partisan generosity towards our species erred in the opposite direction. Aquinas in the chapter of the *Summa contra Gentiles* immediately preceding that of the last quotation seems to be insisting that what he is just going to say about reprobation is inconsistent with what he is resolved to say about the responsibility of human sinners:

Now although God does not convert certain sinners to himself, but leaves them in their sins according to their deserts, nevertheless he does not lead them into sinning. For men sin in as much as they turn away from that which is their ultimate end (as is clear from what has gone before). But, since every agent acts for an end which is proper and suitable to it, it is impossible for anyone by the agency of God to be turned away from his ultimate end, which is God. It is, therefore, impossible for God to cause anyone to sin.

Again, good cannot be the cause of evil. But sin is an evil for man. . . . It is, therefore, impossible for God to be the cause of anyone's sinning. . . .

Furthermore, every fault stems from some deficiency in the proximate agent, but not from the influence of the first agent. Thus the fault of limping stems from the condition of the leg bone, and not from the motive power. For whatever perfection of motion is still apparent in the limping comes from that. But the proximate agent of human sin is the will. The defect of sin, therefore, comes from the will of man, and not from God who is the prime agent. Whatever pertains to the perfection of action in the act is, nevertheless, from him.   (III (clxii))

It is not, surely, only the illustration which is limping in this argument. Certainly anyone familiar with attempts to reconcile the consequences of a doctrine of creation with our undivided responsibility for our faults will appreciate why in the first *Inquiry* the ironic Hume took these as a main pointer to his desired moral about the limitations of the human understanding:

These are mysteries which mere natural and unassisted reason is very unfit to handle; and whatever system she embraces, she must find herself involved in inextricable difficulties, and even contradictions, at every step which she takes with regard to such subjects.

To reconcile the indifference and contingency of human actions with prescience, or to defend absolute decrees and yet free the Deity from being the author of sin, has been found hitherto to exceed all the power of philosophy. Happy, if she be thence sensible of her temerity when she pries into these sublime mysteries, and, leaving a scene so full of obscurities and perplexities, return, with suitable modesty, to her true and proper province, the examination of common life, where she will find difficulties enough to employ her inquiries without launching into so boundless an ocean of doubt, uncertainty, and contradiction.

(§ VIII (ii))

§4 Radical onslaughts: (ii) hard determinism

Suppose we allow that Hume was right about the implications of pre-destination. Still there remains the purely secular problem of determinism and freedom; a problem which Hume himself met, and to his own satis-faction solved, in the first Part of the same Section of the first *Inquiry*. About this problem the first essential is to insist again that predestina-tionism and determinism are not the same thing: on the hypothesis of divine creation there is Someone else who surely must be partly or wholly responsible for our actions; whereas on the atheist determinist view if we are not truly responsible ourselves then there is no one at all who can be. Thus the English philosopher F. H. Bradley (1846–1924), defending a Compatibility Thesis about determinism, wrote in a letter to William James:

> The trouble, I believe, has been mainly caused by the moral (or immoral) Creator. Once tell a man that another fellow, however big, has made him to be and to do what he is and does, and of course he throws it on the other fellow; and his poor morality goes to the devil, or may do so. I don't understand a word of what you say about 'possi-bilities' in connection with this other fellow, unless you mean that he's not a 'Creator' at all, but somehow a limited struggling sort of chap like ourselves, only bigger and better, and loves us and tries to help us, and we ought to stick to him. . . . But go further and I don't think you'll save either the morality of the personal God or ours either, so far as we take him seriously and look on ourselves as his pottery. . . .
>
> (R. H. Parry, II, p. 239)

Bradley in that final sentence is, of course, alluding to the last stanzas of Edward Fitzgerald's translation of 'The Rubaiyat of Omar Khayyam', a poem shaped by the militantly predestinarian theism of Islam:

> *With Earth's first Clay they did the last Man knead,*
> *And there of the Last Harvest sow'd the Seed:*
> *Yea, the first Morning of Creation wrote*
> *What the last Dawn of Reckoning shall read.*

For a bold clear statement of a scientifically oriented determinism, with no predestinarian overtones, consider the manifesto of P.S. de Laplace (1749–1827). It was Laplace who is said, although he was himself by conviction a Catholic, to have replied to Napoleon's question about where God came into his astronomical calculations: "Sir, I have no need of that hypothesis." The present passage comes from his *Philosophical Essay on Probabilities*:

We ought then to regard the present state of the universe as the effect of its previous state and the cause of the one which is to follow. An intelligence knowing at a given instant of time all the forces operating in nature, as well as the position at that instant of all the things of which the universe consists, would be able to comprehend the motions of the largest bodies in the universe and those of the smallest atoms in a single formula – provided that it was sufficiently powerful to submit all these data to analysis. To it nothing would be uncertain and the future would be present to its eyes as much as the past. (I (i))

In this case the radical Incompatibility Thesis is that if such determinism is true then it follows that everyone's every thought and action must be and have been inevitable; that no one ever really has or has had any choice about anything, because everyone always necessarily does as he is thus ineluctably determined to do; and that we cannot but be, for better or for worse, helpless products of ultimately blind forces which have made us what we are. Those who believe this philosophical proposition, and also believe that determinism is in fact true, are sometimes known as hard determinists; by contrast with the soft, whose determinism is linked with a Compatibility Thesis.

Our concern in the present book is with these rival philosophical theses, and not with the first-order question of how far determinism is in fact true. But it is easy to appreciate the importance for anyone unable to accept a Compatibility Thesis of this first-order issue. Thus we have in this century seen some desperate clutching at the Principle of Indeterminacy in particle physics, because this was thought to offer some physical warrant for a measure of indeterminism. It is a response which has been often and aptly compared with the introduction by Epicurus into the original atomism of Leucippus and Democritus of a sort of unpredictable atomic swerve: this was intended, among other things, to make room in the universe for (libertarian) freewill. Again, on the other side, anyone who is attracted by the implications of hard determinism thereby acquires some interest in the truth of determinism as such. Good examples of the practical application of hard determinist ideas can be found in the speeches for the defence of Clarence Darrow, who used most effectively to quote A. E. Housman:

My mother and my father
Out of the light they lie;
The warrant would not find them
And here 'tis only I
Shall hang so high   ('The Culprit).

However, no question of practical application ought to arise unless the presupposition of incompatibility is indeed correct. So the rest of the present chapter will be devoted to considering reasons for thinking that it is not.

First, as a preliminary which is much more than a preliminary, notice that the hard determinist needs to be extremely careful to ensure that his formulations take due account of certain manifest differences. For while it is open to argument that both philosophers and plain men may in some way have misconstrued the nature and implications of these differences; it is not similarly open to anyone to deny that, where distinctions are in practice constantly and systematically made, these must have some basis of actual difference somewhere. Thus it will not do for the hard determinist to conclude, for instance, that we are all always – without qualification – "helpless products of ultimately blind forces which have made us what we are." Products of such forces indeed we may be. But, at least in the ordinary and everyday sense, universally helpless we are not.

The fundamental point is that the term *helpless* always derives its meaning from an implicit or explicit contrast with some excluded opposite. It is used to indicate a difference or differences: between, on the one hand, those cases where we should ordinarily say that someone was helpless – as a polio victim perhaps or, less drastically, as 'a cog in the military machine'; and, on the other hand, those contrasting cases where by the same token he most certainly is not – as a fit man, or as the General or the President controlling that military machine. It cannot, therefore, be right to maintain that we are all of us always – without qualification, and hence presumably in this ordinary sense – helpless. But we can and must say this without prejudice to the still open possibility of urging: either that the differences involved are for some reason really less important than we usually and uninstructedly think; or that some actual or supposed further implication of the application of one or other of the contrasting terms does not in fact obtain.

Consider in this connection an argument from the *Theodicy* of Leibniz. This brilliant book labours to achieve what Hume, "with suitable. modesty", later judged to be beyond the powers of "mere natural and unassisted reason". In the course of his toils Leibniz, from the premise that the universe is the creation of a perfect God, validly argues to the immensely implausible conclusion that this must be the best of all possible worlds. It was this bold and boldly paraded inference – inordinately exacerbated by such claims as that "The work most worthy of the wisdom of God involves . . . the eternal damnation of the majority of men" (§ 236) – which provoked Voltaire's masterly satire *Candide*. The first passage comes from the 'Abridgement', made by Leibniz himself. The second is taken from the full original:

So the necessity which is contrary to morality, which must be avoided, and which would make punishment unjust, is an irresistible necessity which would make all opposition useless; even if we were to wish wholeheartedly to avoid the necessary action, and if we were exercising all our efforts to that end. Now, it is clear that this does not apply to voluntary actions, because we would not do them if we did not actually want to. Also the foreseeing of them and their predetermination are not unconditional, but take the will for granted: if it is certain that we shall do them, it is equally certain that we shall want to do them. These voluntary actions, and their consequences, are not things which will occur no matter what we do, or whether we wish them or not; but they will be results of what we shall do, and of what we shall want to do. This is contained in the foreseeing and in the predetermination, and even constitutes its grounds. . . . Thus it is futile, in the case of what is necessary unconditionally, to prohibit or to command, to propose penalties or to offer prizes, to praise or to blame; it will happen regard-less. In the other case, that of voluntary actions and what depends on them, commands fortified with the power of punishment and reward are very frequently useful, and are among the sorts of causes which pro-duce actions. And this is why not only care and effort but prayer too is useful. . . . This is why . . . not only those who – appealing to the empty excuse of the necessity of events – pretend that the care which business demands may be neglected, but also those who reason against prayer, fall into what the ancients even then called 'the Lazy Sophism'. . . .

. . . for – people would say – if what I ask must happen it will happen even if I do nothing; and if it is not to happen it will never happen, no matter what trouble I take to bring it about. This necessity, supposedly existent in events detached from their causes, might be termed 'Mahom-medan Fate'. . . because the same sort of argument – or so they say – induces the Turks not to avoid at all places ravaged by plague. But the answer is ready to hand: the effect being certain, the cause which will produce it is also certain; and if the effect comes about this will be thanks to a corresponding cause. Thus perhaps your laziness will bring it about that you will get nothing of what you want, and that you will fall into those misfortunes which by acting carefully you would have avoided. We see, therefore, that the connection of causes with effects, far from producing an intolerable rule of fate, instead provides a means of removing this. . . . The sophism, which ends in a decision to trouble oneself over nothing, will perhaps sometimes be useful in inducing some people to go bull-headed into danger. It has been applied particularly to Turkish soldiers. . . .

('Essays on the Goodness of God', I, § 55)

These are rich passages. Their most immediate lessons are two. First, they illustrate the way in which argument which was originally deployed in the religious context may be equally – or even more – relevant in the secular. Second, it can be used to show that whatever determinism – or predestinationism – may imply it quite certainly cannot imply that the differences to which in everyday discourse about human conduct we do so continually refer, do not after all really exist. Or, alternatively, if determinism – or predestinationism – does indeed imply this, then the manifest fact of the existence of these differences must prove, by reversal of the argument, that these hypotheses are false. It is, therefore, totally out of the question that any scientific – or theological – discovery ever could show that there just is no difference between the man who we should ordinarily say could help himself, and the man who we should normally allow could not. Hence it must be wrong to say that we always act subject to what Leibniz would call an unconditional necessity; that we are always – in an ordinary sense – helpless.

Such a conclusion may be reminiscent of Dr Samuel Johnson's famous: "We know our will is free, and there's an end on't" (Boswell's *Journal* for 10 October 1769). But this is philosophical where that was not: first, in the supporting argument just provided; and, second, in the insistence now that this must be the beginning rather than the end. For, granting that the familiar differences cannot be denied, the questions remain of what determinism – or predestinationism – would imply, and whether the expressions which we use every day to mark these differences would on either of these hypotheses be shown to be in some way misleading.

Reverting for a moment to predestination, it should be appreciated that Leibniz was entirely typical of all the ablest predestinarian philosopher theologians in his underlining of the facts of these differences as crucially important. In others you will find also a sustained insistence that our everyday expressions do not in fact carry philosophically libertarian implications. This is especially true of the treatise *Freedom of the Will* by Jonathan Edwards (1703–1757), the earliest philosophical work of the first rank to be produced within the territories which were later to become the United States. These able predestinarians had no wish to deny the differences between those cases in which men are, to the secular eye, helpless and those in which they are not; those in which they would ordinarily be said to act of their own freewill and those in which they act under compulsion; and so on. On the contrary: they affirmed these differences and urged that such distinctions are of terrible consequence in the Divine scheme. Their contention was: not that the supposed fact that we are creatures of an omnipotent and omniscient Creator shows that we are all always – in the ordinary this-worldly sense – utterly helpless, and never able to act of our own freewill; but rather that this same supposed fact of creation is entirely compatible with the subsistence of all these familiar differences and distinctions, which are indeed of the greatest importance, theologically as well as in secular human terms. It was by this road that they reached their conclusion that there is no inconsistency in such formulations as that of the *Westminster Confession* of 1643. (These the poet Robert Burns must have had much in mind in writing such a work as 'Holy Wullie's Prayer'.)

God from all eternity did, by the most wise and holy counsel of his own will, freely and unchangeably ordain whatsoever comes to pass. Yet so as thereby neither . . . is violence offered to the will of the creatures. . . . By the decree of God, for the manifestation of his glory, some men and angels are predestinated unto everlasting life, and others foreordained to everlasting death. . . . Neither are any redeemed by Christ . . . but the elect only. The rest of mankind God was pleased to pass by, and to ordain them to dishonour and wrath. . .   (III)

In this particular contention about compatibility they were, I believe, right. The truly indefensible weakness of their position surely lies elsewhere in phrases which I have omitted from my quotation. It lies in their assumption that these differences and distinctions could retain the same unchanged place within a world perspective deepened by the addition of a predestinarian dimension; and, above all, that consequently even in that perspective we rather than God must be accounted wholly responsible for what we do 'of our own freewill'. The embarrassment of Edwards on this point is as evident as it is significant:

> They who object that this doctrine makes God the author of sin, ought distinctly to explain what they mean by that phrase. . . . I know, the phrase, as it is commonly used, signifies something very ill. If by *the author of sin* be meant the sinner, the agent, or actor of sin, or the doer of a wicked thing; so it would be a reproach and a blasphemy to suppose God to be the author of sin. In this sense, I utterly deny God to be the author of sin; rejecting such an imputation on the most High, as what is infinitely to be abhorred; and deny any such thing to be the consequence of what I have laid down. But if by *the author of sin*, is meant the permitter, or not a hinderer of sin; and, at the same time, a disposer of the state of events, in such a manner, for wise, holy and most excellent ends and purposes, that sin, if it be permitted and not hindered, will most certainly and infallibly follow; I say, if this be all that is meant by being the author of sin, I don't deny that God is the author of sin (though I dislike and reject the phrase, as that which by use and custom is apt to carry another sense); it is no reproach to the most High to be thus the author of sin. This is not to be the actor of sin, but, on the contrary, of holiness. What God doth herein, is holy; and a glorious exercise of the infinite excellency of his nature. And I don't deny, that God's being thus the author of sin, follows from what I have laid down; and I assert, that it equally follows from the doctrine which is maintained by most of the Arminian divines.　　　　　　　　　　　　　　　　(IV, § 9 (ii))

The "Arminian divines" of whom Edwards speaks were followers of the Dutch theologian Jacobus Arminius (1560–1609), and as such opponents of Calvinist doctrines of predestination. The point of reverting to the idea of predestination in the three or four previous paragraphs was to provide what may be a surprising illustration of the main moral of the present section. This moral is that, while any view must be false if it denies the existence of differences which we can and do mark every day of our lives, the overtones and implications carried by the contrasting descriptions which we employ are not by the same token equally sacrosanct. Most certainly there are actual differences which we use these contrasting descriptions to point, yet it is none the less possible that some or all such actual descriptions are in some way misleading. Perhaps, for instance, they imply or presuppose something which the truth of universal determinism would show to be false; and it may be that, alternatively or additionally, they express and excite responses which in a deterministic perspective would be seen to be inappropriate. If this proved to be so then the logical situation with regard to determinism would be very closely analogous to that which, I have just been suggesting, does indeed obtain with regard to predestinationism. This possibility thus constitutes a further reason for giving quite extensive attention in the present chapter to that currently unfashionable doctrine.

§5 *Necessity, avoidability, and foreknowledge*

Consider now the ancient Problem of the Sea-fight – so called in deference to Aristotle's illustration. The originating passage occurs in his *de Interpretatione,* one of the logical treatises which later came to be known as the *Organon* (*Organon* is the Greek word for *instrument*, and the idea was that these works constituted a toolkit for inquiry):

> Propositions about the present or the past must necessarily be either true or false. . . . But with regard to propositions about the future, and with singular subjects, the situation is different. For if every proposition, whether positive or negative, is either true or false, and if every predicate must either apply or not apply, then if one man declares that something will happen and another declares that it will not, it is plain that one or other of them is speaking the truth; provided, that is, that every proposition is either true or false, for both predicates cannot apply simultaneously to such propositions. Now if it is true to say that something is white or that it is not white then necessarily it is either white or not white, and if it is white or not white it was true to affirm or to deny this. And if it is not in fact white this is false, and if it is false then it is not white. It follows necessarily that all affirmations and denials are either true or false.
>
> But then there will be nothing which happens by chance or as may be; nothing will ever so happen, but everything will happen necessarily and not as may be. Either the man who maintains that something will occur or the man who denies it will be speaking the truth. . . .
>
> Furthermore, if something is now white then it was true previously to say that it would be white; with the consequence that it was always true to say of anything whatever which has happened that it is or that it will be. But if it was always true to say that it is or that it will be, then it is not possible for it not to be or not to be about to be. And if it cannot not happen then it is impossible for it not to happen. Yet what cannot not happen, must happen. So everything future necessarily

happens. Then nothing happens as may be, or will come about by chance. For if it happened by chance it would not happen by necessity.

But, nevertheless, it is not on to say that neither proposition is true, that something neither will be nor will not be. . . . If some event, a sea-fight for example, neither will happen nor will not happen tomorrow it still would not be a case of 'as may be'; for on this supposition it would have neither to happen nor not to happen tomorrow.

Yet the following extraordinary consequences, and others, hold if every affirmation or denial . . . is either true or false, and if none of the things which occur are 'whichever may be' but all happen by necessity. The consequence would be that there would be no need to deliberate nor to take trouble on the assumption that if we do this that will happen, and if we do not it will not. There is nothing to prevent one person saying as much as ten thousand years in advance that this will happen and another saying that it will not, with the consequence that whichever thing was truly said then would occur by necessity. Indeed it is no matter whether anyone ever uttered the contradictory predictions, for it is obvious that someone's affirming something and another man's denying it does not bring it about that things are thus or thus. . . .

All this is, however, impossible. For we can see for ourselves that future events depend on our deliberations and on what we do. . . . So it is clear that not everything is or happens by necessity. . . .

Therefore, what is must be when it is, and what is not cannot be when it is not. Yet it is not necessary for everything which does exist to exist, or for what does not not to. For it is not the same thing to say that everything that is is by necessity when it is, and to say that it is – without qualification – by necessity. . . . I mean, for example, that it is necessary that there either will or will not be a sea-fight tomorrow, but yet it is not necessary either that there will be a sea-fight tomorrow or that there will not be. What is necessary is that it will either happen or not happen. And so, since the truth of propositions consists in corresponding with the facts it is clear that wherever the situation is one of 'whichever may be' and where either of two opposite things is possible the two contradictory statements about them must have the same character. . . . It is, therefore, plain that there is no necessity for one of every pair of contradictory affirmations and denials to be true and the other false.

(IX: 18A28–19B3, with excisions as indicated)

Confronted by an argument which seems to prove a universal fatalist conclusion from the premise that all propositions must be either true or false, Aristotle thinks he sees a way of escape in a denial that propositions about future matters of fact – called future contingents – are either true or false. For he had too much sense to accept a universal fatalism, and he was too much the logician to abandon The Law of the Excluded Middle – here to be construed as saying not that every proposition must be either true or false but rather that no proposition may be both true and false. It will help us to focus on the issues most immediately relevant if we look next at the contribution made by Hobbes. It occurs in a pamphlet 'Of Liberty and Necessity'. (The subtitle is, incidentally, too good to miss even though it was apparently not written by Hobbes but added by his piratical publisher: "A treatise wherein all controversy concerning predestination, election, freewill, grace, merits, reprobation, etc. is fully decided and cleared".)

Let the case be put, for example, of the weather. It is necessary that tomorrow it shall rain or not rain. If therefore it be not necessary that it shall rain, it is necessary it shall not rain; otherwise there is no necessity that the proposition, *It shall rain or not rain*, should be true. I know there be some that say it may necessarily be true that one of the two shall come to pass, but not, singly, that it shall rain, or that it shall not rain. Which is as much as to say one of them is necessary, yet neither of them is necessary. And therefore, to seem to avoid that absurdity, they make a distinction, that neither of them is true 'determinate', but 'indeterminate'. Which distinction either signifies no more but this, one of them is true but we know not which, and so the necessity remains though we know it not; or, if the meaning of the distinction be not that, it hath no meaning, and they might as well have said, one of them is true 'Titirice', but neither of them, 'Tu patulice'. (*English Works*, IV, p. 277)

Hobbes, like Aristotle, took the argument to be valid; though, being English, he preferred to talk about the weather. Ever the robust controversialist he rejected Aristotelian subtleties and offered it as a proof not of fatalism but of determinism: "that all events have necessary causes" (p. 276). Yet there has to be something wrong with an argument which proceeds from a purely tautological premise to a substantial conclusion: such a conclusion cannot be contained in, and hence cannot be deduced from, any such premise or premises. So let us apply to it tools of analysis introduced in earlier chapters.

The crux lies in the misplacing and consequent misinterpretation of the term *necessary*; and of its other apodeictic associates such as *possible, impossible, must,* and *cannot*. (*Apodeictic*, meaning 'pertaining to demonstration', is a word one needs to know simply because it was a favourite with Kant.) What is going on, and going wrong, can be brought out clearly by the careful joint employment both of this constellation of apodeictic notions and of the Formal Mode of Speech. (See Chapters V § 1 and VI § 2 and 4, above.) Remember especially that a necessary, or necessarily true, proposition is one the denial of which must involve asserting a self-contradiction, a logical impossibility. Contrariwise a contingent proposition is one which is logically possible, one which whether or not it happens to be true can nevertheless always be denied without actual self-contradiction. And all the terms of this constellation, in this employment, belong to a vocabulary for second-order talk about propositions and their logical relations; rather than to our primary vocabulary for first-order talk about actual things and their factual relations.

Now certainly the proposition, *Either it will rain or it will not rain,* is necessarily true. Equally certainly from the proposition, *It will rain,* it follows necessarily that it will rain; just as from the proposition, *It is raining,* it follows necessarily that it is raining. But from none of this does it even look as if it follows that either *It will rain* or *It is raining* is a necessary, as opposed to contingent, truth; or, as the case may happen to be, falsehood.

Or, to change the example yet again, consider the formulation of the Lazy Sophism used in a song sung by Miss Doris Day in one of her films: "Whatever will be, will be." This is an undeniable tautology, since from *It will be* it must follow necessarily that *It will be,* whatever 'It' may be. But it is no tautology at all to say that whatever will be will occur, necessarily, inevitably, and unavoidably. Nor does this follow necessarily – as the Lazy Sophism requires – from the proposition, *Whatever will be, will be.* For from *It will be* it does not by any means follow that *It will necessarily be,* whatever 'It' may happen to be. The substantial and false conclusion is drawn invalidly from the tautologically true premise by illegitimately inserting into the conclusion a *necessarily* for which there is no warrant in that premise. These unsound proceedings are fundamentally the same, and equally unsound, whether the *necessarily* is then construed in its original sense and taken to refer to the logical status of the conclusion proposition, or whether it is now construed more appropriately to its new context as equivalent to *inevitably as a matter of contingent fact.*

The Problem of the Sea-fight arose for Aquinas as a question about God's providence. As such it offers to the theist peculiar intractabilities. These we can ignore, noticing simply that his treatment is along the lines just suggested although without benefit of any of the modern machinery. (A possible exercise would be to constitute yourself as a one-person technical aid mission!) The passages come from the *Summa contra Gentiles*:

'Furthermore, suppose something is foreseen by God: for example, that such and such a man will be king. Then it is either possible or not possible for it to happen that he will be king. But if it is not possible for him not to be king, then it is impossible for him not to be king; therefore it is necessary that he is king. If, on the other hand, it is possible for him not to be king; then, granted this possibility, it follows that there is no impossibility about it. But then divine providence fails, and so it is not impossible for divine providence to fail. The consequence is, therefore, if all things are foreseen by God, either that divine providence is not certain or that everything happens necessarily.'

From what has just been said it is evident that this conditional proposition is true, *If God foresees that this will happen it will happen.* . . . But it will occur in the way in which God foresaw that it would occur. He, however, foresaw that it would occur contingently. It follows, therefore, infallibly that it will occur contingently and not necessarily.
(III (xciv))

In the more interesting case not of necessity as opposed to contingency but of inevitability as against avoidability a similar answer can be given. From the mere fact that some event is reliably forecast it by no means follows that it will occur inevitably. In the first place it does not follow from the fact that anticipatory words are spoken: "for it is obvious that someone's affirming something does not bring it about that things are thus or thus. . . ."

But there is much more to this than Aristotle appears to have grasped. For, in the second place, nothing relevant follows even from the different fact of the proposition's being, albeit perhaps unspoken and even unknown, true. Just as from *They are shooting* it follows necessarily that *They are shooting*, but nothing follows about the necessity of either the proposition or the shooting; so the implications when the example is transposed into the future tense are, with appropriate alterations, the same, and equally unexciting. If once it is allowed that the truth of propositions in present and past tenses imposes no sort of necessity on anything, we lose any reason we might have thought we had for believing that the future is different; and hence for suggesting that future contingents cannot as such be either true or false. What mainly encourages these illusions about the power of truth is talking and thinking of it as if it were a temporal property of propositions, as if it would make sense to say that one and the same proposition was once true, is now false, but tomorrow will perhaps be true again. Certainly precisely this might seem to hold of our exemplary proposition, *It will rain tomorrow*. But this form of words requires some determinate context of date and place if it is to express a determinate proposition. Once a definite context is provided and we have a specific proposition to discuss, then it is manifestly absurd to suggest that this proposition might be true on some days and not on others or that it will become true or cease to be true on such and such a day.

One uninteresting reason why without a context *It will rain tomorrow* is more an uncompleted form than a fully determinate proposition is that the words by themselves give no indication of an area to which reference is being made. The other and instructive reason is that *tomorrow* is always a token-reflexive term. When we speak of a word or an expression we are normally referring to the type or class of which all the particular individual occasions of its employment are tokens. A word or expression is called token-reflexive when its reference varies with, and is in some way a function of, the situations of its tokens. Thus all the personal pronouns are token-reflexive because to know who I, or you, or he is you have to know who is talking. *Yesterday, today,* and *tomorrow* are all token-reflexive because to know the days to which reference is being made we have to know when the words are being uttered. All tense in verbs used temporally is also token-reflexive. This all makes for philosophical trouble when something non-temporal needs to be said. For since most verb tokens are used temporally, and since the demands of conventional grammar and syntax in all the languages which most of us either know or know about require that all sentences should contain a tensed verb, there is a very strong temptation to think that something temporal must be being asserted whenever anyone claims, for instance, that this proposition is as a matter of fact true or that the square on the hypotenuse is equal to the sum of the squares on the other two sides. By mistaking the *is* in such cases to be temporal we provide ourselves with a reason for drawing two erroneous conclusions. The first is that truth somehow imposes some sort of objective necessity onto things and hence, at one remove, that the only refuge against fatalism is deperately to maintain that future contingents can be neither true nor false. The second is that geometry is a realm of eternal (everlasting) truths, contrasting most favourably with the merely ephemeral truths of everyday life and science.

In the third place, again, nothing relevant follows solely from the fact that someone knew that someone would act in such and such a way. Certainly from *He knows that Mr Truman will vote for Mr Johnson* it follows necessarily that *Mr Truman will vote for Mr Johnson*; because the meaning of the word *know* is such that it is not possible, that is to say it would be contradictory, to assert the former while denying the latter. But such knowledge neither constituted nor needed to be based upon any reason for fearing that President Truman would in some way be unable to help himself. On the contrary, we might, and indeed do, know that nothing but paralysing illness or overwhelming coercion would have induced him either to vote for Mr Goldwater or to abstain. And had anyone said of him, what Martin Luther said of himself before the Diet of Worms, "Here I stand, I can no other. So help me God", then both statements would have to be interpreted as meaning, not that these agents had literally no alternative, but that all actually available alternatives were to their subjects totally unacceptable. What the person making a well-grounded and correct forecast of such behaviour knows is not that the agent will not be able to, but simply that he will not, act otherwise than is foreseen: two totally different things.

In addition to the various confusions already examined another source of the misconception that foreknowledge as such must preclude the contingent possibility of alternative courses of action is that in particular cases there often are additional grounds which would warrant some much stronger conclusion. Thus, suppose Dr Gallup tells us that General Eisenhower will win in a landslide, we cannot infer either that the electors will have to be coerced to support him or that no alternative candidate will be permitted to run. But we are all able, even without the assistance of the findings of Dr Gallup, to forecast with remarkable exactitude the outcome of the election substitutes staged in such states as the irritatingly mistitled German Democratic Republic; precisely because we are aware of how these ritual parades are conducted. Again, and similarly, the apparent antinomy between divine predestination and human responsibility arises because God is thought to be omnipotent as well as omniscient. This point is nicely made by the Renaissance Italian Lorenzo Valla (1405–1457) in his dialogue *On Freewill,* a work mentioned with respect not only by the philosopher Leibniz but also by both Calvin and Martin Luther (1483–1546). In accordance with the new literary conventions of his time Valla attributes omniscience and omnipotence to two separate Greek gods, Apollo and Jupiter, respectively:

LORENZO – Apollo, if we are to believe what was said, knew and fore-saw everything that would happen with respect not only to men but also to gods, and he rendered true and undoubted oracles about these things to those who consulted him. . . . Sextus Tarquinius enquired what his fate would be. Let us suppose that Apollo replied, and in verse as was his wont:

'You will fall as an exile in poverty, killed by an angry city.' To this Sextus responds: 'What are you saying, Apollo? What have I done to deserve this from you, that you proclaim so cruel a fate for me? . . . .' Apollo replies: 'Young man, your gifts are certainly pleasing and acceptable to me, and I have repaid them with that sad and wretched oracle. I could wish it were more cheerful. But it is not in my hands to make it so. I know the fates, I do not decide them; I can proclaim for-tune, not change it; I am the index of destinies, not their arbiter; I would proclaim better things if better things awaited you. . . . Accuse Jupiter, if you like . . . accuse Fortune. . . . Power and control over the fates rests with them, with me foreknowledge and foresaying only. . . .' Could Sextus justly reply to this speech: 'Yes indeed the fault lies in you, Apollo, who in your wisdom foresaw my fate: for if you had not foreseen them these things would not have been going to happen to me'?

ANTONIO – Not only would it be unjust, but he never would reply in such terms.   (454–488)

ANTONIO – Sextus speaks bravely and truly and justly. What does the god say this time?

LORENZO – 'That is how it is, Sextus. Jupiter, as he created the wolf rapacious, the hare timid, the lion spirited, the ass dull, the dog savage, and the sheep harmless, so he made some men hardhearted, and others softhearted, one man he produced more inclined to crime and another to virtue. And, furthermore, he gave to one man a capacity for reform and to another an incapacity. To you, indeed, he assigned a vicious spirit, not by any means to be corrected. So it is the case both that you will do evil because you are the sort of person that you are, and that Jupiter will exact a penalty because you will do what you will do and this will have the effects which it will have; and this is how he has sworn by the Stygian swamp that it will be.'

ANTONIO – Apollo excuses himself splendidly, but accuses Jupiter the more; for I am more on the side of Sextus than of Jupiter. Sextus might with the best of justification protest: 'And why is it my fault rather than that of Jupiter? When I am not permitted to do anything but evil, why does Jupiter condemn me for the fault which is his own? Why does he

251

exact vengeance on me when I am not to blame? Whatever I do . . . I do of necessity. Can I oppose his will and power?'
LORENZO – This is what I wanted to bring forward as my proof, for this is the point of this story. Although the wisdom of God cannot be separated from his will and power I can separate Apollo and Jupiter in this image. What cannot be got with one God can be got with two, each having his own determinate nature – one for creating men's characters and the other for knowing them. Thus it becomes evident that foresight is not the cause of necessity, but all this, whatever it is, must be referred wholly to the will of God.   (556–584)

Before concluding this section, and turning to another and better sort of reason for believing that determinism entails unavoidability, there are two further fairly practical morals to be drawn. The first is that we must never accept that there is something necessarily and obviously discreditable about predictability; which seems to be the assumption behind the increasingly widespread inclination to dismiss unwelcome reactions as 'predictable responses'. For it is in fact very much to my credit if my friends can be sure that I shall be against cruelty, chicanery, and injustice; and this regardless both of the colour and of the ideology of both the agent and the victim. Nor is it anything for you to be proud of if no one can be sure where, if anywhere, you will stand on anything.

Such readiness to dismiss the predictable may perhaps, at least when it is manifested in academic circles, be seen as one form of a polymorphous occupational escapism. For it is generally characteristic of academics to shift eagerly and precipitately from challenging practical questions demanding 'Which side are you on?' to less disturbing theoretical discussions about how you can understand why they acted or reacted in such and such a way. The latter are then treated rather as a substitute for than as a means towards, or a complement to, the answering of the former. To pillory such dangerously congenial changings of the subject I introduce the suitably offensive label, *The But-you-can-understand-why Evasion*.

Let us also now introduce a similarly dyslogistic mnemonic for another intellectual malpractice connected with explanation. Again this is especially common among those whose daily business is with origins and explanations. It is the tendency to suggest, if not actually to state, that the human phenomena which have been thus explained have somehow been shown thereby not to be what they are. If their brutality and mendacity is to be understood as the outcome of a continually brutal and mendacious national tradition, then this somehow shows that there is no need to worry, because these mendacious brutes must really be quite other than what the whole explanatory investigation presupposes that they are. For this I offer the label, *The It-is-not-really-because-it-is-because Suggestion*. (In both cases the exercise of seeking your own real-life examples will simultaneously both fix these labels in mind and show the need for them.)

The second practical moral is to be on the alert for other misplacements of necessities occurring elsewhere. Thus, someone may say that Frank has to support further measures of nationalization, because he is a socialist, or that Gina has to maintain that Jesus bar Joseph was the Son of God and that he rose again on the third day, because she is a Christian. Such statements are often offered as if they were by themselves sufficient to discredit or to vindicate either the believer or his conviction. But, of course, they are not. For they say no more than from *Frank (or Gina) is a socialist (or a Christian)* it follows necessarily that *Frank (or Gina) believes this (or that)*; and these inferences are valid in virtue of the strict meanings of the terms *socialist* and *Christian*. That Frank is a socialist, and that he therefore supports public ownership – in the words of Clause IV of the constitution of the British Labour Party – "of all the means of production, distribution and exchange", constitutes no sort of reason either for or against his Clause IV convictions. (As usual the best way to become persuaded that a moral is worth pointing is to catch someone lapsing in the manner prescribed – yourself, perhaps, as a suitably salutary start!)

§6 *Laws and inevitability*

Section five was concerned with ways in which conclusions containing ideas of necessity are apparently derived from premises which do not. In § 6 we have to consider the more hopefully disturbing contention that determinism itself essentially contains such ideas. The reason for saying that it does is that the word *determinism* is defined in terms of the notions of cause and law: it is not equivalent simply to *predictability*. (See §§ 1 and 4, above.) But now, the suggestion is, these notions covertly contain precisely that idea of inevitability which we were so careful not to include explicitly in those initial definitions. For, surely, causes necessitate; in as much as, once given the causally sufficient conditions of some effect, that effect cannot any longer be prevented: while the determination of a law of nature is equally ineluctable; in that, if you were able to bring about an occurrence incompatible with what had been thought to be such a law, this achievement would be in itself sufficient to show either that this supposed law does not after all obtain or – what for present purposes amounts to the same thing – that it has a scope narrower than had been previously assumed.

This is, perhaps, a good moment to pause for revision and consolidation. The suggestion which we are about to examine threatens, after so much has been done in previous sections to draw the teeth of determinism, to reveal it again as after all a monster which we shall wish, if we can, somehow to restrict or reject. Yet the gains achieved in those sections, though they may need to be rearranged in the light of later discoveries, do already constitute substantial progress; and they also include items, such as the realization of the harmlessness by itself of foreknowledge, which must be indispensable to any satisfactory handling of the formidable problem now arising.

So, taking that refreshing pause as having been made, let us turn to Hume. Hume's treatment of this idea of necessary connection is both a main element in his whole philosophical work and the seminal contribution to its subject. It divides easily into two parts. The first is an epoch-marking denial. The second is a piece of dubious psychological speculation, which nevertheless fitted well into the project of the *Treatise*. What Hume was denying was that there are any logical necessities in things. In particular he maintained that anything may be the cause of anything; that was to say, that we cannot know apriori – in advance of actual investigation of how things in fact are – that any thing or sort of thing either must be or cannot be the cause of any other thing or sort of thing. His psychological speculation was that our misconceptions about necessities in things are projections of the felt force of our own associations of ideas. Like his account of value this was modelled on the story about secondary qualities which he found in Newton and Galileo, and both appeared to him to be trophies of his Copernican revolution in reverse. (See Chapter III § 3, above.) In his first *Inquiry* Hume applies this account to our present problem:

It would seem, indeed, that men begin at the wrong end of this question concerning liberty and necessity when they enter upon it by examining the faculties of the soul, the influence of the understanding, and the operations of the will. Let them first discuss a more simple question, namely, the question of body and brute and unintelligent matter, and try whether they can there form any idea of causation and necessity, except that of constant conjunction of objects and subsequent inference of the mind from one to another. If these circumstances form, in reality, the whole of that necessity which we conceive in matter, and if these circumstances be universally acknowledged to take place in the operations of the mind, the dispute is at an end; or at least, must be owned to be thenceforth merely verbal. But as long as we will rashly suppose that we have some further idea of necessity and causation in the operations of external objects, at the same time as we can find nothing further in the voluntary actions of the mind, there is no possibility of bringing the question to any determinate issue. . . . The only method of undeceiving us is to mount up higher, to examine the narrow extent of science when applied to material causes, and to convince ourselves that all we know of them is the constant conjunction and inference above mentioned. We may, perhaps, find that it is with difficulty we are induced to fix such narrow limits to human understanding, but we can afterwards find no difficulty when we come to apply this doctrine to the actions of the will. (§ VIII (i))

In both method and execution this is excellent. But the premise is false. For there surely is more to the ideas of causation and of natural law than mere actual constant conjunction, and part if not the whole of that something more is an idea of practical inevitability. Also, although Hume is right in thinking that there is some sort of mistaken projection going on, what is being projected to where it does not belong is the quite different idea of logical necessity. Take in evidence a thoroughly Humean passage by Thomas Henry Huxley (1825–1895). This Huxley was a leading biologist, an early and vigorous advocate of Darwin's theory of the origin of species by natural selection, and author of the most sympathetic book on Hume written in the last century. This paragraph comes from his 1868 essay on 'The Physical Basis of Life':

And what is this dire necessity and 'iron' law under which men groan? Truly, most gratuitously invented bugbears. I suppose that if there is an 'iron' law, it is that of gravitation; and if there be a physical necessity, it is that a stone, unsupported, must fall to the ground. But what is all we really know, and can know, about the latter phenomena? Simply, that in all human experience, stones have fallen to the ground under these conditions; and that we have not the smallest reason for believing that any stone so circumstanced will not fall to the ground; and that we have, on the contrary, every reason to believe that it will so fall. It is very convenient to indicate that all the conditions of belief have been fulfilled in this case, by calling the statement that unsupported stones will fall to the ground *a law of nature*. But when, as commonly happens, we change *will* into *must*, we introduce an idea of necessity which most assuredly does not lie in the observed facts, and has no warranty that I can discover elsewhere. For my part I utterly repudiate and anathematize the intruder. Fact I know; and law I know; but what is this Necessity, save an empty shadow of my own mind's throwing?

(I, p. 161)

The account so picturesquely epitomized in that final clause corresponds splendidly with unsound manoeuvres of the sort examined in § 5. Certainly, granted the appropriate laws of nature and the appropriate statements of the values of their variables it follows necessarily that this or that in fact occurs; and, equally certainly, it is fundamentally mistaken to project the logical necessity which characterizes the inference into the propositions linked by that inference and so out onto the world – and the mistake is changed but not diminished if somewhere along the line the logical necessity is transmogrified into practical inevitability. But the suggestion now in this § 6 is that the latter notion is itself an essential element of that of a law of nature: if law you know then this necessity you also know.

Hume elsewhere in the first *Inquiry* unwittingly gives evidence against himself both about practical inevitability and about practical impossibility. The three passages to be quoted are of the greatest interest in other ways too. The first is a summary of his positive account of causality. The second two come from the in his own day most notorious discussion 'Of Miracles'. The gist of this, which is a landmark both in the philosophy of history and the philosophy of religion, is that the assumptions which the historian has to make in order to advance his inquiries into what actually happened preclude the possibility of establishing – upon purely historical evidence – the occurrence of any genuinely miraculous event, and that, in particular and especially, it must be impossible by thus proving the occurrence of real miracles to authenticate the claims of any candidate religious revelation:

> The only immediate utility of all sciences is to teach us how to control and regulate future events by their causes. Our thoughts and inquiries are, therefore, every moment employed about this relation; yet so imperfect are the ideas we form concerning it that it is impossible to give any just definition of *cause*, except what is drawn from something extraneous and foreign to it. Similar objects are always conjoined with similar. Of this we have experience. Suitably to this experience, therefore, we may define *a cause* to be 'an object followed by another, and where all the objects, similar to the first, are followed by objects similar

to the second'. Or, in other words, 'where, if the first object had not been, the second never had existed'. The appearance of a cause always conveys the mind, by a customary transition, to the idea of the effect. Of this also we have experience. We may, therefore, suitably to this experience, form another definition of *cause*, and call it 'an object followed by another, and whose appearance always conveys the thought to that other'. (§ VII (ii))

But in order to increase the probability against the testimony of witnesses, let us suppose that the fact which they affirm, instead of being only marvelous, is really miraculous; and suppose also that the testimony, considered apart and in itself, amounts to an entire proof – in that case there is proof against proof, of which the strongest must prevail, but still with a diminution of its force, in proportion to that of its antagonist.

A miracle is a violation of the laws of nature; and, as a firm and unalterable experience has established these laws, the proof against a miracle, from the very nature of the fact, is as entire as any argument from experience can possibly be imagined. . . . (§ X (i))

There surely never was a greater number of miracles ascribed to one person than those which were lately said to have been wrought in France upon the tomb of the Abbé Paris, the famous Jansenist, with whose sanctity the people were so long deluded. . . . And what have we to oppose to so great a cloud of witnesses but the absolute impossibility or miraculous nature of the events which they relate? And this, surely, in the eyes of all reasonable people, will alone be regarded as a sufficient refutation. (§ X (ii))

From the second two passages it is obvious that, whether or not he could or should provide for this within his system, Hume did – and rightly – wish to distinguish sharply between the merely marvellous, because very unusual and otherwise remarkable, and the sheerly miraculous, and hence practically impossible. Taking the reference to "a firm and unalterable experience as a hint, we can begin to appreciate that and why the second of the two clauses in the first passage which is asserted to be the first "in other words" is, significantly, not. Propositions of the 'If-it-were-to-have-it-would' form of this second are known, reasonably enough, as subjunctive or contrary-to-fact conditionals. Now all statements of laws of nature and of causal connections imply some subjunctive conditionals: if I claim that the cause of the breakdown was sand in the magneto then this implies that – all other things being equal – if there had been no sand there, then there would have been no breakdown. This being so any complete analysis or definition of either of these ideas must warrant such inferences: for if it does not, then that analysis or definition cannot be equivalent to what it purports to analyse or define. But precisely this is lacking in Hume's account of causality, and must also be lacking in any parallel account of a law of nature. For from the proposition that *B's as a matter of fact never have occurred or will occur without antecedent A's* it does not necessarily follow that *If there were not to have been any A's there would not have been any B's*. Nothing is actually said in the former proposition to block the suggestion that this particular correlation is coincidental; and yet precisely that would be precluded by a statement that *A's cause B's* or that *A's are related to B's by a law of nature*.

Now the immediate relevance of all this is that practical inevitability, and practical impossibility, are matters of what cannot be prevented, or of what cannot be brought about, however much and in whatever way we try; and hence we must ultimately refer to practice and experiment, as well as to mere observation, if we are to know the truth of the sorts of proposition which embrace these notions, and of the subjunctive conditionals which are derived from them. It is most significant that, although Hume's official definitions rely entirely upon the purely spectator notion of an observed perfect correlation, he is himself unable altogether to exclude the gatecrashing of these other ideas belonging to the agent rather than the spectator; ideas which, as we have just seen, must be provided for in any fully adequate analysis. It is vital here to heed the advice of the physicist Niels Bohr: "it must never be forgotten that we . . . are both agents and spectators in the drama of existence" (Bohr, p. 318).

Another and very relevant manifestation of this fundamental and general truth, and one which needs to be noticed and named before we return to the question of the implications for human action of determinism, is the Oedipus Effect. The importance of this in the present context was emphasized both by Hume and by Valla before him, but it was left to Sir Karl Popper in our own time to fix the phenomenon more firmly in our attention by attaching to it a memorable label. This Oedipus Effect is the impact of the publication of a prediction upon the subjects of that prediction, whether in making for its fulfilment or for its falsification (Popper (2), p. 13); and the reference is to the Greek legend of Oedipus the King, whose parents' efforts to falsify the prophecy that he would kill his father and marry his mother became partly instrumental in its fulfilment. The first passage is by Valla and the second by Hume, and both are taken from the works just mentioned:

LORENZO – . . . I come now to what you gave as your first reply, that the present and past are unalterable and so can be known, but that the future is alterable and so cannot be foreknown. So I ask whether it can be changed that eight hours from now night will arrive, that after the summer it will be autumn, after the autumn the winter, after the winter the spring, and after the spring the summer?

ANTONIO – Those are natural phenomena, and ones which always run the same course: but I am speaking of voluntary actions. . . . Predict which foot I will move first, and whichever you say you will be wrong, because I will move the other.

LORENZO – I ask you, was there ever such a clever fellow as this Glarea? He thinks he can impose on God like the man in Aesop who for the sake of deceiving him consulted Apollo as to whether the sparrow he was holding under his cloak was alive or dead. For it was not to me but to God that you said, 'Predict' . . . .

ANTONIO – So what would he reply?

LORENZO – Certainly he might tell me, he might tell one of those people over there, he might tell many people what you would do, but not in your hearing: and when he has done that do you not think he will have predicted the truth?

ANTONIO – Yes, indeed. . . .

LORENZO – . . . But let us leave this out, which has nothing to do with foreknowledge. For it is one thing to foreknow and another thing to foresay the future. Say whatever you have to say about foreknowledge, but leave foresaying out of it.

(294–302, 316–322, 373–377, and 382–385)

The prevalence of the doctrine of liberty [libertarian freewill – AF] may be accounted for from another cause, viz., a false sensation, or seeming experience, which we have, or may have, of liberty or in-difference in many of our actions . . . we may observe that though, in reflecting on human actions, we . . . are commonly able to infer them with considerable certainty from their motives, and from the disposition of the agent; yet it frequently happens that, in performing the actions themselves we are sensible of something like it; and . . . this has been employed as a demonstrative or even intuitive proof of human liberty. We feel that our actions are subject to our will on most occasions, and imagine that we feel that the will itself is subject to nothing, because, when by a denial of it we are provoked to try, we feel that it moves easily every way, and produces an image of itself ... even on that side on which it did not settle. This ... we persuade ourselves, could at that time have been completed into the thing itself, because, should that be denied, we find upon a second trial that at present it can. We consider not that the fantastical desire of showing liberty is here the motive of our actions. And it seems certain that, however we may imagine we feel a liberty within ourselves, a spectator can commonly infer our actions from our motives and character; and, even where he cannot, he concludes in general that he might, were he perfectly acquainted with every circumstance of our situation and temper, and the most secret springs of our complexion and disposition. (§ VIII (i))

The Oedipus Effect is the most interesting and humanly important special case of the very general phenomenon of the impact of the investigator upon his objects of inquiry. This has in our century found its place even in the theories of physics, as the Principle of Indeterminacy, or the Uncertainty Principle. But it is, of course, primarily in the human sciences that it constitutes a perennial and pervasive source of methodological difficulty: consider, for instance, the dilemmas which it must present to the anthropologist doing his field work. Hume himself, thinking in a Cartesian way of psychology as essentially introspective, insisted in the 'Introduction' to the *Treatise* that it must render psychological experiment impossible:

> When I am at a loss to know the effects of one body upon another in any situation, I need only put them in that situation, and observe what results from it. But should I endeavour to clear up after the same manner any doubt ... by placing myself in the same case with that which I consider, it is evident this reflexion and premeditation would so disturb my natural principles, as must render it impossible to form any just conclusion from the phenomenon.

But now, at last, what is the bearing of this upon questions about determinism? The first and less disputatious conclusions are about the Oedipus Effect. For surely what Valla and Hume say is correct: that it has no tendency to show that foreknowledge of human behaviour is impossible; but that anyone who aspires to make such warranted forecasts must either, easily, take care that these are not communicated to the persons concerned or, a much trickier business, make allowance in his forecasts for the impact of this communication?

So far the present section has done two things, explained the notion of inevitability which is an essential element in our ideas both of causation and of laws of nature, and drawn attention to the nature and importance of the Oedipus Effect. It is at last time to consider how, if at all, such inevitability is to be reconciled with the presuppositions of human action. It is worth underlining once more that the problem arises because we are agents only and precisely in so far as, in some everyday sense, we could have done other than we did. If their strong-arm men overpower me and fling me out of the window, then there is no question of my needing to excuse my 'action' in thereby smashing your glasshouse and ruining your prize-winning orchids. For I did not do anything. I simply was a helpless missile projected by others. But if, on the other hand, I broadcast an appeal for collaboration with either the German or the Russian occupying forces in Czechoslovakia or wherever, then I do need to try to excuse myself in some way. For certainly I did do it. And even if I did it – I protest – only under compulsion from the men of the Gestapo or the KGB, still I could have refused; as some of my braver compatriots did. So, in so far as a statement of a law of nature is a statement of what happens inevitably, the ideas of human action and of laws of nature seem to be incompatible.

If the resources of philosophical diplomacy prove inadequate to effect any reconciliation here, then the repercussions of the conflict must be very wide indeed. Assuming that we cleave to the truth that we are very often agents, then we shall have to concede that there just are no psychological laws comprehending that largest and most interesting part of human behaviour. Some narrow-minded natural scientists might perhaps accept this implication with equanimity. But it is not only the ambitions of psychologists which would be discomfited. For whenever a person does something all manner of physical, chemical, and physiological occurrences are involved in his action; I cannot make my broadcast unless my lips, and tongue, and larynx move in the appropriate ways; and so on. If therefore, on the present assumptions, we are to save the ideal of universal laws within even the natural sciences it would seem that it can only be by maintaining that the true agent – the person – is really an incorporeal manipulator using the human organism as its instrument. Descartes, as we shall be seeing soon in Part Three, did exactly this. For he urged that, while the material organism is wholly subject to mechanical laws, the springs of our actions are prods intruded from outside the mechanical system of material nature by our immaterial souls.

So, unless we are content to abandon the ambitions of both the natural and the human sciences, or unless we are prepared to pretend that we never really do act, a peace-making formula is required urgently. The best suggestion which I can offer at this stage is that we should take as a hint the fact that the term *inevitable*, in its practical sense and in the context of human activities, is elliptical. We need, therefore, always to be ready to ask, 'Inevitable by whom?'; just as we should be ever alert to demand that too general talk about freedom be made usefully specific by answering the corresponding question, 'Freedom from what?'

Thus, seen from Copenhagen, the German invasion of Denmark in 1940 was no doubt inevitable; in as much as there was absolutely nothing any Dane could have done which would have prevented it. It was, therefore, reasonable for Danes to be at least in this respect fatalists. Yet this is neither to say nor to imply that it was inevitable by anyone. For, in particular, it would obviously be false to assert that for Adolf Hitler who in fact ordered it there was literally no alternative – that he was on that occasion, as he was apt to boast, "simply following his destiny like a somnambulist". Similarly, and notoriously, freedom from colonial rule and freedom from 'capitalist exploitation' are not as such and necessarily guarantees of freedom from hunger or freedom from the tyranny of a self-perpetuating oligarchy of party bosses; and so on.

Certainly both these observations are valuable for our historical and political thinking. The immediate relevance here of the former lies in the possibility of qualifying the notion of a law of nature in such a way that any inevitability involved is interpreted, not as inevitability by absolutely anyone, but as inevitability by everyone with the possible exception of any human agent whose behaviour falls within the scope of the law in question. Given this understanding any physiological, psychological, historical, or other law which happens to cover on some particular occasion some aspect of either my internal economy or my external behaviour, will, in its refer-ence to this, be construed as saying only that such and such will in fact occur; and that, even if this particular such and such happens to be a thing which I could prevent, in fact I will not prevent it.

No doubt, if any such formula is going to provide an acceptable basis for a reconciliation between the deterministic presupposition of science and that possibility of an alternative which is essential to the very idea of human action, then a deal of elaboration, exploration, and precisification will be required. Yet even now and without this we can be sure that these peace talks will break down if it turns out to be impossible to maintain the contention of the end of the previous section, that foreknowledge as such is not compatible with responsible human action. Furthermore, this disruptive conclusion must certainly follow if the philosophical libertarian ever succeeds in showing that his distinctive ideas are essentially involved in the crucial notion of having an alternative. For to allow that some events in this area cannot be foreknown, that they are unpredictable in principle, would for the determinist be not a tolerable concession but total defeat.

If, however, the concession were made quite general it would also be contrary to much familiar fact. For, as Hume insists in his first *Inquiry*, a great deal of successful forecasting of human behaviour does in fact occur: much of our practice is premised on these actual possibilities; while our science presupposes the subsistence of universal regularities everywhere:

> The mutual dependence of men is so great in all societies that scarce any human action is entirely complete in itself, or is performed without some reference to the actions of others, which are requisite to make it answer fully the intention of the agent. The poorest artificer who labours alone expects at least the protection of the magistrate to insure him the enjoyment of the fruits of his labour. He also expects that when he carries his goods to market and offers them at a reasonable price, he shall find purchasers and shall be able, by the money he acquires, to engage others to supply him with those commodities which are requisite to his subsistence. . . . A manufacturer reckons upon the labour of his servants for the execution of any work as much as on the tools which he employs, and would be equally surprised were his expectations disappointed. . . .
>
> Nor have philosophers ever entertained a different opinion from the people in this particular. For, not to mention that almost every action of their life suppose that opinion, there are even few of the speculative parts of learning to which it is not essential. What would become of history had we not dependence on the veracity of the historian according to the experience which we have had of mankind? How could politics be a science if laws and forms of government had not an uniform influence upon society. . . . And with what pretense could we employ our criticism upon any poet or polite author if we could not pronounce the conduct and sentiments of his actors either natural or unnatural to such characters and in such circumstances?   (§ VIII (i))

§7 *Choice and desire*

A comprehensive examination of the subjects of the present chapter would demand a direct and sustained attack on the question whether that notion of having an alternative which is crucial to the whole conception of human action does or does not presuppose philosophical libertarianism. The best tactics for such an attack would probably be to approach the more intractable and hence here more important ideas of regret and remorse by way of easier and so less interesting cases. Thus if I were to boast that I could have killed the whole lot of them with one burst, if only I had been carrying my trusty Sten gun, there is, surely, no reason to think that my claim presupposes libertarianism. But it is perhaps a different as it is certainly a more difficult matter when I say that I could, or would, have been a physicist if only I had chosen to study on the science rather than the humanities side of my boarding school; or when I reproach myself with a failure where it seems that if only I had tried harder I could have been successful.

However, if Chapter VII is to remain introductory and to end soon, that must be left as one of the inquiries which the introduction introduces. So the remaining pages will be devoted instead to suitably introductory yet fundamental points about choice and desire. The main passages for study are drawn from *The Leibniz-Clarke Correspondence*. This is primarily concerned with the metaphysical implications of the physics of Newton. Its importance and interest is greatly increased by the fact that Dr Samuel Clarke wrote with the guidance and tacit approval of Newton himself, who was shy of engaging in controversy directly. The first passages quoted come from the fourth letter by Leibniz. It is both remarkable and quite typical of philosophy that these considerations about choice and desire occur, with perfect relevance, in a discussion of the nature of space and time:

(*i*) Where things are absolutely indifferent there is no such thing as choice, and consequently no such thing as election or will, since a choice requires some reason or principle.

(*ii*) A mere will without any motive is a fiction which is not only contrary to the perfection of God but also chimerical, contradictory, incompatible with the definition of *will*, and sufficiently refuted in the *Theodicy*.

(*iii*) To place three bodies which are equal and alike in all respects in whatever order one wishes is a case of indifference; and, consequently, they will never be so placed by he who does nothing without wisdom. But then, as he is the author of things, he will not produce anything of the sort; and, consequently, there is nothing of the sort in nature.

(*iv*) There is no such thing as two indiscernible individuals. A talented gentleman of my acquaintance, talking with me in the presence of her highness the Elector in the garden of Herrenhausen, believed that he could find two leaves which were perfectly alike. Her highness the Elector defied him to do it, and he ran about for a long time fruitlessly searching. Two drops of water or of milk looked at under the microscope will be discovered to be discernible. This is an argument against atoms, which are just as much confuted by the principles of true metaphysics as is the vacuum.

(*v*) These great principles of Sufficient Reason and of the Identity of Indiscernibles change the condition of metaphysics, which becomes through them genuine and demonstrative where before it consisted of little but empty words.

(*vi*) To postulate two indiscernible things is to postulate the same thing under two names. So the hypothesis that the universe might have had a different position in time and space from that in which it actually was, while yet all the parts of the universe still retained the same relative positions as they then in fact had, is an impossible fiction.

(*vii*) The same reason which shows that space outside the universe is imaginary, proves that all empty space is something imaginary; for they only differ as greater and less.

(*xiii*) To say that God might cause the whole universe to move forward in a straight or other line, without making any other change, is also a chimerical supposition. For two indiscernible states are the same state and, consequently, it is a change which changes nothing. Furthermore, it has no rhyme or reason. But God does nothing without reason, and it is impossible that there should be any here. Besides it would be "doing nothing by doing", as I have just said, because of the indiscernibility.

(*xiv*) These are "idols of the tribe", complete and utter chimeras, superficial imaginations. The whole thing is founded merely on the supposition that imaginary space is real.

(*xv*) It is a similar fiction, that is to say it is impossible, to suppose that God might have created the universe millions of years sooner. Those who entertain fictions of this sort cannot know what to answer to those who would argue for the eternity of the world. For God does nothing without a reason, and, since it is not possible to assign a reason why he did not create the world sooner, it must follow either that he has not created anything at all or that he produced the world before all assignable times, that is to say that the world is eternal. But when one shows that the beginning, whatever it was, is always the same thing the question why it was not other than it was lapses.

(*xvi*) If space and time were something absolute, that is to say, if they were something other than certain arrangements of things, what I say would be a contradiction. But since that is not the case, the hypothesis is contradictory; that is to say, it is an impossible fiction.

(*xviii*) The uniformity of space ensures that there is no reason, either internal or external, by which to distinguish its parts and to make a choice between them. For an external reason could only be grounded on an internal one; otherwise it would be a matter of choosing without discerning. Will without reasons would be the chance of the Epicureans. A God who would act by a will of this sort would be a God only in name. The source of these errors is that people take no pains to avoid what derogates from the divine perfections.

I have quoted more than is immediately relevant in order to give Leibniz the chance to expound and apply the second of the two "great principles"; the first made its entrance in the previous chapter (Ch. VI, § 4). His lucid and compelling argument for a relativist, as opposed to absolutist, view of space and time is characteristic of Leibniz the metaphysician; while the references to "her highness the Elector" and the English allusions in a letter written in French are equally typical of Leibniz the courtier and the diplomat. The phrase "idols of the tribe" is, by the way, borrowed from the *Novum Organum* of Francis Bacon, Lord Chancellor and prophet of empirical science (1561–1626). Bacon's own title embodied in its turn a calculated and challenging comparison with the *Organon* of Aristotle.

Returning to our present main interest, it might perhaps be objected that we can sometimes properly speak of choosing where no differences are discernible; for instance, in drawing lots or in guessing which fist the sweet is in. To this a first response would be that it seems more natural in these cases to use such words as *guess* or *draw* or *pick* instead of *choose*. But, whatever peripheral qualifications may be required, on the central point Leibniz is surely right. For, at least in a choice which is deliberate and rational, there have to be reasons for choosing in this way rather than in that; and, if there are to be any such discriminating reasons, there have to be discernible differences to provide purchase for the discriminations. Furthermore, if these are to be not indifferent reasons in the abstract but reasons for us, they have to engage with our desires and our inclinations.

It was this last and necessarily true contention which constituted Hume's warrant for claiming, in a self-consciously scandalous phrase in the *Treatise*, that "Reason is, and ought only to be, the slave of the passions. . .". When a tautology is dramatized in this way, the claim which is warranted only in its toothless interpretation is easily misconstrued in some much stronger and more disputatious sense. Thus, for instance, there is no harm – if little good – in saying tritely and tautologically that a government must govern, or that it takes two to make a quarrel. The temptation is to slide unwittingly, without further and relevant argument, to the quite different and much less indisputable conclusions that in every conflict there must be some wrong on both sides, or that "the smack of firm government" is both inevitable and desirable. Let us label this, the *Since-it-is-trivially-true-it-must-be-importantly-true Manoeuvre*:

Nothing is more usual in philosophy, and even in common life, than to talk of the combat of passion and reason, to give the preference to reason, and to assert that men are only so far virtuous as they conform to its dictates. . . . In order to shew the fallacy of all this philosophy I shall endeavour to prove, first, that reason alone can never be a motive to any action of the will; and, secondly, that it can never oppose passion in the direction of the will.

The understanding exerts itself after two different ways . . . as it regards the abstract relations of our ideas, or those relations of objects, of which experience only gives us information. I believe it scarce will be asserted that the first species of reasoning alone is ever the cause of any action. As its proper province is the world of ideas, and as the will always places us in that of realities, demonstration and volition seem, upon that account, to be totally removed from each other. . . . Abstract or demonstrative reasoning, therefore, never influences any of our actions but only as it directs our judgement concerning causes and effects; which leads us to the second operation of the understanding.

. . . It can never in the least concern us to know that such objects are causes, and such others effects, if both the causes and effects be indifferent to us. Where the objects themselves do not affect us, their connection can never give them any influence; and it is plain that, as reason is nothing but the discovery of this connection, it cannot be by its means that the objects are able to affect us.

Since reason alone can never produce any action, or give rise to volition, I infer that the same faculty is as incapable of preventing volition, or of disputing the preference with any passion or emotion. This consequence is necessary. . . . Thus it appears that the principle which opposes our passion cannot be the same with reason, and is only called so in an improper sense. We speak not strictly and philosophically when we talk of the combat of passion and of reason. Reason is, and ought only to be, the slave of the passions, and can never pretend to any other office than to serve and obey them. (II (iii) 3)

Whenever such picturesque hypostatizations of human faculties begin to be taken at all literally it becomes tempting – especially to naturally Platonic spirits – to identify themselves with reason, and to proceed thence to think of their passions as compelling them to do things. Seductive though this identification may sometimes be, it is preposterous. When I do something which I want to do because I very much want to do it I am precisely not acting under compulsion. No one is coercing me into doing what I do not want to do. For what I am doing is exactly what I do want to do.

My own desires cannot compel me, since they are not external but integral to the person supposedly being compelled. (If there really are such things as psychological compulsions these can no more be compulsions in the ordinary and primary sense than reflex actions are actions. For the man under a psychological compulsion presumably has literally no alternative, while my knee-jerk reflex – say – is not something which I do but something which I simply feel or observe occurring.)

It is also wrong, for the same and other more interesting reasons, to suggest that we are (not compelled by but) creatures of our passions – that we are puppets on the strings of our desires. The fact that I want, that I should very much prefer, to spend the day reading military history is no guarantee that I will; for I may instead do something else – the job which I am paid to do, for instance. Against this it may be urged that that will only show that some other desire or combination of desires was stronger; and hence it remains true that I am always the creature of whatever happens to be my strongest desire or combination of desires. A similar argument is also used in an attempt to demonstrate that there can be no such thing as a genuinely unselfish and disinterested action: the mere fact that I do whatever I do do shows that this seemingly splendid performance sprang simply from some want of my own – that I wanted to punish myself, perhaps.

This reply will not pass. For both arguments are specimens of the Since-it-is-trivially-true-it-must-be-importantly-true Manoeuvre. So long as the only method proposed for identifying desires as the strongest is to wait and see what is in fact done, the general conclusion – offered as if it were a discovery of empirical psychology – is no more than a tautology in disguise. Nothing at all has been said to show that it was false to say that I should very much prefer to be reading the Manstein memoirs. Similarly, the custom-built sense of *want* in which it becomes necessarily true that all your actions spring from your wants is not the relevant and everyday sense in which you might endearingly admit that you are going to visit your old aunt to cheer her up, although there is nothing which you want to do less.

The point, therefore, still stands that however much I want to do something I am often – perhaps always – able to refrain; and this constitutes a second reason why it must be wrong to suggest that we are (helpless, creatures of our desires. From all that has just been said we should learn to be very wary of talk of 'psychological drives', talk which seems to combine hints both of overwhelming coercion and of absolute literal helplessness in a single phrase. Indeed the uncharitable might suspect that the main appeal of this scientific-sounding terminological innovation just is that it does thus suggest what would more easily be seen to be untrue if we stuck to speaking colloquially of wishes and wants.

A third and final relevant point about desires is that, because these are always integral to the person, it is only to a limited extent that we can ever choose what we shall want. It is a familiar fact that, within limits, we can by taking thought and making efforts both acquire and lose inclinations. People are not, for instance, born with the taste for cigarette smoking; and it is certainly possible, although notoriously hard and unappealing, first to inhibit the habit and later and in consequence to lose even the wish to smoke. But what is not possible is that any agent – even God himself – should have chosen all his own original desires. This is necessarily impossible because, as the latest passages quoted from Leibniz and Hume make clear, choice logically presupposes preference.

So if anyone urges that he cannot properly be held responsible because he did not choose his own original desires, then this must be taken as an attack on the (or a) whole concept or pseudo-concept of responsibility rather than a protest that as a matter of contingent fact the preconditions for the application of that notion are not satisfied. (The exception, already considered sufficiently under the title *predestinationism*, would be if his point was that his original desires had in fact been chosen, but not by him.) The upshot is that we have to choose between: either abandoning such a notion of responsibility as a pseudo-concept, on the grounds that it presupposes the logical absurdity of a choice without desires; or else admitting that it may be entirely proper to hold people responsible for what they do even where their tastes and dispositions are not the outcome of their own original choices. In pondering this challenge it would be well to reread and to reconsider the passages quoted from Aristotle at the very end of § 2, and perhaps also the comments thereon made at the beginning of § 3.

I now conclude Chapter VII with two further passages from Leibniz. These offer useful revision exercise in the employment of almost all the ideas and distinctions explained earlier. Both come from his fifth letter in *The Leibniz-Clarke Correspondence*:

(*ii*) The attempt is often made to impute necessity and fatalism to me, though perhaps no one has better and more fully explained than I have done in the *Theodicy* the true difference between liberty, contingency, and spontaneity on the one hand, and absolute necessity, chance, and coaction on the other. . . .

(*iii*) It is true that reasons in the mind of a wise man, and motives in any mind at all, do what corresponds to the effect which weights produce on a balance. It is objected that this idea leads to necessity and fatalism. But this is said without proof. . . .

(*iv*) And it seems that there is play on equivocations. There are necessities which have to be admitted. For we must distinguish between an absolute necessity and an hypothetical necessity. Also we must distinguish between a necessity which consists in the opposite implying a contradiction, and which is called logical, metaphysical, or mathematical; and a necessity which is moral, by which the wise man chooses the best, and every mind follows its strongest inclination.

(*v*) Hypothetical necessity is the one which the supposition, or hypothesis, of God's foresight imposes on future contingents. And that has to be admitted unless with the Socinians one refuses to God foreknowledge of future contingents, and a Providence which regulates and governs every particular thing.

(*vi*) But neither this foreknowledge nor this predestination derogate from liberty. For God, led by his supreme reason to choose from among several orders of things (or possible worlds) that in which free creatures will take such and such decisions, albeit not without his sustaining causality, has thereby rendered every event certain and determined once for all; and without thereby derogating from the liberty of his creatures. This decree of choice as such does not in any way change but actualizes their natures, which he saw in his ideas.

(*vii*) And as for moral necessity this does not derogate from liberty either. For when the wise man – and above all God who is the sovereignly wise – chooses the best, he is none the less free on that account. . . .

(*viii*) But the good, whether true or apparent, in a word the motive, inclines without necessitating – without, that is to say, imposing an absolute necessity. For when God, for instance, chooses the best what he does not choose and what is inferior in perfection, remains none the less possible. But if what God chooses were absolutely necessary every other option would be, contrary to the hypothesis, impossible. For God chooses among possibles, that is to say, among several options none of which implies a contradiction.

(*ix*) But to say that God can only choose the best, and to try to infer from this that what he does not choose is impossible, is to confound terms – *power* with *will, metaphysical necessity* with *moral necessity, essence* with *existence*. . . .

Certainly, given that God is perfectly good, and that the situation described by the proposition *p* would be the best, it follows necessarily that God will bring about that situation; but, equally certainly, it does not follow that *p* must therefore be necessarily true. The expression "The essence of God" is the MMS analogue of "the definition of the word *God*" in the FMS; and hence we should say, in the former terminology, that the Ontological Argument constitutes an invalid argument from essence to existence. Leibniz continues, a little later:

(*xv*) It must also be recognized that properly speaking motives do not act on the mind like weights on a balance; but rather it is the mind which acts in virtue of its motives, which are its dispositions to act. And so to have it . . . that the mind sometimes prefers weak motives to stronger, and even what is indifferent to motives; this is to separate the mind from its motives, as if they were external to it as the weights are separate from the balance; and as if the mind contained dispositions to action other than motives, in virtue of which it could accept or reject motives. On the contrary the truth is that the motives include all possible dispositions to voluntary action; for they include not only the reasons but also the inclinations which arise from the feelings or other previous impressions. Hence, if the mind were to prefer the weak inclination to the strong it would act against itself and in a way different from that in which it is disposed to act. Which shows that the notions here which are in conflict with mine are superficial, and are revealed as having nothing solid in them when they are properly examined.

(*xvi*) To say too that the mind can have good reasons for acting when it has not got any motives, and when the things are absolutely indifferent . . . is a manifest contradiction; for if there are good reasons for the option which it chooses, then the things are not indifferent to it."

Part Three

CHAPTER VIII

Descartes and the Cartesian Revolution

§1 *Method for a new beginning*

The division of the history of ideas into periods is always and inevitably more or less artificial. Yet of such divisions one of the least arbitrary is that by which modern, as opposed to ancient and medieval, philosophy begins with Descartes (1596–1650); and, more precisely, with the publication in 1637 of his *Discourse on the Method*. This brief, brilliant manifesto was in every way a portent of things to come. It was, for instance, first written and printed in Descartes' native French. Only later was it to be translated into Latin, then just beginning to lose its former status as the sole and international language of learning. Then, again, the *Discourse* is remarkable for its autobiography and for its individualism. A single paragraph may tell you more of the personal life, hopes, and achievements of Descartes than you could expect to learn of Aquinas from a study of the entire *Summa Theologica*. (No doubt these two facts help to explain why many French intellectuals appear to believe that not merely modern philosophy but philosophy itself began with Descartes.)

Far more important, however, than the vernacular language and the personalized style is the shift of interests which Descartes both expressed and encouraged. He always claimed to be loyal to the Roman Catholicism in which he had been reared by his parents and by his Jesuit tutors. Notwithstanding many insinuations to the contrary – Hobbes, for instance, seems to have been characteristically mordant and uncharitable – the protestations of Descartes appear to have been sincere as well often as servile. But his own dominant intellectual concerns were in sharp contrast with those of his Scholastic predecessors and contemporaries. His main personal involvement was with not religion and theology but science and mathematics. The method which he sought, and thought that he had found, was the method for extending and vindicating these kinds of knowledge.

275

We shall never understand Descartes, or appreciate the impact of the *Discourse*, unless we recognize this, and remember that at its first publication it was bound up with three essays in the application of the method. Of these the second – *Dioptric* – was a treatise on optics, exploiting the recent invention of the telescope. The third – misleadingly entitled *Meteorology* – developed Descartes' mechanical ideas, and applied them to many different natural phenomena. But it was the first – called simply *Geometry* – which was epoch-making. For it was here that Descartes presented his invention of analytical geometry. (Hence we still speak of "Cartesian co-ordinates", *Cartesian* being the adjective from *Descartes*.) Let a historian of science sum up the importance of this invention:

> Until Descartes, algebra as the mathematics of discrete quantity was suited only to atomistic presuppositions about the structure of reality. Geometry, on the other hand, traditionally the mathematics of the spatial continuum, served only the Platonistic or the Stoic traditions, which sought to contemplate the unity of nature rather than to number her parts.
>
> Descartes abolished that distinction. The possibilities were too immense for his generation, and he himself was too much the geometer to exploit them. . . . One element in the Newtonian synthesis would be to unite an abstract and continuous conception of space with a concrete and atomistic conception of matter. Even without that hidden implication, however, the invention of analytical geometry was the most momentous contribution to mathematics since Euclid.
>
> (Gillispie, pp. 87–88)

But Descartes did not just happen to be great in both mathematics and philosophy separately. Rather he should be seen as one, and mathematically perhaps the most distinguished, of a long line of philosophers for whom mathematics provides in some way the ideal paradigm of knowledge. This succession begins with Pythagoras and the Plato of *The Republic*; it continues through Descartes, Leibniz, and Spinoza; and in our own century it includes the Bertrand Russell who wrote that introductory classic *The Problems of Philosophy*. In Part I of the *Discourse* Descartes first explains why he attaches such importance to method, and then proceeds to review the several subjects of his very thorough education at the excellent Jesuit College of La Flèche:

> Good sense is of everything in the world the best distributed, for everyone believes that he is so well provided with it that even those who are the most difficult to satisfy in every other respect do not usually

demand more of this than they have. It is not likely that everyone is deceiving himself in this matter, but instead the facts are evidence for the conclusion that the power of judging well and of distinguishing the true from the false – which properly speaking is what we mean by good sense or reason – is naturally equal in all men. Consequently, the diversity of our opinions arises from the fact that we conduct our thoughts along different paths and do not consider the same things, rather than from the fact that some have more reason than others. For it is not enough to have a good mind. The main thing is to apply it well. . . .

I was attracted above all by mathematics, because of the certitude and the evidence of the arguments there. But I did not yet appreciate its true application, thinking that it was of use only to the mechanical arts. I was astonished by the fact that when foundations are so firm and solid no one should have built anything taller on top.

Such certitude and evidence will appear especially attractive against a background of disagreement and confusion. In Part II Descartes provides this background, and draws the moral that he must make his own discovery of a legitimate basis for certainty. No one could infer from reading only this account, even when supplemented by his later *Meditations*, that the possibility of a really radical general scepticism had become an intellectual commonplace in France since the publication in the 1560's of Latin translations of the works of the Hellenistic Greek Sextus Empiricus. The finest exemplar of this influence before Descartes is the captivating and admirable Michel de Montaigne (1533–1592); from whom, incidentally, Descartes and later Hobbes derived the wry notion that common sense is of all things the most satisfactorily distributed. (See Montaigne's *Essays*, II 17; and compare *Leviathan*, Ch. XIII.) Sextus Empiricus (late 100's and early 200's AD) was himself an undistinguished writer, whose great importance lies entirely in the fact that through the accidents of loss and survival his works happen to constitute our main source for the ideas of the classical Greek Sceptics, above all Pyrrho of Elis (c. 360 – c. 270 BC).

Again, and similarly, we could never infer simply from the published philosophical writings of Descartes the even more significant fact that since Luther's great challenge at the Diet of Worms in 1521 the question of the proper criterion of authentic religious knowledge had been, and still was, the fundamental issue in dispute between Reformers and protagonists of "the Old Religion".

Descartes tells us how he met and overcame his personal crisis of scepticism while serving in the Imperial armies. This was in the early phases of what was to be the Thirty Years' War. He was able to withdraw from it all in 1621, shortly after he had participated on the winning side in the Battle of Prague ("the White Mountain"). Clearly the war had not at that stage reached the pitch of ferocity portrayed in Brecht's play *Mother Courage*. Descartes continues:

> I was then in Germany, brought there by the wars which have not yet finished; and, as I was returning to the army from the coronation of the Emperor, the beginning of winter held me up in a place where – having no conversation to divert me, and having besides, fortunately, no cares or passions to trouble me – I stayed all day shut up in a room with a stove where I had complete leisure to occupy myself with my thoughts. . . .
>
> . . . I could not approve of all those restless and interfering characters who, not being called either by their birth or their fortune to the management of public affairs, never cease from making – in thought – some fresh reformation of it. If I believed that there was the slightest thing in this essay to make anyone suspect me of this folly I should be very sorry to permit it to be published. My design has never extended further than the attempt to reform my own opinions, and to build on a foundation which is entirely my own. And although I am sufficiently pleased with my work to be presenting a draft of it here that does not mean that I want to advise anyone to imitate it.

The mixture of extreme individualistic intellectual radicalism with rather tetchy conventionality is typical. He continues, still in Part II of the *Discourse*, to explain why he felt he had to embark on this sort of reconstruction:

> As for me I should undoubtedly have been numbered among these last [those who modestly accept the opinions of other people – AF] if I had had only one teacher or if I had not known of the differences of opinion which have always prevailed among the most learned people. But I had realized from the time I was at college that one cannot imagine anything so strange and so incredible that it has not been said by some sage; and afterwards, on my travels, I had recognized that all those whose opinions are strongly contrary to our own are not on that account either barbarians or savages, but that several of them make as much or more use of reason than we do. I had taken account of the difference there is between the same man with the same heredity brought

up as a child among Frenchmen or Germans and what he would be if he had lived his whole life among Chinese or cannibals; and how, in matters of fashions of dress, what pleased us ten years ago and what may please us again before another ten years are out, now seems extravagant and ridiculous. The implication is that it is much more custom and example than any certain knowledge which persuades us. Yet the voice of a majority carried no weight as a proof where the truths are a little difficult to discover, since it is more likely that one man on his own rather than an entire people has found them. I could not pick out anyone whose opinions seemed to me to deserve to be preferred to those of others. And so I found myself as it were compelled to take charge myself of my own direction.

In what remains of Part II Descartes lays down four principles of method. These appear trite and pedestrian in the extreme. The first was "never to accept anything as true which I did not clearly know to be such"; the second "to divide each difficulty which I examined into as many parts as was possible and as was required for its best resolution"; the third to deal with problems in order of difficulty, starting with the simplest and easiest; and the fourth to make exhaustive general reviews to ensure that nothing had been left out. All this, though no doubt sufficiently sensible as far as it goes, sounds just about as fresh and arresting as the advice poured out on to all comers by Polonius in Shakespeare's *Hamlet*. The only hint of more exciting things to come is the suggestion of vast possibilities for quasi-mathematical deduction. It is this which is the true centre of the methodological vision of Descartes:

> Those long chains of reasons, all of them simple and easy, which geometers are accustomed to employ in order to reach the conclusions of their most difficult demonstrations, had caused me to suppose that everything which can fall under the cognizance of man is connected together in the same way. Provided only that we refrain from receiving anything as true which is not, and that we always preserve the order which is necessary if one thing is to be deduced from another, there can be nothing too remote for us to reach in the end, nor too hidden for us to discover. It was not much trouble for me to discover where one had to begin, for I was already acquainted with the fact that it was with the simplest things and the easiest to know. I took account of the fact that, among those who have hitherto sought for truth in the sciences, only the mathematicians have been able to discover any demonstrations – any certain and manifest reasons, that is to say – and I did not doubt but that they had conducted their inquiries in the same way.

§ 2 *Protestant individualism secularized*

In Part III Descartes considers the principles by which he should live while the work of demolition and reconstruction is in progress. Then in Part IV suddenly in a few paragraphs he unveils what was to become the main frame of reference for a series of great successors:

> I do not know whether I ought to tell you of the first meditations in which I engaged there; for they are so metaphysical and so unusual that perhaps they will not be to everyone's taste. Yet at the same time if people are to be able to judge whether the foundations which I have laid are sufficiently firm I am in a way forced to speak of them. . . . I thought that I must . . . reject as if it were absolutely false everything about which I could suppose there was the least doubt, in order to see if after that there remained anything which I believed which was entirely indubitable. So, on the grounds that our senses sometimes deceive us, I wanted to suppose that there was not anything corresponding to what they make us imagine. And, because some men make mistakes in reasoning – even with regard to the simplest matters of geometry – and fall into fallacies, I judged that I was as much subject to error as anyone else, and I rejected as unsound all the reasonings which I had hitherto taken for demonstrations. Finally, taking account of the fact that all the same experiences which we have when we are awake can also come to us when we are asleep without there being one of them which is then veridical, I resolved to pretend that everything which had ever entered into my mind was no more veridical than the illusions of my dreams.

This is the famous – or notorious – Cartesian doubt. In so far as it is now part of the popular image of the philosopher that he doubts, or pretends to doubt, what no one in his senses consistently and constantly could doubt, we owe this reputation to Descartes. (Or perhaps, in strict historical accuracy, the credit should be at least shared with the now largely forgotten Sextus Empiricus. Certainly it was from the rediscovery – which he dates incorrectly – of these writings that Pierre Bayle in the article 'Pyrrho' in his *Dictionary* reckons the beginning of modern philosophy.) Descartes continues immediately, in the same paragraph:

> But at once I noticed that while I was wishing in this way to think in this way that everything was false it followed necessarily that I who was thinking must be something. And I observed that this truth, *I think,*

therefore I am, was so solid and certain that all the most extravagant suppositions of the sceptics were unable to upset it. I judged that I could receive it without hesitation as the first principle of the philosophy which I was seeking.

For some unknown but surely insufficient reason this principle, first stated in French, is often by an extraordinary miscegenation of English and Latin called either "the *cogito*" or "Descartes' *cogito*". (*Cogito, ergo sum* is Latin for *I think, therefore I am*.) Often too it is urged that, notwithstanding the *therefore*, Descartes' principle should not be construed as embodying an inference. Certainly it is intended as primarily an expression of his own immediate and indubitable awareness of his present consciousness. In consequence of this the word *thought* in Descartes has frequently to be construed very widely, as not necessarily implying ratiocination but covering all but only modes of consciousness. It is thus equivalent to the expression *subjective experience*, in the sense explained earlier (Ch. VI, § 6). His own best explanation occurs as Principle IX of Part I of his *Principles of Philosophy*, first published in Latin in 1644. My translation is of the improved and approved French version (curiously, this work was dedicated to the eldest daughter of the King and Queen whom in the Battle of Prague Descartes had helped to drive from Bohemia):

> By the word *thought* I mean everything in us which is the object of our own immediate awareness. That is why not only understanding, wishing, and supposing, but also feeling are here the same thing as thinking. For if I say that I can see or that I am walking, and from this I infer that I am, and if by this I intend to speak of the action of my eyes or my legs, then this conclusion is not so infallible that I have no basis for doubt about it. The reason is that it is possible for me to believe that I see or am walking, notwithstanding that I do not open my eyes and do not stir from my place. For that does sometimes occur when I am asleep, and the same thing could perhaps happen if I had no body. But if instead I intend to refer only to the occurrence of my thoughts and feelings – to the knowledge which is inside me, that is, makes it seem to me that I see or that I am walking – then that same conclusion is so absolutely true that I cannot doubt it. . . .

In a new paragraph following immediately the last passage quoted from the *Discourse* Descartes continues:

> Next, I examined carefully what I was and I saw that I could suppose that I had no body and that there was no world or place where I was,

but that I could not by the same token suppose that I did not exist. On the contrary, from the very fact that I was thinking to doubt the truth of other things it followed very evidently and very certainly that I was existing. On the other hand, granted only that I had ceased to think, while all the rest of what I had imagined had been the case, I had no reason to believe that I had existed. From this I knew that I was a substance the whole essence or nature of which simply was to think; and which, to exist, needs no place and has no dependence on any material thing. Consequently I, that is to say my mind – what makes me what I am – am entirely distinct from the body; and, furthermore, the former is more easily known than the latter, while if the latter did not exist the former could be all that it is.

The Cartesian view of the nature of man thus falls squarely within the Platonic tradition. Accordingly it is, as we shall see, cherished partly for its promise of similar immortal possibilities; and the word *substance* is employed in the crucial sense explained already and characterized as 'logical' (Ch. IV, § 3). What is distinctive, and what gives ground for speaking of a Platonic-Cartesian stream within that Platonic tradition, is above all the stress on consciousness. It is Descartes and not Plato who wants to begin from and with the immediately present subjective experience of one individual.

Since on his account I am my mind, and since it is also contended that the essence – the defining characteristic – of mind is to think, which is here to say to be conscious, it must follow that for a Cartesian *unconscious mind* is a self-contradictory expression. This consequence was in his own way appreciated by Locke, and taken by him as the basis for an objection to Descartes: "Thus, methinks, every drowsy nod shakes their doctrine who teach that the soul is always thinking" (*Essay* II (i) 13). The whole passage constitutes an admirable example of Locke's characteristic refusal to overlook familiar facts for the sake of any nostrum. By contrast, it was an indication both of the pervasive persuasiveness of Cartesian presuppositions and of a less admirable mental inertia that some two centuries later there were those who took the same consequence as a decisive refutation of then recent psychological findings – above all the early work of Sigmund Freud (1856–1939).

The second main thing to notice about the Cartesian starting-point is that it raises as central and fundamental the epistemological question of whether we can know, and if so how we can know, anything about the universe around us. This question, particularly as set by Descartes, has since come to be labelled *The Problem of Our Knowledge of the External World*. Before proceeding to his own attempted solution it is just worth noticing – with disfavour – the way in which he slips from an epistemological premise to an ontological conclusion. Certainly if I were at any time wholly insensible, I could at that time be aware of "no reason to believe that I had existed"; or, for that matter, to believe anything else either. But this is no ground at all for asserting that I am "a substance the whole essence or nature of which simply is to think"; any more than the parallel facts that I was then also unaware of anything else, constitute reasons for saying that the essences of all other things consist in their being experienced by me. Descartes continues in the *Discourse*:

> After that I examined in general the question of what is required in a proposition for it to be true and certain. For since I had just discovered one which I knew to be such I thought I should also know in what this certitude consists. So, after observing that there was nothing at all in this *I think, therefore I am* which assures me that I am speaking the truth except that I can see very clearly that in order to think it is necessary to exist, I concluded that I could take it as a general rule that the things which we conceive quite clearly and quite distinctly are all true; but just remembering that there is some difficulty about distinguishing properly which are the cases in which we do conceive distinctly.

The reader will need a pause to recover his breath. He should take advantage of this pause also to recognize that what Descartes is offering is a generalized and secularized version of the ultimate criterion defended by the Reformers. Thus Calvin argues in his *Institutes of the Christian Religion* that the Church cannot be the authoritative interpreter of Scripture, since the authority of the Church is itself derived from some verses in the Bible. But then the further questions arise of how we are to know that the Bible itself is authoritative, and that this or that interpretation is correct. Calvin's answer is that it is by an indubitable inner illumination from the Holy Spirit:

> It is, therefore, a persuasion of a kind which requires no reasons; and at the same time a knowledge of a sort which is based on a very good reason. It is a matter of knowing in as much as our mind rests more certain and assured than in any reasons. Finally, it is an experience which could only be the product of a revelation from heaven. I am not saying anything but what each believer puts to the test inside himself, except that the words do such poor justice to the worth of the argument, and are inadequate to explain it properly.   (I (vii))

§ 3 *Cartesian foundations for knowledge*

The next phase in the development of the system of Descartes, now that he has to his own satisfaction established a criterion of truth and validity, is to employ this to test some arguments for the existence of God. The members of this group are chosen for their suitability to the Cartesian starting-point. Thus, whereas all the Five Ways of Aquinas take off from supposed general features of 'the External World', these are intended to provide a "knowledge of God which is easier and more certain than our knowledge of the things of the world". Indeed, by an elegant inversion which must have appealed most strongly to his mathematician's spirit, Descartes proposes to prove that the latter cannot provide a basis for, but rather presupposes, the former. (The last quotation comes from his Dedication of the *Meditations* to "the Dean and Doctors of the Sacred Faculty of Theology at Paris" – part of the Sorbonne.)

Prominent among these putative proofs, which Descartes clearly and distinctly conceives to be sound, is the Ontological Argument (Ch. VI, § 2). This meets his requirements in that its premise, in so far as it has a premise, is that the concept of God as a logically necessary being is a legitimate concept. It should be, though it often is not, distinguished from his first suggestion. This starts from the alleged psychological fact that we possess the idea of a perfect being as an item of our mental furniture. The first passage following continues from Part IV of the *Discourse*, and the second comes from the later version in the third of the *Meditations*:

> In the next place, reflecting on the fact that I was doubting and that, consequently, my being was not wholly perfect – for I saw clearly that it was a greater perfection to know than to doubt – I bethought myself to inquire from where I had learnt to think of something more perfect than I was. And I knew evidently that this must be from some entity which was in reality more perfect . . . for to receive it from nothing was a thing manifestly impossible; and because it is no less repugnant to reason that the more perfect should depend upon and be a consequence of the less perfect than that something should come about from nothing, I could not have received it from myself either. Accordingly the conclusion was that it had been put in me by an entity which was in truth more perfect than I was, and even one which possessed in itself all the perfections of which I could have any idea – that is to say, to put it in a word, which was God.

... but it is necessary to conclude, simply from the facts that I exist and that the idea of a sovereignly perfect being – that is to say, of God – is in me, that the existence of God is very evidently demonstrated.

It only remains for me to investigate how I have acquired this idea. For I did not receive it from the senses. . . . Nor is it a pure product or fiction of my own mind, since it is not in my power to add anything to it or to take anything from it. And, consequently, there is no alternative but to say that – like the idea of myself – it was innate and made part of me from the time of my creation.

Certainly one should not find it strange that God in creating me put this idea in me as the mark of the workman imprinted on his work; and furthermore, it is not necessary that this mark should be something different from the work itself.

Let us christen this the Trademark Argument. It is instructive to observe that Descartes appeals confidently and repeatedly to "the natural light of human reason" as guaranteeing the axioms upon which this argument rests. It is supposed to be thus incontestably and immediately obvious both that nothing can come about without a cause, and that nothing can be produced or sustained by a cause less perfect than itself. These principles appear – as Axioms III and IV, respectively – in a very characteristic exercise included in Descartes' replies to the second set of solicited Objections to the *Meditations*: "Reasons which prove the existence of God and the distinction between the mind and the human body, arranged as geometry." Yet, as I mentioned in the previous chapter, Hume was later to show that there is no contradiction involved in denying either of these allegedly self-evident axioms, since "we cannot know apriori . . . that any thing or sort of thing either must be or cannot be the cause of any other thing or sort of thing" (p. 254).

The modern reader who bridles at this too easily Scholastic talk of perfections will better understand both the appeal of Axiom IV and the scope and significance of Hume's great denial if he reflects for a moment how it may seem obvious that life and consciousness and intelligence could not conceivably be the effects of causes which were not themselves alive, or conscious, or intelligent. The whole Trademark Argument can be compared with Plato's Argument from Recollection in the *Phaedo* (Ch. III, § 2). Those who are making their own collections of Ostensibly Counter-evidential Intuitions will surely wish to acquire as a choice specimen Descartes' insistence that the supposedly unique and unequivocal idea of God cannot be any sort of human invention (Ch. IV, § 5).

In the next and last movement of his epistemology Descartes argues that from a logically prior knowledge of the existence of a good God "who is no deceiver", and from this alone, it is possible to derive a sure ground for confidence that our faculties are generally reliable and that we are not being systematically and inescapably deceived. The following version, taken from the fourth *Meditation*, may be especially interesting for its recognition of a Problem of Error; a special case of the theist's general Problem of Evil (Ch. I, § 2):

And when I reflect that I doubt, that is to say that I am an incomplete and dependent being, the idea of a complete and independent being, that is to say of God, presents itself to my mind with so much distinctness and clearness – and from the mere fact that this idea is found in me, or even that I am or that I exist (I who possess this idea), I conclude so evidently that God exists and that my existence depends entirely on his in every moment of my life – that I do not believe that the human mind can know anything with greater evidence and certainty. And already it seems to me that I am discovering a road which will lead us from this contemplation of the true God . . . to the knowledge of other things in the universe.

For, in the first place, I recognize that it is impossible that he ever deceives me, since there is some kind of imperfection to be found in all fraud and deception. . . .

Then, in the next place, I experience in myself a certain capacity for judging which undoubtedly – like the rest of my possessions – I have received from God. And, as he would not want to do me wrong, it is certain that he has not given me one such that I could ever err when I use it properly.

And no doubt would remain about this truth were it not that it seems that one could draw from it the consequence that, in that case, I never am mistaken. For, if I derive everything that I possess from God, and if he has not given me the capacity to err, it appears that I should never be mistaken. . . . I notice that I am a sort of half way house between God and nothing, that is to say that I am as it were situated between sovereign being and non-existence. There is in truth nothing in me which can lead me into error in so far as a sovereign being has produced me; but, if I think of myself as participating in some way in nothingness or non-existence, that is to say in so far as I am not myself the sovereign being, I find myself prey to such an infinity of deficiencies that I ought not to be surprised if I make mistakes.

This, it may be said, is one of the many places in Descartes where the supposedly natural light would appear to have been switched on artificially by his Jesuit instructors. For there had already been a long Scholastic and pre-Scholastic history of such attempts simultaneously to insist in one context that our deficiencies are terribly real while in another suggesting that they are somehow a matter of simple non-existence; and hence, apparently, not truly features of the work of the one and only and perfect Creator. Very reasonably Descartes himself comments at once: 'All the same that does not yet satisfy me completely . . .''; and proceeds to deploy further, if not better, arguments. Yet the whole performance may seem to some an application of the Ten-leaky-buckets Tactic – presenting a series of severally unsound arguments as if their mere conjunction might render them collectively valid: something which needs to be distinguished carefully from the accumulation of evidence, where every item possesses some weight in its own right.

Descartes' main argument is then applied to The Problem of Our Knowledge of the External World. Thus in the sixth *Meditation* he writes:

> Furthermore there is in me a certain passive faculty of perception, that is to say of receiving and knowing the ideas of sensible objects. But that would be useless to me . . . if there was not in me or elsewhere another and active faculty capable of forming and producing these ideas. But this active faculty cannot be in me, in as much as I am only a thing which is conscious, whereas it does not presuppose my consciousness; also these ideas are often put before my mind without my contributing to this in any way, and even against my will often. So it is necessarily the case that it resides in some substance different from me, in which all the reality subjectively in the ideas produced is formally or eminently contained.

This is one of many moments when the vocabulary of Descartes is more stilted and technical than might at first appear. This contrast between *formally* and *eminently* is Scholastic: the latter means in a pre-eminent manner or degree; the former specifies a straightforward correspondence with what is found in the effect. Descartes continues:

> And this substance is either a body, that is to say a material thing, in which everything which is subjectively and by representation in the ideas is contained formally and in reality; or else it is God himself; or else it is another created thing more splendid than body, in which that itself is contained eminently.

Now, since God is not a deceiver, it is very obvious that he does not despatch these ideas to me himself and without intermediary, and also that it is not done through the interposition of some created thing containing their reality only eminently and not formally. For as he has not given me any faculty to recognize that this is the case, but rather a very powerful inclination to believe that they are sent to me by or come to me from material things, I do not see how one could exonerate him from the charge of deceit if in reality these ideas did come from or were produced by causes other than material things. Hence we must allow that material things do exist.

However, perhaps they are not in all respects like what we perceive by our senses since this perception by the senses is in many instances very obscure and confused. But at least we must admit that everything which I conceive clearly and distinctly to be there – that is to say, everything, generally speaking, which is included among the objects of pure geometry – really is to be found there.

In that last paragraph Descartes is sketching his version of a distinction between primary and secondary qualities. A similar distinction, as we have seen already (Ch. III, § 3), is prominent also in Newton and Galileo and the other Founding Fathers of modern science. The earlier emphasis on the possibility or impossibility of being deceived, as opposed to being simply mistaken, is of course entirely appropriate in this final movement in the Cartesian epistemology. In the previous sceptical development, in the first *Meditation*, he gives this same concern memorably picturesque shape as the Evil Demon ("le malin génie").

This supposition, which seems to have been introduced first by Descartes, brings radical scepticism right to the end of the road. Perhaps he got the idea from considering one of the celebrated cases of the 1630's in France, the judicial persecution of Father Grandier for infesting a convent with devils. The frightful story is retold by the English novelist Aldous Huxley in his *The Devils of Loudun*. The case stimulated interest in the demoniac, and particularly in the evidential problems arising. The Sorbonne, for instance, had to rule on the question of the reliability of testimony given under oath supposedly by devils possessing human victims. For a more recent and secular example compare the occasion in one of the Stalinist show trials in Moscow in the late thirties when the Old Bolshevik Karl Radek, after admitting as required that he was a treacherous liar and total scoundrel, pointed out that the whole prosecution case rested upon his confession (this confession, we may add, had presumably, like those in the Grandier affair, been extracted by threats and by actual torture):

I shall suppose then that there is, not a true God who is the sovereign source of truth, but a certain Evil Demon who is as clever and deceitful as he is powerful and who has employed all his energies to deceive me. I shall consider that the sky, the air, the earth, colours, shapes, sounds, and everything which we see in the external world are nothing but illusions and tricks which he employs to gull my credulity. I shall think of myself as having no hands, no eyes, no flesh, no blood, as having no senses; but falsely believing that I have all these things. I shall remain stubbornly devoted to this supposition; and even if it is not in my power to come to the knowledge of any truth by this means, at least it is in my power to suspend judgement.

§4 *A rationalist vision*

With the completion of § 3 all the main elements of the epistemology of Descartes have made their first entrances. It remains in this fourth section and in the fifth to say something more about his ideas first of a science on the model of mathematics, and then of the person as essentially the incorporeal subject of experience. The notion of mechanism is vital in the distinctively Cartesian development of both.

This is, appropriately enough, introduced very clearly and distinctly in his treatment of the former at the beginning of Part V of the *Discourse*. Yet it appears that most readers fail fully to appreciate the nature, the extent, and consequently the boldness, of the claims which Descartes is making so confidently. Partly this is precisely because these claims are so bold and so extensive. Partly it is because the anxieties generated by the persecution of Galileo led Descartes to express himself in a way which was, for all his lucidity, rather indirect. And partly no doubt it is also because many modern readers, thinking anachronistically of Descartes as a great philosopher only in the narrowest modern sense, tacitly discount his own much wider interests. Yet what he says is:

> I would have been very glad to follow this up, and to display here the whole chain of other truths which I have deduced from these primary ones. But to achieve this I should have had to speak about several questions which are in dispute among the learned, questions in which I do not want to embroil myself. . . . I have always remained firm in my original resolution to postulate no other principle besides the one which I have just used to demonstrate the existence of God and of the soul, and not to accept anything as true which did not seem clearer and more

certain than the demonstrations of the geometers had done formerly. Nevertheless I make bold to say that, not only have I found the means to satisfy myself in short order about all the main difficulties which are customarily treated in philosophy, but I have also become aware of certain laws which God has so established in nature, and of which he has impressed such ideas in our minds, that, given sufficient reflection, we cannot doubt that these are exactly observed in all that exists or occurs in the universe. And, furthermore, it seems to me that by attending to the logical consequences of these laws I have discovered several truths more useful and more important than everything which I had learnt or even which I had hoped to learn previously.

But, because I have undertaken to explain the most important of these in a treatise which certain considerations prevent me from publishing, I cannot think of a better way of making these known than by giving a summary of the contents of that here.

The treatise mentioned thus is *Le Monde* [The Universe], eventually published in 1664 posthumously. The "certain considerations" were considerations of prudence, since Descartes maintains in *Le Monde* that the Earth is in motion. In Part V of the *Discourse*, after explaining that the suppressed work concentrated on light but had something to say on almost everything else as well, he continues:

.. in order to be able to speak my thoughts more freely, without being obliged either to adopt or to refute the opinions which are received among the learned, I resolved to abandon all this present universe to their disputes, and to speak only of what would happen in a new one if God were now to create somewhere, in imaginary space, enough matter to make it, and if he stirred up the different bits of this matter higgledy-piggledy to produce a chaos as complete as the poets ever imagined, and if after that he did nothing else but lend his ordinary concurrence to nature, leaving it to operate according to the laws which he has established. So, in the first place, I described this matter, labouring to represent it in such a way that there is – it seems to me – nothing in the universe more clear and more intelligible save what has just now been said about God and the soul. For I even supposed in as many words that it had in it none of those forms or qualities so debated by the Scholastics, nor, generally, anything the knowledge of which is not so natural to our minds that one could not even pretend not to know it. What is more, I pointed out what the laws of nature are, and, without basing my arguments on any other principle than the infinite perfections of God, I tried to demonstrate all those about which there could be any doubt, and to show that these laws are such that even if God had created several universes he would not have known how to have one in which they were not observed. After that I showed how the greater part of the matter in this chaos must, in accordance with these laws, dispose and arrange itself in a particular way which makes it resemble our heavens; and how at the same time some of its bits must make an Earth, some planets and comets, and others again a Sun and fixed stars. . . .

All the same I did not want to infer from all this that the universe had been created in the manner I was describing; for it is much more likely that, from the beginning, God made it as it must become. But it is certain . . . provided that, having established the laws of nature, he lent it his concurrence to operate in its customary way, that by that alone all things which are purely material could, given time, have got themselves into the condition in which we see them now. And their nature is much more easily conceived when one sees them coming into existence little by little in this way than when one thinks of them only as completely made.

In speaking of "his ordinary concurrence" Descartes postulates God as the universal sustainer, the First Cause without whose support the entire universe must supposedly collapse into non-existence: this is creation in the theologian's sense. In suggesting that, after all, it had not in fact "been created in the manner I was describing" Descartes introduces also the idea of creation in the beginning, creation in the layman's sense (Ch. II, § 2). The whole passage constitutes a paradigm of philosophical rationalism. In this technical but important sense of the word *rationalism* the opposite of a rationalist is not an irrationalist but an empiricist. The philosophical rationalist holds that there are self-evident and non-tautological truths from which we can deduce substantial conclusions about the way things have been, are, and will be. The philosophical empiricist denies this, urging that it is only through objective experience that we can acquire knowledge of the universe around us (Ch. VI, § 6). This technical distinction is made without prejudice to the question which of these alternatives is, in an ordinary sense, more reasonable.

§ 5 *The ghost in the machine*

For Descartes the supposedly self-evident laws of nature are mechanical: it is to him rather than to Newton that we should attribute the first vision of a clockwork universe (Gillispie, pp. 91–92). In the *Discourse* Descartes proceeds at once to apply this vision to man. Significantly he begins with an account of the mechanism of the circulation of the blood. The tribute which he pays to William Harvey (1578–1657), "an English physician", is one of his very few acknowledgements of an intellectual debt either to a contemporary or to a predecessor. It was well deserved, for Harvey's discoveries belong to that very select group of scientific achievements which are both important in themselves and far more important in their wider implications. (Compare Passmore (1) and Ch. XI, §§ 1–2, below.) Descartes writes:

> And, in order that there may be less difficulty in understanding what I am going to say, I should like those who are not versed in anatomy to take the trouble of getting the heart of some large animal with lungs . . . dissected in front of them before they read this. . . . [Descartes then describes the mechanism as he takes it to be.] . . . Now, after that, there is no need for me to say anything more to explain the movement of the heart. . . . Finally, in order that those who are not familiar with the force of mathematical demonstrations, and who are not used to distinguishing true reasons from mere probabilities, should not venture to deny what has been said without examining it, I want them to notice that this movement which I have just explained follows as necessarily, simply from the arrangement which the eye can see of the organs in the heart, and from the warmth which one can feel with one's fingers, and from the nature which one can know by experience of the blood; as does that of a clock from the power, from the position, and from the shape of its counterweights and of its wheels.

It is a remarkable index, both generally of the blinkering effects of jurisdictional rigidity in the academic world and particularly of the strictness of the institutional segregation of the humanities from the sciences in traditional English education, that in a recent pedagogically useful volume of selections from the philosophical writings of Descartes the editors chose to omit the whole of the passage from which that last extract was taken. In an explanatory footnote they describe it as "a long passage on physiology, in particular the circulation of the blood, which is now of merely historical interest" (Anscombe and Geach, p. 41). For, although the details certainly are both inaccurate and of no present concern, it does matter that the work of Harvey encouraged Descartes to believe that mechanical ideas provided the passport to an understanding of the physiology of both man and the brutes. (*The brutes* is a now rather old-fashioned expression for all animals other than men.) After further physiological detail Descartes resumes:

Nor will this appear at all strange to those who know how many automata (moving machines) can be made by human industry – and this using only a very few pieces compared with the great multitude of bones, muscles, nerves, arteries, veins, and all the other parts there are in the body of every animal. For they will think of this body as a machine which, having been made by the hands of God, is incomparably better arranged and possesses in itself movements more admirable than any of those which can be invented by men.

. . . if there were such machines having the organs and shape of a monkey or of some other animal without reason we should have no means of knowing that they were not entirely of the same nature as these animals. On the other hand, if there were those which resembled our bodies and which imitated our behaviour as far as is practically possible, we should always have two very certain ways of telling that they were nevertheless not true men. The first of these is that they could never use words or other signs arranged as we do in order to declare our thoughts to others. For one can easily conceive that a machine may be so made that it emits words, and even that it emits some which are appropriate to corporeal stimuli causing certain changes in its organs; if, for instance, we touch it in one place it asks what we want to say to it, and if in another it cries that we are hurting it, and so on. But one cannot conceive that it arranges them in various ways in order to reply to the sense of everything which is said in its presence, as the stupidest men can do. And the second is that, although they might do several things as well or perhaps better than any of us, they could not but fall short in some others, and thus we should discover that they were not acting from knowledge but only by the arrangement of their organs. For, while reason is an universal instrument which can serve on every kind of occasion, these organs need a particular arrangement for each particular action; and this is the reason why it is practically impossible for there to be sufficient variety in a machine to make it act on all the occasions of life in the same way that our reason makes us act.

Again, by the same tests we can recognize the difference which obtains between men and the brutes . . .

. . . the rational soul . . . cannot in any way be derived from the power of matter, as the other things of which I have spoken can, but must be specially created. And . . . it is not enough for it to be lodged in the human body like a pilot in a ship – except perhaps in order to move its limbs – but it is necessary for it to be joined and united more closely with the body, if it is to have feelings and desires like ours, and thus to constitute a true man. Finally, I here went into the subject of the soul at some length, on the ground that it is one of the most important. For, after the error – which I think I have refuted adequately above – of those who deny God, there is nothing which does more to lead feeble minds astray from the straight path of virtue than to imagine that our souls are of the same kind as those of the brutes, and consequently that we have nothing to fear or to hope for after this life, any more than flies and ants do. Instead, when we know how much they differ we can understand much better the reasons which prove that our souls are of a nature entirely independent of their bodies, and consequently, they are not liable to die with them. Then, because we can see no other causes which might destroy them, we are led naturally to the conclusion that they are immortal.

These words conclude Part V of the *Discourse*; and again, as previously at the end of Part IV, one may be tempted to quote T. S. Eliot:

> *We shall not cease from exploration*
> *And the end of all our exploring*
> *Will be to arrive where we started* ('Little Gidding' § V).

For these findings conform well with traditional Catholic doctrine: not only and obviously in the insistence that men, unlike the brutes, have something "to fear or to hope for after this life"; but also in the contention that human souls are logical substances which "must be specially created". Descartes' possibly confusing talk of the radically different souls of the brutes can best be understood by referring back to the explanations given already of expressions such as *the vegetative soul* in Aristotle (Ch. IV, § 4). The word *creation* in the phrase *special creation* is to be construed in the layman's sense; and the contrast is between particular things or species of things created specially, at later times, and the remainder which evolves or emerges in the ordinary course of a nature created "in the beginning". Thus Pope Pius XII in his Encyclical Letter *Humani Generis* (1930) concedes that "the teaching of the Church leaves the doctrine of Evolution an open question, as long as it confines its speculations to the development, from other living matter already in existence, of the human body". But he then reaffirms that "that souls are immediately created by God is a view which the Catholic faith imposes on us".

Yet the interpreter of Descartes must insist on adding the remainder of that quotation from Eliot:

And know the place for the first time.

For just as it is, in Descartes' view, only at the end of the exercises of Part IV, when we are equipped with proofs of the existence of a God who is no deceiver, that we can really be said to know even the simplest and most familiar truths about the universe around us; so, again in his view, it is only now that we can begin to appreciate the precise truth about ourselves. His account of what this precise truth is constitutes a main area both of tension and of promise within his new system.

The promise lies mainly in the vast possibilities of the idea that both the brutes and our human bodies either are, or can be regarded as, machines. It was an idea which obviously would be, and in fact was, later extended by spirits bolder or rasher than Descartes to cover man as a whole. Thus in the following century Julien de la Mettrie (1709–1751), a Frenchman who spent his last years under the protection of Frederick the Great of Prussia, published a book with the title – more Cartesian than Descartes – *L'Homme Machine* [Man a Machine]. In the century after that and again in our own this extension has become a more or less scandalous commonplace supported on the one hand by enormous advances in physiology and biochemistry, and on the other hand by equally enormous developments in machinery – above all that of those machines which are perhaps strictly not machines, electronic computers. (It is, by the way, not clear whether Descartes himself recognized the significance here of the distinction between actually being, and only being regarded as, a machine: if I say that I will deem you to be, that – for certain purposes – I will regard you as being, married I am precisely not saying that you actually are but, rather, presupposing the contrary!)

The tensions too have proved abundantly stimulating. Thus it was the system of Descartes which set us the modern Problem of Mind and Matter, conceived as the problem of the relations between consciousness and stuff. This, as has been remarked already (Ch. IV, § 5), did not occur to either the ancients or the medievals. It is to this question that such doctrines as Epiphenomenalism and the Mind-Body Identity Thesis are presented as answers. Epiphenomenalism consists in the contention that mental events, conceived as moments of consciousness, are always effects and never causes of physical events, in the brain or wherever. The analogies most frequently suggested are that of phosphorescence on water and – following

Curt Ducasse (1881–1969) – of "the halo on the saint". The Mind-Body Identity Thesis maintains that having a subjective experience just is being in a particular physiological condition, in the way that the morning star just is the evening star, and a flash of lightning just is a discharge of electricity.

Again, it was Descartes who bequeathed to us The Problem of Other Minds. This is the problem of how, if at all, it can be possible validly to draw conclusions about the subjective experience, the private consciousness, of other people from what seem to be the only premises which are, or ever could be, available. These premises must, at best, consist in the sum total of the behaviour of those other people. Yet subjective experience is radically and essentially private. It is private in a sense in which no behaviour, however well concealed, could ever be. Even the political police in George Orwell's *1984*, with devices to uncover my most secret thoughts, could still not inspect these for themselves as both you and I together may join in examining the furniture of the common and public world.

It is as responses to the challenge of this sort of privacy that we can best understand the three kinds of behaviourism. There is, first, metaphysical behaviourism. This is always associated with the name of the American psychologist J. B. Watson (1878–1958). It dares to maintain that really there is no such thing as subjective experience. Second, there is methodological behaviourism. Even Watson himself would probably – most of the time – have been prepared to settle for this. It recommends, without thereby necessarily presupposing metaphysical behaviourism, that psychologists should stop worrying about subjective experience and devote themselves unreservedly to the study of behaviour.

Third, there is what is called either logical or analytic behaviourism. This maintains that words and expressions which have been taken to refer to Cartesian mental events in fact refer only to actual and possible behaviour. Thus, for instance, a claim to have understood would be construed as referring not to the occurrence of a moment of private illumination but to the acquisition of capacities to manifest understanding. The undisputed example of an attempt to push logical behaviourism as far as it will go is Ryle's *The Concept of Mind*; and it might also be argued, but against bitter opposition, that another version is to be found in Wittgenstein's *Philosophical Investigations*. The behaviour to which the term *behaviourism* refers always includes not only what people do but also, what is often and importantly contrasted with this, what they say – their "verbal behaviour".

Descartes himself seems not to have been troubled by The Problem of Other Minds. Like most other innovators both in philosophy and elsewhere he failed fully and thoroughly to recognize and accept the implications of his own novelties. (Remember that folklore figure sighing in self-congratulation, "I'm an atheist now, thank God"!) The novelty here is Descartes' emphasis on consciousness: he is "a substance the whole essence and nature of which is to think"; but in his own new and peculiar sense of *think*, making the word equivalent to *be conscious*.

It is this notion which is crucial in the second of the two latest passages quoted. For, according to Descartes, the brutes are no more conscious than are inanimate objects. This is why they "have nothing to fear or to hope for after this life"; whereas we, on the contrary, precisely because we are, have. Descartes here could echo the conclusion of Shakespeare's Hamlet in the great speech contemplating suicide; where his *conscience* means the same as our *consciousness*:

> ... *the dread of something after death,*
> *The undiscover'd country from whose bourn*
> *No traveller returns, puzzles the will*
> *And makes us rather bear those ills we have*
> *Than fly to others that we know not of?*
> *Thus conscience doth make cowards of us all*...
>
> (*Hamlet* III (i))

In the earlier passage, however, where Descartes is informing us of his "two very certain ways" of telling which bodily machine has the soul in it, the emphasis is not on consciousness. It reverts, traditionally, to rationality. But now, even supposing that we were willing to allow that as a matter of fact no purely corporeal thing could ever possess the responsive versatility of a man, and consequently to hypothesize the existence of incorporeal entities to account for the various responses we were unable to attribute to anything else, still this would by no means compel us to say that these incorporeal components are – in other people – subjects of consciousness. For even if it is contradictory to say that he is rational while denying that he is conscious, it is surely not contradictory to say that this inanimate and insensible machine can match all my responsive behaviour. The price of insisting that rationality entails consciousness is that it must at once become logically possible for some object to exhibit all the behaviour appropriate to a rational being without its in fact being conscious; and hence without its being after all, in this full sense, rational.

The problem which Descartes did see, and to which he gave a prominence which was awkward for all concerned, was that of the relations between the thinking substance or rational soul and the body which was, or could be regarded as, a machine. The body is corporeal and as such, according to Descartes, subject to mechanical laws; whereas the soul is incorporeal and as such, surely, incapable of any mechanical transactions. It would seem, therefore, that any dealings between the two must be, like the dealings of an incorporeal God with his corporeal world, essentially mysterious. But to Descartes with his vision of a comprehensive and mechanistic science this was altogether unacceptable. Besides, Two-way Interactionism – the idea that mind and body each affect the other – seems at least to post-Cartesian common sense obviously true.

Again, and more particularly, a thinking substance being incorporeal cannot significantly be said to have a place in the physical world. It is, in the rather weak formulation of Descartes, one "which, to exist, needs no place and has no dependence on any material thing". Yet it is a distinctive feature of the Cartesian system that, just as thought is the defining characteristic of spiritual substance, so extension is the defining characteristic of the other sort of substance, matter. To say that something is extended is simply to say that it has dimensions. So the obvious conclusion would seem to be that a Cartesian mind cannot be said to be located in its body; and this again conflicts both with the aspirations of Cartesian science and the intuitions of common sense.

What Descartes himself said in response to this challenge is bold, curious, memorable, altogether incredible, and – on his own stated assumptions – contradictory. For all that, and indeed because of that, it is potentially a major contribution to the progress of philosophy. With uninhibited clarity and frankness Descartes reveals some of the final implications of assumptions which generations of his successors, both in philosophy and in science, were going to take absolutely for granted. Consider first two illustrations to show this persisting appeal of Cartesian assumptions. One is taken from Norman Kemp-Smith's *The Credibility of Divine Existence*, the posthumous work of one of the leading philosophical scholars of his generation:

> Those who deny the possibility of an after-life frequently base their denial upon what they consider to be the established results of the natural sciences, and especially of physiology. This ... is a mistaken estimate of what the positive sciences have so far succeeded in proving. I venture the statement – and it would have the support, I think, of

almost all workers in the field of philosophy – that the positive sciences leave us free to affirm or to deny survival after death. There is no evidence that the body has the power of generating thought and feeling; and there is no evidence, except strictly negative evidence, that the consciousness of the individual ceases for ever when the functioning of his brain is at an end.

Certainly we have overwhelming evidence that in our present state of existence our conscious life is conditioned by the body. The relation of mind and body is, however, a two-sided relation. Each influences the other; and the influence can start from either end. The mind is at least sufficiently independent of the body to influence the body; and this being so the possibility remains that it may be sufficiently independent to survive the body. (p. 363)

The second illustration is from an essay on 'The Neurophysiological Basis of Experience' by the Australian Nobel Prizewinner J. C. Eccles. Parallel passages can be found very easily in the writings of many if not most other workers in the same field. I have chosen these, partly in deference to the scientific distinction of its author, but mainly because they bring out especially well that and how the contention that I am essentially an incorporeal subject of experience complements the thesis that I have a fundamental problem of achieving knowledge of the external world. Eccles writes:

> . . . physiological investigation reveals that all perception depends on very complex processes of detection by sense organs and of transmission of signals (nerve impulses) from them to the brain. There is much neurophysiological evidence that a conscious experience arises only when there is some specific cerebral activity. . . . Thus in the case of perception, the sequence of events is that of a stimulus to a sense organ causing the discharge of impulses along afferent nerve fibres which, after various synaptic relays, eventually evoke specific spatio-temporal patterns of impulses in the neuronal network of the cerebral cortex. . . . Yet, as a consequence of these cerebral patterns of activity, I experience sensations (. . . percepts) which in my private perceptual world are 'projected' to somewhere outside the cortex. . . . (p. 268)

When I re-examine the nature of my sensory perceptions, it is evident that these give me the so-called facts of immediate experience, and that the so-called 'objective world' is a derivative of certain types of this private and direct experience. . . . It is built upon spatial relations, but also gives symbolic information in terms of secondary qualities. For example, colours, sounds, smells, heat, and cold, as such, belong only to the perceptual world. Furthermore, it is part of my interpretation of my perceptual experience that my 'self' is associated with a body that is in the 'objective world', and I find innumerable other bodies which appear to be of like nature. (p. 273)

For Eccles as for Descartes the external world begins with his own body; and the problem of knowledge of this external world is, correspondingly, the problem of how, if at all, it is possible validly to proceed from the subjective experience of this 'self' to conclusions about the existence and characteristics of those material things. A useful mnemonic to fix this complementarity in mind is provided by bringing together as question and answer two phrases both coined by Ryle: "What is the External World external to?"; "The Ghost in the Machine". The following passages all come from Descartes' treatise on *The Passions of the Soul*:

But in order to understand all these things more perfectly it is necessary to know that the soul is really joined to the entire body, and that one cannot properly say that it is in one of its parts to the exclusion of the others. The reason is that it is one and in a way indivisible, because of the arrangement of its organs which are so related to one another that when one of them is removed that makes the entire body defective. The reason is also that the nature of the soul has nothing to do with extension or with dimensions or with other properties of the matter of which the body is made, but only with the whole union of its organs; as we can see from the facts that we cannot by any means conceive a half or a third of a soul, nor what space it occupies, and that it is not diminished by the amputation of some part of the body, but separates itself from it as a whole when the union of the organs of the body is dissolved. (I (xxx))

It is perhaps just worth interrupting to remark that Descartes the summer soldier had been much impressed by the fact that people may have feelings 'in' limbs which they have lost; as also, incidentally, was the British naval hero Lord Nelson, who construed it as a proof that people are not truly corporeal. In the next passage the animal spirits flowing through their ducts are, of course, the strictly mechanical precursors of the electrical impulses passing along the nerve fibres. The gland in question is the pineal gland:

It is also necessary to know that, notwithstanding that the soul is joined to the entire body, there is nevertheless one part of the body in which it exercizes its functions more particularly than in all the others. It is commonly believed that this part is the brain, or perhaps the heart: the brain because it is to that that the sense organs are connected; and the heart because it seems as if it is in that that we feel the passions. However, by examining the matter with care, I think that I have clearly identified the part of the body in which the soul exercizes its functions immediately as being, certainly not the heart, nor yet the entire brain, but only its most inward part. This is a certain very small gland, situated in the middle of the stuff of the brain, and so suspended above the duct through which the animal spirits in its anterior cavities communicate with those in the posterior cavities, that the slightest movements in the gland can do a lot to alter the course of these spirits; and, reciprocally, so that the slightest changes which occur in the course of the spirits can do a lot to alter the movements of this gland.   (I (xxxi))

If the essentially non-spatial is to have a place, and if the essentially incorporeal is both to move and to be moved, then no doubt the place as well as the movements had best be little ones! Yet in fairness to Descartes as a philosopher we must end not with his statements but with his arguments:

The argument which persuades me that the soul cannot have in the whole body any other place where it exercizes its functions immediately, is the reflection that the other parts of the brain are all double – just as we have two hands, two eyes, two ears, and in a word all the organs of our exterior senses are double; and that, in as much as we have only a single and simple experience of one and the same thing at any one time, there must necessarily be some place where the two images which come from the two eyes, or the two other sense impressions which come from a single object by the double organs of the other senses, can unite into one before reaching the soul, so that they do not represent two objects to it instead of one. And it is easy to conceive that these images or other sense impressions unite in this gland through the medium of the animal spirits which fill the cavities of the brain; but there is no other place in the body where they can be united in this way if it is not in this gland.
(I (xxxii))

CHAPTER IX

Philosophical Doubt and Cartesian Certainty

§ 1 *Hume opposes Descartes*

Hume's critique of the Cartesian progress from a supposedly all-corroding doubt to irrefragable certainty is found in the first Part of the final Section of his first *Inquiry*. Hume, a notorious sceptic about matters of religion, begins a consideration of scepticism in general with suave and altogether characteristic irony:

> There is not a greater number of reasonings displayed on any subject than those which prove the existence of a Deity and refute the fallacies of atheists; and yet the most religious philosophers still dispute whether any man can be so blinded as to be a speculative atheist. How can we reconcile these contradictions? The knights-errant who wandered about to clear the world of dragons and of giants never entertained the least doubt with regard to the existence of these monsters.
>
> The sceptic is another enemy of religion, who naturally provokes the indignation of all divines and graver philosophers, though it is certain that no man ever met with any such absurd creature, or conversed with any man who had no opinion or principle concerning any subject, either of action or speculation. This begets a very natural question. What is meant by *a sceptic*? And how far is it possible to push these philosophical principles of doubt and uncertainty?
>
> There is a species of scepticism, antecedent to all study and philosophy, which is much inculcated by Descartes and others as a sovereign preservative against error and all precipitate judgement. It recommends a universal doubt, not only of all our former opinions and principles, but also of our very faculties, of whose veracity, say they, we must assure ourselves by a chain of reasoning deduced from some original principle which cannot possibly be fallacious or deceitful. But neither is there any such original principle which has a prerogative above others that are self-evident and convincing. Nor, if there were, could we advance a step beyond it but by the use of those very faculties of which

we are supposed to be already diffident. The Cartesian doubt, therefore, were it ever possible to be attained by any human creature (as it plainly is not), would be entirely incurable, and no reasoning could ever bring us to a state of assurance and conviction on any subject.   (XII (i))

To have recourse to the veracity of the Supreme Being in order to prove the veracity of our senses is surely making a very unexpected circuit. If his veracity were at all concerned in this matter, our senses would be entirely infallible, because it is not possible that he can ever deceive. Not to mention that, if the external world be once called into question, we shall be at a loss to find arguments by which we may prove the existence of that Being or any of his attributes.

This is a topic, therefore, in which the profounder and more philosophical sceptics will always triumph when they endeavour to introduce a universal doubt into all subjects of human knowledge and inquiry.
(XII (i))

In these passages Hume certainly delivers what Berkeley would have called "the killing blow" to any attempt to argue a way out of total Cartesian scepticism. For the systematic doubt of Descartes, whatever its actual inhibitions, officially afflicts not only our sensory but also our reasoning faculties: "And, because some men make mistakes in reasoning – even with regard to the simplest matters of geometry – and fall into fallacies, I judged that I was as much subject to error as anyone else, and I rejected as unsound all the reasonings which I had hitherto taken for demonstrations." Clearly, if this conclusion is indeed correct, then we must by the same token reject simultaneously not only the attempt of Descartes himself, but also all other future attempts, to reason a way out of total Cartesian scepticism.

Hume's further claim, that this is in any case not "possible to be attained by any human creature", is more interesting. The first point to seize is that Hume intends the *possible* here as *possible in fact*, and in particular as *possible psychologically*. His meaning comes out well in a statement on the upshot of his own radical philosophical scepticism at the end of Book I of the *Treatise*:

I am at first affrighted and confounded with that forelorn solitude in which I am placed in my philosophy, and fancy myself some strange uncouth monster who, not being able to mingle and unite in society, has been . . . left utterly abandoned and disconsolate. Fain would I run into the crowd for shelter and warmth; but I cannot prevail with myself to mix with such deformity. I call upon others to join me, in order to make a company apart; but no one will hearken to me.

Most fortunately it happens, that, since reason is incapable of dispelling these clouds, nature herself suffices to that purpose, and cures me of this philosophical melancholy and delirium, either by relaxing this bent of mind, or by some avocation, and lively impression of my senses, which obliterates all these chimaeras. I dine, I play a game of backgammon, I converse, and am merry with my friends; and when after three or four hours' amusement I would return to these speculations, they appear so cold, and strained, and ridiculous, that I cannot find it in my heart to enter into them any further. Here then I find myself absolutely and necessarily determined to live, and talk, and act, like other people in the common affairs of life. (I (iv) 7)

As far as it goes this is all very well; no doubt it is psychologically impossible to play the total Cartesian sceptic consistently. But to insist on this is scarcely to begin to meet the sceptical challenge. For if that is indeed the only sort of impossibility involved, then it still appears that the end of the road of reason must lie in cognitive despair. Precisely this was the moral being urged in France even before Descartes was born by polemicists of the Counter-Reformation. Thus Gentian Hervet, Secretary to the Cardinal of Lorraine, promised in his Preface to the Latin translation of Sextus Empiricus that these Pyrrhonian arguments would provide "a new machine of war" against the Calvinists; reducing heretics to a "forlorn scepticism", from which return to the true Faith would appear the obvious and welcome escape. (See, again, Popkin: Ch. IV and passim.) What for Hervet was a promise constituted for Hume a corresponding threat; and Hume, who was well read in the French literature and actually wrote his *Treatise* in France, was well aware of it. Yet he proposes to proceed almost immediately to "make bold to recommend philosophy, and . . . to give it the preference to superstition of every kind or denomination".

§2 *Two conditions of authentic doubt*

But now, granted that it must be impossible to reason our way out of a total Cartesian scepticism, we do not have therefore to grant that "the profounder and more philosophical sceptics will always triumph when they endeavour to introduce a universal doubt". For there remains the unexplored possibility that such universal doubt either is or presupposes some logical impropriety. Allowing that reason would indeed be powerless to lay the Demon of Descartes, perhaps it is able to show – more fundamentally – that it could not be raised legitimately in the first place. In philosophy – and not in philosophy only – it is a good policy, when confronted by two incompatible theories neither of which is acceptable, to ask whether there is not some unsound framework assumption shared by both parties. Let this, in deference to the pedagogic purposes of the present book, be labelled, *The Search-for-the-shared-assumptions-to-challenge Strategy*.

A first step in this direction is to develop Hume's observation that total Cartesian scepticism is "not possible to be attained by any human creature". One consequence is that what presents itself as Cartesian, or philosophical, doubt cannot really be doubt at all. Consider here the remarks made by Descartes himself in quite a different context at the beginning of Part III of the *Discourse*:

> And, finally, as it is not enough, before starting to rebuild the house in which one lives, to pull it down and to provide materials and builders . . . but you also need to be provided with another in which you can live comfortably in the period while work is in progress; so, in order that I should not be irresolute in my actions while reason compelled me to be in my judgements, . . . I formed a provisional ethic, which consisted in only three or four maxims. . . .
>
> The first was to observe the laws and customs of my country, keeping a steady hold on the religion in which by the grace of God I had been instructed since infancy, and regulating my conduct in every other matter in accordance with the most moderate opinions . . . which were generally received and practiced among the most judicious of those among whom I was going to have to live. . . . And, in order to know what their opinions really were, I needed to pay attention more to what they did than to what they said. Not only because in these corrupt times there are few people who are willing to say everything which they believe, but also because many do not know themselves.

It is just worth remarking in passing that it is a scepticism considerably less than total which involves "keeping a steady hold on the religion in which by the grace of God I had been instructed since infancy." But for us now the significant thing is the final clause, "but also because many do not know themselves." For if Descartes is right about this, as he surely is, then there must be at least some truth in analytical behaviourism: at least part of what it means to say that he believes this or doubts that must be that he is disposed, or not disposed, to behave in certain sorts of ways. If someone says that he believes this or doubts that, while acting as if he did not, then his behaviour is evidence to the contrary; evidence which cannot be discounted by reference solely to facts about his states of consciousness. Suppose that, having carefully shut yourself up in a room with a stove, thereby for a time warding off most of the demanding and revealing tests of action, you report that while in this retreat you doubted almost everything. Then the fact that you were even then always ready to act as if you were utterly confident of all the things which you were persuading yourself that you doubted must constitute a decisive reason for saying that you were never in any straightforward sense doubting at all.

This first point about the nature of doubt is interesting mainly as reinforcing the suggestion that many notions which we think of as distinctively mental may actually refer partly, or primarily, or even – as the analytical behaviourist would have it – wholly and exclusively to behaviour or dispositions to behave. A second point shows that a universal doubt must be logically vicious, and not only psychologically impossible. This second point is that all doubt necessarily presupposes some ground or grounds of doubt. Suppose that I know literally nothing about comparative phlebotomy; a condition which is easily met since, so far as I know, there is no such subject. Then I cannot be in a position, properly speaking, to doubt what is said on a particular page of Dr Deadhead's monumental *Textbook of Comparative Phlebotomy*. For I cannot have any grounds. This second point is tacitly accepted by Descartes in Part IV of the *Discourse*, in a passage quoted already (Ch. VIII, § 2):

> I thought that I must . . . reject as absolutely false everything about which I could suppose there was the least doubt. . . . So, on the grounds that our senses sometimes deceive us, I wanted to suppose that there was not anything corresponding to what they make us imagine. And, because some men make mistakes in reasoning. . . . I judged that I was as much subject to error as anyone else, and I rejected as unsound all the reasonings which I had hitherto taken for demonstrations. Finally, taking account of the fact that all the same experiences which we have when we are awake can also come to us when we are asleep without there being one of them which is then veridical, I resolved to pretend that everything which had ever entered into my mind was no more veridical than the illusions of my dreams.

Certainly Descartes cannot be faulted for failing to offer grounds. So he provides no further purchase here for the charge that it is not authentically doubt. But, precisely in his thus offering the necessary grounds, he finds himself unavoidably committed to claims which not merely do not prove, but are formally inconsistent with, the conclusion which they are deployed to support.

Since Descartes says (he knows that) "some men make mistakes in reasoning", then he cannot consistently claim to doubt, much less to reject as unsound, "all the reasonings which he had hitherto taken for demonstrations". For among these must be those which led him to conclude that other people fall into error – "even with regard to the simplest matters of geometry". Again and similarly with the senses, since Descartes knows that "our senses sometimes deceive us", then presumably he knows this only and precisely because he knows that sometimes we are misled to think that the things around us are not as they in fact are. But this is clearly inconsistent with any claim to doubt, or not to know, whether there is anything there at all. Descartes, therefore, actually did put forward a sophism identical in form with the egregiously fallacious First Cause argument sometimes attributed, incorrectly, to Aquinas (Ch. VI, § 3).

Some may object that the present section has been unduly verbal, too much concerned with the ways in which it would or would not be correct to employ the English word *doubt*. To this the first reply must be similar to that offered earlier in defence of Aristotle (Ch. VII, § 2); that there is no way to elucidate the concept of doubt other than to investigate the use and the correct usage of the word *doubt*, and of its equivalents in other languages. But it is also appropriate to reply that what such an objector might be inclined to dismiss as trivial verbal niceties do bear upon obviously substantial philosophical issues. We have already seen how the first is relevant to the truth of one kind of behaviourism. Both this and the second also carry suggestions of the fundamental criticism of Cartesian method developed by C. S. Peirce in his paper on 'Some Consequences of Four Incapacities':

Descartes is the father of modern philosophy, and the spirit of Cartesianism – that which principally distinguished it from the scholasticism which it displaced – may be compendiously stated as follows:

(*i*) It teaches that philosophy must begin with universal doubt; whereas scholasticism had never questioned fundamentals.

(*ii*) It teaches that the ultimate test of certainty is to be found in the individual consciousness; whereas scholasticism had rested on the testimony of sages and of the Catholic Church. . . . .

In some, or all of, these respects most modern philosophers have been, in effect, Cartesians. Now without wishing to return to scholasticism, it seems to me that modern science and modern logic require us to stand upon a very different platform from this.

(i) We cannot begin with complete doubt. We must begin with all the prejudices which we actually have when we enter upon the study of philosophy. These prejudices are not to be dispelled by a maxim, for they are things which it does not occur to us can be questioned. Hence this initial scepticism will be a mere self-deception, and not real doubt; and no one who follows the Cartesian method will ever be satisfied until he has formally recovered all those beliefs which in form he has given up. It is, therefore, as useless as a preliminary as going to the North Pole would be in order to get to Constantinople by coming down regularly upon a meridian. A person may, it is true, find reason to doubt what he began by believing; but in that case he doubts because he has a positive reason for it, and not on account of the Cartesian maxim. Let us not pretend to doubt in philosophy what we do not doubt in our hearts.

(Vol. V, pp. 156–157)

Since, therefore, doubt to be truly doubt has to have grounds, it would seem to follow that, if we are ever to come to have doubted all that which we happen to believe now, then this could only be through our having doubted all these present beliefs, not collectively and simultaneously, but severally and successively. The Cartesian programme for a once for all and wholesale doubt might thus be compared with a project to test, and possibly remove and replace, all the plates in the hull of a ship at one time and while at sea. And, furthermore, since genuine doubt must manifest itself in conduct on appropriate occasions, we cannot – this time as a matter of psychological fact – doubt everything and entirely at will: "I find myself absolutely and necessarily determined to live, and talk, and act, like other people in the common affairs of life."

This response, however, is not adequate to the Cartesian challenge in its strongest form. Certainly, as we have just seen, Descartes in the *Discourse* does meet the demand for grounds for his wholesale doubt by making claims inconsistent with the conclusion they are supposed to support. But in the *Meditations* he is more subtle. For there, above all in the supposition of the Evil Demon, the doubt is grounded not on references to actual past mistakes, but upon the perennial theoretical possibilities of error (Ch. VIII, § 3). To counter this more subtly grounded scepticism an opponent will have to argue: either that these supposed theoretical possibilities are somehow not even theoretical possibilities; or else – or perhaps additionally – that a theoretical possibility of error cannot constitute a sufficient warrant for doubt. For, as we have also just now remarked, to rest the case upon the psychological point made so memorably by Hume would be to abandon the field of reason to the radical sceptic.

§ 3 *Inexpressible doubt and logically private language*

So let us consider each of these two possible responses in turn, beginning by repeating two key sentences from the first *Meditation*:

> I shall suppose then that there is, not a true God who is the sovereign source of truth, but a certain Evil Demon who is as clever and deceitful as he is powerful, and who has employed all his energies to deceive me. I shall consider that the sky, the air, the earth, colours, shapes, sounds, and everything which we see in the external world are nothing but illusions and tricks which he employs to gull my credulity.

We must now press the question of how precisely it is to be supposed that we may be being deceived. We are all, of course, altogether familiar with some illusions and tricks: the Müller-Lyer illusion; the realistic dummy aircraft deployed on the abandoned airfield in order to deceive enemy aerial reconnaissance; the lump of soap cunningly fashioned to look like a luscious apple; and so on. But in supposing that all those things "which we see in the external world are nothing but illusions and tricks which he employs to gull my credulity" Descartes surely overreaches himself. Certainly we can sensibly suggest that this here may turn out to be a joke soap apple, while that there looking so like a MIG 21 is really only a dummy. But it is not sensible, it is indeed quite unintelligible, to say the same things when you are contentedly munching the one or dashingly piloting the other. To suggestions of this sort what can we do but reply, in the spirit of Mr Damon Runyon, that if the apple which I am eating is not a real apple, if the machine which I am piloting is not a real aircraft, they will both at least do until real apples and real aircraft come along?

The difficulty for Descartes is that, if the supposition of the Evil Demon is to add anything to the argument, then it must involve the idea of an all-inclusive error. Yet to suppose an all-inclusive trick or illusion is to suppose what, for reasons of the kind indicated in the previous paragraph, is manifestly not true. Nor is all the power and ingenuity of the supposed Evil Demon of any avail in this context. Allow that he "is as clever and deceitful as he is powerful", and that he "has employed all his energies to deceive me". Then he must have succeeded in producing dummy aircraft which we cannot in any way distinguish from the real thing. Yet precisely this complete success must be for an Evil Demon failure. For who but the Deceiver is now deceived? And what is what is absolutely indistinguishable from the real thing but the real thing itself? (See Ch. VII, § 7, above; on "the great principle . . . of the Identity of Indiscernibles"!)

Suppose now that the suggestion is, not that the things "which we see in the external world are nothing but illusions and tricks which he employs to gull my credulity", but that I do not really see anything at all. Suppose further that we combine this idea of the Evil Demon with the suggestion made in Part IV of the *Discourse*: "Finally, taking account of the fact that the same experiences which we have when we are awake can also come to us when we are asleep without there being one of them which is veridical, I resolved to pretend that everything which had ever entered into my mind was no more veridical than the illusions of my dreams." It is perhaps possible that an Evil Demon has provided me with all my (subjective) experiences; that I have never truly perceived anything; and even that there is in fact – spirits being incorporeal – nothing to perceive.

One response to this might be to recall that we know a language; that this language contains innumerable words for sorts of material thing; and that we could not have learnt the meanings of any of these words had our seniors not been able to indicate, and we to discern, actual specimens of many of these sorts of thing. There is a passage in the *Confessions* of St Augustine which can be cited here to underline the importance in philosophy of the Wittgensteinian question, 'How would you teach that word?':

> Passing on from infancy I came to boyhood. . . . I was no longer a speechless infant now, but a boy and talking. I remember this, and afterwards I noticed how I had learnt to talk. My seniors did not teach me by presenting me with the words in some set order of teaching, as they did with letters a little later. Instead I myself with the mind which you gave me, O my God, tried to express my internal thoughts through gruntings, through a variety of vocal sounds, and through various movements of my parts, in order that I should get what I desired. But I could not express everything I wanted to express, nor could I express it to everyone to whom I wanted to express it. Then I pondered on my experience: when those elders themselves named something and when

they moved their bodies towards something which had been thus named, I noticed; and I grasped that the thing was called by the sound which they uttered when they intended to show me it. And that this is what they meant was revealed to me by the movements of their bodies, by – so to speak – the natural language of all peoples; which discovers the affections of the mind – to seek, to have, to reject, or to escape – by the expressions of the face, by the cast of the eyes, by the sounds of the voice, and by the movements of the other parts. Thus I came little by little to understand the meanings of the words which I heard used often in context in a variety of sentences; and, after I had disciplined my mouth to them, I expressed my own desires through these words. So I communicated by means of these signs with those around me, using them to express what I wanted. Hence I entered more deeply into the dangerous society of human life, while depending still on the authority of my parents and being at the beck of my elders. (I, § 8)

Certainly in elucidating the meanings of our words it is always important to remember that and how these meanings in fact are and have to be taught. But as an answer to Descartes here it will not do simply to refer, however truly, to the large part which various sorts of showing – Ostensive Definitions – do in fact play in our teaching and learning of words. It will not do because the proposal of Descartes concerns, not what actually is the case, but what it is logically possible to suppose; what, that is to say, can be suggested significantly and without self-contradiction. And surely, Descartes might reply, a sufficiently powerful Evil Demon could have created me as an adult, fully-armed with my present knowledge of language? Could I not in that event have understood the Cartesian suggestion that whatever I now take to be my waking experience is really only subjective, "no more veridical than the illusions of my dreams"? For certainly, as things actually are, I can understand what it would mean to say 'I can see a unicorn' – notwithstanding that none of my tutors has ever been able to introduce me to a flesh-and-blood specimen of that fabulous beast.

To avoid this defence the critic of radical scepticism has to show: not just that the terms employed in expressing this radical scepticism could in fact only have been learnt in ways inconsistent with the truth of its suppositions; but rather that these terms cannot be employed at all without logically presupposing some knowledge incompatible with radical Cartesian doubt. The difference is crucial, and needs to be laboured. For the doubts of such a radical sceptic must, of course, embrace all our present certainties about what is and is not possible, the world being as we normally suppose it to be. To appeal, therefore, for his refutation to these practical impossibilities would be no more – and no less – adequate than to stand pat on any other certainty about any other matter of logically contingent fact.

But now reread yet again that key passage from the *Discourse* quoted for the second time in the previous section (p. 306). Compare too what was said much earlier about the 'What is X?' form of question, which is so characteristic of Plato's 'Socrates' (Ch. II, § 2). By arguments like that of the concluding sentence of Book I of *The Republic* the 'Socrates' of Plato's earlier dialogues wrought havoc: "For when I do not know what justice is I can scarcely know whether it is a virtue or not, and whether he that possesses it is unhappy or happy." This, surely, is undeniable? And yet in dialogue after dialogue we are shown how someone, who is of all people the exemplar and standard of some particular virtue, cannot nevertheless satisfy the demand of 'Socrates' to know what that particular virtue is.

To resolve this paradox, to expose what has earned the label *The 'Socratic' Fallacy*, we have to make a distinction between two senses of *know what X is*. For 'Socrates' to know what X is always is – or would be – to be able to produce a satisfactory definition of the word *X*. (It is no doubt ultimately to him that philosophers owe their reputation for asking for definitions of words which the layman does not think require elucidation.) But this definitional employment of the expression is not its only or primary use. For in that, the recognitional, sense of *know what X is* it is necessary and sufficient to such knowledge simply to be able to use the word *X* correctly in ordinary and typical contexts. There is, therefore, no call to be surprised that the hero Laches, who will unfailingly recognize courage or the lack of it when he meets them, should lack the facility to frame a definition of the word *courage* able to survive the probing cross-examination of the philosopher. (And there is still less call to be surprised when that philosopher demands – as 'Socrates' did – a definition adequate not only to actual, ordinary, and typical cases but also to possible, extra-ordinary, and marginal ones.)

Applying all this to radical Cartesian scepticism, it becomes clear that in order to formulate his doubts the sceptic has to presuppose some recognitional knowledge of what certain things are. In this interpretation the Socratic truism is undoubtedly true. Even the radical sceptic requires to know what he is talking about, at least in the absolutely minimal sense of knowing the meanings of his own words. So when Descartes tells us, "I rejected as unsound all the reasonings which I had hitherto taken for demonstrations", he is clearly by saying this in some way presupposing that he knows what a fallacy is, and how fallacies are to be distinguished from valid arguments. But now, waiving all questions about how in fact we did learn or must have learnt the meanings of these terms, a claim not to be able even in the simplest text-book case to recognize a valid argument and to detect a fallacy cannot consist with a claim to know the meaning of the two key expressions *fallacious argument* and *valid argument*. Again, and similarly, it will scarcely do to confess to a complete inability to distinguish the "experiences which we have when we are awake" from those "which come to us when we are asleep" if you are proposing in the same breath to suggest, in the words of Shakespeare's Prospero, that perhaps

> *. . . the baseless fabric of this vision,*
> *The cloud-capped towers, the gorgeous palaces,*
> *The solemn temples, the great globe itself,*
> *Yea, all which it inherit shall dissolve,*
> *And, like this insubstantial pageant faded,*
> *Leave not a wrack behind. We are such stuff*
> *As dreams are made on. . . .* (*The Tempest* IV (i))

Had any criticism on these lines been put to Descartes he would probably have tried to dismiss it too as irrelevant. For in that room with a stove, he might have said, I never attempted in any way to communicate my systematic doubts to anyone else. Indeed part of what I was then so systematically doubting was the existence of anything else, whether other things or other people or even my own body. I was just thinking my own thoughts privately to myself; and, furthermore, I was "thinking of myself as having no hands, no eyes, no flesh, no blood" and "as having no senses".

But now, if this reply is to be allowed to be apt, Descartes must be interpreted to be assuming that what he then said to himself was, or at least could have been, said in a logically private language. Certainly if it was, and had to be, said in a logically public language then the mere fact that Descartes chose to talk only to himself would be irrelevant; just as it would be equally irrelevant had he chosen – as Locke later did – to render his secret thoughts from his own tongue into a code which he alone happened to know. What is definitionally essential to a logically public language is that the criteria determining the applicability of its expressions must be, in principle if not always in practice, publicly available. Correspondingly, it would be essential to a logically private language that it must be possible to explain the meaning of its terms by reference only to the subjective experience of the user.

Of course, Descartes himself did not formulate either of these two notions. It has been left to the successors of Wittgenstein to display the enormous and pervasive importance of the latter as a covert assumption, after Wittgenstein in his posthumously published *Philosophical Investigations* had massively assaulted it as radically incoherent. Incidentally he there mentions the passage which I quoted just now from St Augustine, and remarks: "Augustine describes the learning of human language as if the child came into a strange country and did not understand the language of the country, that is, as if it already has a language, only not this one" (§ 32). (Characteristically Wittgenstein provides no reference; and, equally characteristically, his Editors fail to repair this omission.)

As an illustrative introduction both to this idea, or pseudo-idea, of a logically private language, and to the structuring concepts of his own *Essay concerning Human Understanding*, consider some passages from Locke. Locke was an undergraduate at Oxford at a time when the latest revolution in philosophy, had anyone then employed that phrase, was that of Descartes; and later, in his *First Letter to Stillingfleet*, Locke acknowledged to Descartes "the great obligation of my first deliverance from the unintelligible way of talking in philosophy in use in the schools in his time". Locke himself tells us, in an introductory 'Epistle to the Reader', how the *Essay* was conceived:

> . . . five or six friends meeting at my chamber, and discoursing on a subject very remote from this, found themselves quickly at a stand, by the difficulties that rose on every side. After we had awhile puzzled ourselves, without coming any nearer a resolution of those doubts which perplexed us, it came into my thoughts that we took a wrong course; and that before we set ourselves upon inquiries of that nature, it was necessary to examine our abilities, and see what objects our understandings were, or were not, fitted to deal with. This I proposed to the company, who all readily assented. . . . Some hasty and undigested thoughts . . . which I set down against our next meeting gave the first entrance into this discourse; which, having been thus begun by chance, was continued . . . and at last, in a retirement where an attendance on my health gave me leisure, it was brought into that order thou now seest it.

Later, in the 'Introduction' proper, Locke presents his key notion of an idea. Even here the reader may want to interrupt in order to insist upon a distinction made by Descartes in his Preface to the *Meditations*: ". . . in this term *idea* there is an equivocation: for it can be taken either intrinsically, as a phenomenon of my understanding . . . ; or it may be taken objectively, as what is represented by this phenomenon . . .". Locke proceeds:

> I must here in the entrance beg pardon of my reader for the frequent use of the word *idea*, which he will find in the following treatise. It being that term which, I think, serves best to stand for whatsoever is the object of the understanding when a man thinks, I have used it to express whatever is meant by *phantasm, notion, species,* or *whatever it is which the mind can be employed about in thinking;* and I could not avoid frequently using it.
>
> I presume it will be easily granted me, that there are such ideas in men's minds: every one is conscious of them in himself; and men's words and actions will satisfy him that they are in others.
>
> Our first inquiry then shall be – how they come into the mind.

Locke's findings on this first question, reported in Book I of the *Essay*, are that all our ideas must ultimately be derived from our own individual experience. Although the opponents whom he had most in mind were lesser men Locke thus rejected anything like the Platonic doctrine that the ideas of perfect equality and so on could not have originated from experience which is always of the imperfect, and the Cartesian contention that that most splendid idea of God must have been stamped on our souls as the trademark of our Maker. (See Ch. II, § 2 and Ch. VIII, § 3, above.) Having concluded in Book I that the mind begins "white paper, void of all characters, without any ideas", Locke starts in Book II to investigate "How comes it to be furnished?", and to classify the furniture (II (i) 2). It is in Book III, after he has found to his surprise that his inquiries have developed into an investigation 'Of Words', that the notion of a logically private language emerges from its opposite:

> God, having designed man for a sociable creature, made him not only with an inclination, and under a necessity to have fellowship with those of his own kind, but furnished him also with language, which was to be the great instrument and common tie of society. Man, therefore, had by nature his organs so fashioned as to be fit to frame articulate sounds, which we call words. But this was not enough to produce language; for parrots, and several other birds, will be taught to make articulate sounds distinct enough, which yet by no means are capable of language.

Besides articulate sounds, therefore, it was further necessary that he should be able to use these sounds as signs of internal conceptions; and to make them stand as marks for the ideas within his own mind, whereby they might be made known to others, and the thoughts of men's minds be conveyed from one to another. (III (i) 1–2)

Man, though he have great variety of thoughts, and such from which others as well as himself might receive profit and delight, yet they are all within his own breast, invisible and hidden from others, nor can of themselves be made to appear. The comfort and advantage of society not being to be had without communication of thoughts it was necessary that man should find some external sensible signs, whereof these invisible ideas, which his thoughts are made up of, might be made known to others. For this purpose nothing was so fit, either for plenty or quickness, as those articulate sounds which with so much ease and variety he found himself able to make. Thus we may conceive how words, which were by nature so well adapted to that purpose, come to be made use of by men as the signs of their ideas; not by any natural connection that there is between particular articulate sounds and certain ideas, for then there would be but one language amongst all men; but by a voluntary imposition, whereby such a word is made arbitrarily the mark of such an idea. The use, then, of words is to be sensible marks of ideas; and the ideas they stand for are their proper and immediate signification.

The use men have of these marks being either to record their own thoughts, for the assistance of their own memory; or, as it were, to bring out their ideas, and lay them before the view of others; words, in their primary or immediate signification, stand for nothing but the ideas in the mind of him that uses them. . . . When a man speaks to another it is that he may be understood; and the end of speech that those sounds, as marks, may make known his ideas to the hearer. That then which words are the marks of are the ideas of the speaker; nor can anyone apply them as marks, immediately, to anything else but the ideas that he himself hath: for this would be to make them signs of his own conceptions, and yet apply them to other ideas; which would be to make them signs and not signs of his ideas at the same time, and so in effect to have no signification at all. Words being voluntary signs, they cannot be voluntary signs imposed by him on things he knows not. That would be to make them signs of nothing, sounds without signification. A man cannot make his words the signs either of qualities in things, or of conceptions in the mind of another, whereof he has none in his own. (III (ii) 1–2)

But though words, as they are used by men, can properly and immediately signify nothing but the ideas that are in the mind of the speaker, yet they in their thoughts give them a secret reference to two other things.

First, they suppose their words to be marks of the ideas in the minds also of other men, with whom they communicate: for else they should talk in vain, and could not be understood, if the sounds they applied to one idea were such as by the hearer were applied to another; which is to speak two languages. But in this men stand not usually to examine whether the idea which they, and those they discourse with, have in their minds be the same; but think it enough that they use the word, as they imagine, in the common acceptation of that language; in which they suppose that the idea they make it a sign of is precisely the same to which the understanding men of that country apply that name.

Secondly, because men would not be thought to talk barely of their own imagination, but of things as they really are, therefore they often suppose the words to stand also for the reality of things. But ... give me leave here to say, that it is a perverting the use of words, and brings ... obscurity and confusion into their signification, whenever we make them stand for anything but those ideas we have in our own minds. (III (ii) 4–5)

§4 *Possible error and actual knowledge*

Locke thus provided a classically excellent account of a logically private language, a conception – or pseudo-conception – to which he was led from premises which to him appeared to be altogether incontestable. For, surely, no one could be immediately acquainted with anything else but his own ideas, the objects of his own understanding; and, equally surely, no one can understand a language except in so far as its terms can be explained by reference to his own experience? Locke also indicates, just as decisively, the devastating implications of this conception. The presently relevant corollary is that in such a language a Cartesian scepticism could not even be formulated. For it necessarily lacks words, both for an external world, and for all possible contents of such a world: "this is certain, their signification, in his use of them, is limited to his ideas, and they can be signs of nothing else" (III (ii) 8).

So we can now turn from the question of § 3, which was whether the theoretical possibility that it is all a dream really is a theoretical possibility, to the question of § 4, which is whether a merely theoretical possibility of error could in any case constitute a sufficient warrant for doubt. To think that this must be so is one of the hardy perennial philosophical temptations. To achieve immunity provides a paradigm of progress in philosophy. So consider another typical statement in the hypnotically seductive voice of Descartes. It comes from *Meditation* III:

I shall now close my eyes, I shall stop my ears, I shall disengage all my senses . . . and so, concerning myself only with myself, and paying attention to the subjective, I shall try little by little to make myself more familiar and better known to myself. I am a thing which thinks, that is to say, which doubts, which affirms, which denies, which knows a few things, which is ignorant of a lot, which loves, which hates, which wants and which does not want. . . .

I shall now reflect more nicely, to see whether there is any other knowledge in me which I have not yet noticed. I am certain that I am a thing which thinks, but do I not also know what is necessary to make me certain of something? In this first knowledge there is nothing but a clear and distinct perception of what I know; which would not indeed be sufficient to give me a guarantee that this is the truth if it could ever happen that something which I conceived so clearly and distinctly turned out to be false. Consequently it seems to me that already I can set it up as a general rule that the things which we conceive very clearly and very distinctly are one and all true.

However, I have in the past received and admitted as very certain and very obvious several things which later I have nevertheless recognized to be doubtful and uncertain. What then were these things? They were the earth, the sky, the stars, and all the other things which I perceived through the instrumentality of my senses. But what is it that I clearly and distinctly conceived in these? Nothing, surely, but that the ideas or thoughts of these things presented themselves to my mind? And even now I do not deny that these ideas are found in me. . . .

But when I considered something very simple and very easy in the sphere of arithmetic and geometry – that, for example, two and three make five and so on – did I not conceive them at least sufficiently clearly to guarantee their truth? Certainly, if I have formed the opinion since that one can doubt these things the only reason has been that it occurred to me that perhaps some God could have so made me that I could have been mistaken even about things which seem to me most obvious. . . . Of course, since I have no reason to believe that there is a deceiver God, and as indeed I have not yet considered the reasons which prove that there is a God, the ground for doubt which depends solely upon this opinion is very slight and – to coin a phrase – metaphysical. But in order to be able to remove it altogether I must, as soon as occasion arises, inquire whether there is a God; and, if I find that there is, I must also inquire whether he can be a deceiver. For without knowing these two truths I do not see that I can ever be certain of anything.

This passage provides further illustration of several points made already. Thus at the beginning we see again the characteristically Cartesian approach from the subjective and the solipsistic, while at the end Descartes is underlining that the role given to the knowledge of God in his epistemology is both crucial and fundamental. But our immediate concern is with the assumption that knowledge – or, at any rate, real knowledge – must preclude even the most theoretical possibility of error. If we know, the implicit argument runs, then we cannot be wrong. If we know, then it is not possible for us to be mistaken. So if it remains possible that we may be mistaken then we cannot really know. Put in that way the argument is likely to appear absolutely compulsive; but also perhaps, as Descartes hinted, far-fetched and in some bad sense metaphysical. Let us therefore bring into evidence a passage from an extremely practical piece of political theorizing. It comes from that liberal classic the essay *On Liberty* by John Stuart Mill; who was also author of an important and very influential treatise, *A System of Logic*, and whom we have already noticed as a spokesman of ethical Utilitarianism (Ch. III, § 6):

The time, it is to be hoped, is gone by, when any defence would be necessary of the liberty of the press as one of the securities against corrupt or tyrannical government. . . . Let us suppose, therefore, that the government is entirely at one with the people, and never thinks of exerting any power of coercion unless in agreement with what it conceives to be their voice. But I deny the right of the people to exercise such coercion, either by themselves or by their government. The power itself is illegitimate. . . .

We can never be sure that the opinion we are endeavouring to stifle is a false opinion . . . the opinion which it is attempted to suppress by authority may possibly be true. Those who desire to suppress it, of course, deny its truth; but they are not infallible. . . . To refuse a hearing to an opinion, because they are sure that it is false, is to assume that their certainty is the same thing as absolute certainty. All silencing of discussion is an assumption of infallibility. Its condemnation may be allowed to rest on this common argument, not the worse for being common.
(Ch. II)

Unfortunately it may not. For what is wrong with the argument is not at all that it is vulgar, but rather that it is unsound. The claim to know that this in particular is the case is by no means the same as the far stronger claim to be in general infallible. The nub of the difference becomes clear in a passage from another great Victorian, John Henry, Cardinal Newman (1801–1890). As in the previous case of J. S. Mill part of the point of this citation is to show that what might for some be frivolous logic-chopping or idly speculative metaphysics is essentially connected with big issues of ideology and practice. The passage comes from Newman's *A Grammar of Assent*:

> I will take one more instance. A man is converted to the Catholic Church from his admiration of its religious system, and his disgust with Protestantism. That admiration remains; but, after a time, he leaves his new faith, perhaps returns to his old. The reason, if we may conjecture, may sometimes be this: he has never believed in the Church's infallibility; in her doctrinal truth he has believed, but in her infallibility, no. He was asked, before he was received, whether he held all that the Church taught, he replied that he did; but he understood the question to mean, whether he held those particular doctrines 'which at that time the Church in matter of fact formally taught', whereas it really meant 'whatever the Church then or at any future time should teach'. Thus, he never had the indispensable and elementary faith of a Catholic, and was simply no subject for reception into the fold of the Church. This being the case, when the Immaculate Conception is defined, he feels that it is something more than he bargained for when he became a Catholic, and accordingly he gives up his religious profession. The world will say that he lost his certitude of the divinity of the Catholic Faith, but he never had it.
>
> (VII 2, § 5)

The claim simply to know is thus weaker than, and therefore cannot imply, the claim to be infallible. Yet we still have somehow to come to terms with the seemingly incontestable contention that if we know then it is not possible that we are mistaken, that if we know then we cannot be wrong; and hence, it would seem inevitably, that knowledge must imply infallibility. Here we face a typically philosophical dilemma. (It is entirely fitting that the Greeks who first needed, should have had, and bequeathed to us, the word for it!) It is from precisely this sort of difficulty that philosophical questions about meanings arise. For, in order to untie the knot, we have to ask what knowledge is; what is, and what is not, implied by the claim to know.

One wrong but popular way to tackle such issues is to treat them as occasions for some sort of introspection; asking yourself what you mean, what you have in mind, and what you intend to imply, when you employ the words. But now, although the answers may happen to be the same, these are quite different questions. Indeed, most typically these arise exactly when there is reason to think that your usage is eccentric; for instance, that when you said *glory* you meant not glory but – following Lewis Carroll's Humpty Dumpty – "there's a nice knock-down argument for you". A good, and possibly the best, way to get clear about the meaning of a statement is to consider what would constitute a rejection of that statement. Consider these passages, which are interesting also in ways not immediately relevant. They come from the beginning of *de Interpretatione*, one of the works by which Aristotle first established logic as an independent discipline:

> Let us begin by defining *noun* and *verb*, and then explain what is meant by *denial, affirmation, proposition*, and *sentence*.
> Words spoken are symbols of what is going on in the mind; and words written of those spoken. And just as writing is not the same for all men, neither is speech. However what the symbols are in the first instance symbols of – the things which go on in the mind – are the same for all men; and so are the things of which these in their turn are representations. . . .
> Furthermore, just as sometimes the thoughts in our minds are neither true nor false whereas at other times they are necessarily the one or the other, so too the same applies with speech. For combination and division are needed before you can have truth and falsity. Nouns and verbs by themselves – the word *man*, for example, or *white* without anything put with it – are like thoughts without combination and division; and there is no truth or falsity yet. Witness the fact that while the word *goat-stag* means something what it means is neither true nor false until you predicate existence or non-existence of it, whether in general or in a particular tense.
> So, now, a noun is a word with a meaning established by convention and involving no reference to time. . . . A verb is a word which also includes a reference to time in its meaning. . . .
> (16A1–9, 16A10–21, 16B6)

Every sentence has meaning . . . but not every sentence constitutes a proposition – only those which are capable of being either true or false. Not all can be. For instance, a prayer is a sentence but it is neither true nor false. So let us dismiss all other sorts of sentence but the proposition, since this is what concerns the present inquiry. The investigation of the others belongs rather to Rhetoric or Poetics. (17A1–8)

One kind of propositions is the simple, which affirm or deny something of something, while the other is the composite, which is compounded of the simple. A simple proposition is a significant utterance which affirms or denies some predicate to some subject in the past or the present or the future. An affirmation is a positive assertion of something about something, a denial is a negative assertion.

Now since it is possible to declare that what is is not, that what is not is, that what is is, and that what is not is not, and correspondingly for times other than the present, it would be possible for someone to deny anything which anyone affirmed and to affirm anything which anyone denied. Thus it follows that for every affirmation there is an opposite denial, and for every denial an affirmation. Let us call an affirmation and its opposite denial a pair of contradictories. (17A21–34)

There are here three things to notice by the way. First, the first of the passages quoted seems again to be taking for granted that curiously potent idea – discussed in the previous section – of a universal private language prior to all public languages. Second, the second passage quoted rules magisterially that the proposition is the only sort of utterance which merits the attention of the logician. This became for centuries accepted doctrine. Thus even Hobbes, who was in general outspokenly hostile to Aristotle, finds it obvious that "In philosophy there is but one kind of speech useful which . . . most men call proposition, and is the speech of those that affirm or deny . . ." (*Works*, Vol. I, p. 30). Third, the third passage quoted makes explicit an assumption fundamental to Aristotelian logic. This is the principle that "every premise is of the form which says that some predicate either does or must or may apply to some subject" (*Prior Analytics* 25A1–3. It was to the subject of this part of Aristotle's *Organon* that Marlowe's Dr Faustus was referring when he sighed, improbably: "Sweet Analytics, 'tis thou hast ravished me . . .").

To confine logic strictly to propositions is to overlook that such paradigmatically logical concepts as presupposition, fallacy, and incompatibility have some application to questions and commands also. For instance, a pair of commands as well as a pair of propositions can be logically contradictory: *Get to Hell out of here!* obviously contradicts *Stay here!* Possible wider implications both of the traditional limitation and of its rejection will begin to emerge when we recall Kant's hint that sentences about what ought to be should be seen as covertly imperative (Ch. III, § 4). Introducing an illuminating distinction, which was not formulated by Kant, we may perhaps want to say they are grammatically indicative but logically imperative. Compare the way in which the sentence *All ranks will parade in battle order at 0600 hours* is in battalion orders employed to express not a prediction but a command. (*Indicative* is the British English equivalent of the American English *declarative*.)

The principle that every proposition must affirm or deny some predicate to some subject would no doubt be unexceptionable if it could be construed as a grammatical – or should it be syntactical? – remark about correctly formed sentences in most Indo-European languages. But interpreted, as it was meant, as a logical thesis it meets difficulties which have been made notorious. Above all, it would seem that it cannot compass propositions about relations. The logical subject of the relational proposition *New York is north of Buenos Aires* is, surely, as much or as little Buenos Aires as it is New York: for this proposition is equivalent to, it entails and is entailed by, *Buenos Aires is south of New York*.

This fundamental, but apparently merely technical, defect in the traditional Aristotelian logic becomes philosophically important in so far as philosophers schooled in that discipline have been inclined to draw metaphysical morals. If all propositions consist of subject and predicate, then perhaps all that there ultimately is must be substances and their attributes. Hence, it will seem, relations can subsist only in the mind of the observer; or they must be somehow reducible to attributes of the objects between which they obtain; or if not either of these then they must in some other way be not in the last analysis real. The most brilliant as well as the most bizarre fruits of this subject-predicate assumption are the metaphysics of Leibniz and of Spinoza (1632–1677), expressed chiefly in the *Monadology* of the former and the *Ethics* of the latter.

However, to return to our present muttons, the moral for us now of these passages from Aristotle is that every proposition must be equivalent to the denial of its contradictory. (For those who like symbolism this can be rendered as $p \equiv \sim \sim p$: where p is any proposition; $\sim$ is read as 'not'; and $\equiv$ means 'is formally equivalent to'.) So in order to get clearer about the meaning of *He knows p* we can begin by asking what would show this proposition to be false. For any logically, as opposed to causally, sufficient condition of its falsity must by the same token be the contradictory of a logically, as opposed to causally, necessary condition of its truth; and the meaning of any proposition just is the sum of the logically necessary conditions of its truth. This general method, and also the two technical expressions *logically necessary* and *logically sufficient condition*, will probably be most easily mastered by pressing on now to see its, and their, application to the particular problem of the meaning of *He knows p*. Two answers to the question what would show this to be false suggest themselves immediately, and this list does not pretend to be complete.

First, *He knows p* must be false if p itself is false. For if he claims to know that Lover Boy will win the Derby, and if Lover Boy does not even run, then necessarily he did not know. The truth of the proposition alleged to be known is a logically necessary condition of true knowledge. So he did not know, but only 'knew'; and the point of the sneering inverted commas precisely is that the claim to have known was false. This idiomatic usage can be instructively compared with that in which we may say of the dipsomaniac during his lost weekend that he 'saw', but not of course that he actually saw, the customary non-existent pink rats. Both *know* and *see* may then be labelled, as a mnemonic, *Cognitive Achievement Words*. (Compare what was said about *know* and *refute* in § 3, also about *prove* in § 2, of Chapter I, above.)

Second, it is a logically sufficient condition of the falsity of *He knows p* that he is not in a position to know. Thus the claim to have known that Lover Boy would win must be false, even if Lover Boy does in fact win, if this claim rests upon nothing better than the picking of that name out of a list of runners with a random pin. The difference between this second way in which a claim to know can be false and the first is practically important. For to err is human, and no precautions can save us all from sometimes making knowledge claims which turn out to have been mistaken. But our mortal fallibility provides no similar excuse for making claims which though not necessarily mistaken are certainly improper. Thus, in even the best judicial system, operated by the most competent and conscientious men, there will surely be at least very occasional miscarriages; when, for instance, all the available evidence pointed, apparently decisively, to the guilt of someone who was nevertheless innocent. But this unfortunate fact provides, of course, no sort of justification for those who condemn a victim improperly: whether without sufficient grounds; or whether – still worse – against the weight of the evidence; or whether – worst of all – on the pretext of 'evidence' which they themselves have reason to know was faked.

Now it is the first of these two elements of the meaning of *He knows p* which generates the ideas that knowledge implies and requires infallibility in the knower, and that it must presuppose the elimination of even the most theoretical and remote possibility of error. For it is precisely and only in as much as *He knows p* entails *p is true* (i.e., p), that we are also and alternatively entitled to say: that if a man knows then he cannot be wrong; and that if a man knows then it is not possible that he is mistaken. Trouble arises here from misplacements and misunderstandings of apodeictic terms. (Compare the similar troubles about choice and inevitability discussed in Chapter VII, § 5, above.)

Certainly, if *He knows p* it follows necessarily that *p is true*. But it does not by the same token follow necessarily that *p is necessarily true*. There is, therefore, no warrant here for the notion that knowledge – true knowledge – can be of necessary truths only. Equally certainly, because alternatively, we are licensed to argue – once granted that *He knows p* – that, since *p is true*, it is impossible that *p is false*. But from this logical incompatibility of *p is true* with *p is false* we cannot legitimately draw the conclusion that if any proposition is truly to be said to be known its contradictory must be inconceivable.

Again, since from *He knows p* it follows necessarily that *p is true,* then suppose he both knows and asserts p it also follows necessarily that he is not mistaken, and that it is impossible that he is mistaken. But this conclusion is in substance only that he happens in fact to be right; and that, since being right is logically incompatible with being wrong, he is also in fact not wrong. But to say this is not to say, nor does it entitle us to infer, that, either quite generally or else in some more restricted area, he is infallible. These, as reflection on passages from J. S. Mill and Newman has reminded us, would be very different and much stronger claims.

The moral will by now have become evident. It is that it will not do to adduce as your ground for doubting – as a reason for challenging his claim to know – some merely theoretical possibility of error. It will not do, that is, to urge that it is always – or perhaps only almost always – conceivable that he may be mistaken. Instead you need to show reason for thinking either that he actually is in fact mistaken or that, whether mistaken or not, he is in no position to know.

§ 5 *Certainty and conception, clear and distinct*

To this conclusion of § 4 a first Cartesian reply might be that so long as any such theoretical possibility of error remains no one is in a position to know; or, at any rate, not really to know – in some supposed true and ultimate sense of *know*. Thus, as we saw in the passage of *Meditation* III quoted in that section, Descartes was perfectly prepared to allow that, "since I have no reason to believe that there is a deceiver God . . . the ground of the doubt which depends on this supposition only is very slight and – to coin a phrase – metaphysical". Nevertheless this does, he insists, provide a sufficient ground for doubt. So, "in order to be able to remove it completely I need to enquire whether there is a God. . . . And . . . whether he is capable of being a deceiver. For without the knowledge of these two truths I do not see that I can be certain of anything." However, in *Meditation* V, "after I have discovered that there is a God . . . and that he is no deceiver, and after I have inferred from this that nothing which I clearly and distinctly conceive can fail to be true . . . then I really do have true and certain science."

It thus appears that Descartes might be prepared to allow that a merely theoretical possibility of error does not constitute a sufficient reason to deny that someone does, by ordinary standards, know. His point would then be that these ordinary standards are ultimately inadequate, that real knowledge must be proof against even metaphysical doubt.

To this someone might be inclined, as many in our century have been, to reply that it is precisely and only these ordinary standards which determine what knowledge is; and, hence, that it is simply preposterous to maintain that what is by these standards undoubtedly knowledge in the last analysis really is not knowledge at all. The man harassed by such metaphysical doubt may thus be made to cut the same sort of figure as the old French Marshal Saxe who, shortly after the discovery of that further planet, asked anxiously: "What guarantee is there that what we call Uranus really is Uranus?"

The Marshal's question was indeed absurd. For in as much as this is the name conventionally attached it must be the correct name. As Wittgenstein once remarked, in a rather different connection: "What is and is not a cow is for the public to decide." But the present case is surely different. For our Cartesian is not committed to disputing that the word *know* has whatever meaning is determined by its conventionally correct usage. Rather he is insisting that we should demand a much higher standard before conceding that the second of the two conventionally correct logically necessary conditions of knowledge has been satisfied. We are, he might urge, altogether too generous with our awards of the diploma title *knowledge*.

We are far too willing to allow that people are in a position to know what they believe that they know.

This is a powerful defence. For it is true that most of us are chronically disposed to admit too many claims to knowledge: to maintain, for instance, for no better reason than that we should like our country to reduce its military spending, that there is no country which threatens us; or to allow, simply because they are so incorrigibly convinced, that those enthusiasts do know that of which they are so passionately persuaded. It is also true, and well worth stressing, that it is one of the most proper functions of the philosopher to try to maintain or to raise intellectual standards. Yet this is not done by demanding the necessarily unattainable.

Already in the first section of the present chapter we saw general reason to agree with Hume: "The Cartesian doubt . . . were it ever possible to be attained . . . would be entirely incurable, and no reasoning could ever bring us to a state of assurance and conviction on any subject" (Ch. IX, § 1). Now, to conclude the chapter, we have to look more closely at the weapon with which Descartes hopes to remove even the theoretical possibility of error; and then to show that what he wants, and what he believes he has discovered, cannot be provided.

What he wants is a sort of sign satisfying three quite different conditions simultaneously. The first is that it must be exclusively mental, in the Cartesian sense; for nothing else could be available to a person reduced by Cartesian doubt to an awareness only of his own consciousness. Second, it must be impossible to be mistaken about its presence. And, third, when it is present it must be impossible for what is thereby endorsed to be untrue. Unless these conditions are satisfied, and perhaps even if they are, Descartes cannot attain his chosen objective of removing even the most theoretical possibility of error.

What Descartes produces as his discovered sign is, surely, luminously inadequate. But it is instructive, and rather more difficult, to see why no one else can hope to do any better. So consider three passages. The first comes from Part IV of the *Discourse*, and has been quoted earlier (Ch. VIII, § 2). The second is the second version of the same thing, from *Meditation* III. The third comes from *Meditation* V:

> After that I examined in general the question of what is required in a proposition for it to be true and certain. For since I had just discovered one which I knew to be such I thought I should also know in what this certitude consists. So, after observing that there was nothing at all in this *I think, therefore I am* which assures me that I am speaking the truth

except that I can see very clearly that in order to think it is necessary to exist, I concluded that I could take it as a general rule that the things which we conceive quite clearly and quite distinctly are all true; but just remembering that there is some difficulty about distinguishing properly which are the cases in which we do conceive distinctly.

Now I will think more carefully to see whether perhaps there are not some other items of knowledge in me which I have not noticed yet. I am certain that I am a thing which is conscious, but does not that mean that I also know what is required to make me certain of something? In this first item of knowledge there is nothing to be found but a clear and distinct perception of what I know; which in truth would not be enough to guarantee to me that it is true, if it could ever happen that something which I conceived clearly and distinctly in this way turned out to be false. Accordingly it seems that already I can take it as a general rule that the things which we conceive quite clearly and quite distinctly are all true.

All the same I have in my time received and admitted many things as very certain and very obvious which yet I afterwards recognized to be uncertain and doubtful. . . .

. . . and I have already fully demonstrated above that everything which I clearly and distinctly know is true. And even if I had not demonstrated it, still the nature of my mind is such that I could not stop myself judging them to be true so long as I conceived them clearly and distinctly. And I recollect that, even while I was still strongly attached to the objects of sense, I reckoned as among the most certain those truths which I clearly conceived about shapes, numbers, and arithmetic and geometry generally.

Briefly, and brutally, the "clear and distinct conception (or perception)" of Descartes seems to be nothing more than a deceptively high-faluting synonym for *certainty*. It then emerges that the crucial distinction is that between a person's feeling certain and a proposition's being certain. To say that Rebecca feels certain is to make a psychological claim about Rebecca. To say that some proposition is certain is to make an epistemological claim about the truth of that proposition. To achieve what he wants to achieve Descartes needs to identify feeling certain that p with its being certain that p; while also taking it that you cannot conceivably be mistaken as to whether or not you feel certain.

Certainly, if I feel certain then I cannot help believing. Just that is at least part of what is meant by *feel certain*: "the nature of my mind is such that I could not stop myself judging them to be true so long as I conceived them clearly and distinctly". But then this feeling certain is, notoriously, no guarantee of truth: "I have in my time . . . admitted many things as very certain . . . which yet I afterwards recognized to be . . . doubtful . . ." So now if certainty is to constitute the infallible sign of truth we have somehow to ensure that it could not conceivably "happen that something which I conceived clearly and distinctly in this way turned out to be false". This can surely be arranged. But it can be arranged only by stipulating that it is to be true by the definition of *clearly and distinctly conceived* that, if p is clearly and distinctly conceived, then necessarily p. But this is where we came in. For precisely this stipulation applies already in the case of knowledge. We should not, therefore, now be surprised to learn "that there is some difficulty about distinguishing properly which are the cases in which we do conceive distinctly"!

The dilemma for Descartes is this. When he gets hold of a sign which, it seems, cannot itself be misidentified – such as a feeling of certainty – then its presence fails to provide the desired guarantee of the truth of the proposition in question. But when he arranges or finds something the presence of which definitionally necessitates the truth of the proposition – like its being known – then it immediately becomes at least theoretically possible that this is not genuinely a case of that something. In fact, and not surprisingly, Descartes time after time makes the truth or falsity of the proposition, rather than the presence of some internal illumination, a criterion of whether it is clearly and distinctly conceived.

Again we should not be surprised. For the search has been for a guarantee G from the presence of which the truth of the proposition p follows necessarily. But to specify this is to specify that G must be a logically sufficient condition of p; and, hence, reciprocally, that p must be a logically necessary condition of G. And where p is a logically necessary condition of G it is altogether proper to use p as a criterion of the authentic presence of G. But in so far as you do this, and have to do this, your proposal to confine your belief to what you clearly and distinctly conceive to be true can have no more substantial value than the advice: "To win at roulette, bet only on the numbers which are going to come up at the next turn of the wheel!"

Perhaps it was some glimmering awareness of the irreparable inadequacy of clear and distinct conception for the impossible task which he had proposed for it that sometimes encouraged Descartes to try to infer its reliability from something else: "after I have discovered that there is a

God . . . and that he is no deceiver, and after I have inferred from this that nothing which I clearly and distinctly conceive can fail to be true . . . then I really do have true and certain science." Since "these two truths" are, in the system of Descartes, supposedly established with the help of precisely this conclusion it is a desperate manoeuvre. It was first challenged by an extremely sympathetic yet no less acute critic, Antoine Arnauld (1612–1694), in the fourth set of solicited 'Objections' to the *Meditations*. Arnauld was later to become, with Pierre Nicole (1625–1695), co-author of the famous Port-Royal *Logic*. Port-Royal was the Jansenist Convent with which Pascal too was associated. The restraint of Arnauld's comment may remind us of James Thurber's fencer who, having decapitated his opponent, cries only "Touché":

> My one remaining hesitation is about how it is possible to avoid circularity when our author says that 'our only guarantee that the things which we clearly and distinctly conceive are true is the fact that God exists'. For our only guarantee that God exists is that we conceive very clearly and very distinctly that he does exist; so before being convinced of the existence of God we need to be convinced that everything which we clearly and distinctly conceive is true.

CHAPTER X

Perception and 'the External World'

§1 *Representative and causal theories*

The examination in Chapter IX of Descartes' progress from a supposedly all-corroding doubt to irrefragable certainty began with passages from Hume's first *Inquiry*. The same source provides an excellent statement of the Problem of the External World, as it presented itself to successors of Descartes unable to accept a Cartesian answer:

> It seems that men are carried by a natural instinct or prepossession to repose faith in their senses, and that without any reasoning, or even almost before the use of reason, we always suppose an external universe which depends not on our perception but would exist though we and every sensible creature were absent or annihilated. . . .
>
> It seems also evident that when men follow this blind and powerful instinct of nature, they always suppose the very images presented by the senses to be the external objects, and never entertain any suspicion that the one are nothing but representations of the other. This very table which we see white, and which we feel hard, is believed to exist independently of our perception and to be something external to our mind which perceives it. . . .
>
> But this universal and primary opinion of all men is soon destroyed by the slightest philosophy, which teaches us that nothing can ever be present to the mind but an image or perception, and that the senses are only the inlets through which these images are conveyed, without being able to produce any immediate intercourse between the mind and the object. The table which we see seems to diminish as we remove farther from it; but the real table, which exists independent of us, suffers no alteration. It was, therefore, nothing but its image which was present to the mind. These are the obvious dictates of reason; and no man who reflects ever doubted that the existences which we consider when we say *this house* and *that tree* are nothing but perceptions in the mind. . . .
>
> So far, then, are we necessitated by reasoning to contradict or depart

from the primary instincts of nature and to embrace a new system with regard to the evidence of our senses. But here philosophy finds herself extremely embarrassed, when she would justify this new system and obviate the cavils and objections of the sceptics. (XII (i))

She does indeed, as we shall be seeing. For one thing, this "new system", as Hume indicates in the last sentence of the penultimate paragraph, includes the notion of a logically private language; a notion which we have already seen developed clearly and disastrously in Locke (Ch. IX, § 3). But consider now three passages from Locke's *Essay*; noting that *idea* here is roughly equivalent to Hume's *perceptions of the mind,* or our own *subjective experiences*:

Since the mind, in all its thoughts and reasonings, hath no other immediate object but its own ideas, which it alone does or can contemplate, it is evident that our knowledge is only conversant about them.
(IV (i) 1)

I have given a short, and, I think, true history of the first beginnings of human knowledge; whence the mind has its first objects; and by what steps it makes its progress to the laying in and storing up those ideas, out of which is to be framed all the knowledge it is capable of.... external and internal sensation are the only passages I can find of knowledge to the understanding. These alone, as far as I can discover, are the windows by which light is let into this dark room. For, methinks, the understanding is not much unlike a closet wholly shut from light, with only some little openings left, to let in external visible resemblances, or ideas of things without.... (II (xi) 15 and 17)

Whatsoever the mind perceives in itself, or is the immediate object of perception, thought, or understanding, that I call *idea*; and the power to produce any idea in our mind I call *quality* of the subject wherein that power is. Thus a snowball having the power to produce in us the ideas of white, cold, and round, – the power to produce those ideas in us, as they are in the snowball, I call qualities; and as they are sensations or perceptions in our understandings, I call them ideas....

Qualities thus considered in bodies are, first, such as are utterly inseparable from the body, in what state soever it be, and such as in all the alterations and changes it suffers, all the force that can be used upon it, it constantly keeps; and such as sense constantly finds in every particle of matter which has bulk enough to be perceived; and the mind finds inseparable from every particle of matter though less than to make itself singly to be perceived by our senses.... These I call *original* or *primary qualities* of body, which I think we may observe to produce simple ideas in us, viz. solidity, extension, figure, motion or rest, and number.

Secondly, such qualities which in truth are nothing in the objects themselves but powers to produce various sensations in us by their primary qualities, i.e. by the bulk, figure, texture, and motion of their insensible parts, as colours, sounds, tastes, etc. These I call *secondary qualities*. . . . (II (viii) 8–10)

The next thing to be considered is, how bodies produce ideas in us; and that is manifestly by impulse, the only way which we can conceive bodies to operate in. . . . And since the extension, figure, number and motion of bodies of an observable bigness may be perceived at a distance by the sight, it is evident some singly imperceptible bodies must come from them to the eyes, and thereby comes to the brain some motion; which produces these ideas which we have of them in us.

(II (viii) 11–12)

. . . the ideas of primary qualities of bodies are resemblances of them, and their patterns do really exist in the bodies themselves, but the ideas produced in us by these secondary qualities have no resemblance of them at all. There is nothing like our ideas, existing in the bodies themselves. They are, in the bodies we denominate from them, only a power to produce those sensations in us: and what is sweet, blue or warm in idea is but the certain bulk, figure and motion of the insensible parts, in the bodies themselves which we call so. (II (viii) 15)

Let us consider the red and white colours in porphyry. Hinder light from striking on it, and its colours vanish; it no longer produces any such ideas in us: upon the return of light it produces these appearances on us again. Can anyone think any real alterations are made in the porphyry by the presence or absence of light; and that those ideas of whiteness and redness are really in porphyry in the light, when it is plain it has no colour in the dark? (II (viii) 11)

Both the rhythms and the vocabulary of Locke's prose are a little archaic now. But the basic conception is not. This is the conception that we – our minds, that is, or our souls – are somehow located in our brains; and that the physiological machinery of our senses brings information in to us from outside. Though characteristically Cartesian this is older than Descartes. Shakespeare's Prince Henry, for instance, mentions:

> . . . *his pure brain* –
> *Which some suppose the soul's frail dwelling house* –
> (*King John* V (vii))

333

And though characteristically Cartesian it is also the one which still seems obviously correct to most working scientists and to most scientifically informed laymen. The images and the vocabulary change, the emphases vary, but the essentials remain hardy perennial: the objects of my immediate awareness are perceptions of my own mind, my sensory impressions, my subjective experiences, my percepts, or my sense-data; and in my awareness I am irremediably removed from the world outside – confined to the isolated Dark Room of the Understanding, solitary in my own private Sensorium Cinema, or trapped in a one-man Operations Control; a place which is, in the most literal sense, a nerve centre.

I have already quoted one passage to illustrate the continuing popularity of this sort of view at the highest scientific level (Ch. VIII, § 5). I can add here some words from Einstein's *The World as I See it*: "The belief in an external world independent of the perceiving subject is the basis of all natural science. Since, however, sense perception only gives information of this external world or of 'physical reality' indirectly, we can only grasp the latter by speculative means" (p. 60). Lenin, as a professional revolutionary and not a scientist, can serve here as spokesman for the scientifically informed layman. For he took time off from his more obviously political activities to write what has become – along with *The Dialectics of Nature* by Engels – one of the only two canonical Marxist-Leninist books on general, as opposed to social, philosophy. In this, *Materialism and Empirio-Criticism*, Lenin states: "Matter is a philosophical category denoting the objective reality which is given to man by his sensations; and which is copied, photographed, and reflected by our sensations, while existing independently of them" (p. 127).

In so far as these sensations – or sense-data – are supposed to be effects brought about, albeit indirectly, by objects outside, this perennially attractive view is aptly labelled *The Causal Theory of Perception*; while in so far as the sensory impressions are said to resemble, or be representations of, these objects the customary description is *The Representative Theory of Perception*. Strictly, therefore, Locke generally adhered to the former; and to the latter only as regards primary qualities. Lenin is inclined to accept both, without qualification or distinction; and to insist upon the combination as essential (not to "a" but) to "the" materialist theory of knowledge. Einstein seems to be hinting at some sort of distinction between what common sense uninstructedly believes about objects in the external world, and what science has to tell us about the true nature of "physical reality".

Certainly, as we have already seen (Ch. III, § 3), a distinction between

334

primary and secondary qualities was one of the commonplaces of the new science in the 1600's. This is a fact of which Locke, as a Fellow of the Royal Society and an admiring friend of both Boyle and Newton, was very well aware; and his awareness led him to conclude his account with the apology: "I have in what . . . goes before been engaged in physical inquiries a little further than perhaps I intended" (II (viii) 22). It was perhaps largely the implications of the second term of this distinction which led John Keats to echo Charles Lamb's toast: "Newton's health, and confusion to mathematics"; and shortly afterwards himself to write:

> . . . *Do not all charms fly*
> *At the mere touch of cold philosophy?* ('Lamia', 229–30)

Certainly they were in the mind of William Blake when he framed the unhappy couplet:

> *The Sun's light when he unfolds it*
> *Depends on the organ that beholds it* (*To Venetian Artists*, p. 1018).

These same implications are spelt out with mischievous good humour by A. N. Whitehead (1861–1947) in his *Science and the Modern World*:

> Thus Nature gets credit which should in truth be reserved for our-selves: the rose for its scent: the nightingale for his song: the sun for his radiance. The poets are entirely mistaken. They should address their lyrics to themselves, and should turn them into odes of self-congratu-lation on the excellency of the human mind. Nature is a dull affair, soundless, scentless, colourless. . . . (pp. 68–69)

These implications as regards secondary qualities might be acceptable, or at any rate just have to be accepted. The decisive objection to any Representative Theory of Perception bears fundamentally against the contention that "the ideas of primary qualities of bodies are resemblances of them, and their patterns do really exist in the bodies themselves". Curiously this decisive objection was well put by Locke himself, in a critique of the views of Nicholas Malebranche (1638–1715).

A few words can usefully be said here about these views before I end this section by quoting the relevant passage of Locke. The French Oratorian Father Malebranche was, along with Arnold Geulincx (1625–1669), one of several who responded to the challenge of a problem set by Descartes by arguing that really there is no psycho-physical interaction in man; and hence no intractable problem about how such a thing can occur. Instead it is the infinite God himself, the one and only true cause, who carefully puts appropriate representations of physical objects into our minds on every appropriate occasion. This view is labelled *Occasionalism,* precisely because it does thus insist that these representations are not caused but only occasioned by the objects we think we perceive.

A response on these lines will appeal most strongly to two sorts of people: first, those who take it to be axiomatic that elements so radically dissimilar cannot enter into direct causal transactions, and, second, those who – perhaps additionally and not alternatively – insist on so defining either *mind* or *matter* that such relations are made to involve a contradiction. Descartes, as we have seen (Ch. VIII, § 5), had manoeuvred himself into the second camp. Hume, applying his general thesis about the impossibility of apriori causal knowledge (Ch. VII, § 6), had in the *Treatise* this to say to the perhaps more numerous members of the first:

> If you pretend, therefore, to prove apriori that such a position of bodies can never cause a thought; because, turn it which way you will, it is nothing but a position of bodies; you must by the same course of reasoning, conclude that it can never produce motion; since there is no more apparent connection in one case than in the other. But as this latter conclusion is contrary to evident experience, and it is possible we may have a like experience in the operations of the mind, and may perceive a constant conjunction of thought and motion; you reason too hastily when, from the mere consideration of the ideas, you conclude that it is impossible motion can ever produce thought, or a different position of parts give rise to a different passion or reflection. Nay, it is not only possible we may have such an experience, but it is certain we have it; since every one may perceive that the different positions of his body change his thoughts and sentiments. (I (iv) 5)

The stock illustration for any Occasionalist position was introduced by Geulincx. This was apparently borrowed and certainly without acknowledgement by Leibniz, who employed it for what he was careful to distinguish as his own original purposes. It is one of those rare illustrations so perfect as to become itself part of the progress of philosophy. The passage to be quoted was composed by Leibniz in French, and first published in the *Histoire des Ouvrages des Savans* for February 1696:

> Imagine two clocks or watches which agree perfectly with each other. That can come about in three ways. The first is the mutual influence of one clock upon the other; the second is the care of a man who looks after them; the third is their own exactitude. The first way, that of

influence, has been tried by the late M. Huygens, with results which greatly astonished him. . . .

The second way to make the two clocks always to agree, even though they are bad ones, would be to ensure that they were constantly looked after by a skilled workman, who is adjusting them all the time; and this is what I call the path of assistance.

Finally the third way would be make the two movements with so much technique and precision in the first place that one could ensure their future agreement; and this is the path of pre-established harmony.

Now substitute the soul and the body for these two clocks. Their accord or agreement too will come about in one of these three ways. The path of influence is that of the philosophy of the plain man; but as we cannot conceive of material particles, nor yet of immaterial things or qualities, which could pass from one of these substances to the other, this notion has to be jettisoned. The path of assistance is that of the system of occasional causes; but I hold that this introduces a *Deus ex machina* [a special divine intervention – AF] into something natural and everyday, where reason requires that God should be involved only in the way in which he is with everything else in nature – by giving his concurrence. So only my hypothesis remains, that is the path of pre-established harmony. From the beginning God, by an anticipatory exercise of the divine skill, has formed each of these substances so perfectly and has regulated it with such exactitude, that it harmonizes with the other by simply observing its own laws which it received with its being. It is all as if there was mutual influence, or as if God did always take a special hand in this over and above providing his general concurrence.

What Leibniz calls "the way of influence" is, of course, the modern two-way interactionism. His objection to this view, as requiring intermediate machinery, can be seen as a special case of his rejection of any suggestion of action at a distance. This is something which in the *Leibniz-Clarke Correspondence* he urges against Newton's account of gravity. He also has this objection there to the idea of God as the mechanic on duty, in as much as the Newtonian system still left some particular work for God to do. God's "general concurrence", or general concourse, is just the same as what I distinguished earlier as "creation in the theologian's sense" (Ch. II, § 2): it is a matter of claiming, as Miss Mahalia Jackson sings, "He's got the whole world in his hands". The notion of a pre-established harmony explained here Leibniz in his metaphysics applies quite generally to all ostensible transactions between substances; and the subsistence of such

337

remarkable harmonies is then, of course, seen as a pointer to the existence of a Pre-established Harmonizer. One final point can be wryly instructive before we return to perception. Notice that this illustration of the two clocks, introduced by Geulincx and exploited by Leibniz to show how there could conceivably be a perfect correlation without any direct causal connection, will serve equally well to bring out what Hume means by "constant conjunction". And yet, as we have seen (Ch. VII, § 6), it is mainly in terms of constant conjunction that Hume attempts to analyse causation.

But now at last we have the decisive objection to any Representative Theory of Perception. This is provided by Locke himself in his *Examination of Father Malebranche's Opinion*:

> ... he says 'he is certain that the ideas of things are unchangeable'. This I cannot comprehend, for how can I know that the picture of anything is like that thing, when I never see that which it represents? For if these words do not mean that ideas are true unchangeable representations of things, I know not to what purpose they are. And if that be not their meaning, then they can only signify, that the idea I once had will be unchangeably the same as long as it recurs the same in my memory. ... Thus the idea of a horse, and the idea of a centaur, will, as often as they recur in my mind, be unchangeably the same; which is no more than this, the same idea will always be the same idea; but whether the one or the other be the true representation of anything that exists, that, upon his principles, neither our author nor anybody else can know. (§ 52)

To this we can now add, as Locke could not, that unless we can actually perceive things – and not just visual, tactual, gustatory and other representations of such things – then we cannot know that we are employing our words in accordance with the conventions of a public language. It is, for instance, only in so far as it is possible to refer to yellow objects as standards that I can be sure that my use of the word *yellow* is the same as that of everyone else. Indeed, since people are surely a sort of things, if I really never can perceive any things it is hard to see how I can know that there is anyone else.

§ 2 *The idealist vision of George Berkeley*

We are now going to look at the most remarkable product of the notion that we can be immediately aware only of our own ideas. This is the system of the Irishman George Berkeley (1685–1753). Berkeley later became a practically minded bishop within the Anglican communion. Like Hume but unlike Locke and Kant he was philosophically precocious. Most of his main philosophical works were published before he was thirty; while his most distinctive and original thoughts seem to have occurred to him first in his early twenties, in the course of studies of Locke made at Trinity College, Dublin. These thoughts Berkeley saw as developments of what Locke's early critic Stillingfleet – another bishop – called "the new way of ideas". So at the very beginning of *The Principles of Human Knowledge* Berkeley lays down a Lockean principle; from which even before the end of the first paragraph he has already drawn a peculiarly Berkeleyan conclusion:

> It is evident to any one who takes a survey of the objects of human knowledge, that they are either ideas actually imprinted on the senses, or else such as are perceived by attending to the passions and operations of the mind, or lastly ideas formed by help of memory and imagination, either compounding, dividing, or barely representing those originally perceived in the aforesaid ways. By sight I have the ideas of light and colours with their several degrees and variations. By touch I perceive, for example, hard and soft, heat and cold, motion and resistance, and of all these more and less either as to quantity or degree. Smelling furnishes me with odours; the palate with tastes, and hearing conveys sounds to the mind in all their variety of tone and composition. And as several of these are observed to accompany each other, they come to be marked by one name, and so to be reputed as one thing. Thus, for example, a certain colour, taste, smell, figure and consistence having been observed to go together, are accounted one distinct thing, signified by the name *apple*. Other collections of ideas constitute a stone, a tree, a book, and the like sensible things. . . . (§1)

Hume was later to offer a terminological improvement here: replacing Locke's *ideas* by *perceptions of the mind*; introducing *impressions* as a label for the first two sorts of ideas in Berkeley's list; and restricting *ideas* to the third only. Hume also hoped, though that is rather a different story, to distinguish ideas from impressions purely phenomenologically; by reference solely to the alleged lesser vivacity of the former, and without mention of any supposed external causes of the latter. But let Berkeley continue:

> But besides all that endless variety of ideas or objects of knowledge, there is likewise something which knows or perceives them, and exercises divers operations, as willing, imagining, remembering about

them. This perceiving, active being is what I call *mind, spirit, soul* or *my self*. By which words I do not denote any one of my ideas, but a thing entirely distinct from them, wherein they exist, or, which is the same thing, whereby they are perceived; for the existence of an idea consists in being perceived.

That neither our thoughts, nor passions, nor ideas formed by the imagination, exist without the mind, is what every body will allow. And it seems no less evident that the various sensations or ideas imprinted on the sense, however blended or combined together (that is, whatever objects they compose) cannot exist otherwise than in a mind perceiving them. I think an intuitive knowledge may be obtained of this, by any one that shall attend to what is meant by the term *exist* when applied to sensible things. The table I write on, I say, exists, that is, I see and feel it; and if I were out of my study I should say it existed, meaning thereby that if I was in my study I might perceive it, or that some other spirit actually does perceive it. There was an odour, that is, it was smelled; there was a sound, that is to say, it was heard; a colour or figure, and it was perceived by sight or touch. This is all that I can understand by these and the like expressions. . . .

It is indeed an opinion strangely prevailing amongst men, that houses, mountains, rivers, and in a word all sensible objects have an existence natural or real, distinct from their being perceived by the understanding. But with how great an assurance and acquiescence soever this principle may be entertained in the world; yet whoever shall find in his heart to call it in question, may, if I mistake not, perceive it to involve a manifest contradiction. For what are the forementioned objects but the things we perceive by sense, and what do we perceive besides our own ideas or sensations; and is it not plainly repugnant that any one of these or any combination of them should exist unperceived? (§§ 2–4)

This, stated characteristically with lucidity and brilliance, is Berkeley's basic contention. It is essential to appreciate both the nature of his fantastic conclusion and the quality of the argument by which from apparently uncontestable premises this conclusion is compulsively deduced. One premise was supplied by Locke: that a person can be immediately aware only of his own ideas, including especially ideas of sense – what Berkeley liked to call "ideas of sensible things", or even simply "sensible things". The other occurred to the young Berkeley as a fresh illumination: that ideas so understood can be said to exist only in so far as someone has them. The essence of such entities must be to be experienced: hence the Latin slogan *Esse* (to be) *est percipi* (is to be perceived). For just as it would make no sense at all to talk of a toothache which was not the toothache of any person, so it cannot make sense to talk of a sensible idea existing un-sensed.

Granted these two premises the final conclusion should be, surely, some form of Solipsistic Idealism: whether epistemological, asserting that all I can ever know is myself and my ideas; or metaphysical, claiming that this is all that – in the last analysis – there actually is; or perhaps analytical, contending that all the propositions which I can understand must deal exclusively with this rather limited subject matter. (That this is indeed the consequence, and that it is intolerable, is, incidentally, what Lenin maintained in the book mentioned in the previous section; vehemently, persistently, but in the case of Berkeley respectfully.) Understandably, however, Berkeley sought, and judged that he had found, a way of keeping the Metaphysical Idealism – the belief that all there is is ideas and (in most versions) spiritual substances to have them – while escaping from the Solipsism – the belief that he alone existed. His argument continues:

> ... whatever power I may have over my own thoughts, I find the ideas actually perceived by sense have not a like dependence on my will. When in broad daylight I open my eyes, it is not in my power to choose whether I shall see or no, or to determine what particular objects shall present themselves to my view; and so likewise as to the hearing and other senses, the ideas imprinted on them are not creatures of my will. There is therefore some other will or spirit that produces them.
>
> The ideas of sense are more strong, lively, and distinct than those of the imagination; they have likewise a steadiness, order, and coherence, and are not excited at random, as those which are the effects of human wills often are, but in a regular train or series, the admirable connexion whereof sufficiently testifies the wisdom and benevolence of its Author. Now the set rules or established methods, wherein the mind we depend on excites in us the ideas of sense, are called the *Laws of Nature*: and these we learn by experience, which teaches us that such and such ideas are attended with such and such other ideas, in the ordinary course of things. (§§ 29–30)

The ideas imprinted on the senses by the Author of Nature are called *real things*: and those excited in the imagination being less regular, vivid and constant, are more properly termed *ideas,* or *images of things,* which they copy and represent. But then our sensations, be they never so vivid and distinct, are nevertheless *ideas,* that is, they exist in the mind, or are perceived by it, as truly as the ideas of its own framing. The ideas of sense are allowed to have more reality in them, that is, to be more strong, orderly, and coherent than the creatures of the mind; but this is no argument that they exist without the mind. They are also less dependent on the spirit, or thinking substance which perceives them, in that they are excited by the will of another and more powerful Spirit; yet still they are ideas, and certainly no idea, whether faint or strong, can exist otherwise than in a mind perceiving it. (§ 33)

If any man thinks this detracts from the existence or reality of things, he is very far from understanding what hath been premised in the plainest terms I could think of. Take here an abstract of what has been said. There are spiritual substances, minds, or human souls, which will or excite ideas in themselves at pleasure: but these are faint, weak, and unsteady in respect of others they perceive by sense, which being impressed upon them according to certain rules or laws of nature, speak themselves the effects of a mind more powerful and wise than human spirits. These latter are said to have more reality in them than the former: by which is meant that they are more affecting, orderly, and distinct, and that they are not fictions of the mind perceiving them. And in this sense, the sun that I see by day is the real sun, and that which I imagine by night is the idea of the former. In the sense here given of *reality*, it is evident that every vegetable, star, mineral, and in general each part of the mundane system, is as much a real being by our principles as by any other. Whether others mean any thing by the term *reality* different from what I do, I entreat them to look into their own thoughts and see. (§ 36)

Certainly we have to ask whether this is indeed what is meant by *the existence or reality of things*. And the answer – whatever fault has to be found with Lenin's conception of sense-data as copies, reflections, or photographs – must surely be that he was wholly right to insist that "objective reality" must be something "existing independently of them". Admittedly Berkeley's system does allow for a distinction between "real things" and "images of things"; and this perhaps would be enough to entitle him to disclaim the admiring description of his compatriot W. B. Yeats:

> ... *God-appointed Berkeley that proved all things a dream*
> *That this pragmatical, preposterous pig of a world* ...
> *Must vanish on the instant if the mind but change its theme*
> ('Blood and the Moon', II)

Yet the distinction for which Berkeley does thus provide is not the distinction which he needs if he is to make good here his own surprising assertions that he is "recalling men to common sense" (*Philosophical Commentaries,*

§ 751). Nor is the situation in this respect improved when the final and in his view vital innovation is brought into account.

Anyone meeting for the first time only the passages quoted so far, and not knowing the famous antiphonal limericks, would take it that Berkeley was without qualification a phenomenalist about material things. For it would be hard to give a better statement of what is meant by the word *phenomenalism* than that sentence from § 3 of Berkeley's *Principles*: "The table I write on I say exists, that is, I see and feel it; and if I were out of my study I should say it existed – meaning thereby that if I was in my study I might perceive it, or that some other . . . actually does perceive it."

Now one stock objection to phenomenalism, as this doctrine has been developed by secular successors to Berkeley, is that it implies that a material thing must cease to exist whenever it is not actually being perceived by man or brute, and that there could not have been any material things when there were no creatures capable of perception. This is the consequence accepted boldly by J. S. Mill in his definition of "Matter" as "a permanent possibility of sensation" (*An Examination of Sir William Hamilton's Philosophy*, Ch. XI). It is put dramatically as an objection in the first of the two limericks:

> *There once was a man who said, 'God*
> *Must think it exceedingly odd*
> *If he finds that this tree*
> *Continues to be*
> *When there's no one about in the Quad.'*

The word *Quad*, it should perhaps be explained, is a slang abbreviation for *Quadrangle*. It is the term used in Oxford for grassed courtyards surrounded by college buildings. This challenging verse is traditionally credited to Monsignor Ronald Knox. Despite the rather different internal attribution the response on behalf of Bishop Berkeley, also in limerick form, probably came from the same witty pen:

> *'Dear Sir*
> *Your astonishment's odd:*
> *I am always about in the Quad*
> *And that's why the tree*
> *Will continue to be,*
> *Since observed by,*
> *Yours faithfully,*
> *God'*

343

The two limericks together constitute an excellent mnemonic. For Berkeley does indeed have his own way of avoiding the outrage to common sense presented by any atheist phenomenalism. By one of those brilliant judo moves which help to make the study of his works the intellectual treat that it is, he converts the stock objection to phenomenalism into what he takes to be a decisive and peculiarly direct proof of the existence of God:

> Some truths there are so near and obvious to the mind that a man need only open his eyes to see them. Such I take this important one to be, viz. that all the choir of heaven and furniture of the earth, in a word all those bodies which compose the mighty frame of the world, have not any subsistence without a mind – that their being is to be perceived or known; and that consequently so long as they are not actually perceived by me, and do not exist in my mind or that of any other created spirit, they must either have no existence at all, or else subsist in the mind of some Eternal Spirit. . . . (§ 6)

> For, though we hold . . . the objects of sense to be nothing else but ideas which cannot exist unperceived, yet we may not hence conclude that they have no existence except only while they are perceived by us; since there may be some other spirit that perceives them though we do not. Wherever bodies are said to have no existence without the mind, I would not be understood to mean this or that particular mind but all minds whatsoever. It does not therefore follow from the foregoing principles that bodies are annihilated and created every moment, or exist not at all during the intervals between our perception of them.
> (§ 48)

> . . . it is plain that we cannot know the existence of other spirits, otherwise than by . . . the ideas by them excited in us. I perceive several motions, changes, and combinations of ideas, that inform me there are certain particular agents like my self, which accompany them, and concur in their production. Hence the knowledge I have of other spirits is not immediate, as is the knowledge of my ideas; but depending on the intervention of ideas, by me referred to agents or spirits distinct from myself, as effects or concomitant signs.

> But though there be some things which convince us human agents are concerned in producing them; yet it is evident to every one, that those things which are called the works of nature, that is, the far greater part of the ideas or sensations perceived by us, are not produced by, or dependent on the wills of men. There is, therefore, some other spirit

that causes them, since it is repugnant that they should subsist by themselves. . . . But if we attentively consider the constant regularity, order, and concatenation of natural things, the surprising magnificence, beauty, and perfection of the larger, and the exquisite contrivance of the smaller parts of the creation, together with the exact harmony and correspondence of the whole . . .; I say if we consider all these things, and at the same time attend to the meaning and import of the attributes, one, eternal, infinitely wise, good, and perfect, we shall clearly perceive that they belong to the aforesaid Spirit 'who works all in all', and by whom all things consist [*I Corinthians*, 12 : 6 and *Colossians*, 1 : 17].

Hence it is evident, that God is known as certainly and immediately as any other mind or spirit whatsoever, distinct from our selves. We may even assert, that the existence of God is far more evidently perceived than the existence of men; because the effects of nature are infinitely more numerous and considerable, than those ascribed to human agents.   (§§ 145–147)

§ 3 *The agnosticism of Hume and Kant*

Now we have heard Berkeley we can allow Hume to continue with the argument from which I quoted at the beginning of § 1. The omission in the following passages is a terse paragraph against Descartes, which has been given already as the second of two extracts from the first *Inquiry* in the previous chapter (Ch. IX, § 1):

By what argument can it be proved that the perceptions of the mind must be caused by external objects, entirely different from them though resembling them (if that be possible), and could not arise either from the energy of the mind itself or from the suggestion of some invisible and unknown spirit or from some other cause still more unknown to us? It is acknowledged that in fact many of these perceptions arise not from anything external, as in dreams, madness, and other diseases. And nothing can be more inexplicable than the manner in which body should so operate upon mind as ever to convey an image of itself to a substance supposed of so different and even contrary a nature.

It is a question of fact whether the perceptions of the senses be produced by external objects resembling them. How shall this question be determined? By experience, surely, as all other questions of a like nature. But here experience is and must be entirely silent. The mind has never anything present to it but the perceptions, and cannot possibly reach any experience of their connection with objects. The supposition of such a connection is, therefore, without any foundation in reasoning. . . .

This is a topic, therefore, in which the profounder and more philosophical sceptics will always triumph when they endeavour to introduce a universal doubt into all subjects of human knowledge and inquiry. Do you follow the instincts and propensities of nature, may they say, in assenting to the veracity of sense? But these lead you to believe that the very perception or sensible image is the external object. Do you disclaim this principle in order to embrace a more rational opinion that the perceptions are only representations of something external? You here depart from your natural propensity and more obvious sentiments, and yet are not able to satisfy your reason, which can never find any convincing arguments from experience to prove that the perceptions are connected with any external objects. (XII (i))

The position supported by the uninstructed "instincts and propensities of nature" is by instructing philosophers labelled contemptuously, *Naïve Realism*. Hume, however, in his account of this position makes a mistake which is as common as it is often difficult to avoid. He introduces into this account the sophisticated notion with which the uninitiated are as such not equipped. For the truly naïve realist must think: not that "the very perception or sensible image is the external object"; but rather that people can – and often do – see, touch, hear, taste, or smell things. Let us do another bit of offensive labelling, and christen this *The Describing-them-as-thinking-in-your-terms-although-they-do-not Misrepresentation*. (The *do* in this label has to be construed as temporally neutral, since we misrepresent the men of old in this way at least as often as we do our contemporaries.)

The second point to notice is that Hume is here applying once again his great negative insight about causality: "If we reason a priori, anything may appear able to produce anything. The falling of a pebble may, for aught we know, extinguish the sun, or the wish of man control the planets in their orbits. It is only experience which teaches us the nature and bounds of cause and effect and enables us to infer the existence of one object from that of another" (ibid., XII (iii); compare Ch. VII, § 6 and Ch. VI, § 5, above). Hume is thus, in terms of an important distinction explained earlier (Ch. VIII, § 4), approaching the question of an external world as an empiricist rather than a rationalist.

Berkeley in this sense and on this issue was not an empiricist but a rationalist. For he, working of course without benefit of Hume's analysis of causality, was firmly and fundamentally convinced that he did know a priori that the only things which can be causes are incorporeal spiritual substances. Hence it was out of the question for him to suggest that ideas which we cannot say we produce ourselves might be in some way generated by matter – "a stupid thoughtless Somewhat" (*Principles*, § 75). Hence too Berkeley became committed to saying that those things – or, rather, those "sensible ideas" – which are normally thought to cause others are not in truth causes at all, but signs. They are signs providentially provided by God, who is alone the real cause of every natural event, in order to give us "a sort of foresight which enables us to regulate our actions for the benefit of life. And without . . . which we should be all in uncertainty and confusion, and a grown man no more know how to manage himself in the affairs of life than an infant just born" (Ibid., § 31).

Berkeley was thus persuaded that, though there certainly cannot be any such thing as matter capable of existing unperceived, we equally certainly can know what – or, rather, who – produces our "ideas of sensible things". By contrast Hume was agnostic by conviction. Though it is psychologically impossible to doubt the existence of the external world, it is equally impossible to find any logically adequate justification for this belief; and so the only profitable investigations here will be psychological. These Hume broaches in the *Treatise*:

> . . . the sceptic still continues to reason and believe, even though he asserts that he cannot defend his reason by reason; . . . he must assent to the principle concerning the existence of body, though he cannot pretend by any arguments of philosophy to maintain its veracity. Nature has not left this to his choice, and has doubtless esteemed it an affair of too great importance to be trusted to our uncertain reasonings and speculations. We may well ask, 'What causes induce us to believe in the existence of body?', but it is vain to ask, 'Whether there be body or not?' That is a point which we must take for granted in all our reasonings. (I (iv) 2)

To conclude this third section I will quote for comparison a statement by Kant, the other great classical philosopher who was in this respect agnostic. Kant himself, as has been said already (Ch. VI, § 2), was generous in his tributes to Hume. He "gave my investigations in the field of speculative philosophy quite a new direction". Yet, because Kant's *Critique of Pure Reason* is enormously different from Hume's *Treatise of Human Nature* in style and tone, students often believe that there is more difference in substance than there actually is. Kant, while envying "the subtlety and . . . the grace of David Hume", described his own masterpiece as "dry, obscure, opposed to all ordinary notions, and moreover long-winded"; though he did then proceed to insist upon the salutary thought that "this much abused obscurity" of its subject frequently serves "as a mere pretext under which people hide their own indolence or dullness".

However, both the *Treatise* and the first *Critique* are works in the same genre as Locke's *Essay*; and both Hume and Kant saw themselves as thereby achieving a sort of Copernican revolution in reverse – showing how and how far our knowledge must be limited and conditioned by the nature of the human mind (Ch. III, § 3). The phrases quoted in the previous paragraph come from the Introduction to *Prolegomena to any Future Metaphysics*, and the statement which follows is taken from the main body of the same work. This constitutes Kant's own guidebook to the first *Critique,* and may be compared with Hume's much shorter and slighter *Abstract of a Treatise of Human Nature.* The present quotation explains the famous Kantian notion of a thing-in-itself, the label for which is often affectedly left in the original German as *Ding-an-sich.* The translation is by P. G. Lucas:

> As the senses, according to what has now been demonstrated, never and in no single instance enable us to know things in themselves, but only their appearances, and as these are mere representations . . . 'all bodies, together with the space in which they are, must be held to be nothing but mere representations in us, and exist nowhere else than merely in our thoughts.' Now is this not manifest idealism?
>
> Idealism consists in the assertion that there are none other than thinking beings; the other things which we believe we perceive . . . are only representations in the thinking beings, to which in fact no object outside the latter corresponds. I say on the contrary: things are given to us as objects of our senses situated outside us, but of what they may be in themselves we know nothing; we only know their appearances, i.e. the representations that they effect in us when they affect our senses. Consequently I do indeed admit that there are bodies outside us, i.e. things which, although wholly unknown to us as to what they may be in themselves, we know through the representations which their influence on our sensibility provides for us, and to which we give the name of bodies. This word therefore merely means the appearance of that for us unknown but none the less real object. Can this be called idealism? It is the very opposite of it.
>
> That it can be said of many of the predicates of outer things, without detriment to their real existence, that they belong not to those things in themselves but only to their appearances and have no existence of their

own outside our representations, is something that was generally accepted and admitted long before Locke's time, but more so afterwards. To these predicates belong heat, colour, taste, etc. But that I . . . also count as mere appearances, in addition to these, the remaining qualities of bodies which are called *primary*, extension, place, and space in general with all that depends on it . . . is something against which not the slightest ground of inadmissibility can be adduced. A man who will not allow colours to be attached to the object in itself as qualities, but only to the sense of sight as modifications, cannot be called an idealist for that; equally little can my doctrine be called idealistic merely because I find that more of, indeed all, the qualities that make up the intuition of a body belong merely to its appearance; for the existence of the thing that appears is not thereby cancelled, as with real idealism, but it is only shown that we cannot know it at all through the senses as it is in itself. (§ 13, Note II)

§4 *The Argument from Illusion*

The outcome of the first three sections may seem wholly negative. For all the three philosophical accounts of perception considered so far – the qualified photographic theory of Locke, the idealism of Berkeley, and the agnosticism of Hume and Kant – appear to be intolerably paradoxical. They are intolerably paradoxical, for two main reasons. First, because they all imply a rejection of naïve realism. They put a theoretically impenetrable screen of sense-data between the (Cartesian) person and the realities around him. Second, and consequently, by removing all knowable public reference points, they rob us each and all of the possibility of communicating with one another in a common, public language and knowing that we are doing so.

Negative in a sense this outcome may be. Yet decisively to establish that some tempting line of exploration is after all a blind alley does constitute a positive achievement; and full credit must be given to those who have contributed, however unintentionally and unwittingly, to this sort of progress. Thomas Reid (1710–1796) was therefore entirely right, though not perhaps very tactful, when he acknowledged a great debt of this kind to Hume:

> I have learned more from your writings . . . than from all others put together. Your system appears to me not only coherent in all its parts, but likewise justly deduced from principles commonly received among

philosophers; principles which I never thought of calling in question, until the conclusions you draw from them in the *Treatise of Human Nature* made me suspect them. [Personal letter, dated 18 March 1763]

It is a case calling for The Search-for-the-shared-assumptions-to-challenge Strategy; and it was not necessary for Reid to look very far since, as we saw in the first section, Hume had already emphasized what is the fatal but apparently unavoidable assumption. By challenging this systematically Reid became the founder of the Scottish Philosophy of Common Sense. The first extract below comes again from a personal letter, this time to a Dr James Gregory, while the rest are taken from Reid's *Essays on the Intellectual Powers of Man*:

> The merit of what you are pleased to call my philosophy lies, I think, chiefly in having called in question the common theory of ideas, or images of things in the mind, being the only objects of thought; a theory founded on natural prejudices, and so universally received as to be interwoven with the structure of language. . . . The discovery was the birth of time not of genius; and Berkeley and Hume did more to bring it to light than the man that hit upon it. I think that there is hardly anything in the philosophy of mind that does not follow with ease from the detection of this prejudice.

> The ideas, of whose existence I require the proof, are not the operations of any mind, but supposed objects of these operations. They are not perception, remembrance, or conception, but things that are said to be perceived, or remembered, or imagined.
> Nor do I dispute the existence of what the vulgar call the objects of perception. These, by all who acknowledge their existence, are called real things, not ideas. But philosophers maintain that, besides these, there are immediate objects of perception in the mind itself: that, for instance, we do not see the sun immediately, but an idea; or, as Mr Hume calls it, an impression in our own minds. This idea is said to be the image, the resemblance, the representative of the sun, if there be a sun. It is from the existence of the idea that we must infer the existence of the sun. But the idea being immediately perceived, there can be no doubt, as philosophers think, of its existence. (II 14)

> Mr Locke, in the Introduction to his *Essay*, tells us that he uses the word *idea* to signify whatever is the immediate object of thought; and then adds, 'I presume it will be easily granted me that there are such ideas in men's minds; everyone is conscious of them in himself; and

men's words and actions will satisfy him that they are in others.' I am indeed conscious of perceiving, remembering, imagining; but that the objects of these operations are images in my mind, I am not conscious. I am satisfied, by men's words and actions, that they often perceive the same objects which I perceive, which could not be if those objects were ideas in their own minds. (II 14)

This is all very fine, as far as it goes. Certainly Reid did much better than either Lenin or G. E. Moore. For Lenin – truly one of Plato's Giants (Ch. II, § 1) – set boldly out to slay Berkeley's God when equipped only with "the materialist theory of knowledge" explicitly defined in terms of precisely the ruinous assumption which must make impossible any knowledge of matter as existing independently. Moore too, who wrote two properly famous articles, 'A Defence of Common Sense' and 'A Refutation of Idealism', seems never once in his long and devoted philosophical career to have questioned this disastrous dogma that what we are immediately aware of in perception is sense-data. But to see how impossibly paradoxical are the consequences of accepting this dogma, and to challenge it, is only a beginning. The next and far more extensive task is to confront and to overcome the arguments which have made it seem that "the slightest philosophy . . . teaches us that nothing can ever be present to the mind but an image or perception, and that the senses" are unable "to produce any immediate intercourse between the mind and the object" (Ch. X, § 1).

To this further and greater task of the philosophy of perception Reid's own contribution was small; partly perhaps because he appears to have been curiously unaware of the size of the arsenal of such arguments. But to the one argument explicitly deployed by Hume in the passage quoted in § 1 Reid's reply is exemplary:

Hitherto I see nothing that can be called an argument. . . . The argument, the only argument, follows: 'The table which we see seems to diminish as we remove farther from it; but the real table, which exists independently of us, suffers no alteration. It was, therefore, nothing but its image which was presented to the mind. These are the obvious dictates of reason'. . . .

Let us suppose, for a moment, that it is the real table that we see. Must not this real table seem to diminish as we remove farther from it. It is demonstrable that it must. How then can this apparent diminution be an argument that it is not the real table? When that which must happen to the real table, as we remove further from it, does actually happen to the table we see, it is absurd to conclude from this, that it is not the real table we see. It is evident, therefore, that this ingenious author has imposed upon himself by confounding real magnitude with apparent magnitude, and that his argument is a mere sophism.

... Mr Hume's argument not only has no strength to support his conclusion, but ... it leads to the contrary conclusion – to wit, that it is the real table that we see; for this plain reason, that the table we see has precisely the apparent magnitude which it is demonstrable that the real table must have been when placed at that distance.   (*Ibid.*, II 14)

That Reid is right on this particular point can be appreciated best by pondering an alternative perceptual possibility. Suppose that I had thought that I could see a table, and that then, as I removed myself further from the place where I had thought it to be, the appearance of that supposed table continued to occupy exactly the same proportion of my whole visual field. This would indeed be a powerful reason for suspecting: either that what I had taken to be a table was some sort of trick object; or that I was subject to some very curious hallucination. But where Reid is quite wrong, and most extraordinarily wrong, is in his conclusion that, having disposed of this Humean argument and a few other oddments besides, "I have considered every argument I have found advanced to prove the existence of ideas, or images of external things, in the mind."

For Reid was plainly familiar with the *Discourse* of Descartes. He must therefore, like us, have read there: "So on the grounds that our senses sometimes deceive us, I wanted to suppose that there was not anything corresponding to what they make us imagine ... all the same experiences which we have when we are awake can also come to us when we are asleep without there being one of them which is veridical. ...." Reid too, again like us, must have been familiar with physico-physiological accounts of the mechanics of perception. For these can be found in Descartes and in Locke as well as in the *Opticks* of Newton. And such accounts are usually thought to establish some kind of Causal Theory of Perception.

The argument which Hume offers, and of which Reid disposes, should be taken not as a lonesome individual but as a representative of a vast class. The argument type of which this specimen is only one of innumerable tokens is nowadays labelled *The Argument from Illusion*. This label is not completely apt, since the phenomena cited could not all be described naturally as illusions. It is also possibly misleading in that it may suggest that these phenomena have always been summoned in support of exactly the same conclusions. But with these warnings and in the present context we can characterize the Argument from Illusion as the attempt to show that, because appearances are or might be in some way deceptive, what we actually see is never things but only the appearances of things; and then, crucially, that these appearances are essentially mental not physical – that they are in the mind not in the external world. Several of the phenomena which have become favourite starting-points were noticed already by Plato; and these, and many others, were lovingly listed by Sextus Empiricus. Thus there is, for instance, mention in *The Republic* of the straight stick which when plunged partly into water appears through refraction bent (§ 602C); while the towers "frequently observed" by Descartes in *Meditation* VI may well have been borrowed from the *Outlines of Pyrrhonism* (I (xiii) 32):

> But, afterwards, several observed phenomena by degrees destroyed all the trust which I had given to my senses. For I frequently observed that towers which from a distance had looked round to me appeared from close by to be square; and that colossi raised on the topmost summits of these towers appeared to me like statuettes when I looked at them from below. So, in an infinity of other instances, I discovered error in judgements based on the external senses. And not only in those based on the external senses but even in those relying on the internal senses. For is there anything more private and more internal than pain? And yet I have sometimes been told by people who have had their arms or their legs amputated that it still sometimes seemed to them that they felt pain in the part which had been cut off; which gave me cause to think that I also could not be certain that there is something wrong with one of my limbs even though I can feel pain in it.
>
> And to these grounds for doubt I shortly afterwards also added two other very general ones. The first is that I have never believed that I perceived anything when awake which I could not also sometimes believe that I perceived when asleep; and as I did not believe that the things which I seemed to be perceiving while sleeping proceeded from things in the external world, I did not see why I ought to have this conviction any more about those which it seems to me that I perceive when I am awake. The second is that, while I was not yet acquainted – or, rather, while I was pretending not to be acquainted – with the Author of my being, I did not see anything to stop my having been made of such a nature that I could be mistaken even about the things which seemed to me most authentic.

Discounting for the moment the second "very general" ground this constitutes an exemplary statement of the Argument from Illusion.

Obviously the conclusion intended is: that we can be sure of the existence and the characteristics of our subjective experiences; but that, at this stage, we cannot be sure of the characteristics or even the existence of anything further to which these may seem to point. Descartes' statement is instructively typical of most presentations of the argument in its failure to insist upon a basic distinction. This is the distinction between cases in which one is, or may be, mistaken about what one is in fact perceiving; and cases in which the mistake is, or would be, to believe that one is perceiving anything at all.

The Cases of the Diminishing Table, the Bent Stick, the Square Tower, the Colossal Statuettes, and such other old favourites as the round coin which when viewed askew allegedly looks elliptical, all fall unequivocally into the first of these two categories. But they are for that very reason inadequate foundations for the conclusion proposed. To point to such possibilities might justify a demand for greater caution in making claims about what we can perceive 'out there in the external world'. But it can scarcely be by itself a ground for saying that all we ever can perceive is objects which are essentially 'in the mind'. So what, if anything, these cases by themselves would warrant is that inhibition on outright assertion prescribed by the Army Instructor in Henry Reed's 'Judging Distances':

> *. . . you know*
> *How to report on a landscape . . .*
> *That things only seem to be things.*
> *A barn is not called a barn, to put it more plainly,*
> *Or a field in the distance, where sheep may be safely grazing.*
> *You must never be over-sure. You must say, when reporting:*
> *'At five o'clock in the central sector is a dozen*
> *Of what appear to be animals'; whatever you do,*
> *Don't call the bleeders* sheep.

The powerful independent Argument from Illusion starts from cases which fall into our second category: such as, for instance, the pain felt as being in a limb which is in fact no longer there at all; or the eidetic imagery which some people sometimes experience even when awake, and which is defined as possessing the vivacity of a genuine perceptual experience. For in these cases we apparently enjoy subjective experiences which are phenomenologically indistinguishable from those which occur in authentic perception; and this suggests that perhaps all that we ever are directly acquainted with is these private experiences; and hence that perception, if there really is such a thing, must be an indirect matter of inference from these as evidence.

§5 *Seeing things and having experiences*

This second kind of Argument from Illusion complements and reinforces a causal argument. This causal argument, which may be presented with more or less scientific sophistication, starts from the contention that when I perceive something the presence of that something must be an essential part of the cause of my having, on that occasion, the appropriate subjective experience. This premise at least is not merely true but necessarily true. For suppose someone were to enjoy the sort of subjective experience which normally goes with actually seeing a kipper; and suppose further that this was in no way a result of the presence of a kipper – perhaps because his eyes had been blinded and the experience was being produced by the manipulation of electrodes within the visual area of his brain; then even if there did happen in fact to be a kipper right in front of his eyes it must still be contradictory to describe this blind man as seeing – as opposed to 'seeing' – a kipper. And it would be even more outrageous to maintain that he could see not just a kipper but that particular kipper.

So much can and must be conceded to the Causal Theory of Perception; and in so far as this is all that is meant then that theory is true. But the crucial move, both for the present argument and for The Causal Theory as usually construed, is the step from an unexceptionable premise to the catastrophic conclusion that all we can perceive – or, at any rate, all we can directly perceive – is our own subjective experiences. It is possible to derive some help towards dealing with this move from a series of passages taken from Reid's *Essays*:

> *To perceive, to remember, to be conscious,* and *to conceive* or *imagine,* are words common to philosophers and to the vulgar. They signify different operations of the mind, which are distinguished in all languages, and by all men that think. I shall endeavour to use them in their most common and proper acceptation, and I think that they are hardly capable of strict definition. But as some philosophers, in treating of the mind have taken the liberty to use them very improperly, so as to corrupt the English language and to confound things which the common understanding of mankind hath always led them to

distinguish, I shall make some observations on the meaning of them that may prevent ambiguity or confusion in the use of them.

First, we are never said to perceive things of the existence of which we have not full conviction. I may conceive or imagine a mountain of gold or a winged horse; but no man says that he perceives such a creature of imagination. Thus perception is distinguished from conception or imagination. Secondly, *perception* is applied only to external objects, not to those that are in the mind itself. When I am pained, I do not say that I perceive pain, but that I feel it, or that I am conscious of it. Thus perception is distinguished from consciousness. Thirdly, the immediate object of perception must be something present, and not what is past. We may remember what is past, but not perceive it. I may say, *I perceive such a person has had the smallpox*; but this phrase is figurative, although the figure is so familiar that it is not observed. The meaning of it is that I perceive the pits in his face, which are certain signs of his having had the smallpox. We say we perceive the thing signified when we only perceive the sign. But when the word *perception* is used properly, and without any figure, it is never applied to things past. And thus it is distinguished from remembrance. (I (i) 5–6)

This passage is interesting not only for the immediate relevance of its contribution to the logical analysis of perception but also and perhaps even more as an illustration of how and why all philosophers – and indeed everyone with any concern for clarity and truth – ought to be concerned about correct English (or French, or Choctaw, or whatever). It is also worth noticing that Reid's third point here is what gives purchase to The Time-lag Argument. This is one more token of the Argument from Illusion; and it is special both in not fitting happily into either of our two categories and in not having been known to Sextus Empiricus. Bertrand Russell provided a succinct formulation in his *Human Knowledge*: ". . . though you see the sun now, the physical object to be inferred from your seeing existed eight minutes ago; if, in the intervening minutes, the sun had gone out, you would still be seeing exactly what you are seeing. We cannot, therefore, identify the physical sun with what we see" (p. 204). In the second of the present series of passages Reid proceeds to a logical analysis of the concept of sensation, once again presenting this as if it were a piece of psychological observation:

Sensation is a name given by philosophers to an act of mind which may be distinguished from all others by this, that it hath no object distinct from the act itself. Pain of every kind is an uneasy sensation.

When I am pained, I cannot say that the pain I feel is one thing, and that my feeling is another thing. They are one and the same thing, and cannot be disjointed, even in imagination. Pain when not felt has no existence. It can be neither greater nor less in degree or duration, nor anything else in kind than it is felt to be. It cannot exist by itself, nor in any subject but a sentient being. (I (i) 12)

Reid's point is that the essence of sensations is not – as Berkeley would have had it – to be perceived; but, rather, to be had. It makes no sense to speak of a pain existing unfelt. Yet despite his desire to employ words "in their most common and proper acceptation" Reid proceeds, like so many other philosophers since, to give to the word *sensation* an extremely wide sense. Whereas it is, surely, ordinarily applied only to things like itches, throbbings, prickly feelings, and thrills running up and down the spine, Reid seems to be willing to employ it wherever I might use the expression *subjective experience*:

The external senses have a double province – to make us feel and to make us perceive. They furnish us with a variety of sensations, some pleasant, others painful, and others indifferent; at the same time they give us . . . an invincible belief of the existence of external objects. . . . This . . . belief which nature produces by means of the senses we call *perception*. The feeling which goes along with the perception we call *sensation*. The perception and the corresponding sensation are produced at the same time. (II (xvii) 5)

That we perceive certain disorders in our own bodies by means of uneasy sensations, which nature hath conjoined with them, will not be disputed. Of this kind are toothache, headache, gout, and every distemper and hurt which we feel. . . .

In the toothache, for instance, there is, first, a painful feeling; and, secondly, a . . . belief of some disorder in the tooth which is believed to be the cause of the uneasy feeling. The first of these is a sensation, the second is perception; for it includes a . . . belief of an external object. But these two things, though of different natures, are so constantly conjoined in our experience and in our imagination that we consider them as one. We give the same name to both; for *the toothache* is the proper name of the pain we feel, and it is the proper name of the disorder in the tooth which causes that pain. If it should be made a question whether the toothache be in the mind that feels it, or in the tooth that is affected, much might be said on both sides, while it is not observed that the word has two meanings. But a little reflection satisfies us that the pain is in the mind, and the disorder in the tooth. If some philosopher should pretend to have made the discovery that the toothache, the gout, the headache, are only sensations in the mind, and that it is a vulgar error to conceive that they are distempers in the body, he might defend his system in the same manner as those who affirm that there is no sound, no colour, no taste, in bodies defend that paradox. But both these systems, like most paradoxes, will be found to be only an abuse of words.

We say that we feel the toothache, not that we perceive it. On the other hand, we say that we can perceive the colour of a body, not that we feel it. Can any reason be given for this difference of phraseology? In answer to this question I apprehend that, both when we feel the toothache and when we see a coloured body, there is sensation and perception conjoined. But, in the toothache, the sensation being very painful, engrosses the attention; and therefore we speak of it as if it were felt only, and not perceived: whereas, in seeing a coloured body, the sensation is indifferent and draws no attention.   (II (xviii))

Cases sometimes happen which give occasion even to the vulgar to distinguish the painful sensation from the disorder which is the cause of it. A man who has had his leg cut off, many years after feels pain in a toe of that leg. . . .

The same phenomenon may lead the philosopher, in all cases, to distinguish sensation from perception. We say that the man had a deceitful feeling, when he felt a pain in his toe after his leg was cut off; and we have a true meaning in saying so. But, if we will speak accurately, our sensations cannot be deceitful; they must be what we feel them to be, and can be nothing else. Where, then, lies the deceit? I answer, it lies not in the sensation, which is real, but in the seeming perception he had of a disorder in his toe. . . .

The same reasoning may be applied to every phenomenon that can, with propriety, be called a deception of sense. As when one who has the jaundice sees a body yellow, which is really white; or when a man sees an object double, because his eyes are not both directed to it. . . .

(II (xviii))

I have allowed this third group of extracts to extend rather further than is immediately necessary, in c :der to provide occasion to bring out two instructive extras. The first of these bonuses can be earned by attending thoughtfully to Reid's speculation, in the last paragraph of the second of this group of extracts, about the possible basis of one of our verbal habits. The moral to take to heart is that verbal habits are indeed habits. So where there is a difference in the conditioned response there must, surely, be some corresponding difference between the occasioning stimuli. It is this consideration which offers the best theoretical foundation for that respect for all existing forms of speech which was so striking a feature of the philosophical work of John Austin (1911–1960).

Again, verbal habits, just like any other habits, may be both hard to acquire and harder still to shift. It is, therefore, only to be expected that doctrines wrapped up in some gratuitously strange terminology may escape objections which would leap to mind had the expression been more familiar. This is the basis of the Translation Test which Hobbes advocates as a sovereign weapon against supposedly empty technicalities. The following passages come from Chapters VIII and XLVI of *Leviathan*, respectively. The Suarez quoted is the Spanish Jesuit Francisco Suarez (1548–1617); and the vehement abusiveness of Hobbes is typical of the Protestant reaction in the 1600's against Scholasticism:

> But to be assured that their words are without any thing correspondent to them in the mind, there would need some examples; which if any man require, let him take a Schoolman into his hands, and see if he can translate any one chapter concerning any difficult point . . . into any of the modern tongues, so as to make the same intelligible; or into any tolerable Latin, such as they were acquainted with all that lived when the Latin tongue was vulgar. What is the meaning of these words, *The first cause does not necessarily inflow anything into the second, by force of the essential subordination of the second causes, by which it may help it to work*? They are the translation of the title of the sixth chapter of Suarez's first book *Of the Concourse, Motion, and Help of God*. When men write whole volumes of such stuff, are they not mad, or intend to make others so?

> More examples of vain philosophy, brought into religion by the Doctors of school-divinity, might be produced. . . . I shall only add this, that the writings of school-divines are nothing else for the most part but insignificant trains of strange and barbarous words, or words otherwise used than in the common use of the Latin tongue – such as would pose Cicero, and Varro, and all the grammarians of ancient Rome. Which if any man would see proved let him (as I have said once before) see whether he can translate any school-divine into any of the modern tongues, as French, English, or any other copious language. For that which cannot in most of these be made intelligible is not intelligible in the Latin. Which insignificancy of language, though I cannot note it for false philosophy, yet it hath a quality not only to hide the truth, but also to make men think they have it, and desist from further search.

The same fundamental consideration about the force of speech habits makes it inept – or worse – arbitrarily to prescribe for a familiar phrase some fresh interpretation going against the grain of existing verbal usage; and, consequently, of established habits. Thus, for example, if you really want to speak as a detached scientist and without any evaluating commitments, you will be scrupulous to eschew the bad example of the American sociologist Thorstein Veblen (1857–1929); who first insists on introducing the strongly offensive expression "conspicuous waste", and then immediately protests that in his usage it is not intended to carry the customary overtones of condemnation. (See his *The Theory of the Leisure Class*, pp. 97 ff.) Such verbal arbitrariness is, I want to add, peculiarly scandalous in those with pretensions to the diploma title *social scientist*. For they above all should be constantly aware of how much men are creatures of habit.

The second bonus to be derived from the extension of the last set of extracts from Reid is more immediately relevant. For the third of these spells out some of the implications of those amputational phenomena which so intrigued Descartes. It is also just worth mentioning incidentally that Reid here falls into an error into which philosophers have been sheepishly following one another for what is now literally centuries. For he mistakes it that things look yellow to the man with jaundice – apparently for no better reason than that the jaundiced man certainly does look yellow to other people.

The main thing for us, however, is to exploit Reid's contributions to the logical analysis of sensation and perception. He brings out well: that it is essential to the notion of perception that any objects perceived must be such as could exist separately, quite independently of their being perceived; whereas it is equally essential to the concept of sensation – or, better, of subjective experience in general – that its objects have to be such as cannot significantly be said to exist independently of their being had. From this a major conclusion follows; although it is altogether typical of the way in which progress is, and is not, made in philosophy that Reid himself seems never to have drawn this conclusion clearly, explicitly, and decisively. The conclusion, which follows necessarily from this understanding of the meanings of *perception* and *sensation*, is that sensations or sensible ideas or sense-data or subjective experiences cannot be all that we ever directly perceive. They cannot be, for the radical and decisive reason that they are not the sorts of things which could significantly be said to be perceived at all.

Berkeley, as we have seen, urged that the essence of "ideas of sensible things" is to be perceived. The truth is rather that it is of the essence of all subjective experiences, including sensible ideas or sense-data, not to be perceived but instead to be had. Consequently, as Berkeley himself always rightly insisted, to suggest that these might "exist otherwise than in a mind" necessarily must be absurd. Certainly it is as senseless to speak of an unfelt pain as it would be to talk of a grin without a face. But perception is crucially and diametrically different. This case is not the same, but contrasting and complementary. For it is as senseless to speak of perceiving entities which cannot "exist otherwise than in a mind perceiving them" as it would be to talk of some subjective experience occurring unexperienced. We may, therefore, view Berkeley's idealism as the outcome of a sustained attempt to assimilate perception to something which is in truth essentially and characteristically contrasted with it. Berkeley's fatal first step was to try to interpret the perceiving of (public) things on the perversely inappropriate model of the having of (private) subjective experiences. This is disastrous, because really to see things precisely is not to 'see' things.

And yet, though it may be perversely inappropriate it is also perennially and almost irresistibly tempting. It is one measure both of the greatness of Berkeley as a philosopher, and of the abiding value of his works for succeeding generations, that he brings out with shining clarity the generally intolerable consequences of yielding to a temptation which will always be with us. Before concluding the present section let us illuminate the nature of this mistake further by considering a second example of misinterpreting the notions of one category by construing them on an inappropriate model provided by another. It comes from *The Republic*. What Plato does there, with bizarre results, is to take perceptual concepts as his model for the interpretation of the ideas of knowledge, belief, and even ignorance:

SOCRATES – Shall we say that capacities are a class of entities in virtue of which we, and all other things which are capable, are capable of what we are capable? What I am saying is that sight and hearing, for example, are capacities. Do you understand what I am driving at? ... In a capacity I cannot see any colour or shape or anything else of that sort, such as in many other cases I regard in distinguishing in my thought between one sort of thing and another. With a capacity I look to one thing only, its field and what it does, and in this way I come to call each of them a capacity. What is addressed to the same field and does the same work I call the same, and where the field and the work is different I call it another one. How about you, what do you do?

GLAUCON – The same.

SOCRATES – To return then, my dear chap, to knowledge. Would you say that it is a capacity, or would you put it into some other genus?

GLAUCON – No, into this one; and it is the most powerful of all capacities.

SOCRATES – Well then, what about opinion, shall we put it as a capacity or shall we put it into another genus?

GLAUCON – Certainly not, for opinion is nothing else but that in virtue of which we are capable of opining.

SOCRATES – But not long ago you agreed that knowledge and opinion are not the same.

GLAUCON – However could anyone with a mind put the infallible down as the same as the fallible?

SOCRATES – Excellent, and we are clearly agreed that opinion is something different from knowledge.

GLAUCON – It is different.

SOCRATES – Each of them then since it is a different capacity naturally has a different object?

GLAUCON – Necessarily.

SOCRATES – Knowledge presumably has as its sphere reality, to know reality as it is?

GLAUCON – Yes.

SOCRATES – But opinion, we say, opines?

GLAUCON – Yes.

SOCRATES – And does it opine the same object which knowledge knows, and is what is known and what is opined the same thing? Or is that impossible?

GLAUCON – It is impossible, granted our agreed premises. For if different capacities naturally have different fields, and if knowledge and opinion are both capacities but different the one from the other, as we said, then this leaves no room for the conclusion that the spheres of knowledge and of opinion are the same.

(§§ 477C–478B)

So much the worse then for these agreed premises. For, as Plato himself seems later to have begun to recognize, this earlier conclusion is false. (See, e.g., *Theaetetus*, §§ 195E–196C.) I can at one time be cautiously of the opinion that, for instance, it was German aircraft, and aircrew seconded by Hitler to the service of General Franco, that were responsible for the destruction of the ancient Basque capital of Gernika. But subsequently, after familiarizing myself with more of the available evidence, I may properly claim to know this same proposition to be true. One and the same proposition can, at different times by the same person, and at the same time by different people, be both known and only believed or opined. It can also and similarly, for that matter, be conjectured, presupposed, asserted, imagined, entertained, supposed, denied, or made the object of many other – as they used to be called – *Propositional Attitudes*.

In *The Republic*, however, following the false scent of the perceptual model, Plato deploys a hierarchy of different sorts of object or supposed object to correspond with a hierarchy of different sorts of cognitive capacity and incapacity. True knowledge naturally holds the place at the top; and its objects are, of course, the Forms. But materials and work are provided for the cognitive lower orders also. Thus as the proper objects of conjecture we have "shadows . . . reflections in water and on close-grained, smooth, bright things, and everything of that kind . . ." (§ 510A). Curiously, despite his liking for analogies of crafts and techniques it does not now occur to Plato that two capacities might be distinguished by differences in either or both their fields and their tasks: as horse-riding and horse-butchery share their objects – horses – but differ in their tasks – riding and butchery, respectively.

The model of perception is perhaps misleading in as much as one can specify peculiar objects for each of the five senses – sights for seeing, sounds for hearing, and so on. But the most important way in which it misleads is by suggesting that the objects of knowledge, and indeed of all other 'propositional attitudes' likewise, must always be present and actual. Certainly – with the one notorious exception aforementioned, which Plato could not have known – if I am to see something it surely must be here now to be seen. I cannot now, in any literal sense, see or hear either what is past or what is yet to come. This is where propositions, and the knowledge of propositions, is essentially and vitally different from perception. For I may know, as in the Spanish example just given, that something did happen. I may know that the next eclipse of the sun will occur on such and such a date. I may also know hypothetical or disjunctive or negative truths: that if you take this much aspirin it will kill you; or that either Jack or Jill is the guilty agent; or that there is as yet no real hospital in the Northern Region. And while there is perhaps little temptation to follow Plato in trying to find different sorts of objects for different 'propositional attitudes', many successors have succumbed to the more subtle enticements of the perceptual model. It provides, for instance, one source of the appeal of the ideas that knowledge of the past or of the future must presuppose that the one is still and the other is already in some mysterious way here.

For Plato the attractions of the perceptual model were reinforced by an antecedent inclination to take as his paragon not knowledge by description but knowledge by acquaintance. Thus, acquaintance with the Form of Virtue is supposed to be a necessary condition of any knowledge that virtue is or is not teachable, or whatever (Ch. II, § 2). The distinction between these two sorts of knowledge is one of which Russell in particular has made much, in *The Problems of Philosophy* and elsewhere. It is one marked in some languages by different words: *cognoscere* and *scire* in Latin, for instance, and *connaître* and *savoir* in French. Indeed English too used to have its *ken* and *wiss*, equivalent to the German *kennen* and *wissen*. Compare "D' ye ken John Peel?" with "I wist not, brethren, that he was the High Priest" in the King James version of *Acts*, 23 : 5. Perhaps the best account to remember is that given by Miss Jane Austen in Chapter XXII of *Sense and Sensibility*, where Lucy says:

'I was afraid you would think I was taking a great liberty with you in telling you this. I have not known you long, to be sure, personally at least, but I have known you and all your family by description a great while; and as soon as I saw you I felt almost as if you was an old acquaintance.'

§6 *Philosophical analyses and scientific accounts*

The upshot of § 5 is that perception can only be of objects which may significantly be said to exist unperceived. It must, consequently, be equally wrong: either to lament that we can see (nothing else but our own) sense-data; or to attempt to interpret all perceiving on the model of having a pain. To have appreciated these truths constitutes progress. Yet, of course, it does not go as far as we should wish to go. For, allowing that I cannot significantly be said to perceive sense-data, the persistent sceptic may still urge that my own subjective experiences are all I ever have. So, these being necessarily all in my own mind, and perception being necessarily of independent objects only, how can it ever be possible for me to perceive anything? Our clearer recognition of what perception, if it occurs, must involve thus appears to be transformed into a reason for saying that in fact it does not happen and cannot.

And yet, surely, no one but a madman has ever genuinely doubted that it does? This unshakeable conviction of common sense has already in earlier sections been buttressed with more sophisticated arguments. Thus, I have urged that our telling one another about our private sense-data is possible only in as much as we are able to refer to some public objects; and I have suggested that the well-worn sceptical instances presuppose a measure of the very sort of knowledge which they are here summoned to undermine. (See Ch. IX, §§ 2 and 3; and compare Ch. X, § 4.) Our present problem, like so many in philosophy, can be presented in a form favoured especially by Kant; that of asking how something certainly actual can be possible. Let us start with a passage from Locke's *Essay*:

> Those who tell us that light is a great number of little globules, striking briskly on the bottom of the eye, speak more intelligibly than the Schools. But yet these words never so well understood would make the idea the word *light* stands for no more known to a man that understands it not before, than if one should tell him that light was nothing but a company of little tennis-balls, which fairies all day long struck with rackets against some men's foreheads, whilst they passed by others. For, granting this explication of the thing to be true, yet the idea of the cause of light, if we had it never so exact, would no more give us the idea of light itself, as it is such a particular perception in us, than the idea of the figure and motion of a sharp piece of steel would give us the idea of that pain which it is able to cause in us. For the cause of any sensation, and the sensation itself, in all the simple ideas of one sense, are two ideas; and two ideas so different and distant one from another that no two can be more so. And therefore, should Descartes' globules strike never so long on the retina of a man who was blind . . . he would thereby never have any idea of light, or anything approaching it, though he understood never so well what little globules were, and what striking on another body was. And therefore the Cartesians very well distinguish between that light which is the cause of that sensation in us, and the idea which is produced in us by it, and is that which is properly light.
>
> (III (iv) 10)

The English of Locke is obsolete, and both the scientific and the semantic notions attributed to Descartes require some revision (Ch. XI, § 6). But the fundamental distinction between giving a scientific account of light and giving the meaning of the word *light* remains, and always will remain, indispensable. It is one thing to know the meanings of the words *yellow, magenta,* and *aquamarine*. It is another thing altogether to know facts and theories about the structure of the light involved in these three cases. Knowledge of the second clearly presupposes knowledge of the first kind. For no one could understand a statement about the wavelength of yellow light and its position in the spectrum unless he already knew the meaning of the word *yellow*. It is, once it has been pointed out, equally obvious that the first neither presupposes nor entails the second kind. Someone could know the meanings of all the colour-words while being wholly innocent of light waves and spectra, and many intelligent people in previous periods did.

Now, in order to begin to put this basic distinction to work, consider a characteristic passage from Russell's *Human Knowledge*. It should be compared with the paragraphs from Eccles and from Descartes quoted at the end of Chapter VIII, above. Russell maintains that it is a complete mistake to think "that a man can see matter":

Not even the ablest physiologist can perform this feat. His percept when he looks at a brain is an event in his own mind, and has only a causal connection with the brain that he fancies he is seeing. When, in a powerful telescope, he sees a tiny luminous dot, and interprets it as a vast nebula existing a million years ago, he realizes that what he sees is different from what he infers. The difference from the case of a brain looked at through a microscope is only one of degree: there is exactly the same need of inference, by means of the laws of physics, from the visual datum to its physical cause. And just as no one supposes that the nebula has any close resemblance to a luminous dot, so no one should suppose that the brain has any close resemblance to what the physiologist sees.

What, then, do we know about the physical world? Let us first define more exactly what we mean by 'a physical event'. I should define it as an event which, if known to occur, is inferred, and is not known to be mental. And I define 'a mental event' . . . as one with which someone is acquainted otherwise than by inference.   (p. 245)

These two short paragraphs contain several instructive errors. First, as the reader will surely have noticed, Russell following Berkeley mistakes it that all we ever see is perceptions in our own minds. The truth is, as I argued in the previous section, that, whatever we do or do not in fact perceive, one sort of thing which we never could see is such perceptions. Second, it is, though perhaps tempting, wrong to construe the fact that all stars other than the sun appear as just so many luminous dots to be a reason for concluding that we can never see them at all. What else, at these distances, would you expect? Certainly, if only you could approach a few billion light years nearer – but not too near – you might get a better view. But even as things are you can see stars; just as one may still see a departing plane when it has become only a black dot against a distant cloud. Marlowe's Dr Faustus in medieval Wertenberg drew his image from what all men knew when he addressed the conjured Helen:

> O *thou art fairer than the evening air*
> *Clad in the beauty of a thousand stars.*

Nor, third, is the inference which may be required if I am to identify one particular luminous dot as Epsilon Eridani inference from some purely mental event. Fortunately, since I shall need astronomical help for this identification, other people can look through the same telescope and inspect the same photographs. It is philosophically important here and elsewhere to notice that talk about how things look or appear is typically not self-centred and autobiographical. If I claim to discern what looks like a three-stage rocket on its launching pad I shall normally be concerned with the furniture of the world rather than with some purely mental visual datum.

The relevance of the basic distinction between scientific questions and questions about the meanings of words is this. It is one thing to enquire what is meant by the generic word *perception*; and by the specific *see, hear, smell, taste,* and so on. It is quite another matter to give accounts of the mechanisms involved in seeing, hearing, smelling, tasting, or what have you. It must, therefore, be wrong to confound the two in any way. So how much more wrong it becomes when the confusion takes the form of providing a scheme which makes impossible the very achievement which it is designed to explain. Yet it is precisely this ruinous implication which Russell flaunts as if it were a trophy. For his sketch of the mechanics of perception opens with the reckless claim: "Not even the ablest physiologist can perform this feat".

Recklessly paradoxical though it surely is, such does seem to be the outcome of scientific investigation. In particular the physiology of perception sets a typically philosophical problem of showing how its own subject is possible. For its investigations, which are of course all ultimately based upon direct observation, appear to show that there can be no such thing. We have already noticed how these findings presented themselves to the two great physiologically-oriented philosophers of the 1600's and to two very distinguished scientists of our own time (Ch. VIII, § 5 and Ch. X, § 1). Russell in effect takes the problem as I have stated it to be insoluble; while proceeding with attempts to show that, although perception as the uninstructed laymen might think of it does not occur, it is nevertheless possible to acquire knowledge of the external world by a less direct route. He writes in *The Analysis of Matter*:

> So long as naïve realism remained tenable, perception was knowledge of a physical object, obtained through the senses, not by inference. But in accepting the causal theory of perception we have committed ourselves to the view that perception gives no immediate knowledge of a physical object, but at least a datum for inference. (p. 218)

In the light of the basic distinction being developed in the present section we can see that this will not do. For if the findings of physics and physiology have really shown that there is no "knowledge of a physical object, obtained through the senses, not by inference", then the moral is: not "that perception gives no immediate knowledge of a physical object"; but rather that there is in truth no such thing as perception. And, since the scientists do and must rely for the ultimate vindication of their discoveries upon direct observation, this consequence necessarily undermines the findings from which it is here derived. Interestingly too, besides thus removing the bases of all scientific inference, this same paradoxical conclusion simultaneously both exploits and repudiates the ordinary antithesis between the direct and the indirect knowledge of things. We commonly contrast, for instance, my actually seeing him do it with your less direct knowledge of the event – knowledge based partly perhaps on my testimony. The idiom *the evidence of my own eyes* thus derives its piquancy from a slight flavour of contradiction. For to see it myself is for me not – because it is so much better than – to know upon evidence.

In Russell's world, however, there is officially no such thing as seeing it happen. Perhaps, he thinks, we see only our own sense-data: or, better, maybe we do not see at all but only have visual and other subjective experiences. Sometimes he presses the distinction between knowledge by acquaintance and knowledge by description into service here: with the former limited to sensory and other purely subjective experiences; and the latter extending, hopefully, to the great universe around the solitary Cartesian subject. To apply this distinction in this way is again, as in the case of that between perceiving and inferring from evidence, simultaneously both to exploit and to repudiate an ordinary antithesis. For in Russell's world there cannot really be any such thing as being personally acquainted with anybody. No wonder that in a rather similar connection in *The Problems of Philosophy* he himself said: "This seems plainly absurd; but whoever wishes to become a philosopher must learn not to be frightened by absurdities" (p. 31).

Yes, it does seem absurd; "but", as Groucho Marx would have it, "don't be misled. It is absurd." And while the philosopher must not be frightened from entertaining absurdities, he should nevertheless strive to avoid embracing them. The secret here is to deploy once more, and more fundamentally, the same key distinction: between philosophical questions about the meaning of perceptual words, and the logical presuppositions of their correct employment; and scientific questions about the various mechanisms involved in the different kinds of perceptual achievement. The previous section of the present chapter began with an insistence that the Causal Theory of Perception is right to maintain that in normal conscious perception I must have an appropriate sensory experience, and that if anything is truly to be said to have been perceived that thing must have been part of the cause of my having that experience. The rest of that section showed why it must be wrong to say that such experiences are themselves perceived. The present section therefore began with the reformulated sceptical question: "these being necessarily all in my own mind, and perception being necessarily of independent objects only, how can it ever be possible for me to perceive anything?"

The answer now falls into place. Certainly sense-data cannot be perceived. Hence they cannot be alternative objects of perception. It is a nonsense to proclaim: "I never see material things, only sense-data!" But now, neither is having such subjective experiences an alternative which excludes perceiving. For, when I hear or see a hammer driving in a piton, having the appropriate auditory or visual experiences is part of what it is to hear or to see. Having such experiences, which are "necessarily all in my own mind", does not preclude but is instead a precondition "for me to perceive anything".

To be in this way a logically necessary condition is not, of course, to be temporally prior (see pp. 140–141). Nor is to be necessary by the same token to be sufficient. There is, as Descartes has been at pains to remind us, no contradiction in maintaining that on some particular occasion someone had perceptual or quasi-perceptual experience without in fact perceiving anything (Ch. VIII, § 2). The anonymous alcoholic on his lost weekend may 'see' a nightmare Hamelin of rats without truly seeing even one.

Perhaps the very fact that so many perceptual terms are thus – like *see* – Cognitive Achievement Words helps to encourage this curious but beguiling notion that having perceptual or quasi-perceptual experience is an exclusive substitute for authentic perception (Ch. IX, § 4). The idea may be that, since the subjective experience can conceivably be had without cognitive achievement, then we should infer that such achievement is not a matter of the occurrence of the appropriate sort of subjective experience under certain essential contextual conditions, but instead involves something altogether different; and that something, unfortunately but not surprisingly, something which is not specified and never occurs. Alternatively, or even additionally, the idea may be that, since in authentic perception there must be an object perceived, and since the occurrence of sense-data does not logically guarantee the presence of corresponding objects, then (merely) to have sense-data is never (really) to perceive. The hopeless quest for some infallible sign internal to our sense-data is the perceptual special case of an insatiable and general Cartesian longing for an inexpugnable guarantee of knowledge (Ch. IX, § 5).

Consider in this connection a passage from *Mind, Perception and Science* by a distinguished British neurologist, the aptly named Lord Brain. He is himself well aware that it must be self-refuting to cite physiological evidence in support of idealist conclusions:

> In so far as neurologists base any theory of knowledge upon their observations, they seem usually to adopt physiological idealism. The neurologist . . . discovers that when an object is perceived, a series of events occurs successively in time, beginning with an event in the object and ending with an event in the subject's brain. If the series is interrupted at any point between the object and the cerebral cortex . . . of the subject, the object is not perceived. If the relevant area of the cortex is destroyed, the object again is not perceived. But if the relevant area of the cortex is electrically stimulated while the subject is conscious, sense-data of a kind aroused by an object are perceived by the subject. Thus it is held that the event immediately preceding, or perhaps synchronous with, the perception of the object, is an event of a physico-chemical kind in the subject's cerebral cortex. The cortical neurones are normally excited, in the way just described, from the external world, but if they should exceptionally be excited in some other way – for example, by electrical stimulation or by an epileptic discharge – the appropriate sense-data would still be experienced. The only independently necessary

conditions for the awareness of sense-data ... is thus an event in the cerebral cortex. (p. 133)

To conclude the previous section and to press home the idea of mis-construing the notions of one category on a wrong model provided by another I introduced a curious passage from *The Republic*. I now conclude both the present section and the whole chapter with three extracts from the intellectual autobiography provided by 'Socrates' in the *Phaedo*. The aim is again to reinforce a lesson taught in one area by suggesting some implications for another (Ch. VII, especially § 7). Both exercises thus show that progress here helps progress there, and that points well made remain permanently relevant:

> Well, Cebes, when I was young I was enormously eager for this kind of wisdom, which they call the investigation of nature. I thought it was a magnificent thing to know the causes of everything, why it comes into existence and why it exists and why it ceases to be. I was all the time upsetting myself by looking into one question of this sort after another: Do heat and cold, as some people say, bring about the nourishment of animals by a sort of putrefaction? Is it the blood, or air, or fire, which enables us to think; or is it none of these, but the brain, which provides the senses of hearing and sight and smell, and do memory and belief arise from these. . .? And again I looked into the ways in which these things decay, and into the phenomena of heaven and earth, until in the end I decided that I am unfitted by nature for this sort of investigation and useless at it. (§ 96A–C)

> But then one day I heard a man reading from a book, which he said was by Anaxagoras, and he said that it is mind which arranges every-thing and is the cause of everything. I was delighted to have a cause of this kind, and I thought that it is in some way right for mind to be the cause of all things. And I considered that, if this is so, then mind in arranging and ordering everything sees to it that everything is as it is best for it to be. So if anyone wants to discover the cause of anything's coming into existence or existing or ceasing to exist then he has to discover how it is best for that thing to exist and what it is best for it to do or to suffer or what have you. (§ 97B–C)

Anaxagoras of Clazomenae flourished around 450 BC. Like such predecessors in the previous century as Thales, Anaximander, and Anaximenes – all from Miletus – he thus counts as a Pre-Socratic. As is usual with these, our few fragments of almost wholly second-hand evidence are buried beneath mountains of speculative scholarship. But we can claim to know that Anaxagoras was while working at Athens prosecuted for the impiety of what in fact were his radically naturalistic views, and that this was part of a political campaign against his friend the great democratic leader Pericles. The idea that the brain is the seat of the mind seems to have been suggested first by the Pythagorean Alcmaeon of Croton, who flourished probably in the high 500's BC. (British readers may here reflect ruefully that our television Sophist Malcolm Muggeridge recently denounced heart transplants in terms which would have been sensible had the functions of the heart in fact been those of the brain.) 'Socrates', who is of course in prison awaiting execution, continues:

My splendid hope, my friend, was taken away from me. When I went on with my reading I saw that the man made no use of mind and did not assign any reasons for the ordering of things. Instead he attributed them to air and ether and water and many other odd things. And it seemed to me that this was very much like someone's saying that it is by mind that Socrates does everything which he does, and then, when he tries to say what are the reasons for my several actions, saying first that I am sitting here now because my body is composed of bones and sinews. Then he goes on to say that the bones are hard and have joints which separate them from one another, and that the sinews can be contracted and relaxed, and that along with the flesh and the skin which contains them they surround the bones. So, as the bones are suspended in their ligaments, the sinews by relaxing and contracting, make me able to bend my limbs now in that certain way; and that is the reason why I am sitting here with my legs bent. Or again it is as if he should give as reasons for my talking to you other similar things, attributing it to vocal noises and air currents and hearings of sounds and innumerable other ongoings of the same sort, and should fail to mention what really are reasons – that since the Athenians thought fit to condemn me I responded by thinking fit to sit here, believing that it is better to stay and to submit to whatever penalty they order. For – gracious me – if I did not think it better and nobler to submit to any penalty which it may command at the hands of the city rather than to run away into exile I imagine that these bones and these sinews would have been in Megara or Boeotia long ago, carried there by an opinion of what is best. But it is excessively absurd to call things of that sort reasons. If anyone were to say that I would not be able to do what I thought proper without having such things as bones and sinews and all the rest of what I have got, then he would be right. But to say that that is why I do what I do, and that I act as I do intelligently yet without choosing what is best, would be a grossly sloppy way of talking. For it would be to be unable to make a distinction between, on the one hand, what really is a reason, and, on the other, that without which the reason would never be a reason. And so it seems to me that most people, by using the wrong word and characterizing the latter as a reason, are, as it were, groping in the dark. (§§ 98B–99B)

CHAPTER XI

Rationalism and Empiricism

§1 *Mathematics and the rationalist hope*

In the fourth section of Chapter VIII I quoted from Part V of the *Discourse* in order to show that Descartes hoped to derive his whole elaborate and detailed mechanical conception of nature from supposedly self-evident principles. Descartes there wrote of "knowledge . . . so natural to our minds that one could not even pretend not to know it"; and then, referring to his earlier suppressed treatise *Le Monde*, he claimed that "I pointed out what the laws of nature are, and, without basing my arguments on any other principle than the infinite perfections of God, I tried to demonstrate all those about which there could be any doubt, and to show that these laws are such that even if God had created several universes he would not have known how to have one in which they were not observed". Descartes thus becomes a paradigm case of "the philosophical rationalist", who, it will be remembered, "holds that there are self-evident and non-tautological truths from which we can deduce substantial conclusions about the way things have been, are, and will be."

Descartes is again a paradigm of the rationalist hope in that his inspiration was drawn from a vision of mathematics. Thus in Part II of the *Discourse,* in a passage quoted at the end of the first section of the same chapter, he wrote: "Those long chains of reasons, all of them simple and easy, which geometers are accustomed to employ in order to reach the conclusions of their most difficult demonstrations, had caused me to suppose that everything which can fall under the cognizance of man is connected together in the same way." It is indeed literally apt to speak here of a Cartesian vision. For Descartes, like his contemporary and rival Pascal, had had his own visionary conversion experience. On the night of 10 November 1619 Descartes enjoyed a dream which he took to be a revelatory endorsement of his burgeoning beliefs in both rationalism and the idea that mathematics provides the key to the secrets of nature.

The second of these two ideas in its first form was the great historical contribution of the school of Pythagoras. The founder himself came from the Aegean island of Samos. But his main work was done in the then Greek coastal city of Croton in southern Italy. He flourished, as has been remarked in an earlier chapter (Ch. IV, § 1), a little over a century before Plato. Yet already for Plato he seems to have been a figure wrapped in mystery and legend. As usual with Pre-Socratics our scanty knowledge depends on secondary sources. Aristotle in the *Metaphysics*, after a short digression on the physical speculations of Leucippus and Democritus, reports:

> At the same time or even earlier the Pythagoreans, as they are called, applied themselves to, and were the first to advance, mathematics. Through this involvement they came to believe that the principles of these studies are the principles of nature. And since numbers are inherently the first of the mathematical principles they fancied that they could discern in these – rather than in fire and in earth and in water – numerous likenesses to what is and what comes into being. Thus such and such a property of numbers is justice, another is soul and thought, another opportunity, and similarly – more or less – with everything else. And since, again, they saw that the attributes and ratios of the musical scales are expressible in numbers, and since indeed other things seemed to be naturally likened entirely to numbers while numbers are the first principles of the whole of nature, they took it that the elements of numbers are the elements of everything and that the whole heavens are a harmony and a number.
>
> They collected and fitted into their scheme whatever properties of numbers and ratios they could show to correspond with the attributes and parts of the heavens and with the whole order of things. And if there was a gap anywhere they were eager to fill it so as to make their whole theory coherent. For example, in as much as ten is thought to be the perfect number, and to embrace the whole essence of numbers, they maintain that there are ten things which move in the heavens. But since we can only observe nine they postulate an Anti-Earth as the tenth.
>
> (985B24–986A12)

It is not possible nor – fortunately – necessary to get from this passage alone a full understanding of what precisely Pythagoras did teach about number. But two points can be brought out. To grasp the first it helps to know that the surprising total of nine is reached by counting the whole supposed sphere of the fixed stars as one and adding it to the list of Earth, Sun, Moon, and the five then known planets. The Anti- or Counter-Earth whose existence is deduced from the theory is not observed because it revolves round the central Fire, "the watchtower of Zeus", in such a way as to be always in opposition to the Earth. It is tempting, but rash, to identify this central Fire with the Sun; and hence to credit the Pythagoreans – as Kepler did – with being the first advocates of a heliocentric system. What, however, we can allow quite safely is that this curious piece of speculative inference represented a major step in perhaps the greatest of all the achievements of the ancient Greeks. "To them", as two recent historians of science have argued, "belongs the glory of having invented the very idea of scientific theory" (Toulmin and Goodfield, p. 59; and compare their whole chapter on 'The Invention of Theory').

To grasp the second point it helps to know that it was most probably Pythagoras himself who discovered – presumably by measuring the required lengths of string on a monochord – that the chief musical intervals are expressible in simple numerical ratios between the first four integers: the octave as two to one, the fifth as three to two, and the fourth as four to three. This was another of those epoch-making discoveries, like that of William Harvey, which are much more important in their wider suggestions than in themselves (Ch. VIII, § 5). For it was this which planted the seminal thought that nature is in some way fundamentally mathematical – a thought which was one of the indispensables for the development of science.

Pythagoras, however, was as much or more the guru of a religious ashram as the head of a research institute: his school constituted a sort of order, the Pythagorean Brotherhood. It is therefore neither surprising nor incongruous that the huge crops which have grown from his first seeds should contain superstition as well as science. He was a true intellectual ancestor of both the mystic numerology of Nostradamus and Kepler's three laws of planetary motion (Gillispie, p. 18; compare, for instance, Koestler, Ch. I and Pt. IV). It is to Pythagoras that our poets owe the haunting notion of the music of the spheres, for "the whole heavens are a harmony and a number". So Shakespeare's Lorenzo explains to Jessica:

> . . . *Look, how the floor of heaven*
> *Is thick inlaid with patines of bright gold;*
> *There's not the smallest orb which thou behold'st*
> *But in his motion like an angel sings*

Still quiring to the young-eyed cherubins, –
Such harmony is in immortal souls;
But, whilst this muddy vesture of decay
Doth grossly close it in, we cannot hear it   *(Merchant of Venice* V (i))

Legend of course had it that the Master himself was a privileged exception. By contrast it is also, ultimately, thanks to Pythagoras that Galileo was able in *The Assayer* to claim that the Book of Nature "is written in the language of mathematics, and its letters are triangles, circles, and other geometric figures; without which it is humanly impossible to understand a single word of it . . .".

I characterized this as the first form of the second of two ideas to be found in Descartes. For the second form we have to move from Pythagoras to Plato. The difference lies in the fact that the emphasis in the first version is metaphysical or ontological and in the second methodological or epistemological. In Pythagoras we have a contention about the nature of the universe. From Plato we get rather a suggestion that the highest method of enquiry is like, though improving upon, that of mathematics. Thus in *The Republic* mathematical studies are prescribed as the essential propaideutic:

SOCRATES – Then these, as it seems, would be among the studies which we are seeking. For a soldier must learn them in order to marshal his troops, and a philosopher in order to escape from the world of becoming and get a grasp on being ...

GLAUCON – That is so.

SOCRATES – And our Guardian is both a soldier and a philosopher?

GLAUCON – Of course.

SOCRATES – So it is appropriate, Glaucon, to prescribe this by law; and to induce those who are destined to participate in the highest matters of state to go in for the study of arithmetic, embracing it in no amateur spirit. Instead they should press on until by pure thought they reach a vision of the nature of numbers, doing this not for the purposes of buying and selling as if they were training to become retail or wholesale merchants, but for the sake of both war and the facilitation of the conversion of the soul itself from the world of becoming to that of being and truth.

GLAUCON – Excellently said.

SOCRATES – And furthermore it occurs to me, now that the study of calculation has been mentioned, how elegant it is and in how many ways it is useful for our purposes provided that it is pursued for the sake of knowledge and not for commercial ends.

GLAUCON – In what way?

SOCRATES – In this very way of which we were speaking, in that it powerfully draws the soul upward and forces it to reason about the numbers themselves – not allowing anyone to proffer to it in the discussion numbers with visible or tangible embodiment.   (§§ 525B–D)

'Socrates' proceeds to commend pure arithmetic for a further reason besides this abstract quality – a reason which will not endear it or him to advocates of soft but of course 'relevant' syllabuses, oriented towards the lowest common denominators of the academic market place:

SOCRATES – And furthermore, in my view, we shall not easily find disciplines which are more difficult for the student and the practitioner than this one, nor many of them.

GLAUCON – Indeed you will not.

SOCRATES – So for all these reasons we must not neglect this study, but those best endowed by nature must be educated in it.   (§ 526C)

Elsewhere in *The Republic* Plato explains where he puts both pure arithmetic and other branches of pure mathematics in his cognitive hierarchy, and why (Ch. X, § 5). Here we see the first example of a rationalist programme; and it is, as usual, inspired by an understanding – or misunderstanding – of the nature of mathematics. The passage comes immediately before the development of the image of The Cave (Ch. II, § 2), and immediately after a comparison between the Sun and the supreme Form of the Good. This glorification of the Sun had, by the way, a great appeal both for the ancient Neo-Platonists and for some early Copernicans: "In the centre of all rests the Sun. For who would place this lamp of a very beautiful temple in another or better place than this wherefrom it can illuminate everything at the same time" (Copernicus, pp. 526–527; compare Burtt, pp. 47–48 on Kepler). Plato writes:

SOCRATES – Consider then that, as we were saying, the Form of the Good and the Sun are two; and the one is sovereign over the world of the intelligible and the other correspondingly over that of the visible. . . . You are, surely, seized of the distinction between these two categories of the visible and the intelligible?

GLAUCON – I am.

SOCRATES – Now take a line divided into two unequal parts, the one representing the sphere of what is seen and the other that of the thought, and divide each of these again in the same proportion. You will have then a representation of their relative clearness and obscurity, with, in the second section of the seen, likenesses. By likenesses I mean first shadows, then reflections in water and on close-grained, smooth, bright things, and everything of that kind – if you get me.

GLAUCON – Yes, I get you.

SOCRATES – Then make the first section of which this is a likeness the living things around us and the entire class of everything which is planted or made.

GLAUCON – Right.

SOCRATES – And so you would be willing to say that in respect of truth and falsehood the division has been made in such a way that what is opined is to what is known as the likeness is to that of which it is a likeness?

GLAUCON – I certainly would.

SOCRATES – Then consider now how we are to make the division of the intelligible part. (§§ 509D–510B)

A preliminary explanation proves almost unintelligible. So 'Socrates' tries again, starting with his account of the nature of pure mathematics. This fits into the second, lower, section of the upper, intelligible, part:

SOCRATES – I think that you know that those who make it their business to do geometry and arithmetic and so on hypothesize the odd and the even, and geometrical figures, and the three kinds of angles, and other similar things in each particular inquiry; and, having made these their hypotheses, they take them as obvious to all, and they do not see fit to render any further account of them to themselves or to other people. Starting from these they proceed systematically and consistently until they finally reach the original object of their investigation.

GLAUCON – Certainly, I know that.

SOCRATES – And of course you also know that they press visible things into service and base their arguments on them, though these are not the objects of their thought but rather those things of which these are likenesses. For their arguments are concerned with the real square and the real diagonal, and not with this which they draw. And so in all cases; for the very things which they mould and draw, which have shadows and likenesses in water, these things they use as likenesses as they seek to get a sight of the actual realities which can be seen only by the mind. (§§ 510C–511A)

In itself this is quite straightforward. But it gives rise by what it does not say to one of the traditional cruces of Platonic exegesis. All that has gone before leads one to expect Plato to produce a class of peculiar mathematical objects, supposedly bearing the same relation to the Forms as the objects of true knowledge as the likenesses bear to the material things which they reflect. And Aristotle, who was presumably well placed to know, tells us that Platonists did indeed postulate a special class of mathematical objects (*Metaphysics* 987B14 ff.). Yet the text of *The Republic* as it stands does not clearly warrant such an interpretation. Instead mathematics is distinguished from true knowledge in an entirely different way:

SOCRATES – Understand then that by the other section of the intelligible I mean that which reason itself grasps by the power of dialectics, treating its hypotheses not as first principles but really as hypotheses – footholds and starting places, as it were – to enable it to get right up to the unhypothetical first principle of everything and, after grasping it, to take hold again of its immediate consequences and so to proceed downwards to the end making no use whatever of any object of sense but only of abstract Forms, moving through Forms and to Forms and ending with Forms.

GLAUCON – I understand, although not fully, for you seem to be describing a mighty labour. But I appreciate that you want to distinguish the aspect of the real and the thinkable which is contemplated by the knowledge of dialectic from that which is the concern of what are labelled as skills. These have their hypotheses as first principles, and though those who study them are forced to do so with their minds rather than with their senses, still because they do not go back to discover a foundation but work from hypotheses you think that they do not possess true knowledge of them – notwithstanding that given a foundation they would be objects of true knowledge.   (§ 511C–D)

The precise nature of the dialectics recommended here is a matter of scholarly dispute, into which we need not enter; though it is perhaps just worth mentioning that Plato's interest is in some pattern of argument, whereas the dialectics paraded by Engels and his followers are putative laws of universal change. The thing which does have to be understood, before we can proceed in the next section to confront philosophical rationalism with its most formidable enemy, is the function proposed for "the unhypothetical first principle of everything". Clearly what Plato wants, and what presumably he hopes that the Form of the Good will in some at present not fully explicable way provide, is an extremely rich and self-certifying first premise from which among many other things all mathematics can be deduced. It has to be rich if satisfactorily lavish conclusions are to be deducible from it (Ch. V, § 1). It has to be somehow self-certifying if it is to be ultimate, and warranted as opposed to hypothetical.

Hindsight now reveals this specification as tailored to accommodate the Ontological Argument (Ch. VI, § 2). It is fitting that the three great rationalists of the 1600's – Descartes, Leibniz, and Spinoza – all gave this a fundamental place in their systems. For if the existence of God as a perfect being is thus a logically necessary truth, and if this also involves that existence must be better than non-existence, then it would seem to follow, both that that God must necessarily have created a universe, and that this universe must necessarily be the best of all logically possible universes. Descartes' use of the Ontological Argument, which we have already considered (Ch. VIII, § 3), stopped short of drawing and developing these two generous consequences. However, Leibniz and Spinoza – each in his own distinctive way – appreciated both.

Both men produced metaphysical systems in which all truths must ultimately be logically necessary truths. But Leibniz always wanted to seem to be, and perhaps even to be, an ecumenical Christian. He was, therefore, forever embarrassed by the difficulties of reconciling this vision of the universal logical necessity of everything with the notion of the whole creation as a gratuitous expression of the Divine Will. Spinoza by contrast was at an early age expelled from the Synagogue of Amsterdam. His God was in fact Nature: the key tag is "God or Nature", often quoted in the original Latin *Deus sive Natura*. When he speaks, in another famous phrase, of "the intellectual love of God" what he means is joyous awareness of the systematic logical necessity of everything.

Again, both Leibniz and Spinoza drew the further conclusion that every genuine possibility of existence must in fact be actualized. This perennially important idea was in Arthur Lovejoy's masterpiece *The Great Chain of Being* finally christened, "the principle of plenitude" (p. 52). A characteristically austere presentation is found in Part I of the *Ethics* of Spinoza:

> Proposition XVI. From the necessity of the divine nature must follow an infinite number of things in infinite ways – all things, in fact, which can be conceived by an infinite intellect.
>
> Proof. This proposition should be clear to everyone who remembers that from the definition given to anything the intellect infers several properties which actually follow from it necessarily – that is, from the very essence of the thing. And it infers more properties in proportion as the essence of the thing defined contains more reality. Hence, since the divine nature possesses absolutely infinite attributes (by Definition vi),

of which each also expresses infinite essence in its own kind, from the necessity of that nature there must therefore follow necessarily an infinite number of things in infinite ways – all things in fact, which can be conceived by an infinite intellect.   Q.E.D.

In the Appendix to the same Part Spinoza rebukes "those demented enough to believe that even God takes pleasure in harmony", and especially "the philosophers who have persuaded themselves that the celestial motions produce a harmony". But he has already there epitomized his own magnificent metaphysical achievement, which represents a mathematical infatuation of another kind:

I have now explained the nature and properties of God; that he exists necessarily; that he is one; that he exists and acts solely from the necessity of his own nature; that he is the free cause of all things, and in what sense this is so; that all things are in God, and so depend on him that without him they could neither exist nor be conceived; and, finally, that all things have been predetermined by God, not of course by his own freewill or absolute fiat but from the very nature of God or infinite power. I have further, wherever occasion offered, taken care to remove prejudices which could have hindered the comprehension of my demonstrations ... those prejudices to which I am going to draw attention here spring from a single source, that men commonly suppose that all things in nature act, as they do themselves, with an end in view. So they take it as certain that God himself directs everything to some definite end. For they say that God made everything for man, and man in order that man might worship God. . . .

And although experience protested day by day, and showed by innumerable examples that satisfactory and unsatisfactory things happen indiscriminately to the pious and the impious alike, still this did not lead them to abandon their inveterate prejudice. For it was easier for them to classify this fact along with other things of which they were ignorant and the use of which they did not know, and thus to keep their present and original ignorance, than to destroy the whole fabric and think out a fresh one. Thus they laid down as an axiom that the judgements of the Gods far exceed human understanding. This could surely have been enough to conceal the truth from the human race for all eternity, had not Mathematics – which deals not with final causes but only with the essences and properties of figures – provided men with another standard of truth.

For the apostate Jew Spinoza to insist on using the word *God* as he did constitutes a paradigm case of what is now usefully docketed as Persuasive

Definition. This was once in a similar context vehemently but nonetheless accurately characterized by a leading Christian fundamentalist, in a quotation which I borrow from the columnist Walter Lippman, as "that weasel method of sucking the meaning out of words, and then presenting the empty shells in an attempt to palm them off as giving the Christian faith a new and another interpretation". It is partly such ambiguities which encourage strangely discordant readings of Spinoza: on the one hand he has been famously hailed as "the God-intoxicated man"; on the other hand he is rated – especially by Soviet and other Marxist scholars – one of the founding fathers of modern atheist materialism.

To conclude § 1 with a less abstract account of the Principle of Plenitude, and of the consequent Great Chain of Being, I turn not to a philosopher but to a poet. Pope sings in a Leibnizian rather than in a Spinozist strain:

> *Of systems possible, if 'tis confess'd,*
> *That Wisdom infinite must form the best,*
> *Where all must fall, or not coherent be,*
> *And all that rises rise in due degree;*
> *Then in the scale of reas'ning life, 'tis plain*
> *There must be, somewhere, such a rank as man:*
> *And all the question (wrangle e'er so long)*
> *Is only this, if God has placed him wrong?*   (*Essay on Man* I 43–50)

> *Vast chain of being! which from God began,*
> *Natures ethereal, human, angel, man,*
> *Beast, bird, fish, insect, what no eye can see,*
> *No glass can reach; from infinite to thee,*
> *From thee to nothing. – On superior pow'rs*
> *Were we to press, inferior might on ours;*
> *Or in the full creation leave a void,*
> *Where, one step broken, the great scale's destroy'd:*
> *From Nature's chain whatever link you strike,*
> *Tenth, or ten thousandth, breaks the chain alike.*   (*Ibid.*, 1237–246)

§2 Hume's Fork

The classical challenger for empiricism against rationalism is Hume. His chosen weapon is the distinction since nicknamed Hume's Fork. Though there were hints in the *Treatise* it is deployed fully only in the first *Inquiry*:

All the objects of human reason or enquiry may naturally be divided into two kinds, to wit, Relations of Ideas and Matters of Fact. Of the first kind are the sciences of geometry, algebra, and arithmetic; and in short, every affirmation which is either intuitively or demonstratively certain. *That the square of the hypothenuse is equal to the square of the two sides,* is a proposition which expresses a relation between these figures. *That three times five is equal to the half of thirty,* expresses a relation between these numbers. Propositions of this kind are discoverable by the mere operation of thought, without dependence on what is anywhere existent in the universe. Though there never were a circle or triangle in nature, the truths demonstrated by Euclid would for ever retain their certainty and evidence.

Matters of fact, which are the second objects of human reason, are not ascertained in the same manner; nor is our evidence of their truth, however great, of a like nature with the foregoing. The contrary of every matter of fact is still possible; because it can never imply a contradiction, and is conceived by the mind with the same facility and distinctness, as if ever so conformable to reality. *That the sun will not rise tomorrow* is no less intelligible a proposition, and implies no more contradiction than the affirmation, *That it will rise.* We should in vain, therefore, attempt to demonstrate its falsehood. Were it demonstratively false, it would imply a contradiction, and could never be distinctly conceived by the mind. (IV (i))

If all propositions must indeed be of one or other of these two kinds then, certainly, the rationalist hope is without foundation. For it follows that there are no premises of the kind required: there are no "self-evident and non-tautological truths from which we can deduce substantial conclusions about the way things have been, are, and will be". So, wielding his absolute weapon against the foundations of rationalism, Hume rejects the principle of the Ontological Argument:

Whatever is may not be. No negation of a fact can involve a contradiction. The non-existence of any being, without exception, is as clear and distinct an idea as its existence. The proposition which affirms it not to be, however false, is no less conceivable and intelligible than that which affirms it to be. The case is different with the sciences, properly so called. Every proposition which is not true is there confused and unintelligible. *That the cube root of 64 is equal to the half of 10* is a false proposition, and can never be distinctly conceived. But *That Caesar, or the angel Gabriel, or any being never existed,* may be a false proposition, but still is perfectly conceivable, and implies no contradiction.

The existence, therefore, of any being can only be proved by arguments from its cause or its effect; and these arguments are founded entirely on experience. If we reason apriori, anything may appear able to produce anything. The falling of a pebble may, for aught we know, extinguish the sun; or the wish of a man control the planets in their orbits. It is only experience which teaches us the nature and bounds of cause and effect, and enables us to infer the existence of one object from that of another. *(Ibid.,* XII (iii))

No wonder perhaps that Hume proceeded to an exultant peroration:

When we run over libraries, persuaded of these principles, what havoc must we make? If we take in our hand any volume – of divinity or school metaphysics, for instance – let us ask, 'Does it contain any abstract reasoning concerning quantity or number?' No. 'Does it contain any experimental reasoning concerning matter of fact and existence?' No. Commit it then to the flames, for it can contain nothing but sophistry and illusion. *(Ibid.,* XII (iii))

It was a similar promise of intellectual devastation which attracted the old original Logical Positivists of the Vienna Circle to their Verification Principle. These were a group of scientifically-minded philosophers who gathered round Moritz Schlick (1882–1936) in the twenties and early thirties of our century – until they were dispersed in exile by men who believed in literal bonfires of books. The most brilliant presentation of Logical Positivist ideas is *Language, Truth and Logic* by their English convert A. J. Ayer (b. 1910), and their most elaborate development is seen in the life's work of Rudolf Carnap (b. 1891). In its first explicit formulation the principle stated that the meaning of a sentence lies in its method of verification; and it was immediately explained that all significant assertions must be either contingent, synthetic, and verifiable in experience, or else necessary and analytic.

The meaning of the terms *analytic* and *synthetic* can be fixed by giving examples. Questioned about the ghost Hamlet replies:

> *There's ne'er a villain dwelling in all Denmark*
> *But he's an arrant knave.*

Horatio responds:

> *There needs no ghost, my lord, come from the grave*
> *To tell us this.* (*Hamlet* I (v))

There needs no ghost because Hamlet's proposition is analytic and, of course, logically necessary. What makes it analytic is that its truth can be known simply by knowing the meanings of its terms, and what makes it logically necessary is that to deny it would involve self-contradiction. What Horatio wants is the opposite, a synthetic proposition; one which makes an assertion – the phrase is Hume's – about a "matter of fact and real existence". Had Hamlet claimed, unpoetically and anachronistically, that all Danish villains are the products of maternal deprivation, then his proposition would have been not analytic but synthetic. It would also have been aposteriori, in as much as it could be known to be true – if it were true – only by reference to some actual empirical study of the home background of Danish villains.

One of the crucial questions here, as we shall see soon, is whether three expressions which certainly differ in connotation – *contingent, synthetic,* and *aposteriori proposition*, and of course their respective opposites correspondingly – do nevertheless have exactly the same denotations. For, as I explained when I introduced Mill's terms, this though not necessary is entirely possible (pp. 146–147). It is this possibility, that two expressions which differ in meaning may in fact apply to the same thing, which provides room for the Masked Man Fallacy. From the facts that my father knew Lloyd George, and that my father did not know who the masked man was, it does not follow that the masked man was not Lloyd George. (As an exercise consider whether Descartes, who wrote in his private notebook "I come forward wearing a mask", committed this fallacy in his argument, quoted in § 2 of Chapter VIII, to the conclusion that he "was a substance the whole essence or nature of which simply was to think; and which, to exist, needs no place and has no dependence on any material thing"; and compare § 3 of Chapter IV.)

Our next extract is drawn from the *Monadology* of Leibniz:

Our reasonings are founded on two great Principles: that of Contradiction, in virtue of which we judge what involves this to be false, and what is opposed or contradictory to the false to be true; and that of Sufficient Reason, in virtue of which we take it that nothing could occur or be real, and no proposition could be true, unless there was a sufficient reason for its being thus and not otherwise – although these reasons most often cannot be known to us.

There are also two kinds of truths, those of reason, and those of fact. The truths of reason are necessary and their opposites impossible, those of fact are contingent and their opposites are possible.

When a truth is necessary its reason can be found by analysis, by resolving it into simpler ideas and truths until you reach those which are primitive. It is in this way that mathematicians reduce speculative theorems and rules of practice by analysis to definitions, axioms, and postulates. In the end one has simple ideas which are indefinable. There are also axioms and postulates – in a word, primary principles – which cannot be proved and do not need to be either. These are identical propositions, the opposites of which contain explicit contradictions.

But there also has to be a sufficient reason for contingent truths – truths of fact; for the sequence of things spread out through the whole creation, that is, where the resolution into particular reasons could run into unlimited detail on account of the immense variety of things in nature and the infinite divisibility of bodies. An infinity of figures and movements, present and past, enter into the efficient cause of my writing at this time; and an infinity of slight inclinations and dispositions, present and past, of my soul enter into the final cause.

However, since all this detail only embraces other previous or more detailed contingents, each of which still requires a similar analysis for its own explanation, one is no forrader; the ultimate sufficient reason must be outside the sequence or series of this detail of contingencies, be it never so infinite. Hence the ultimate reason for things has to lie in a necessary substance, in which the particularity of change exists only eminently, as in its source; and it is this that we call God.

Now this substance, being a sufficient reason of all this detail, which is also everywhere connected, there is only one God, and this God is sufficient. We can further infer that this supreme substance – which is unique, universal, and necessary, which has nothing external independent of it, and which is an immediate consequence of its own possibility – must be incapable of limitation and must contain every reality which is possible. And from this it follows that God is absolutely perfect; perfection being nothing else but the magnitude of positive reality taken in its strict sense, and setting aside the limits or bounds of the things which have them. And where there are no limits, that is in God, perfection is absolutely infinite. (§§ 31–41)

Since this was one of the few works published by Leibniz in his own lifetime, and, since Hume was a scholar, we can be sure that he had studied the *Monadology*. Yet it would be wrong to accuse Hume of plagiarism. Certainly, given our own stricter conventions, it would have been proper to make some acknowledgement to Leibniz here. What however distinguishes Hume's Fork is not just the basic division but its aggressive employment. Leibniz was totally inhibited from putting it to such use by his commitment to the principle of the Ontological Argument, which involves that there is at least one incomparably important "matter of fact and real existence" the negation of which must involve a contradition (Ch. VI, § 2). And, this once granted, it becomes impossible to deny that all truths are logically necessary. Certainly this conclusion is presupposed by one of the most interesting of the many projects of Leibniz – that translated literally from his Latin as "the universal character". This idea, to which he was throughout his life devoted, was to develop a logically perfect language in which the truth or falsity of any proposition would be obvious from the symbols alone. Since he also believed – along with almost all other logicians from Aristotle until the revolution in Logic marked by the publication of *Principia Mathematica* (pp. 190 and 322–323) – that all correctly formed propositions must attribute some predicate to a subject, this involved that in this language every possible assertion would be and be easily seen to be either analytic and necessarily true or necessarily false: like, in our own less perfect natural language, *All orthodox Roman Catholics believe in the possibility of a positive natural theology* and *Some orthodox Roman Catholics deny the possibility of a positive natural theology* (p. 178).

The essentially aggressive character of Hume's Fork makes it closely comparable with another famous Humean dichotomy, discussed in an earlier chapter (Ch. III, § 4). For just as it must be completely beside the point to produce "words, or expressions, or whole utterances which either are ambiguous as between, or simultaneously combine," both descriptive and prescriptive meaning, so it would be equally misguided to try to collect specimen utterances which bridged the gap between "relations of ideas" and "matters of fact". Hume is not attempting a classification of all actual assertive utterances. Here too, as in that other case, he is urging: not that the distinction always is made; but that it always can be, and that it should be.

This recommendation is one which has point not merely within philosophy but quite generally. For people everywhere – being too human – constantly fail to be and to make clear which sort of claim they are supposed to be urging. Worse still, having started with an assertion of the one sort we then illicitly – and often unwittingly – reinterpret it in the other way. Let us pillory this particular form of intellectual delinquency by dubbing it, *The No-true-Scotsman Move*. Someone says: 'No Scotsman would beat his wife to a shapeless pulp with a blunt instrument'. He is confronted with a falsifying instance: 'Mr Angus McSporran did just that'. Instead of withdrawing, or at least qualifying, the too rash original claim our patriot insists: 'Well, no true Scotsman would do such a thing!' By this evasive essay in persuasive definition, what started as a contention about a supposed matter of fact is shiftily transmogrified into the expression of a factitious necessary truth. For if Angus McSporran is to be disqualified as a true Scot for no better reason than that he has savagely maltreated his wife, it is clear that it has been made part of the meaning of *true Scot* that no true Scot can so misbehave. The remaining temptation is to mistake it – especially once the pressure of opposition has eased – that this verbal manoeuvre constitutes an adequate defence of the original claim; whereas, of course, to resort to so desperate a measure is tacitly to concede that the contention thus defended is really indefensible.

§3 *Arguments from experience*

But Hume with his new weapon was interested chiefly in bigger game. The first two passages quoted in the previous section show the attack developing immediately on two different versions of the rationalist notion that it is possible to know some matters of fact and real existence apriori: first, "The non-existence of any being, without exception, is as clear and distinct an idea as its existence"; and, second, "If we reason apriori, anything may appear able to produce anything". One application of this second negative insight, and one which went far to warrant the exultation of the third passage quoted, has been considered already in an earlier chapter (Ch. VI, § 5; cf. pp. 346–347, 285, and 254). But its most radical implication is drawn out only in the *Treatise*. It is equally impossible to know apriori: not only "that any thing or sort of thing either must be or cannot be the cause of any other thing or sort of thing" (p. 254, above); but also that there has to be any cause at all:

> It is a general maxim in philosophy, that whatever begins to exist must have a cause of existence. This is commonly taken for granted in all reasonings, without any proof given or demanded. It is supposed to be founded on intuition, and to be one of those maxims which, though they may be denied with the lips, it is impossible for men in their hearts really to doubt of. But, if we examine this maxim by the idea of knowledge above-explained, we shall discover in it no mark of any such intuitive certainty; but, on the contrary, we shall find that it is of a nature quite foreign to that species of conviction. (I (iii) 3)

Hume, after applying cruder versions of ideas refined in the first *Inquiry*, goes on to deal very faithfully with three contrary arguments. The first of these is by Hume credited to Hobbes. But something very like it is prominent in the *Leibniz-Clarke Correspondence*:

> Accordingly we shall find upon examination that every demonstration, which has been produced for the necessity of a cause, is fallacious and sophistical. All the points of time and place, say some philosophers, in which we can suppose any object to begin to exist, are in themselves equal; and unless there be some cause, which is peculiar to one time and to one place, and which by that means determines and fixes the existence, it must remain in eternal suspense; and the object can never begin to be, for want of something to fix its beginning. But, I ask, 'Is there any more difficulty in supposing the time and place to be fixed without a cause, than to suppose the existence to be determined in that manner?' The first question that occurs on this subject is always whether the object shall exist or not; the next, when and where it shall begin to exist. If the removal of a cause be intuitively absurd in the one case, it must be so in the other: and if that absurdity be not clear without a proof in the one case, it will equally require one in the other. The absurdity, then, of the one supposition can never be a proof of that of the other; since they are both upon the same footing, and must stand or fall by the same reasoning.   (*Ibid.*, I (iii) 3)

Hume attributes a second argument to Clarke and an almost indistinguishable third to Locke. I quote Hume's treatment of the former mainly for its relevance to some discussions of the idea of God as a first cause, and follow this immediately with Hume's summary:

> The second argument ... labours under an equal difficulty. Everything, it is said, must have a cause; for if any thing wanted a cause, it would produce itself, that is, exist before it existed; which is impossible. But this reasoning is plainly unconclusive; because it supposes, that in our denial of a cause we still grant what we expressly deny, viz. that there must be a cause; which therefore is taken to be the object itself; and that, no doubt, is an evident contradiction. But to say that any thing is produced or, to express myself more properly, comes into existence, without a cause is not to affirm that it is itself its own cause. . . . An object, that exists absolutely without any cause, certainly is not its own cause. . . .

> I believe it will not be necessary to employ many words in shewing the weakness of this argument, after what I have said of the foregoing. They are all of them founded on the same fallacy, and are derived from the same turn of thought. It is sufficient only to observe that when we

exclude all causes we really do exclude them, and neither suppose nothing nor the object itself to be the causes of the existence; and consequently can draw no argument from the absurdity of these suppositions to prove the absurdity of that exclusion. If every thing must have a cause, it follows, that upon the exclusion of other causes we must accept of the object itself or of nothing as causes. But it is the very point in question, whether every thing must have a cause or not; and therefore, according to all just reasoning, it ought never to be taken for granted.

They are still more frivolous who say that every effect must have a cause, because it is implied in the very idea of effect. Every effect necessarily presupposes a cause; *effect* being a relative term, of which *cause* is the correlative. But this does not prove, that every being must be preceded by a cause; no more than it follows, because every husband must have a wife, that therefore every man must be married. The true state of the question is, whether every object, which begins to exist, must owe its existence to a cause; and this I assert neither to be intuitively nor demonstratively certain, and hope to have proved it sufficiently by the foregoing arguments. (*Ibid.,* I (iii) 3)

From this treatment of causality Hume presses on to raise a still more fundamental question. I quote from the improved presentation in the first *Inquiry*:

When it is asked, 'What is the nature of all our reasonings concerning matter of fact?' the proper answer seems to be that they are founded on the relation of cause and effect. When again it is asked, 'What is the foundation of all our reasonings and conclusions concerning that relation?' it may be replied in one word, 'Experience'. But if we still carry on our sifting humour, and ask, 'What is the foundation of all conclusions from experience?' this implies a new question, which may be of more difficult solution and explication. Philosophers, that give themselves airs of superior wisdom and sufficiency, have a hard task when they encounter persons of inquisitive dispositions, who push them from every corner to which they retreat, and who are sure at last to bring them to some dangerous dilemma. The best expedient to prevent this confusion, is to be modest in our pretensions; and even to discover the difficulty ourselves before it is objected to us. By this means, we may make a kind of merit of our very ignorance.

I shall content myself, in this section, with an easy task, and shall pretend only to give a negative answer to the question here proposed. I say then, that, even after we have experience of the operations of cause and effect, our conclusions from that experience are not founded on reasoning, or any process of the understanding. (IV (ii))

Hume's modesty here befits his programme to determine the limits of the human understanding. Other "philosophers and graver divines" have been inclined to appeal to such limitations only in order to disarm criticism of their own rash claims to know of the existence and – often in extraordinary detail – of the wishes and plans of a supposedly infinite and incomprehensible God. Hume, by contrast, took the moral to be a humanist agnosticism. Thus in the same *Inquiry* he concludes his discussion of the topics of our Chapter VII with characteristically mischievous irony:

> To reconcile the indifference and contingency of human actions with prescience, or to defend absolute decrees and yet free the Deity of being the author of sin, has been found hitherto to exceed all the power of philosophy. Happy, if she be thence sensible of her temerity when she pries into these sublime mysteries, and, leaving a scene so full of obscurities and perplexities, return, with suitable modesty, to her true and proper province, the examination of common life, where she will find difficulties enough to employ her inquiries without launching into so boundless an ocean of doubt, uncertainty, and contradiction.
>
> (VIII (ii))

But now, what is the irremediable weakness which Hume discerns in the foundations of argument from experience?

> As to past experience, it can be allowed to give direct and certain information of those precise objects only, and that precise period of time, which fell under its cognizance. But why this experience should be extended to future times, and to other objects, . . . is the main question on which I would insist. The bread which I formerly ate nourished me. . . . But does it follow that other bread must also nourish me a another time. . .? The consequence seems nowise necessary. At least, it must be acknowledged that there is here a consequence drawn by the mind, that there is a certain step taken, a process of thought, and an inference which wants to be explained. These two propositions are far from being the same: *I have found that such an object has always been attended with such an effect;* and *I foresee that other objects which are in appearance similar will be attended with similar effects.* I shall allow, if you please, that the one proposition may justly be inferred from the other. I know, in fact, that it always is inferred. But if you insist that the inference is made

by a chain of reasoning, I desire you to produce that reasoning. The connection between these propositions is not intuitive. There is required a medium which may enable the mind to draw such an inference, if indeed it be drawn by reasoning and argument. What that medium is I must confess passes my comprehension; and it is incumbent on those to produce it who assert that it really exists and is the original of all our conclusions concerning matter of fact.   (IV (ii))

The challenge thus thrown down by Hume has since his time come to be known as The Problem of Induction. It provides a particularly good illustration of the truth of Russell's claim that logic is the essence of philosophy. For the challenge as Hume presents it is to find a suitable minor premise to complete a valid syllogism; and *syllogism,* like *medium* or *middle term,* is a semi-technicality from traditional, Aristotelian, formal logic. The problem thus set can be appreciated best by introducing a modicum of self-evident symbolism. How are we to get from the major premise *All observed X's are or have been* ϕ to the conclusion *All X's have been, are and will be* ϕ?

One possibly tempting resort is to make the ungracious No-true-Scotsman Move: if – to work with Hume's own example – we were to come across what was to all appearances ordinary bread, but possessing none of the expected nutritive properties, then we always could insist that it was, for that reason only, not real or true bread. This is tantamount to making ϕ one of the defining characteristics of an X. This once granted then obviously the desired conclusion follows immediately, and without benefit of any minor premise: "The connection between these propositions is", in Hume's terminology, "intuitive". (I introduced the Greek letter ϕ – pronounced phi – in order to mark in my symbolism the categorial distinction between characteristics and things.)

Now, certainly there is a proper place in the development of science for a manœuvre of this sort. Something which to the layman may be indistinguishable from ordinary water is, because of its special structure and characteristics, distinguished as heavy water; and so on. But this is nothing to the present philosophical point. For where it already is, or is made, true by definition that all X's are ϕ, there is no call for argument from experience: it would be absurd to ground the dull conclusion that all husbands are married upon the findings of some laborious social survey. What such empirical investigation might, of course, do is to provide us with reason for abandoning one concept – one definition – and introducing another. In a country like Jamaica, for instance, the sociologist who really

393

is concerned with description rather than prescription will find far more application for the concept of man cohabiting than for that of husband in any stricter sense.

A similarly irrelevant but equally instructive answer to Hume's question is to offer as a minor premise, *All X's are or have been observed*. The insertion of this would again produce a valid syllogism. But its validity would be bought only at the price of becoming a misrepresentation of the nerve of the argument from experience. We need to grasp the distinction: between analyses of the findings of experience; and arguments from them. Certainly if we have weighed a hundred six-month-old babies it is easy by a very primitive statistical analysis to deduce their average weight. But a true argument from experience must go beyond such data to some conclusion covering also some other babies not similarly studied.

The third possible answer, and the only one actually examined by Hume, is to suggest a second premise expressing some supposed universal uniformity of nature. The objection to this is epistemological. Here and elsewhere the reference to the future is inessential: Hume's main thesis is logical, and as such timeless; and as a future historian he was himself at least equally interested in arguments from experience to conclusions about the past:

> We have said that all arguments concerning existence are founded on the relation of cause and effect; that our knowledge of that relation is derived entirely from experience; and that all our experimental conclusions proceed upon the supposition that the future will be conformable to the past. To endeavour, therefore, the proof of this last supposition by probable arguments, or arguments regarding existence, must be evidently going in a circle, and taking that for granted which is the very point in question.
>
> ... all inferences from experience suppose, as their foundation, that the future will resemble the past, and that similar powers will be conjoined with similar sensible qualities. If there be any suspicion that the course of nature may change, and that the past may be no rule for the future, all experience becomes useless, and can give rise to no inference or conclusion. It is impossible, therefore, that any arguments from experience can prove this resemblance of the past to the future; since all these arguments are founded on the supposition of that resemblance. Let the course of things be allowed hitherto ever so regular; that alone, without some new argument or inference, proves not that, for the future, it will continue so. In vain do you pretend to have learned the nature of bodies from your past experience. Their secret nature, and

consequently all their effects and influence, may change, without any change in their sensible qualities. This happens sometimes, and with regard to some objects. Why may it not happen always, and with regard to all objects? What logic, what process of argument secures you against this supposition? My practice, you say, refutes my doubts. But you mistake the purport of my question. As an agent, I am quite satisfied in the point; but as a philosopher, who has some share of curiosity, I will not say scepticism, I want to learn the foundation of this inference.

(IV (ii))

If we refuse to talk largely and loosely of the Uniformity of Nature (with initial capitals, naturally!), and instead think of a precise formulation which would satisfactorily close the gap, then it emerges that the epistemological picture is even blacker than Hume painted it. For even if we did know in general that everything which occurs can in principle be subsumed under universal laws, still this would not be enough to enable us in a particular case validly to deduce from *All observed X's are or have been φ* the desired conclusion that *All X's have been, are and will be φ*: the behaviour of X's might be fully determined by laws though these did not include what we – misguided by our too limited experience – had mistakenly conjectured to be one such law. Adequately to fill the gap in the syllogism we need something relatively specific: *Whenever all observed X's are or have been φ, all X's have been, are and will be φ.*

The trouble with this is not that it can be known to be true only by employing argument from experience. It is that it is already, and without any such here illegitimate resource, known to be false. Consider, for piety's sake, a traditional example. Until Abel Tasman and his crew discovered the black swans of Western Australia all those observed by Europeans had been white. And if for austere tastes this illustration smacks too much of natural history, it is easy to summon others from the development of theoretical science. ("In science", as the atomic physicist Lord Rutherford used to say, "there is only physics – and stamp collecting!")

References to the development of physical science are very much in place. For in setting his problem Hume, who described his *Treatise* as "an attempt to introduce the experimental method of reasoning into moral subjects" (Ch. III, § 3), was certainly thinking of Newton's "Rules of Reasoning in Philosophy", and aware that these ideas had themselves been developed in fruitful opposition to the methodological proposals of Descartes (Ch. VIII, § 4). These "Rules" are found in Book III of *Principia*, the work which once and for all defined classical physics. The full title in the original Latin, *Philosophiae Naturalis Principia Mathematica,* itself constituted an allusion to Descartes' *Principles of Philosophy.* To appreciate Newton's comments on Rule III you need to know that one of the Cartesian fundamentals – clearly and distinctly conceived by him to be true – is that while the essence of mind is consciousness the essence of matter is extension. Again out of piety, I quote in the translation published by Andrew Motte in 1729:

Rule I. We are to admit no more causes of natural things than such as are both true and sufficient to explain their appearances.

To this purpose the philosophers say that Nature does nothing in vain, and more is in vain when less will serve; for Nature is pleased with simplicity and affects not the pomp of superfluous causes.

Rule II. Therefore to the same natural effects we must, as far as possible, assign the same causes.

As to respiration in a man, and in a beast; the descent of stones in Europe and in America; the light of our culinary fire, and of the Sun; the reflection of light in the earth, and in the planets.

Rule III. The qualities of bodies, which admit neither intensification nor remission of degrees, and which are found to belong to all bodies within the reach of our experiments, are to be esteemed the universal qualities of all bodies whatsoever.

For since the qualities of bodies are only known to us by experiments, we are to hold for universal all such as universally agree with experiments; and such as are not liable to diminution can never be quite taken away. We are certainly not to relinquish the evidence of experiments for the sake of dreams and vain fictions of our own devising.... We no otherways know the extension of bodies than by our senses, nor do these reach it in all bodies; but because we perceive extension in all that are sensible, therefore we ascribe it universally to all others also. That abundance of bodies are hard we learn by experience. And because the hardness of the whole arises from the hardness of the parts, we therefore justly infer the hardness of the undivided particles, not only of the bodies we feel, but of all others. That all bodies are impenetrable, we gather not from reason but from sensation. The bodies which we handle we find impenetrable, and thence conclude impenetrability to be an universal property of all bodies whatsoever.... And this is the foundation of all philosophy....

Rule IV. In experimental philosophy we are to look upon propositions collected by general induction from phenomena as accurately or very nearly true, notwithstanding any contrary hypotheses that may be imagined, till such a time as other phenomena occur by which they may either be made more accurate or liable to exceptions.

This rule we must follow, that the argument of induction may not be evaded by hypotheses.

It is worth rereading this passage, and pondering it a little at large, before returning to the challenge put by Hume. Rule I is a restatement of Ockham's Razor (Ch. VI, § 1). Such rules of procedure are very often given gratuitous ontological support; and in this case, surely, the claim about Nature is rash as well as unnecessary. Certainly it is unnecessary, for this rule is one which would be followed by any cautious and systematic investigator, even if he had positive reason to fear that Nature may be exhibitionist and lavish.

Rule II some may want to dismiss as trite. But one lesson which the history of ideas, if nothing else, should teach us is that obviousness is a relative matter; that what is obvious now to anyone was perhaps once a radical insight, which may one day be lost; and hence that what is at this time obvious to me is not, for that reason only, to be despised. The uniformitarian principle upon which Newton is insisting had once, in the rejection of the Aristotelian cosmology, had to be fought for. (Aristotle had taught, and of course not without reason, that the Earth alone is stationary in the centre of a system of concentric shells; that the innermost of these spheres, carrying the moon, makes the boundary between our 'sublunary', earthly region of change, growth, and decay and the un- corruptible, 'superlunary', heavenly spheres; and that the latter are exclusively composed of a special and peculiar sort of matter, called quintessence.) It was left to a later century – the century of Lyell (1797– 1875) and Darwin (1809–1882) – to apply the same uniformitarian principle to the development of geological structures and to the origin of species. *Hamlet* may seem now a string of quotations; but to write it was, and it remains, a work of genius.

Rules III and IV together constitute a deliberate and total rejection of the Cartesian programme for a rationalist science. *Hypothesis* in Newton is a very bad word, suggesting wanton and arbitrary speculation unwarranted and unchecked by proper empirical enquiry. There is, therefore, a studied piquancy in Hume's choice of the expression "the religious hypothesis". The ironic Hume recognized and relished the fact that he was using Newton's own methodological principles to undermine precisely the kind of empirical natural theology which Newton himself had favoured (Ch. VI, § 5).

Where Descartes had boasted of founding all our knowledge of nature on a prior knowledge of God, Newton – and it was to be a sign of the times – preferred to reverse that order. So in the General Scholium to the same Book of *Principia* he wrote: "This most beautiful system of the sun, planets and comets could only proceed from the counsel and dominion of an intelligent and powerful Being . . . to discourse of whom from the appearances of things does certainly belong to natural philosophy"; and "whatever is not deduced from the phenomena is to be called a hypothesis, and hypotheses, whether metaphysical or physical, whether of occult qualities or mechanical, have no place in experimental philosophy. In this philosophy particular propositions are collected from the phenomena and afterward made general by induction. Thus it was that the impenetrability, the mobility, and the impulsive force of bodies, and the laws of motion and of gravitation, were discovered." Later, in his First Letter to Bentley, Newton claimed sincerely: "When I wrote my treatise about our system, I had an eye on such principles as might work with considering men for the belief of a Deity; and nothing can rejoice me more than to find it useful for that purpose."

But it is high time to come directly to grips with Hume's challenge. There are some things which, standing on the shoulders of tall predecessors, we can now see fairly clearly. First, it should have become obvious that what Hume has produced is a compulsive demonstration. It is of the essential nature of argument from experience that its conclusions must go beyond its premises. For the whole point and purpose of such argument precisely is to enable us to employ our knowledge of the examined to shape our expectations of the unexamined; and, by the same token, these conclusions cannot be deducible from those premises. As appeared earlier, in our probing of Hume's incomplete syllogism, to supply a second premise which yielded a valid deduction would be thereby to disqualify the result as a representation of what is here meant by *argument from experience*.

Nor will it do to suggest that, though the possible premises cannot be made to prove the desired conclusions, they can at least give them some degree of probability. This is a blind alley which has been very thoroughly explored, often with the aid of fine mathematical equipment which might have been put to some better use. Of course there is a sense, into which Hume himself lapses, in which all "these arguments must be probable only, or such as regard matter of fact and real existence"; though if we too are inclined to speak in this way we might also remember his advice that "to conform our language more to common use, we ought to divide arguments into demonstrations, proofs, and probabilities; by *proofs* meaning such arguments from experience as leave no room for doubt or opposition". ("Mr Locke", Hume notes in section VI of the first *Inquiry*, "divides all arguments into 'demonstrative' and 'probable'. In this view we must say that it is only probable that all men must die, or that the sun will rise tomorrow.") But in the present context the resort to probability is wholly misguided. An invalid syllogism, or one wanting a second premise, does not make its conclusion to some degree probable while failing quite to prove it. It supplies no rational support whatsoever.

Second, once we are fully seized of the first point we are in position to try the Search-for-the-shared-assumptions-to-challenge Strategy. What all the responses so far considered have in common is accepting Hume's representation of the nerve of all argument from experience. But now look at Newton's Rule III and Rule IV again. Newton is not telling us that universal conclusions about all cases without restriction can validly be deduced from premises covering only the few or many instances actually examined. He is not saying: that "The qualities of bodies . . . found to belong to all bodies within reach of our experiments" necessarily are "the universal qualities of all bodies whatsoever"; or that "propositions collected by general induction from phenomena" must always be true. What he is urging is something quite different: that such qualities "are to be esteemed the universal qualities of all bodies whatsoever"; and that "In experimental philosophy we are to look upon" these propositions "as accurately or very nearly true". One does not recommend that this should be esteemed or looked upon as that if there is no question but that it genuinely is; any more than one graciously deems someone to be properly qualified when they manifestly and indubitably are. Very significantly, Newton in Rule IV adds the proviso: "till such time as other phenomena occur by which they may either be made more accurate or liable to exceptions".

The second suggestion, therefore, is that, accepting Hume's demonstration that the ultimate basis of argument from experience cannot be deductive, we should take the moral as being that the final nerve of such argument has to be represented as a matter of following a tentative, undogmatic, and self-correcting rule. This rule would be something like: Where all known X's are ϕ, and where you have no particular experiential reason to the contrary, to take it that all X's are ϕ until you find experiential reason to revise or to abandon this conclusion. The parenthetical clause is inserted to take care of the swans. For, even before Tasman's discoveries, any European who took it that all swans are white would have been ignoring "particular experiential reason to the contrary". For it was common knowledge, both that the Earth at that time had not been fully explored, and that in many other species there are varieties with different pigmentation.

The qualifications *ultimate* and *final* in the previous paragraph require attention. It may prove – indeed it very often has proved – misleading to speak here, in the accepted way, of the Problem of Induction. For this suggests that Hume's challenge threatens only a particular method, that of proceeding from examinations of available instances to generalizations covering all cases – "propositions collected by general induction from phenomena". The response then comes that this does scant justice to the practice of creative scientists, that the method of science is not inductive but hypothetico-deductive, and so on.

All this is both important and true; so long as no one goes on – as some enthusiasts have – to make rash claims that there is no place at all for inductive procedures in scientific work or that no competent scientist has ever believed that there was. (Long-range weather forecasting surely provides one counter-example against the former, while the phrase just quoted from Newton constitutes a formidable rebuttal of the latter.) The important truth is expressed memorably in Kant's Preface to the second edition of his first *Critique* (trans. N. Kemp Smith):

> When Galileo caused balls, the weights of which he had himself previously determined, to roll down an inclined plane; when Torricelli made the air carry a weight which he had calculated beforehand to be equal to that of a definite column of water; or in more recent times, when Stahl changed metal into lime, and lime back into metal, by withdrawing something and then restoring it, a light broke upon all students of nature. They learned that reason . . . must not allow itself to be kept, as it were, in nature's leading strings, but must itself show the way with principles of judgement based upon fixed laws, constraining nature to give answer to questions of reason's own determining. . . . Reason must approach nature in order to be taught by it. It must not, however, do so in the character of a pupil who listens to everything that the teacher chooses to say, but of an appointed judge who compels the witnesses to answer questions which he has himself formulated. Even physics, therefore, owes the beneficent revolution in its point of view entirely to the happy thought, that while reason must seek in nature, not fictitiously ascribe to it, whatever as not being knowable through

reason's own resources has to be learnt, if learnt at all, only from nature, it must adopt as its guide, in so seeking, that which it has itself put into nature. It is thus that the study of nature has entered on the secure path of a science, after having for so many centuries been nothing but a process of merely random groping.

This need for rational creativity on the part of the scientist is, it is worth pointing out, a direct consequence of the logical nature of explanation and of the basic aims of the whole scientific quest. Those aims are to discover what happens and why; for where the object is application we have not pure science but technology. But an explanation must tell us more; it cannot as such be deduced from statements of the facts to be explained; hence the explainer must introduce something which is not simply contained already in the facts themselves. It is for this reason that we join with Molière in laughing at the comic doctors in his *Le Malade Imaginaire* who pretend to explain the soporific power of opium by reference to its dormitive virtue.

So far so good. But none of this does anything to meet Hume. For if it really is as irrational to be guided by experience as his representation would suggest that it must be, then the most sophisticated hypothetico-deductive procedures are as much at risk as the crudest inductions. Grant that hypotheses are formed by leaps of the imagination; that their logical consequences are deduced; and that some, because these deduced consequences are found in fact to obtain, survive our testing. We then, until and unless these hypotheses are falsified by further tests, "look upon" them as "propositions . . . accurately or very nearly true". And this just is the conclusion of what Hume meant by an argument from experience; though not, of course, represented as he would have represented it.

Before proceeding at last to § 4 a word or two about the idea of faith in the uniformity of nature. It is often maintained that science somehow presupposes this; and morals are then drawn about the need for faith as well as reason, and so on. We have seen that in a formulation fitted to plug the gap in Hume's syllogism such faith would be ill-founded. But it might also be an absolutely general and unspecific conviction that there are everywhere lawful regularities to be discovered. In this form it would of course be safely unfalsifiable, while the whole previous success of scientific investigation provides it with ever-increasing warrant. Such a conviction can, as a matter of psychology, boost the morale of research workers. As one of the most distinguished – the German physicist Max Planck – once cried: "Without this faith the enormous labours of the scientists would be without hope!"

But even if such a conviction is psychologically necessary to some or all scientific workers, this is not to say that it is a logical presupposition of science. For for it to be rational to look for natural laws or for anything else it is not essential to know or to believe that these are in fact there to be found. It is sufficient to want to discover them if they are, and to have no reason to believe that they are not. So, as in the case of Newton's Rule I and the supposed simplicity of nature, it is perfectly reasonable for those who are prepared to travel metaphysically light to do so. In the words of the hero Stadtholder William the Silent: "It is not necessary to hope in order to act, nor to succeed in order to persevere."

§4 *Proposed epistemological foundations for mathematics*

In the first section of the present chapter I repeated my earlier definition of what it is to be a rationalist, and I then developed the point that mathematics has always provided the main inspiration for such hopes. The fact of this inspiration thus gives controversial edge to investigations of the general nature of the apriori, and of the status of pure mathematics in particular. We have looked at certain contributions to this enquiry already in other contexts. For instance, Plato's Argument from Recollection appeared first in Chapter II as a pointer to the existence of Forms, and then it was considered again in Chapter IV as a candidate proof for personal pre-existence. We are concerned now with its third aspect, as an answer to the question, 'How is apriori knowledge possible?'

In giving his answer Plato observed, but did not himself make, a distinction between apriori concepts and apriori propositions. For in the *Phaedo* version, quoted earlier (pp. 53–55), 'Socrates' proceeds: from the fact that we have concepts which are never perfectly instantiated in the universe around us, to the conclusion that our souls must have been previously acquainted with the appropriate Forms as actual ideal exemplars of whatever it may be. But in the *Meno* he reaches a similar conclusion starting from the apriori knowledge of propositions. The stated object of the exercise is to make out the claim that: "Since all nature is interrelated, and since the soul has learned all things, there is no reason why one should not by remembering – what people insist on calling learning – one single thing discover everything else. It is a matter of being courageous and not wearying of the search. For research and learning are, it would seem, wholly recollection" (§ 81D). The example employed is the conclusion of the Theorem of Pythagoras, and 'Socrates' shows how a slave boy who has never learnt any geometry can nevertheless be got to 'remember' this:

SOCRATES – What do you think, Meno? Was there any opinion which this lad did not give as an answer from his own resources?

MENO – No, they were his own.

SOCRATES – And yet, as we were saying a little while back, he certainly did not know.

MENO – That is true.

SOCRATES – Still he had these opinions in him, did he not?

MENO – Yes.

SOCRATES – So someone who has no knowledge in some area may have true opinions about these things which he does not know.

MENO – So it seems.

SOCRATES – As of now these opinions have just been stirred up in him, as if he were in a dream. But if someone were to ask him these same questions repeatedly and in a variety of forms, you realize that in the end he will have as exact a knowledge of them as anyone.

MENO – So it seems.

SOCRATES – Without anyone having taught him, then, but just through being asked questions he will know? By himself recovering the knowledge out of himself?

MENO – Yes.

SOCRATES – And is not this recovery of knowledge in himself and by himself, precisely, recollection?

MENO – Absolutely.

SOCRATES – So then this lad either at some time acquired or else always had the knowledge which he now has?

MEMO – Yes.

SOCRATES – If, therefore, he always had it then he was always in a state of knowing. But if he acquired it some time it could not have been in this present life. Or has someone taught this fellow to do geometry? For he will be able to do the same with all geometry and with all the other branches of knowledge. Now is there someone who has taught him all this? You are surely the one to know, the more so since he was born and bred in your household.

MENO – But I know that no one has ever taught him.   (§§ 85B–E)

Meno's last statement here is, of course, false. But to concentrate on the fact that 'Socrates' has himself been teaching Meno's slave is to miss lessons which we should ourselves learn. Nor, for the same reason, must we be too much disturbed by the rash reference to "all other branches of knowledge". Presumably if pressed 'Socrates' would have conducted a fighting withdrawal; since for Plato knowledge – true knowledge! – consists at most in what we, but not he, would call apriori knowledge (Ch. X, § 5). What has to be recognized is that whoever taught Meno's slave, no one taught Pythagoras. For it was he who first through some internal dialectic – some dialogue, as Plato would have put it, of the soul with itself – formed the proof by which a mere opinion, that the square on the hypoteneuse of a right-angled triangle is equal to the sum of the squares on the other two sides, can be promoted into the knowledge that it must be. And what also has to be recognized is that, whatever may be thought of the supposed hypothesis of personal pre-existence, to compare the production of this sort of knowledge with remembering is to choose what is perhaps the best of all available analogies. For, surely, producing conclusions without empirical investigation but somehow derived from something we already have is very like remembering what we had forgotten?

Now consider again, in the light of the suggestions about mathematics made in Hume's Fork, the passages from *The Republic* quoted in § 1. These are even more significant in what they do not say than in what they do. Plato is eloquently insistent: first, that pure mathematics is not about either "numbers with visible or tangible embodiment" or the diagrams which geometricians sometimes draw in aid; and, second, that mathematicians, starting from various postulates of which "they do not see fit to render any further account", then "proceed systematically and consistently until they reach the original object of their investigation". But what Plato does not say is: first, that pure mathematics as such cannot be about anything, or at any rate not in the way that biology – for instance – is about living things; and, second, that there is no call for anyone "to render any further account" of the postulates and the primitive notions since pure mathematics just is knowledge of the logical consequences of such things. Plato makes neither of these two further statements because, as he clearly shows, he does not believe them to be true. So he surely could not have agreed with the Hume of the first *Inquiry* that: "Though there never were a circle or a triangle in nature, the truths demonstrated . . . would forever retain their certainty and evidence".

Nowadays the two things which Plato did not say will seem obvious to many with only a smattering of mathematics or philosophy. It is therefore salutary to try to think ourselves back into the positions of outstanding thinkers who would have rejected one or both of these supposed truisms. Leibniz provides perhaps the most interesting example. On the second count, as the passage quoted in § 2 showed, he anticipated a modern view. He was also himself a creative mathematician of the first rank, able in a notorious controversy to challenge Newton's claim to priority in the invention of the Infinitesimal Calculus. The following passage comes from *New Essays concerning Human Understanding*, a critical running commentary by Leibniz on Locke's *Essay*:

> Your division seems to amount to the same as mine, between propositions of fact and propositions of reason. . . . As regards the eternal truths it is necessary to remark that they are at bottom all conditional, and state in effect: given such a thing, such another thing is. For example, in saying *Every figure which has three sides will also have three angles* I am saying nothing else but that, granted a figure with three sides, this same figure will have three angles. . . . The Scholastics disputed strongly, *de constantia subjecti* as their phrase was; that is to say, about how a proposition about a subject can have a real truth if this subject does not exist. The fact is that the truth is only conditional, and consists in the statement that in the event that the subject does ever exist it will be found to be such. But, it will be asked further, in what is this connection founded since there is in it some reality which does not deceive? The reply will be that it lies in the connection between the ideas. But, it will be asked in answer, where would these ideas be if no mind existed, and what would become then of the real foundation of this certitude of the eternal truths? That brings us at last to the ultimate foundation of truths, that is, to that Supreme and Universal Mind which cannot fail to exist. His understanding, to tell true, is the sphere of the eternal truths; as St Augustine recognized, and expressed it vividly enough. And in order that it should not be thought unnecessary to revert to this, we must reflect that these necessary truths contain the determining reasons and the regulative principles of the actual existents, and – in a word – the laws of the universe. So, since these necessary truths are anterior to the existence of contingent beings it is entirely necessary that they should be grounded in the existence of a necessary substance. It is there that I discover the original of the ideas and the truths which are engraved in our minds – not formulated as propositions, but as the materials whose opportune use will give rise to actual assertions.
>
> (IV (xi) 14)

The *New Essays* were published only in the last decade of Hume's life. But this thesis that necessary truths require some actual ground, and that they find it in the relations of the ideas of God, must already have been known to Hume from other sources while he was working on the *Treatise*. His project for "a sort of Copernican revolution in reverse" demanded that any such grounding should be in human rather than in Divine psychology (Ch. III, § 3). He took desperate steps:

> It appears, then, that the ideas which are most essential to geometry, viz. those of equality and inequality, of a right line and a plane surface, are far from being exact and determinate, according to our common method of conceiving them. Not only are we incapable of telling, if the case be in any degree doubtful, when such particular figures are equal; when such a line is a right one, and such a surface a plane one; but we can form no idea of that proportion, or of those figures, which is firm and invariable. Our appeal is still to the weak and fallible judgement, which we make from the appearance of the objects, and correct by a compass or common measure; and if we join the supposition of any farther correction, it is of such a one as is either useless or imaginary. In vain should we have recourse to the common topic, and employ the supposition of a Deity, whose omnipotence may enable him to form a perfect geometrical figure, and describe a right line without any curve or inflexion. As the ultimate standard of these figures is derived from nothing but the senses and imagination, it is absurd to talk of any perfection beyond what these faculties can judge of; since the true perfection of anything consists in its conformity to its standard.
>
> Now since these ideas are so loose and uncertain, I would fain ask any mathematician what infallible assurance he has, not only of the more intricate and obscure propositions of his science, but of the most vulgar and obvious principles? How can he prove to me, for instance, that two right lines cannot have one common segment? Or that it is impossible to draw more than one right line betwixt any two points. Should he tell me that these opinions are obviously absurd, and repugnant to our clear ideas, I would answer that I do not deny, where two right lines incline upon each other with a sensible angle, but it is absurd to imagine them to have a common segment. But supposing these two lines to approach at the rate of an inch in twenty leagues, I perceive no absurdity in asserting that upon their contact they become one. . . .
>
> I desire therefore our mathematician to form, as accurately as possible, the ideas of a circle and a right line; and I then ask if, upon the conception of their contact, he can conceive them as touching in a mathematical point, or if he must necessarily imagine them to concur for some space. (I (ii) 4)

A century later J. S. Mill had similar overall aims in *A System of Logic*. He developed a full account of mathematics on lines only indicated in the *Treatise*. But where Hume's emphasis was on the limitations of mental imagery, Mill stressed his thesis that fundamental mathematical propositions are to be construed as generalizations from our experience of the world:

> It remains to inquire, what is the ground of our belief in axioms – what is the evidence on which they rest? I answer that they are experimental truths; generalizations from observation. The proposition, *Two straight lines cannot inclose a space* – or in other words, *Two straight lines which have once met, do not meet again, but continue to diverge* – is an induction from the evidence of our senses. (II (v) 4)

> The expression *two pebbles and one pebble*, and the expression *three pebbles*, stand indeed for the same aggregation of objects, but they by no means stand for the same physical fact. . . . Three pebbles in two separate parcels, and three pebbles in one parcel, do not make the same impression on our senses; and the assertion that the very same pebbles may by an alteration of place and arrangement be made to produce either the one set of sensations or the other, though a very familiar proposition, is not an identical one. It is a truth known to us by early and constant experience: an inductive truth; and such truths are the foundation of the science of Number. (II (vi) 2)

Anyone accepting this kind of account still has to allow that many of the putative generalizations fit very loosely to the facts they are supposed to describe. This lack of correspondence is what was by Plato construed as an indication of the grossness and inferiority of the corporeal as compared with the ideal and truly real. Mill sees it rather as a matter of calculated scientific misrepresentation:

> The peculiar accuracy, supposed to be characteristic of the first principles of geometry, thus appears to be fictitious. The assertions on which the reasonings of the science are founded do not, any more than in other sciences, exactly correspond with the fact; but we suppose that they do so, for the sake of tracing the consequences which follow from the supposition. . . .
> When, therefore, it is affirmed that the conclusions of geometry are necessary truths, the necessity consists in reality only in this, that they correctly follow from the suppositions from which they are deduced. These suppositions are so far from being necessary that they are not even true; they purposely depart, more or less widely, from the truth. (II (v) 1)

§ 5 *The nature of the apriori*

Sections 5, 6 and 7 will touch on three morals suggested by § 4. These morals may usefully be approached by emphasizing – although this is not exactly what Mill has just said – that there can be no doubt but any valid deductive argument can be expressed as a single logically necessary truth, and that this remains so regardless of the status of the component premises and conclusion. This possibility is a consequence of the essential nature of deductive argument (Ch. I, § 2). It was indeed appreciation of the implications of the definitional fact, that it must be self-contradictory to assert the premises while denying the conclusion of a valid deductive argument, which led Mill to press his complaint that such argument necessarily begs the question (Ch. V, § 1). So any correct piece of mathematics, whatever the status of its axioms and other first principles, can be represented as a structure of analytic propositions. You may, therefore, if you like, speak of it when so represented as a system of tautologies. But if in this kind of context you do want to talk dashingly of tautologies you must remember that tautologies are not as such and necessarily either trivial or obvious.

The first moral is the need to get absolutely clear about the present meaning of *apriori knowledge*. Leibniz, Hume, and Mill in passages quoted in § 4 all give accounts of some or all our supposed apriori knowledge which would make it immediately, or ultimately, something else. Perhaps the same could be said of Plato also. Three perennial misconceptions call for exorcism.

First, *apriori knowledge* does not here refer to any sort of knowledge of human psychology, however basic or universal, as opposed to knowledge of what goes on out there in a Cartesian external world. It would, therefore, seem that Kant too lies open to the charge just levelled at Leibniz, Hume, and Mill. For his account, in terms of our inescapable "forms of sensibility", of what he picks out as our synthetic apriori knowledge does sound like a psychological speculation. (Russell once compared it, mischievously, with a suggestion that we are all forever forced to look out at reality through irremovable blue spectacles!) Kant's critical philosophy is thus perhaps more closely than he realized within the tradition of such ostensibly psychological works as Locke's *Essay* and Hume's *Treatise*. The following all comes from the *Prolegomena*, in the translation of P. G. Lucas:

But whatever origin judgements may have . . . there is in them a distinction according to content, by virtue of which they are either merely explicative and add nothing to knowledge, or ampliative and enlarge . . . knowledge; the former can be called *analytic judgements*, the latter *synthetic judgements*. (§ 2 (a))

All analytic judgements rest wholly upon the principle of contradiction, and it is in their nature to be knowledge apriori, whether the concepts that serve as matter for them be empirical or not. (§ 2 (b))

There are synthetic judgements aposteriori, which have an empirical origin; but there are also synthetic judgements which have apriori certainty, and have their origin in pure understanding and reason. Both agree in that they can never originate according to the principle of analysis alone, namely the principle of contradiction. They require another quite different principle, although whatever principle they are deduced from, they must always be deduced in conformity with the principle of contradiction. (§ 2 (c))

Mathematical judgements are all without exception synthetic. This proposition, though incontestably certain and in its consequences very important, seems to have wholly escaped hitherto the analyzers of human reason, indeed to be directly opposed to all their conjectures. . . .

One might indeed think that the proposition $7 + 5 = 12$ is a merely analytic proposition which follows according to the principle of contradiction from the concept of the sum of seven and five. But if we look more closely we find that the concept of the sum of 7 and 5 contains nothing further than the unification of the two numbers into a single number, and in this we do not in the least think what this single number may be which combines the two. . . .

Nor is any principle of pure geometry analytic. That the straight line between two points is the shortest is a synthetic proposition. For my concept of straight contains nothing of quantity but only a quality. The concept of the shortest is therefore wholly an addition, and cannot be drawn by any analysis from the concept of a straight line. Intuition, by means of which alone the synthesis is possible, must therefore be called in here to help. (§ 2 (c) 2)

If our intuition had to be of such a nature that it represented things as they are in themselves, no intuition apriori would ever take place and intuition would be empirical every time. . . . There is thus only one way in which it is possible for my intuition to precede the reality of the object, and take place as knowledge apriori, namely if it contains nothing else than the form of sensibility which in me as subject precedes all real impressions through which I am affected by objects. That objects of the senses can only be intuited in accordance with this form of sensibility is something that I can know apriori. From this it follows that propositions which concern merely this form of sensible intuition will be possible and valid for objects of the senses. . . .   (§ 9)

Second, it is wrong to think that to possess apriori knowledge it is sufficient to be armoured with an unshakable elementary conviction that things inescapably must be thus and thus. It is necessary, but still not sufficient, both to be right and to be in a position to know. For instance, many of the claims of Descartes clearly and distinctly to conceive such and such have to be disqualified as apriori knowledge upon one or both of these two counts (Ch. VIII, § 3 and Ch. IX, § 5).

Nor, third and finally, is apriori knowledge confined to that involving concepts – if such there be – which could not have been derived from experience, or beliefs which were originally acquired without benefit of any sort of empirical investigation. That $7 + 5 = 12$ is nonetheless an item in the inventory of my apriori knowledge for the fact, if it be a fact, that I could never have acquired any of the concepts involved without the help of patent instructional toys providing "numbers with visible and tangible embodiment". That pious favourite Theorem of Pythagoras still remains an achievement in pure mathematics notwithstanding that its conclusion was probably first suggested by the coarsely impure practical dodges of Egyptian surveyors. For it is not a matter of how a proposition in fact originally came to be believed, but of how the claim to know it could now be warranted. The distinction between apriori and aposteriori knowledge belongs not to the context of discovery but to that of justification. From all three points taken together it should begin to be clear why it was neither sufficient nor necessary, in order to show the comparatively limited scope and content of our apriori knowledge, for Locke to make out that, as a matter of psychological fact, our minds are at first "white paper, void of all characters, without any ideas" (*Essay*, II (i) 2). However, in fairness remember that Locke was arguing against people – especially followers of Lord Herbert of Cherbury (1581–1648) – who assumed that if there are, on the contrary, any innate ideas then these must be irrefragably guaranteed by the Maker. (Compare, again, § 3 of Chapter VIII.)

Obviously both Mill and the Hume of the *Treatise* intended to deny that certain pretended items of apriori knowledge are truly such. The case of Leibniz is less straightforward. First, if it really were a logically necessary condition of the truth of any eternal truth that God must have the appropriate thought in mind, then it must surely follow that these truths cannot after all be known apriori. For that God, or anyone else, is at this time or at all times thinking certain thoughts would appear to be very obviously a matter of contingent fact; the contrary of which "is still possible, because it can never imply a contradiction. . . ." But, second, what then becomes of the supposed ultimate logical necessities upon which Leibniz founds his entire metaphysics? For, as we have seen, he insists that it is itself one of the logically necessary eternal truths that God exists. Yet if this is so, and if what must surely be a contingent fact about the Divine psychology is a condition of the truth of all such truths, it would appear that everything must after all depend on its being contingently true both that there is a God and that he does think the required thoughts.

For a modern view of what apriori knowledge is, as opposed to suggestions implying that ultimately there is no such thing, we can turn to Wittgenstein's *Tractatus Logico-Philosophicus*. Wittgenstein was by birth Austrian, and started training as an engineer before abandoning this to go to Cambridge to study under Russell. To Wittgenstein Russell's appeal lay in his work on the foundations of mathematics. First in his *Principles of Mathematics* and then, jointly with Whitehead, in the monumental *Principia Mathematica* Russell had been trying to reduce mathematics to logic. This involved, first, the analysis of the fundamental notions of mathematics into purely logical terms, and, second, the elaboration of a system of logic adequate to furnish premises from which the propositions of mathematics could be deduced.

The *Tractatus*, written it seems while Wittgenstein was held as a prisoner of war in an Italian camp, is the defining work of his first philosophical period. The very different second period began in the early thirties after his return to Cambridge, although no work of this period was actually printed until the unfinished *Philosophical Investigations* came out, posthumously, in 1953. The title *Tractatus Logico-Philosophicus* was contributed by G. E. Moore. This was in its allusion to Spinoza, who wrote both a *Tractatus de Emendatione Intellectus* and a *Tractatus Theologico-Politicus,* an inspired suggestion. For not only was this first work a piece of high and systematic metaphysics, but Wittgenstein's whole achievement – like that of Spinoza – has been subject to flatly contrary interpretations; and for similar reasons (Ch. XI, § 1). Wittgenstein's later ideas about meaning – already embryonic in some of the following passages – should, surely, side him with the Giants against the Gods (Ch. II, § 1). Yet Wittgenstein personally, though he too neither lived nor died in the faith in which he had been reared, had like Spinoza the sort of temperament which many wanted nevertheless to call religious. In this and in other ways the spirit of the Vienna Circle was utterly alien to Wittgenstein. Two short passages from Carnap's 'Intellectual Autobiography' are worth quoting for what they reveal both about Wittgenstein and about the Vienna Circle. The first will also serve as a defining statement of *Scientific Humanism*. Carnap first remarks that "All of us in the Vienna Circle took a strong interest in the political events in our country, in Europe, and in the world", and then proceeds:

> I think that nearly all of us shared the following three views as a matter of course which hardly needed any discussion. The first is the view that man has no supernatural protectors or enemies and that therefore whatever can be done to improve life is the task of man himself. Second, we had the conviction that mankind is able to change the conditions of life in such a way that many of the sufferings of today may be avoided and that the external and the internal situation of life for the individual, the community, and finally for humanity will be essentially improved. The third is the view that all deliberate action presupposes knowledge of the world, that the scientific method is the best method of acquiring knowledge, and that therefore science must be regarded as one of the most valuable instruments for the improvement of life. In Vienna we had no names for these views; if we look for a brief designation in American terminology for the combination of these three convictions, the best would seem to be 'scientific humanism.'   (p. 83)

> Our attitude towards philosophical problems was not very different from that which scientists have toward their problems. For us the discussion of doubts and objections of others seemed the best way of testing a new idea in the field of philosophy just as much as in the fields of science; Wittgenstein, on the other hand, tolerated no critical examination by others, once the insight had been gained by an act of inspiration. I sometimes had the impression that the deliberately rational and unemotional attitude of the scientist, and likewise any ideas which had the flavour of 'enlightenment', were repugnant to Wittgenstein.
> (p. 26)

The following passages from the *Tractatus* are in the translation of C. K. Ogden, slightly revised by me. This first translation has in general the merits and demerits of the Authorized Version of the Bible, as compared with the later Revised Version of D. F. Pears and B. McGuiness. It is no doubt thanks to the *Tractatus* that all logically necessary propositions are now called truths of logic:

3.328   If a sign is not necessary then it is meaningless. That is the significance of Ockham's Razor.

(If everything in the symbolism works as though a sign had meaning, then it has meaning.)

5.551   Our fundamental principle is that every question which can be decided at all by logic can be decided without further machinery.

(And if we get into a situation where we need to answer such a problem by looking at the world, this shows that we are on a fundamentally wrong track.)

6.112   The correct explanation of logical propositions must give them a peculiar position among all propositions.

6.113   It is the characteristic mark of logical propositions that one can perceive in the symbol alone that they are true; and this fact contains in itself the whole philosophy of logic. And so also it is one of the most important facts that the truth or falsehood of non-logical propositions can not be recognized from the propositions alone.

6.1222   This throws light on the question why logical propositions can no more be empirically confirmed than they can be empirically refuted. Not only must a proposition of logic be incapable of being contradicted by any possible experience, but it must also be incapable of being confirmed by any such.

6.1223   It now becomes clear why we often feel as though 'logical truths' must be 'postulated' by us We can in fact postulate them in so far as we can postulate an adequate notation.

Wittgenstein has earlier distinguished two sorts of "logical proposition", the necessary truths and the necessary falsehoods:

4.46   Among the possible groups of truth-conditions there are two extreme cases. . . .

In the first case we call the proposition a tautology, in the second case a contradiction.

4.461   The proposition shows what it says, the tautology and the contradiction that they say nothing.

The tautology has no truth conditions, for it is unconditionally true; and the contradiction is on no condition true.

Tautology and contradiction are without direction.

(Like the point from which two arrows go out in opposite directions.)

(I know, for example, nothing about the weather, when I know that it rains or it does not rain.)

4.4611   Tautology and contradiction are, however, not nonsensical;

they are part of the symbolism in the same way that 'o' is part of the symbolism of arithmetic.

4.462 Tautology and contradiction are not pictures of reality. They present no possible state of affairs. For the one allows every possible state of affairs, the other none. . . .

The next passage adds little to Wittgenstein's account of the apriori. It earns its space here more as a wonderfully succinct refutation of any idea of clear and distinct conception as a guarantee of truth (Ch. IX, § 5):

5.1363 If from the fact that a proposition is obvious to us it does not follow that it is true, then obviousness is no justification for our belief in its truth.

5.14 If a proposition follows from another, then the latter says more than the former, the former less than the latter.

5.141 If p follows from q and q from p then they are one and the same proposition.

5.142 A tautology follows from all propositions; it says nothing.

What comes next for us is slightly more technical, and it spells out what Wittgenstein meant when he said earlier: "My fundamental thought is that the 'logical constants' do not stand for anything" (4.0312). The logical constants are the symbols of which the verbal equivalents used to be called syncategorematic words. Of the three appearing below, 'V' is read as 'or', and '∼' as 'not'. The third, '⊃', is the sign for material implication. To say that p materially implies q is to say that p is never as a matter of fact true without that q is true also. The popular Belfast saying, 'That is true or the Pope's a Jew', provides a helpfully mischievous mnemonic. (It was not without reason that Moore, in his paper on 'External and Internal Relations', characterized Russell's equation of *is materially implied by* with *is deducible from* as "simply an enormous howler". To get this straight Moore introduced the word *entails*, for the relation of deducibility which obtains when to assert p and deny q would be to contradict yourself.) Wiggenstein proceeds:

5.42 That V, ⊃, etc. are not relations, in the sense in which right and left etc. are, is obvious.

The possibility of crosswise definition of the logical 'primitive signs' of Frege and Russell shows by itself that these are not primitive signs and that they signify no relations.

And it is obvious that the '⊃' which we define by means of '∼' and 'V' is identical with that by which we define 'V' with the help of '∼', and that this 'V' is the same as the first, and so on.

5.43   That from a fact p an infinite number of others should follow, namely ~ ~p, ~ ~ ~ ~p, etc. is indeed hardly to be believed, and it is no less wonderful that the infinite number of propositions of logic (of mathematics) should follow from half a dozen 'primitive propositions'.

But all the propositions of logic say the same thing. That is, nothing.

6.1262   Proof in logic is only a mechanical expedient to facilitate the recognition of tautology, where it is complicated.

6.1263   . . . It is clear from the beginning that the logical proof of a proposition with direction and a proof in logic must be two quite different things.

6.2   Mathematics is a logical method.

The propositions of mathematics are equations, and therefore pseudo-propositions.

6.21   Mathematical propositions express no thoughts.

6.211   In life it is never a mathematical proposition which we need, but we use mathematical propositions only in order to infer from propositions which do not belong to mathematics to others which equally do not belong to mathematics.

(In philosophy the question, 'For what purpose do we use that word, that proposition?' constantly leads to valuable results.)

6.22   The logic . . . which the propositions of logic show in tautologies, mathematics shows in equations.

6.23   If two expressions are connected by the sign of equality, this means that they can be substituted for one another. But whether this is the case must show itself in the two expressions themselves . . .

6.2321   And, that the propositions of mathematics can be proved means nothing else than that their correctness can be seen without our having to compare what they express with the facts as regards correctness.

6.2322   The identity of the meaning of two expressions cannot be asserted. For in order to be able to assert something about their meaning, I must know their meaning, and if I know their meaning, I know whether they mean the same or something different.

§6 *The logical and the psychological*

The second moral which needs to be drawn out from passages quoted in § 4 is to obey the first of the three principles advanced by Frege in *The Foundations of Arithmetic*, "always to separate sharply the psychological from the logical" (Ch. VI, § 2). We have studiously not to confound: on the one side the fact that someone – whether with or without accompanying mental illustrations – says certain words aloud or to himself; with, on the other side, assertions about the meanings of those words or the validity of any argument which they may have been used to express.

A particular and strong temptation is to mistake it that somehow the meanings of words are mental images, or that our understanding of these meanings is necessarily dependent upon the occurrence of such images. These misunderstandings, which were by Locke and Hume elevated into philosophical principles, are encouraged by many common idioms. We say: "That so-called strategic expert keeps employing the phrase *second strike capability* without having any idea what it means"; and it is easy to assume that what this charlatan lacks is some corresponding psychological occurrence. The extract from the *Treatise* in § 5 displays these misunderstandings flagrantly. A more testing but a useful exercise is to uncover them in the passage from Locke's *Essay* quoted in the previous chapter (Ch. X, § 6). The following polemic is by Frege, in the translation of J. L. Austin:

When Stricker, for instance, calls our ideas of numbers motor phenomena, and makes them dependent on muscular sensations, no mathematician can recognize his numbers in such stuff or knows where to begin to tackle such a proposition. An arithmetic founded on muscular sensations would certainly turn out sensational enough, but also every bit as vague as its foundation. No, sensations are absolutely no concern of arithmetic. No more are mental pictures, formed from the amalgamated traces of earlier sense-impressions. All these phrases of consciousness are characteristically fluctuating and indefinite, in strong contrast to the definiteness and fixity of the concepts and objects of mathematics. It may, of course, serve some purpose to investigate the ideas and changes of ideas which occur during the course of mathematical thinking; but psychology should not imagine that it can contribute anything whatever to the foundation of arithmetic. To the mathematician as such these mental pictures, with their origins and transformations, are immaterial. Stricker himself states that the only idea he associates with the word *hundred* is the symbol 100. Others may have the idea of the letter C or something else; does it not follow, therefore, that these mental pictures are, so far as concerns us and the essentials of our problem, completely immaterial and accidental – just as accidental as it is that a blackboard and a piece of chalk do not by any means qualify to be called ideas of the number a hundred? Then let us cease to suppose that the essence of the matter lies in such ideas. Never again let us take a description of the origin of an idea for a definition, or an account of the mental and physical conditions on which we become conscious of a proposition for a proof of it. A proposition may be thought, and again it may be true; never again let us confuse these two things. We must remind ourselves, it seems, that a proposition no more ceases to be true when I cease to think of it than the Sun ceases to exist when I shut my eyes. Otherwise, in proving Pythagoras' theorem we should be reduced to allowing for the phosphorus content of the human brain; and astronomers would hesitate to draw any conclusions about the distant past, for fears of being charged with anachronism – with reckoning twice two as four regardless of the fact that our idea of number is a product of evolution and has a history behind it.   (pp. v–vi)

Those final sentences should, I think, in a sociologically minded and relativistically inclined age make a lot of ears burn. The next passage comes from the fifth of the *Meditations* of Descartes. I use the fastidious word *imaging* where other translators have said *imagination* for the good reason that the latter does not carry the implication, essential to Descartes' point, of the occurrence of mental imagery:

. . . I notice in the first place the difference which there is between imaging and conceiving. For example, when I image a triangle I do not only conceive it as a figure composed of and comprehended by three lines but apart from this I contemplate these three lines as present through the application of the internal power of my mind; and this is, strictly, what I call imaging. But suppose I want to think about a chiliagon, I certainly conceive truly that it is a figure composed of a thousand, as easily as I conceive that a triangle is a figure composed of only three, sides. But I cannot image the thousand sides of a chiliagon as I do the three sides of the triangle nor, so to speak, look at them with my mind's eyes as if they were present. And although, following my habit of making use of my powers of imaging when I think of corporeal things, it may happen that in conceiving a chiliagon I do confusedly represent some figure to myself; still it is very clear that this figure is not a chiliagon, since it does not differ at all from the one which I should represent to myself if I were thinking of a myriagon or of some other figure with an abundance of sides; and that it is no use at all for discovering the properties which make the difference between the chiliagon and the other polygons.

A third group of extracts comes from Berkeley's dialogue *Alciphron*. They anticipate remarkably several notions which it was left to our own century to develop; in particular the suggestion, usually credited exclusively to the later Wittgenstein, that the meaning of a word may be identified with its use – the job, that is to say, which it does when correctly employed. These anticipations seem to have been generally overlooked: not just by Wittgenstein himself, who was for a professional philosopher quite extraordinarily ill read in his own subject; but even by those, such as Hume and Peirce, who might have been expected to do better. Berkeley is thus frequently put down as advocating just the sort of view which he here puts into the mouth of Alciphron, and criticizes through his own spokesman Euphranor:

ALCIPHRON – Words are signs: they do or should stand for ideas, which so far as they suggest they are significant. But words that suggest no ideas are insignificant. He who annexeth a clear idea to every word he makes use of speaks sense; but where such ideas are wanting, the speaker utters nonsense. In order therefore to know whether any man's speech be senseless and insignificant, we have nothing to do but lay aside the words, and consider the ideas suggested by them. Men, not being able immediately to communicate their ideas one to another, are obliged to make use of sensible signs or words; the use of which is to raise those ideas in the hearer which are in the mind of the speaker; and if they fail of this end they serve to no purpose. He who really thinks hath a train of ideas succeeding each other and connected in his mind; and when he expresseth himself by discourse each word suggests a distinct idea to the hearer or reader; who by that means hath the same train of ideas in his which was in the mind of the speaker or writer. As far as this effect is produced, so far the discourse is intelligible, hath sense and meaning. Hence it follows that whoever can be supposed to understand what he reads or hears must have a train of ideas raised in his mind, correspondent to the train of words read or heard.   (VII 2)

EUPHRANOR – Words, it is agreed, are signs: it may not therefore be amiss to examine the use of other signs, in order to know that of words. Counters, for instance, at a card-table are used, not for their own sake, but only as signs substituted for money, as words are for ideas. Say now, Alciphron, is it necessary every time these counters are used throughout the progress of a game, to frame an idea of the distinct sum or value that each represents?

ALCIPHRON – By no means: it is sufficient the players at first agree on their respective values, and at last substitute those values in their stead....

EUPHRANOR – From hence it seems to follow, that words may not be insignificant, although they should not, every time they are used, excite the ideas they signify in our minds; it being sufficient that we have it in our power to substitute things or ideas for their signs when there is occasion. It seems also to follow that there may be another use of words besides that of marking and suggesting distinct ideas, to wit, the influencing our conduct and actions; which may be done either by rules for us to act by, or by raising certain passions, dispositions, and emotions in our minds. A discourse, therefore, that directs how to act or excites to the doing or forbearance of an action may, it seems, be useful and significant, although the words whereof it is composed should not bring each a distinct idea into our minds.

ALCIPHRON – It seems so. (VII 5)

Berkeley proceeds to his most drastic general contention, "that words may be significant, although they do not stand for ideas. The contrary whereof having been presumed seems to have produced the doctrine of abstract ideas." Alciphron replies:

ALCIPHRON – Will you not allow then that the mind can abstract?

EUPHRANOR – I do not deny it may abstract in a certain sense, inasmuch as those things that can really exist, or be really perceived asunder, may be conceived asunder, or abstracted one from the other; for instance, a man's head from his body, colour from motion, figure from weight. But it will not thence follow that the mind can frame abstract general ideas, which appear to be impossible.

ALCIPHRON – And yet it is a current opinion that every substantive name marks out and exhibits to the mind one distinct idea separate from all others.

EUPHRANOR – Pray, Alciphron, is not the word *number* such a substantive name?

ALCIPHRON – It is.

EUPHRANOR – Do but try now whether you can frame an idea of number in abstract, exclusive of all signs, words, and things numbered. I profess for my own part I cannot.

ALCIPHRON – Can it be so hard a matter to form a simple idea of number, the object of a most evident demonstrable science? Hold, let me see if I can't abstract the idea of number from the numerical names and characters, and all particular numerable things. (VII 5)

Here the narrator comments: "Upon which Alciphron paused a while, and then said, 'To confess the truth I do not find that I can.' " Alciphron's method seems to be exactly that which in the previous section we saw Kant employing to investigate $7 + 5 = 12$. Berkeley's own findings are later summarized:

Thus much, upon the whole, may be said of all signs: that they do not always suggest ideas signified to the mind; that when they suggest ideas, they are not general abstract ideas; that they have other uses besides barely standing for and exhibiting ideas, such as raising proper emotions, producing certain dispositions or habits of mind, and directing our actions in pursuit of that happiness which is the ultimate end and design, the primary spring and motive, that sets rational agents at work; that signs may imply or suggest the relations of things – which relations, habitudes or proportions, as they cannot be by us understood but by the help of signs, so being thereby expressed and confuted, they direct and enable us to act with regard to things; that the true end of speech, reason, science, faith, assent, in all its different degrees, is not merely, or principally, or always, the imparting or acquiring of ideas, but rather something of an active operative nature, tending to a conceived good – which may sometimes be obtained, not only although the ideas marked are not offered to the mind, but even although there should be no possibility of offering or exhibiting any such idea to the mind. For instance, the algebraic mark, which denotes the root of a negative square, hath its use in logistic operations, although it be impossible to form an idea of any such quantity. And what is true of algebraic signs is also true of words or language, modern algebra being in fact a more short, opposite, and artificial sort of language, and it being possible to express by words at length, though less conveniently, all the steps of an algebraical process. And it must be confessed that even the mathematical sciences themselves, which above all others are reckoned the most clear and certain, if they are considered, not as instruments to direct our practice, but as speculations to employ our curiosity, will be found to fall short in many instances of those clear and distinct ideas which, it seems, the minute philosophers of this age, whether knowingly or ignorantly, expect and insist upon in the mysteries of religion.   (VII 14)

§7 *Mathematics, pure and applied*

The final moral to be drawn from passages in § 4 is the need to make a radical distinction between pure and applied mathematics. Suppose that we take some simple arithmetical example, such as those favoured by Mill; and suppose that we recognize and use, as Mill did not, both this further distinction and the one spelt out earlier between the context of discovery and the context of justification. It should at once become obvious that no piece of pure arithmetical calculus makes any assertion about what does or does not happen, or could or could not happen. No such piece of calculus could, therefore, be refuted by any conceivable occurrence: "*That three times five is equal to the half of thirty* expresses a relation between these numbers"; and as a piece of pure calculus it can be known "by the mere operation of thought, without dependence on what is anywhere existent in the universe."

The temptation to believe the contrary springs from failure to appreciate the two basic distinctions just mentioned. For what holds of pure mathematics does not obtain with its applications. To deny that (to take the simplest possible example!) $1 + 1 = 2$ is to involve yourself in self-contradiction. But it is easy to imagine cases to falsify its application in the proposition that if you put one alongside another you will find you have two of the same. This very modest piece of applied arithmetic would, surely, be explosively false of two suitably large lumps of uranium 235? Nor, again, does what holds as regards discovery necessarily obtain of justification also. It may well be that no one could ever have acquired the notions of pure arithmetic without some initiation through "numbers with visible and tangible embodiment". But this would have no tendency to show that what you know if you know that $2 + 1 = 3$ "is a truth known to us by early and constant experience: an inductive truth."

Hume in the first *Inquiry* says the same about what has traditionally been felt to be the more difficult case of geometry. His expression *mixed mathematics,* where we would say *applied*, seems to have been derived from Francis Bacon:

> Every part of mixed mathematics proceeds upon the supposition that certain laws are established by nature in her operations, and abstract reasonings are employed either to assist experience in the discovery of these laws or to determine their influence in particular instances where it depends on any precise degree of distance and quantity. Thus it is a law of motion, discovered by experience, that the moment of force of any body in motion is in the compound ratio or proportion of its solid contents and its velocity and, consequently, that a small force may remove the greatest obstacle or raise the greatest weight if by any contrivance or machinery we can increase the velocity of that force so as to make it an overmatch for its antagonist. Geometry assists us in the application of this law by giving us the just dimensions of all the parts and figures which can enter into any species of machine, but still the discovery of the law itself is owing merely to experience; and all the abstract reasonings in the world could never lead us one step toward the knowledge of it. (IV (i))

Time spent labouring to give Hume's second sentence a precise interpretation in modern terms would probably be wasted. Yet it is worth remarking, especially after what was said in § 1 about the enormous shadow of Pythagoras, that science needs mathematical notions not merely in calculations of consequences but within its very laws themselves. How, for instance, could any inverse square law be formulated anumerically?

Our immediate concern is with geometry, as possibly being a special case. This has, I think, been by many regarded as the inner citadel of rationalist aspirations because, as compared with arithmetic and algebra, its applications are relatively specific and its ideas relatively concrete. It has appeared, therefore, rather easier here than there to give a persuasively this-worldly answer to the question: 'What is it that it gives us logically necessary and apriori information about?' For the plausible answer leapt to the tongue: 'Space'.

Thus, above all, Kant thought that the geometry which there was as yet no reason to qualify as Euclidean constituted knowledge which is both synthetic and apriori: "Geometry is a science which determines the properties of space synthetically, and yet apriori" (A25). It was in these terms that he characterized the problem upon which, he thought, the future of metaphysics depended. The following statement, like the sentence just quoted, comes from the *Critique of Pure Reason* – again in Kemp Smith's translation:

> Much is already gained if we can bring a number of investigations under the formula of a single problem. For we not only lighten our task, by defining it accurately, but make it easier for others, who would test our results, to judge whether or not we have succeeded in what we set out to do. Now the proper problem of pure reason is contained in the question: 'How are synthetic judgements apriori possible?'

> That metaphysics has hitherto remained in so vacillating a state of uncertainty and contradiction, is entirely due to the fact that this problem, and perhaps even the distinction between analytic and synthetic judgements, has never previously been considered. Upon the solution of this problem, or upon a sufficient proof that the possibility which it desires to have explained does not exist at all, depends the success or failure of metaphysics. Among philosophers, David Hume came nearest to envisaging this problem, but still was very far from conceiving it with sufficient definiteness and universality. He occupied himself exclusively with the synthetic proposition regarding the connection of an effect with its cause ... and he believed himself to have

shown that such an apriori proposition is entirely impossible. If we accept his conclusions, then all that we call metaphysics is a mere delusion whereby we fancy ourselves to have rational insight into what, in actual fact, is borrowed solely from experience, and under the influence of custom has taken the illusory semblance of necessity. If he had envisaged our problem in all its universality, he would never have been guilty of this statement, so destructive of all pure philosophy. For he would have recognized that, according to his own argument, pure mathematics, as certainly containing apriori synthetic propositions, would also not be possible; and from such an assertion his good sense would have saved him. ('Introduction', B19–B20)

There are two things worth noticing by the way. First, Kant's first paragraph is a model of the scientific temper; for the author of the passage quoted in § 5 knows what science is, and shares its ideals. He wishes to present his results in a form in which they can conveniently be tested by fellow workers. Though Kant often is, he never intends to be, obscure or indeterminate. In the words of the French aphorist, the Marquis de Vauvenargues (1715–1747): "For the philosopher clarity is a matter of good faith."

Second, handicapped though he obviously was by not knowing the *Treatise* Kant seems fully seized of what Hume's theses about causality actually were (Ch. VII, § 6 and Ch. XI, § 3). Yet the moment Kant begins to develop his own account of what synthetic apriori knowledge is supposed to be, the necessity we are offered appears to be psychological rather than logical. The first extract comes from the very beginning of the 'Introduction'. The second two are taken from Section I of 'The Transcendental Dialectic', and explicate the distinctive Kantian thesis that, "Space does not represent any property of things in themselves, nor does it represent them in their relation to one another" (A26):

There can be no doubt that all our knowledge begins with experience. For how should our faculty of knowledge be awakened into action, did not objects affecting our senses partly of themselves produce representations, partly arouse the activity of our understanding to compare these representations, and, by combining or separating them, work up the raw material of the sensible impressions into that knowledge of objects which is entitled experience. In the order of time, therefore, we have no knowledge antecedent to experience, and with experience all our knowledge begins.

But though all our knowledge begins with experience, it does not follow that it all arises out of experience. For it may well be that even our empirical knowledge is made up of what we receive through impressions and of what our own faculty of knowledge (sensible impressions serving merely as the occasion) supplies from itself. If our faculty of knowledge makes any such addition, it may be that we are not in a position to distinguish it from the raw material, until with long practice of attention we have become skilled in separating it.   (B1–B2)

What, then, are space and time? Are they real existences? Are they only determinations or relations of things, yet such as would belong to things even if they were not intuited? Or are space and time such that they belong only to the form of intuition, and therefore to the subjective constitution of our mind, apart from which they could not be ascribed to anything whatsoever?   (A23)

Space is not an empirical concept which has been derived from outer experiences. For in order that certain sensations be referred to something outside me (that is, to something in another region of space to that in which I find myself) and similarly in order that I may be able to represent them as outside and alongside one another, and accordingly as not only different but as in different places, the representation of space must be presupposed. The representation of space cannot, therefore, be empirically obtained from the relations of outer appearance. On the contrary, this outer experience is itself possible at all only through that representation.

Space is a necessary apriori representation, which underlies all outer intuitions. We can never represent to ourselves the absence of space though we can quite well think it as empty of objects. It must therefore be regarded as the condition of the possibility of appearances, and not as a determination dependent upon them. It is an apriori representation, which necessarily underlies all outer appearances. The apodeictic certainty of all geometrical propositions, and the possibility of their apriori construction, is grounded in this apriori necessity of space. Were this representation of space a concept acquired aposteriori, and derived from outer experience in general, the first principles of mathematical determination would be nothing but perceptions. They would therefore share in the contingent character of perception; that there should be only one straight line between two points would not be necessary, but only what experience always teaches.   (A24)

Had Kant known the *Treatise* – which, fallen "dead-born from the press", had not yet been translated into German – he would have been shocked to discover how Hume there had been prepared to claim, in the passage I quoted in § 4, that the first principles of geometrical determination precisely are "nothing but perceptions". But it is obvious that Kant would have been immeasurably more disturbed had he known that the century following the publication of the first *Critique* – in 1787 – would see the development of several systems of non-Euclidean geometry.

These developments constituted another of that special category of epoch-making intellectual break-throughs to which I have already twice drawn attention in other contexts (Ch. VIII, § 5 and Ch. XI, § 1). The first publications were by the Russian N. I. Lobachevsky (1793–1856) and the Hungarian J. Bolyai (1802–1860), working quite independently. We who have the advantage of living after these events may find it much too easy to discuss the supposed errors of bigger men handicapped by being born too soon. Of course, we may brashly interject, we know: that, as such, no sort of pure mathematics can be about anything; that it is better to think of all mathematical moves as a special sort of ratiocinative activity than as attempts to describe some highly idiosyncratic subject-matter; that it is applied, if any sort of, mathematics whose business it is to be about things; and so on.

Even if this is all quite right – and certainly the precise nature of the foundations of mathematics is still a question as controversial as it is difficult – it is bound to be misleading too. For it tends to conceal how enormous was the historical achievement by which *Euclid* ceased to be a synonym for *geometry*, and how very difficult it was to achieve this particular great leap forward. With reason Bolyai gloried: "I have made such wonderful discoveries that I am myself lost in astonishment; out of nothing I have created a new and another world." Before him 'the prince of mathematicians', the German K. F. Gauss (1775–1855), had begun to explore that world, but he had not dared to publish. And much earlier still an Italian Jesuit mathematician, Giorolamo Saccheri, had in part anticipated all three; but he had persisted in believing that his inconceivable conclusions simply must contain contradictions, which he himself had altogether failed to find.

Even judged as philosophy, and not as a failure in historical understanding, the now too ready response is at least insufficient. For one thing, this very development of non-Euclidean geometries must itself and directly make it more difficult to give an account of all mathematics on the lines sketched by Leibniz in the *Monadology*, quoted in § 2: "There are also axioms and postulates – in a word, primary principles – which cannot be proved and do not need to be either. These are identical propositions, the opposites of which contain explicit contradictions."

The first of these statements is perhaps true. But the second is very hard to square with the fact that, although the development of the non-Euclidean geometries began with attempts to prove that there would be a contradiction in denying the parallel postulate of Euclid, it was consummated on the basis of the recognition that there is not, and hence that alternatives are legitimate. It was partly, but only partly, for reasons of this sort that Frege, while giving a Leibnizian account of *The Foundations of Arithmetic*, remained unrepentantly Kantian about geometry (the translation is, as before, that of J. L. Austin):

> I do not wish to incur the reproach of picking petty quarrels with a genius to whom we must all look up with grateful awe; I feel bound, therefore, to call attention to my agreement with him, which far exceeds any disagreement. . . . I consider Kant did great service in drawing the distinction between synthetic and analytic judgements. In calling the truths of geometry synthetic and apriori he revealed their true nature. . . . If Kant was wrong about arithmetic that does not seriously detract, in my opinion, from the value of his work.
>
> (pp. 101–102)

Elsewhere in the same book Frege gives his reasons. Where in the following extract he speaks of an intuition "not taken at its face value" (as when "we call straight or plane what we actually intuite as curved"), Frege presumably had in mind suggestions of the sort developed brilliantly by the German scientist Hermann von Helmholz (1821–1894) in his 1870 lecture 'On the origin and significance of geometrical axioms'. For instance: given the definition of *straight line* as meaning the shortest distance between two points, then on the surface of a sphere the Euclidean axiom that there is only one straight line between any two points has to be drastically changed to meet the case of great circles, intersecting in the limiting points of the diameters of that sphere; while every pair of great circles provides a case of two straight lines, or perhaps two 'straight lines', which do enclose spaces. Frege writes:

> Empirical propositions hold good of what is physically or psychologically existent, the truths of geometry govern all that is spatially intuitable, whether existent or product of our fancy. The wildest vision of delirium, the boldest inventions of legend and poetry, where animals speak and stars stand still, where men are turned to stone and trees turn into men, where the drowning haul themselves out of swamps by their

own topknots – all these remain, so long as they remain intuitable, still subject to the axioms of geometry. Conceptual thought alone can after a fashion shake off their yoke, when it postulates a space, say of four dimensions or positive curvature. To study such conceptions is not useless by any means; but it is to leave the ground of intuition entirely behind. If we do make use of intuition even here, as an aid, it is still the same old intuition of Euclidean space, the only space of which we have any picture. Only then the intuition is not taken at its face value, but as symbolic of something else; for example, we call straight or plane what we actually intuite as curved. For purposes of conceptual thought we can always postulate the contrary of one or other of the geometrical axioms, without involving ourselves in any self-contradictions when we proceed to our deductions, despite the conflict between our postulates and our intuition. The fact that this is possible shows that the axioms of geometry are independent of one another and of the primitive laws of logic, and consequently are synthetic. (pp. 20–21)

The fact that even Frege, the great protagonist of this fundamental distinction, appears here to be ignoring his own embargo on the admission into the investigation of the logical foundations of mathematics of the psychological, can be seen as revealing how Kant has got into the bones of all the best who think in German. That his ideas have achieved this sort of status provides one of the best indirect reasons for us to study such a thinker directly. And yet, surely, we can now say – whatever should be salvaged from Kant's account, and however intricate and baffling the remaining technical problems – that there is no longer any question of defending the ancient and long-recurring rationalist hope that geometry gives us knowledge which is both synthetic and apriori. There is no one who can on this be quoted more aptly than Einstein. For he was the first to give a physical application to a non-Euclidean geometry, that of Riemann: "As far as the laws of mathematics refer to reality, they are not certain; and as far as they are certain, they do not refer to reality."

Epilogue

CHAPTER XII

Words and the World

§1 *Confronting Plato with Locke*

Back in Chapter II, in expounding the One over Many Argument, I quoted a remarkable statement by the Platonic 'Socrates': "We have regularly assumed a Form for all the manys to which we apply the same name, one Form for each Many" (*The Republic*, § 596A). It is time now to bring out just how remarkable this statement is. The richness of the vocabulary of Classical Greek is, of course, proverbial: 'The Greeks had a word for it'. But what Plato is here presupposing is: not so much that Greek in his day had contrived to keep in step with the inordinate richness of reality, which would itself be a sufficiently bold assumption; but rather that the ultimate realities themselves in some way are – how he would have hated this inversion of his employment of a favourite image! – shadows cast by language.

Certainly, this correspondence is required by Plato's Theory of Forms. For this is, in the first instance, offered to explain predication – hence the One over Many Argument (Ch. II, § 1). But if it is to do this in the way proposed there has to be a Form for every actual and possible predicate. The introduction of such a theory to our hindsight now appears to manifest at one and the same time, both a truly magnificent assurance of man's central place in some scheme of things, and a total lack of critical self-consciousness about his linguistic equipment. The latter here reinforces the former, although that had plenty of independent strength in Plato as in all the leaders of those few Classical generations of incomparable achievement. No one, for example, knew the tragic possibilities of human life better than Sophocles; and yet it was he who wrote the tremendous choral panegyric beginning:

> *Many are the wonders of the world, but none more wonderful than man*
> (*Antigone*, ll.332 ff.)

431

Our present concern, however, is with critical self-consciousness about linguistic equipment. The spokesman to show what this phrase means is Locke. He has already in an earlier citation explained in his own words how the *Essay* arose (Ch. IX, § 3). We also noticed there his later recognition that "to see what objects our understandings were, or were not, fitted to deal with" he would have to write a whole Book 'Of Words'. For, as he puts it, "it is impossible to speak clearly and distinctly of our knowledge, which all consists in propositions, without considering first the nature, use, and signification of language" (II (xxxiii) 19).

It was especially with this Book III in mind that Locke introduced into his prefatory 'Epistle to the Reader' a homespun image for what was to become a popular conception of the proper relations between philosophy and science. It was, for instance, a conception shared by the Vienna Circle. Robert Boyle (1626–1691), primarily *The Sceptical Chemist*, and Thomas Sydenham (1624–1689), one of the major figures in the history of medicine, were with Locke Fellows of the Royal Society. Huygenius was the Dutch mathematician and physicist Christian Huygens (1629–1693):

> I shall always have the satisfaction to have aimed sincerely at truth and usefulness, though in one of the meanest ways. The commonwealth of learning is not at this time without master-builders, whose mighty designs, in advancing the sciences, will leave lasting monuments to the admiration of posterity: but every one must not hope to be a Boyle or a Sydenham; and in an age that produces such masters as the great Huygenius and the incomparable Mr Newton, with some others of that strain, it is ambition enough to be employed as an under-labourer in clearing the ground a little, and removing some of the rubbish that lies in the way to knowledge. . . .
>
> Vague and insignificant forms of speech, and abuse of language, have so long passed for mysteries of science; and hard and misapplied words, with little or no meaning, have, by prescription, such a right to be mistaken for deep learning and height of speculation; that it will not be easy to persuade either those who speak or those who hear them, that they are but the covers of ignorance, and hindrance of true knowledge. To break in upon the sanctuary of vanity and ignorance will be, I suppose, some service to human understanding. . . .

After an ill-starred beginning in which, as we have seen (Ch. IX, § 3), he explicates the idea of a logically private language Locke moves to consider general terms:

All things that exist being particulars, it may perhaps be thought reasonable that words, which ought to be conformed to things, should be so too, – I mean in their signification. But yet we find quite the contrary. The far greatest part of words that make all languages are general terms; which has not been the effect of neglect or chance, but of reason and necessity. (III (iii) 1)

§ 2 General words and Locke's abstract general images

Indeed it has not. But Locke in the three subsequent supporting paragraphs never quite manages to state what that reason and necessity is – that in a language consisting entirely of proper names we could only indicate what we wanted to say something about, without ever being able actually to say it. The account which he goes on to give of the possibilities and limitations of these indispensable general terms is throughout bedevilled by the seducing notion that to understand the meaning of a word, to possess the concept, is to have some appropriate mental image. This disastrous misconception so pervades Locke's account of language that it is sensible to spend a little more time on it, and on Berkeley's criticisms, before we go on to take the positive lessons which that account has to teach. Thus Locke tells us how children begin to form abstract ideas. (The indications of social context within this extract give purchase for those who – perhaps because Locke's devotion to constitutional checks and balances offends their own attachment to a Leninist 'democratic centralism' – want to denounce Locke as "an English bourgeois philosopher"!):

The idea of the nurse and the mother are well framed in their minds; and, like pictures of them there, represent only those individuals. The names they first give to them are confined to these individuals; and the names *nurse* and *mamma*, which the child uses, determine themselves to those persons. Afterwards, when time and a larger acquaintance have made them observe that there are a great many other things in the world, that in some common agreements of shape, and several other qualities, resemble their father and their mother, and those persons they have been used to, they frame an idea, which they find these many particulars do partake in; and to that they give, with others, the name *man*, for example. And thus they come to have a general name, and a general idea. Wherein they make nothing new; but only leave out of the complex idea which they had of Peter and James, Mary and Jane, that which is peculiar to each, and retain only what is common to them all. (III (iii) 7)

The particular passage upon which Berkeley seized triumphantly is one where Locke himself seems unable fully to believe his own story, while also unable to reject it:

> For abstract ideas are not so obvious or easy to children, or the yet unexercized mind, as particular ones . . . when we nicely reflect upon them, we shall find that general ideas are fictions and contrivances of the mind, that carry difficulty with them, and do not so easily offer themselves as we are apt to imagine. For example, does it not require some pains and skill to form the general idea of a triangle, (which is yet none of the most abstract, comprehensive, and difficult,) for it must be neither oblique nor rectangle, neither equilateral, equicrural, nor scalenon; but all and none of these at once. In effect, it is something imperfect, that cannot exist; an idea wherein some parts of several different and inconsistent ideas are put together. It is true, the mind, in this imperfect state, has need of such ideas, and makes all the haste to them it can, for the conveniency of communication and enlargement of knowledge; to both which it is very much inclined. (IV (vii) 9)

It is a rueful spectacle of an able and honest thinker tormented by an antinomy from which he can see no escape. For though the abstract, general idea as specified by Locke "is something imperfect, that cannot exist" it apparently has to, if understanding, "communication and enlargement of knowledge" are to be possible. And they obviously are, since they do in fact occur. Berkeley in the *Principles* quotes this passage, and comments:

> If any man has the faculty of framing in his mind such an idea of a triangle as is here described, it is in vain to pretend to dispute him out of it, nor would I go about it. All I desire is that the reader would more fully and certainly inform himself whether he has such an idea or no. And this, methinks, can be no hard task for anyone to perform. What more easy than for anyone to look a little into his own thoughts, and there to try whether he has, or can attain to have, an idea that shall correspond with the description that is here given of the general idea of a triangle – which is neither oblique nor rectangle, equilateral, equicrural nor scalenon, but all and none of these at once?" (Introduction, § 13)

Since Locke has already himself displayed his specification as contradictory, and hence as not a possible description at all, this should be a "killing blow". But, of course, Locke's thesis about abstract general ideas was not reached as a finding of introspection. It was in fact left to Francis Galton (1822–1911), a cousin of Charles Darwin, to make the first thorough investigation of mental imagery. This Galton published in his *Inquiries into Human Faculty*. Galton's most interesting discoveries were that individuals vary enormously in their image lives, or lack of them; and that there is no obvious correlation between the vividness and variety of men's private imagery, and those public qualities which lead us to describe them as imaginative or unimaginative. Locke, however, postulated his abstract general ideas – just as Plato postulated his Forms – because these seemed to him to be necessarily presupposed by the possibility of something else, which undoubtedly does occur.

In philosophy, as in science, a theory is usually killed only by a better theory. And this Berkeley provided. Locke, he says, puts the question: "Since all things that exist are only particulars, how come we by general terms?" Berkeley responds:

His answer is: 'Words become general by being made the signs of general ideas'. . . . But it seems that a word becomes general by being made the sign, not of an abstract general idea, but of several particular ideas, any one of which it indifferently suggests to the mind.

(Introduction, § 11)

By observing how ideas become general, we may the better judge how words are made so. And here it is to be noted that I do not deny absolutely that there are general ideas, but only that there are any abstract general ideas . . . an idea which, considered in itself, is particular, becomes general by being made to represent or stand for all other particular ideas of the same sort.   (Ibid., § 12)

It was this move which Hume in the *Treatise* hailed as "one of the greatest and most valuable discoveries that has been made of late years in the republic of letters" (I (i) 7). Berkeley proceeds with reference to the last passage quoted from Locke, to drive his point home:

Much is here said of the difficulty that abstract ideas carry with them and the pains and skill requisite to forming them. . . . From all which the natural consequence should seem to be, that so difficult a thing as the forming abstract ideas was not necessary for communication, which is so easy and familiar to all sorts of men. But, we are told, if they seem obvious and easy to grown men, it is only because by constant and familiar use they are made so. Now, I would fain know at what time it is men are employed in surmounting that difficulty, and furnishing themselves with those necessary helps for discourse. It cannot be when they are grown up, for then it seems that they are not conscious of any such painstaking; it remains therefore to be the business of their childhood. And surely the great and multiplied labour of framing abstract notions will be found a hard task for that tender age. Is it not a hard thing to imagine that a couple of children cannot prate together of their sugar plums and rattles and the rest of their little trinkets, till they have first tacked together numberless inconsistencies, and so framed in their minds abstract general ideas, and annexed them to every common name they make use of?

Nor do I think them a whit more needful for the enlargement of knowledge than for communication. It is, I know, a point much insisted on, that all knowledge and demonstration are about universal notions, to which I fully agree. But then it does not appear to me that those notions are formed by abstraction in the manner premised – universality, so far as I can comprehend, not consisting in the absolute, positive nature or conception of anything, but in the relation it bears to the particulars signified or represented by it; by virtue whereof it is that things, names, or notions, being in their own nature particular, are rendered universal. Thus when I demonstrate any proposition concerning triangles, it is to be supposed that I have in view the universal idea of a triangle; which ought not to be understood as if I could frame an idea of a triangle which was neither equilateral, nor scalenon, nor equicrural; but only that the particular triangle I consider, whether of this or that sort it matters not, doth equally stand for and represent all rectilinear triangles whatsoever, and is *in that sense* universal. All which seems very plain and not to include any difficulty in it. (*Ibid.*, §§ 14–15)

The first of the two previous paragraphs is quoted partly for the delight of Berkeley's polemical style. But it can also be seen as an anticipation of one of the insights characteristic of the later Wittgenstein; that in philosophy it is often profitable to ask, 'How would you teach that word?' For no word, surely, in a public language can have meaning which could not have been taught. The second paragraph underlines the way in which Locke and Berkeley together succeeded in erecting a decisive 'No through road' sign against one tempting opening.

But even in the published version of the Introduction to his *Principles* there are hints – which, as we have seen (Ch. XI, § 6), Berkeley later began to develop in the *Alciphron* – of something far better than his own first rival theory. Berkeley starts this time from Locke's criticism of the Cartesian insistence on drawing one particular hard and fast line between men and the brutes (Ch. VIII, § 5):

'The having of general ideas', saith he, 'is that which puts a perfect distinction betwixt men and brutes, and is an excellency which the faculties of brutes do by no means attain unto. For, it is evident we observe no footsteps in them of making use of general signs for universal ideas; from which we have reason to imagine that they have not the faculty of abstracting, or making general ideas, since they have no use of words or any other general signs.' And, a little after: 'Therefore, I think, we may suppose that it is in this that the species of brutes are discriminated from men, and it is that proper difference wherein they are wholly separated, and which at last widens to so wide a distance. For, if they have any ideas at all, and are not bare machines (as some would have them) we cannot deny them to have some reason. It seems as evident to me that they do, some of them, in certain instances reason as that they have sense; but it is only in particular ideas, just as they receive them from their senses. They are the best of them tied up within those narrow bounds, and have not (as I think) the faculty to enlarge them by any kind of abstraction' [*Essay*, II (xi) 10–11]. I readily agree with this learned author, that the faculties of brutes can by no means attain to abstraction. But then if this be made the distinguishing property of that sort of animal, I fear that a great number of those that pass for men must be reckoned into their number. The reason that is here assigned why we have no grounds to think brutes have abstract general ideas is, that we observe in them no use of words or other general signs; which is built on this supposition – that the making use of words implies the having general ideas. From which it follows that men who use language are able to abstract or generalize their ideas.   (§ 11)

'The next step is to urge that all ideas, construed as mental images, and not just Locke's abstract general ideas, are altogether inessential. This is a short, but a bold and crucial step; and one which Berkeley did not himself complete. Taking it from here, the argument goes: 'If, for both man and beast, the criterion for possessing such general ideas is having the capacity to use correctly the corresponding general words, then why not make bold to say that to know the meaning of any term precisely and only is to be able to employ that term correctly?' If this is right, then presumably the meaning known is the use; something which, as has been explained earlier (Ch. VI, § 2), must necessarily be the same for all synonyms and equivalents in all languages. Certainly, were the actual occurrence of appropriate imagery, or even the capacity to summon it at need, any part of what is meant by saying that someone possesses the concept of over-determination, or knows the meaning of the word *oligopoly*; then it would become wholly incredible that the discoveries of Francis Galton were made so late in the day, and that their content remains so little known.

§ 3 *Two tests for souls and two concepts of soul*

In order to reinforce understanding of the nature of this "next step", while at the same time improving the occasion by explaining another basic distinction, let us in what may seem to be a digression consider again those two very certain ways of telling "that even the most manlike of robots are nevertheless not true men" (Ch. VIII, § 5). Descartes, it will be remembered, affirmed: "that they could never use words or other signs arranged as we do in order to declare our thoughts to others". For although, he allows, "one can easily conceive that a machine may be so made that it emits words, and even that it emits some which are appropriate to corporeal stimuli causing certain changes in its organs", still "one cannot conceive that it arranges them in various ways in order to reply to the sense of everything which is said in its presence, as the stupidest men can do." Descartes' proposed second way of telling is based on the similar claim that: "although they might do several things as well or perhaps better than any of us they could not but fall short in some others, and thus we should discover that they were not acting from knowledge but only by the arrangement of their organs."

These two tests are really two aspects of the same. Translated into contemporary terms Descartes' thesis is that no robot could be programmed to manifest the same versatility and adaptability of either verbal or non-verbal behaviour as is shown by even "the stupidest men". A weighing machine may be made to fulfil its promise, 'I speak your weight', but it cannot then reply to questions about the time of day or the sports news. The steam hammer may put the labours of John Henry into the shade, a digital computer may do sums faster than any 'wonder calculating boy'; but if you want something which can both drive in the nails for the pictures and check the addition in a garage bill, then you still need a man about the house.

But now, how come that Descartes can be so sure? The first distinction, which is essential if any progress at all is to be made in any such discussion of men and machines, is that between logical and contingent impossibilities (Ch. V, § 1). To any philosophical rationalist this is likely to be an unwelcome dichotomy. So we must be alert for attempts by too sympathetic interpreters to effect an obfuscating That-is-his-blind-spot-so-he-is-not-vulnerable-there Transformation (Ch. III, § 4). What Descartes is doing is – to put it anachronistically – vouchsafing to us a piece of his supposed synthetic apriori knowledge. Thus in the first of his *Rules for the Direction of the Mind* – his first work, published only posthumously, and usually given its original Latin title *Regulae* – Descartes writes:

> In the subjects we propose to investigate we must look, not to what others have thought nor to what we ourselves hypothesize, but to what we can clearly and evidently intuit or what we can with certainty deduce; for knowledge is not won in any other way. . . .
>
> By *intuition* I understand, not the changing testimony of the senses, nor the misleading judgement of an imagination which puts its objects together wrongly, but the conception of an unclouded and attentive mind, conception which is so distinct and so effortless that no doubt remains of what we comprehend. Or, what comes to the same thing, it is the firm conception of an unclouded and attentive mind, which is born from the light of reason alone, and which, since it is simpler is consequently surer than deduction itself (although that too, as we have noted above, a man cannot do wrongly). Thus each person can see by intuition that he exists, that he thinks, that the triangle is bounded by only three lines, the sphere by a single surface, and things of this sort. These are more numerous than most people can bring themselves to believe, because they disdain to direct their minds to matters which are so easy.

Among them Descartes would, presumably, wish us to number the putative impossibilities alleged as the bases for his "two very certain ways of telling". Yet certainly neither he nor anyone else would be contented to be assured that a man-made organism, for that sole reason, could not truly be a man; that it is – or should be – a defining characteristic of a true man that he was not constructed artificially. Or, at any rate, no one would be contented once they became apprised of the barmecidal character of the proffered guarantee. We must, therefore, construe Descartes' contentions as contingent. The point is, substantially and straightforwardly, that it is as a matter of fact impossible for what consists only of flesh and blood to possess the degree of versatility and adaptability of even "the stupidest men". It is in itself an advance in philosophy to have seen that this Empirical Intuition is Ostensibly Counter-evidential.

Taking this intuition as certain truth, what in effect Descartes then does is to hypothesize rational souls in order to account for all the versatile adaptive behaviour which in fact occurs, and which must otherwise appear inexplicable. In this respect he resembles the scientists who first postulated the then still undetected genes, in terms of which the hereditary transmission of characteristics might be explained; or even the detectives who form the theory that all the recent bank robberies have been the work of a gang whose members have had no previous criminal records. The main differences are: first, that Descartes believes that he has produced independent philosophical proof that we all have, or indeed really are, such rational souls (Ch. VIII, § 2); and, second, that in his case the hypothetical entities are defined as being incorporeal.

One crucial consequence is that there is no possibility of verifying this hypothesis later by any observational confrontation. There can be no question here of analogues to pointing out the place of one particular gene on a chromosome, and unravelling the chemistry of the DNA molecule. Nor can we hope to hear that a band of rational souls have been put in the dock for all to see. Another and much less obvious consequence, which unfortunately we cannot pursue within the present book, is to raise possibly insoluble problems of identity and individuation. How, that is to say, could one incorporeal thinking substance at time two be even in principle identifiable with some predecessor at time one; what would it mean to say that these were the same? And how at either time one or time two could different incorporeal thinking substances be individuated; what would it mean to speak of this as one, as opposed to others?

But now suppose that we can see no sufficient reason to allow that Descartes' suggested impossibilities really are known to be such, or that they genuinely are ultimate impossibilities. Alternatively or additionally, suppose that we believe that the problems of giving suitable sense to the expression *incorporeal thinking substance* cannot be solved. It then becomes easy and natural to take another "next step", parallel to that proposed in the case of Locke's abstract general ideas. Instead of trying to explain the occurrence of the versatile adaptive behaviour by reference to the activities of these hypothetical pseudo-entities, we now more economically attribute both that and all other human behaviour – and all the subjective experiences as well, including in most cases some mental imagery – to the flesh and blood human person. All explanation of these characteristics has, consequently, to be ultimately in terms of the material constituents and organization of the human organism.

In both the Lockean and the Cartesian cases such moves can be supported by appealing to the meanings of certain key terms, as these meanings are determined by correct and common usage. Teachers of chemistry every day settle definitively the question whether their pupils have yet mastered the meaning of the word *titration* by public tests of their capacity or incapacity to employ it. The richness or poverty of any private image lives is totally irrelevant either way. Similarly it is by equally public, though not always and necessarily by such formal, tests that we daily establish truths about people's qualities of mind. We find no call first to seek out any incorporeal entities for our study.

At this point we can at last make that promised further basic distinction. Descartes, as we have seen, employs the expression *a mind* as equivalent to *a rational soul*, and both are clearly construed as referring to a supposed logical substance. It is indeed essential to one of his ideologically important arguments that it should make sense to say that souls can survive death. But in the interpretation suggested in the previous paragraph a mind is just as clearly not a logical substance. To say that someone has a first-class mind simply is to say that he possesses the appropriate capacities; the expression *a mind* becomes in principle definable in terms of such capacities; and it must be nonsense to suggest that any mind might outlast the flesh-and-blood individual of whose capacities it must thus be a logical function. The sorts of notion of which these radically different interpretations of *a mind* are representative have been christened not very happily by two Minnesotan psychologists: the Cartesian kind are labelled *hypothetical constructs*; the others *intervening variables* (P. Meehl and K. McCorquodale).

The importance of this antithesis for the philosophy of science, the particular area in which it was first forged, lies in the parts which the two sorts of notion are or are not fitted to play in the explanation of the related phenomena. To attempt to explain his good philosophical performance by saying that he has, in the second interpretation, a sound philosophical mind, would be like appealing to its dormitive virtue in order to account for the soporific powers of opium (Ch. XI, § 3). But, whatever the other difficulties of the Cartesian hypothesis, there is no doubt on this count that it is constitutionally suited to do an explicatory job. For to postulate an incorporeal thinking substance behind, and responsible for producing, our rational behaviour is emphatically not merely to redescribe it.

Two final notes before we at last return to the confrontation between Locke and Plato. First, in suggesting a non-Cartesian interpretation of *a mind*, I was careful to talk of meanings as "determined by correct and common usage". The point is that this is one of the cases where you must expect to get different answers according to which of two methods of enquiry you choose to adopt. Certainly I have found in my own investigations with students that if I ask, 'What do you mean by *a mind*?' and thus perhaps suggest that they undertake some sort of conceptual introspection;

then I am most likely to get a Cartesian answer. Yet those same students will ordinarily, when there is nothing to make them philosophically self-conscious, follow the common usage. And this, surely, determines a meaning of the second kind. It is much the same with the expression *of his own freewill*. Although conceptual introspection usually yields a libertarian answer, the meaning as determined by ordinary unphilosophical usage is, as I have argued in earlier chapters, significantly different. (See Ch. I, § 2 and Ch. VII, § 1; and for an especially flagrant application of the – to coin another pillory-phrase – *Method of Conceptual Introspection*, compare Kant in Ch. XI, § 5.)

Second, this can help us to appreciate one of the reasons why philosophers need to be alert to the ordinary meanings of the words which they employ. If when doing philosophy you unwittingly make use of some everyday expression in what is not its ordinary sense, then there is a risk that you will confuse the two in some way which matters. Thus, for instance, you may – on the sole ground that there is indeed no question but that in another and quite different sense we do all have minds – fallaciously take it to be established that we all have, or are, Cartesian thinking substances. Or again, just because you are rightly confident that we all of us do on occasion act not under compulsion but of our own freewill, you may wrongly presume that these performances must by the same token be manifestations of freewill in the other sense, that of the philosophical libertarian.

§ 4 *Classification as a human activity*

We are now in position to consider Locke's self-consciousness about language, while all the time discounting his unfortunate assumption that the actual or possible occurrence of mental imagery is part or the whole of what all words when meaningfully used mean. For with Locke here, as with Hume on causality (Ch. VII, § 6), the positive contribution lies not in the psychologizing speculations but in the part which might – albeit misleadingly – be characterized as negative. So take the following extract from the *Essay* as a first challenge to such an exercise in discounting:

> To return to general words: it is plain, by what has been said, that *general* and *universal* belong not to the real existence of things; but are the inventions and creatures of the understanding, made for its own use, and concern only signs, whether words or ideas. Words are general, as has

been said, when used for signs of general ideas, and so are applicable indifferently to many particular things; and ideas are general when they are set up as the representatives of many particular things: but universality belongs not to things themselves, which are all of them particular in their existence, even those words and ideas which in their signification are general. When, therefore, we quit particulars the generals that rest are only creatures of our own making; their general nature being nothing but the capacity they are put into, by the understanding, of signifying or representing many particulars. For the signification they have is nothing but a relation that, by the mind of man, is added to them.

(III (iii) 11)

Locke in this paragraph gives us a clinically pure specimen of metaphysical assertion (Ch. II, § 1). He is telling us what ultimately there is, and there is not. What there is is nothing but particulars; and what there is not is anything general, because whatever might uninstructedly be thought to be general is ultimately – in itself – also particular. These metaphysical claims are, as usual, tied up with questions and answers about meaning, presupposition, contradiction, and entailment. Specifically the involvement is with the area of dispute traditionally labelled, *The Problem of Universals*. This is one of the very many regions in philosophy in which the greatest difficulty is perhaps the first, that of achieving satisfactory formulations of the problems. But it is certainly best to begin, as we have done, with Plato; and to conceive of the problem as being that which led Plato via the One over Many Argument to his Theory of Forms. The question then becomes one of the conditions of predication, of what is logically presupposed and entailed by the fact of our ability to employ general words.

Plato's own answer is, of course, given in terms of the Forms. In its metaphysical aspect the answer is that particular everyday things can only possess a characteristic in as much as the appropriate Form makes them possess it, and they all participate in that common Form (whatever *make* and *participate* may mean here). In its semantic aspect Plato's answer is that to be able to say with understanding that this possesses a certain characteristic logically presupposes some kind of prior acquaintance with the corresponding Form. Views of this sort, asserting that a general word somehow names or necessarily refers to some very peculiar object are called, in yet another sense of a much overburdened word, *realist*. They are called realist views of universals, rather than of general words, in deference ultimately to Aristotle. Thus he wrote in *de Interpretatione*:

443

Some things are universal, others individual. By the term *universal* I mean that which is of such a nature as to be predicated of many subjects, by *individual* that which is not thus predicated. Thus *man* is a universal, *Callias* is an individual.

Propositions necessarily either affirm or deny something, either about a universal or about an individual subject.

If, then, a man states a positive and a negative proposition of universal character about a universal, these two propositions are called *contrary*. By the expression *a proposition of universal character about a universal,* such propositions as *Every man is white* and *No man is white* are meant. . . .

An affirmation is opposed to a denial in the sense which I give to the term *contradictory* when, while the subject remains the same, the affirmation is of universal character and the denial is not. The affirmation *Every man is white* is the contradictory of the denial *Not every man is white*; or, again, the proposition *No man is white* is the contradictory of the proposition *Some man is white*. But propositions are opposed as contraries when both the affirmation and the denial are universal, as in the sentences *Every man is white* or *No man is white,* and *Every man is just* or *No man is just.* (17A39–17B7 and 17B17–17B23)

Aristotle's pellucid exposition of his technical distinction between contraries and contradictories is a bonus. The immediate point to grasp is that while not all propositions are "of universal character" – they are not all concerned with all or none – every proposition must contain at least one universal: one general word or expression, that is. Besides showing how such general terms come to be known as universals the passage also brings out that subject expressions as well as predicates may be general. This fact, especially in so far as it is expressed in a Material Mode of Speech (Ch. VI, § 2), encourages realist views. For if "Propositions necessarily either affirm or deny something, either about a universal or about an individual subject"; then, surely it may seem, there must be universal as well as particular things; some special kind of objects, that is, to which general words may refer. Thus Aristotle himself first gave good reasons for rejecting Plato's suggestion of Forms separate from and additional to their particulars, what are sometimes called real universals. But Aristotle then offered his own rather elusive notion of real universals not separable from their particulars but somehow embodied in them. (These postulates are often spoken of in the Latin as *universales in re.*)

Flatly opposed to any Platonic realism about general words are the views called *nominalist*. This term, like too many others in philosophy, contrives to be technical without being precise. It is perhaps best understood as involving simply a rejection of realism combined with an insistence that the only subject which can in this context be said to be universal is a sort of word. The best way to appreciate a nominalism is to relish a few choice sentences from Chapter IV of *Leviathan*. It should be remembered that the main purpose of Hobbes in this book is to establish a science, which shall at the same time be a justification, of the all-powerful sovereign state:

> But the most noble and profitable invention of all other was that of speech, consisting of names or appellations, and their connexion; whereby men register their thoughts; recall them when they are past; and also declare them to one another for mutual utility and conversation; without which there has been amongst men neither commonwealth, nor society, nor contract, nor peace – no more than amongst lions, bears, and wolves. The first author of speech was God himself, that instructed Adam as to how to name such creatures as he presented to his sight . . . the Scripture goeth no further in this matter. . . . For I do not find anything in the Scripture out of which, directly or by consequence, can be gathered that Adam was taught the names of all figures, numbers, measures, colours, sounds, fancies, relations; much less the names of words and speech, as *general, special, affirmative, negative, interrogative, optative, infinitive*, all of which are useful; and least of all, of *entity, internationality, quiddity*, and other insignificant words of the School.

> Of names, some are proper, and singular to one only thing; as *Peter, John, this man, this tree*; and some are common to many things; as *man, horse, tree*; every of which though but one name is nevertheless the name of divers particular things; in respect of all of which together it is called *an universal*; there being nothing in the world universal but names, for the things named are every one of them individual and singular.
> One universal name is imposed on many things, for their similitude in some quality, or other accident. And, whereas a proper name bringeth to mind one thing only, universals recall any one of these many.

> Fourthly, we bring into account, consider, and give names to, names themselves, and to speeches. For *general, universal, special, equivocal*, are names of names. And *affirmation, interrogation, commandment, narration, syllogism, sermon, oration*, and many such are names of speeches.

Hobbes, like most of the new men of the 1600's, was much given to expressing contempt for Scholasticism – "the School". Yet the important distinction which he is using at the end of the first and in the third of these passages is one which he might have learnt from Scholastic predecessors, and perhaps originally did. In their barbarous terminology it appears as a contrast between terms of first and second intention. In the equally barbarous terminology introduced by Carnap the antithesis is between object-language and meta-language. The crux is that although most of our discourse is logically first-order, some is at least second-order, and some of our vocabulary is peculiar to the higher orders of talk about talk. (*Meta* in this case is Greek for not *after* but *about*.)

The third sort of view about universals is labelled *conceptualist*. Conceptualism perhaps arises typically from dissatisfaction with available forms of nominalism. Surely, the conceptualist says to himself, although of course I cannot stomach anything like Platonic Forms, there must be something involved more than mere words. His suggestion then is that our application of general words must in some way be mediated by corresponding concepts or by appropriate mental images. Apart from Locke himself the most famous thinker rated as a conceptualist is Peter Abélard (1079–1142); more famous still for his romantic but costly association with Héloïse.

Not only does conceptualism as a middle way typically arise from dissatisfaction with nominalism as an alternative to realism; it also tends under the pressure of criticism to revert to nominalism, albeit perhaps to a nominalism made more sophisticated by the detour. We have already seen in § 2 that there is no future in postulating abstract general images; and that, where it seems that mere words are not enough, the remedy lies not in adding mental images but rather in thinking of the uses of words. The same section taken with its successor should have made it clear also that it must be absurd to appeal to my possession of a concept in order to explain my abilities correctly to employ the corresponding word, and to make related discriminations. For to say that I possess the concept is nothing but to say that I have these abilities.

Nor, finally, can the conceptualist profitably urge against the nominalist – nor, for that matter, the realist against either or both – that he has to admit that there must actually be similarities and differences between things if we are legitimately to classify and to distinguish as we do. Indeed there must be, and are. But this, surely, is one thing which all parties must have in common. If anyone insists – as some have done – on implicitly so defining *nominalist* or *conceptualist* as to require a denial of this, then he sets up a futile class with no respectable member. We have just seen how the paradigm of nominalism, Thomas Hobbes: first, asserts that there is "nothing in the world universal but names"; and then at once adds in explanation, that "One universal name is imposed on many things, for their similitude in some quality, or other accident".

That the same is true of Locke, our paradigm conceptualist, emerges when we continue the quotation begun at the start of the present section. It is worth remarking now that in this sort of context – as for instance, a moment ago in Hobbes – the words *general* and *special* are sometimes intended not in their derivative modern senses but directly as the adjectives of *genus* and *species*. (Compare the adjective *genial* as applied to J. V. Stalin in Soviet and Soviet-inspired publications in English, and intended to suggest genius rather than affability.)

The next thing, therefore, to be considered is: 'What kind of signification do general words have?'. . . . That then which general words signify is a sort of things; and each of them does that by being a sign of an abstract idea in the mind; to which idea, as things existing are found to agree, so they come to be ranked under that name, or, which is all one, be of that sort. Whereby it is evident that the essences of the sorts, or, if the Latin word pleases better, species of things, are nothing else but these abstract ideas. For the having the essence of any species, being that which makes anything to be of that species; and the conformity to the idea to which the name is annexed being that which gives a right to that name; the having the essence, and the having that conformity, must needs be the same thing: since to be of any species, and to have a right to the name of that species, is all one. As, for example, to be a man, or of the species man, and to have right to the name *man*, is the same thing. Again, to be a man, or of the species man, and have the essence of a man, is the same thing. Now, since nothing can be a man, or have a right to the name *man*, but what has a conformity to the abstract idea the name *man* stands for, nor anything be a man, or have a right to the species *man*, but what has the essence of that species; it follows, that the abstract idea for which the name stands, and the essence of the species, is one and the same. From whence it is easy to observe, that the essences of the sorts of things, and, consequently, the sorting of things, is the workmanship of the understanding that abstracts and makes those general ideas.

I would not here be thought to forget, much less to deny, that Nature, in the production of things, makes several of them alike: there is nothing more obvious, especially in the races of animals, and all things propagated by seed. But yet I think we may say the sorting of them under names is the workmanship of the understanding, taking occasion, from the similitude it observes amongst them, to make abstract general ideas, and set them up in the mind, with names annexed to them, as patterns or

forms, (for, in that sense, the word *form* has a very proper signification,)
to which as particular things existing are found to agree, so they come
to be of that species, have that denomination, or are put into that [class].
For when we say this is a man, that a horse; this justice, that cruelty;
this a watch, that a jack; what do we else but rank things under different
specific names, as agreeing to those abstract ideas, of which we have
made those names the signs? And what are the essences of those species
set out and marked by names, but those abstract ideas in the mind;
which are, as it were, the bonds between particular things that exist, and
the names they are to be ranked under? And when general names have
any connexion with particular beings, these abstract ideas are the
medium that unites them: so that the essences of species, as distinguished
and denominated by us, neither are nor can be anything but those
precise abstract ideas we have in our minds. And therefore the supposed
real essences of substances, if different from our abstract ideas, cannot
be the essence of the species we rank things into. . . .   (III (iii) 12–13)

Nor will any one wonder that I say these . . . abstract ideas (which are
the measures of name, and the boundaries of species) are the workmanship of the understanding, who considers that at least the complex ones
are often, in several men, different collections of simple ideas; and
therefore that is covetousness to one man, which is not so to another.
Nay, even in substances, where their abstract ideas seem to be taken
from the things themselves, they are not constantly the same; no, not in
that species which is most familiar to us, and with which we have the
most intimate acquaintance: it having been more than once doubted,
whether the foetus born of a woman were a man, even so far as that it
hath been debated, whether it were or were not to be nourished and
baptized: which could not be, if the abstract idea or essence to which
the name man belonged were of nature's making; and were not the
uncertain and various collection of simple ideas, which the understanding put together, and then, abstracting it, affixed a name to it. So that, in
truth, every distinct abstract idea is a distinct essence; and the names
that stand for such distinct ideas are the names of things essentially
different. . . .   (*Ibid.*, 14)

These passages show decisively that Locke's conceptualism included a
positive assertion, rather than a denial, that it is on the basis of actual
similarities or dissimilarities that we are able to subsume objects under the
same or different concepts. They also provide further bracing exercise in
the discounting of all suggestions that our ideas should be construed as
mental images. But what makes this exercise more than a mere intellectual

gymnastic is that it can help us to get a better hold on the main lesson which Locke has to teach, a lesson which is first outlined in these passages. This lesson has two aspects: first, that genera, species, essences, classes, and so on are human creations; and, second, that we have no right to expect – and will in fact often be disappointed if we do expect – that the realities will always fit neatly into the slots which we have made.

As is so often the case – as, for instance, we saw it to be with Hume's great 'negative' thesis about causality (Ch. VIII, § 3), the best way of coming to appreciate what a thesis involves is at the same time a way of getting to realize why it matters. And, as always when the suggestion is made that something is a matter of human convention, it has immediately to be emphasized that to say this is not to say that it is trivial, or that there cannot be decisive good reasons both for having some conventions and for having this convention rather than that (Ch. III, § 2). Nor does the fact that words obtain their meanings by convention imply that, once these meanings are given, we are still entitled to choose just as our whimsy takes us what any word shall imply, and what objects may be subsumed under what concept. For, for any given meaning, certain entailments follow necessarily: these are indeed what determine that meaning (Ch. I, § 2). Although you may choose to be so tiresome as to operate not with the concept of Scot but with that of true Scot, you cannot choose whether or not Mr Angus McSporran is a Scot. You can only choose whether to say what is false, that he is not (Ch. XI, § 2).

In order to develop some insight into what Locke is maintaining, and why it matters, contrast the Biblical picture, to which Hobbes was content to refer without protest, with remarks made by Darwin in the final, recapitulatory chapter of *The Origin of Species*. In the Biblical scene – so engagingly illustrated by William Blake – the kinds are natural, and the members of each are decisively divided from all others in accordance with the unfrustratable intentions of Omnipotence. What Adam does is simply to think up labels for these natural kinds: "And out of the ground the Lord God formed every beast of the field, and every fowl of the air; and brought them unto Adam to see what he would call them: and whatsoever Adam called every living creature, that was the name thereof. And Adam gave names to all cattle, and to the fowl of the air, and to every beast of the field . . ." (*Genesis*, 2: 19–20). It was in accordance with this profoundly attractive picture that the Swedish Academy honoured the great classifying naturalist Carl von Linnaeus (1707–1778) for having, among other things, "discovered the essential nature of insects". But compare Darwin:

When the views advanced by me in this volume . . . are generally admitted . . . there will be a considerable revolution in natural history. Systematists will be able to pursue their labours as at present; but they will not be incessantly haunted by the shadowy doubt whether this or that form be a true species. This, I feel sure and I speak after experience, will be no slight relief. The endless disputes whether or not some fifty species of British brambles are good species will cease. Systematists will have only to decide (not that this will be easy) whether any form be sufficiently constant, and distinct from other forms, to be capable of definition; and if definable, whether the differences be sufficiently important to deserve a specific name. This latter point will become a far more essential consideration than it is at present; for differences, however slight, between any two forms, if not blended by intermediate gradations, are looked at by most naturalists as sufficient to raise both forms to the rank of species.

Hereafter we shall be compelled to acknowledge that the only distinction between species and well-marked varieties is, that the latter are known, or believed, to be connected at the present day by intermediate gradations, whereas species were formerly thus connected. Hence, without rejecting the consideration of the present existence of gradations between any two forms, we shall be led to weigh more carefully and to value higher the actual amount of difference between them. It is quite possible that forms now generally acknowledged to be merely varieties may hereafter be thought worthy of specific names; and in this case scientific and common language will come into accordance. In short, we shall have to treat species in the same manner as those naturalists treat genera, who admit that genera are merely artificial combinations made for convenience. This may not be a cheering prospect; but we shall at least be freed from the vain search for the undiscovered and undiscoverable essence of the term *species*.

(Sixth edition)

To put it still in theological terms, the moral is: 'God makes the spectrum; man makes the pigeonholes.' Returning now to Locke, whom I have no reason to believe that Darwin had read, we are ready to recognize part of the point and importance of the distinction between the delusive notion of a real essence and the reality of the nominal. The one is, surely, an empty shadow cast by the other. Locke writes:

But since the essences of things are thought by some (and not without reason) to be wholly unknown, it may not be amiss to consider the several significations of the word *essence*.

First, *essence* may be taken for the very being of anything, whereby it is what it is. And thus the real internal, but generally . . . unknown constitution of things, whereon their discoverable qualities depend, may be called their *essence*. This is the proper original signification of the word, as is evident from the formation of it; *essentia*, in its primary notation, signifying properly, being. . . .

Secondly, the learning and disputes of the Schools having been much busied about genus and species, the word *essence* has almost lost its primary signification: and, instead of the real constitution of things, has been almost wholly applied to the artificial constitution of genus and species. It is true, there is ordinarily supposed a real constitution of the sorts of things; and it is past doubt there must be some real constitution, on which any collection of simple ideas co-existing must depend. But, it being evident that things are ranked under names into sorts of species, only as they agree to certain abstract ideas, to which we have annexed those names, the essence of each genus, or sort, comes to be nothing but that abstract idea which the general, or sortal (if I may have leave so to call it from sort, as I do general from genus,) name stands for. And this we shall find to be that which the word *essence* imports in its most familiar use.

These two sorts of essences, I suppose, may not unfitly be termed, the one the *real*, the other *nominal essence*.

Between the nominal essence and the name there is so near a connexion, that the name of any sort of things cannot be attributed to any particular being but what has this essence, whereby it answers that abstract idea whereof that name is the sign.

Concerning the real essences of corporeal substances (to mention these only) there are, if I mistake not, two opinions. The one is of those who, using the word *essence* for they know not what, suppose a certain number of those essences, according to which all natural things are made, and wherein they do exactly every one of them partake, and so become of this or that species. The other and more rational opinion is of those who look on all natural things to have a real, but unknown, constitution of their insensible parts; from which flow those sensible qualities which serve us to distinguish them one from another, according as we have occasion to rank them into sorts, under common denominations. The former of these opinions, which supposes these essences as a certain number of forms or moulds, wherein all natural things that exist are cast, and do equally partake, has, I imagine, very much perplexed the knowledge of natural things. The frequent productions of monsters, in all the species of animals . . . carry with them difficulties, not possible to consist with this hypothesis; since it is as impossible that two things

partaking exactly of the same real essence should have different properties, as that two figures partaking of the same real essence of a circle
should have different properties. But were there no other reason against
it, yet the supposition of essences that cannot be known; and the making
of them, nevertheless, to be that which distinguishes the species of
things, is so wholly useless and unserviceable to any part of our
knowledge, that that alone were sufficient to make us lay it by, and
content ourselves with such essences of the sorts or species of things
as come within the reach of our knowledge: which, when seriously
considered, will be found, as I have said, to be nothing else but, those
abstract complex ideas to which we have annexed distinct general names.
(III (iii) 15–17)

To conclude. This is that which in short I would say, viz. that all the
great business of genera and species, and their essences, amounts to no
more but this: That men making abstract ideas, and settling them in
their minds with names annexed to them, do thereby enable themselves
to consider things, and discourse of them, as it were in bundles, for the
easier and readier improvement and communication of their knowledge,
which would advance but slowly were their words and thoughts
confined only to particulars.   (*Ibid.*, 20)

In these passages Locke is taking issue with a long and powerful tradition extending right back to Aristotle. For that first sense of *essence* – "the
very being of anything, whereby it is what it is" – is none other than
Aristotle's " 'the-what-it-is-to-be' of such and such a thing", the Scholastic
quidditas (Ch. IV, § 4). It is this quiddity, or Aristotelian form, which is
sometimes also known as the substantial form. So we need to be quite
clear that such a form certainly is not in our sense, as opposed to that of
Aristotle, a substance.

The power which this ancient notion possesses to suggest some mysterious non-verbal reality is at this stage best illustrated by considering again
how Aquinas, although he did once put his finger on the nerve of the fallacy
in the Ontological Argument, persisted nevertheless in maintaining that
the uniquely favoured essence of God (with which, apparently God alone
is privileged to be acquainted) does entail – indeed is – existence (Ch. VI,
§ 2). If the real essence really is reducible to the nominal, then the claim of
Aquinas that neither he nor anyone else knows that of God, must constitute an utterly ruinous confession. For it implies that, although his massive
works purport to provide a vast amount of detailed information on
the ways and wishes of Deity, still, in the most literal sense, neither

Aquinas nor any of his fellow theologians know what they are talking about.

Locke, once he is sure that he has said enough to establish that even if there are real essences the only kind we can know is the nominal, proceeds to draw out some possibly disturbing implications. The first such consequence is that there will be questions of the form, 'Is this a such and such or is it not?', to which there is no antecedently correct answer. The passage in which Locke applies this moral to the most sensitive case of our own species becomes no less interesting and instructive to us for the fact that the innovator himself momentarily loses confidence in his own radical convictions:

Monsieur Menage furnishes us with an example worth the taking notice of on this occasion: 'When the Abbot of Saint Martin', says he, 'was born, he had so little of the figure of a man that it bespake him rather a monster. It was for some time under deliberation whether he should be baptized or no. However he was baptized, and declared a man provisionally till time should show what he would prove. Nature had moulded him so untowardly that he was called all his life the Abbot Malotru; i.e., ill-shaped. He was of Caen' (*Menagiana*, 278, 430). This child, we see, was very near being excluded out of the species of man, barely by his shape. He escaped very narrowly as he was; and, it is certain, a figure a little more oddly turned had cast him, and he had been executed, as a thing not to be allowed to pass for a man. And yet there can be no reason given why, if the lineaments of his face had been a little altered, a rational soul could not have been lodged in him; why a visage somewhat longer, a nose flatter, or a wider mouth, could not have consisted, as well as the rest of his ill figure, with such a soul, such parts, as made him, disfigured as he was, capable to be a dignitary of the church.

Wherein, then, would I gladly know, consist the precise and unmovable boundaries of that species? It is plain, if we examine, there is no such thing made by Nature, and established by her amongst men. The real essence of that or any other sort of substances, it is evident, we know not; and therefore are so undetermined in our nominal essences, which we make ourselves, that, if several men were to be asked concerning some oddly-shaped fœtus, as soon as born, whether it were a man or no, it is past doubt one should meet with different answers. Which could not happen, if the nominal essences, whereby we limit and distinguish the species of substances, were not made by man with some liberty; but were exactly copied from precise boundaries set by nature, whereby it distinguished all substances into certain species. Who would undertake to resolve what species that monster was of which is mentioned by Licetus . . . with a man's head and hog's body? Or those others which to the bodies of men had the heads of beasts, as dogs, horses, etc. If any of these creatures had lived, and could have spoke, it would have increased the difficulty. Had the upper part to the middle been of human shape, and all below swine, had it been murder to destroy it? Or must the Bishop have been consulted, whether it were man enough to be admitted to the font or no? As I have been told it happened in France since, in somewhat a like case. So uncertain are the boundaries of species of animals to us, who have no other measures than the complex ideas of our own collecting: and so far are we from certainly knowing what a man is; though it will be judged great ignorance to make any doubt about it. And yet I think I may say, that the certain boundaries of that species are so far from being determined, and the precise number of simple ideas which make the nominal essence so far from being settled and perfectly known, that very material doubts may still arise about it. And I imagine none of the definitions of the word *man* which we yet have, nor descriptions of that sort of animal, are so perfect and exact as to satisfy a considerate inquisitive person; much less to obtain a general consent, and to be that which men would everywhere stick by, in the decision of cases, and determining of life and death, baptism or no baptism, in productions that might happen. (III (vi) 26–27)

Locke's momentary failure of nerve occurs in dealing with the Abbot Malotru when he appears to retreat from ontology to epistemology. Here Locke seems to be taking it, in the special case of our own species, that the impossibility is only that of being legitimately sure of the answer. The question itself, it is suggested, is susceptible in principle – but not in practice by us – of an absolutely clear-cut and unqualified answer: yes or no. The tests which fail in this puzzle case are, apparently, tests for the presence or absence of a substantial soul. In so far as this remains the crux the actual line between men and the brutes presumably retains – independent of our discernment – all the clarity and distinctness for which Descartes longed.

The expression *puzzle case* is a worthwhile label for those actual or imaginary cases which may raise decision issues about the meanings of words. By *a decision issue* I here mean one in which what has to be settled is: not so much, 'What was the antecedently correct answer to the question, "Is this one?" '; but rather, 'In what way are we now to deal with the indeterminateness revealed by putting that question in a puzzle case?'

Equipped with these two technical expressions we now become better able to understand a sort of issue very prominent in the Law Reports of the serious newspapers. For instance: the courts are asked to decide whether, 'within the meaning of the Act', a flying boat is a ship; or whether a locked car is a locked receptacle. Obviously no one, including the original legislators, would naturally, and without hesitation or qualification, call a flying boat a ship or a locked car a locked receptacle. On the other hand, and equally clearly, there was something in the contention of the prosecution; that the pre-Wright Brothers Act, which – we will assume – forbids a ship to anchor athwart a harbour entrance, must be taken to apply equally to these new-fangled flying boats. Similarly there was something in the claim of the defence; that the doctor did satisfy the requirement to secure all drugs in a locked receptacle, when he left the barbiturates not in his antique surgery cupboard but on the passenger seat of his Rolls-Royce.

There are three main points for us to seize here. First, in a puzzle case raising an authentic decision issue there is by definition no antecedently correct answer, already determined by previously established proper linguistic usage, to the questions whether it is or is not a so-and-so. But, second, in deciding such a decision issue there can be good and bad reasons. Hence the decision itself may properly be hailed as correct or incorrect, in as much as the balance of these reasons tips in this way or in that. The admissibility of different sorts of reason varies with the system. Thus all British courts are required to respect previous court decisions as determinants of present legal meanings, whereas the Supreme Court of the United States is supposed to defer only to the Constitution itself. Third, a decision which is both correct and valid in one context is not necessarily either in another. The recent Pope who after weighing all the reasons relevant in that context ruled that, for the purposes of Friday abstinence, whalemeat is to count as fish, neither bound nor intended to bind biologists to misclassify whales as anything but mammals.

So far we have been considering Locke's insight only as applied to the classification of what he calls substances. Locke proceeds immediately to another sort of term. For "though these nominal essences of substances are made by the mind, they are not yet made so arbitrarily as those of mixed modes" (III (vi) 28). The meaning of the expression *mixed mode* will emerge sufficiently from the following passage, again from the *Essay*:

> Because the names of mixed modes . . . want standards in nature, whereby men may rectify and adjust their significations; therefore they

are very various and doubtful. They are assemblages of ideas put together at the pleasure of the mind, pursuing its own ends of discourse, and suited to its own notions; whereby it designs not to copy anything really existing, but to denominate and rank things as they come to agree with those archetypes or forms it has made. . . . Names, therefore, that stand for collections of ideas which the mind makes at pleasure must needs be of doubtful signification, when such collections are nowhere to be found constantly united in nature, nor any patterns to be shown whereby men may adjust them. What the word *murder*, or *sacrilege*, . . . signifies can never be known from things themselves: there be many of the parts of those complex ideas which are not visible in the action itself; the intention of the mind, or the relation of holy things, which make a part of murder or sacrilege, have no necessary connexion with the outward and visible action of him that commits either: and the pulling the trigger of the gun with which the murder is committed, and is all the action that perhaps is visible, has no natural connexion with those other ideas that make up the complex one named murder. They have their union and combination only from the understanding which unites them under one name: but, uniting them without any rule or pattern, it cannot be but that the signification of the name that stands for such voluntary collections should be often various in the minds of different men, who have scarce any standing rule to regulate themselves and their notions by, in such arbitrary ideas.

It is true, common use, that is, the rule of propriety may be supposed here to afford some aid, to settle the signification of language; and it cannot be denied but that in some measure it does. Common use regulates the meaning of words well for common conversation; but, nobody having an authority to establish the precise signification of words, nor determine to what ideas any one shall annex them, common use is not sufficient to adjust them to philosophical discourses. . . . Besides, the rule and measure of propriety itself being nowhere established, it is often matter of dispute, whether this or that way of using a word be propriety of speech or no. From all which it is evident, that the names of such kind of very complex ideas are naturally liable to this imperfection, to be of doubtful and uncertain signification; and even in men that have a mind to understand one another, do not always stand for the same idea in speaker and hearer. Though the names *glory* and *gratitude* be the same in every man's mouth through a whole country, yet the complex collective idea which every one thinks on or intends by that name, is apparently very different in men using the same language.

The way also wherein the names of mixed modes are ordinarily learned, does not a little contribute to the doubtfulness of their signification. For if we will observe how children learn languages, we shall find that, to make them understand what the names of simple ideas or substances stand for, people ordinarily show them the thing whereof they would have them have the idea; and then repeat to them the name that stands for it; as *white, sweet, milk, sugar, cat, dog*. But as for mixed modes, especially the most material of them, moral words, the sounds are usually learned first; and then, to know what complex ideas they stand for, they are either beholden to the explication of others, or (which happens for the most part) are left to their own observation and industry; which being little laid out in the search of the true and precise meaning of names, these moral words are in most men's mouths little more than bare sounds; or when they have any, it is for the most part a very loose and undetermined and, consequently, obscure and confused signification.

(III (ix) 7–9)

As always throughout the present section we have, in order to learn the lessons which Locke has to teach, to discount all references to ideas conceived as mental imagery. A second point, which arises for the first time out of this last passage, is that simply to draw attention to disagreements about denotation is not a sufficient demonstration of a difference in connotation (Ch. IV, § 3). The mere fact that one man characterizes Czechoslovakia and Kazakhstan as both parts of the Russian colonial empire, while another insists that there have not since 1917 been any Russian colonies, by no means shows that these two attach different meanings to the expression *colonial empire*: indeed the very fury of the latter's rejection suggests that, on the contrary, the nature of the charge is well understood and agreed by both parties. Again, to take an example which may be felt to be closer to Locke's own *glory* and *gratitude*, the fact that that man denounces as licence some of the liberties which you and I hold dear, does not by itself show that we are not all three agreed in meaning by *licence* – roughly – 'freedoms which people ought not to have'. Milton should thus be seen as making a semantic remark when he writes, in his *Tenure of Kings and Magistrates*: 'None can love freedom but good men; the rest love not freedom but licence."

It is over mixed modes that Locke confronts Plato most directly and fundamentally. For Plato takes it for granted that there must always be antecedently correct answers to all possible questions about what Locke would have called mixed modes; and Plato, furthermore, insists that these answers could actually be provided by a Guardian élite adequately acquainted with the relevant Forms (Ch. II, § 2: compare Ch. IX, § 3). Indeed one of the first definitions of *justice* suggested in *The Republic* is rejected partly because of its inadequacy to compass what we, but not of course Plato, would call a puzzle case (§§ 331C–332B). But Locke has become committed to saying that there can and will be questions involving moral notions, or other ideas of mixed modes, to which there simply are not any antecedently correct answers. This is of course, as I have just now argued in a legal context, something which can be asserted without prejudice to the possibility that a decision in some one particular sense may nevertheless on the basis of the weight of the supporting argument be adjudged the correct decision.

Consider, for instance, the puzzle case of artificial insemination from a donor (AID). This, like most biological inventions, raises both moral and legal decision issues. When these were first debated by the British House of Lords the then Archbishop of Canterbury asked rhetorically: "If AID is not adultery, what is it?" (16 March 1949). Now that we have studied some Locke we can easily see, what was certainly not obvious to everyone from the beginning, that the correct answer is: "AID is AID, an entirely new development raising radical issues for decision." The pat response of the Archbishop can, surely, be defended only by allowing an appeal to the supposed wishes of the Deity, who must as omniscient have anticipated all inventions; and, furthermore, by conceding that ecclesiastical authorities have an access to the mind of God paralleling the acquaintance with the Forms definitionally enjoyed by Plato's Guardians.

Certainly AID, like what we should perhaps now qualify as conventional or mainstream adultery, may produce offspring who are not biologically the children of the husband; and this fact is by itself sufficient to raise decision issues about adultery, and paternity, and so on. But also and obviously AID is very different from mainstream adultery: most importantly, it does not necessarily involve any direct physical contact or any personal relationship between donor and recipient; and it usually requires from the donor, and certainly offers to him no more than, an act of masturbation. My purpose here, however, is not, what it would be elsewhere, to argue that these differences either are or are not sufficient to warrant a decision in one particular sense. It is to show only and in general that Locke's insight into – as he would have put it – the nature of our ideas of mixed modes opens up a new dimension of moral disagreement.

At the beginning of the chapter on 'The Nature of Value' I quoted passages from Herodotus and Thucydides in order to illustrate that background of conflict and uncertainty about standards against which Plato's objectivism has to be set (Ch. III, § 1). This turmoil may be contrasted with the stability happily represented by Mrs Farebrother in George Eliot's *Middlemarch*: "Keep hold of a few plain truths, and make everything square with them. When I was young, Mr Lydgate, there never was any question about right and wrong." Now both the confusion and uncertainty illustrated in that earlier chapter, and the tranquil conviction represented by Mrs Farebrother, can be independent of any awareness of a perennial need to make new decisions to meet radically new problems. A paragraph or so back I said that "Plato takes it for granted that there must always be antecedently correct answers to all possible questions about . . . mixed modes." This is, I believe, true. But it is also misleading if it suggests that Plato himself, or most of those contemporaries who did not share his moral certainties, were aware of puzzle cases as such, and of the sort of problems which these raise. In a period of relatively stagnant technology such problems were not so obtrusive as they have since become. On the other hand, it could be perfectly consistent to combine a conviction as strong as that of Mrs Farebrother about "a few plain truths" with a lively awareness that new situations, and particularly the new situations created by technical change, will present fresh problems for their application. We might, for instance, insist that adultery is always (at least presumptively) wrong, while still allowing questions of the morality of AID to be put on the agenda for decision.

Finally, before starting the next section and on another tack, one distinction remains to be made and one fallacy to be identified and named. The distinction is between vagueness and open texture. I have already insisted on the difference between ambiguity and vagueness (Ch. IV, § 2). But now, a term is vague in as much as it is imprecise in some direction indicated within its own meaning. *Bald* is a stock example because, although to say that I am bald is to say something about my shortage of hair, this statement carries no precise quantitative implications. Were we now by stipulation to demand precision we should thereby be removing the vagueness; and by the same token, changing the present vague meaning of the word *bald*. 'To remove vagueness is to outline the penumbra of a shadow: the line is there after we have drawn it, and not before.'

Open texture is a contrasting and perhaps less satisfactory expression introduced by Friedrich Waismann, another charter member of the Vienna Circle (Waismann (1)). A term has open texture in so far as there are directions of uncertainty about its possible application, which are not suggested within its meaning. Waismann works with the example *gold*. Suppose we make the meaning more precise than it at present is by stipulating, within specified limits of tolerance, the acceptable atomic weight as actually measured, the acceptable spectroscopic pattern, and so on. Still there will always be conceivable cases to which all these careful stipulations provide no clear-cut answer. Suppose, and this suggestion too comes from Waismann, that we find some stuff which satisfies the entire previous specification but gives off a hitherto unknown form of radiation. Locke himself in his discussion of real and nominal essences provides examples of both vagueness and open texture, without of course making the distinction.

Statements are so often – and so often rightly – denounced as vague or indeterminate that it is worth emphasizing that neither vagueness nor open texture is necessarily a fault. There are times when all we can say or need to say is not, precisely, "at sixteen hundred hours on the dot", but instead, vaguely, "fourish"; and certainly few of us who find occupation for the word *bald* will ever have occasion to utter the findings of a precise haircount on anyone. Open texture cannot be done away with, since it is not possible to anticipate every conceivable case; and it would be silly to try to deal in advance with problems which we have no positive reason to expect, and the details of which we cannot yet know.

The fallacy to be identified may be given the name, *The Logically-black-is-white Slide*. One effect of the Lockean discussion which we have been considering is to draw attention to differences of degree. To say that this differs from that in degree is – I suggest – to say that both this and that could be members of a continuous series of actual or possible cases, arranged in order of more or less in respect of whatever it is with regard to which they differ in degree. Our differences in height, or weight, or age are thus in this understanding all differences of degree. If, therefore, we wish to draw a sharp line of division across any such series of possibilities, the choice of point through which to draw it is bound to be more or less arbitrary. That is why we have all those familiar complaints, that if only she had been one day older she would have been above the age of consent; that if only he had been a fraction taller he would have qualified to enter the corps d'élite; and so on.

The temptation, to which those who commit the fallacy succumb, is to mistake it that a difference of degree should not matter; that it can be dismissed as a mere difference of degree; that ultimately it is not any real difference at all. This temptation is often strengthened by also arguing, fallaciously, that if the choice of point through which to draw a line is arbitrary then it must be equally arbitrary to choose to draw a line at all, and to insist on sticking to it. The label proposed for the main fallacy already indicates what is wrong with it. For the very differences about which men care most are, in my interpretation, differences of degree: those, for instance, between age and youth; between riches and poverty; between sanity and insanity; between a free society and one where – in an old phrase – everything which is not forbidden is compulsory.

§ 5 *Essence and existence (i) existentialism*

The whole of § 4 has been, although I have not so far described it in exactly these terms, a discussion of the relations between essence and existence. This is a theme which has indeed been appearing and re-appearing in various guises throughout the entire book. Thus Plato's Theory of Forms, from which we began, is an account of how real essences – albeit ones which are, unlike their Aristotelian successors, separate from their instances – must be logically presupposed by and prior to ordinary everyday existences. These Forms then serve as ideals and standards, which are themselves allegedly more real than any actuality, of what we and all things ought to be. It is again from these separate real essences of his that Plato, through an argument which constitutes a major landmark in intellectual history, tries to infer that persons – conceived as incorporeal souls – must be immortal. In response to this set-piece, would-be, proof in the *Phaedo* we had to make a fundamental distinction between two senses of *eternal*. In one the word is equivalent to *everlasting*; and it applies, if it applies to anything, only to concrete individuals. But in the other sense eternity is a matter of non-temporality; and this is a prerogative of the realm of essences (Ch. IV, § 2).

Then in Part Two, in order to appreciate why contradictions must be intolerable to anyone who cares about truth, and why it would be no limitation on Omnipotence to be unable to compass the logically impossible, we began to deepen our understanding of these and other inseparably associated notions: "contradictions refer to the significant or insignificant employment of words rather than to the objective realities or unrealities of things" (Ch. V, § 1). Later in the same Part the Ontological Argument was introduced as the classic attempt to infer existence from essence. It is as such a manoeuvre of basically the same type as that first

461

epoch-marking attempt in the *Phaedo,* and it fulfils the role sketched in *The Republic* for an "unhypothetical first principle of all things" (Ch. VI, § 2 and Ch. XI, § 1). The same fundamental distinction between essence and existence appeared again repeatedly in Part Three, especially in the final chapter on 'Rationalism and Empiricism'. Hume's Fork, for instance, could perfectly well be reformulated as a dichotomy between propositions about the relations of nominal essences, and propositions about matters of fact and real existence: where the pure mathematician offers us an 'existence theorem', what he proves is a conceptual possibility only; not the actuality, or real existence, of anything.

The background reviewed in the two previous paragraphs facilitates a quick appreciation of what is meant by *Existentialism.* This is not the name for a system of doctrine in the way that *Christianity* and *Marxism* are. Even the description *Existentialist* itself has apparently been repudiated by most of the leading contemporary figures to whom it has been applied. Nevertheless the term has been widely employed and, given a sensibly limited interpretation, is useful. Crucially an existentialist is one who insists upon and develops the notion that existence is prior to essence, particularly with regard to man. This development brings with it an enormous emphasis on the scope and significance of human decision. It is presumably this which has given existentialism its special appeal both for professional playwrights and for all those who have a taste for – in a very broad sense – dramatics. (This broad sense is illustrated perfectly though mischievously in the surely apocryphal tale of President Eisenhower's reply to a question about General MacArthur: "Yes, I served under him for two years in the Philippines; studying dramatics.")

The best introductory source is a lecture given in 1946 by the French man of letters J.-P. Sartre (b. 1905). The original title was *L'existentialisme est un humanisme,* but it is published in the United States as *Existentialism and Humanism* and in England simply as *Existentialism.* It is from this translation, by Philip Mairet, that I quote:

> . . . in truth this is of all teachings the least scandalous and the most austere: it is intended strictly for technicians and philosophers. All the same it can easily be defined.
>
> The question is only complicated because there are two kinds of existentialists. There are, on the one hand, the Christians, amongst whom I shall name Jaspers and Gabriel Marcel, both professed Catholics; and on the other the existential atheists, amongst whom we must place Heidegger as well as the French existentialists and myself. What

they have in common is simply the fact that they believe that existence comes before essence – or, if you will, that we must begin from the subjective. What exactly do we mean by that?

Before hearing the answer which Sartre gives we must notice that Martin Heidegger (b. 1889) and Karl Jaspers (b. 1883) are both German academics, and that the Frenchman Gabriel Marcel (b. 1889) is a playwright as well as a philosopher. Sartre's statement that Jaspers is a professing Catholic is false. This specific correction provides a convenient occasion to warn that, although Sartre was once employed as a teacher of philosophy, this in France provides no guarantee of even a minimal acquaintance with those philosophical classics which were written originally in English. (Thus, for instance, the third section of the Introduction to his massive *Being and Nothingness* faults Berkeley for maintaining that to be is to be perceived. Sartre urges against him that if there is to be a perceived, there must also be a perceiver. But Berkeley is in fact most careful to claim only that the existence of sensible things is to be perceived. For the very good reason which Sartre presents as an objection, Berkeley himself insists that existence in general must be: either to be perceived; or to perceive. The word *perceive* has, of course, to be construed throughout in the same broad sense as Descartes' *think*.) Sartre may now continue his own explanation:

If one considers an article of manufacture – as, for example, a book or a paper-knife – one sees that it has been made by an artisan who had a conception of it; and he has paid attention, equally, to the conception of a paper-knife and to the existent technique of production which is a part of that conception and is, at bottom, a formula. Thus the paper-knife is at the same time an article producible in a certain manner and one which, on the other hand, serves a definite purpose, for one cannot suppose that a man would produce a paper-knife without knowing what it was for. Let us say, then, of the paper-knife that its essence – that is to say the sum of the formulae and the qualities which made its production and its definition possible – precedes its existence. The presence of such and such a paper-knife or book is thus determined before my eyes. Here then we are viewing the world from a technical standpoint, and we can say that production precedes existence.

When we think of God as the creator, we are thinking of him, most of the time, as a supernatural artisan. Whatever doctrine we may be considering, whether it be a doctrine like that of Descartes, or of Leibniz himself, we always imply that the will follows, more or less, from the understanding or at least accompanies it, so that when God creates he knows precisely what he is creating. Thus the conception of man in the mind of God is comparable to that of the paper-knife in the mind of the artisan: God makes man according to a procedure and a conception, exactly as the artisan manufactures a paper-knife, following a definition and a formula. Thus each individual man is the realization of a certain conception which dwells in the divine understanding. In the philosophical atheism of the eighteenth century, the notion of God is suppressed, but not, for all that, the idea that essence is prior to existence; something of that idea we still find everywhere, in Diderot, in Voltaire and even in Kant. Man possesses a human nature; that 'human nature', which is the conception of human being, is found in every man; which means that each man is a particular example of an universal conception, the conception of Man. In Kant, this universality goes so far that the wild man of the woods, man in the state of nature and the bourgeois are all contained in the same definition and have the same fundamental qualities. Here again, the essence of man precedes that historic existence which we confront in experience.

Denis Diderot (1713–1784) was at first co-editor and later sole editor of the great French Encyclopaedia, intended as a new *Summa* of all knowledge and enlightenment. F.M.A. de Voltaire (1694–1778) was another major figure – perhaps the major figure – of that movement known as the Enlightenment. Although strongly anti-Christian, Voltaire, like Kant later, would certainly have rejected the label *atheist*. Both were, rather, in their very different ways, deists: they believed, that is to say, in some sort of largely unknowable and non-interventionist Supreme Power. Voltaire is relevant here especially as the author of the satire *Candide*, attacking the ideas epitomized in the *Theodicy* of Leibniz. Just as existentialism in general can perhaps be characterized most illuminatingly as a rejection of all these ideas of the priority of essence to existence which are developed in *The Republic* of Plato, so the atheist existentialism of Sartre is a rejection of the whole world-picture of Leibnizian rationalism. This, it will be remembered, takes it that everything is, if not immediately then – surely – ultimately, logically necessary; and also that whatever was or is or is to be is for the best in what must be the best of all possible worlds. To quote again from Pope's *Essay on Man*:

> *God sends not ill, if rightly understood;*
> *Or partial ill is universal good,*
> *Or change admits, or nature lets it fall,*
> *Short, and but rare, 'till man improved it all.*

We just as wisely might of Heaven complain
That righteous Abel was destroy'd by Cain,
As that the virtuous son is ill at ease
When his lewd father gave the dire disease.   (IV 113–120)

Sartre now proceeds at once to indicate what he takes to be the consequences of this fundamental rejection:

Atheistic existentialism, of which I am a representative, declares . . . that if God does not exist there is at least one being whose existence comes before its essence, a being which exists before it can be defined by any conception of it. That being is man or, as Heidegger has it, the human reality. What do we mean by saying that existence precedes essence? We mean that man first of all exists, encounters himself, surges up in the world – and defines himself afterwards. If man as the existentialist sees him is not definable, it is because to begin with he is nothing. He will not be anything until later, and then he will be what he makes of himself. Thus, there is no human nature, because there is no God to have a conception of it. Man simply is. Not that he is simply what he conceives himself to be, but he is what he wills, and as he conceives himself after already existing – as he wills to be after that leap towards existence. Man is nothing else but that which he makes of himself. That is the first principle of existentialism. And this is what people call its 'subjectivity', using the word as a reproach against us. But what do we mean to say by this, but that man is of a greater dignity than a stone or a table? For we mean to say that man primarily exists – that man is, before all else, something which propels itself towards a future, and is aware that it is doing so. Man is, indeed, a project which possesses a subjective life, instead of being a kind of moss, or a fungus or a cauliflower. Before that projection of the self nothing exists; not even in the heaven of intelligence: man will only attain existence when he is what he purposes to be. Not, however, what he may wish to be. For what we usually understand by wishing or willing is a conscious decision taken – much more often than not – after we have made ourselves what we are. I may wish to join a party, to write a book or to marry – but in such a case what is usually called my will is probably a manifestation of a prior and more spontaneous decision. If, however, it is true that existence is prior to essence, man is responsible for what he is. Thus, the first effect of existentialism is that it puts every man in possession of himself as he is, and places the entire responsibility for his existence squarely on his own shoulders.

This idea of the enormous and inalienable responsibility of the human individual is first qualified and then illustrated. But the qualification, which consists in applying the distinctively Kantian notion of the individual will legislating for all mankind (Ch. III, § 7), does not weaken but intensifies:

> And, when we say that man is responsible for himself, we do not mean that he is responsible for his own individuality, but that he is responsible for all men. . . . When we say that man chooses himself, we do mean that every one of us must choose himself; but by that we also mean that in choosing for himself he chooses for all men. For in effect, of all the actions a man may take in order to create himself as he wills to be, there is not one which is not creative, at the same time, of an image of man such as he believes he ought to be. To choose between this or that is at the same time to affirm the value of that which is chosen; for we are unable ever to choose the worse. What we choose is always the better; and nothing can be better for us unless it is better for all. . . . Our responsibility is thus much greater than we had supposed, for it concerns mankind as a whole. If I am a worker, for instance, I may choose to join a Christian rather than a Communist trade union. And if, by that membership, I choose to signify that resignation is, after all, the attitude that best becomes a man, that man's kingdom is not upon this earth, I do not commit myself alone to that view. Resignation is my will for everyone, and my action is, in consequence a commitment on behalf of all mankind. Or if, to take a more personal case, I decide to marry and have children, even though this decision proceeds simply from my situation, from my passion or my desire, I am thereby committing not only myself but humanity as a whole, to the practice of monogamy. I am thus responsible for myself and for all men, and I am creating a certain image of man as I would have him to be. In fashioning myself I fashion man.

This is a moment to note that, whereas the prophet Heidegger hailed Hitler's accession to power in a notorious Rectorial Address, and dissociated himself from Husserl because Husserl was a Jew, Sartre served in the French Resistance and has remained an avowed Communist fellow-traveller ever since. Sartre proceeds to explain some admittedly rather dramatic technical terms. Those who have learnt their lessons from Hume will notice here Sartre's subtle but unwitting shifts from *is* to *ought* and back again:

> First, what do we mean by *anguish*? The existentialist frankly states that man is in anguish. His meaning is as follows – When a man commits himself to anything, fully realizing that he is not only choosing what he

will be, but is thereby a legislator deciding for the whole of mankind – in such a moment a man cannot escape from the sense of complete and profound responsibility. There are many, indeed, who show no such anxiety. But we affirm that there are many who are merely disguising their anguish or are in flight from it. Certainly, many people think that in what they are doing they commit no one but themselves to anything; and if you ask them, 'What would happen if everyone did so?' they shrug their shoulders and reply, 'Everyone does not do so.' But in truth, one ought always to ask oneself what would happen if everyone did as one is doing; nor can one escape from that disturbing thought except by a kind of self-deception.

And when we speak of 'abandonment' – a favourite word of Heidegger – we only mean to say that God does not exist, and that it is necessary to draw the consequences of his absence right to the end. . . . The existentialist . . . finds it extremely embarrassing that God does not exist, for there disappears with Him all possibility of finding values in an intelligible heaven. . . . It is nowhere written that 'the good' exists, that we must be honest and must not lie, since we are now upon the plane where there are only men. Dostoievsky once wrote 'If God did not exist, everything would be permitted'; and that, for existentialism, is the starting point. Everything is indeed permitted if God does not exist, and man is in consequence forlorn, for he cannot find anything to depend upon either within or outside himself. He discovers forthwith that he is without excuse. For if indeed existence precedes essence, one will never be able to explain one's action by reference to a given and specific human nature. . . . Nor, on the other hand, if God does not exist, are we provided with any values or commands that could legitimize our behaviour. Thus we have neither behind us, nor before us in a luminous world of values, any means of justification or excuse. We are left alone, without excuse. That is what I mean when I say that man is condemned to be free. Condemned, because he did not create himself, yet is nevertheless at liberty, and from the moment he is thrown into this world he is responsible for everything that he does.

The phrases "finding values in an intelligible heaven" and "a luminous world of values" must, surely, allude to the Forms which are, as Plato once put it, "laid up in heaven". Perhaps too the emphasis on our being in a Godless world "without excuse" is intended to echo a similar claim made by Spinoza about the situation of man in his deterministic but not pre-destinarian world (Ch. XI, § 1; and compare Ch. VII, §§ 3–4). Certainly in referring here to the Russian novelist Dostoievsky (1821–1881) Sartre is saluting one of the acknowledged precursors of his own explicit existential-ism. Another and even more important inspiration, who was himself enormously impressed by Dostoievsky's *Notes from Underground,* is the prophetic German-born Swiss moralist Friedrich Nietzsche (1844–1900). To represent this extraordinarily influential writer I will here, before proceeding to some of Sartre's illustrations of the scope of human decision, quote for comparison a passage made famous by contemporary Protestant theology. It is called 'The Madman'. Surprisingly it comes from a book entitled *The Gay Science.* The translation is by Walter Kaufmann:

Have you not heard of that madman who lit a lantern in the bright morning hours, ran to the market place and cried incessantly, 'I seek God! I seek God!' As many of those who do not believe in God were standing around just then, he provoked much laughter. 'Why, did he get lost?' said one, 'Did he lose his way like a child?' said another. 'Or is he hiding? Is he afraid of us? Has he gone on a voyage? or emigrated?' They yelled and laughed. The madman jumped into their midst and pierced them with his glances.

'Whither is God?' he cried. 'I shall tell you. *We have killed him* – you and I. All of us are his murderers. But how have we done this? How were we able to drink up the sea? Who gave us the sponge to wipe away the entire horizon? What did we do when we unchained this earth from its sun? Whither is it moving now? Whither are we moving now? Away from all suns? Are we not plunging continually? Backward, sideward, forward, in all directions? Is there any up or down left? Are we not straying as through an infinite nothing? Do we not feel the breath of empty space? Has it not become colder? Is not night and more night coming on all the while? Must not lanterns be lit in the morning? Do we not hear anything yet of the noise of the grave diggers who are burying God? Do we not smell anything yet of God's decomposition? Gods too decompose. God is dead. God remains dead. And we have killed him. How shall we, the murderers of all murderers, comfort ourselves? What was holiest and most powerful of all that the world has yet owned has bled to death under our knives. Who will wipe this blood off us? What water is there for us to clean ourselves? What festivals of atonement, what sacred games shall we have to invent? Is not the greatness of this deed too great for us? Must we not ourselves become gods simply to seem worthy of it? There has never been a greater deed: and whoever will be born after us – for the sake of this deed he will be part of a higher history than all history hitherto.'

Here the madman fell silent and looked again at his listeners; and they too were silent and stared at him in astonishment. At last he threw his lantern on the ground, and it broke and went out. 'I come too early', he said then; 'my time has not come yet. This tremendous event is still on its way, still wandering – it has not yet reached the ears of man. Lightning and thunder require time, the light of the stars requires time, deeds require time even after they are done, before they can be seen and heard. This deed is still more distant from them than the most distant stars – *and yet they have done it themselves.*'

It has been related further that on that same day the madman entered divers churches and there sang his *requiem aeternam deo* [eternal rest for God – AF]. Led out and called to account, he is said to have replied each time, 'What are these churches now if they are not the tombs and sepulchres of God?' (§ 125 : italics original)

Sartre employs many, often memorable, illustrations to display the full scope of individual decision and individual responsibility. He sees this as discovered through a recognition of Nietzsche's "tremendous event". But it is worth remarking – the more so since such atheist dramatics will be as uncongenial to some as they are appealing to others – that the content of this existentialist discovery is logically independent of this or any theological occasion. The present book has already, albeit in a less histrionic idiom, had a lot to say about the logical relations and lack of relations between questions of fact and questions of value (Ch. III, especially § 3). This should be enough to show that it was not inconsistent for Kant to believe in God and yet to insist that "Even the Holy One of the Gospels must first be compared with our ideal of moral perfection before we can recognize Him as such" (*Foundations of the Metaphysics of Morals*, II).

One of Sartre's illustrations, in the same lecture as before, is that of a Jesuit friend who had suffered various misfortunes before deciding to enter that Order. Just as, Sartre would say, we choose our own obstacles by setting for ourselves the aims which these obstruct; so it is we who choose the interpretations we put upon what we decide to see as signs:

This young man, then, could regard himself as a total failure: it was a sign – but a sign of what? He might have taken refuge in bitterness or despair. But he took it – very cleverly for him – as a sign that he was not intended for secular successes, that only the attainments of religion, those of sanctity and faith, were accessible to him. He interpreted his record as a message from God and became a member of the Order. Who can doubt but that this decision as to the meaning of the sign was his, and his alone? One could have drawn quite different conclusions from such a series of reverses – as, for example, that he had better become a carpenter or a revolutionary. For the decipherment of the sign, however, he bears the entire responsibility. That is what 'abandonment' implies, that we ourselves decide our being. And with this abandonment goes anguish.

Another, and deservedly famous, illustration is that of the young man who came to Sartre during the German Occupation for advice on whether he should stay to look after his mother, or try to escape to join the Free French Forces. Sartre points an austere moral; which is, in a secular sense, radically protestant:

> . . . if you seek counsel – from a priest, for example – you have selected that priest; and at bottom you already know, more or less, what he would advise. In other words, to choose an adviser is nevertheless to commit oneself by that choice. If you are a Christian, you will say, 'Consult a priest'; but there are collaborationists, priests who are resisters, and priests who wait for the tide to turn: which will you choose? Had this young man chosen a priest of the resistance, or one of the collaboration, he would have decided beforehand the kind of advice he was to receive. Similarly, in coming to me, he knew what advice I should give him. . . .

A third illustration, which must be mentioned, reaches Sartre by way of the Danish religious writer Soeren Kierkegaard (1813–1855). "You know the story: An angel commanded Abraham to sacrifice his son; and obedience was obligatory if it really was an angel who had appeared and said, 'Thou, Abraham, shalt sacrifice thy son!' But anyone in such a case would wonder, first, whether it was indeed an angel and, secondly, whether I am really Abraham." In the original account of what Kierkegaard calls "the anguish of Abraham", which occurs in *Genesis* 22, the voice was not of an angel but of God himself. It is, of course, for this sort of emphasis on agonizing decisions that both the arch-Protestant Kierkegaard and the Catholic Pascal are regarded as existentialist forerunners. For, as we have seen, although belief in the possibility of a positive natural theology is essential to Roman Catholicism, Pascal's Wager begins from the concession "Reason can decide nothing here . . ." (Ch. V, § 2 and Ch. VI, § 7).

§6 *Essence and existence (ii) essentialism*

In a passage quoted in the previous section Sartre remarked: "In the philosophic atheism of the eighteenth century, the notion of God is suppressed, but not, for all that, the idea that essence is prior to existence;

something of that idea we can still find in Diderot, in Voltaire, and even in Kant." The same could be said of the following century, and even of our own. For in general, and not of course just in this special case, it is in rejecting one belief very difficult not to continue to accept others warranted only as supposed implications of the first. Thus, for instance, you may with some sense of emancipation reject belief in a God; but you are unlikely at the same time to abandon that old optimistic faith in the fundamental friendliness of nature. Yet this faith could perhaps have been justified – if at all – only by appealing to some Divine Providence. Thus we find the young Friedrich Engels (1820–1895) protesting in 1844 against Malthusian theses concerning the pressures of population: "Am I to go on any longer elaborating this vile, infamous theory, this revolting blasphemy against nature and mankind?" ('Outlines of a Critique of Political Economy').

We must not, therefore, be surprised to discover essentialist vestiges in thinkers who consciously would reject Plato and all his works. In order to deal with these remnants consider first a distinction between four senses of *the nature of* or *the essence of*. Let us for ready reference label them: *definitional*; *empirical*; *normative*; and *theological*. In the first, the definitional sense, to speak of the nature or essence of – for instance – the state would be to speak of the nominal essence, the defining characteristics, the meaning of the word *state*. In the second, the empirical sense, an investigation of the nature of the state would – taking some meaning of the word *state* as given – enquire about the contingent characteristics of states: how they work; how far they resemble, and how far they differ from, one another; and so on. In the third, the normative sense, talk about what will in this case often be significantly qualified as the true or the real nature of the state will be talk about what states ought to be rather than about what – whether supposedly or in actual fact – they are. The distinguishing mark of our fourth, theological, sense is a reference to the alleged intentions for states harboured by the Deity.

That these four senses are all in themselves different is, once the distinctions have been made, obvious. The theoretical possibilities of confusion are equally obvious. In particular a terminology which is in this way multiply ambiguous appears well suited to encourage two developments of which much has been said already. First, by confounding the definitional with the empirical, and perhaps mixing in the theological too, it should be easy to generate a belief in some sort of real essence. Second, a terminology which collapses the crucial distinction between *is* and *ought* is bound to facilitate illegitimate shifts from one to the other and back again.

These strong possibilities of trouble become virtual certainties when we bring into account three other features of the logical geography of this region of discourse. The first of these is the notion of function. This is, as everyone who has ever tried to repair any piece of machinery can quickly see, ambiguous as between prescriptive and descriptive: my sparking plugs may not in fact be fulfilling their proper function. Apparently too it is here more than usually tempting to confuse an *a* with a *the*. People are thus inclined – committing both confusions simultaneously – to argue: that since reproduction certainly is a function of sexual intercourse, in as much as reproduction is that for which sexual intercourse is "the indispensable instrument, or the best" (Ch. IV, § 2); therefore it cannot have any other actual or proper function, and hence it must in all circumstances be wrong to participate while taking effective precautions to prevent reproduction.

The second feature is the concept of purpose. Although this introduces the fresh idea of intention it can be almost irresistibly easy to assume that to show function is necessarily to reveal purpose. For this false assumption Darwin's theory of evolution by natural selection constitutes the historic remedy. Two further complications, additional to those noticed in the case of function, are: that the expression *has a purpose* can have either a primary or a derivative application; and that my purposes may not be yours. Thus to have purposes is primarily characteristic of persons; but then the things for which people entertain these purposes can also be said, derivatively, to possess purposes. My purpose in accumulating stones of that size may be to throw them at intruding dogs; but then the point of that heap of stones becomes – for me – to serve as missiles in my war against dogs.

Despite the abstract and general way in which I have so far been presenting them, both these complicating points, and indeed all the other distinctions indicated earlier in the present section, are very relevant to all discussions of the purpose either of one man in particular or of mankind in general. But I propose with these hints and helps already given to leave the reader to pursue his own enquiries in that direction; adding only two further suggestive reflections. The first is that it would, I think, usually and rightly be thought insulting to ask of an individual person, 'What is this man for?' Yet it is often assumed that it is not merely not insulting but a necessary condition of human dignity that there should be an answer to the question, 'What is the purpose of all mankind, of all human life?' The second suggestion consists simply in explaining what is meant by *The*

Fallacy of Many Questions. This is best done with the stock example. For it is easy to recognize that it must be not merely socially but also logically improper to press the question, 'When did you stop beating your wife?', except where we can take for granted all of three things: that he has a wife; that he has started to beat her; and that he has since abandoned this practice. Where the purpose in question is more than the sum of actual or possible human purposes it will often be similarly fallacious to demand, 'What is the purpose of human life?' And it can be correspondingly misleading to try to reinforce this requirement by urging that, failing some satisfactory answer, human life must be meaningless, pointless, purposeless. For the lack of any extraneous Purposer, such as is here taken for granted, by no means necessitates that our individual human lives are without purpose or purposes for us.

The third feature of the local logical geography adding to the danger of the terminology of *the nature of* and *the essence of* is the idea that the essence is necessarily connected with the origin, that nothing can in its development be really and fundamentally transformed. Appropriately enough this historical form of essentialism can also be found in *The Republic*. For there, after the withdrawal of Thrasymachus, Glaucon offers his account of "the nature and origin of justice" as if the two must be linked necessarily. Embryonic in the same passage, from which I can here afford to quote only a brief extract, are the ideas of a state of nature and of a social contract. Since these important ideas fall outside the scope of my book I simply note them in passing. I will add only that the first crucial distinction is: between interpretations – such as that of Locke – which demand actual historical states and historical social contracts; and other, more sophisticated interpretations – such as those of Hobbes and the Frenchman J. J. Rousseau (1712–1778) – which treat these not as historical realities but as theoretical fictions. Plato writes:

GLAUCON – And now listen to what I said I would say first, about the nature and origin of justice. By nature, they say, to commit injustice is a good thing and to suffer it is bad. But the bad of the latter exceeds the good of the former. So when men do injustice to one another and suffer it, and have experience of both, those who have not been able to escape the one and to inflict the other think that it will pay better to make a compact with everyone else neither to do nor to suffer injustice. And this is how laws came to be established and mutual agreements, and they called what was commanded by the law lawful and just; and this is the origin and nature of justice – a compromise between the best, which is to

473

do wrong with impunity, and the worst, which is to suffer wrong and to be unable to obtain satisfaction. (§§ 358E–359A)

To Plato himself the question, 'Is this supposed to be historical or not?' did not occur with the force and persistence which we have learnt to give it. Anyone who wishes to explore some of the possible ramifications of an historical essentialism must apply to those who have been to school with the German G. W. F. Hegel (1770–1831), the great metaphysician of historical development. For us the most important of these are Karl Marx (1818–1883) and his followers. For historical essentialism as applied to our original example *The Origin of the Family, Private Property, and the State* by Engels and Lenin's pamphlet *State and Revolution* are excellent sources. But remembering the stated limitations of the present book, which excludes social philosophy as such, and in order to provide useful and testing exercise for more of the distinctions sketched earlier in this section, I turn to Marx himself. The three passages which follow all come from 'Estranged Labour', one of *The Economic and Philosophic Manuscripts of 1844*. The whole essay is important as a first outline of several of the structuring ideas of his central work *Capital*. The translation, from the original German, is by Martin Milligan:

When we ask, then, what is the essential relationship of labour we are asking about the relationship of worker to production.

Till now we have been considering the estrangement, the alienation, of the worker only in one of its aspects, i.e. the worker's relationship to the products of his labour. But the estrangement is manifested not only in the result but in the act of production, within the producing activity, itself. How could the worker come to face the product of his activity as a stranger, were it not that in the very act of production he was estranging himself from himself? If then the product of labour is alienation, production itself must be active alienation, the alienation of activity, the activity of alienation. In the estrangement of the object of labour is merely summarized the estrangement, the alienation, in the activity of labour itself.

What then constitutes the alienation of labour?

First, the fact that labour is external to the worker, i.e. it does not belong to his essential being; that in his work, therefore, he does not affirm himself but denies himself, does not feel content but unhappy, does not develop freely his physical and mental energy but mortifies his body and ruins his mind. The worker therefore only feels himself outside his work, and in his work feels outside himself. He is at home when he is not working, and when he is working he is not at home. His labour is therefore not voluntary but coerced; it is forced labour. It is therefore not the satisfaction of a need; it is merely a means to satisfy needs external to it. Its alien character emerges clearly in the fact that as soon as no physical or other compulsion exists, labour is shunned like the plague. External labour, labour in which man alienates himself, is a labour of self-sacrifice, of mortification. Lastly, the external character of labour for the worker appears in the fact that it is not his own, but someone else's, that it does not belong to him, that in it he belongs, not to himself, but to another. Just as in religion the spontaneous activity of the human imagination, of the human brain and the human heart, operates independently of the individual – that is, operates on him as an alien, divine, or diabolical activity – so is the worker's activity not his spontaneous activity. It belongs to another; it is the loss of his self.

As a result, therefore, man (the worker) only feels himself freely active in his animal functions – eating, drinking, and procreating, or at most in his dwelling and in dressing up, etc.: and in his human functions he no longer feels himself to be anything but an animal. What is animal becomes human and what is human becomes animal.

Certainly eating, drinking, procreating, etc., are also genuinely human functions. But abstractly taken, separated from the sphere of all other human activity and turned into sole and ultimate ends, they are animal functions.   (pp. 110–111: italics removed)

It is a passage which has to be read more than once and very carefully if one is to get the hang of this nowadays much talked about notion of alienation. Before the second reading it will help to know that the reference to religion is shaped by the ideas of Ludwig Feuerbach (1804–1872). Feurbach's early writings on religion made an enormous impression on Marx and Engels, and on all the other young Hegelian radicals of the time. Feuerbach's key idea, developed most fully in his *The Essence of Christianity*, is that in religion men project onto imaginary beings qualities which really belong to themselves: ". . . religion alienates our own nature from us, and represents it as not ours . . ."; and "The impoverishing of the real world and the enriching of God is one act. Only the poor man has a rich God" (Ch. XXV and Ch. VI; the translation is by George Eliot, the authoress of *Middlemarch*). The aim of Feuerbach consequently became, as he put it in the conclusion of his Heidelberg lectures in 1848, to change "the friends of God into the friends of man, believers into thinkers, worshippers into workers, candidates for the other world into students of this world,

Christians, who on their own confession are half-criminal and half-angel, into men, whole men".

The two aspects of Feuerbach's thought which need to be stressed here are: that its content is an atheist humanism, for us adequately defined in the previous paragraph; and that its form is emphatically and heavily essentialist. The word *essentialist* is simply the opposite of *existentialist*. I describe Feuerbach's thought as in this sense essentialist because – although his essences, like those of Aristotle, are immanent in things – for him as so often later for Marx the species seems to be prior to and more real than the flesh-and-blood individuals. Thus Feuerbach writes in the Preface to the Second Edition of *The Essence of Christianity*: "This philosophy has for its principle, not the Substance of Spinoza, not the Ego of Kant . . . not the Absolute Mind of Hegel, in short, no abstract, merely conceptual being, but a real being, the true *Ens realissimum* [Most Real Being – AF] – man; its principle, therefore, is in the highest degree positive and real."

So now, after that first rereading of the first passage from Marx, we can go on to the second two:

> Through estranged, alienated, labour then the worker produces the relationship of this labour of a man alien to labour and standing outside it. The relationship of the worker to labour creates the relation to it of the capitalist (or whatever one chooses to call the master of labour). Private property is thus the product, the result, the necessary consequence, of alienated labour, of the external relation of the worker to nature and to himself.
>
> Private property thus results by analysis from the concept of alienated labour, i.e., of alienated man, of estranged labour, of estranged life, of estranged man. (pp. 116–117: italics removed)

> Just as we have derived the concept of private property from the concept of estranged, alienated labour by analysis, so we can develop every category of political economy with the help of these two factors; and we shall find in each category, e.g. trade, competition, capital, money, only a definite and developed expression of these first elements. (p. 118: italics removed)

The relevance of distinctions made earlier becomes apparent as soon as we begin to challenge this abstract general analysis by reference to concrete particular facts. Certainly work in modern mass-production industries too often is, in a quite untechnical sense, dehumanizing: truly human life begins only at the factory gates, or when the conveyor belt stops. But is there any solid reason to believe that this wretched fact is the consequence of private ownership rather than of the division of labour? In the century before Marx Adam Smith himself, who in his *The Wealth of Nations* first gave prominence to the idea even if he was not the first to forge the phrase *division of labour*, deplored that what is so good for productivity is so bad for people. The decisive test of Marx's implausible suggestion would presumably be found in comparative studies of mass-production workers in factories under different kinds of ownership. The hostility of Marxists in power to this, and indeed most other lines of free sociological enquiry, within their bailiwicks cannot but suggest a fear that its results might falsify their theories.

Again, this analysis of alienation in work is supposed to apply to all work for an employer if not to all work absolutely. So what is Marx to say about those employees of private firms and private individuals who actually do feel content and happy in their work; who – as the significantly not uncommon phrase goes – live for their work, and who have great difficulty in making a satisfactory adjustment even to a tolerably well-endowed retirement? It would be ruinous to the theory to admit frankly that there are, as there manifestly are, many such people who do feel satisfied and who do not feel coerced. For the sake, therefore, of the abstract analysis it becomes necessary in one way or another to pretend that really there are not any such happy people; or, which is an utterly different thing, that, although they are, they have no business to be so content. Sartre shifted, we saw: from claiming that people do all feel "the sense of complete and profound responsibility"; to maintaining that they ought to; or that, if they do not, they are "merely disguising their anguish or are in flight from it". So the essential and endemic disease of alienation becomes for the Marxist similarly elusive or supposedly obligatory. Yet the insistence on the proposed cure – the nationalization of all the means of production, distribution, and exchange – retains always the same confident prominence. It is as if what was wanted was not a cure to fit the complaint, but a complaint to justify the cure.

§7 *Linguistic philosophy and philosophy*

At this stage, if not much much sooner, someone is sure to make some hostile reference to linguistic philosophy. For instance: criticism directed at that cherished panacea-provoker alienation has been dismissed for no better reason than that such is said to be the typical reaction of a linguistic philosopher. Or perhaps this entire book will be characterized either as a linguistic introduction to philosophy or as an introduction only to linguistic philosophy. There are valuable lessons to be learnt or relearnt from these complaints.

First, here as always the point of inserting a qualifying adjective must lie in whatever it is that this qualification is supposed to exclude (compare, for instance, Ch. III, § 2 and Ch. VII, § 4). This fact has a general moral, worth fixing with one of our mnemonic labels. Confronted with some lament that we have only, or merely, or nothing but, this particular sort of so and so; respond by putting *The Precisely-what-have-we-not-got? Challenge.* Employed against unthinking clichés this move can be as instructive as it is astringent. Austin once set the examination question: " 'Power politics'. What other sorts of politics are there?" It would be similarly salutary, if not safe, to ask those demonstrators and propagandists who denounce American imperialism, whose imperialism it is which, by inserting this qualification, they intend to excuse. (In this example the discovery of the true answer is unlikely to be intellectually demanding!)

So I respond by asking: " 'Linguistic philosophy'. What other sorts of philosophy are there?" Right from the beginning I explained: that "philosophy, as the word is understood here, is concerned first, last, and all the time with argument"; and that "Such works of the classical Chinese Sages as the *Analects* of Confucius are in their own kind great. But that does not make them in the present sense philosophy" (Ch. I, § 3). If, therefore, what is wanted is philosophy in this other sense – philosophy, that would seem to be, as the enunciation without argument of a world-outlook and a way of life – then of course the reader has all this time been reading the wrong book. Yet just before you put it down in belated disillusionment notice two things. First, if *linguistic philosophy* is to be construed as excluding only philosophy in this other, unargumentative, sense; then Plato and Aristotle, Descartes, Leibniz, and Hume, all go onto the same dump with Ryle and Austin. Second, if *linguistic* is interpreted as opposed not to *unargumentative* but only to *relevant to questions of world-outlook and way of life*; then it becomes false to describe the contents of this book as linguistic philosophy. For, to go no further, all the discussions of Part One and Part Two are so relevant.

But now consider how Hume in the first *Inquiry* introduces his contribution 'Of liberty and necessity':

It might reasonably have been expected, in questions which have been canvassed and disputed with great eagerness since the first origin of science and philosophy, that the meaning of all the terms, at least, should have been agreed upon among the disputants, and our inquiries, in the course of two thousand years, been able to pass from words to the true and real subject of the controversy. For how easy may it seem to give exact definitions of the terms employed in reasoning, and make these definitions, not the mere sound of words, the object of future scrutiny and examination? But if we consider the matter more narrowly, we shall be apt to draw a quite opposite conclusion. From this circumstance alone, that a controversy has long been kept on foot and remains still undecided, we may presume that there is some ambiguity in the expression, and that the disputants affix different ideas to the terms in the controversy. . . .

This has been the case in the long-disputed question concerning liberty and necessity, and to so remarkable a degree that, if I be not much mistaken, we shall find that all mankind, both learned and ignorant, have always been of the same opinion with regard to this subject, and that a few intelligible definitions would immediately have put an end to the whole controversy. . . .

I hope, therefore, to make it appear that all men have ever agreed in the doctrine both of necessity and of liberty, according to any reasonable sense which can be put on these terms, and that the whole controversy has hitherto turned merely upon words. (VIII (i))

Compare this with Kant's protest in the second *Critique*, the *Critique of Practical Reason*. This passage was presumably written with Hume among others in mind. The translation is by T. K. Abbott:

When I say of a man who commits a theft that, by the physical law of causality, this deed is a necessary result of the determining causes in preceding time, then it was impossible that it could not have happened; how then can the judgment, according to the moral law, make any change, and suppose that it could have been omitted, because the law says that it ought to have been omitted: that is, how can a man be called quite free at the same moment, and with respect to the same action in which he is subject to an inevitable physical necessity? Some try to evade this by saying that the causes that determine his causality are of such a kind as to agree with a comparative notion of freedom. According to this, that is sometimes called a free effect, the determining physical cause of which lies within in the acting things itself, e.g. that which a projectile performs when it is in free motion, in which case we use the word "freedom", because while it is in flight it is not urged by anything external; or as we call the motion of a clock a free motion, because it moves its hands itself, which therefore do not require to be pushed by external force; so although the actions of man are necessarily determined by causes which precede in time, we yet call them free, because these causes are ideas produced by our own faculties, whereby desires are evoked on occasion of circumstances, and hence actions are wrought according to our own pleasure. This is a wretched subterfuge with which some persons still let themselves be put off, and so think they have solved, with a petty word-jugglery, that difficult problem, at the solution of which centuries have laboured in vain, and which can therefore not be found so completely on the surface.

(I (i) 3: 'Critical Examination of the Analytic of Pure Practical Reason')

Certainly Hume is rather brash and flash in his presentation of the position to which Kant is here objecting. Already in Chapter VII we saw sufficient reason to agree with Kant's rebuke to those who assume that a complete answer to all the problems is to "be found so completely on the surface". But that is not at all the same thing as to agree with Kant and, for that matter, with Hume himself that to be a "word-jugglery" or to turn "merely upon words" is, in this context, a fault. Once again we have to press the question: 'What is the supposed alternative?' In the case of Hume the answer would pretty clearly be that real, and not merely verbal, philosophy must be psychology. For, as we have seen, Hume's great ambition in the *Treatise* was to become a Galileo or a Newton of the study of man. Nevertheless, as again we have seen, to the extent that a question really is a question of psychological or other scientific fact, that question is precisely not philosophical. If the problem of the freedom of the will, for instance, is to be construed as a problem about the possible predictability of human behaviour, then the problem is not philosophical at all (Ch. VII, § 1).

To realize that, and how, and in what sense logical and conceptual issues are necessarily verbal itself constitutes progress in philosophy. It is a theme to which we have in this book returned again and again. Thus in the very first chapter I started to bring out the essential connections between the concepts of meaning, deduction, logical necessity, logical impossibility, and contradiction. In the second I had to notice that the prime argument for that most highly metaphysical of philosophical doctrines, Plato's Theory of Forms, takes off from a question about the possibility of applying the same predicate to several subjects. Throughout the third it was clear that an enquiry into the nature of value could not be separated from a study of the meaning of moral and other value terms. And so it went on, right up to and including this final chapter on 'Words and the World'. But it must be complementary to this same progressive realization to recognize that, in as much as the logical and conceptual issues of philosophy are simultaneously and necessarily verbal, so the philosopher's professional interest in language is limited correspondingly to its logical and conceptual aspects. When, therefore, some contemporary philosopher speaks in a perhaps provocatively linguistic way about *God*-sentences or the word *God*, what he is talking about is the use or meaning of that word. This, as we have seen, is not linked exclusively to English or to any other particular natural or artificial language (Ch. V, § 2). His subject precisely is the concept of God and the logical relations thereof (Ch. XI, § 6).

Suppose then, following what seems to be the only established usage, we take the expression *linguistic philosopher* to be implicitly defined as meaning 'a philosopher who possesses, and is inclined to parade, a realization of the verbal aspect of the logical and conceptual'. It must now become preposterous: either to ask for non-linguistic philosophy as a possibly superior substitute; or to complain that linguistic philosophy is trivial and trifling in some way in which this other sort is not. Non-linguistic philosophy, in this interpretation, is as such necessarily inferior. For its defining characteristic is the lack of a constellation of insights the acquisition of which surely constitutes progress in philosophy. This does not, of course, prevent such non-linguistic philosophy having other and perhaps compensating merits. It implies only that what makes it non-linguistic is in itself a deficiency. It is not, for instance, a merit in Jaspers that he can apparently see nothing wrong with self-contradiction; that he is capable of maintaining that a philosophy which tries to get rid of circularities and self-contradictions "falls flat on its face and becomes totally empty". Nor, on the other hand, can philosophical problems lose whatever importance they previously had just because we may have come to realize: first, that such problems are not factual but logical and conceptual; and, second, that the logical and conceptual must have always its verbal aspect.

A philosophical interest in words is not, however, to be detached from some concern with the actual and possible practices of human life. The familiar contrast between words and things cannot here be absolute. For the use of words is their use for men, and their use in some sort of human context. To bring this out consider for a moment two independently interesting matters: one, the conscious and systematic application in philosophy of techniques first developed by the historians of ideas; and, two, the provision of a philosophical account of the nature of promising.

We noticed in Chapter VII how Aristotle in the *Nicomachean Ethics* in his analyses of choice, deliberation, and so on, was all the time tacitly appealing to the correct usage of the Greek terms. I put there the rhetorical question: "How else, indeed, could the conservative analysis of a concept proceed?" Notice now also that such appeals to correct usage must necessarily involve reference to actual and possible contexts. The interest is in the sort of situations in which a man could correctly be said to have acted voluntarily, or by mistake, or by accident, or involuntarily, or under compulsion, or what have you. Exactly the same applies to the familiar and accepted technique of the historian of ideas. As a first step to understanding – say – the development of Greek ideas of the soul he assembles and examines occurrences of the word *psyche* in all the available texts. Yet this examination involves continual reference to all his knowledge of the historical and social context. It is significant that John Austin, who is for most of those who employ this unfortunate phrase the archetypal linguistic philosopher, and who in our day took the lead in the systematic, articulate, and explicit application of this technique to the philosophical elucidation of current notions, was in his first training like most Oxford philosophers a Classical scholar.

It is also instructive to ponder in this connection two very similar accounts of promising. The first comes from Hume's *Treatise*:

In order, therefore, to distinguish those two different sorts of commerce, the interested and the disinterested, there is a certain form of words invented for the former, by which we bind ourselves to the performance of any action. This form of words constitutes what we call a promise, which is the sanction of the interested commerce of mankind. When a man says he promises anything, he in effect expresses a resolution of performing it; and, along with that, by making use of this form of words, subjects himself to the penalty of never being trusted again in the case of failure. A resolution is the natural act of the mind, which promises express. But were there no more than a resolution in the case, promises would only declare our former motives, and would not create any new motive or obligation. They are the conventions of men, which create a new motive, when experience has taught us that human affairs would be conducted much more for mutual advantage were there certain symbols or signs instituted, by which we might give each other security of our conduct in any particular incident. After these signs are instituted, whoever uses them is immediately bound by his interest to execute his engagements, and must never be expected to be trusted any more if he refuse to perform what he promised. . .

It is evident that the will alone is never supposed to cause the obligation, but must be expressed by words or signs in order to impose a tie on any man. The expression, being once brought in as subservient to the will, soon becomes the principal part of the promise; nor will a man be less bound by his word, though he secretly give a different direction to his intention and withhold himself both from a resolution and from willing an obligation. But though the expression makes on most occasions the whole of the promise, yet it does not always so; and one who should make use of any expression of which he knows not the meaning, and which he uses without any intention of binding himself, would certainly not be bound by it. Nay, though he knows its meaning, yet if he uses it in jest only, and with such signs as show evidently that he has no serious intention of binding himself, he would not lie under any obligation of performance; but it is necessary that the words be a perfect expression of the will, without any contrary signs. Nay, even this we must not carry so far as to imagine that one whom, by our quickness of understanding, we conjecture, from certain signs, to have an intention of deceiving us, is not bound by his expression or verbal promise, if we accept of it; but must limit this conclusion to those cases where the signs are of a different kind from those of deceit.   (III (ii) 5)

Hume himself proceeds to compare this crucial importance of a conventional form of words in promising with the ceremonial employment of formulae, which he obviously despises as magic, in such religious practices as Ordination and the Mass. Austin discussed such ritual or performatory employments of words in 1946 in a classic paper on 'Other Minds': " 'I promise' is quite different from 'He promises': if I say 'I promise', I don't say I *say* I promise, I *promise*, just as if he says he promises, he doesn't say he says he promises, he promises: whereas if I say 'He promises', I do (only) say he *says* he promises. . . . I *describe* his promising, but I *do* my own promising and he must do *his* own" (p. 67 n: italics original). Later, in his William James lectures on *How to do things with words*, Austin returned to the charge:

Surely the words must be spoken 'seriously' and so as to be taken 'seriously'? This is, though vague, true enough in general – it is an important commonplace in discussing any utterance whatsoever. I must not be joking, for example, nor writing a poem. But we are apt to have a feeling that being serious consists in their being uttered as (merely) the outward and visible sign, for convenience or other record or for information, of an inward and spiritual act: from which it is but a short step to go on to believe or to assume without realizing that for many purposes the outward utterance is a description, *true or false*, of the occurrence of the inward performance. The classic expression of this idea is to be found in the *Hippolytus* (1.612), where Hippolytus says 'my tongue swore to, but my heart (or mind or other backstage artiste) did not'. Thus 'I promise to . . .' obliges me – puts on record my spiritual assumption of a spiritual shackle.

It is gratifying to observe in this very example how excess of profundity, or rather solemnity, at once paves the way for immorality. For one who says 'Promising is not merely a matter of uttering words! It is an inward and spiritual act!' is apt to appear as a solid moralist standing out against a generation of superficial theorizers: we see him as he sees himself, surveying the invisible depths of ethical space, with all the distinction of a specialist in the *sui generis*. Yet he provides Hippolytus with a let-out, the bigamist with an excuse for his 'I do' and the welsher with a defence for his 'I bet'. Accuracy and morality alike are on the side of the plain saying that *our word is our bond*.   (pp. 9–10: italics original)

By now, surely, it is beginning to seem as if the demand for a non-linguistic philosophy amounts in the end to a disguised appeal either for bad philosophy or for no philosophy at all; at least in the sense of *philosophy* in which, by common consent, Plato, Aristotle, Aquinas, Descartes, Locke, Leibniz, Spinoza, Hume, and Kant score as philosophers. On the one hand: to ask for worse philosophy rather than better is obscurantism, and inexcusable. On the other hand: to insist only that philosophy is not everything, that there are and ought to be other things in life, is realistic, robust, and altogether unexceptionable. But Shakespeare's Romeo did not pretend to reject one supposed sort in favour of another:

. . . Hang up philosophy!
Unless philosophy can make a Juliet,
Displant a town, reverse a prince's doom,
It helps not, it prevails not: talk no more.   (*Romeo and Juliet, III (iii)*)

PARTICULARS OF BOOKS MENTIONED

AESCHYLUS *The Agamemnon,* tr. L. MacNeice (Faber and Faber: London, 1936).

ANSCOMBE, G. E. M. and GEACH, P. T. *Descartes' Philosophical Writings* (Nelson: London, 1954).

ANSELM, ST *Proslogion,* tr. M. J. Charlesworth (O.U.P: Oxford, 1965).

AQUINAS, ST THOMAS (1) *Summa contra Gentiles,* tr. Pegis (Doubleday Image Paperbacks: New York, 1955).

AQUINAS, ST THOMAS (2) *Summa Theologica,* new translation and edition by various hands under Fr Thomas Gilby as General Editor (McGraw-Hill: New York and Eyre and Spottiswoode: London, 1963 onwards).

ARISTOTLE *The Basic Works of Aristotle,* ed. R. McKeon (Random House: New York, 1941). This contains every work mentioned in this book, and many more.

ARNAULD, A. and NICOLE, P. *La Logique, ou l'Art de Penser* (Paris, 1662).

AUGUSTINE of HIPPO, ST (1) *Confessions,* tr. E. B. Pusey and ed. A. H. Armstrong (Dutton: New York and Dent: London, 1907 and onwards).

AUGUSTINE of HIPPO, ST (2) *The Enchiridion on Faith, Hope, and Love,* tr. J. F. Shaw and ed. H. Paolucci (H. Regnery: Chicago, 1961).

AUSTIN, J. L. (1) *Philosophical Papers* (O.U.P: Oxford, 1961). This contains both 'Other Minds' and 'A Plea for Excuses'.

AUSTIN, J. L. (2) *Sense and Sensibilia* (O.U.P: Oxford, 1962).

AUSTIN, J. L. (3) *How to do things with Words* (O.U.P: Oxford and Harvard U.P: Cambridge (Mass.), 1962).

AYER, A. J. *Language, Truth and Logic* (Second Edition. Gollancz: London, 1946).

BACON, F. *Works,* ed. J. Spedding, R. L. Ellis, and D. D. Heath (Longmans etc.: London, 1870).

BAYLE, P. *Historical and Critical Dictionary* (Selections, ed. R. H. Popkin. Bobbs-Merrill: New York, 1965. The original was first published in French in 1697 and there were many printings in English in the 1700's).

BENEDICT, R. *Patterns of Culture* (New American Library: New York, 1946).

BERKELEY, G. *Works,* ed. T. Jessup and A. Luce (Nelson: London and Edinburgh, 1948 onwards).

BOHR, N. 'On the Notions of Causality and Complementarity', in *Dialectica* for 1948.

BRAIN, R. (Lord Brain) *Mind, Perception and Science* (B. Blackwell: Oxford, 1951).

BREWSTER, D. *Memoirs of the Life, Writings, and Discoveries of Sir Isaac Newton* (T. Constable: Edinburgh, 1850).

BURTT, E. A. *Metaphysical Foundations of Modern Physical Science* (Second Edition. Harcourt Brace: New York and Routledge and Kegan Paul: London, 1932).

BUTLER, J. *Works*, ed. W. E. Gladstone (O.U.P: Oxford, 1896).

BUTTERFIELD, H. *The Origins of Modern Science* (G. Bell: London, 1949).

CAJETAN (Thomas de Vio) *The Analogy of Names*, tr. A. E. Bushinski and H. J. Koren (Dusquesne U.P: Pittsburgh, 1953).

CALVIN, J. *Institutes of the Christian Religion*, tr. F. J. Battles and ed. J. T. McNeill (Westminster Press: Philadelphia and S.C.M. Press: London, 1961).

CARNAP, R. 'Autobiography' in *The Philosophy of Rudolf Carnap,* ed. P. A. Schilpp (Open Court: La Salle (Illinois), 1963).

COPERNICUS, N. *de Revolutionibus*, in Vol. 16 of the Great Books Series (W. Benton and Encyclopaedia Britannica: Chicago, 1939).

DARWIN, C. *The Origin of Species* (Sixth Edition. John Murray: London, 1872).

DENZINGER, H. *Encheiridion Symbolorum* (Twenty Ninth Revised Edition. Herder: Freiberg im Breisgau, 1953).

DESCARTES, R. *Philosophical Works*, tr. and ed. E. S. Haldane and G. R. T. Ross (C.U.P: Cambridge, 1931, and now in paperback from Dover: New York).

ECCLES, J. C. 'The Neurophysiological Basis of Experience' in *The Critical Approach to Science and Philosophy*, ed. M. Bunge (Free Press of Glencoe: New York and Collier-MacMillan: London, 1964).

EDWARDS, J. *The Freedom of the Will*, ed. P. Ramsey (Yale U.P: New Haven and London, 1957).

EDWARDS, P. 'Tillich's Confusions' in *Mind*, 1965.

EDWARDS, P. (Editor) *The Encyclopaedia of Philosophy* (MacMillan and The Free Press: New York and Collier-MacMillan: London, 1967).

EDWARDS, P. and PAP, A. *A Modern Introduction to Philosophy* (Revised Edition. Free Press of Glencoe: New York and Collier-MacMillan: London, 1965).

EINSTEIN, A. (1) 'Autobiographical Notes' in *Albert Einstein: Philosopher-Scientist*, ed. P. A. Schilpp (Harper Torchbooks: New York, 1959).

EINSTEIN, A. (2) *Out of My Later Years* (Thames and Hudson: London and The Philosophical Library: New York, 1950).

ELIOT, T. S. *Four Quartets* (Faber and Faber: London and Harcourt, Brace and World: New York, 1944).

ENGELS, F. (1) *Origin of the Family, Private Property, and the State* (Lawrence and Wishart: London, 1940).

ENGELS, F. (2) *The Dialectics of Nature* (International Publishers: New York, 1940).

FARRER, A. *Finite and Infinite* (Second Edition. A. C. Black-Dacre Press: London, 1959).

FEUERBACH, L. *The Essence of Christianity*, tr. G. Eliot (Harper Torchbooks: New York, 1957).

FIELD, G. C. *Plato and His Contemporaries* (Third and Paperback Edition. Methuen: London and New York, 1967).

FREGE, G. *The Foundations of Arithmetic*, tr. J. L. Austin (Blackwell: Oxford, 1950).

GALILEO, G. *Discoveries and Opinions of Galileo*, tr. and ed. S. Drake (Doubleday Anchor Paperback: New York, 1957).

GALTON, F. *Inquiries into Human Faculty* (MacMillan: London, 1883).

GILLISPIE, C. C. *The Edge of Objectivity* (Princeton U.P: Princeton, 1960 and paperback 1966).

HARE, R. M. *The Language of Morals* (O.U.P: Oxford and New York, 1952).

HELMHOLZ, H. VON 'On the Origin and Significance of Geometrical Axioms', in *Popular Scientific Lectures*, ed. M. Kline (Dover: New York, 1962).

HICKS, R. D. *Aristotle: de Anima* (C.U.P: Cambridge, 1907).

HOBBES, T. *English Works of Thomas Hobbes*, ed. W. Molesworth (Bohn: London, 1839–1840).

HOUSMAN, A. E. *Collected Poems* (Jonathan Cape: London, 1939 and Holt, Rinehart and Winston: New York, 1950).

HUME, D. (1) *A Treatise of Human Nature*, ed. L. A. Selby-Bigge (O.U.P: Oxford, 1906).

HUME, D. (2) *An Inquiry concerning Human Understanding*, ed. C. W. Hendel (Bobbs-Merrill: New York, 1955). This also contains *An Abstract of a Treatise of Human Nature*.

HUME, D. (3) *An Inquiry concerning the Principles of Morals*, ed. C. W. Hendel (Bobbs-Merrill: New York, 1957).

HUME, D. (4) *Dialogues concerning Natural Religion*, ed. N. Kemp Smith (O.U.P: Oxford, 1935. There was a new edition from T. Nelson in 1947, and the same is now available in paperback from Bobbs-Merrill: New York).

HOOK, S. 'The Atheism of Paul Tillich' in *Religious Experience and Truth*, ed. S. Hook (New York U.P: New York, 1961).

HOSPERS, P. *An Introduction to Philosophical Analysis* (Prentice Hall: New York, 1953 and Routledge and Kegan Paul: London, 1956).

HUXLEY, T. H. 'On the Physical Basis of Life' in *Collected Essays* (MacMillan: London, 1894).

JAMES, W. 'The Will to Believe' in *The Will to Believe* (Longmans Green: London, 1897).

KANT, I. (1) *A Critique of Pure Reason,* tr. N. Kemp Smith (MacMillan: London, 1929).

KANT, I. (2) *Prolegomena to any Future Metaphysics,* tr. P. G. Lucas (Manchester U.P: Manchester, 1953).

KANT, I. (3) *Critique of Practical Reason,* tr. T. K. Abbott (Longmans, Green: London, 1873). This includes Kant's *Foundations of the Metaphysics of Morals,* but for a better edition of this alone see under Paton, H. J., below.

KAUFMANN, W. *Existentialism from Dostoievsky to Sartre* (World Publishing Co: Cleveland and New York, 1956).

KEMP SMITH, N. *The Credibility of Divine Existence* (MacMillan: London, 1967).

KEYNES, J. M. *Two Memoirs,* introduced by D. Garnett (R. Hart-Davis: London, 1949 and Augustus M. Kelly Inc.: New York).

KIRK, G. S. and RAVEN, J. F. *The Presocratic Philosophers* (C.U.P: Cambridge, 1957).

KOESTLER, A. *The Sleepwalkers* (London: Hutchinson, 1959 and Penguin Books, 1964).

LAPLACE, P. S. DE *A Philosophical Essay on Probabilities,* tr. F. W. Truscott and F. L. Emery (Dover: New York, 1951).

LEE, D. D. 'Conceptual implications of an Indian language' in *Philosophy of Science* for 1940.

LEIBNIZ, G. W. (1) *Theodicy* tr. E. M. Huggard and ed. A. Farrer (Routledge and Kegan Paul: London, 1951).

LEIBNIZ, G. W. (2) *The Monadology etc.,* tr. and ed. A. Latta (O.U.P: Oxford, 1898). This contains the 'Principles of Nature and of Grace, founded on Reason'.

LEIBNIZ, G. W. (3) *New Essays concerning Human Understanding,* tr. and ed. A. G. Langley (MacMillan: London and New York, 1896).

LEIBNIZ, G. W. (4) *Discourse on Metaphysics,* tr. P. G. Lucas and L. Grint (Manchester U.P: Manchester, 1953).

LEIBNIZ, G. W. and CLARKE, S. *The Leibniz-Clarke Correspondence,* tr. S. Clarke and ed. H. G. Alexander (Manchester U.P: Manchester, 1956).

LENIN, V. I. (1) *Materialism and Empirio-Criticism* (Foreign Languages Publishing House: Moscow, 1952).

LENIN, V. I. (2) *State and Revolution* (Lawrence and Wishart: London, undated).

LOCKE, J. (1) *An Essay concerning Human Understanding* ed. A. C. Fraser (O.U.P: Oxford, 1894, and now in paperback from Dover: New York).

LOCKE, J. (2) *Works* (Seventh Edition. London, 1768). There is no modern edition containing all the minor philosophical pieces.

LOVEJOY, A. D. *The Great Chain of Being* (Harvard U.P: Cambridge (Mass.), 1936 and now in paperback as a Harper Torchbook).

MCCORQUODALE, K. and MEEHL, P. 'On a Distinction between Hypothetical Constructs and Intervening Variables' in *The Psychological Review* for 1948.

MAIMONIDES, M. (MOSES BEN MAIMON) *The Guide for the Perplexed*, tr. M. Friedlander (Routledge and Kegan Paul: London, 1904 and now in paperback from Dover: New York).

MARX, K. *The Economic and Philosophic Manuscripts of 1844*, ed. D. K. Struik, and tr. M. Milligan (International Publishers: New York, 1964).

MEAD, M. (1) *Coming of Age in Samoa* (Penguin Books: Harmondsworth, 1943).

MEAD, M. (2) *Sex and Temperament in three Primitive Societies* (New American Library: New York, 1950).

MEAD, M. (3) *Growing up in New Guinea* (New American Library: New York, 1953).

METTRIE, J. DE L. *Man a Machine*, tr. G. M. Bussey etc. (Open Court Publishing Co: La Salle (Illinois), 1961).

MILL, J. S. (1) *On Liberty,* in *Utilitarianism etc.* (E. P. Dutton: New York and J. M. Dent: London, 1910).

MILL, J. S. (2) *Utilitarianism,* see above.

MILL, J. S. (3) *A System of Logic* (Seventh Edition. Longmans, Green: London, 1868).

MILL, J. S. (4) *An Examination of Sir William Hamilton's Philosophy* (Fourth Edition. Longmans, Green: London and New York, 1872).

MILL, J. S. (5) *Mill on Bentham and Coleridge*, ed. F. R. Leavis (Chatto and Windus: London, 1950).

MOHAMMED, The Prophet *The Koran*, tr. N. J. Dawood (Penguin Books: Harmondsworth and Baltimore, 1956).

MOORE, G. E. (1) *Principia Ethica* (C.U.P: Cambridge, 1903).

MOORE, G. E. (2) 'The Refutation of Idealism' in his *Philosophical Studies* (Routledge and Kegan Paul: London, 1922).

MOORE, G. E. (3) 'A Defence of Common Sense' in *Contemporary British Philosophy* (Second Series), ed. J. H. Muirhead (Allen and Unwin: London and MacMillan: New York, 1925).

MOTTRAM, V. H. *The Physical Basis of Personality* (Penguin Books: Harmondsworth and Baltimore, 1944).

NEWMAN, J. H. *A Grammar of Assent* (Longmans, Green: London and New York, 1891).

NEWTON, I. (1) *Principia Mathematica*, ed. F. Cajori (California U.P: Berkeley, 1946).

NEWTON, I. (2) *Opticks*, ed. L. B. Cohen (Dover: New York, 1952).

O'CONNOR, D. J. (Ed.) *A Critical History of Western Philosophy* (MacMillan: New York and G. Allen and Unwin: London, 1964).

PALEY, W. *Works*, ed. E. Paley (Longmans: London, 1838).

PASSMORE, J. A. (1) 'William Harvey and the Philosophy of Science' in *Australasian Journal of Philosophy* for 1958.

PASSMORE, J. A. (2) *A Hundred Years of Philosophy* (Second Edition. Penguin Books: Harmondsworth and Baltimore, 1968).

PASCAL, B. *Pensées*, tr. W. F. Trotter (Dutton: New York and Dent: London, 1931).

PATON, H. J. *The Moral Law* (Hutchinson: London and Harper and Row: New York, 1947). This contains a translation of *The Foundations of the Metaphysics of Morals*. The U.S. edition has the more informative title *Immanuel Kant: Groundwork of the Metaphysic of Morals*.

PATTERSON BROWN 'St. Thomas' Doctrine of Necessary Being' in *The Philosophical Review* for 1964.

PEIRCE, C. S. 'Some consequences of four incapacities' in *Collected Papers*, ed. C. Hartshorne and P. Weiss (Harvard U.P: Cambridge (Mass.), (Vol. V) 1934).

PERRY, R. B. *Thought and Character of William James* (Little, Brown and Co: Boston and Toronto, 1935).

PIUS XII *Humani Generis* (Catholic Truth Society: London, 1950).

PLATO *Collected Dialogues*, ed. E. Hamilton and H. H. Cairns (Princeton U.P: Princeton, 1961).

POPPER, K. R. (1) *The Open Society* (Routledge and Kegan Paul: London, 1945).

POPPER, K. R. (2) *The Poverty of Historicism* (Routledge and Kegan Paul: London, 1957).

POPPER, K. R. (3) *Conjectures and Refutations* (Routledge and Kegan Paul: London, 1963).

REED, H. *A Map of Verona* (Jonathan Cape: London and Harcourt, Brace and World: New York, 1946).

REID, T. *Essays on the Intellectual Powers of Man,* in *The Powers of the Human Mind* (Bell and Bradfute: Edinburgh, 1819).

RUSSELL, B. A. W. (1) *The Principles of Mathematics* (G. Allen and Unwin: London, 1903).

RUSSELL, B. A. W. (2) *The Problems of Philosophy* (O.U.P: London and New York, 1912).

RUSSELL, B. A. W. (3) *The Analysis of Matter* (Kegan Paul: London and Harcourt Brace: New York, 1927).

RUSSELL, B. A. W. (4) *Religion and Science* (O.U.P: London and New York, 1935).

RUSSELL, B. A. W. (5) *Human Knowledge* (G. Allen and Unwin: London, 1948).

RUSSELL, B. A. W. (6) *The Practice and Theory of Bolshevism* (Second Edition. G. Allen and Unwin: London, 1949).

RUSSELL, B. A. W. (7) *Human Society in Ethics and Politics* (G. Allen and Unwin: London and Simon and Schuster: New York, 1954).

RUSSELL, B. A. W. and WHITEHEAD, A. N. *Principia Mathematica* (C.U.P: Cambridge, 1913).

RYLE, G. *The Concept of Mind* (Hutchinson: London, 1949).

SARTRE, J-P. (1) *Being and Nothingness*, tr. H. E. Barnes (Philosophical Library: New York, 1956).

SARTRE, J-P. (2) *Existentialism and Humanism*, tr. P. Mairet (Methuen: London and Philosophical Library: New York, 1948).

SCHOPENHAUER, A. *The World as Will and Idea,* tr. R. B. Haldane and J. Kemp (Trübner: London, 1883–1886).

SCRIVEN, M. *Primary Philosophy* (McGraw-Hill: New York and London, 1966).

SPINOZA, B. (1) *The Chief Works*, tr. R. H. M. Elwes (G. Bell: London, 1889, and now in paperback from Dover: New York).

SPINOZA, B. (2) *Principles of Cartesian Philosophy*, tr. H. E. Wedeck (P. Owen: London and Philosophical Library: New York, 1961).

TILLICH, P. *Systematic Theology* (Chicago U.P: Chicago, 1951 and Nisbet: London, 1953. The reference in the text is to the latter, which is differently paginated. The relevant section is on the 'Possibility of the Question of God and the So-called Ontological Argument').

TOULMIN, S. E. and GOODFIELD, J. *The Fabric of the Heavens* (Hutchinson: London, 1961, and now in paperback from Penguin Books: Harmondsworth and Baltimore).

URMSON, J. O. (Ed.) *A Concise Encyclopaedia of Philosophy and Philosophers* (Hutchinson: London and New York, 1960).

VALLA, L. 'On Freewill', tr. C. E. Trinkaus in *The Renaissance Philosophy of Man*, ed. E. Cassirer, P. O. Kristeller, and J. H. Randall (Chicago U.P: Chicago, 1956).

VEBLEN, THORSTEIN *The Theory of the Leisure Class* (MacMillan: London and New York, 1899).

WAISMANN, F. (1) 'Verifiability' in *Logic and Language* (First Series), ed. A. G. N. Flew (Blackwell: Oxford, 1951).

WAISMANN, F. (2) 'How I see philosophy' in *Contemporary British Philosophy* (Third Series), ed. H. D. Lewis (G. Allen and Unwin: London and MacMillan: New York, 1956).

WHITEHEAD, A. N. *Science and the Modern World* (C.U.P: Cambridge, 1926).

WITTGENSTEIN, L. (1) *Tractatus Logico-Philosophicus*, tr. C. K. Ogden (Routledge and Kegan Paul: London, 1922. There is now another translation, by D. F. Pears and B. McGuiness, from the same publishers).

WITTGENSTEIN, L. (2) *Philosophical Investigations*, tr. G. E. M. Anscombe (Blackwell: Oxford, 1953).

WITTGENSTEIN, L. (3) *The Blue and Brown Books* (Blackwell: Oxford, 1958).

SUGGESTIONS FOR FURTHER READING

For anyone who has started by studying a modern introductory textbook the most urgent need now is to work straight through two or three of the philosophical classics. Of the numerous possibilities mentioned already in the present book none will be equally right for all comers. But the samples provided by the extracts, and the supporting information, should help you to choose the ones which will be best in your case.

Plato you might start with the *Laches* or the *Euthyphro*, and then proceed by way of the *Meno* to *The Republic* or the *Phaedo*, and from there perhaps to the *Theaetetus* and *The Sophist*. The beginner attempting any of the later and harder dialogues on this list should use one of the editions providing summaries and some discussion as well as a translation of the text: *Plato's Meno*, translated by B. Jowett and edited by A. Sesonske and N. Fleming (Wadsworth: Belmont (California), 1965); *Plato's Republic*, translated and edited by F. M. Cornford (O.U.P.: Oxford, 1941); *Plato's Phaedo*, translated and edited by R. Hackforth (C.U.P.: Cambridge, 1953); or *Plato's Theory of Knowledge*, by F. M. Cornford (Routledge and Kegan Paul: London, 1953 and now in paperback from Bobbs-Merrill: New York, 1957. This book contains Cornford's translations of both the *Theaetetus* and *The Sophist*).

There is nothing similarly suitable to recommend from either Aristotle or Aquinas. But anyone determined to come to terms immediately with Aristotle had perhaps best try the *Nicomachean Ethics*. For Aquinas start with F. C. Copleston's *Aquinas* (Penguin Books: Harmondsworth and Baltimore, 1955) and let Copleston be your guide into the massive *Summae*. The chapters on Aristotle and Aquinas in O'Connor's *A Critical History of Western Philosophy* are both excellent.

Among the moderns read the *Discourse on the Method* first, and then the *Meditations*. One excellent introductory book is A. Kenny's *Descartes: a Study of his Philosophy* (Random House: New York, 1968). There are two very useful collections of critical papers: one, edited by W. Doney, is in the 'Modern Studies in Philosophy' series, and is called simply *Descartes* (Doubleday Anchor: New York, 1967 and Macmillan: London, 1968); and the other, edited by A. Sesonske and N. Fleming, is – like the *Plato's Meno* mentioned earlier – one of the 'Wadsworth Studies in Philosophical Criticism', and entitled *Metameditations* (Wadsworth: Belmont (California), 1965).

Of the other two great modern philosophical rationalists Spinoza is really too hard for beginners. But the thing to read from Spinoza is the

Ethics; perhaps in the version included complete in the *Spinoza Selections*, edited by J. Wild (Charles Scribner's Sons: New York, 1958). For interpretation and criticism try the essay by P. H. Nidditch in O'Connor's *Critical History* and S. N. Hampshire, *Spinoza* (Penguin Books: Harmondsworth and Baltimore, 1951). The system of Leibniz is much more accessible. Here too perhaps the best thing to use is *Leibniz Selections* in 'The Modern Sudent's Library', edited by P. P. Wiener (Charles Scribner's Sons: New York, 1951). This contains the *Discourse on Metaphysics* and the *Monadology*, both agreeably short and succinct works, complete; as well as a great deal of other useful material, much of which is hard to get elsewhere. The chapter on 'Leibniz' in Bertrand Russell's *A History of Western Philosophy* (G. Allen and Unwin: London, 1946) is short and sharp; the work of a major philosopher whose own *The Philosophy of Leibniz* (G. Allen and Unwin: London, 1900) constitutes a landmark in Leibniz studies. Another thing to read along with one or two of the rationalist classics is A. O. Lovejoy's *The Great Chain of Being*, a work which is itself one of the classics of the history of ideas. (Here and later where no bibliographical information is given it is because this can be found in the 'Particulars of Books Mentioned', above.)

Of the three chief British empiricists Locke wrote only one work within our present scope. But this, the *Essay concerning Human Understanding*, is, as Locke himself was the first to admit, excessively long and repetitious. The standard edition by A. C. Fraser with abundant critical material is in two solid Victorian volumes (O.U.P.: Oxford, 1894). So in this one case it is perhaps excusable to go first to an abridgement: for instance that by A. D. Woozley (Collins Fontana: London, 1964). From Berkeley the first things to read are the *Principles* and *Three Dialogues between Hylas and Philonous*. These two brief and brilliant books are both included, with an excellent 'Introduction' by G. J. Warnock, in *The Principles of Human Knowledge, and other writings* (Collins Fontana: London, 1962). Hume is perhaps best approached through the first *Inquiry*, of which the only edition acceptable now is that by C. W. Hendel. The standard edition of the *Treatise* has for long been that by L. A. Selby-Bigge. But a possible alternative now is the Pelican Classic done by Hume's biographer E. C. Mossner (Penguin Books: Harmondsworth and Baltimore, 1969). Book I 'Of the Understanding' can be got by itself, edited by D. G. C. Macnabb, in the Collins Fontana series mentioned twice already in this paragraph (London, 1962).

There are valuable collections of critical essays in the 'Modern Studies in Philosophy' series on *Locke and Berkeley*, edited by C. B. Martin and D. M. Armstrong (Doubleday Anchor: New York, 1968 and Macmillan: London, 1969), and on *Hume*, edited by V. C. Chappell (Doubleday Anchor: New York, 1966 and Macmillan: London, 1968). On the first

Inquiry alone there are *Human Understanding*, edited by A. Sesonske and N. Fleming (Wadsworth: Belmont (California), 1965) and A. Flew's *Hume's Philosophy of Belief* (Routledge and Kegan Paul: London, and Humanities Press: New York, 1961). The surveys of Locke, Berkeley and Hume in O'Connor's *Critical History* can be recommended; also the volumes on *John Locke*, by D. J. O'Connor, and on *Berkeley*, by G. J. Warnock, in the Pelican Philosophy Series (Penguin Books: Harmondsworth and Baltimore, 1952 and 1953, respectively. The first of these has since been reissued by Dover Publications of New York).

Kant, like Spinoza, is not generally for beginners. But with Kant there is the *Prolegomena*, which was specially written as an introduction to the *Critique of Pure Reason*; Kemp Smith himself produced an abridged edition of his standard English translation of that first *Critique*; and the *Foundations of the Metaphysics of Morals* is short, great, and not too agonizingly difficult. G. J. Warnock's study of Kant in O'Connor's *Critical History* is a dry masterpiece of critical illumination; and there is a *Kant* volume, edited by R. P. Wolff, in the 'Modern Studies in Philosophy' series (Doubleday Anchor: New York, 1967 and Macmillan: London, 1968).

Coming to our own century G. E. Moore is very much a philosophers' philosopher. But anyone who has done some reading in Descartes, Locke, Berkeley, and Hume should be ready for Moore's *Philosophical Studies* (Routledge and Kegan Paul: London, 1922). Bertrand Russell, on the other hand, has written many books with a wider public in mind. The problem here is to choose from the riches. One possible beginning here is *The Problems of Philosophy*, to be followed perhaps by *Our Knowledge of the External World* (Open Court: La Salle, 1914 and reissued by G. Allen and Unwin: London, 1922); *Mysticism and Logic* (G. Allen and Unwin: London, 1910. This was first published as *Philosophical Essays*, and has since been reissued by Penguin Books); and the *Analysis of Mind* (G. Allen and Unwin: London, 1921 and Macmillan: New York, 1924). The studies of Moore and Russell in O'Connor's *Critical History* are both valuable exercises in discerning compression. There are massive volumes on *The Philosophy of G. E. Moore* and *The Philosophy of Bertrand Russell* in 'The Library of Living Philosophers': both are edited by P. A. Schilpp and both, along with the whole series, have had a chequered publishing history resting now with the Open Court Company of La Salle, Illinois.

Wittgenstein's *Tractatus* is an esoteric work, and the labours of the commentators have been to some extent confused and distracted by a cult of personality. My advice to readers who have no ambitions themselves to become Wittgenstein scholars is to use the original translation (A.V.); to dip into *Essays on Wittgenstein's Tractatus*, edited by I. M. Copi and R. W. Beard (Routledge and Kegan Paul: London, 1966); and to have close at hand M. Black's *A Companion to Wittgenstein's Tractatus* (C.U.P.: Cambridge, 1964). The work of Wittgenstein's second period is less esoteric. But the *Philosophical Investigations*, which does not really succeed in actually being a book, is best approached via the more finished *Blue and Brown Books*. The *Wittgenstein* volume in the 'Modern Studies in Philosophy' series, edited by G. Pitcher, confines itself to what came after the *Tractatus*.

So far these 'Suggestions for Further Reading' have concentrated on the study of philosophical classics by the great masters. Another and complementary approach is to mention some books for those who want to pursue an interest in the subject of a particular chapter. Thus from Chapter III one might go on to the two short, lucid, and much discussed books of R. M. Hare, *The Language of Morals* and *Freedom and Reason* (O.U.P.: Oxford and New York, 1963); to P. H. Nowell-Smith, *Ethics* (Penguin Books: Harmondsworth and Baltimore, 1954); to A. C. McIntyre, *A Short History of Ethics* (Macmillan: New York, 1966 and Routledge and Kegan Paul: London, 1967); and to the edition of J. S. Mill's *Utilitarianism, etc.*, edited by Mary Warnock.

From Chapter IV, on 'Survival and Immortality', you could go to the volume in the 'Problems of Philosophy' series on *Body, Mind and Death* (Collier Macmillan: New York, 1964); though this is edited by A. Flew, and contains some extracts from the classics which are also included in the present volume. Three other books are C. J. Ducasse, *The Belief in a Life after Death* (C. C. Thomas: Springfield (Illinois), 1961), S. Shoemaker, *Self-Knowledge and Self-Identity* (Cornell U.P.: Ithaca (N.Y.), 1963), and R. Puccetti, *Persons* (Macmillan: London, 1968). Of these three the first is a little old-fashioned but very relevant, while the last two bear only rather indirectly on survival and immortality. The third will surely be found more immediately exciting and less difficult than the second.

For Chapters V and VI try a volume of papers such as *Faith and the Philosophers*, edited by J. Hick (Macmillan: London, 1964); *Talk of God*, edited by G. N. A. Vesey (Macmillan: London, 1969); or *New Essays in Philosophical Theology*, edited by A. Flew and A. McIntyre (S.C.M. Press: London, and St Martin's Press: New York, 1956). Two impressive books by single authors are R. W. Hepburn, *Christianity and Paradox* (C. A. Watts: London, 1958) and W. Kaufmann, *Critique of Religion and Philosophy* (Faber and Faber: London, 1959). And if you can bear the thought of any more from the present writer, there is his *God and Philosophy* (Hutchinson: London and Harcourt, Brace and World: New York, 1966. Also Dell Delta paperbacks, 1969).

For Chapter VII start with the whole of Valla's short dialogue 'On Freewill', and then dip into two collections of papers: *Determinism and Freedom in the Age of Modern Science*, edited by S. Hook (New York U.P.:

New York, 1958); and *Freedom and Determinism*, edited by K. Lehrer (Random House: New York, 1966). This will be a good time to read J. L. Austin's 'A Plea for Excuses' and to go on from there to others of his *Philosophical Papers*. For those with theological interests the *Theodicy* of Leibniz and *The Freedom of the Will* by Jonathan Edwards can also be recommended strongly.

For Chapter IX, apart from books dealing specifically with Descartes, try A. D. Woozley, *Theory of Knowledge* (Hutchinson: London and New York, 1949); A. J. Ayer, *The Problem of Knowledge* (Macmillan: London, and St Martin's Press: New York, 1956); and the collection in the 'Oxford Readings in Philosophy' series on *Knowledge and Belief*, edited by A. P. Griffiths (O.U.P.: London and New York, 1967).

For Chapter X try: in the 'Problems of Philosophy Series' *Perception and the External World*, edited by R. J. Hirst (Collier Macmillan: London and New York, 1965); in the 'Oxford Readings in Philosophy' series *The Philosophy of Perception*, edited by G. J. Warnock (O.U.P.: London and New York, 1967); perhaps A. J. Ayer, *The Foundations of Empirical Knowledge* (Macmillan: London, 1940); and certainly J. L. Austin, *Sense and Sensibilia* (O.U.P.: London and New York, 1962).

Chapter XI and XII do not either of them determine a single line of further reading. But if you want to explore existentialism further, try W. Kaufmann's selections, *Existentialism from Dostoievsky to Sartre* (World Publishing: Cleveland and New York, 1956); and perhaps Mary Warnock, *The Philosophy of Sartre* (Hutchinson: London and New York, 1965). The best first introduction to Marxism is surely S. Hook's *Marx and the Marxists* in the useful 'Anvil Original' series (Van Nostrand: Princeton and London, 1955). Apart from existentialism and Marxism all the themes of the last two chapters, and many more, are treated in one or other of the papers collected (again, I fear, by the present writer) in two volumes of essays on *Logic and Language* (Blackwell: Oxford, First Series, 1951 and Second Series, 1953. The two have since been republished as one paperback by Doubleday Anchor) and in a third volume of *Essays in Conceptual Analysis* (Macmillan: London, and St Martin's Press: New York, 1956). The Introduction to the first *Logic and Language* was written far too long ago, but Chapter I of *Essays in Conceptual Analysis* on 'Philosophy and Language' has worn better.

Index of Names

Note. Neither of the two indices attempts to cover pp. 1–12 and 485–497. This first is almost completely confined to personal names, and it also excludes the names of fictitious or mythological human persons and of gods. Where, as with most of the dialogues of Plato, real people are represented with artistic licence, these references are not included either. The word *God* is construed as a description rather than as a name, and therefore appears only in the second index. I wish to thank my wife for her help in compiling this first index.

Index of Notions

Note In accordance with the aims of the whole book, as stated in Chapter I, this index has been compiled mainly as an aid to reinforcement in learning. It should serve for revision purposes as a check list of the most important ideas, distinctions, and arguments introduced in the text. Shorter lists within this list will be found under the four headings: 'Arguments, labelled'; 'Fallacies, labelled'; 'Principles, labelled'; and 'Tactical and strategic moves, labelled and legitimate'. Numerals in italic type indicate pages providing explanations of the word or expression concerned, and these are the references which should normally be pursued first.